ACCOUNTING THEORY

ACCOUNTING THEORY
A Conceptual and
Institutional Approach

Harry I. Wolk
Drake University

Jere R. Francis
University of Missouri-Columbia

Michael G. Tearney
University of Kentucky

**KENT
PUBLISHING
COMPANY**
A Division of Wadsworth, Inc.
Boston, Massachusetts

Senior Editor: John B. McHugh
Production Editor: Nancy J. Crow
Interior Design: Nancy Blodget
Cover Design: Outside Design
Production Coordinator: Linda Siegrist

Kent Publishing Company
A Division of Wadsworth, Inc.

Printed in the United States of America

3 4 5 6 7 8 9 — 88 87 86 85

Library of Congress Cataloging in Publication Data

Wolk, Harry I.
  Accounting theory.

  Includes bibliographical references and index.
  1. Accounting. I. Francis, Jere R. II. Tearney,
Michael G. III. Title.
HF5625.W64   1984   657   83-23883
ISBN 0-543-03046-7

PREFACE

During the last two decades, standard-setting in accounting has become both more extensive and complex. Paralleling this regulatory development has been a growth in the importance and sophistication of accounting research. Indeed this period has seen an increased respectability accorded to accounting and other business disciplines as academic subjects by other members of the university community and the public at large.

As a result of these developments, courses in accounting theory have arisen with the purpose, broadly speaking, of synthesizing approaches to and developments in financial accounting. With this book, we join a small but hardy band of accounting scholars who have attempted to provide an overview of accounting theory and policy to sharpen the understanding and analytical abilities of our students.

This book is intended for one-semester accounting theory courses at both the senior and graduate levels. Students should be thoroughly grounded in intermediate accounting as well as business combinations (for Chapter 17 on Investments in Equity Securities and Foreign Currency Translations and Chapter 18 on Business Combinations) prior to delving into accounting theory. At the graduate level the book is applicable to courses in MBA programs with accounting concentrations and MS in accounting programs.

The aim of this text is to identify the elements of accounting theory in the first part of the book and then relate these elements to significant problem areas in accounting in the second part. As a result, it is hoped that an appreciation of the linkages between theory and policy will be gained by the reader. This has proven to be a difficult and elusive task in the past.

Each chapter contains a fairly lengthy group of questions and several cases or problems which attempt to either reinforce the textual material or expand upon it. More teaching materials are contained in the instructor's manual. There is a very extensive list of referenced works and additional readings at the end of each chapter. We would presume that all users would assign the first seven chapters which are concerned with the elements of accounting theory as well as material on the structure and development of accounting policy formulating agencies. Beyond this point, any order can be used although Chapters 11 and 12 (accounting for inflation and changing prices) are linked together as are Chapters 17 and 18.

We have accumulated many debts arising from this project. The following individuals provided very valuable reviews and comments of the chapter materials: R. Glen Berryman, University of Minnesota, Minneapolis; Sharon McKinnon, Northeastern University; G. Edward Philips, University of New Mexico; Gary A. Porter, Loyola University (Chicago); H. Lee Schlorff, Bentley College; and Weldon H. Walker, Bentley College. In addition, Pam Blewer of Drake provided many useful insights from the student perspective. We would like to thank David S. McEttrick, Nancy Crow, Cathy Labresh, and other members of the staff at Kent Publishing Company. We found them to be highly competent and dedicated professionals as well as being a pleasure to work with. We would also like to express our appreciation to the Peat, Marwick & Mitchell Foundation for financial support. Ginger Wheeler, our typist, managed to cheerfully and efficiently turn our often illegible drafts into finished manuscript form. Finally, our wives—Barbara, Candis, and Barbara—not only put up with our sometimes agonized outpourings about accounting theory, they also paid the opportunity cost of foregone evenings out and lost vacations. To them we dedicate the book.

CONTENTS

CHAPTER 3

The Regulation of Financial Reporting   71

CHAPTER 4

Postulates, Principles, and Concepts   107

CHAPTER 5

Objectives and Standards   143

CHAPTER 6

The Usefulness of Accounting Information 187

CHAPTER 7

Uniformity and Disclosure: Some Policy-Making Directions 219

PART I

Theoretical and Institutional Background of Accounting Theory

THE ELEMENTS OF ACCOUNTING THEORY

The first part of the text is concerned with what accounting theory is and identifying important current issues pertaining to it. Accounting theory developments play an important part in the formulation of accounting standards (rules), as well as providing guidance for "constitutions" that are intended to underlie accounting standards such as the Conceptual Framework Project of the Financial Accounting Standards Board. The intention of this book is to show the links existing between theoretical issues and institutional developments in the area of financial accounting.

The term **accounting theory** is commonly used in financial accounting, but it has no single standardized definition. Theory itself helps to explain and predict phenomena that exist in a given field, and the same is true in accounting. Therefore, a broad approach is taken relative to the interpretation of accounting theory in this text. The concern of Chapter 1 is with the definition of accounting theory and its role in the standard-setting process. Accounting theory includes a sizable array of concepts, models, hypotheses, and theories (in the narrow sense) whose subject matter is concerned with financial accounting. Many of these concepts have been developed in response to needs arising from practice, such as the realization rules for recognizing revenues. Also included would be valuation models such as current valuation and general price level adjustment approaches that have arisen as a result of changing prices and purchasing power of the measurement unit. A newer orientation to accounting theory involves the application of formalized research techniques for the purpose of analyzing data and providing insights. This is called empirical research.

An important concern of Chapter 1 is the role that accounting theory plays in the standard-setting process. Accounting theory provides one important input into the policy-making process because of the insights it provides in terms of identifying issues and solving problems. Political factors and economic conditions are two other important sources of influence upon the standard-setting process.

Very closely related to the accounting theory domain is the area of measurement. Measurement is concerned with the process of assigning numbers to the attributes or characteristics of the elements being measured. The process of measurement is clearly an activity in which accountants are engaged. It is also of great concern in the formulation of rules by standard-setting agencies. The relation of measurement to accounting theory is considered not only in Chapter 1, but throughout the book.

The concern of Chapter 2 is institutional matters. The creation of the Securities and Exchange Commission in 1934 empowered that agency to make the accounting rules for enterprises whose securities are publicly traded. As a result of the possibility that accounting rules would be made in the public sector, the Committee on Accounting Procedure of the American Institute of Certified Public Accountants took a much more active role in the setting of accounting standards. A good working relationship was established between the private sector group and the public agency that was charged with the power to make accounting rules. Despite occasional clashes, a close connection has been maintained to this day between the public and private sector agencies engaged in making financial accounting rules.

The Committee on Accounting Procedure has been succeeded by two other private sector rule-making agencies: the Accounting Principles Board and the Financial Accounting Standards Board. How these three groups have operated and developed, including their similarities and differences and relations with the Securities and Exchange Commission and other external groups, is the main subject matter of Chapter 2.

Accounting information is a commodity which is produced by the enterprise itself and, in the case of publicly traded firms, consumed by a wide variety of outside users. This economic analysis of accounting information, a relatively new outlook, is presented in Chapter 3. The nature of this market is that accounting information is prepared by a monopoly supplier, the firm itself, for consumers—financial analysts—who do not pay for the commodity.

In light of this theoretical background, certain important issues have been raised. One important question concerns whether the cost of regulatory agencies in accounting exceed the benefits. Another important related issue concerns the economic consequences of accounting standards: the impact that accounting standards have upon the behavior of those who are affected by financial reporting.

An extensive analysis is made in Chapters 4 and 5 of important documents and committee reports published by the American Accounting Association, American Institute of Certified Public Accountants, and the Financial Accounting Standards Board. These publications highlight standard-setting developments and summaries of research issues which have occurred during the last twenty-five years.

Included in these works are the attempt to establish a system of postulates and principles for the Accounting Principles Board and the Conceptual Framework Project of the Financial Accounting Standards Board. The transition period between these two attempts to establish a guiding theoretical structure saw a rise in emphasis on the importance of users of financial statements and their perceived information needs. Two committee reports of the American Accounting Association included in this survey provide an excellent summary of the state of accounting theory at the time of the issuance of these documents. Also included in Chapter 4 is a brief analysis of the concepts that have been used, albeit in an informal and unorganized fashion, as a guide for financial accounting rule making within a historical cost context.

Important new theoretical work centered largely on the usefulness of accounting information is covered in Chapter 6. Much of this work originated in fields outside of accounting but has important implications for the standard-setting process.

Information economics provides a broad framework for understanding the value of information where uncertainty exists. It is presented in the context of measuring the probabilities and values of the payoffs stemming from the various choices facing the decision maker.

Capital market research is concerned with the response of security prices to accounting information. Of particular importance within capital market research are studies that have attempted to determine whether securities markets are "efficient." While the issue is by no means closed, these studies have generally shown that new information is rapidly and unbiasedly reflected in security prices. Furthermore, the market does not appear to be "fooled" by changes in accounting method that merely have a cosmetic effect upon income. However, changes in accounting policy that do have either direct or indirect effect upon enterprise cash flows influence security prices. Studies have also shown that accounting information is useful for assessing risk: the degree of expected variability of accounting earnings.

Complementary to capital market research has been the interest in the allocation problem in accounting. Allocations are the methods used by accountants to divide costs or revenues among different affected periods. A strict interpretation maintains that there is no way to logically justify one allocation method over another. Nevertheless, income numbers containing allocations still influence security prices and are useful to investors.

The theory section of the text concludes in Chapter 7 with an extensive look at two concepts: uniformity and disclosure. Since one of the objectives of the Financial Accounting Standards Board, particularly in light of its Conceptual Framework Project, is to bring about greater uniformity in financial accounting, it is a potentially important topic. However, uniformity is a concept that has not been appropriately resolved, though extensively discussed in accounting literature. There appear to be two formulations of uniformity. One type ignores the presence of different economic circumstances in broadly similar transaction situations. The other approach attempts to take into account these differences in underlying circumstances. The two conceptions of uniformity are analyzed in broad cost-benefit terms as well as seeing how they have been applied in some situations by standard-setting agencies.

The other main topic examined in Chapter 7 is disclosure. Recent developments in capital markets research, increasing complexity of transactions, and an inability to resolve theoretical issues indicates that disclosure is becoming more important as a means of communicating financial and economic information.

The first seven chapters form a framework that is useful in terms of analyzing and assessing the important accounting issues examined in the second part of the text.

CHAPTER 1

An Introduction to Accounting Theory

Accounting information has been useful for hundreds, if not thousands, of years. The double-entry framework was first described in a book written by Luca Pacioli, a fifteenth-century Italian monk and mathematician, though its origins can be traced back another 300 years. Hence, the formal structure for processing transactions of business entities is at least 700 years old. It should be no surprise that financial and economic information relative to enterprises has always been important to owners and managers. What is surprising, however, is the durability of the double-entry approach during a period of history in which man's technology and social institutions—including business itself—have become increasingly complex.

The enormity of these complex changes directly affecting business includes the following:

1. Growth of absentee ownership and increasing importance of stock exchanges, where securities of firms can be bought and sold.
2. Increase in the power of national governments, including the right to tax, to regulate, and (in socialist countries) to own and operate business enterprises.

3. Catastrophic financial upheavals, the greatest of which was the depression of the 1930s, which have undermined the confidence of the public in financial reporting.

4. Prolonged inflationary periods, in which the utility of traditional historical cost-based accounting has come under sharp attack.

In view of the fact that the last fifty years have been particularly susceptible to all the preceding conditions, it should not be surprising that a movement has arisen to provide some amount of uniformity for recording business transactions and presenting financial statements of publicly owned companies. This movement came about in the United States by means of the Securities Act of 1933 and the Securities and Exchange Act of 1934. The latter law created the Securities and Exchange Commission (SEC) and empowered it to prescribe accounting principles for firms whose securities are registered for trading on national and regional stock exchanges. Since the creation of the SEC, three groups have arisen in the private sector; they have been entrusted with the task of developing and implementing accounting principles for publicly traded corporations: the Committee on Accounting Procedure (CAP, 1935–59), the Accounting Principles Board (APB, 1959–73), and the Financial Accounting Standards Board (FASB, 1973 to the present).

The development and accomplishments of these private-sector groups will be discussed in Chapter 2. We would all undoubtedly agree that since these groups and the SEC have been engaged in formulating financial accounting policy, they must somehow be concerned with something identifiable as "accounting theory."

Though the last statement is undoubtedly correct, a theory ideally precedes the work of rule-making bodies. The subject of accounting theory is concerned with the whole complex of the concepts, models, hypotheses, and theories that underlie and influence the work of the rule-making groups.

The term "accounting theory" has been used for many years.[1] However, it has no standard definition. The term is being used here in a very broad sense. It includes concepts that have evolved in response to practical needs, such as realization and objectivity. "Models" is a general term comprising valuation methods and other types of accounting alternatives such as, for example, purchase and pooling. "Hypotheses and theories" refers to a more formalized method of investigation and analysis of subject matter coming from the academic discipline of philosophy. These newer and more formal approaches to accounting theory development are a relatively recent innovation in our field. They permeate much of the accounting research going on today. Results of the research process are published in books and academic and professional journals devoted to advancing the state of financial accounting by disseminating the results of the research process.

---

[1]For example, the title of a famous work originally published in 1922 was *Accounting Theory.* See Paton (1922).

Various facets of accounting theory are discussed throughout this book. The present chapter, as its title indicates, provides an introduction to accounting theory.

The main part of this chapter commences by briefly examining the relation between accounting theory and the institutional structure of accounting. One of the objectives of this book is to assess the influence of accounting theory upon the rule-making process. Hence, the approach adopted here is concerned with the linkages (and often the lack thereof) between accounting theory and the institutions charged with developing the rules that are intended to improve accounting practice.

The formal approach to theory development, frequently called **scientific method,** is the next subject we take up. Scientific method refers to the formal procedures that are used to derive the laws and principles that govern operations in "hard" scientific disciplines, such as physics and chemistry. Application of scientific methodology to "softer" disciplines, such as accounting—which involves the human behavior of rule makers, preparers, and auditors of financial statements, and of the users of accounting information—has become an important topic in recent years.

Another aspect of scientific method and its relationship to accounting concerns the process of measurement. **Measurement** is the assignment of numbers to properties or characteristics of objects. Measurement and how it applies to accounting are an important part of the accounting theory picture discussed in this chapter.

The role and meaning of theory to a given discipline are affected by whether the discipline is a science. Therefore, we need to consider the questions of whether accounting is, or can be, a science and of the relation of art to science.

Accounting theory is largely derived from the research process. Therefore, the main part of the chapter is rounded out by examining what appear to be the main directions of current accounting research.

The appendix to the chapter briefly illustrates the principal valuation approaches to accounting. These are examples of broad or global concepts of accounting theory. While they are discussed in more depth in Chapter 11, reference is made to them in the intervening chapters on accounting theory.

ACCOUNTING THEORY AND POLICYMAKING

The relationship between accounting theory and the standard-setting process must be understood within its wider context, as shown in Exhibit 1-1. Bodies such as the FASB and the SEC, which have been charged with making financial accounting rules, perform a policy type of function. This policy function is also called standard setting or rule making and specifically

EXHIBIT 1-1.

The Financial Accounting Environment

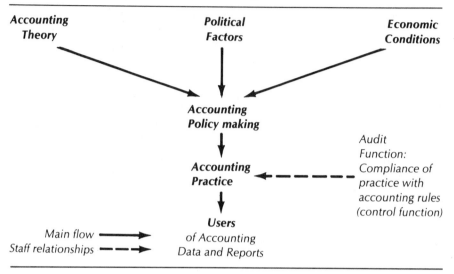

refs to the process of arriving at pronouncements issued by the FASB or SEC.

The inputs to the policy-making function come from three main (though not necessarily equal) sources. A classic example of an economic condition that impinged on policy making was the steep inflation of the 1970s, which was undoubtedly the catalyst that forced the FASB to take action leading to disclosure of information concerning changing prices.

The *political factors* influence refers to the effect upon the policymaking by those who are subject to it. Included in this category would be auditors who are responsible for assessing whether the rules have been followed; preparers of financial statements, who would be represented by organizations such as the Financial Executives Institute; investors, who would be represented by organizations such as the Chartered Financial Analysts; and the public itself, who might be represented by governmental groups such as Congress or by departments or agencies of the executive branch of government. In addition, corporate management of major firms and industry trade associations are important political components of the policy-making process.

Accounting theory is developed and refined by the process of accounting research. It is carried out mainly by accounting professors, but many individuals from policy-making organizations, public accounting firms, and private industry also play an important part in the research process.

Standards and other pronouncements of policymaking organizations are interpreted and put into practice at the firm level. Hence, the output of the policy level is implemented at the accounting practice level.

Users are made up of many groups, including both actual and potential shareholders and creditors, as well as the public at large. It is important to remember not only that users employ financial statements and reporting in making decisions, but that they are also affected by the policymaking function and its implementation at the accounting practice level.

While all facets of the accounting policy environment are important and are considered in this book, our primary focus is on that part of the track running between accounting theory and the accounting policy function. Finally, it should be cautioned that Exhibit 1-1 is extremely simplistic. In reality, numerous feedback relationships exist, for example, among the components of the accounting policy environment. Nevertheless, it is a good starting point for bringing out how ideas and conditions eventually coalesce into policymaking decisions that shape financial reporting.

ACCOUNTING RESEARCH AND SCIENTIFIC METHOD

While accounting theory embraces a wide collection of philosophical elements relating to the ideas of accounting, we are particularly concerned in this chapter with formally developed theories that result from the research process. Theories can be extremely useful because they attempt to explain relationships or predict phenomena.

In terms of scientific method, a theory is, first of all, nothing more than sentences.[2] It must contain a basic set of premises (also called assumptions or postulates). The premises may be self-evident or they may be constructed so that they can be tested by statistical inference, in which case they are usually called hypotheses. Some of the terms in premises may be undefined but other terms may need precise definitions. The words **debit** and **credit** are so well understood by accountants that no definition is necessary. However, the word **liabilities** as used in a theory should be carefully defined because several different conceptions of it occur in practice. In the narrowest context, liabilities can be defined strictly in the legal sense—as amounts presently due other parties for goods, services, or other consideration already received. However, the definition can be extended to include future cash disbursements for estimated income tax liabilities—straight-line depreciation is used for published financial statement purposes, and accelerated depreciation is used for tax purposes (a legal liability does not exist in this situation). Finally, a theory contains a set of conclusions derived from the premises. The conclusions can be determined either by deduction or induction.

---

[2]Scientific method cannot be precisely defined and restricted to a given set of rules or procedures. See AAA (1972, pp. 403–406).

DEDUCTIVE AND INDUCTIVE REASONING

Deductive systems require logical reasoning to go from premises to conclusions. Empirical data are not analyzed in purely deductive systems. A simple example of a deductive system would be:

Premise 1:   A horse has four legs.
Premise 2:   John has two legs.
Conclusion 1:   John is not a horse.

In this simple case only one conclusion can be derived from the premises. In a more complex system, more than one conclusion can be derived. However, conclusions must not be in conflict with each other. Notice that no other conclusion relative to John could possibly be reached from the given premises.

Of course, assuming that this theory pertained to a real being named John, as opposed to sentences whose logic is being analyzed, we would have to see and, if necessary, examine John to determine his status. At this point we would be in the inductive realm—because we would be judging the theory not simply by its internal logic but rather by observing the evidence itself. For example, John might be a horse that had two legs amputated. Assuming that the reasoning is valid, a deductive theory can be challenged only by empirically questioning premises or conclusions.

Different income models proposed by accounting and economic theorists have been developed by means of deductive reasoning. The main source of income is an increase in the wealth of the firm resulting from operations during the period. It has often been defined as the maximum amount that can be distributed to owners and still leave the firm as well off at the end of a period as it was at the beginning of the period.[3] Income thus arises, in the definitional sense, in accordance with maintaining intact the firm's capital at the beginning of the period. This concept is known as **capital maintenance.** There are at least three different ways to approach well-offness in capital maintenance terms. If we assume that the dollar is stable, historical cost income measurement is appropriate and capital maintenance is ascertained in unadjusted dollars. In a period of inflation, if we desire to take into account the shrinking general purchasing power of the dollar, revenues and expenses can be measured by restating historical cost figures by appropriate general price level adjustments. Similarly, income measured by calculating expenses in terms of current replacement costs is geared to a physical capacity concept of capital maintenance.

These concepts of income were deduced from the basic premise of the type of capital maintenance protection desired. A more extensive look at capital maintenance and other goals and premises of various income systems appears in Chapter 11.

[3]Hicks (1961, p. 172).

Inductive theories attempt to gather data or make observations in support of a premise or hypothesis.[4] If an individual were testing a pair of dice to see that they were not loaded, he might throw each die 100 times in order to check that all sides come up approximately one-sixth of the time as a test of the "fairness" of the dice. In accounting research, data is gathered by many methods, including questionnaires of practitioners or other appropriate parties, laboratory experiments involving individuals in simulation exercises, numbers from published financial statements, and prices of publicly traded securities.

In a complex environment such as the business world, a good inductive theory must carefully specify the problem that is being examined. The research must propound a hypothesis that is capable of being tested, select an appropriate sample from the population under investigation, gather and scrutinize the needed data, and employ the requisite tools of statistical inference to test the hypothesis.

One of the criticisms that has been made of early examples of inductive or empirical research is that the relationships expressed were "mechanistic" in nature. For example, empirical tests were made relative to the relationship between security prices and changes in accounting methods. However, the question of *why* particular alternatives are chosen by standard setters or financial managers largely remained unanswered. Empirical research that attempts to answer the question of why particular standards are selected by policymakers or why management selects the particular accounting alternatives they choose has been called **positive research** in accounting.[5] Positive research attempts to explain behavioral relationships in accounting. It attempts to describe "what is" without making any value judgments as to how things should be in accounting.

Many examples of inductively derived theories are present in the accounting literature. Watts and Zimmerman, as an example of positive research, were concerned with the question of how corporate management responds to new standards proposed by the FASB (the Board invites written responses from interested parties to exposure drafts of proposed new standards).[6] One of their premises is that management acts in its own self-interest, one benefit of which might be increased personal compensation, if reported net income increases. However, this is not necessarily the case in large firms if they are subject to antitrust action or regulation because of their dominant market position. In these firms it may be in management's best long-run interests to have standards that result in lower reported net

---

[4]Deductive reasoning prevailed over the inductive form from Ancient Greece down through the Middle Ages. One of the individuals most responsible for bringing inductive reasoning to the forefront was the famous Elizabethan statesman and scholar, Sir Francis Bacon. See Eiseley (1962).

[5]A discussion of positive research in accounting and a critique of previous empirical work appears in Zimmerman (1980).

[6]Watts and Zimmerman (1978).

income. As a result, Watts and Zimmerman hypothesized that managment has more incentive to favor standards that lower reported net income where the firm is subject to "political pressure." They examined submissions to the Board's exposure draft requiring general price-level adjusted income calculations in corporate annual reports (the exposure draft was eventually withdrawn). Their findings tended to corroborate the hypothesis that the proposal was supported by larger firms that would have lower income as a result of general price-level adjustment. Similarly, those larger firms having higher income using general price-level adjustment tended to be against the proposal.

NORMATIVE AND DESCRIPTIVE THEORIES

In addition to theories being classified as deductive or inductive, they may also be categorized as normative (prescriptive) or descriptive. Normative theories employ a value judgment: contained within them is at least one premise saying that this is the way things *should be*. For example, a premise stating that accounting reports should be based on net realizable value measurements of assets would indicate a normative system. By contrast, descriptive theories attempt to find relationships that actually exist. The Watts and Zimmerman study, discussed previously, is an excellent example of a descriptive theory applied to a particular situation.

While there are exceptions, it is usually the case that deductive systems are normative and inductive approaches attempt to be descriptive. This categorization derives from the nature of the deductive and inductive methods. The deductive method is basically a closed, nonempirical system. Its conclusions are based strictly on its premises. The inductive approach, conversely, because it tries to find and explain real-world relationships, is in the descriptive realm by its very nature. Two recent journal articles—one by Tinker, Merino, and Neimark and the other by Christenson—raise a very important question about theories because they challenge whether positive research can be "value free" (neutral) in its findings because implicit value judgments underlie the form and content of the research itself.[7] In other words, all research has an inevitable bias which reflects the personal value of the researcher.

GLOBAL AND PARTICULARISTIC THEORIES

Another difference between deductive and inductive systems is that the former are sometimes global (macro) in terms of content, whereas the latter are usually particularistic (micro). Where premises of deductive systems are total or all-encompassing in nature, their conclusions must be sweeping. Within the context of accounting, examples of the global approach are the

---

[7]Tinker, Merino, and Neimark (1982); and Christenson (1983).

theories previously mentioned advocating one type of valuation system for all accounts. These systems are illustrated in Appendix 1-A of this chapter. Inductive systems, because they are grounded in real-world phenomena, can realistically focus on only a small part of the relevant environment. In other words, inductive research tends to examine rather narrowly defined questions and problems. Again, the Watts and Zimmerman paper provides a representative example of the particularistic scope of inductive theory.

Many individuals (Nelson, for example) see global theorizing as reaching an impasse in accounting.[8] The *Statement of Accounting Theory and Theory Acceptance* of the American Accounting Association saw the conflict between global accounting theories as unresolvable at this particular time.[9] Caplan saw the future of accounting research as one in which inductive theory would become predominant because it could shed light on particular questions.[10] Nevertheless, there continue to be important advocates of normative approaches.[11] In fact, the distinction between deductive and inductive research is simply not as clear-cut as might be thought.

COMPLEMENTARY NATURE OF DEDUCTIVE AND INDUCTIVE METHODS

The deductive–inductive distinction, while a good concept for teaching purposes, often does not apply as research is actually practiced. Far from being either/or competitive approaches, deduction and induction are complementary in nature and are often used together.[12] Hakansson, for example, suggests that the inductive method can be used to assess the appropriateness of the set of originally selected premises in a primarily deductive system.[13] Obviously, changing the premises can change the logically derived conclusions. The research process itself does not always follow a precisely laid out pattern. Individuals often work backwards from the conclusions of other studies by developing new hypotheses that appear to fit the data. They then attempt to test the new hypotheses.

An excellent example of the complementary nature of deductive and inductive reasoning is provided by the greatest detective created in all literature, Sherlock Holmes, renowned for his extraordinary powers of deductive reasoning. An interesting specimen of Holmes's approach involved Silver Blaze, a famous race horse that mysteriously disappeared when its trainer was murdered. One element of the case is that the watchdog did not bark when the horse disappeared. Dr. Watson, Holmes's somewhat slow-witted sidekick, saw nothing unusual about the dog not barking. Holmes,

[8]Nelson (1973, p. 16).
[9]AAA (1977).
[10]Caplan (1972, pp. 437–443).
[11]See Hakansson (1969).
[12]See Carnap (1951, pp. 199–202) and Rudner (1966, p. 66).
[13]Hakansson (1969, p. 37).

however, immediately deduced that the horse was taken from the stable by someone from the household rather than by an outsider. Thus, his list of suspects was immediately narrowed.

Holmes was also keenly aware of induction: he practiced a systematic observation of elements that would increase his knowledge and perceptions. His studies included extensive classification of such diverse items as cigar ashes, the influence of various trades upon the form of the hand, and the uses of plaster of Paris for preserving hand and footprints. Thus, the vast knowledge that Holmes was able to draw upon from these and other studies added considerable depth to his deductive abilities.

In a not dissimilar fashion in accounting, inductive research can help to shed light on relationships and phenomena existing in the business environment. This research, in turn, can be useful in the policy-making process in which deductive reasoning helps to determine prescribed rules. Hence, it should be clear that inductive and deductive methods can be used together and are not mutually exclusive approaches.

THE ROLE OF MEASUREMENT

As research progresses in accounting, it has also brought up a concern for measurement theory. Although there is a link between theory formulation and measurement, they are separate problems. Larson has stated this relationship well:

> First, there is a conceptual category of problems involving the isolation and precise definition of the properties that will be measured. Second, there is a separate category of methodological problems involving the determination of appropriate measurement procedures to be employed in assigning numbers to represent those properties.
>
> Evaluating the explanatory significance of the numbers which ensue from any measurement process depends on having resolved the problems of both categories . . . if the two types of problems are confused with each other and treated as being essentially one, it is likely that one or the other of the problem areas will go generally unresolved.[14]

Measurement is defined as the assignment of numbers to the attributes or properties of objects being measured, which is exactly what accountants do. Objects themselves have numerous attributes or properties. Assume a manufacturing firm owns a lathe. The lathe has properties such as length, width, height, and weight. If we eliminate purely physical attributes (because accounting measures are made in dollars), there are still several possibilities. These would include historical cost, replacement cost of the lathe

---

[14]Larson (1969, p. 44).

in its present condition, selling price of the lathe in its present condition, and present value of the future cash flows that the lathe will help to generate.

Attributes or properties are particular characteristics of objects. It should be clear that we do not measure objects themselves but rather something that might be termed the dollar "numerosity" or "how-much-ness" that relates to a particular attribute of the object.

DIRECT AND INDIRECT MEASUREMENTS

If the number assigned to an object is an actual measurement of the desired property, it would be called a direct measurement. This does not necessarily mean that it is accurate, though. An indirect measurement is one that must use roundabout means for measuring the desired attribute. For example, a "blue book" price for a lathe of the same type and condition would be a direct measure of its selling price. However, an attempt to arrive at the lathe's selling price, in the absence of a blue book, by using the weighted average of the ten most recent selling prices, would constitute an indirect measure. Direct measures are usually preferable to indirect ones.

ASSESSMENT AND PREDICTION MEASURES

Another way of categorizing measurements is to classify them as assessment or prediction measurements. Assessment measures are concerned with particular attributes of objects. They can be either direct or indirect. Prediction measures, on the other hand, are concerned with factors that may be indicative of conditions at a future point in time.[15] Hence, there is a functional relationship between the predictor (prediction measure) and the future condition. For example, income of a present period might be used as a predictor of dividends of the following period. Cost of ending inventory would be an example of an assessment measure.

THE MEASUREMENT PROCESS

Several elements are brought together in the measurement process. Even when dealing with a direct assessment measure, there is no guarantee that there is one absolutely correct measure. A simple measure of this type, such as a count of cash, depends on several factors:

1. The object itself.
2. The attribute being measured.
3. The measurer.

---

[15]Chambers does not believe that prediction measures should fall within the scope of measurement theory. Chambers (1968, p. 246).

4. Counting or enumerating operations.
5. Instruments available for the measuring task.
6. Constraints affecting the measurer.

Objects themselves and their attributes differ vastly in type and complexity. How much cash does a small retail firm have? What is the size of the grape harvest in the Napa Valley during the current year? How many inches of topsoil did Iowa lose in 1983? The measurers themselves might have different qualifications. An ambitious junior accountant and a clerk who is somewhat shaky in arithmetic and not overly concerned about the job could bring markedly different talents to a measuring task. Counting and enumerating operations vary from simple arithmetic in a cash count to statistical sampling in inventory valuation. Instruments used by the measurer would include everything from a large computer installation to a hand calculator to nothing more than pencil and paper. The most obvious type of constraint would be that of time. Hence it is clear that even a direct assessment measure is not as simple a matter as might first be thought.

TYPES OF MEASUREMENTS

This category is concerned with the relationship between the measuring system itself and the attributes of the objects being measured.[16] The simplest type of measuring system is the nominal scale. A *nominal* scale is nothing more than a simple classification system, a system of names. Assume that all the students at a university come from Massachusetts, Connecticut, or Rhode Island. If we wish to classify students by state, a 1 might be assigned to Massachusetts students, a 2 to those from Connecticut, and a 3 to Rhode Islanders. In this example, the numbering system serves no other purpose than the state classification. The same purpose could be carried out by a different number assignment for the state of origination—as long as the assignment of numbers to students is done consistently in accordance with the new nominal scale. A chart of accounts provides a good example of nominal classification in accounting.

Next in the order of measurement rigor is the ordinal scale. Numerals assigned in *ordinal* rankings indicate an order of preference. However, the degree of preference between ranks is not necessarily the same. Assume that three candidates are running for office. A voter's ranking might be Abel first, Baker second, and Charles third. However, the voter may see a virtual toss-up between Abel and Baker, either of whom is vastly preferable to Charles. Ordinal measurement is used to determine liquidity in the balance sheet.

The interval scale goes one step beyond the ordinal scale. Unlike ordinal rankings, the change in the attribute must be equal between assigned

---

[16]Excellent coverage of this topic is given by Mattessich (1964, pp. 57–74).

numbers in *interval* scales. The Fahrenheit temperature scale is an example. The increase in warmth from 9° to 10° is the same as that from 19° to 20° or any other increase in temperature of 1°.

The ratio scale has one additional feature beyond the interval scale. In the *ratio* scale, the zero point must have a unique quality. It does *not* in the Fahrenheit scale. Therefore, we cannot say that 8° is twice as warm as 4°. Furthermore, 8° divided by 4° is not "equal" to 16° divided by 8°.

Accounting has at least the potentiality for a ratio scale type of measurement because the zero point implies nothingness in terms of dollar amounts. In contrast, the zero point on a Fahrenheit thermometer does not imply absence of temperature. Thus, in accounting, both $100,000 of current assets divided by $50,000 of current liabilities and $200,000 of current assets divided by $100,000 of current liabilities indicate the property of $2 of current assets for each $1 of current liabilities. This is possible only because of the uniqueness of the zero point in accounting.

QUALITY OF MEASUREMENTS

In attempting to analyze the worth of a measure, several qualities might be considered. Since measurers and their skills, tools, and measuring techniques are so important, we might consider agreement among measurers, in the statistical sense, as one criterion. Ijiri and Jaedicke view **objectivity** as the degree of consensus among measurers in situations where a given group of measurers having similar instruments and constraints measure the same attribute of a given object.[17] Objectivity is then defined as

$$V = \frac{1}{n} \sum_{i=1}^{n} (x_i - \bar{x})^2 \tag{1.1}$$

where

n = the number of measurers in the group;

x_i = measurement of the ith measurer;

$\bar{x}$ = mean of all x_i for all measurers involved.

In Equation (1.1), Ijiri and Jaedicke have used the statistical measure of variance as a means of quantifying the degree of agreement among measurers. The closer each x_i is to $\bar{x}$, the more objective is the measure and the smaller will be V. A comparison among competing measures in terms of

---

[17]Ijiri and Jaedicke (1966). *Objectivity*, prior to the Ijiri and Jaedicke paper, referred to the quality of evidence underlying a measurement. In the statistical sense developed by Ijiri and Jaedicke, the word *verifiability* has tended to supplant *objectivity*.

objectivity could thus be made by comparing the *V*s in controlled experiments.[18]

In the case of prediction measures, an obvious criterion is how well the task of prediction is accomplished. Assume that users of accounting data for a particular firm presume that dividends are equal to 50 percent of the income of the preceding period. This can be stated as

$$D_{j2} = f(.50I_{j1}) \tag{1.2}$$

where

$$D_{j2} = \text{dividends of firm } j \text{ for period 2;}$$

$$I_{j1} = \text{income of firm } j \text{ for period 1.}$$

Very often the predictor—the right-hand term in Equation (1.2)—cannot be known because users are diverse and make predictions in vastly different ways. In these cases, how well prediction is accomplished cannot be quantified. Where it can be, a measure of predictive ability—called **bias** by Ijiri and Jaedicke—can be determined by the following equation:

$$B = (\bar{x} - x^*)^2 \tag{1.3}$$

where

x^* = the value the predictor should have been, given the actual value of what was predicted and the predictive model—such as (1.2)—of users.

While (1.3) is a less operational measure than (1.1), it is, nevertheless, an interesting conception for both theory formulation and policy-making purposes.[19]

Two other qualities that are pertinent to both assessment and prediction measures are timeliness and the cost constraint.[20] In terms of financial accounting, timeliness means that financial statement data—which are aggregations of many measurements—should be up to date and ready for quarterly announcements of earnings (forms 10-K and 10-Q requirements of the SEC,) as well as for annual published financial statement purposes. Oftentimes the need for information on a timely basis may conflict with the cost constraint problem.

It is easy to lose sight of the fact that data are costly to produce. Many costs are fixed in the form of computer information systems and accounting staffs. Nevertheless, more "precise" or "accurate" measurements, as well as

---

[18]Objectivity tests have been applied by McDonald (1968) and Sterling and Radosevich (1969). Both studies used standard deviation of alternate measurements rather than the variance of Equation (1.1).

[19]Ijiri and Jaedicke (1966, p. 481) combine the objectivity and bias measures into one formula. Objectivity and bias together add up to the relevance of the measure (R = V + B).

[20]McDonald (1967, pp. 676–677).

more timely measures, involve additional resources. Timeliness and costliness must be borne in mind in the policy-setting process if not in the theory formulation area.

We will be referring again to problems of measurement throughout this text. However, one observation must immediately be made. Many of the measurements made in traditional financial accounting are of neither the assessment nor the prediction variety. Historical cost depreciation and LIFO inventory valuations are numbers which admittedly do not represent any real attributes. Whether or not these are really "measurements" is not the primary issue. The important question is whether or not measurements made by totally arbitrary methods have utility for users.

IS ACCOUNTING AN ART OR A SCIENCE?

In looking at both the rule-making structure of accounting and its practice, a question that occasionally arises is whether accounting is an art or a science. At least one early look at this question (in the 1940s) perceived it to be a science.[21] However, that author did not really set up criteria for defining a science, except his own particular prejudices in terms of valuation issues. A slightly later effort saw accounting as very closely related to the liberal arts.[22] Accounting itself was seen as a "practical art." But that author did not present any real criteria for distinguishing between an art and a science. Certainly we can see that to discuss accounting along with scientific method and the role of measurement theory relative to accounting indicates the potential of classifying accounting within the scientific domain.

In an important article and a follow-up book, Sterling has attempted to specify more clearly the position of accounting relative to science.[23] Subjects that are classified as arts rely heavily on the personal interpretations of practitioners. For example, one painter might represent a model as having three eyes whereas another painter might use the conventional two eyes—and a green nose—to represent the same subject. In a science, however, there should be a relatively high amount of agreement among practitioners in regard to the phenomena being observed and measured (notice the relationship of Sterling's definition of a science to the concept of measurement).

Sterling believes that accounting, as presently practiced, is far closer to an art than a science—owing to the way we define our problems. In the case

---

[21]Kelley (1948).
[22]Cullather (1959).
[23]Sterling (1975 and 1979).

of depreciation, for example, in our measurements (if that is even the appropriate word) a great deal of latitude is allowed in terms of selecting a depreciation method as well as deciding on an estimated number of years of life and a salvage value. The result is a low degree of objectivity, as well as the fact that no real attribute of the asset or the related expense measurement can result except for the vague terms "unamortized historical cost" and "depreciation expense." A science, on the other hand, would strive to institute rigorous measurement procedures resulting in economically meaningful attributes, such as replacement cost or net realizable value of the asset or other elements being measured. The intention would be to provide information useful for either predictive or assessment purposes, whereas this is clearly not the case under our presently existing rules.

Whether rigidly specified measurement procedures can be instituted to bring about a high degree of consensus among measurers in accounting is, of course, an extremely important question. However, it must not be supposed that scientists always come up with uniform measurements or interpretations of what they are measuring. Two examples from other disciplines should help to clarify this point.

One of the principal functions of econometricians (literally economic measurers) is predicting gross national product and related variables, such as the percentage of unemployment. There are several large models that have been constructed to attempt to predict these variables. The models employ hundreds of simultaneous equations that must be solved by computer to generate the predictions. However, there has been considerable disagreement among the models and they are often far from accurate when the actual results are tabulated. A further complicating factor is that the predictions interact with the results because many large corporations, as well as the federal government, use the services of econometric forecasters which, of course, influences their actions. Nevertheless, the term "economic science" has been used to describe what econometricians do, though some individuals may dispute the characterization.

Going further afield, human anthropology is concerned with the study of ancient people and their forebears. In the mid-1970s, an unprecedented discovery of an almost complete female skeleton was made in a remote desert in Ethiopia. This particular species has been named Australopithecus Afarensis (the skeleton itself is affectionately and unscientifically known as "Lucy" because its discoverers jubilantly played "Lucy in the Sky with Diamonds" and other Beatles songs after the discovery was made).

The skeleton has been subjected to many scientific measurements, including carbon dating which puts Lucy's age at approximately 3,500,000 years. In addition, careful scrutiny of the structure of the leg and thigh bones indicates that the creature walked upright like humans rather than with the shambling gait of members of the ape family.

Nevertheless, a huge controversy surrounds Australopithecus Afarensis. Some anthropologists, particularly its discoverers, maintain that this species is a true ancestor of the line that eventually became humankind.

Other anthropologists, though, are of the opinion that the species is not a true progenitor of humans. It should be noted that the arguments surrounding the species' place are largely deductive in nature. The answer may never be known for certain unless more evidence is forthcoming. However, no one would dispute that human anthropology is a science. Despite the indeterminacy of the outcome, the measurement techniques are carefully specified though they are often applied in new and ingenious ways.

These two examples demonstrate that science is not always exact and scientists are not always in agreement over the results of their work. Bearing this in mind, we can say, along with Sterling, that accounting has the potential to move closer to the scientific realm, an outcome that should be pleasing to all involved. It must be remembered, though, that accounting is largely concerned with the human element, which is less controllable than the physical phenomena measured in the natural sciences. Consequently, accounting, along with economics and other social sciences, cannot be expected to be as precise in its measurements and predictions as the natural sciences.[24]

ACCOUNTING RESEARCH DIRECTIONS

The approaches discussed below represent particular orientations or directions of accounting research. They represent a significant advance over what passed as "research" a mere generation ago.

DECISION MODEL APPROACH

The decision model approach asks what information is needed for making decisions. Financial statements based on entry values, exit values, and discounted cash flows all qualify as useful possibilities (see Appendix 1-A). This approach does not ask what information users want but rather concentrates on what information is useful for particular decisions. Thus, its orientation is normative. A premise underlying this research is that decision makers must be taught how to use this information if they are unfamiliar with it. Sterling advocates the exit-value approach in terms of its decision usefulness because selling price of assets is relevant to the decision of keeping or disposing.[25] Also, aggregated exit values of all assets provide a measure of total liquidity available to the firm.

---

[24]See Stamp (1981) for an extended discussion of this point.
[25]See Sterling (1979, p. 89 and pp. 95–124).

CAPITAL MARKET RESEARCH

A significant amount of research has shown that prices of publicly traded securities react rapidly and in an unbiased manner to new information. Hence market prices are assumed to reflect fully all publicly available information. This proposition, which stems principally from the discipline of finance, is known as the efficient markets hypothesis. It has some potentially significant implications for accounting. As a result of information being rapidly impounded into security prices, there has been an impetus toward increased disclosure with less concern for choice among accounting alternatives, for example.[26] Since the efficient markets hypothesis states that return of a security is equated with its risk, other research has attempted to assess the relationship between accounting-based measures of risk (financial statement ratios, for example) and market-based risk measures.[27] The effect of accounting policy choices on security prices has also been extensively tested.

BEHAVIORAL RESEARCH

Another important area of investigation involves behavioral research. The main concern here is how users of accounting information make decisions and what information they need. Notice that this approach is descriptive whereas the decision model approach is normative. Much of this research attempts to use laboratory subjects, such as students, in carefully controlled experimental situations. McIntyre, for example, attempted to ascertain whether replacement cost information is more useful than historical cost information in evaluating actual annual rate of return.[28] His subjects were graduate and undergraduate students. Some subjects received replacement cost financial statements, others received historical cost statements, and still others received both. The companies examined were four middle-sized firms in the tire and rubber industry, analyzed over a three-year period. The subjects were asked to select the firm that would produce the highest actual annual rate of return during the three years. Actual annual rate of return was defined as

$$r = \frac{1}{n}\left(\frac{\Delta M + D}{M}\right) \tag{1.4}$$

where

n = length of the assumed holding period in years;

D = dividends received during the holding period;

---

[26]See Beaver (1973).

[27]For example, see Beaver, Kettler, and Scholes (1968); and Bildersee (1975).

[28]McIntyre (1973). For an extended critique of McIntyre's research design see Dyckman (1975).

M = market value of the stock at the beginning of the holding period;

ΔM = change in the market value of the stock during the holding period.

While there were considerable qualifications, McIntyre's findings failed to show any advantage to users of replacement cost financial statements. The question might be raised as to how representative McIntyre's student subjects are relative to the broad population of real decision makers. This problem pervades virtually all behavioral research employing student subjects in laboratory experiments.

AGENCY THEORY

A promising new direction of research is called **agency theory.** The corporation is the locus or intersection point for many contractual-type relationships which exist among various parties such as management, owners, creditors, and government. Agency theory is concerned with the various costs of monitoring and enforcing relations among these various groups.[29] The audit, for example, can be viewed as an instrument for ensuring that the firm's financial statements have been subject to a certain amount of scrutiny from the standpoint of internal control. In addition, the statements themselves—presuming an unqualified opinion—are assumed to meet the criterion of being in accordance with generally accepted accounting principles. The audit, therefore, attempts to give assurances to outsiders, such as owners and creditors, about the governance of the enterprise by management. Many agency relationships between parties are defined or governed by accounting numbers. These include bond covenants which prescribe the maximum level of ratios such as debt to equity, management compensation contracts where bonuses are based on income, and income taxes. As a result, choice among accounting methods by firms may be influenced by their effect on agency costs.

One hypothesis of agency theory is that management attempts to maximize its own welfare by minimizing the various agency costs. Notice that this is not quite the same as saying that management attempts to maximize the value of the firm. As in the Watts and Zimmerman study discussed previously, managers would presumably select that accounting alternative which maximizes the measurement of income if their own compensation is tied to reported income, provided they perceive that no adverse political effects such as antitrust action would result.

Agency theory studies may be deductive or inductive in nature. It should also be noted that agency theory is a special example of behavioral research, though its roots lie in finance and economics rather than in psychology and sociology.

---

[29]See Watts (1977) for more on agency relationships and the role of audited financial statements in an unregulated economy.

INFORMATION ECONOMICS

Finally, accountants are becoming increasingly conscious of the cost of producing accounting information. This has led to a relatively new field of inquiry for accounting researchers: information economics. With the exception of cash flow accounting, alternatives to the historical cost accounting model would, prima facie, appear to impose additional information production costs upon firms. Whether the benefits of alternative information sets or larger information sets are worth their costs is an important question. The nature of this problem has been succinctly stated by Beaver and Demski:

> . . . . the crux of the argument on behalf of accrual accounting rests on the premise that (1) reported income under accrual accounting conveys more information than a less ambitious cash flow-oriented accounting system would, (2) accrual accounting is the most efficient way to convey this additional information, and, as a corollary, (3) the "value" of such additional information system exceeds its "cost."[30]

This brief summary by no means covers all directions of financial accounting research. While some approaches may be more promising than others, we believe that all approaches are capable of contributing to our knowledge and providing important insights for the policy process.[31] A similar view has also been expressed by Sterling and by May and Sundem.[32] Many of these approaches will be discussed throughout the text.

SUMMARY

The main concern of this chapter is with the relation between accounting theory and accounting policymaking. The former is an input, though certainly not the only one, to the latter. Accounting theory may be descriptive or normative, depending largely on whether inductive or deductive approaches are used. Accounting policymaking, however, must be normative since it is concerned with prescribing choices among accounting methods and requiring particular disclosures.

Closely related to accounting theory is measurement. Accounting theory is ultimately concerned with what information is needed by users

[30]Beaver and Demski (1979, p. 43).

[31]This view is apparently shared by the FASB. At a recent FASB meeting (September 26, 1980), the Board stated it was going to employ all available research methodologies to evaluate the usefulness of Statement of Financial Accounting Standards No. 33 (SFAS 33) disclosures (accounting for changing prices). The Board indicated that the various approaches it planned to use include both security–price studies and behavioral studies. FASB made it quite clear that no approach to accounting research would be excluded in evaluating SFAS 33.

[32]Sterling (1979, p. 53) and May and Sundem (1976).

whereas measurement is involved with what is being measured and how it is being measured. As a result, there are often trade-offs between objectivity and the usefulness of the numbers being generated by the measurement process. Costliness and timeliness of the information are other important considerations underlying the measurement process.

Accounting research has taken many directions. These include the decision model approach, capital market research, behavioral research, agency theory, and information economics. The viewpoint adopted here is that all these approaches are potentially valuable in terms of adding to our knowledge about accounting and its environment.

Finally (in Appendix 1-A), the principal valuation approaches to accounting are briefly illustrated and discussed. These include historical costs, general price level, exit and entry value models of current value accounting, and discounted cash flows. These valuation approaches are examples of global types of models that have been developed in accounting.

APPENDIX 1-A: VALUATION SYSTEMS

Much of the debate in accounting today centers on the issue of valuation of accounts appearing in the balance sheet and income statement. We believe that many other theoretical issues should precede any attempt to come to grips with the valuation question. However, a basic familiarity with valuation systems enriches the preceding theoretical discussion in this chapter.

Consequently, an extremely simple example will be used as a vehicle for illustrating five valuation systems that have been extensively discussed in the literature. Simplicity is seen as a means for crystallizing the assumptions and workings of the valuation methods while holding aside, for the moment, many difficult problems which will surface later. The main aspects of each system will be discussed and critiqued here.

THE SIMPLE COMPANY

1. Simple Company was formed on December 30, 1984, by stockholders who invested a total of $90,000 in cash.
2. The owners operate the company and receive no salary for their services.
3. On December 31, 1984, the owners acquired for $90,000 cash a machine that provides a service which customers pay for in cash.
4. The machine has a life of three years with no salvage value.
5. All services provided by this machine occur on the last day of the year.
6. No other assets are needed to run the business nor are there any other expenses aside from depreciation.

7. Dividends declared equal income for the year.
8. The remaining cash is kept in a checking account that does not earn interest.
9. The general price index stands at 100 on December 31, 1984. It goes up to 105 on January 1, 1986, and 110 on January 1, 1987.
10. Budgeted revenues and actual revenues are the same. They are $33,000 for 1985; $36,302 for 1986; and $39,931 for 1987.
11. Replacement cost for a new asset of the same type increases to $96,000 on January 1, 1986; and $105,000 on January 1, 1987.
12. Net realizable value of the asset is $58,000 on December 31, 1985; and $31,000 on December 31, 1986. It has no value on December 31, 1987.
13. Simple Company is dissolved on December 31, 1987. All cash is distributed among the owners.
14. There are no income taxes.

The balance sheet for Simple Company after acquiring its fixed asset is shown in Exhibit 1-2.

EXHIBIT 1-2.

SIMPLE COMPANY
Balance Sheet
December 31, 1984

Fixed Assets	$90,000	Capital Stock	$90,000

VALUATION APPROACHES TO ACCOUNTING FOR THE SIMPLE COMPANY

Historical Cost

Historical cost has been the accepted orthodoxy in published financial statements throughout the financial history of the United States. The severe inflation in this country, as well as in many other nations of the industrial and third worlds, has led to an extensive search for a viable alternative to either replace historical costing or serve as a supplement to it.

In a period of rising prices, attributes measured under historical costing generally have limited relevance to economic reality. The major exception to this is accounts that are either receivable or payable in cash during the short run, such as accounts receivable and payable, as well as cash itself.

The presumed saving graces of historical costing are the suppositions that valuation systems are both more objectively determinable and better understood than are competing valuation systems. However, the objectivity issue is by no means to be taken for granted. Even in our simple example, sum-of-the-years'-digits or fixed-percentage-of-declining-balance depreciation (among other methods) might have been selected. Further differences could arise from the estimated depreciable life and salvage value factors. Understandability of historical costing is largely a function of familiarity. Introduction of new valuation methods obviously requires an attempt to familiarize users with their underlying assumptions and limitations.

Historical costing has also been defended on the grounds of being more suitable as a means for distributing income among capital providers, officers and employees, and taxation agencies because it is not based on hypothetical opportunity cost figures. Hence, the presumption is that there would be less conflict among competing groups over the distribution of income. However, this argument is by no means conclusive. As with the depreciation case, there can easily be dispute over methods selected for income measurement. Furthermore, opportunity cost valuations may be "hypothetical" in one sense but they are surely far more indicative of economic valuation than are historical costs.

Income statements and balance sheets under historical costing are summarized in Exhibit 1-3.

EXHIBIT 1-3.

SIMPLE COMPANY
Income Statements
Historical Costs

	1985	1986	1987	Total
Revenues	$33,000	$36,302	$39,931	$109,233
Depreciation	30,000	30,000	30,000	90,000
Net Income	$ 3,000	$ 6,302	$ 9,931	$ 19,233

Balance Sheet
December 31, 1985

Cash	$30,000		
Fixed asset (net)	60,000	Capital Stock	$90,000
Total Assets	$90,000	Total Equities	$90,000

Balance Sheet
December 31, 1986

Cash	$60,000		
Fixed asset (net)	30,000	Capital Stock	$90,000
Total Assets	$90,000	Total Equities	$90,000

General Price Level Adjustment

Historical cost financial statements combine dollars that were expended or received at different dates. For example, a balance sheet on December 31, 1984, would add together cash that is on hand at that date with the unamortized cost of a building that was acquired, say, in 1960. It is, of course, very well known that a 1960 dollar had considerably greater purchasing power than a 1984 dollar. Consequently, there is a very serious additivity problem under historical costing because dollars of different purchasing power are added to or subtracted from each other. The additivity issue is an aspect of measurement theory.

One possible response to this problem is general price level adjustment. This term refers to the purchasing power of the monetary unit relative to all goods and services in the economy. Obviously measurement of this phenomenon is a considerable task. Adjustment is accomplished by transforming historical cost dollars by an index such as the Consumer Price Index compiled by the Department of Labor. This index is not really broad enough, as its name implies, to be a true general price index but it has been advocated as a meaningful substitute.

Except for monetary assets and liabilities—all items receivable or payable in a specific and unalterable number of dollars as well as cash itself—all amounts in the financial statements will be restated in terms of the general purchasing power of the dollar at a given date, either as of the financial statement date itself or the average purchasing power of the dollar during the current year.

Assume that land was purchased on January 1, 1970, for $50,000 when the general price index stood at 120. On December 31, 1984—the balance sheet date—the general price index stands at 240. The transformation to bring forward the historical cost is accomplished in the following manner:

$$\$50,000 \times \frac{240}{120} = \$100,000 \tag{1.5}$$

Since it takes twice as many dollars to buy the same general group of goods and services in 1984 as in 1970, the general price-level adjusted cost of the land is, likewise, twice the historical cost.

Adjustments of this type are seen as restoring the additivity of the dollar amounts on the 1984 statements. However, one very important point must be stressed. In no way should it be construed that the $100,000 figure represents the "value" of the land on December 31, 1984. It is merely the bringing forward or adjusting of the historical cost of the land so that it is expressed in terms that are consistent with the purchasing power of 1984 dollars. Consequently, some individuals see it as a natural extension of the historical cost approach rather than being a separate valuation system.

Income statements and balance sheets using general price-level adjustments are shown in Exhibit 1-4. Calculations for general price-level ad-

---

EXHIBIT 1-4.

SIMPLE COMPANY
Income Statements
General Price-Level Adjustment

	1985	1986	1987	Total
Revenues	$33,000	$36,302	$39,931	$109,233
Depreciation	30,000	31,500[a]	33,000[b]	94,500
Operating Income	3,000	4,802	6,931	14,733
Purchasing Power Loss	—	1,500[c]	3,000[d]	4,500
Net Income	$ 3,000	$ 3,302	$ 3,931	$ 10,233

Balance Sheet
December 31, 1985

Cash	$30,000		
Fixed Asset (net)	60,000	Capital Stock	$90,000
Total Assets	$90,000	Total Equities	$90,000

Balance Sheet
December 31, 1986

Cash	$63,000		
Fixed Asset (net)	31,500	Capital Stock	$94,500[e]
Total Assets	$94,500	Total Equities	$94,500

---

[a] $\$30,000 \times \dfrac{105}{100} = \$31,500$

[b] $\$30,000 \times \dfrac{110}{100} = \$33,000$

[c] $(\$30,000 \times \dfrac{105}{100}) - \$30,000 = \$1,500$

[d] $(\$63,000 \times \dfrac{110}{105}) - \$63,000 = \$3,000$

[e] $(\$90,000 \times \dfrac{105}{100}) = \$94,500$

justed depreciation are shown in footnotes below the income statements. Purchasing power loss on monetary items is an element that arises during inflation where holdings of monetary assets exceed monetary liabilities. Calculation of the purchasing power loss is very similar to the adjustment of depreciation. In the Simple Company case, the cash holding prior to the price-level change is multiplied by a fraction consisting of the general price-level index *after* change in the numerator divided by the general price-level index in the denominator *before* change.

While a purchasing power loss is very real, it is totally different from other losses and expenses. The latter represent actual diminutions in the firm's assets of either an unproductive or productive nature. Purchasing power losses do not result in a decrease in monetary assets themselves but rather in a decline in their purchasing power when the general price-level index increases. Consistent with the "will-o-the-wisp" nature of the loss, if an entry were booked it would take the following form:

Purchasing Power Loss	XXX	
Retained Earnings		XXX

The direct effect in the accounts is thus nil even though a very real type of loss has occurred. Calculations for purchasing power losses on monetary assets are shown below the income statements in Exhibit 1-4.

Current Value Systems

Current value, as the name implies, refers to approaches that try to assign numbers to financial statement components that correspond to some existing attribute of the elements being measured. There are two valuation systems that fall into the current value category: exit value (also called "net realizable value") and replacement cost (also called "entry value"). As we shall see, entirely different purposes and philosophy underlie each system.

Exit Valuation. This approach is primarily oriented toward the balance sheet. Assets are valued at the net realizable amounts that the enterprise would expect to obtain from them if they were disposed of in the normal course of operations rather than in a bona fide liquidation. Hence, the method is frequently referred to as a process of "orderly liquidation." Liabilities would be similarly valued at the amounts it would take to pay them off as of the statement date.

The income statement for the period would be equal to the change in the net realizable value of the firm's net assets occurring during the period, excluding the effect of capital transactions. Expenses for elements such as depreciation represent the decline in net realizable value of fixed assets during the period.

Proponents of exit-value accounting see this type of system providing relevant information because the balance sheet becomes a huge statement of net liquidity available to the enterprise in the ordinary course of operations. It thus portrays the firm's "adaptability," or ability to shift its presently existing resources into new opportunities.

A point in the system's favor is that all of the measurements are additive because valuations are at the same time point for the balance sheet (and for the same period of time on the income statement) and consist of the same attribute being measured.

The principal criticism of exit valuation concerns the same question of relevance: how useful are net realizable value measurements for fixed assets if the firm intends to keep and utilize the great bulk of them during the foreseeable future for revenue production purposes.

Exit-value income statements and balance sheets are shown in Exhibit 1-5. As noted above, depreciation amounts represent the decline in net realizable value of the fixed asset occurring during each period.

EXHIBIT 1-5.

SIMPLE COMPANY
Income Statements
Exit Valuation

	1985	1986	1987	Total
Revenues	$33,000	$36,302	$39,931	$109,233
Depreciation	32,000	27,000	31,000	90,000
Net Income	1,000	9,302	8,931	19,233

Balance Sheet
December 31, 1985

Cash	$32,000		
Fixed Asset (net)	58,000	Capital Stock	$90,000
Total Assets	$90,000		$90,000

Balance Sheet
December 31, 1986

Cash	$59,000		
Fixed Asset (net)	31,000	Capital Stock	$90,000
Total Assets	$90,000		$90,000

Replacement Cost or Entry Value. As the name implies, this system uses current replacement cost valuations in the financial statements. Replacement cost and exit values are both current market values. Replacement cost will usually be higher for two reasons. Firstly, selling an asset which a firm does not ordinarily market usually results in a lower price than a regular dealer would be able to obtain. A good example is provided by the automobile market. If an individual buys a new car and immediately decides to sell it, he usually cannot recover full cost because of limited access to the buying side of the market. Secondly, "tearing out" and other disposal costs are deducted from selling price in determining net realizable values. Hence, the two different markets can result in significantly different current values.

Replacement cost is ideally measured where market values are available for similar assets. This is often the case for acquired merchandise inventories and stocks of raw materials that will be used in the production process. However, market values are often unavailable for unique fixed assets such as land, buildings, and heavy equipment that are specially designed for a particular firm. The same is true even for used fixed assets that are not unique, although second-hand markets often exist for these assets. These same considerations of measurement difficulty, however, also apply to exit valuation.

In the absence of firm market prices, replacement cost can be estimated by either appraisal or specific index adjustment. Cost constraints may inhibit the wider usage of appraisals. Specific indexes are applicable to particular segments of the economy such as machinery and equipment used in the steel industry, for example. Indexes are essentially averages and if calculated for too wide a segment of the economy, they may not be good representations of replacement cost.

The principal argument that is used to justify replacement cost over exit values is that if the great majority of the firm's assets were not already owned, it would be economically justifiable to acquire them. On the other hand, fixed assets are sold mainly when they become obsolete or their output is no longer needed.

It should be pointed out that there are some significant differences within the replacement cost school. The main one concerns the disposition of holding gains and losses. These are the designations for the differences between replacement cost of assets and their historical costs. The point at issue is whether these elements should be run through income or closed directly to capital. This problem will be discussed in Chapter 11.

Finally, replacement cost can be combined with general price-level adjustment in order to accomplish a more complete analysis of inflationary effects upon the firm. Coverage of this issue will likewise occur in Chapter 11.

Replacement cost income statements and balance sheets appear in Exhibit 1-6. When replacement costs changed, depreciation was calculated by taking one-third of the new cost. Current value depreciation is a much more complex phenomenon to measure in practice. The holding gain adjustment on the balance sheet offsets the excess depreciation above historical cost.

Discounted Cash Flows

Only the discounted cash flow approach, of the systems discussed, is a purely theoretical method with virtually no operable practicability on a statement-wide basis. In this system, valuation of assets is a function of discounted cash flows and income is measured by the change in the present value of cash flows arising from operations during the period. Thus, both asset valuation and income measurement are anchored to future expectations.

In the example, the internal rate of return of the asset is found by discounting the future cash flows at that rate which will make them just equal the cost of the asset (10% in this case). Thereafter, income is equal to 10% of the beginning of period asset valuation and depreciation is "plugged" to

---

EXHIBIT 1-6.

SIMPLE COMPANY
Income Statements
Replacement Cost

	1985	1986	1987	Total
Revenues	$33,000	$36,302	$39,931	$109,233
Depreciation	30,000	32,000	35,000	97,000
Net Income	$ 3,000	$ 4,302	$ 4,931	$ 12,233

Balance Sheet
December 31, 1985

Cash	$30,000		
Fixed Asset (net)	60,000	Capital Stock	$90,000
	$90,000		$90,000

Balance Sheet
December 31, 1986

Cash	$62,000		
Fixed Asset (net)	32,000	Capital Stock	$90,000
		Holding Gain Adjustment	4,000
Total Assets	$94,000	Total Equities	$94,000

---

bring about this result. Income is also equal to the change in the present value of the cash flows measured at the beginning and end of the period.

In a real situation, the method would be virtually impossible to apply because many assets contribute jointly to the production of cash flows, so individual asset valuation could not be determined. Also, the future orientation of asset valuation and income determination leads to very formidable estimation problems which would undoubtedly lead to low objectivity in terms of the degree of consensus among measurers.

Because of the insuperable measurement problems, the discounted cash flow approach can be implemented only for a very restricted group of assets and liabilities: those where interest and principal payments are directly stipulated or can be imputed. For other assets, a substitute approach has been advocated, whereby assets of the firm would be valued in terms of those attributes assumed to approximate most closely their discounted cash flow in terms of their expected usage.[33] A mixed bag of discounted cash flows, net realizable values, and replacement costs results.

Income statements and balance sheets are shown in Exhibit 1-7.

---

[33]For more detail, see Staubus (1967).

EXHIBIT 1-7.

SIMPLE COMPANY
Income Statements
Discounted Cash Flows

	1985	1986	1987	Total
Revenues	$33,000	$36,302	$39,931	$109,233
Depreciation	24,000	29,702	36,298	90,000
Net Income (10% of beginning-of-period asset value	9,000	6,600	3,630	19,230
Beginning-of-period Asset Value	$90,000	$66,000	$36,298	

Present Value of Cash Flows
December 31, 1984

$39,931 × .7513	$30,000	
36,302 × .8264	30,000	
33,000 × .9091	30,000	$90,000

December 31, 1985

$39,931 × .8264	$32,999		$ 9,000
36,302 × .9091	33,002		
33,001 × 1	33,000	$99,000[a]	

December 31, 1986

$39,931 × .9091	$36,301		$ 6,603
36,302 × 1	36,302		
33,000 × 1	33,000	$105,603	

December 31, 1987

$39,931 × 1	$39,931		$ 3,630
36,302 × 1	36,302		
33,000 × 1	33,000	$109,233	

Balance Sheet
December 31, 1985

Cash	$24,000	Capital Stock	$90,000
Fixed Asset (net)	66,000	Total Equities	$90,000
Total Assets	$90,000		

EXHIBIT 1-7. *(continued)*

Balance Sheet
December 31, 1986

Cash	$53,700		Capital Stock	$90,000
Fixed Asset (net)	36,300		Total Equities	$90,000
Total Assets	$90,000			

---

a$1 rounding error

QUESTIONS

1. Do you think that the work of a policymaking organization such as FASB or the SEC is normative (value judgment oriented) or positive (oriented toward value-free rules)? Discuss.

2. An individual who was appraising accounting education had the following premises (assumptions):
   (a) Accounting professors used to do more consulting with accounting practitioners than they do today.
   (b) Accounting professors have become more interested in research that is abstract and not practical than used to be the case.
   He therefore concluded that accounting students are not as well prepared to enter the accounting profession as they used to be. What kind of reasoning was the individual using? What is your assessment of his conclusion? Discuss in depth.

3. In 1936 the country was still suffering from the Great Depression. During the presidential election campaign, a polling organization took an extensive survey of voter attitudes to find out whether the public preferred the incumbent, Franklin Delano Roosevelt, or the challenger, Alf Landon. The sample was gathered randomly from telephone book listings throughout the country. A preference was found for Alf Landon. However, Roosevelt won re-election by a huge landslide. What type of research was being conducted? Why do you think it failed to make an accurate prediction?

4. Do you think that deductive reasoning, in general, is normative in nature? In accounting, deductive approaches to accounting are generally normative. Why do you think this is the case?

5. It is often held that inductive reasoning is value free because it is simply investigating empirical evidence. Yet the charge has been raised that it is not value free. What do you think is the basis for this charge?

6. Several years ago an author stated that corporate income could be scientifically ascertained. He felt that it could be, but any type of inflation adjustment would be pure folly because measurements would tend to become very subjective. Do you agree with the author's appraisal? Comment in detail.

7. Of the four disciplines in the following list, which do you think qualify as sciences and which do not? State your reasons very carefully.

    Law
    Medicine
    Cosmetology
    Accountancy

8. In reference to the preceding question, several occupations *within* two of the above named disciplines are listed below. Which do you think come closest to the role of being "scientists" and which do not?

    Accounting researcher
    Chief accountant for an industrial firm
    Medical researcher
    General practitioner doctor

9. A great deal of interest is generated each week during the college football and college basketball seasons by the ratings of the teams by the Associated Press and United Press International. Sports writers or coaches are polled on what they believe are the top ten teams in the country. Weightings are assigned (ten points for each first place vote, nine for each second place vote, ... one for each tenth place vote) and the results are tabulated. The results appear as a weekly listing of the top twenty teams in the nation. Do you think that these polls are engaged in the process of measurement? Discuss.

10. Accounting practitioners have criticized some proposed accounting standards on the grounds that they would be difficult to implement because of measurement problems. They therefore concluded that the underlying theory was inappropriate. Assuming that they are correct about the implementational difficulties, would you agree with their thinking? Discuss.

11. Some individuals believe that valuation methods proposed by a standard-setting body such as FASB should be based on those measurement procedures having the highest degree of objectivity as defined by Equation (1.1). Thus some assets might be valued on the basis of replacement cost and others on net realizable value. Do you see any problems with this proposal? Discuss.

12. What type of measurement scale (nominal, ordinal, interval, or ratio) is being used in the following situations?

    Musical scales
    Insurance risk classes for automobile insurance
    Numbering of pages in a book
    A grocery scale
    A grocery scale deliberately set ten pounds too high
    Assignment of students to advisors, based on major

13. Why, in practical terms, is it impossible to separate deductive and inductive approaches to theoretical reasoning?
14. What are the elements of accounting theory and how do they differ from each other?
15. What is the relationship among scientific method, accounting research, and accounting policymaking?

CASES AND PROBLEMS

1. Assume that three accountants have been selected to measure the income of a firm under two different income measurement systems. The results for the first income system (M_1) were incomes of $3,000, $2,600, and $2,200. Under the second system (M_2), results were $5,000, $4,000, and $3,000. Assume that users of accounting data believe that dividends of a year are equal to 75% of income determined by M_1 for the previous year. Users also believe that dividends of a year are equal to 60% of income determined by M_2 for the previous year. Actual dividends for the year following the income measurements were $3,000. Determine the objectivity and bias of each of the two measurement systems for the year under consideration. On the basis of your examination, which of the two systems would you prefer?

2. J & J Enterprises is formed on December 31, 1982. At that point it buys one asset costing $2,487. The asset has a three-year life with no salvage value and is expected to generate cash flows of $1,000 on December 31 in the years 1983, 1984, and 1985. Actual results are exactly the same as plan. Depreciation is the firm's only expense. All income is to be distributed as dividends on the three dates mentioned. Other information:
   • The price index stands at 100 on December 31, 1982. It goes up to 104 and 108 on January 1, 1984 and 1985.
   • Net realizable value of the asset on December 31 in the years 1983, 1984, and 1985 is $1,500, $600, and 0.
   • Replacement cost for a new asset of the same type is $2,700, $3,000, and $3,300 on the last day of the year in 1983, 1984, and 1985.

   Required: Income statements for the years 1983, 1984, and 1985 under
   Historical costing
   General price-level adjustment
   Exit valuation
   Replacement cost
   Discounted cash flows

BIBLIOGRAPHY OF REFERENCED WORKS

American Accounting Association (1972). "Report of the Committee on Research Methodology in Accounting," *Accounting Review Supplement*, pp. 399–520.

American Accounting Association (1977). *Statement on Accounting Theory and Theory Acceptance* (American Accounting Association).

Beaver, William (1973). "What Should Be the FASB's Objectives?", *Journal of Accountancy* (August 1973), pp. 49–56.

Beaver, William, and Joel Demski (1979). "The Nature of Income Measurement," *The Accounting Review* (January 1979), pp. 38–46.

Beaver, William; Paul Kettler; and Myron Scholes (1970). "The Association Between Market Determined and Accounting Determined Risk Measures," *The Accounting Review* (October 1970), pp. 654–682.

Bildersee, John (1975). "The Association Between a Market-Determined Measure of Risk and Alternative Measures of Risk," *The Accounting Review* (January 1975), pp. 81–98.

Blaug, Mark (1980). *The Methodology of Economics*, (Cambridge University Press).

Caplan, Edward (1972). "Accounting Research as an Information Source for Theory Construction," *Accounting Review Supplement*, pp. 437–444.

Carnap, Rudolf (1951). *The Nature and Application of Inductive Logic* (University of Chicago Press).

Chambers, Raymond J. (1968). "Measures and Values: A Reply to Professor Staubus," *The Accounting Review* (April 1968), pp. 239–247.

Christenson, Charles (1983). "The Methodology of Positive Accounting," *The Accounting Review* (January 1983), pp. 1–22.

Cullather, James (1959). "Accounting: Kin to the Humanities," *The Accounting Review* (October 1959), pp. 525–527.

Dyckman, Thomas R. (1975). "The Effects of Restating Price-Level Changes: A Comment," *The Accounting Review* (October 1975), pp. 796–808.

Eiseley, Loren (1962). *Francis Bacon and the Modern Dilemma* (University of Nebraska Press).

Hakansson, Nils (1969). "Normative Accounting Theory and the Theory of Decision," *International Journal of Accounting* (Spring 1969), pp. 33–48.

Hicks, John R. (1961). *Value and Capital*, 2nd ed. (Oxford University Press).

Ijiri, Yuji, and Robert Jaedicke (1966). "Reliability and Objectivity of Accounting Methods," *The Accounting Review* (July 1966), pp. 474–483.

Kelley, Arthur (1948). "Definitive Income Determinations: The Measurement of Corporate Income on an Objective Scientific Basis," *The Accounting Review* (April 1948), pp. 148–153.

Larson, Kermit (1969). "Implications of Measurement Theory on Accounting Concept Formulation," *The Accounting Review* (January 1969), pp. 38–47.

Mattessich, Richard (1964). *Accounting and Analytical Methods* (Richard D. Irwin).

May, Robert, and Gary Sundem (1976). "Research for Accounting Policy: An Overview," *The Accounting Review* (October 1976), pp. 747–763.

McDonald, Daniel (1967). "Feasibility Criteria for Accounting Measures," *The Accounting Review* (October 1967), pp. 662–679.

McDonald, Daniel (1968). "A Test Application of the Feasibility of Market Based

Measures in Accounting," *Journal of Accounting Research* (Spring 1969), pp. 38–49.

McIntyre, Edward (1973). "Current-Cost Financial Statements and Common-Stock Investment Decisions," *The Accounting Review* (July 1973), pp. 575-585.

Nelson, Carl (1973). "A Priori Research in Accounting," in *Accounting Research 1960–1970: A Critical Evaluation*, ed. N. Dopuch and L. Revsine (University of Illinois), pp. 3–19.

Paton, William A. (1922). *Accounting Theory* (Accounting Studies Press, Ltd., reprinted in 1962).

Rudner, Richard (1966). *Philosophy of Social Science* (Prentice-Hall).

Stamp, Edward (1981). "Why Can Accounting Not Become a Science Like Physics?" *Abacus* (Spring 1981), pp. 13–27.

Staubus, George (1967). "Current Cash Equivalent for Assets: A Dissent," *The Accounting Review* (October 1967), pp. 650–661.

Sterling, Robert R. (1975). "Toward a Science of Accounting," *Financial Analysts Journal* (September–October 1975), pp. 28–36.

Sterling, Robert R. (1979). *Toward a Science of Accounting* (Scholars Book Co.)

Sterling, Robert R., and Raymond Radosevich (1969). "A Valuation Experiment," *Journal of Accounting Research* (Spring 1969), pp. 90–95.

Tinker, Anthony; Barbara Merino; and Marilyn Neimark (1982). "The Normative Origins of Positive Theories: Ideology and Accounting Thought," *Accounting, Organizations and Society* 7 no. 2: 167–200.

Watts, Ross L. (1977). "Corporate Financial Statements, a Product of the Market and Political Processes," *Australian Journal of Management* (April 1977), pp. 33–75.

Watts, Ross L., and Jerold L. Zimmerman (1978). "Towards a Positive Theory of the Determination of Accounting Standards," *The Accounting Review* (January 1978), pp. 112–134.

Zimmerman, Jerold L. (1980). "Positive Research in Accounting," in *Perspectives on Research*, ed. R. Nair and T. Williams (University of Wisconsin), pp. 107–128.

ADDITIONAL READINGS

RESEARCH IN ACCOUNTING

Abdel-Khalik, A. Rashad (1983). "Accounting Research and Practice: Incompatible Twins?", *CA Magazine* (March 1983), pp. 28–34.

Mautz, Robert K., and Jack Gray (1970). "Some Thoughts on Research Needs in Accounting," *Journal of Accountancy* (September 1970), pp. 54–62.

Sterling, Robert R. (1973). "Accounting Research, Education, and Practice," *Journal of Accountancy* (September 1973), pp. 44–52.

Wolk, Harry I., and Roger Briggs (1975). "Accounting Research, Professors, and Practitioners: A Perspective," *International Journal of Accounting* (Spring 1975), pp. 47–56.

THEORY APPROACHES AND PROBLEMS

Abdel-Khalik, A. Rashad, and Bipin Ajinkya (1979). *Empirical Research in Accounting: A Methodological Viewpoint* (American Accounting Association).

American Accounting Association (1971). "Report of the Committee on Accounting Theory Construction and Verification," *Accounting Review Supplement*, pp. 31–80.

Buckley, John; Paul Kircher; and Russell Mathews (1968). "Methodology in Accounting Theory," *The Accounting Review* (April 1968), pp. 274–286.

Carlson, Marvin L., and James W. Lamb (1981). "Constructing a Theory of Accounting—An Axiomatic Approach," *The Accounting Review* (July 1981), pp. 554–573.

Devine, Carl (1960). "Research Methodology and Accounting Theory Formation," *The Accounting Review* (July 1960), pp. 387–399.

Gordon, Myron (1960). "Scope and Method of Theory and Research in the Measurement of Income and Wealth," *The Accounting Review* (October 1960), pp. 603–618.

Ijiri, Yuji (1971). "Logic and Sanctions in Accounting," in *Accounting in Perspective: Contributions to Accounting Thought by Other Disciplines*, ed. R. Sterling and W. Bentz (Southwestern Publishing Co.), pp. 3–28.

Mattessich, Richard (1972). "Methodological Preconditions and Problems of a General Theory of Accounting," *The Accounting Review* (July 1972), pp. 469–487.

Sterling, Robert R. (1970). "On Theory Construction and Verification," *The Accounting Review* (July 1970), pp. 444–457.

Watts, Ross L., and Jerold L. Zimmerman (1979). "The Demand for and Supply of Accounting Theories: The Market for Excuses," *The Accounting Review* (April 1979), pp. 273–305.

Williams, Thomas, and Charles Griffin (1969). "On the Nature of Empirical Verification in Accounting," *Abacus* (December 1969), pp. 143–178.

MEASUREMENT IN ACCOUNTING

American Accounting Association (1971). "Report of the Committee on Foundations of Accounting Measurements," *Accounting Review Supplement*, pp. 1–48.

American Accounting Association (1975). "Report of the Committee on Accounting Valuation Bases," *Accounting Review Supplement*, pp. 535–573.

Bierman, Harold (1963). "Measurement and Accounting," *The Accounting Review* (July 1963), pp. 501–507.

Chambers, Raymond J. (1965). "Measurement in Accounting," *Journal of Accounting Research* (Spring 1965), pp. 32–62.

Chambers, Raymond J. (1972). "Measurement in Current Accounting Practices: A Critique," *The Accounting Review* (July 1972), pp. 488–509.

Ijiri, Yuji (1967). *The Foundations of Accounting Measurement: A Mathematical, Economic, and Behavioral Inquiry* (Prentice-Hall).

Ijiri, Yuji (1972). "Measurement in Current Accounting Practices: A Reply," *The Accounting Review* (July 1972), pp. 510–526.

Ijiri, Yuji (1975). "Theory of Accounting Measurement," *Studies in Accounting Research* #10 (American Accounting Association).

Jaedicke, Robert; Yuji Ijiri; and Oswald Nielsen, editors (1966). *Research in Accounting Measurement* (American Accounting Association).

Mock, Theodore (1976). "Measurement and Accounting Information Criteria," *Studies in Accounting Research* #13 (American Accounting Association).

Vickrey, Don (1970). "Is Accounting a Measurement Discipline," *The Accounting Review* (October 1970), pp. 731–742.

CHAPTER 2

Development of the Institutional Structure of Financial Accounting

In Chapter 1, we looked at the role of accounting theory relative to the standard-setting process. In this chapter, we examine the evolution of the policy-making process in the United States, from the first formal attempts to establish standards to the present day. The history of the accounting profession and the formal financial reporting function covers a longer period than is reviewed in this chapter. (For example, regulation of disclosure and the audit function in the United Kingdom is over one hundred years old.) The prime focus in this book, however, is on major events in the United States which have led to the present institutional arrangements for development of accounting standards.

Accounting in the United States prior to 1930 was largely unregulated. The accounting practices and procedures used by a firm were generally considered confidential. Thus, one firm had little knowledge about the procedures followed by other companies. Obviously, the result was a considerable lack of uniformity in accounting practices among companies from year to year, even within the same industry. The only real direction provided in accounting practices was established by bankers and other creditors because they were the primary users of financial reports. Bank and creditor pressure was aimed primarily at the disclosure of cash and near-cash resources that could be used for repayment of debt.

The emphasis on debt-paying ability can be traced back to the social and economic conditions existing in the United States. Prior to the end of World War I, the American public typically did not invest large sums in private corporations. This began to change rapidly in the 1920s. When the federal government made lump-sum payments for retirement of Liberty Bonds, the public suddenly had large amounts of available cash. Private corporations were expanding; and both they and government leaders encouraged the public to invest in American business. A "people's capitalism" concept took hold and the number of individual shareholder investors grew tremendously. Unfortunately, financial reporting development lagged behind investor needs, so reports continued to be prepared primarily for creditors.[1]

Not until the stock market crash of 1929 did shareholder investors begin to question whether accounting and reporting practices were adequate to assess investments. Financial reports were based on widely diversified accounting practices and frequently were misleading to current and prospective investors. This realization led to the first of three distinct time periods of great interest and productivity in the development of accounting standards.[2]

The three time periods will be examined carefully in this chapter:

The formative years, 1930–46.

The postwar period, 1946–59.

The modern period, 1959–present.

THE FORMATIVE YEARS, 1930–46

As a result of the stock market crash, 1930 to 1946 was the first period of great interest and productivity in the development of accounting standards. This period had a more significant influence on accounting practices in the United States than any other comparable period in our history. The first attempt to develop accounting standards was an agreement brought about by the joint efforts of the American Institute of Certified Public Accountants (AICPA) and the New York Stock Exchange (NYSE).

[1]Bedford (1970, pp. 69–70).
[2]Storey (1964, pp. 3–8).

NYSE/AICPA AGREEMENT

In 1930, the AICPA began a cooperative effort with the NYSE that eventually led to the preparation of one of the most important documents in the development of accounting rule making.[3] The AICPA's Special Committee on Co-operation with the Stock Exchange worked closely with the NYSE's Committee on Stock List to develop a document on accounting principles to be followed by all companies listed on the Exchange.

The situation that was of concern to the NYSE was the fact that listed companies were using a large variety of undisclosed accounting practices. Initially the AICPA thought that the best solution was a dual approach: (1) education of the users of accounting reports regarding limitation of the reports and (2) improvement of reports to make them more informative to users.

Ultimately the AICPA's Committee suggested the following general solution to the NYSE Committee:

> The more practical alternative would be to leave every corporation free to choose its own methods of accounting within . . . very broad limits. . . , but require disclosure of the methods employed and consistency in their application from year to year. . . .
>
> Within quite wide limits, it is relatively unimportant to the investor which precise rules or conventions are adopted by a corporation in reporting its earnings if he knows what method is being followed and is assured that it is followed consistently from year to year. . . .[4]

A formal draft of "five broad accounting principles" was prepared by the AICPA's Committee and approved by the NYSE's Committee on September 22, 1932. This document represented the first formal attempt to develop "generally accepted accounting principles." In fact, the AICPA's Committee coined the phrase "accepted principles of accounting." The first five principles were later incorporated as Chapter 1 of Accounting Research Bulletin (ARB) 43.

The joint effort of the NYSE and AICPA had a profound influence upon accounting policymaking in the United States during the next fifty years. Reed K. Storey described it this way:

> . . . The recommendations [all aspects of the original NYSE/AICPA document] were not fully implemented, but the basic concept which permitted each corporation to choose those methods and procedures which were most appropriate for its own financial statements within the basic framework of "accepted accounting principles" became the focal point of the development of principles in the United States.[5]

[3]Zeff (1972, p. 119).
[4]American Institute of Accountants (1934, p. 9).
[5]Storey (1964, p. 12).

FORMATION OF THE SECURITIES AND EXCHANGE COMMISSION (SEC)

The SEC was created by Congress in 1934. Its defined purpose was (and is) to administer the Securities Act of 1933 and the Securities and Exchange Act of 1934. The two acts were the first national securities legislation in the United States. The 1933 act regulates the issuance of securities in interstate markets, while the 1934 act is primarily concerned with the trading of securities. The 1933 and 1934 acts conferred on the SEC both broad and specific authority to prescribe the form and content of financial information filed with the SEC.

The SEC initially allowed the accounting profession to set accounting principles without interference. However, in statements made by the SEC in 1937 and 1938, it became evident that they were growing impatient with the profession. In December, 1937, SEC Commissioner Robert Healy addressed the American Accounting Association (AAA):

> It seems to me, that one great difficulty has been that there has been no body which had the authority to fix and maintain standards [of accounting]. I believe that such a body now exists in the Securities and Exchange Commission.[6]

Finally, on April 25, 1938, the message the SEC was sending the profession became quite clear. They issued Accounting Series Release (ASR) No. 4, which said

> In cases where financial statements filed with the Commission . . . are prepared in accordance with accounting principles for which there is no substantial authoritative support, such financial statements will be presumed to be misleading or inaccurate despite disclosures contained in the certificate of the accountant or in footnotes to the statements provided the matters are material. In cases where there is a difference of opinion between the Commission and the registrant as to the proper principles of accounting to be followed, disclosure will be accepted in lieu of correction of the financial statements themselves only if the points involved are such that there is substantial authoritative support for the practices followed by the registrant and the position of the Commission has not previously been expressed in rules, regulations, or other official releases of the Commission, including the published opinions of its chief accountant.[7]

The implicit message was that unless the profession established an authoritative body for the development of accounting standards, the SEC would determine acceptable accounting practices and mandate methods to be employed in reports filed with them.

---

[6]Healy (1938, p. 5).
[7]SEC (1938, p. 5).

COMMITTEE ON ACCOUNTING PROCEDURE, 1933–46

The AICPA had formed a Committee on Accounting Procedure (CAP) in 1933. The CAP had seven members. It was relatively inactive until 1938. However, in 1938, prompted primarily by the SEC's new policy embodied in ASR 4, the CAP was expanded to twenty-one members and became much more active.

The CAP originally wanted to develop a comprehensive statement of accounting principles that would serve as a general guide to the solution of specific practical problems. However, most felt it would take at least five years to develop such a statement and by that time the SEC undoubtedly would have lost its patience. Thus, the CAP decided to adopt a plan of attacking specific problems and recommend preferred methods of accounting whenever possible.[8]

The CAP, acting in response to ASR 4, began in 1939 to issue statements on accounting principles that, prima facie, had "substantial authoritative support." During the two-year period of 1938–39, twelve Accounting Research Bulletins (ARBs) were issued. The CAP was cognizant of the SEC looking over its shoulder and frequently consulted with the SEC to determine whether proposed ARBs would be acceptable to the Commission.[9]

The SEC was initially satisfied with the accounting profession's efforts to establish accounting principles. However, it had always let it be known that it was prepared to take over the rule-making process if the profession lagged. The following quotation from the Commission's 1939 report to Congress indicates their position clearly:

> One of the most important functions of the Commission is to maintain and improve the standards of accounting practices. . . . the independence of the public accountant must be preserved and strengthened and standards of thoroughness and accuracy protected. I [Chairman Jerome N. Frank] understand that certain groups in the profession [CAP] are moving ahead in good stride. They will get all the help we can give them so long as they conscientiously attempt that task. That's definite. But if we find that they are unwilling or unable . . . to do the job thoroughly, we won't hesitate to step in to the full extent of our statutory powers.[10]

Not all accounting constituents were happy with the development of accounting rules during this period. Members of the AAA favored a deductive approach to the formulation of accounting rules—as opposed to the predominantly informal inductive approach employed by the CAP. Regarding the first four ARBs, the editor of *The Accounting Review* wrote:

> It is unfortunate that the four pamphlets thus far published give no evidence of extensive research nor of well-reasoned conclusions. They reflect,

[8]Zeff (1972, pp. 135–137).
[9]Zeff (1972, p. 139).
[10]SEC (1939, p. 121).

on the other hand, a hasty marshaling of facts and opinions, and the derivation of temporizing rules to which it is doubtless hoped that a professional majority will subscribe. As models of approach in a field already heavily burdened with expedients and dogmatism, they leave much to be desired.[11]

This era did not produce a comprehensive set of accounting principles. However, two very important contributions were made. First, accounting practices, especially in terms of uniformity, improved significantly. Second, accounting policymaking in the United States was firmly established in the private sector.[12]

When World War II began, the development of accounting rules slowed down significantly. During the war years, the CAP dealt almost exclusively with accounting problems involving war transactions. Of the thirteen ARBs issued between January 1942 and September 1946, seven dealt with war-related problems and three with terminology.

THE POSTWAR PERIOD, 1946–59

The postwar period experienced an even greater economic boom than had the 1920s. Industry required massive amounts of capital in order to expand. The expansion, in turn, created more jobs and more money in the economy. At the encouragement of stock exchanges, industry began to actively tap available money from the public. In 1940 there were an estimated four million stockholders in the United States. By 1952 the number had grown to seven million and in 1962 it reached seventeen million.

A large portion of the American public had a direct financial interest in corporations. Corporate financial reports were an important source of information for financial decisions. Thus, financial reports and the accounting rules used to prepare them gained national attention.

For the first time, accounting policymaking became an important topic in the financial press. The primary problem was one of uniformity or comparability of reported earnings between different companies. Increasingly heavy pressure was brought on the accounting profession by the financial press and the SEC to eliminate different methods of accounting for similar transactions that significantly affected reported net income.

ARB 32 AND THE SEC

The CAP was busy during this time period. In total, eighteen ARBs were issued from 1946 to 1953. Although the Committee had been quite

[11]Kohler (1939, p. 319).
[12]Storey (1964, p. 5).

successful in eliminating many questionable accounting practices of the 1930s, this strategy resulted in a new set of problems during the late 1940s and early 1950s.

While eliminating suspect accounting practices, the CAP failed to make positive recommendations regarding general accounting principles. As a result, there was an oversupply of "good" accounting principles. Many alternative practices continued to flourish because there was no underlying accounting theory. This situation led to conflicts between the CAP and the SEC.

The most publicized conflict dealt with the all-inclusive income statement versus current operating performance. The CAP felt that utilizing current operating performance would enhance comparability of earnings reports between companies and between years for the same company. Any extraordinary gains and losses, they pointed out, are excluded from net income under the current operating performance concept. Consequently, ARB 32 was issued recommending the current operating performance concept. Upon issuance of ARB 32, the SEC chief accountant wrote:

> [The] Commission has authorized the staff to take exception to financial statements which appear to be misleading, even though they reflect the application of ARB 32.[13]

In 1950, the SEC proposed in an amendment to Regulation S-X the use of the all-inclusive concept. This proposal was in direct conflict with ARB 32. Subsequently, the CAP and the SEC reached a compromise agreement regarding the authority of ARB 32. Thus, the prominence of the CAP in the policy-making arena was maintained. However, it was very definitely subject to the oversight of the SEC.

THE PRICE-LEVEL PROBLEM

By the end of 1953 the accounting profession became increasingly concerned with accounting under conditions of changing price levels. The profession turned its attention almost entirely to this problem. As a result, for approximately three years, little if any progress was made regarding the development of accounting principles.

The main thrust of the price-level debate dealt with depreciation charges. Depreciation charges based on historical costs did not accurately measure the attrition of fixed-asset values in terms of current purchasing power. The result was an overstatement of reported net income. In general, the profession decided that to reflect changes in purchasing power would confuse users of financial statements. As a result, the price-level debate was put on the shelf for many years and attention was again directed to the development of standards of financial accounting.

---

[13]King (1947, p. 25).

THE CLOSING YEARS OF THE CAP

The years 1957 to 1959 represented a period of transition in the development of accounting standards in the United States. Criticism directed toward the CAP increased, and even pillars of the accounting establishment were critical of its operations. Finally, a president of the AICPA, Alvin R. Jennings, called for a new approach to the development of accounting principles.

Increasing Criticism

During the middle and late 1950s, the interest in accounting principles was growing both within and outside the profession. Unfortunately, much of this interest was negative criticism directed toward the CAP. Financial executives and accounting practitioners in the smaller firms complained that they were not given an adequate hearing to express their opinions on proposed ARBs. Many felt that the CAP worked too slowly on pressing issues and refused to take unpopular positions on controversial topics.

Leonard Spacek, the managing partner of Arthur Andersen & Co., shocked the accounting profession with these remarks:

> The partners of our firm believe that the public accounting profession is not in important respects carrying its public responsibility in the certification of financial statements at the present time. We believe that the profession's existence is in peril. Until the profession establishes within its framework (a) the premise of an accepted accounting principle, (b) the principles of accounting that meet those premises, and (c) a public forum through which such principles of accounting may be determined, our firm is dedicated to airing in public the major shortcomings of the profession.[14]

Spacek seemed to be calling for the profession to prepare a comprehensive statement of basic accounting principles. In this light, he was not alone. In 1957 the AAA had published a statement of underlying concepts and definitions.[15] The deductive approach was at least attempted in arriving at the results in this statement. From its very inception, the CAP had discarded a formalized deductive approach because it was too time consuming. In fact the Committee had devoted its time to solving specific problems by prescribing rules on a piecemeal approach—without developing fundamental principles of financial accounting, much less a comprehensive theory.

A New Approach

Alvin R. Jennings delivered a historic speech in 1957 at the AICPA's annual meeting. He suggested a reorganization of the AICPA to expedite

---

[14]Spacek (1969, p. 21).
[15]AAA (1957, pp. 1–12).

development of accounting principles. Jennings emphasized the need for research as part of this process. In other words, he called for a conceptual approach to replace the piecemeal method that had been followed for twenty years by the CAP.

The accounting profession was ready to consider Jenning's new approach. The AICPA set up a Special Committee on Research Program. The committee report was finished in less than a year. This report became the "articles of incorporation" for the Accounting Principles Board (APB) and the Accounting Research Division. The report emphasized the importance of research in establishing financial accounting standards:

> Adequate accounting research is necessary in all of the foregoing [establishing standards]. Pronouncements on accounting matters should be based on thorough-going independent study of the matters in question, during which consideration is given to all points of view. For this an adequate staff is necessary. . . . Research reports or studies should be carefully reasoned and fully documented. They should have wide exposure to both the profession and the public.[16]

The CAP was heavily criticized, perhaps deservedly so, but it represented the profession's first sustained attempt to develop workable financial accounting rules. A total of fifty-one ARBs had been issued during its existence. One of these, No. 43, represented a restatement and revision of the first 42 bulletins. Large parts of ARB 43 remain in force to this day. Throughout the CAP's life, ARBs began to be increasingly recognized as authoritative and had a pronounced effect on accounting practice.

THE MODERN PERIOD, 1959 TO THE PRESENT

The "charter" that brought the APB and the Accounting Research Division into existence called for a two-pronged approach to the development of accounting principles. The research division was to be semiautonomous. It had its own director who had authority to publish the findings of the research staff. The division was to be exclusively devoted to development of accounting principles and had no responsibilities to the technical committees of the AICPA. In establishing what research projects to undertake, the director of research had to confer with the chairman of the APB. If the two disagreed, the APB, as a whole, determined what projects the research division would undertake. Results of the projects of the research division would be published in the form of Accounting Research Studies (ARSs).

---

[16]AICPA (1958, pp. 62–63).

These studies would present detailed documentation, all aspects of particular problems, and recommendations or conclusions. At the outset, two projects were called for in the Special Committee's report: (1) the "basic postulates of accounting" and (2) a "fairly broad set of coordinated accounting principles" based on the postulates.

In form, the APB was very similar to the CAP. It had from eighteen to twenty-one members, all of whom were members of the AICPA. They represented large and small CPA firms, academe, and private industry. As an innovation, it was hoped that the APB's Opinions would be based on the studies of the research division. It required a two-thirds majority for the issuance of an opinion and disclaimers of dissenting members were to be published.

EARLY YEARS OF THE APB

The early years of the APB were characterized by failure and doubt. Research studies called for in the original charter were not accepted by the profession and the investment credit controversy resulted in a serious challenge to the Board's authority by large CPA firms.

ARSs 1 and 3

ARS 1, *The Basic Postulates of Accounting*, by Maurice Moonitz was published in 1961. This ARS did not initially result in much reaction, favorable or unfavorable, by either the APB or the profession generally. Apparently, everyone was awaiting the publication of the companion study on principles before passing judgment.

ARS 3, *A Tentative Set of Broad Accounting Principles for Business Enterprises*, by Robert Sprouse and Moonitz, appeared in April 1962. To say the least, this study provoked criticism from all areas. In fact, following the publishing of the text of the study, nine of the twelve members of the project advisory committees on the postulates and principles studies provided personal comments. Only one of the comments was positive. APB Statement 1 expressed the APB's views of the study. The statement said, in part:

> The Board believes, however, that while these studies [1 and 3] are a valuable contribution to accounting thinking, they are too radically different from present generally accepted accounting principles for acceptance at this time.[17]

By issuing that statement, the APB seriously weakened the two-pronged approach to development of accounting standards.

---

[17]APB (1962).

Investment Credit

Another problem occurred in 1962. In November of that year APB 2, which dealt with the investment tax credit, was issued. The profession as a whole was divided on how to account for the investment credit. Two alternatives existed: (1) recognizing the tax benefit in the year received, designated the "flow-through method," and (2) recognizing the tax benefit over the life of the related asset, called the "deferral method." The Board chose not to commission a research study on the subject and issued APB 2 which opted for the deferral method.

Almost immediately, three large CPA firms made it known that they would not require their clients to follow the opinion. Furthermore, in January 1963 the SEC issued ASR 96 which allowed registrants to employ either the flow-through or deferral methods. Obviously, these large CPA firms and the SEC had challenged the APB's authority. As a result, APB 4 was issued, which permitted the use of either method.

As a result of this successful challenge, the binding authority of APB opinions was questioned in the press for several years. Finally, in late 1964 the AICPA's Council (the organization's governing body) declared the authority of APB opinions in an Appendix to APB 6. They unanimously agreed that departures from APB opinions must be disclosed in financial statements audited by a member of the AICPA. If the independent accountant concludes that a method being employed has substantial authoritative support, even though not contained in a specific accounting principle, this support must be disclosed in footnotes or the auditor's report. Furthermore, the auditor must, if possible, disclose the effect of the departure. If the principle employed does not have substantial authoritative support, the auditor must qualify the opinion, give an adverse opinion, or disclaim the opinion.[18]

Thus as 1964 drew to a close the authoritative nature of APB opinions had been established. However, the two-pronged approach to the development of accounting principles had not been employed.

THE EMBATTLED APB

The years 1965 to 1967 saw further criticisms of the Board in the press. The period of "high profile" for the accounting profession had arrived. Diversity of accounting practices was discussed in *Barron's*, *Business Week*, *Dun's Review*, *Forbes*, *Fortune*, *The New York Times*, and the *Wall Street Journal*. Despite the public controversy, the APB was silently at work and compiled an impressive list of accomplishments.

[18]Although the term is not defined in APB 6, it has developed a meaning over the years which encompasses—in addition to pronouncements of rule-making bodies and the SEC—opinions of regulatory commissions provided they do not conflict with statements from other sources, recognized textbooks, leading CPAs, and practices that are commonly followed by business. See Grady (1965, p. 16).

During this period seven opinions were issued. Included in the list were at least three of noteworthy achievement. Accounting for the employer's cost of pension plans successfully utilized the desired approach embodied in the charter. In ARS 8, *Accounting for the Cost of Pension Plans,* by Ernest L. Hicks, the arguments for and against various accounting alternatives and the practical problems of each alternative were reviewed. Using the Research Study as a source document, APB 8 was issued. Not only did this effort represent the first real application of the two-pronged approach but it also resulted in unanimous approval by the Board.

APB 9 was also adopted unanimously by the Board. It embraced the areas of extraordinary items and earnings per share. This opinion eliminated widely diversified practices that had existed for handling extraordinary items. Also, the all-inclusive concept of the income statement was approved.

In another controversial area, income tax allocation, the dual approach was again employed. ARS 9, *Interperiod Allocation of Corporate Income Taxes,* by Homer Black, was used as a source of information in the deliberations of the Board. Although controversial, APB 11, which requires comprehensive income tax allocation, did significantly curtail alternative procedures in practice. Thus, by the close of 1967, the Board had finally demonstrated it could function in a meaningful manner.

ARS 7 and APB Statement 4

When the accounting profession failed to accept ARS 1 and ARS 3, another research study was commissioned. Its objectives were to discuss the basic concepts of accounting principles and summarize existing acceptable principles and practices. For this purpose, ARS 7, *Inventory of Generally Accepted Accounting Principles for Business Enterprises,* by Paul Grady was successful. Although the study was well received by the profession, it fell short of the original task assigned to the Board by the Special Committee on Research Program in 1958. Grady codified existing pronouncements (over fifty percent of the study was reproductions of pronouncements) and then tried to derive the profession's existing structure of principles. The study blended inductive and deductive approaches because it took the existing pronouncements and then attempted to deduce accounting principles from the body of accepted pronouncements.

Possibly because of the failure of the APB to accomplish their original task on accounting principles, another committee recommendation was made. The Special Committee of the Accounting Principles Board made several recommendations, some of which were that "at the earliest possible time" the Board should set forth the purposes and limitations of financial statements, determine acceptable accounting principles, and define "generally accepted accounting principles."[19]

[19]The CPA Letter (1965, p. 3).

To accomplish that task, a committee was established. The Committee worked for five years and, in 1970, the APB approved Statement 4, *Basic Concepts and Accounting Principles Underlying Financial Statements of Business Enterprises*. The statement had two purposes:

> (1) to provide a foundation for evaluating present accounting practices, for assisting in solving accounting problems, and for guiding the future development of financial accounting; and, (2) to enhance understanding of the purposes of financial accounting, the nature of the process and the forces which shape it, and the potential and limitations of financial statements in providing needed information.[20]

APB Statement 4 covered many of the same topics included in ARS 7, but it went beyond that study (as Chapter 5 will show). The statement had no authoritative position in the profession. Being an APB *statement*, as opposed to an *opinion*, "it is binding on no one for any purpose whatsoever."[21] Thus, the APB failed in its original charge to set forth the basic postulates and broad principles of accounting, at least in any binding and coherent manner.

Continuing Criticism

Criticism of the standard-setting process continued in two separate areas: (1) exposure for tentative APB opinions was too limited and occurred too late in the process and (2) the problems with business combinations showed the standard-setting process was too long and subject to too many outside pressures which were not appropriately channeled into the formulation process.

In response to considerable criticism of the exposure process, several important changes that have been carried forward to the Financial Accounting Standards Board (FASB) were initiated in the latter years of the APB. Public hearings were introduced in 1971. Discussion memorandums had circulated to interested parties several months prior to the drafting of proposed opinions. These memorandums discussed all aspects of the particular accounting problem and invited interested parties to send written comments as well as to voice their views at the public hearing. After the public hearing, outlines of the proposed opinion were distributed to interested parties for "mini-exposure" in order to determine initial reaction to the proposed opinion. Following that stage, an official exposure draft of the proposed opinion was given wide distribution throughout the profession and comments were requested. Ultimately the opinion required at least a two-thirds favorable vote to be issued. The broadened exposure process prior to issuance of an accounting standard allowed interested parties to be involved in the standard-setting process and tended to alleviate criticism, other than that of timeliness, of the APB.

[20]The CPA Letter (1970, p. 1).
[21]Moonitz (1974, p. 22).

The controversy over business combinations and goodwill was the most time-consuming and extensively discussed problem the APB faced. In 1963, ARS 5, *A Critical Study of Accounting for Business Combinations*, by Arthur Wyatt, was published while ARS 10, *Accounting for Goodwill*, by George Catlett and Norman Olson, appeared in the latter part of 1968. Both of these studies reached conclusions that were at variance with existing accounting principles. ARS 5 concluded that pooling of interests accounting should be discontinued and that goodwill may have two components—one with limited life requiring periodic amortization, the other with unlimited life to be carried forward indefinitely to future periods. ARS 10 concluded that goodwill does not qualify as an asset and should be immediately subtracted from stockholders' equity upon completion of the combination.

Business combinations and goodwill received more publicity and discussion than any other subject taken up by the APB. News publications such as *Time* and *Newsweek* had several articles on the subject. Three Congressional committees and the Federal Trade Commission, as well as the SEC, were concerned with the merger accounting problem.[22]

A brief review of the various drafts of the proposed opinion on business combinations and goodwill indicates the difficulty in establishing accounting principles on this subject. The initial draft opinion, in July 1969, proposed that pooling of interests be eliminated and goodwill be amortized over a period no longer than forty years. In February 1970, another draft opinion was issued, this one allowing pooling of interests when a 3-to-1 size test was met and also requiring amortization of goodwill over a maximum of forty years. The APB was unable to obtain a two-thirds majority on the draft. Finally, a two-thirds majority was obtained in June 1970, allowing pooling of interests with a 9-to-1 size test and goodwill amortization restricted to the forty-year maximum. When the APB met again in July, one member changed his vote. Thus the Board was again at an impasse. Finally the business combination and goodwill subjects were split into two opinions: APB 16, on business combinations, eliminating the size test for a pooling of interests, passed 12 to 6; APB 17, on goodwill, requiring amortization over a maximum of forty years, passed 13 to 5.

The extreme difficulty in arriving at definitive standards of accounting for business combinations and goodwill was certainly in part responsible for the decision to begin a comprehensive review of the procedures for establishing accounting principles. In April 1971 the AICPA formed two special study groups. One group, "The Study Group on Establishment of Accounting Principles," was chaired by Francis M. Wheat. Wheat was a former SEC commissioner and a long-time critic of the accounting profession. The other group, "The Study Group on the Objectives of Financial Statements," was chaired by Robert M. Trueblood. Trueblood was a prominent CPA and managing partner of Touche Ross & Co.

---

[22]Zeff (1972, p. 213).

Wheat and Trueblood Committee Reports

The Wheat Committee report was completed in March, 1972. It called for significant changes in the establishment of financial accounting standards. The report made the following recommendations:

1. The establishment of a Financial Accounting Foundation. This foundation would have nine trustees whose principal duties would be to appoint members of the FASB and raise funds for its operation.
2. The establishment of the FASB. The Board would have seven full-time members and would establish standards of financial reporting.
3. The establishment of the Financial Accounting Standards Advisory Council. This Council, with twenty members, would consult with the FASB for establishing priorities and task forces as well as reacting to proposed standards.[23]

The recommendations were accepted by the AICPA's Council in June 1972, so the FASB became a reality on July 1, 1973.

The Trueblood Study Group report was not completed until October 1973, after the formation of the FASB. The report identified several objectives of financial statements. However, the Study Group's report did not provide any suggestions regarding the implementation of its recommendations. It concluded with the following statement:

> The Study Group concludes that the objectives developed in this report can be looked upon as attainable in stages within a reasonable time. Selecting the appropriate course of action for gaining acceptance of these objectives is not within the purview of the Study Group. However, the Study Group urges that its conclusions be considered as an initial step in developing objectives important for the ongoing refinement and improvement of accounting standards and practices.[24]

The FASB has considered the Trueblood Study Group Report in its Conceptual Framework Project. Progress on this project will be reviewed in the next section.

THE CONTEMPORARY PERIOD

The charge to the newly formed FASB was different in one important respect from that given to the APB in 1959. Whereas the APB was to work toward standard setting with a two-pronged approach, the new FASB, although it had a research division, was to establish standards of financial accounting and reporting in the most efficient and complete manner possible. Thus, FASB was not required to stipulate the postulates and principles of accounting as an underlying framework. Perhaps a trade-off between "efficiency" and "completeness" was intended. Ironically, FASB statements are more thoroughly researched than prior standards of either the CAP or the APB. The FASB also launched the conceptual framework project, a ma-

---

[23] AICPA (1972, pp. 69–82).
[24] AICPA (1973, p. 66).

jor task which is attempting to provide a "constitution" for the standard-setting function.

FASB Mechanics of Operations

The structure of establishing financial accounting standards has been modified somewhat since the FASB's initial conception in 1973. The modifications were the result of recommendations made by the Structure Committee of the Financial Accounting Foundation (FAF) in 1977. The organizational structure and its relationship to its constituency is depicted in Exhibit 2-1.

EXHIBIT 2-1.
The Structure of the Board's Constituency Relationships

THE CONSTITUENCY

The FAF includes members of the six sponsoring organizations. These organizations are the AAA, AICPA, Financial Analysts Federation, Financial Executives Institute (FEI), National Association of Accountants (NAA), and Securities Industry Association. The responsibility of the FAF is to elect the Board of Trustees. The Board of Trustees has been expanded to accommodate up to two additional members at large from organizations not included in the six sponsoring organizations. To date, one such member has been elected, representing the banking industry. The Board of Trustees selects FASB members, funds the Board's activities, and performs the oversight role.

The FASB includes seven members, each serving a term of five years. A maximum of two terms can be served by any individual member. During their terms of office, the members of the Board must maintain complete independence. This not only applies to other employment arrangements (past, present, or future), but also to investments. "There must be no conflict, real or apparent, between the members' private interest and the public interest."[25] The background requirement of members of the Board is simply a knowledge of accounting, finance, and business; and a concern for the public interest. The appointment of a new member in March 1979 resulted for the first time in a Board that had a majority of its members with backgrounds primarily in areas other than public accounting.

The Financial Accounting Standards Advisory Council (FASAC) is instrumental in the establishment of financial accounting standards. It is also appointed by the Board of Trustees. The FASAC advises the FASB on its operating and project plans, agenda and priorities, and appointment of task forces as well as on all major technical issues.

The standard-setting procedure starts with the identification of a problem. A task force is then formed to explore all aspects of the problem. It produces a discussion memorandum which identifies all issues and possible solutions. The discusssion memorandum is widely circulated to interested parties. The FASB then convenes a public hearing where interested parties may make their views known to the Board. Subsequently, an exposure draft of the final standard is issued and written comments are requested. After consideration of written comments either another exposure draft is issued (if significant changes are deemed necessary) or a final vote is taken by the Board. A simple majority (four votes) is needed for a final standard to be issued.

Assessment of the FASB

The FASB experiment in standard setting is perhaps the last opportunity to establish financial accounting standards in the private sector. From its earliest beginnings, the SEC has allowed the accounting profession to set standards. However, the fact remains that the SEC has the legal authority

---

[25] AICPA (1972, p. 72).

to establish standards whenever it chooses. Both the CAP and the APB made important progress in eliminating bad accounting practices and in standardizing existing practices, but they were not successful in developing a theoretical basis for standard setting.

In the early years of the FASB's existence, criticism of its process was quite vocal. Some said it issued too many pronouncements, while others complained that not enough had been issued. Some critics said the Board was too conceptual in its approach, but others said it had ignored research and accounting theory. Furthermore, some felt the FASB did not have a significant effect on financial reporting, although others maintained that changes had been too radical.

With all this in mind, a comprehensive review of the Board was undertaken by the Structure Committee of the Board of Trustees of the FAF in late 1976. The basic charge of the committee was to "make recommendations to the Board of Trustees regarding any changes in the basic structure of the FASB and the FASAC."[26]

The report of the Committee included seventeen major findings. They found overwhelming support for maintaining the standard-setting process in the private sector and that the FASB was the right body to discharge that responsibility. Regarding the standard-setting process, the committee found

1. the process of establishing a new accounting standard requires careful consideration of the views of all elements of the constituency,
2. the process requires research to assess the possible effects of a proposed standard,
3. a successful standard cannot be imposed by the standard setter, it must be assimilated by the constituency,
4. the assimilation process may require an educational effort to demonstrate the overall value of the proposed new standard.[27]

As a result of the various findings of the Structure Committee, significant changes have occurred since 1977. Basically these changes have increased the involvement of the constituency. Meetings of the FASB, FASAC, the Foundation, task forces, and the Screening Committee on Emerging Problems are now open to the public. Additionally, the Board has begun publication of a weekly news bulletin called *Action Alert*. Furthermore, the Board has increasingly been utilizing available resources outside the FASB staff and making greater use of task forces. A result of the process has been that the Board is sensitive to the potential economic consequences of proposed standards prior to issuance.

To date FASB has been quite productive when compared with predecessor standard-setting bodies. It has issued over 70 Statements of Financial Accounting Standards as well as numerous interpretations and technical

[26]FAF (1977, p. 55).
[27]FAF (1977, p. 18).

bulletins. If a trend in philosophy can be derived from these standards, it would be that there is a move to "clean up the balance sheet." This has resulted in a more conservative balance sheet with immediate, as opposed to delayed, recognition of events on the income statement.

In June 1974 the Board issued a discussion memorandum entitled *Conceptual Framework for Accounting and Reporting: Consideration of the Report of the Study Group on the Objectives of Financial Statements.* This discussion memorandum and subsequent public hearings were based primarily on the Trueblood Committee Report. As a result of the public hearings and written comments it was decided that the Board would issue a series of Statements of Financial Accounting Concepts. Statements in this series do not establish accounting standards but rather describe concepts that will underlie future financial accounting standards and practices and in due course serve as a basis for evaluating existing standards and practices. The four thus far issued have dealt with the objectives of financial reporting by business enterprises, qualitative characteristics of accounting information, elements of financial statements of business enterprises, and objectives of financial reporting by nonprofit organizations.

Congressional Investigations

Although a good case can be made that the standard-setting process is operating better than in the past, this view is not universally held. Two Congressional subcommittee reports were circulated in late 1976 and early 1977 that were highly critical of the accounting profession. Congressman John E. Moss was chairman of a subcommittee whose report was particularly critical of the diversity of existing generally accepted accounting principles. The report of the Senate subcommittee, chaired by Senator Lee Metcalf, was directed toward the institutional structure of financial accounting. The report was critical of the concentration of power by the FASB, SEC, AICPA, and the "Big Eight" CPA firms. In essence, the report called for government regulation of the entire profession. Following public hearings, the report was modified significantly to allow standard setting to remain in the private sector.

Many organizational changes have occurred because of these Congressional investigations. The principal purpose of these changes within the profession are to

1. strengthen the auditing process and the independence of auditors,
2. assure compliance with high standards of performance not only of individual CPAs but of CPA firms under an effective self-regulatory system,
3. assure greater participation by public representatives in the affairs of the profession,
4. establish distinctions between public and smaller nonpublic companies for purposes of applying technical standards,

---

[28] AICPA (1978, p. 15).

5. enhance the overall effectiveness of the profession in serving public needs.[28]

Furthermore, the SEC must now include a specific section on the accounting profession in their annual report to Congress. In general these reports have been complimentary to the profession in terms of standard setting and self-governance since the time of the Congressional investigation.

Finally, despite the allegation of undue influence over the FASB by the Big Eight public accounting firms, no concrete evidence has yet been presented that substantiates this position.[29] Brown's research did, however, show a similarity of responses by seven of the Big Eight firms to twelve discussion memorandums of the FASB appearing between October 1974 and December 1977.[30] Similarity of responses assuredly shows a general agreement on issues, but absolutely nothing more in terms of the possibility of collusive conduct. It is interesting to note that the resulting FASB statements appeared to be evenly split in terms of "closeness" between the attestors (Big Eight firms) and preparers of financial statements (as evidenced by corporate respondents and interest groups).[31]

Current Role of the AICPA

With the creation of the FASB, the AICPA created a senior technical committee to serve as its policy-setting body on financial accounting and reporting matters. This committee, Accounting Standards Executives Committee (AcSEC), issues two official pronouncements: (1) Statements of Position (SOP) and (2) Industry Accounting Guides (Guides). Generally SOPs and Guides deal with specialized, narrower subjects than FASB Statements. Neither the SOPs nor the Guides are considered mandatory accounting standards under the AICPA's Rule 203 of the Rules of Conduct, as are FASB Statements. The FASB has embarked on a program (see Statement of Financial Accounting Standards No. 32) to incorporate the majority of the SOPs and Guides in FASB statements. In addition to these pronouncements, AcSEC periodically prepares Issue Papers covering various accounting practice problems. These Issue Papers are forwarded to the FASB and frequently become the basis of a subject's being added to the Board's agenda.

Finally, the AICPA has exclusive authority in the private sector for promulgating auditing rules. The committee responsible for this task is the Auditing Standards Board. This board issues Statements on Auditing Standards. Rule 202 of the Rules of Conduct requires AICPA members to adhere to all applicable Statements on Auditing Standards in conducting audits.

---

[29]See Meyer (1974), Rockness and Nikolai (1977), and McEnroe and Nikolai (1983).
[30]Brown (1981, pp. 240–241).
[31]Brown (1981, p. 243). Brown noted (p. 241) that the FASB's position appeared to be closest to the Financial Analysts' Federation, a group representing user interests.

Current Role of the SEC

As mentioned earlier, the SEC is legally empowered to regulate accounting practices. It has, as a matter of policy, been supportive of private sector standard setting in general and the FASB in particular. In ASR 150, the SEC stated that financial statements based on accounting practices for which there is no substantial authoritative support will be presumed to be misleading. For the first time, accounting standards set in the private sector were formally recognized as having substantial authoritative support. Prior to ASR 150, this support was informal.

The SEC and FASB have had differences of opinion—as in the case of oil and gas accounting, which is examined in Chapter 14. In general, though, their relationship has been cordial and mutually beneficial. The primary differences in accounting standards promulgated by the two groups has been in the area of disclosures. The Annual Report filed with the SEC, form 10-K, as well as the 8-Q quarterly report, require significantly more disclosure of nonfinancial statement information than does the typical annual report to stockholders.

Other Groups

At least three professional associations other than the AICPA have an interest in the standard-setting process in the United States today: the AAA, the FEI, and the NAA.

The AAA has been concerned with accounting standards for many years. They sponsored several statements on accounting principles from 1936 to 1957. In 1966, a committee appointed two years earlier to develop an integrated statement on basic accounting theory published *A Statement of Basic Accounting Theory*. Parts of this statement subsequently appeared in APB Statement 4, which has become significant in the development of the FASB's Conceptual Framework project. An AAA Committee issued a report calling for a special commission to study the organizational structure of establishing accounting standards at about the same time the Wheat Committee was being formed. Due to the formation of the Wheat Committee, the AAA never formed the commission, but the initial Committee report reflects the AAA's obvious interest in the development of accounting standards. Today, the AAA sponsors various research studies on accounting problems. These studies, of which there have been eighteen to date, represent a significant contribution to the development of accounting theory. AAA subcommittees also respond to FASB exposure drafts.

The FEI formed a subsidiary, the Financial Executives Research Foundation, specifically to fund various research projects in accounting and related areas. Numerous projects have been published to date. Furthermore, FEI's technical committee on corporate reporting reviews all FASB discussion memorandums and exposure drafts and develops the official FEI position, which is communicated to FASB. They also frequently participate in FASB public hearings.

The NAA, since its formation in 1919, has always conducted research and published reports in the cost and managerial accounting area. Recently they have become more interested in external financial reporting and, as a consequence, formed a Committee on Accounting and Reporting Concepts. This Committee responds to various FASB projects.

Most countries in the English-speaking world have societies that are similar in nature to the AICPA. These societies—the Institute of Chartered Accountants in England and Wales, the Canadian Institute of Chartered Accountants, and the Institute of Chartered Accountants in Australia—issue accounting rules (similar to FASB standards) and publish research studies on all facets of financial accounting.

The International Accounting Standards Committee (IASC) was formed on June 29, 1973, as a result of an agreement between the leading accounting bodies of Australia, Canada, France, Germany, Japan, Mexico, the Netherlands, the United Kingdom and Ireland, and the United States. IASC activity is conducted by an eleven-member board made up of a member from each of the nine countries above and two additional representatives from member countries. They issue Statements of International Accounting Standards (SIAS). Although SIASs do not override local regulations, the hope is that local regulations will eventually conform to SIAS's, thus harmonizing accounting standards at the international level.

SUMMARY

A brief history of the three financial accounting policy-making bodies that have existed in the United States since 1930 has been the main subject matter of this chapter. Prior to that year, published accounting information in this country was unregulated.

As a result of cooperation between the AICPA and NYSE, work on drafting accounting principles was begun. A major impetus was, of course, the creation of the SEC because this body was given the power by Congress to prescribe accounting principles. As a result, the CAP was formed and the brunt of the policy-making function has remained in the private sector. The CAP in its life issued a total of 51 ARBs, the most famous being ARB 43. Toward the close of its life, the CAP was being increasingly criticized because its rules attempted to solve problems on a piecemeal basis without having a coherent, underlying theory.

The APB was conceived in a period of high optimism. Opinions were to be based upon in-depth research studies which, in turn, were to be grounded in a set of underlying postulates and principles: in other words, the deductive approach was to come into flower. Unfortunately, the rejection of ARS 3, the broad principles study, virtually put an end to the formalized deductive approach—despite the publication of the conservative ARS 7 which attempted to extract principles from existing rules.

Despite considerable progress on many fronts, the very shaky start of the APB combined with its own institutional weaknesses and the fumbling of the business combination issue signalled the demise of the APB.

The work of two important committees, one concerned with the organization of the new body and the other with the objectives of financial accounting, preceded the formation of the FASB. There was much greater independence by Board members and the organization itself was separate from the AICPA. The FASB appears to have weathered a great deal of criticism in its early years, including that stemming from two Congressional subcommittees. Whether the Conceptual Framework Project satisfies the long-felt need for a formalized theoretical underpinning of financial accounting, only time will tell.

QUESTIONS

1. How did the APB pave the way for the FASB?
2. In what ways does the FASB differ most markedly from its two predecessor organizations?
3. What is the weakness of the approach used by Grady in arriving at principles in ARS 7?
4. Do you think that the nonbinding status of FASB's statements of financial accounting concepts (like APB Statement 4 before it) is a good idea or not?
5. Discuss the significance of the SEC's ASR 150.
6. What has been the SEC's role in the evolution of the rule-making process? Why do you think it has generally not had a high profile?
7. What were the "politics" that led to the demise of both the CAP and the APB?
8. Do you think the conceptual framework project is important to the long-run success of the FASB?
9. Should constituents have input into FASB decisions, or should FASB neutrally and independently set standards?
10. Explain how the role and form of research used by the APB and FASB differ.
11. What is the importance of the FAF and FASAC to the success of the FASB?
12. The three attempts at standard setting in the private sector (CAP, APB, and FASB) have all dealt with the need for a theoretical foundation. Why were the CAP and the APB not successful at this endeavor?

13. Can any overall trend be detected in FASB pronouncements? Explain and cite examples to substantiate your opinion.
14. In terms of financial reporting in the future, do you expect greater refinement of measurements appearing in the body of the financial statements or increasing disclosure with less effort directed toward refinement of measurements?
15. Do you believe that financial reporting is better today than it was thirty years ago?

CASES AND PROBLEMS

1. A Look at the Committee on Accounting Procedure.

    During its long tenure, this group produced a total of 51 ARBs. While the CAP was in existence, another committee, the Committee on Terminology of the American Institute of Accountants (the previous name of the AICPA) prepared certain definitions. Assess their definitions of **assets** and **liabilities** (See Chapter 8 for the definitions). Do you see any problems relative to one committee preparing rules and another making definitions?

    Read Chapter 15 of ARB 43 on unamortized discount, issue cost, and redemption premium on bonds refunded. Why do you think this was an issue that concerned the Committee? What are the two acceptable alternatives for dealing with the costs at any issue? Why would the definition of assets be helpful in analyzing a situation of this type? Are there any other situations that might be somewhat analogous to the bond redemption situation?

2. Five so-called "broad principles of accounting" were prepared by the AICPA's Special Committee on Co-operation with the Stock Exchange and approved by the NYSE's Committee on Stock List in 1932. They were to be followed by all firms listed on the Exchange.

    Subsequently these principles (along with a sixth item) were codified as Chapter 1 of ARB 43 and are printed below.

    (a) Unrealized profit should not be credited to income account of the corporation either directly or indirectly, through the medium of charging against such unrealized profits amounts which would ordinarily fall to be charged against income account. Profit is deemed to be realized when a sale in the ordinary course of business is effected, unless the circumstances are such that the collection of the sale price is not reasonably assured. An exception to the general rule may be made in respect of inventories in industries (such as the packing-house industry) in which owing to the impossibility of determining costs it is a trade custom to take inventories at net selling prices, which may exceed cost.

(b) Capital surplus, however created, should not be used to relieve the income account of the current or future years of charges which would otherwise fall to be made thereagainst. This rule might be subject to the exception that where, upon reorganization, a reorganized company would be relieved of charges which would require to be made against income if the existing corporation were continued, it might be regarded as permissible to accomplish the same result without reorganization provided the facts were as fully revealed to and the action as formally approved by the shareholders as in reorganization.

(c) Earned surplus of a subsidiary company created prior to acquisition does not form a part of the consolidated earned surplus of the parent company and subsidiaries; nor can any dividend declared out of such surplus properly be credited to the income account of the parent company.

(d) While it is perhaps in some circumstances permissible to show stock of a corporation held in its own treasury as an asset, if adequately disclosed, the dividends on stock so held should not be treated as a credit to the income account of the company.

(e) Notes or accounts receivable due from officers, employees, or affiliated companies must be shown separately and not included under a general heading such as notes receivable or accounts receivable.

(f) If capital stock is issued nominally for the acquisition of property and it appears that at about the same time, and pursuant to a previous agreement or understanding, some portion of the stock so issued is donated to the corporation, it is not permissible to treat the par value of the stock nominally issued for the property as the cost of that property. If stock so donated is subsequently sold, it is not permissible to treat the proceeds as a credit to surplus of the corporation.

Listed below are two principles coming from ARS 7 as well as some additional comments. This study was done under the auspices of the APB and was published in 1965.

Principle B-1

In case there are two or more classes of stock, account for the equity capital invested for each and disclose the rights and preferences to dividends and to principal in liquidation.

Principle B-4

Retained earnings should represent the cumulative balance of periodic earnings less dividend distributions in cash, property or stock, plus or minus gains and losses of such magnitude as not to be properly included in periodic earnings. The entire amount may be presumed to be unrestricted as to dividend distributions unless restrictions are indicated in the financial statements.

This principle is closely parallel to the definition of earned surplus in *Accounting Terminology Bulletin No. 1*, paragraph 34, which follows:

> The balance of net profits, income, gains and losses of a corporation from the date of incorporation (or from the latest date when a deficit was eliminated in a quasi-reorganization) after deducting distributions therefrom to shareholders and transfers therefrom to capital stock or capital surplus accounts.

Terms such as "principles of accounting" have been frequently used since 1932. Describe what you think principles might be. Do any of the principles coming from ARB 43, Chapter 1 or ARS 7 qualify as principles as you have construed them? How similar are these two partial groups of principles?

BIBLIOGRAPHY OF REFERENCED WORKS

Accounting Principles Board (1962). "Statement by the Accounting Principles Board," *Statement No. 1* (Accounting Principles Board).

American Accounting Association (1957). *Accounting and Reporting Standards for Corporate Financial Statements and Preceding Statements and Supplements* (American Accounting Association).

American Institute of Accountants (1934). *Audits of Corporate Accounts* (American Institute of Accountants).

American Institute of Certified Public Accountants (1958). "Report of Council of the Special Committee on Research Programs," *Journal of Accountancy* (December 1958), pp. 62–68.

———— (1972). *Establishing Financial Accountants Standards: Report of the Study on Establishment of Accounting Principles* (American Institute of Certified Public Accountants).

———— (1973). *Objectives of Financial Statements: Report of the Study Group on the Objectives of Financial Statements* (American Institute of Certified Public Accountants).

———— (1978). *Report of Progress: the Institute Acts on Recommendations for Improvements in the Profession* (American Institute of Certified Public Accountants).

Bedford, Norton (1970). *The Future of Accounting in a Changing Society* (Stipes Publishing Co.).

Brown, Paul R. (1981). "A Descriptive Analysis of Select Input Bases of the Financial Accounting Standards Board," *Journal of Accounting Research* (Spring 1981), pp. 232–246.

The CPA Letter (1965). "Accounting Principles: Committee Identifies the Major Professional Considerations," *The CPA Letter* (June 1965), pp. 3–4.

——— (1970). "APB Approves Fundamental Statements," *The CPA Letter* (November 1970), p. 1.

Financial Accounting Foundation (1977). *The Structure of Establishing Financial Accounting Standards: Report of the Structure Committee, the Financial Accounting Foundation* (Financial Accounting Foundation).

Grady, Paul (1965). "Inventory of Generally Accepted Accounting Principles for Business Enterprises," *Accounting Research Study No. 7* (American Institute of Certified Public Accountants).

Healy, Robert E. (1938). "The Next Step in Accounting," *The Accounting Review* (March 1938), pp. 1–9.

King, Earle C. (1947). "SEC May Take Exception to Financial Statements Reflecting Application of Bulletin No. 32," letter to Carmen G. Glough dated December 11, 1947, *The Journal of Accountancy* (January 1948), p. 25.

Kohler, Eric L. (1939). "Theories and Practice," *The Accounting Review* (September 1939), pp. 316–321.

McEnroe, John E., and Loren A. Nikolai (1983). "Voting Patterns of Big Eight Representatives in Setting Accounting and Auditing Standards," *Journal of Business Research* (March 1983), pp. 77–89.

Meyer, Philip E. (1974). "The APB's Independence and Its Implications for the FASB," *Journal of Accounting Research* (Spring 1974), pp. 188–196.

Moonitz, Maurice (1974). "Obtaining Agreement on Standards in the Accounting Profession," *Studies in Accounting Research No. 8* (American Accounting Association).

Rockness, Howard O., and Loren A. Nikolai (1977). "An Assessment of APB Voting Patterns," *Journal of Accounting Research* (Spring 1977), pp. 154–167.

Securities and Exchange Commission (1938). "Administrative Policy on Financial Statements," *Accounting Series Release No. 4* (Securities and Exchange Commission).

——— (1939). *Fifth Annual Report Fiscal Year Ended June 30, 1939* (Government Printing Office).

Spacek, Leonard (1957). "Professional Accountants and Their Public Responsibility," in *A Search for Fairness in Financial Reporting to the Public* (Arthur Andersen & Co., 1969), pp. 17–26.

Storey, Reed K. (1964). *The Search for Accounting Principles—Today's Problems in Perspective* (American Institute of Certified Public Accountants).

Zeff, Stephen A. (1972). *Forging Accounting Principles in Five Countries* (Stipes Publishing Co.).

ADDITIONAL READINGS

HISTORY AND DEVELOPMENT OF REGULATION IN THE PRIVATE SECTOR

Burton, John C. (1973). "Some General and Specific Thoughts on the Accounting Environment," *Journal of Accountancy* (October 1973), pp. 40–46.

Carey, John L. (1969 and 1970). *The Rise of the Accounting Profession*, Vols. 1 and 2 (American Institute of Certified Public Accountants).

"History of the Accounting Procedure Committee—from the Final Report," *Journal of Accountancy* (November 1959), pp. 70–71.

Schuetze, Walter P. (1979). "The Early Days of the FASB," *World* (Peat, Marwick & Mitchell, Summer 1979), pp. 34–39.

Spacek, Leonard (1959). *Business Success Requires an Understanding of Unsolved Problems of Accounting and Financial Reporting* (Arthur Andersen & Co.).

Sprouse, Robert T., and Detley F. Vagts (1965). "The Accounting Principles Board and Differences and Inconsistencies in Accounting Practice: An Interim Appraisal," *Law and Contemporary Problems* (Autumn 1965), pp. 706–726.

Trueblood, Robert M. (1969). "Ten Years of the APB: One Practitioner's Appraisal," *Tempo* (Touche Ross, September 1969), pp. 4–8.

THE SECURITIES AND EXCHANGE COMMISSION

Blough, Carmen (1967). "Development of Accounting Principles in the United States," *Berkeley Symposium on the Foundations of Financial Accounting* (University of California), pp. 1–14.

Chatov, Robert (1975). *Corporate Financial Reporting* (The Free Press).

Pines, J. Arnold (1965). "The Securities and Exchange Commission and Accounting Principles," *Law and Contemporary Problems* (Autumn 1965), pp. 727-751.

Previts, Gary John (1978). "The SEC and Its Chief Accountants: Historical Impressions," *Journal of Accountancy* (August 1978), pp. 83–91.

Skousen, K. Fred (1982). *An Introduction to the SEC*, 3rd ed. (South-Western Publishing Co.).

VOTING PATTERNS AND POWER IN REGULATORY ORGANIZATIONS

Haring, J. R., Jr. (1979). "Accounting Rules and the 'Accounting Establishment'," *Journal of Business* (October 1979), pp. 507–519.

Newman, D. Paul (1981). "Coalition Formation in the APB and the FASB: Some Evidence on the Size Principle," *The Accounting Review* (October 1981), pp. 897–909.

———— (1981). "An Investigation of the Distribution of Power in the APB and FASB," *Journal of Accounting Research* (Spring 1981), pp. 247–262.

CHAPTER 3

The Regulation of Financial Reporting

Financial reporting has been regulated in the United States since the 1930s. Congress empowered the Securities and Exchange Commission (SEC) to regulate financial reporting. However, as noted in Chapter 2, the SEC has delegated a great deal of accounting policy-making power to the private sector; first to the American Institute of Certified Public Accountants (AICPA) which operated the Committee on Accounting Procedure and the Accounting Principles Board, and then to the Financial Accounting Standards Board (FASB). Oversight is maintained by the SEC, and the authority of the private sector to set accounting policy is derived from the SEC mandate.

Even though financial reporting is a regulated activity and is likely to continue as such, it is useful to evaluate the arguments both for and against formal regulation. Such an evaluation helps us understand the nature of accounting regulation and some of the consequences which flow from it. Remember that this chapter is presenting only a set of arguments, not facts. Arguments for unregulated markets are presented first, followed by arguments for regulated markets. At the conclusion of the first two sections, there is an assessment of the merits of the two arguments. Because regulation does exist and is likely to continue, we need to examine next the nature of regulatory decision making and its influence on parties affected by regulation. This examination aids in understanding how the regulatory process works. Finally, we look at an important concept in assessing the impact of accounting regulation—**economic consequences,** which will be extensively referred to in subsequent chapters.

UNREGULATED MARKETS FOR ACCOUNTING INFORMATION

A recent body of literature has considered the possibility that financial reporting need not be regulated. Several different arguments have been developed to support the case for unregulated markets. The arguments all relate to the incentives for a firm to report information about itself to owners and to the capital market in general. Agency theory is employed for the purpose of explaining why incentives exist for reliable and voluntary reporting to owners. Wider voluntary reporting to the capital market is attributed to competitiveness in the capital markets. Finally, it is argued that any information not reported voluntarily could be obtained through private contracting.

AGENCY THEORY

The economic theory of agency is used to predict and explain the behavior of parties involved with the firm. In law, an agent is a person employed to represent another person's interests. The economic theory of agency builds on the legal concept of agency. The firm itself is conceived of as a nexus (intersection) of agency relationships. Agency theory seeks to understand organizational behavior by examining how parties to agency relationships within the firm maximize their own utility.

One of the major agency relationships is between the management group and the owners of the firm. Managers are hired by the owners of a firm to administer the firm's activities, thus establishing an agency relationship. Goals of managers and owners may not be in perfect agreement. It is easy to see how the utility maximizing behavior of managers could be in conflict with ownership interests. Owners are interested in maximizing return on investment, while managers have a wider range of economic and psychological needs, which are satisfied by the employment contract. Because of this potential conflict, owners are motivated to contract with managers in such a way as to minimize conflict between the goals of the two groups. Costs are incurred in monitoring agency contracts with management; and these costs, it is argued, reduce managers' compensation. Therefore, managers have an incentive to keep the costs low by not being in conflict with owners.

Agency theory describes a conflict between owners and managers which is mitigated to some extent by routine financial reporting. Routine financial reporting is one means by which owners can monitor employment contracts with their managers. Accountants refer to this traditional type of reporting as stewardship, or accountability to the owners of the firm. Agency theory has also been used to explain the demand for audits. The auditor functions in the role of a policeman or independent verifier of financial reports submitted by managers to owners.[1] The historical development of both financial reporting and auditing supports the agency theory argument.[2]

In order to minimize agency monitoring costs, there is an economic incentive for managers to report accounting results reliably to the ownership.[3] The incentive exists because managers are judged and rewarded, at least in part, by how well they report. The reputation of a manager will be enhanced by good reporting; and a good reputation should result in higher compensation because agency monitoring costs are minimized if owners perceive the accounting reports are more reliable. Agency theory applied in this way is also an example of positive theory because it seeks to explain why managers choose the reporting policies they do.

COMPETITIVE CAPITAL MARKETS

Agency theory provides a framework for analyzing financial reporting incentives between managers and owners.[4] An argument can also be made that firms would have an incentive to report voluntarily to the capital market, even if there were no mandatory reporting requirements: firms compete with one another for scarce risk capital, and voluntary disclosure is necessary in order to compete successfully in the market for risk capital. The ability of the firm to raise capital will be improved if the firm has a good reputation for financial reporting. In addition, it is argued that good reporting would also lower a firm's cost of capital because there is less uncertainty about firms that report more extensively and reliably: therefore there is less investment risk and a lower required rate of return.

There would be incentives to prepare a prospectus voluntarily when raising capital. In addition there would be incentives to report regularly in order to maintain continued investor interest in the firm. Companies that perform well have a strong incentive to report their operating results. Competitive pressures would also force other companies to report even if they

---

[1] See Ng (1978) and Wallace (1980) for extensions of agency theory to auditing.
[2] Watts and Zimmerman (1981).
[3] Holthausen and Leftwich (1982).
[4] The owners of the firm include both debt holders and stockholders under agency theory (Jensen and Meckling, 1976).

did not have good results. Silence (a failure to report) would be interpreted as bad news. Companies with neutral news would be motivated to report their results in order to avoid being suspected of having poor results. This would leave only firms with bad news which would not report. Such a situation would also force "bad news" firms to disclose results in order to maintain credibility in the capital market.[5]

There has been some empirical evidence that SEC reporting requirements are not a significant improvement over voluntary reporting existing prior to the 1933 and 1934 Acts. One study concluded that the SEC's prospectus requirements has not significantly affected the quality of securities offered for public subscription. A recent SEC commissioner acknowledged that this conclusion was difficult to refute.[6] A study has also been made of voluntary annual reporting prior to the Securities Exchange Act of 1934.[7] This law required the 10-K annual report. The basic conclusion in the study was that the reporting requirements mandated by the SEC were already being done on a voluntary basis. This finding says nothing about the quality or usefulness of the disclosures, but it supports the argument that voluntary disclosure would occur in a competitive capital market.

PRIVATE CONTRACTING OPPORTUNITIES

An argument in favor of unregulated markets is the presumption that anyone would be able to obtain information about a firm if it were genuinely desired, even in the event unregulated markets resulted in less free public disclosure. Any party could privately contract for information with the firm itself, with the firm's owners, or indirectly with information intermediaries such as brokers. If information is truly desired beyond that which is publicly available and free of charge, private individuals would be able to buy the desired information. In this way market forces should result in the optimal allocation of resources to the production of information.

An examination of the stock market reveals that people are willing to contract privately for information. The securities market is really a market for information as much as a market for securities. Investor newsletters available only by subscription are a good example of paying for private information. A somewhat less formal purchase of information is the use of brokerage firms for investment advice. The cost of investment advice is hidden in commission rates, but it is still a real cost.

Because of private contracting opportunities for additional information, market intervention in the form of mandatory disclosure rules is argued to be both unnecessary and undesirable. In this view, the demand for information is optimally met when market forces determine the production

---

[5]See Ross (1979) for an excellent summary of this argument.
[6]Stigler (1975, pp. 78–100). The comments of SEC Commissioner Roderick Hills were quoted in an article which appeared in *The Wall Street Journal,* January 8, 1976, p. 5.
[7]Benston (1973).

(supply) and disclosure of accounting information. There is some evidence of a philosophical shift in this direction by the SEC. An SEC commissioner was recently quoted as saying the mandatory disclosure system may not be an effective route for transmission of information to the capital markets—and that it serves no purpose to force-feed the investment community with information it does not want.[8] It remains, however, for the SEC to implement a major program of disclosure deregulation.[9]

REGULATED MARKETS

Market regulation can be justified on the grounds that it is in the public interest. In this context two reasons are normally used to defend regulation. One reason is the possibility of a failure in the free market system to achieve a competitive equilibrium price. This is referred to as market failure, and indicates a suboptimal allocation of resources. Natural monopolies, such as occur in the utilities industry, are an example of market failures requiring regulatory intervention to prevent monopoly pricing. The second reason is the possibility that free markets may be optimal but contrary to social goals. For example, welfare programs come into existence from need; they represent income redistributions that modify market-based income distributions. These programs are undertaken to meet social goals of minimum family income.

MARKET FAILURES

There are several arguments favoring regulation because of market failures. The arguments concern the firm as a monopoly supplier of information, the failure of financial reporting to prevent frauds and bankruptcies, and the public-good nature of accounting information.

The Firm as a Monopoly Supplier of Information

Market failure is argued to occur because the firm is a natural monopoly supplier of information about itself. This situation creates the opportunity for restricted production and monopolistic pricing if the market is un-

---

[8]SEC Commissioner Stephen Friedman, as quoted in *Executive Newsletter* (Peat, Marwick, Mitchell & Co., June 3, 1981), p. 3.

[9]A step toward deregulation is the experimental shelf-registration (SEC rule 415). This temporary rule permits the speedier sales of routine offerings of debt and equity securities by large companies. It is not necessary to file a specific prospectus with the SEC for each individual offering of securities. One prospectus can be used for multiple issues within the time period covered by the shelf-registration.

regulated. Mandatory disclosure would result in more information and a lower cost to society than would be achieved in an unregulated market. Since the firm is a natural monopoly, it enjoys economies of scale in the production of firm-specific information. However, being a monopoly producer, the firm can underproduce (underreport) information and charge monopolistic prices. A similar situation exists in the utilities industry. The regulatory solution in the utilities industry is to permit monopolistic production, but to regulate prices.

With accounting regulation, the argument is that it is better to force mandatory reporting, rather than to have individuals competing to buy information privately and at monopolistic prices. In other words, mandatory public disclosure is a cost-effective method of getting firm-specific information to those demanding it. It is a waste of social resources for everyone to be buying the same information about firms.

It has been suggested that production costs of mandatory reporting requirements may be quite small since most of the basic information is produced as a byproduct of internal accounting systems.[10] If marginal information production costs are low, as has been theorized, then the social costs associated with mandatory financial reporting requirements may be small. And as previously noted, mandatory public disclosures could save investors a great deal of money if the alternative is private contracting. The argument is very appealing, though lacking in empirical verification.

If the production costs are not low, however, then there is the question of who bears the cost of producing free public disclosure. Companies will either absorb or pass on regulation costs to consumers; therefore the owners of the company or the firm's consumers will be subsidizing the information costs. This reality raises the question of fairness concerning the costs of regulation.

Failures of Financial Reporting and Auditing

Accounting and auditing have had their critics over the years. Some criticisms of accounting practice and the standard-setting process were reviewed in Chapter 2. The criticisms have focused on the alleged low quality of financial reporting, even under regulation. Reasons cited are poor accounting and auditing standards, too much management flexibility in the choice of accounting policies, and occasional laxity by auditors.[11] Corporate frauds undetected by auditors, and corporate failures not signaled in advance by either financial statements or audit reports are usually cited as evidence that the financial reporting system is failing to protect the public interest.[12] The argument is that more and better regulation is necessary to

---

[10]Hakansson (1977).

[11]For example, see Briloff (1972) and (1976).

[12]One of the most publicized frauds was Equity Funding. See Seidler, Andrews, and Epstein (1977).

raise the quality of financial reporting in order to protect the public from frauds and failures.

A capitalist economy relies on a competitive private sector capital market. Information is an important part of the capital market infrastructure. Good financial reporting is essential to create investor confidence in the fairness of the capital market so that savings will be channeled into investments. In addition, good information leads to better investment decisions and capital allocation, both of which are socially beneficial. The corollary is that bad financial reporting has the opposite effect. Advocates of regulation doubt if companies can really be trusted to report fully and accurately. In fact, the competitive nature of the capital market could even induce misleading reporting, at least by some companies during the short term. Therefore, regulation of accounting is both necessary and in the public interest to prevent some companies from bad or misleading reporting. This is a counterargument to the notion that a competitive capital market produces good voluntary reporting.

A useful function is served by this type of criticism because it raises questions about the value of accounting information, and can serve as an impetus for reviewing accounting and auditing standards. It can also be a catalyst for discussing the quantity and quality of mandatory accounting and auditing which would be in the public interest, as well as the amount of regulation needed to achieve these goals. Caution is necessary, however, because corporate frauds and failures by themselves do not necessarily mean a failure exists in the financial reporting system. Accounting regulation is not going to prevent frauds and failures. Risk cannot be eliminated in investments, no matter how much accounting and auditing is required. Risk is something which inherently exists in investments. Increased regulation of financial reporting may reduce the likelihood of undetected frauds and failures, but it can never eliminate them. Finally, any argument favoring expanded regulation must also consider the costs of regulation. In all control or regulatory systems there exists a point where the marginal benefits from more control are less than the marginal costs. It is by no means clear if benefits exceed costs under existing requirements, let alone under potentially expanded regulation.

Accounting as a Public Good

Market failures can also occur with what are called **public goods.** Public goods are commodities that, once produced, can be consumed without reducing the opportunity for consumption by others.[13] This condition exists because of the soft property rights associated with such goods. Classic examples of pure public goods are television and radio signals. By contrast, private goods possess hard property rights so that nonpurchasers are, by definition, excluded from consuming the good.

---

[13]See Bowers (1974) for a good review of the public-good problem.

Public goods are underproduced in a free market—owing to what are called externalities. An **externality** exists if a producer is unable to internalize (or impose) production costs on all users of the good. In slightly less technical language, the effect of an externality is that the producer of a public good has a limited incentive to produce it because all consumers cannot be charged for the good. The people who consume public goods without paying for them are called **free riders.** True market demand for public goods is not revealed in the marketplace because free riders are able to use the goods at no cost. Magazine and newspaper publishers face this situation. The result is that production is less than true market demand.

Underproduction of public goods is regarded as a market failure because producers are not motivated to meet the real demand for public goods. The only way in which production can be increased is through regulatory intervention. Inevitably, the cost of free riders must be borne by society as a whole if production is subsidized to meet true demand for public goods.

Accounting information has been argued to be a public good.[14] All information has very soft property rights and can be freely passed from person to person; each person can consume or absorb the content of the information. Because of this characteristic, accounting information has the qualities of a public good. If accounting information really is a public good, companies would not have a strong incentive to produce and sell accounting information about themselves in a free market. The opportunities to contract privately for firm-specific information would be restricted, and the heart of one argument supporting unregulated markets is seriously challenged. The outcome would be an underproduction of accounting information in an unregulated market. Intervention in the form of mandatory reporting requirements is considered necessary to ensure that the real demand for accounting information is met.

SOCIAL GOALS

The other reason for imposing regulation is the desire to achieve social goals that are not met by a free market, even if there is no market failure. This approach is also justified by a public-interest argument and inevitably involves a normative judgment about how society ought to allocate its resources.

The SEC has always been concerned with what might be termed fair reporting and the protection of investors. Fairness of the capital market is a public-interest type of argument. It is believed that the stock market will be fair only if all potential investors have equal access to the same information. This situation is referred to as **information symmetry.** An extension of this is the belief that the market will be fair only if information is equally com-

---

[14]Gonedes and Dopuch (1974), and May and Sundem (1976).

prehended by all investors. This condition is called **equal endowments.** It is an ideal which is unattainable because people do not have equal abilities.

While the SEC cannot do anything about unequal endowments, it can try to ensure that all investors have access to the same information. This is a laudable goal because the more widely information is distributed, the more competitive the capital market will be. After all, perfect and costless information is an assumption of the economic model of perfect competition. Regulation of insider trading is an application of the information symmetry philosophy. Such regulation attempts to prevent those with unfair access to private information from taking advantage of it. This behavior, it is argued, undermines investor confidence in the fairness of the capital market.

The goal of having a strong capital market cannot be disputed. But the real question is whether it is necessary to regulate financial reporting in order to achieve a fair market that has the confidence of investors. It should also be pointed out that no matter how much free public disclosure is required by the SEC or FASB, there will always be an incentive to search for new private information in order to "beat the market."[15]

ASSESSMENT OF THE REGULATION ARGUMENTS

Arguments against regulation are speculative and based on deductive reasoning. Since we live in a regulated environment, empirical tests of the free-market position are rather difficult. This is why the arguments for an unregulated market are largely deductive. Two empirical studies were cited, which offer weak support for the free-market position. And in spite of the fact that accounting is regulated, precious little is really known about the costs and benefits of regulation. What this means is that the proregulation arguments are also deductively reasoned, rather than empirically researched. In short, it is impossible to accept either argument as correct. What follows is an attempt to assess the merits of the two arguments, and to compare them on points where they address the same issues.

One of the arguments for regulation is that firms are monopoly suppliers of information about themselves. Prima facie, this could be viewed as a market failure. Since the firm is a monopoly supplier of information about itself, it may be cheaper to society to require mandatory free disclosure rather than to have all investors privately contracting for the same information and paying monopolistic prices. The free-market counterargument to this is that, owing to competitive pressure for capital, firms have

---

[15]Hirschleifer (1971) argues that information intended solely to beat the market is a waste of social resources because it can only create wealth transfers between individuals. His argument is rather simplistic, however, because all information has the potential of revising investor assessments of stocks and can affect the valuation of securities and the allocation of capital in the market.

an incentive to report information voluntarily about themselves. Because of alternative investment opportunities, companies are not really able to impose monopolistic prices. They have incentives to report freely in order to attract capital and to lower their cost of capital by being perceived to be a good reporting firm. The argument is that where there is perceived information risk due to poor quality reporting, investors penalize such companies by requiring a higher rate of return (to compensate for the extra risk they think they are taking). Proregulators counter that the competitive nature of the capital market provides an incentive for misleading reporting, at least in the short term. The implication is that managers of companies may not pay the penalty for poor or misleading reporting, and for this reason may be tempted to manipulate reporting in the short term. If this is true it would also indicate that owners have not developed good mechanisms for monitoring agency contracts with managers.

Another argument against regulation is that information not voluntarily disclosed by the firm could be obtained through private contracting. However, the viability of private contracting opportunities is questionable because of the public good nature of accounting information and the free-rider problem.

Finally, on social grounds it can be argued that mandatory reporting is desirable because it creates fairness in the capital market. The less private information there is (and the more that's public), the less wealth transfers between those who have information and those who do not. It is this same principle which is behind insider trading regulations. The criticism to be made of all proregulation arguments, but especially of the ones related to social goals, is that they call for regulation while ignoring the costs of regulation, as well as who ultimately has to pay for regulation.

The arguments for and against regulation represent deliberate extremes. In reality, voluntary disclosure would probably be substantial for the reasons already cited. Yet there is merit in mandating accounting policies. For example, standardization of accounting policies may lead more quickly to uniformity between companies than would occur in an unregulated market. This may improve the quality of financial reporting and reduce criticisms of it. Mandatory public reporting also enhances the perceived fairness of the capital market and may reduce the total cost to society of acquiring the information. And since most regulated information is produced as a byproduct of the firm's accounting system, regulatory costs to the firm appear to be low, while benefits to society could be substantial.

Much of the economic argument against regulation maintains that there are incentives for voluntary reporting. However, the focus of accounting regulation is not on mandatory reporting, per se; it is on improving the quality of reported information. Accounting regulation is mainly concerned with refining and unifying the rules of recognition and measurement used in the preparation of financial statements. An important implication is that accounting regulation requires a theoretical foundation—

given that it is mainly the quality of information which is being regulated. As was evident in Chapter 2, the lack of a theoretical foundation was directly responsible for the collapse of both the Committee on Accounting Procedure (CAP) and the Accounting Principles Board (APB) as standard-setting bodies. By contrast, the FASB is attempting to develop a conceptual framework as the basis for future accounting standards. This shows an awareness of the need for a normative theoretical framework in accounting regulation to justify policies.

THE PARADOX OF REGULATION

If free-market pricing does not work because of market failures or is deliberately abandoned, it is impossible to know if resources are used to maximize social welfare, or even to achieve optimality in the more restrictive sense of Pareto-optimality.[16] Market regulation can be justified if there is a market failure (as in the case of public goods) or if the free market produces a result incompatible with social goals. Ironically, though, regulated production and pricing decisions cannot provide an optimal answer to the problem left unsolved by the free-market pricing system. This is one paradox of regulation.

Economists have concluded that it is impossible to derive deductively or empirically any regulatory policies which will knowingly maximize social welfare. This somewhat gloomy conclusion is the subject of Arrow's well-known **Impossibility Theorem**.[17] Once the free-market pricing system is abandoned, there is no way of determining aggregate social preferences. If the pricing system is working, aggregate social preferences are revealed indirectly through supply–demand equilibria, and resources are allocated according to market prices. There is no comparable rule in a regulated market, and for this reason it is difficult to evaluate the benefits of market regulation. Because of this paradox, it is also impossible to know if accounting regulation is producing the optimal quantity and quality of financial reporting.[18]

---

[16]Pareto-optimality occurs when it is not possible to make anyone better off without making someone else worse off. A Pareto-optimal economy is considered to be efficient. If it is possible to make someone better off at no cost, then the existing allocation of resources is inefficient and involves a waste of resources due to suboptimality.

[17]Arrow (1963).

[18]Gonedes (1972) argued that it was possible to determine optimal accounting regulation. Later thinking, however, has reversed that conclusion. See Demski (1973) and Gonedes and Dopuch (1974). Recently, Watts (1980) suggested that optimal regulation may be determinable, but only if information-contracting costs can be specified.

Economists argue that public goods supplied under regulation tend to be overproduced. This contrasts with underproduction in unregulated markets and gives rise to a second paradox of regulation. The reason for overproduction is that demand is overstated because public goods supplied under regulation are normally subsidized (or even costless) goods. Users overstate their real demand or preference because the good is costless. Since accounting information has public-good characteristics, there is a very real danger that overproduction of accounting information occurs in a regulated market. Users of accounting information, such as financial analysts, probably have an insatiable demand for free information about firms.

In determining accounting policy, the FASB could easily be deceived about the level of real demand for new or alternative accounting policies since users do not pay directly. The ever-increasing set of accounting requirements imposed on public corporations tends to support the proposition that such a situation has in fact occurred. The FASB may also be cognizant of the overproduction problem. In recent years increasing attention has been given to what is called **standards overload,** particularly as it affects smaller, nonpublicly traded companies. To date the only relief has been the exemption of some supplemental disclosures for closely held firms. However, the problem of standards overload is still under consideration by the FASB.

The tendency for overproduction under regulation can be avoided only if a pricing system can be imposed on public goods, creating nonpurchasers who are effectively excluded from consuming the good.[19] Cable television is an example of how this imposition can be accomplished with television signals. The key is to strengthen property rights over the good so that nonpurchasers are excluded from freely consuming the good. One means of doing this in accounting would be to file company reports with the SEC and charge users to receive copies of the information. If accounting information is purchased, there may be incentives for users *not* to pass on the information to free riders. In this way real economic demand for the information could be determined and production costs could be recovered from the real users of accounting information. The present disclosure system imposes costs on companies rather than on users. Assuming that firms recover the costs indirectly through product pricing, the users of accounting information are being subsidized by the users of the firms' products. This consequence of regulation can be criticized on the grounds of fairness.

In summary, the consequences of regulating accounting, given its public-good nature, are (1) a potential overallocation of social resources to the production of free publicly available accounting information, and (2) a wealth transfer from nonusers to users of accounting information. A wealth transfer occurs because users are receiving the benefits of free accounting information while nonusers are implicitly incurring the production costs.

---

[19]Demsetz (1970).

The wealth transfer is small if the costs of regulation are low, as has been conjectured. However, this is only conjecture.

THE REGULATORY PROCESS

In regulated markets, economic resource allocation is partially determined as a result of a political process. Regulation is essentially a political activity. This is not intended as a criticism, nor is it surprising since regulation is undertaken in the so-called public interest. Ironically, it is unclear exactly what is meant by public interest. Since social welfare cannot be measured (the Arrow Impossibility Theorem), there is no economic criterion for determining what policy will maximize the public interest. Consequently, public interest is best understood in a political context referring to the particular redistribution of income and wealth being advocated. What this means is that there is no way of determining optimal accounting regulation and that regulation will be the outcome of a political as much as an economic process.

Self-interest is the underlying rationale for analyzing regulatory behavior. In a regulated market, individuals or groups of individuals who have any stake in the market will be motivated to lobby for their vested interests, to form coalitions with other parties to further strengthen their influence, and generally to try to influence the political system to their advantage. This basic process occurs in all political systems.

THE POLITICAL NATURE OF REGULATION

The democratic tradition in the United States means that due process is an important ingredient to the regulatory process. In setting policy, **due process** means that a regulatory agency seeks to involve all affected parties in the deliberations; this is important in maintaining the legitimacy of the regulatory process. In other words, people affected by regulation have an opportunity to make input to the regulatory decision-making process. The due-process tradition goes back to one of the first federal agencies, the Interstate Commerce Commission.[20] It has even been suggested that the method of operation by a regulatory body (which includes the principle of due process) is more important to its own political survival than the actual decisions made.

There is a belief by some members of the accounting profession that accounting policy setting should be neutral and apolitical.[21] The more

---

[20]Krislov and Musolf (1964, p. 185).
[21]For examples of this position see Armstrong (1977) and Kirk (1978).

widely held view, however, is that accounting policy is inevitably political because of its regulatory nature.[22] In reflecting back on Chapter 2, it is easy to see why both the CAP and the APB failed as regulatory bodies. The two AICPA committees were regulatory bodies but they lacked the necessary structure to ensure their survival. For one thing, they had a weak mandate to regulate financial reporting. Until the issue of Accounting Series Release (ASR) 150 in 1973, the SEC did not officially endorse private-sector standard setting.[23] What existed was an informal alliance in which the SEC tacitly accepted accounting standards as acceptable for SEC filings. Occasionally, though, the SEC would challenge a specific standard. The investment tax credit produced such a situation. Because of this arrangement, the AICPA's authority to regulate was very weak.

From the SEC's perspective, the arrangement prior to ASR 150 provided security and flexibility. By permitting self-regulation in the private sector, the SEC was shielded from the politics of actually setting accounting policy except when it was expedient to do so. It has also been suggested that the private sector was in a position to be used as a scapegoat by the SEC if Congress were to challenge the work of the SEC.[24]

The other fatal characteristic of the AICPA committees was the closed-door nature of policy setting. It appeared that there was no due process in the determination of accounting and disclosure rules. While there was undoubtedly some informal fact gathering and solicitation of the views of interested parties, it was not until late in the life of the APB that formal due process procedures were applied. The lack of due process, or at least the apparent lack of due process, sometimes led to a low level of acceptance by affected parties. Ironically, the accounting profession believed a closed-door approach was good because it insulated policymaking from outside influence. This attitude reflected a belief at the time that accounting policy was primarily a process of identifying the true and correct normative accounting methods. With hindsight, this seems naive; but it was a strongly held conviction by accounting researchers and policymakers through the 1960s.

From a regulatory viewpoint the FASB is functioning much more successfully. Its standards were endorsed by the SEC in ASR 150. Due process has been adopted as standard procedure in debating and evaluating accounting policy. As with the legal system, decision making under due process is extremely slow, but this is the nature of democratic politics. Arrow refers to this tendency as **democratic paralysis**.[25] Regulation under a system of due process is slow, but the consensus gained is what gives legitimacy to the regulation as being in the public interest. Accounting regulation has evolved to a mature model of regulation—as reflected in the

---

[22]Horngren (1973) and Solomons (1978).
[23]SEC (1973). Accounting standards of the FASB were officially sanctioned as the basis for statutory reports filed with the SEC.
[24]Watts and Zimmerman (1978).
[25]Arrow (1963).

structure and operations of the FASB. This is consistent with the fact that accounting policy is a matter of public interest and a social decision.

Even though accounting regulation is a political process and accounting policy a social decision, a theoretical framework is very important. It provides a logical and unified structure to the standard-setting process and mitigates the effect of lobbying by vested-interest groups, which is not in the public interest. In other words, theory can help the FASB remain neutral and objective in setting accounting policy. Another aspect of the Conceptual Framework Project is that the FASB is seeking a consensus on the framework by the constituency. This contrasts sharply with earlier theory efforts which were derived without due process, and which were rejected. Accounting theory is not self-evident, nor is it easily testable as is theory in the physical sciences. For these two reasons, it is important that a consensus exist on the theoretical foundation of financial reporting and accounting policy. The FASB is establishing this consensus through a political process. It must be stated, though, that research still plays an important role in the process of theory acceptance. Theory, even in an area like accounting, cannot be derived solely by a political process. Theories are derived and tested through research. However, because of the unique regulatory nature of accounting, it is important that theories gain acceptance beyond the narrow confines of the research community. This acceptance can be achieved through a political process—as is occurring with the FASB's Conceptual Framework Project.

REGULATORY BEHAVIOR

Given that financial reporting is regulated, some consideration must be given to how regulation affects behavior. **Capture theory** and the **life-cycle theory** of regulation both argue that the group being regulated eventually comes to use the regulatory process to promote its own self-interests.[26] When this occurs, the regulatory process is considered to be captured. The life-cycle theory of regulation develops the argument that a regulatory agency goes through several distinct phases. While starting out in the public interest, regulation often becomes an instrument used to protect the group being regulated.

Regulation is often created as a political vehicle to win votes. For example, the SEC was created following a political mandate for stock market reform in the wake of the 1929 crash.[27] However, once the mandate for regulation recedes, the parties being regulated and the regulatory agency come to see that their interests converge. It becomes very difficult for a regulator to remain truly independent because survival of the regulatory agency itself may depend on how well the policies are accepted by the group being regulated. What often happens is that the regulatory body pro-

---

[26] Stigler (1971) and Bernstein (1955).
[27] Watts (1980).

tects the regulated group from competition. This behavior has been observed in older regulatory agencies—such as the Interstate Commerce Commission, which regulates land transportation; the Federal Aviation Agency, which regulates air transportation; and the Federal Communications Commission, which regulates radio and television licenses. This behavior, by both the regulator and the regulated parties, is perfectly rational and is explained by the self-interest theory of political behavior.

Capture theory and the life-cycle theory have been applied to accounting regulation. From 1976 to 1978, financial reporting was under investigation by the United States Congress.[28] The allegation was made in Congress that accounting regulation had been captured by the Big Eight group of accounting firms. As the predominant auditors of publicly listed corporations, this group has a large stake in the regulation game. In addition, prior to the FASB, accounting regulation was done primarily by AICPA subcommittees, which were undoubtedly heavily influenced by the Big Eight accounting firms. With the implementation of the independent FASB, however, the capture theory argument lost much of its validity. At the time of the Congressional hearings, the FASB had been in operation for several years.

Some changes were made in response to the Congressional hearings—for example, restructuring of the AICPA to lessen Big Eight dominance and to increase self-regulation by the AICPA.[29] But accounting regulation survived the scrutiny of Congress because capture theory and the life-cycle theory are not applicable to the nature of financial reporting. The number of parties directly affected by accounting regulation is much larger and more diverse than in older regulated industries. A recent study of submissions to the FASB found that even the Big Eight group of accounting firms does not have a unified viewpoint, and the group does not dominate policy at the FASB.[30] The conclusion was that decision making at the FASB is pluralistic. Other parties affected by accounting regulation are companies that must comply with regulations, along with free riders who use the costless information for investment analyses. There is a divergence of interests

[28]The Congressional hearings conducted by Senator Lee Metcalf in 1977, and Congressman John E. Moss in 1978, were discussed in Chapter 2. The staff reports prepared for both hearings were highly critical of financial reporting and accounting regulation. After the hearings, the status quo of accounting regulation was maintained, although the SEC, FASB, and AICPA all responded positively to some of the criticisms made during the hearings.

[29]Some of the fallout from the Watergate Congressional investigations was the discovery of corporate slushfunds which were used to make political contributions. Direct corporate political contributions are of course illegal. It was also discovered that some of these funds were used to make bribes in foreign countries. Auditors were held publicly accountable for failing to detect these slushfunds in their audits. There were also several well-publicized corporate failures in the 1970s in which the auditors' performance was seriously questioned. To some degree then, the Congressional investigations of the accounting profession reflected a genuine public-interest concern, but they were also part of the post-Watergate politics.

[30]Hussein and Ketz (1980) and Brown (1981).

among the three groups, which places the accounting regulator in a more naturally neutral posture than occurs in other regulated industries. The independent structure of the FASB helps to maintain the neutral position and to reach decisions which are thought to be in the best interests of society as a whole.

The three groups affected by accounting regulation—companies, auditors, and free riders—are discussed now in greater detail. Management of companies can be expected to respond to regulatory proposals that will affect either their companies or themselves personally. All accounting regulation imposes some amount of production cost on firms. One could argue, a priori, that there would be a natural tendency for management to oppose new disclosures or rules that will impose a cost on the firm. On the other hand, some rules may cause specific firms to increase reported net income. Management could have an incentive to support those new proposals which would positively affect reported income and which might increase their own compensation (especially where employment contracts use accounting numbers for bonuses). However, one study found the opposite result. Large regulated companies supported proposed accounting rules that would lower reported net income.[31] The suggested reason was that the self-interest of this type of company was to minimize political costs, such as the possibility of future regulatory intervention, and that lower profits were consistent with this goal. So, even within the management group there is likely to be a range of reactions to accounting policy proposals.

Auditors are concerned with the auditing implications of financial reporting rules. It would be naive to think the opinion of large accounting firms is not seriously considered in accounting policy deliberations. Many accounting firms maintain regular liaison with FASB personnel and routinely attend policy hearings at the FASB. Auditors could be expected to support regulation that reduces the riskiness of audits—for example, rules that clarify or standardize financial reporting. There has been a tendency among auditors to oppose proposed policies which would expand the audit function into areas of subjectivity. Two such areas are supplemental disclosures of inflation accounting data and profit forecasts.[32] The reason for this opposition is fairly obvious. If less objective information is required to be reported, the auditor will incur a greater risk in auditing the information.

---

[31]Watts and Zimmerman (1978).

[32]Two areas where the AICPA membership balked were the proposals by the SEC for mandatory financial forecasts (proposed rule No. 33–581 issued in 1975), and ASR 177, also issued in 1975, which required auditors to comment on the preferability of a reported change in accounting policy. Because of the resistance by accounting firms to these two proposed requirements, they were subsequently dropped by the SEC. Auditors would have been placed in the position of attesting to information which was very subjective in the case of forecasts, and to comment on the preferability of accounting standards when there were no official guidelines for making such a determination (for example, FIFO versus LIFO inventory methods).

This would increase the possibility of litigation. Assuming that auditors are risk averse, they would prefer to avoid such risky ventures, if possible.

Finally, free riders may also try to influence the outcome of accounting policy deliberations. Any group or individual is motivated to pursue its self-interests only if there is a benefit greater than the cost of participation. This principle is true in all lobbying activity in politics. It would not normally pay individuals to try and influence accounting regulation. However, financial analysts have a sufficiently strong interest to lobby. As sellers of investment advice, they have a strong motivation to demand new accounting information which they can incorporate into investment counseling and newsletters. As information intermediaries, they can make money simply by summarizing public information for investors who do not have time to sift through it themselves.

The lobbying behavior of free riders needs to be watched closely by the FASB because free riders do not have the direct economic interests in information production that management and auditors have. Because they do not, it could be easy to get into an overproduction situation. It is politically difficult to deal with free riders because they can claim to be acting in the public interest. Their argument suggests that the capital market will be fairer and more competitive if there is free public reporting. While this is true, it ignores the question of information production costs and who pays for accounting regulation. The danger of bowing to pressures from special-interest groups has been noted.[33] Accounting policymaking should not serve special-interest groups to the detriment of society as a whole. When this does happen, the mandate for regulation no longer exists because the regulation process has been captured by a vested-interest group.

Accounting regulation is likely to continue. For this reason it is important to understand the nature of regulatory processes. It is hoped that accounting regulation produces a net social benefit, but there is no real evidence either to support or to reject this hope. The predominant types of accounting regulations deal with financial statement refinement and standardization of practices rather than with expanded disclosure.[34] This may mean that the overproduction problem is exaggerated by the critics of regulation. However, as noted before, there is a paucity of hard evidence to support arguments either for or against accounting regulation, so this belief is also offered more hopefully than conclusively.

---

[33]Solomons (1978).

[34]Four accounting standards by the FASB require major supplemental disclosure not readily available as a byproduct of the firm's accounting system. These are: (1) SFAS 14, which requires segmental disclosures; (2) SFAS 33, which deals with inflation accounting; (3) SFAS 36, which requires pension plan disclosures; and (4) SFAS 69, which requires disclosures by oil and gas companies. The overproduction tendency does not appear to be a serious problem in the private sector regulation of accounting. On the other hand, the SEC requires more supplemental disclosures in statutory 10-Q, 8-K and 10-K filings. The overproduction tendency may be more of a problem at the SEC.

ECONOMIC CONSEQUENCES

Economic consequences is an important concept which has emerged with respect to accounting policymaking. It has been defined in the following manner:

> The impact of accounting reports on the decision-making behavior of business, government, unions, investors, and creditors.[35]

In the broadest sense, economic consequences refer to the costs and benefits of financial reporting regulation. All accounting policies impose costs on companies in the form of compliance. The effect of accounting reports on decision making may be internal (on company management), or external (on investors, creditors, unions, and government). An important part of the regulatory process is to assess carefully the impact of existing and proposed policies. Such an evaluation can be used to assess the net benefits of regulation, who bears the costs, who benefits, and the discovery of any unforeseen consequences.

One extensively researched type of economic consequence is the effect of accounting reports and accounting policies on stock prices. This research is reviewed in Chapter 6. Such research can provide insight into the usefulness of accounting information as well as the effect of accounting policies on stockholder wealth. For example, a mandatory change in accounting policies that causes stock prices to drop would cause a decrease in stockholder wealth. There is some evidence that this occurred with respect to oil and gas accounting. This issue is considered further in Chapter 14.

Economic consequences cannot be avoided in accounting regulation. After all, regulation is a political means of economic resource allocation. There will be costs and benefits accruing to the different parties affected by regulation. Studying the economic consequences simply means that we will understand more about the nature of these costs and benefits. However, one special type of economic consequence should definitely be avoided. It has been called an extraneous consequence. An **extraneous consequence** occurs when an accounting policy motivates an economic transaction for the sole purpose of financial reporting effects, which is contrary to the firm's normal profit-making behavior. If accounting policy causes management decision making to be contrary to normal profit maximization, an extraneous impact has occurred.

One area where it is alleged this occurs is in leasing. It is argued that the FASB has created incentives to structure leases in such a way that they do not have to be capitalized under SFAS 13.[36] The benefit to companies

---

[35]Zeff (1978, p. 56).
[36]FASB (1976a).

lies in off-balance sheet financing (a financial reporting effect), while there would be legal costs incurred in structuring leases this way. It can be argued that the benefit of noncapitalization is purely illusory rather than economic, intended solely to "fool" the securities market concerning a company's debt level. The lease problem is examined in Chapter 16. Another area where extraneous consequences are alleged to have occurred is foreign exchange gains and losses under SFAS 8.[37] It is argued that companies were motivated to hedge against accounting-created risks, rather than real economic risks. This issue is discussed in detail in Chapter 17.

The FASB incorporates consideration of economic consequences in two ways. One way is the due-process phase in which affected parties may provide input to policy deliberations. Such a procedure can help policy makers identify costs, benefits, and extraneous consequences at an early stage of the standard-setting process. The other way is to review the effects of past policies. This monitoring is both informal and formal. An example of the informal type is the open request by the FASB in 1978 for feedback on its first twelve accounting standards.[38] An example of formal monitoring is the commissioning of research to evaluate the economic consequences of specific accounting standards.[39]

SUMMARY

Accounting regulation will probably continue. But the arguments against regulation force us to consider why we regulate, who benefits, and who pays the costs. These are good questions to pose of any regulatory process. Since regulation is a matter of public interest, the benefits of regulation should clearly be in the public interest and the benefits should exceed costs. In the case of accounting regulation, the benefits are in the form of improving the fairness and competitiveness of the capital market. Society as a whole benefits indirectly from a well-functioning capital market. However, certain individuals benefit directly, while others incur the cost. An analysis of the economic consequences of regulation helps to evaluate these benefits and costs and their fairness.

Regulation is a political process and it is self-interest which motivates individuals and groups to participate. Behavior occurs in the form of furthering self-interest through the regulatory process. This places the regu-

---

[37] FASB (1975).

[38] In 1978, the FASB extended an open invitation to comment on any aspects of the first twelve accounting standards which had been issued. The purpose was to gain feedback on the effects of the standards.

[39] See, for example, FASB (1978) and Abdel-Khalik (1981).

lator in the role of weighing sometimes conflicting positions and trying to determine what is in the best interests of society as a whole. Due process and neutrality are critical to regulatory success if the regulation is to retain the support of both the regulated parties and society generally. All these requirements are difficult for a regulatory agency to accomplish, and there is always the danger that vested-interest groups may capture the regulatory process and divert it to private.ends.

The rationale or justification for regulation rests on the public-interest argument. However, a paradox exists. There is no way of determining optimal regulatory policies which maximize social welfare or the public interest. The best that regulators can do is to try to determine that a net benefit exists—that is, an excess of benefits over costs. Benefits are difficult to identify and measure because they relate to the usefulness of accounting information for investors in the capital market. There is evidence that information is useful to investors. This research is examined in Chapter 6. Yet, it is not known if regulation is really necessary to create disclosure, or whether regulation is the optimal way of meeting the real demand for information. Costs are somewhat easier to quantify. There is some reason to believe regulation costs are low because most of the information contained in financial reports is produced as a byproduct of firms' accounting systems. Overall, then, there is reason to believe that accounting regulation produces a net benefit to society. But it is unknown if regulation produces a socially optimal allocation of resources to the production of accounting information.

QUESTIONS

1. What are the arguments favoring regulation of financial reporting?
2. What are the arguments against regulation of financial reporting?
3. Why is it difficult to evaluate the regulation question?
4. Why does accounting information have the qualities of a public good? What are the implications for production in both unregulated and regulated markets?
5. Why is optimal regulation not determinable? Given that optimal accounting regulation cannot be determined, how can a regulatory body such as the SEC or FASB make good decisions?
6. A distinction was made in the chapter between two types of regulation: (a) the refinement and standardization of financial statements, and (b) expanded disclosure. Why is the distinction important in evaluating the regulation question?
7. Who pays for accounting regulation and who benefits?
8. Can accounting standards and policy-making be neutral? In what sense is neutrality really important?

9. Arrow (1963) warns that public participation and a consensual approach to social issues can lead to democratic paralysis; that is, to a failure to act due to an inability to agree on goals or objectives. Is this danger applicable to accounting regulation? How did such a situation lead to the demise of the APB (review Chapter 2)?

10. Horngren (1973) argues that accounting policies are a social decision and a matter of public interest. Evaluate this statement.

11. Horngren (1973) also believes that accounting standards must be "marketed" by regulatory bodies. By this he means that affected parties need to be sold on the benefits of standards. How is this concept consistent with the nature of regulation?

12. It was suggested many years ago that an accounting "court" should be created to resolve disputes in accounting. In what ways does the FASB function as an accounting court? In what ways is it different?

13. What benefit is the conceptual framework project to the FASB if (a) there is no way of determining optimal accounting regulation, and (b) regulatory decision making is a political process?

14. What is meant by economic and extraneous consequences? Why are they important to the regulation question?

15. Do you think accounting should be regulated? Defend your answer. What do you think should be the purpose or goal of accounting regulation, if it is regulated? How can this best be achieved?

CASES AND PROBLEMS

1. The table opposite was presented in Hussein and Ketz (1980, p. 365). It summarizes written responses of Big Eight accounting firms to proposals in exposure drafts, proposals that were eventually adopted in SFASs. An *A* indicates agreement, *D* indicates disagreement, and *N* indicates no opinion.

   Required:
   1. Why might different positions be taken by accounting firms?
   2. Is there any evidence from this table that policymaking has been captured by the Big Eight? Support your answer with an analysis of the responses in this table.
   3. Does the FASB appear to be responsive to the Big Eight? Should it be?
   4. What are the limitations of the evidence from this analysis?

2. Presented on the following pages are extracts from the 1931 annual report of General Electric Company. This company was considered to be at the forefront of progressive voluntary reporting during this time period.

Big Eight Responses to FASB Statements									
		Big Eight							
Issue	Proposal	AA	AY	CL	DHS	EW	PMM	PW	TR
1	FASB No. 2: R&D Costs Expenses	A	N	N	D	D	A	A	A
2	FASB No. 2: R&D Under Contract	N	N	N	A	A	A	A	A
3	FASB No. 5: Overall Reaction	A	D	D	N	A	D	D	A
4	FASB No. 5: Self-Insured Risks	A	A	N	N	N	A	D	A
5	FASB No. 5: Catastrophe Losses of Casualty Insurers	N	A	D	D	N	A	D	A
6	FASB No. 5: Expropriations of Foreign Assets	A	N	N	A	N	A	N	A
7	FASB No. 7: Overall Reaction	N	N	N	D	D	N	D	N
8	FASB No. 7: Same Standards	A	A	A	D	D	A	D	N
9	FASB No. 7: Certain Industries Exempt	A	N	D	N	N	N	N	N
10	FASB No. 7: Start-Up and Similar Costs First	D	D	D	D	D	D	N	D
11	FASB No. 8: Modified Temporal Method	A	D	D	D	N	A	D	D
12	FASB No. 8: Exchange Adjustment to Income	A	D	D	N	N	A	N	N
13	FASB No. 8: Forward Exchange Contract	D	A	A	N	N	N	A	A
14	FASB No. 9: Tax Allocation	A	A	A	A	A	A	A	A
15	FASB No. 9: Transition Method	D	D	A	D	D	D	D	D
16	FASB No. 12: Overall Reaction	A	N	D	D	D	A	A	A
17	FASB No. 12: Lower of Cost or Market	A	A	D	D	D	A	A	A
18	FASB No. 12: All Declines in Income	D	A	A	A	A	D	D	D
19	FASB No. 13: Overall Reaction	D	D	A	A	A	D	N	N
20	FASB No. 13: Lease Classification Criteria	D	D	D	D	D	D	D	A
21	FASB No. 13: Operating Leases on Face of B/S	A	A	N	A	A	A	N	N
22	FASB No. 13: Implementation	A	A	N	N	N	N	N	N
23	FASB No. 14: Overall Reaction	A	A	N	A	D	A	N	N
24	FASB No. 14: Annual Statements	N	N	D	N	N	N	N	D
25	FASB No. 14: Interim Statements	N	N	N	N	N	N	N	D
26	FASB No. 14: Exemption for Small Co.	N	D	D	N	D	D	N	A
27	FASB No. 14: Assets	A	N	N	N	D	D	N	N
28	FASB No. 14: Major Customers	A	N	N	A	A	N	N	N

Compare the report to a contemporary annual report with respect to (1) form, (2) content, (3) explanations of accounting policies, and (4) supplemental disclosures. What effects have fifty years of accounting regulations had on financial reporting? Why is this comparison inadequate in assessing the impact of regulation (that is, the costs and benefits) as well as the question of optimality?

Schenectady, N. Y., March 26, 1932.

To the Stockholders of the
  General Electric Company:

Orders received during the year 1931 were $252,021,496, compared with $341,820,312 in the year 1930, a decrease of 26 per cent.

Unfilled orders at the end of the year were $49,308,000, compared with $56,062,000 at the end of 1930, a decrease of 12 per cent.

COMPARATIVE STATEMENT OF INCOME AND EXPENSES

	1931	1930
Net sales billed	$263,275,255.37	$376,167,428.42
Less: Costs, expenses, and all charges except interest	234,884,372.57	335,717,167.11
Net income from sales	$ 28,390,882.80	$ 40,450,261.31
Income from other sources: Associated companies and miscellaneous securities	$ 8,657,110.67	$ 13,453,654.25
Interest and discount	3,819,280.21	3,258,498.99
U.S. Government and other marketable securities	21,533.46	1,757,715.15
Royalties and sundry revenue	501,422.20	1,605,334.28
	$ 12,999,346.54	$ 20,075,202.67
Total income	$ 41,390,229.34	$ 60,525,463.98
Less: Interest payments	$ 433,233.73	$ 313,078.69
Addition to general reserve		2,721,470.03
	$ 433,233.73	$ 3,034,548.72
Profit available for dividends	$ 40,956,995.61	$ 57,490,915.26
Less: 6% cash dividends on special stock	2,575,005.15	2,574,952.95
Profit available for dividends on common stock	$ 38,381,990.46	$ 54,915,962.31
Less: Cash dividends on common stock	46,150,256.80	46,150,203.60
Deficit (1931) and surplus (1930) for the year	$ 7,768,266.34	$ 8,765,758.71

CONDENSED BALANCE SHEET
December 31, 1931 and 1930

ASSETS

	1931	1930
Fixed investments:		
Manufacturing plants at cost, including land, buildings, and machinery	$199,129,732.92	$198,303,962.66
Less: General plant reserve and depreciation	153,068,713.66	152,436,033.08
	$ 46,061,019.26	$ 45,867,929.58
Other property	228,445.67	252,609.47
Furniture and appliances (other than in factories)	1.00	1.00
Patents	1.00	1.00
Total fixed investments	**$ 46,289,466.93**	**$ 46,120,541.05**
Associated companies and miscellaneous securities	**179,308,010.36**	**204,810,328.13**
Current assets:		
Inventories	57,335,498.53	60,063,418.56
Installation work in progress	10,063,820.42	16,229,589.20
Notes and accounts receivable	39,192,433.60	41,676,727,47
Marketable securities (at the lower of par or market) ..... $ 7,122,820.00		
Cash .. 115,056,113.22	122,178,933.22	141,717,851.25
	$228,770,685.77	$259,687,586.48
Less: Advance payments on contracts	9,684,175.13	17,123,037.38
Total current assets:	**$219,086,510.64**	**$242,564,549.10**
Deferred charges	**241,948.86**	**476,403.83**
	$444,925,936.79	**$493,971,822.11**

CONDENSED BALANCE SHEET
December 31, 1931 and 1930

LIABILITIES AND CAPITAL

	1931	1930
3½% Debenture bonds due 1942	$ 2,047,000.00	$ 2,047,000.00
Current liabilities:		
Accounts payable and accrued liabilities	16,301,469.11	28,422,154.65
Dividends payable	12,181,318.95	12,181,296.35
Total current liabilities	$ 28,482,788.06	$ 40,603,451.00
Reserves for self-insurance, workmen's compensation, etc.	4,063,496.81	7,974,385.38
Charles A. Coffin Foundation	400,000.00	400,000.00
General reserve	14,517,597.21*	39,763,664.68
Special stock: Authorized 5,500,000 shares, par value $10; issued 4,292,963½ shares	42,929,635.00	42,929,635.00
Common stock and earned surplus:		
Common stock (authorized 29,600,000 shares no par value; issued 28,845,927 36/100 shares)	180,287,046.00	180,287,046.00
Earned surplus on January 1st	179,966,640.05	171,200,881.34
Deficit (1931) and surplus (1930) for the year (page 5)	7,768,266.34	8,765,758.71
Total common stock and earned surplus	$352,485,419.71	$360,253,686.05
	$444,925,936.79	$493,971,822.11

*After applying $25,246,067.47 in reduction of book value of "Associated companies and miscellaneous securities."

Committees of the Board of Directors reviewed the valuation of manufacturing plants, investments in associated companies and miscellaneous securities, inventories, and notes and accounts receivable, and the figures used in this report are the result of such reviews.

MANUFACTURING PLANTS

From the formation of the General Electric Company in 1892, there had been expended on manufacturing plants to December 31, 1930		$327,225,297.35
Added during 1931		9,600,173.80
		$336,825,471.15
Dismantled, sold or otherwise disposed of to December 31, 1930	$128,921,334.69	
Dismantled, sold or otherwise disposed of during 1931	8,774,403.54	137,695,738.23
Cost of present plants	....	$199,129,732.92
General plant reserve and depreciation, December 31, 1930	$152,436,033.08	
Added by charges to income during 1931	8,859,062.05	
Proceeds from sale of dismantled equipment, etc., during 1931	548,022.07	
	$161,843,117.20	
Less: Cost of plants dismantled, sold or otherwise disposed of during 1931	8,774,403.54	153,068,713.66
Net book value, December 31, 1931		$ 46,061,019.26

ASSOCIATED COMPANIES AND MISCELLANEOUS SECURITIES

Investments in associated companies and miscellaneous securities were increased during 1931 by $17,782,549.22, and amounted to $222,592,877.35 before revaluation on December 31, 1931. This amount has been reduced by reappraisal, according to methods stated below, to

$179,308,010.36. These investments include advances to associated companies as well as securities, inasmuch as most of the advances are required permanently in the business. The decrease resulting from revaluation was charged in part to the General reserve (page 12) and to other reserves set aside from earnings of previous years.

The larger investments during the year were in Electrical Securities Corporation, United Electric Securities Company, and International General Electric Company, Inc.

Interest and dividends received from associated companies in the United States, and from Canadian General Electric Company, Ltd., and International General Electric Company, Inc., are included in the "Statement of income and expenses" as part of "Income from associated companies and miscellaneous securities." Total income from associated companies and miscellaneous securities amounted to $8,657,110.67, which is 4.5 per cent of the average net value of these investments at the beginning and end of the year. This compares with 6.9 per cent returned in 1930.

Your Company's share of income earned by associated companies during 1931 (disregarding revaluations of their securities) exceeded your Company's share of the dividends distributed by approximately $5,000,000, which is equivalent to 17 cents per share of the common stock of your Company outstanding on December 31, 1931.

Investments in associated companies are of a more or less permanent character, and may well be considered as investments in plant and working capital of companies closely associated with your Company in the development of its business on a broader base and in a more effective manner than could be done by your Company itself. Accordingly, investments in associated companies in which your Company has a majority interest are appraised on a basis similar to that used in the valuation of your Company's assets. Investments in other companies are appraised after consideration of cost, net worth, return on investment, market price, if any, and foreign exchange, but in no case is an investment or security appraised at a higher valuation than the market price on a recognized exchange on December 31, 1931, with due allowance for foreign exchange rates.

In determining the value of your Company's investment in International General Electric Company, Inc., these same methods of appraisal were applied to securities of foreign companies held by International General Electric Company, Inc. and its subsidiaries.

Foreign Business

Canadian General Electric Company, Ltd. reported net profit for the year 1931 of $2,308,155, compared with $3,765,798 for 1930. Dividends of 7 per cent were paid on $8,557,750 of preference stock, and 8 per cent on $9,442,250 of common stock outstanding.

International General Electric Company, Inc. conducts the export and foreign business of your Company outside of Canada, and, for 1931, reported a profit available for interest on capital advances and dividends of $2,963,222, compared with $3,897,818 for 1930. Interest and dividends paid in 1931 amounted to $2,846,667, compared with $3,878,619 in 1930.

Electrical Securities Corporation

The capital of Electrical Securities Corporation was reduced $18,750,000 in December 1931, by the surrender by your Company of 750,000 of the 1,000,000 shares of common stock without par value outstanding. As your Company owned all of the common shares, the surrender did not affect its equity position. This action was taken as a result of depreciation in the market price of securities owned by Electrical Securities Corporation, and the amount of the capital reduction was set aside as a reserve against losses on securities.

Earnings of Electrical Securities Corporation for 1931 were $2,675,199, compared with $2,399,048 for 1930, and regular dividends were paid out of earnings at the annual rate of 5 per cent on the preferred stock, and 50 cents per share on the common stock during each of the first three quarters and $2 per share (on the reduced number of shares) in the last quarter.

CURRENT ASSETS

Inventories

Inventories in factories and warehouses and on consignment have been valued, in accordance with the custom of your Company, at the lower of cost or market. After deducting reserves, they were carried at $57,335,498.53, compared with $60,063,418.56 at the end of 1930.

The following table shows the relation of inventories to shipments billed in each of the last twelve years:

Year	Inventories at end of year	Net billing	Per cent of inventories to billing
1920	$118,109,173.99	$275,758,487.57	42.8
1921	64,848,188.87	221,007,991.64	29.3
1922	75,334,561.79	200,194,294.09	37.6
1923	83,746,031.05	271,309,695.37	30.9
1924	68,485,161.08	299,251,869.15	22.9
1925	67,798,190.20	290,290,165.97	23.4
1926	65,295,154.88	326,974,103.84	20.0
1927	67,213,705.87	312,603,771.53	21.5
1928	63,776,149.05	337,189,422.43	18.9
1929	80,835,545.38	415,338,094.39	19.5
1930	60,063,418.56	376,167,428.42	16.0
1931	57,335,498.53	263,275,255.37	21.8

CURRENT AND CONTINGENT LIABILITIES

Total current liabilities amounted to $28,482,788.06, compared with $40,603,451.00 at the end of 1930. Your Company had no notes payable or any obligation bearing its endorsement outstanding, and none of the companies in which your Company owns a majority interest had any funded debt or any loans owing to banks or to the public. Your Company's only contingent liability was that of guarantor for $1,846,724 in connection with the employees home ownership plan (reviewed on page 15), which was adequately secured.

WORKING CAPITAL

Working capital (total current assets less total current liabilities) amounted to $190,603,722.58, compared with $201,961,098.10 at the end of 1930, a decrease of $11,357,375.52.

GENERAL RESERVE

The general reserve, which amounted to $39,763,664.68 on December 31, 1930, has been drawn upon in 1931 in connection with the revaluation of associated companies and miscellaneous securities, and on December 31, 1931, amounted to $14,517,597.21.

CAPITAL STOCK AND DIVIDENDS

There were no changes during the year in the special or common stock outstanding. Regular dividends of 15 cents per share on the special stock and 40 cents per share on the common stock were paid quarterly.

STOCKHOLDERS

On December 18, 1931, there were 150,073 holders of common and special stock, half of this number (exclusive of corporations, institutions, etc.) being women. This compares with 116,750 on December 19, 1930, and 60,374 on December 16, 1929, an increase in 1931 over 1929 of 149 per cent.

ORGANIZATION CHANGES

Theodore W. Frech, who was given leave of absence on January 1, 1930, resumed his position as Vice President in charge of the Incandescent Lamp Department in April 1931.

Dana R. Bullen, Assistant Vice President, retired on pension July 1, 1931.

EMPLOYEES AND PAYROLLS

The average number of employees of your Company during 1931, not including those of associated companies, was 65,516, compared with 78,380 during 1930. Total earnings of these employees amounted to $106,656,000 for 1931 and $140,905,000 for 1930. Average annual earnings per employee were $1628 and $1798 respectively, a decrease of 9.5 per cent. The cost of living, according to the index of the National Industrial Conference Board, decreased 9.9 per cent from 1930.

Compared with the year 1923, average annual earnings of employees for 1931 were 1.2 per cent more and the cost of living was 13.3 per cent less.

The several plans of extra compensation (or profit sharing), referred to in previous reports, yielded $1,940,257 payable to 1,731 employees for 1931, compared with payments of $3,971,153 to 2335 employees for 1930.

VARIOUS EMPLOYEE PLANS

Plans dealing with group life and disability insurance, home ownership, savings, pensions, unemployment, and employment guarantee were described at length in the 1930 Annual Report.

Pensions and Retirement Payments

Company pension and retirement payments aggregating $1,517,667 were made during 1931 to 2141 retired employees, the larger share of which was paid by the Pension Trust. On December 31, 1931, there were 1953 on the pension and retirement rolls, whose average age was 68.0 years, average active service to date of retirement 29.6 years, and average annual payment $885. Pension and retirement payments amounting to $5,513,400 have been made since the inauguration of the plans in 1912.

The General Electric Pension Trust on December 31, 1931 held assets of $20,125,255, compared with $16,505,168 on December 31, 1930.

Contributions by employees to the Additional Pension Plan during the three and one-half years since its establishment amounted, with interest, to $4,098,382. This amount is deposited in a trust fund to the credit of 50,037 employees.

The Additional Pension Plan added $43,275 to pensions paid during 1931.

The Trustees of these two Trusts hold title to their respective assets, which are therefore not reflected in your Company's balance sheet.

PEAT, MARWICK, MITCHELL & CO.
Accountants and Auditors

40 Exchange Place, New York, March 4, 1932.

To the Board of Directors of the
  General Electric Company,
    120 Broadway, New York.

Dear Sirs:

We have examined the accounts of the General Electric Company for the year ended December 31, 1931, and certify that the Condensed statement of income and expenses and Balance sheet appearing on pages 5–7 of this report are in accordance with the books and, in our opinion, set forth the results of the operations of the Company for the year and the condition of its affairs as at December 31, 1931.

We have confirmed the cash and securities by count and inspection or by certificates which we have obtained from the depositories. The valuations at which the investments in Associated companies and miscellaneous securities are carried have been approved by a Committee of the Board of Directors and, in our opinion, are conservative. Our examination has not included the accounts of companies controlled through stock ownership (other than International General Electric Company, Inc. and G. E. Employees Securities Corporation), but financial statements of these Companies have been submitted to us.

We have scrutinized the notes and accounts receivable and are satisfied that full provision has been made for possible losses through bad and doubtful debts.

Certified inventories of merchandise, work in progress, and materials and supplies have been submitted to us and we have satisfied ourselves that these inventories have been taken in a careful manner, that ample allowance has been made for old or inactive stocks, and that they are conservatively stated on the basis of cost or market, whichever is lower. Provision has also been made for possible allowances or additional expenditures on completed contracts.

Expenditures capitalized in the property and plant accounts during the year were properly so chargeable as representing additions or improvements. Adequate provision has been made in the operating accounts for repairs, renewals and depreciation, and for contingencies.

Yours truly,

PEAT, MARWICK, MITCHELL & CO.

BIBLIOGRAPHY OF REFERENCED WORKS

Abdel-Khalik, A. Rashad (1981). *The Economic Effects on Lessees of FASB Statement No. 13, Accounting for Leases* (Financial Accounting Standards Board).

Armstrong, Marshall S. (1977). "The Politics of Establishing Accounting Standards," *Journal of Accountancy* (February 1977), pp. 76–79.

Arrow, Kenneth (1963). *Social Choice and Individual Values* (John Wiley).

Benston, George J. (1973). "Required Disclosure and the Stock Market: An Evaluation of the Securities Act of 1934," *American Economic Review* (March 1973), pp. 132–155.

Bernstein, Marver H. (1955). *Regulating Business by Independent Commission* (Princeton University Press).

Bowers, Patricia F. (1974). *Private Choice and Public Welfare, the Economics of Public Goods* (The Dryden Press).

Briloff, Abraham J. (1972). *Unaccountable Accounting* (Harper & Row).

——— (1976). *More Debits than Credits* (Harper & Row).

Brown, Paul R. (1981). "A Descriptive Analysis of Select Input Bases of the Financial Accounting Standards Board," *Journal of Accounting Research* (Spring 1981), pp. 232–246.

Demsetz, Harold (1970). "The Private Production of Public Goods," *The Journal of Law and Economics* (October 1970), pp. 293–306.

Demski, Joel S. (1973). "The General Impossibility of Normative Accounting Standards," *The Accounting Review* (October 1973), pp. 718–723.

Financial Accounting Standards Board (1975). "Accounting for the Translation of Foreign Currency Transactions and Foreign Currency Financial Statements," *Statement of Financial Accounting Standards No. 8* (Financial Accounting Standards Board).

—— (1976a). "Accounting for Leases," *Statement of Financial Accounting Standards No. 13* (Financial Accounting Standards Board).

—— (1976b). "Financial Reporting for Segments of a Business Enterprise," *Statement of Financial Accounting Standards No. 14.* (Financial Accounting Standards Board).

—— (1978). *Economic Consequences of Financial Accounting Standards* (Financial Accounting Standards Board).

—— (1979). "Financial Reporting and Changing Prices," *Statement of Financial Accounting Standards No. 33* (Financial Accounting Standards Board).

—— (1980). "Disclosure of Pension Information," *Statement of Financial Accounting Standards No. 36* (Financial Accounting Standards Board).

—— (1982). "Disclosures About Oil and Gas Producing Activities," *Statement of Financial Accounting Standards No. 69* (Financial Accounting Standards Board).

Gonedes, Nicholas J. (1972). "Efficient Capital Markets and External Accounting," *The Accounting Review* (January 1972), pp. 11–21.

Gonedes, Nicholas J., and Nicholas Dopuch (1974). "Capital Market Equilibrium, Information Production, and Selected Accounting Techniques: Theoretical Framework and Review of Empirical Work," *Studies on Financial Accounting Objectives* (Supplement to *Journal of Accounting Research*), pp. 48–129.

Hakansson, Nils H. (1977). "Interim Disclosure and Public Forecasts: An Economic Analysis and Framework for Choice," *The Accounting Review* (April 1977), pp. 396–416.

Hirshleifer, Jack (1971). "The Private and Social Value of Information and the Reward to Inventive Activity," *American Economic Review* (September 1971) pp. 561–573.

Holthausen, Robert W., and Richard W. Leftwich (1982). "The Economic Consequences of Accounting Alternatives: Frictions in the Monitoring, Contracting and Information Processes" (Paper presented at the 1982 annual meeting of the American Accounting Association).

Horngren, Charles T. (1973). "The Marketing of Accounting Standards," *Journal of Accountancy* (October 1973), pp. 61–66.

Hussein, Mohamed E., and J. Edward Ketz (1980). "Ruling Elites of the FASB: A Study of the Big Eight," *Journal of Accounting, Auditing and Finance* (Summer 1980), pp. 354–367.

Jensen, Michael, and William Meckling (1976). "Theory of the Firm: Managerial Behavior, Agency Costs and Ownership Structure," *Journal of Financial Economics* (October 1976), pp. 305–360.

Kirk, Donald J. (1978). "How to Keep Politics Out of Standard Setting: Making Private Sector Rule-Making Work," *Journal of Accountancy* (September 1978), pp. 92–94.

Krislov, Samuel, and Lloyd D. Musolf (1964). *The Politics of Regulation* (Houghton Mifflin).

May, Robert G., and Gary L. Sundem (1976). "Research for Accounting Policy: An Overview," *The Accounting Review* (October 1976), pp. 747–763.

Ng, David S. (1978). "An Information Economics Analysis of Financial Reporting and External Auditing," *The Accounting Review* (October 1978), pp. 910–920.

Ross, Steven A. (1979). "Disclosure Regulation in Financial Markets," in *Issues in Financial Regulation*, ed. F. Edwards (McGraw-Hill), pp. 177–202.

Securities and Exchange Commission (1973). "Statement of Accounting Policy on the Establishment and Improvement of Accounting Principles and Standards," *Accounting Series Release No. 150* (Securities and Exchange Commission).

———— (1975). "Notice of Adoption of Amendments to Form 10-Q and Regulation S-X Regarding Interim Reporting," *Accounting Series Release No. 177* (Securities and Exchange Commission).

Seidler, Lee J.; Frederick Andrews; and Marc J. Epstein (1977). *The Equity Funding Papers, Anatomy of a Fraud* (John Wiley & Sons).

Solomons, David (1978). "The Politicalization of Accounting," *Journal of Accountancy* (November 1978), pp. 65–72.

Stigler, George J. (1971). "The Theory of Economic Regulation," *Bell Journal of Economics and Management Science* (Fall 1971), pp. 3–21.

———— (1975). *The Citizen and the State: Essays on Regulation* (University of Chicago Press).

Wallace, Wanda A. (1980). *The Economic Role of the Audit in Free and Regulated Markets* (University of Rochester).

Watts, Ross L. (1980). "Can Optimal Information Be Determined by Regulation," in *Regulation and the Accounting Profession*, ed. John W. Buckley and J. Fred Weston (Lifetime Learning Publication, 1980), pp. 153–162.

Watts, Ross L., and Jerold L. Zimmerman (1978). "Toward a Positive Theory of the Determination of Accounting Standards," *The Accounting Review* (January 1978), pp. 112–134.

———— (1981). "The Markets for Independence and Independent Auditors" (Paper presented at the 1981 annual meeting of the American Accounting Association).

Zeff, Stephen A. (1978). "The Rise of Economic Consequences," *Journal of Accountancy* (December 1978), pp. 56–63.

ADDITIONAL READINGS

Abdel-Khalik, A. Rashad, ed. (1980). *Government Regulation of Accounting, Accounting Series No. 11* (University Presses of Florida).

Advisory Committee on Corporate Disclosure (1977). *Report of the Advisory Committee on Corporate Disclosure to the Securities and Exchange Commission* (U.S. Government Printing Office).

Bejan, Mary (1981). "On the Application of Rational Choice Theory to Financial Reporting Controversies: A Comment on Cushing," *The Accounting Review* (July 1981), pp. 704–712.

Benston, George J. (1979). "The Market for Public Accounting Services: Demand, Supply and Regulation," *The Accounting Journal* (Winter 1979–1980), pp. 2–46.

———— (1980a). "Disclosure under the Securities Acts and the Proposed Federal Securities Code," *Journal of Accountancy* (October 1980), pp. 34–45.

—— (1980b). "The Establishment and Enforcement of Accounting Standards: Methods, Benefits, and Costs," *Accounting and Business Research* (Winter 1980), pp. 51–60.

Breyer, Steven G. (1982). *Regulation and Its Reform* (Harvard University Press).

Chatov, Robert (1975). *Corporate Financial Reporting: Public or Private Control* (The Free Press).

Cushing, Barry E. (1977). "On the Possibility of Optimal Accounting Principles," *The Accounting Review* (April 1977), pp. 308–321.

Demski, Joel S. (1974). "Choice Among Financial Reporting Alternatives," *The Accounting Review* (April 1974), pp. 221–232.

Fama, Eugene F., and Arthur B. Laffer (1971). "Information and Capital Markets," *Journal of Business* (July 1971), pp. 289–298.

Foster, George (1980a). "Externalities and Financial Reporting," *Journal of Finance* (May 1980), pp. 521–533.

—— (1980b). "Accounting Policy Decisions and Capital Market Research," *Journal of Accounting and Economics* (June 1980), pp. 29–62.

Fromm, Gary, ed. (1981). *Studies in Public Regulation* (The MIT Press).

Horngren, Charles T. (1972). "Accounting Principles: Private or Public Sector?" *The Journal of Accountancy* (May 1972), pp. 37–41.

Kelly-Newton, Lauren (1980). *Accounting Policy Formulation, the Role of Management* (Addison-Wesley).

Leftwich, Richard W. (1980). "Market Failure Fallacies and Accounting Information," *Journal of Accounting and Economics* (December 1980), pp. 193–211.

Marshall, John M. (1974). "Information Accuracy and Public Information," *American Economic Review* (June 1974), pp. 373–390.

Moonitz, Maurice (1974). "Obtaining Agreement on Standards in the Accounting Profession," *Studies in Accounting Research No. 8* (American Accounting Association).

Owen, Bruce M., and Ronald Braeutigam (1978). *The Regulation Game* (Ballinger).

Peltzman, Sam (1976). "Toward a More General Theory of Regulation," *Journal of Law and Economics* (October 1976), pp. 211–240.

Posner, Richard A. (1974). "Theories of Economic Regulation," *Bell Journal of Economics and Management Science* (Autumn 1974), pp. 335–358.

Sterling, Robert R., ed. (1974). *Institutional Issues in Public Accounting* (Scholars Book Company).

Watts, Ross L. (1977). "Corporate Financial Statements: Product of the Market and Political Processes," *Australian Journal of Management* (April 1977), pp. 53–75.

White, Lawrence J. (1981). *Reforming Regulation: Processes and Problems* (Prentice-Hall).

CHAPTER 4

Postulates, Principles, and Concepts

In Chapter 3 the possible benefits of accounting regulation, including the need for a theoretical framework, were discussed. The Committee on Accounting Procedure (CAP) was not concerned with the task of deriving an underlying framework. However, both the Accounting Principles Board (APB) and the Financial Accounting Standards Board (FASB) have attempted to develop theoretical foundations as a guide to formulating accounting rules. In the case of the APB, it was the system of postulates and principles that was briefly mentioned in Chapter 2. For the FASB, it is the conceptual framework project. The APB's works proved to be unsuccessful; whereas the FASB effort, a much longer term endeavor, is still unfolding.

Despite the lack of acceptance of Accounting Research Studies (ARSs) 1 and 3 on postulates and principles, these studies represent a milestone in the attempt to provide a unified theoretical underpinning for financial accounting rules. Consequently, it is important to assess why these studies fell short of the goal of obtaining a framework for the derivation of opinions by the APB. Part of the story has already been told: the project advisors, not to mention the profession at large, felt the principles were too much in conflict with existing notions to serve as a frame of reference for the rules that were sure to follow. A closer look at these studies will enable us to gain a better understanding of FASB's conceptual framework and its prospect for success.

A discussion of postulates and principles would be incomplete without analyzing those concepts that have formed an important basis for contemporary historical cost accounting. No matter what form financial statements may take in the future, it is quite likely that many of these ideas will be retained, refined, or modified because they have proved useful in an informal but pragmatic fashion.

Finally, we look at another group of concepts, which have long played a role in interpreting accounting relationships. These are the so-called equity theories of accounting. They are concerned with the relationship that exists between the firm itself and its ownership interests. Various inferences can be drawn from these relationships, which can have an influence on standard setting. A discussion of these concepts and their implications for policy-making conclude the chapter.

Two appendices are also provided. They are the postulates of ARS 1 and the broad principles of ARS 3. They should be read in conjunction with the discussion of these documents.

POSTULATES AND PRINCIPLES

The watershed nature of the formation of the APB relative to accounting theory development and the role of research cannot be overstressed. However, Alvin R. Jennings, in his important speech advocating this new approach to the development of accounting principles, did not propose formation of a new rule-making body. What he did envision was a new research organization within the American Institute of Certified Public Accountants (AICPA) which would issue statements that would be subject to a two-thirds vote of the Council of the AICPA.[1]

SPECIAL COMMITTEE ON RESEARCH PROGRAM

The actual resultant mechanism came from the Special Committee on Research Program, which reported the need for articulating the basic set of postulates underlying accounting. In turn, the principles were to be logically derived from the postulates. The Committee thus advocated a deductive approach. It was noted in Chapter 1 that deductive approaches to theory are basically normative in outlook. The Committee gave only a slight

---

[1]Jennings (1958, p. 32).

mention to the fact that it was dealing with a normative approach and the implications thereof.

> The general purpose of the Institute . . . should be to advance the written expression of what constitutes generally accepted accounting principles, for the guidance of its members. . . . *This means something more than a survey of existing practice.* It means continuing efforts to *determine appropriate practice* and to narrow the areas of difference and inconsistency in practice. . . . The Institute *should take definite steps to lead in the thinking on unsettled and controversial issues* (emphasis added).[2]

While the need for securing the approval of those who would be subject to the rules of the new APB was noted, the storm of protest that would erupt in the wake of ARS 3 was not foreseen by the Committee.[3] Further problems arose in terms of the Committee's conception of postulates and principles.

Postulates were seen as being few in number and stemming from the economic and political environments as well as from the customs and underlying viewpoints of the business community. The Committee in its report had thus virtually defined postulates, and the fact that there were presumably few of them, for the author of ARS 1. One committee member revealed shortly thereafter that it was not the intention of the committee to define postulates.[4]

Postulates have been defined as basic assumptions that cannot be verified. In addition, they form a basis for inference, serving as a foundation for a theoretical structure that consists of propositions deduced from them.[5] In systems using formal logical techniques, the basic premises are called **axioms** and consist of symbolic notation, with the operations for deducing propositions being mathematically based.[6]

Broad principles, on the other hand, were not defined by the Committee though they were compared in scope to definitions and pronouncements that had been issued in four different reports by the American Accounting Association (AAA). These documents and several supplements were published in 1936, 1941, 1948, and 1957. The first two reports contain the word "principles" in their titles but the word was replaced by "standards" in the 1948 and 1957 reports (the 1948 revision also uses "concepts" in its title).[7] These reports contain definitions of basic accounting terms, proposed rules for presentation and measurement of accounting data, and concepts to be applied to published financial reports. The material in these reports thus covers a wide variety of topics, only some of which might

---

[2]Special Committee on Research Program (1958, pp. 62–63).
[3]See "Comments on 'A Tentative Set of Broad Accounting Principles'" (1963).
[4]Mautz (1965).
[5]Mautz and Sharaf (1961, p. 37).
[6]Morgenstern (1963, pp. 23–24). Some examples of axiomatic deductive systems in accounting include Mattesich (1964, pp. 446–465), Ijiri (1975, pp. 71–84), and Carlson and Lamb (1981).
[7]AAA (1957).

legitimately fall under the topic of principles for the basic study (the basic definitions and concepts, such as disclosure and uniformity).

There is no mention made, however, of the definition of **principles** put forth in Accounting Terminology Bulletin No. 1 of the AICPA:

> A general law or rule adopted or professed as a guide to action, a settled ground or basis of conduct or practice. . . .[8]

This definition is quite close in substance to the definition made in the philosophy of science, a discipline concerned with scientific method. A principle is also closely related to a law. Both are considered to be true statements of a generalized nature, containing referents to the real world as opposed to purely analytic statements whose truth or falsity is self-contained by their internal logic (as in Chapter 1, for example).[9] A law differs from a principle in that the former contains elements observable by empirical techniques, whereas the latter does not. Of course a principle can be empirically tested and, if proven true (or at least not proven false), would become a law. The "truth" of a law or principle does not mean that they are not capable of being replaced by newer systems. However, changes—particularly in the case of laws—should be extremely infrequent.

ACCOUNTING RESEARCH STUDY NO. 1

Given his charge by the Special Committee, Moonitz adopted a frame of reference or outlook that was oriented to the problems dealt with by accountants. He had rejected a deductive type of approach that was rooted in reasoning alone because it was not broad enough to encompass experiential and empirical aspects of accounting. Deinzer has correctly pointed out that Moonitz did come back to the axiomatic (meaning deductive) method.[10] He indeed uses a deductive type of approach—but without employing symbolic terminology and formal logical methods—in terms of reasoning to a second level of postulates and some of the principles. However, the postulates themselves are of two decidedly different types. One category (the A and B groups) is made up of general descriptive types of postulates that appear to coincide with the Committee's charge that postulates should be derived from the economic and political environment and modes of thought and customs from all segments of the community. The second category (the C group) is value judgments. It is this latter type which may have gone against the Committee's desires and definitely labels Moonitz's work as deductive–normative in scope.

The postulates themselves (see Appendix 4–A) are in three groups: the environmental group (A), those stemming from accounting itself (B), and the imperatives (C). Some postulates in the B group appear to stem from the A category. This has led to the criticism that no postulates should be

[8]AICPA (1953, pp. 9505–9506).
[9]Caws (1965, p. 85).
[10]Deinzer (1965, p. 111).

reasoned from any others and a similar criticism that a ranking among postulates exists. While these criticisms may have some validity, these problems could easily be overcome by relabeling. There is no rule that only two levels (postulates and principles) can be used in deductive reasoning. A complex environment, such as that in which accounting operates, can have numerous levels.

A far more telling criticism is that postulates that are self-evident may not be sufficiently substantive to enable the reasoning process to lead to a unique and meaningful set of accounting principles. This unquestionably appears to be the case with both the A and B groups. If postulates are indeed defined as self-evident generalizations from a particular environment, the question must be raised as to what their role is in a deductively oriented system where principles form the basis for more specific rules to improve the practice of accounting. Of necessity, it appears that they must play a more passive role. The principles and rules should not be in conflict with them, but alone they are not sufficiently important to lead to the desired principles and rules.[11] They are thus necessary but not sufficient to lead to a viable outcome.

Hence the key group is the imperatives. These appear to be more in the nature of what Mautz has called "concepts" because (1) they are normative in nature and (2) they have developed within the context of accounting practice.[12] The imperatives have the flavor of being objectives that should be strived for, which is also a result of their normative aspect. The key postulate appears to be C-4, stability of the monetary unit. This postulate appears to have two possible outcomes. If purchasing power of the monetary unit is, in fact, not stable, the postulate implies that some form of inflation accounting should be instituted. If, on the other hand, purchasing power of the monetary unit is relatively stable, two further consequences of the postulate arise—one is that retention of historical cost is justified, owing to stability of the dollar; the other is that a system of current values is still justified, despite general stability of the monetary unit, because considerable price fluctuation can occur on account of demand changes that occur despite general monetary stability. The dual nature of the interpretation of C-4 is a definite weakness of this very important postulate. Perhaps Postulate A-1, usefulness of quantitative data, should lead to current values, but this is certainly not self-evident from the Moonitz postulates. At any rate, the profession was generally silent when the postulates appeared. It was undoubtedly awaiting the appearance of the broad principles study.

ACCOUNTING RESEARCH STUDY NO. 3

There are a total of eight broad principles in the study (see Apppendix 4-B). At least three of them (A, B and D) are related to the problem of changing prices, which was the point of departure leading to the profession's

[11]Vatter (1963, pp. 185–186).
[12]Mautz (1965, p. 47).

rather stinging rejection of the study. It is interesting to note that the summary of the eight principles covers some four and one-half pages, two and one-half of which are devoted to Principle D, the asset valuation principle.

Deinzer has very appropriately noted that Principle A—which states that revenue is earned by the entire process of operations of the firm rather than at one point only, usually when sale occurs—was not reasoned from any of the fourteen postulates.[13] As such, it would appear to belong in the B group of postulates. More importantly, it appears that Sprouse and Moonitz needed it to pave the way for their value-oriented principles because it underlies the recognition of changes in replacement cost, which leads to holding gains or losses (Principle B-2).

One of the most pointed criticisms of the asset valuation measures prescribed in Principle D is that they are not "additive." That is, although current value dollars are being used, different attributes or characteristics are being measured; hence they cannot theoretically be combined by means of the addition operation because different current-value characteristics are advocated by Sprouse and Moonitz for different asset classes. For example, if inventory can easily be sold at a given market price, net realizable value (selling price less known costs of disposal) should be used (D-2). On the other hand, the value of fixed assets, which are not intended for sale, is rooted in terms of the service they can provide over present and future periods. As a result, Sprouse and Moonitz opt for replacement cost as the appropriate characteristic of measurement for this class of assets (D-3). Obviously the additivity question, where different attributes are being measured, has strong overtones of measurement theory.

The principal opponent of lack of additivity of asset values put forth by the broad principles of ARS 3 is Chambers.[14] Chambers is a very strong advocate of the exit-value approach illustrated in Chapter 1.[15] His own position has been blurred because he would accept replacement cost as a secondary valuation if exit values were unavailable.[16] However, it should be clear that Chambers is attempting to separate conceptual or theoretical issues from measurement problems. Hence it would almost appear that the additivity issue can be breached only if one's heart is in the right place: the basic theoretical system must be unified in terms of one primary characteristic of assets and liabilities to be measured. Nevertheless, the primacy of conceptual issues over measurement problems cannot be ignored. The answer probably lies in determining which current value elements have most utility for financial statement users, an issue not addressed by Sprouse and Moonitz.

---

[13]Deinzer (1965, p. 131).
[14]Chambers (1964, p. 409).
[15]For a complete exposition see Chambers (1966).
[16]See Chambers (1966, p. 249). For additional coverage, see Wright (1967) and Chambers (1970).

A last criticism to be leveled at ARS 1 and ARS 3 is that a set of postulates should be complete enough to allow no conflicting conclusions to be derived from them. Postulate C-4 says that the monetary unit should be stable. From it, Principle D was derived advocating various current values for different categories of assets. The various choices espoused in Principle D cannot be justified to the exclusion of other possibilities. Hence the postulate system is not theoretically tight enough to justify it, whether or not one agrees with the resulting principles.

A PERSPECTIVE OF ARS 1 AND ARS 3

ARS 1 and ARS 3 failed for a variety of reasons, in addition to the most obvious one—the inability of the profession to abandon historical costs. There were several weaknesses of the postulates and principles themselves: The postulates were not complete and therefore could not exclude all value systems other than the one prescribed in the principles. Additionally, at least one of the principles, Principle A, was not derived from any of the postulates. Finally, the question of whether resulting valuations of various assets should be additive (because they advocated different attributes) became an interesting, and probably moot, point.

Even beyond the questions of logic and adequacy of ARS 1 and ARS 3, a number of issues have since made it clear that the Moonitz–Sprouse efforts could not succeed. It appears that Moonitz and Sprouse were commissioned to find those postulates and principles that would lead to "true income," to use a single concept of income that would show itself superior to all other challengers. In retrospect, it has become evident that no income measurement can presently be deemed to have such an advantage over competing concepts (see Chapter 5 for further coverage).

Aside from Postulate A-1, which states that "quantitative data are helpful in making rational economic decisions," virtually nothing is said in either study about who are the outside users of accounting data and what their particular information needs and abilities might be. It is generally conceded today that users of financial data (with their underlying information needs and abilities to understand and manipulate financial data) cover a broad spectrum of heterogeneous categories. However, emphasis on users was not a particularly prominent theoretical accounting issue when ARSs 1 and 3 were published. (User diversity and its implications are discussed later in Chapter 5.)

The postulates and principles approach tended to overlook a theoretical area that has since then received a great deal of attention. The rise of the user-needs outlook has produced a new focus on the objectives of published financial statement data. Indeed, as was previously mentioned, several of the imperative postulates actually began to spill over into the area of financial statement objectives. Formulating objectives of financial statements and reporting has become an extremely important part of theory formulation; they will be extensively discussed in Chapter 5.

Finally, we note that the commissioning of ARS 1 and ARS 3 occurred at a time when little formal attention was given to what might be called the "politics" of rule making. By this we mean that there is more opportunity to react to potential accounting rules by those who will be subject to them under the FASB than was the case with the APB.

Some might say that the postulates and principles studies were a dismal failure. As we view events from the perspective of twenty years, we realize that this is not the case. These studies would hold an important place in the history of accounting theory if for no other reason than the fact that they were the first attempt in the United States by the practicing arm of the profession to provide a conceptual underpinning for the rule-making function. Furthermore, by facing the difficulties of drafting a theoretical statement that would meet the approval of those who would be governed by it, the FASB learned valuable lessons which they eventually put to good use in their Conceptual Framework Project.

BASIC CONCEPTS UNDERLYING HISTORICAL COSTING

Accounting has long had many concepts that have influenced the resulting rules. While these concepts have largely developed in a pragmatic fashion from practical operating necessities, including income tax laws, they have frequently been the subject of works written largely in the formative years (1930–46) of accounting policy-making groups in the United States.[17] Perhaps the most outstanding of these was the monograph by Paton and Littleton, *An Introduction to Corporate Accounting Standards*.[18] While this work was not revolutionary in nature, it did attempt to provide a basic framework that the accounting entity could use to assess its practices. It was hoped that a greater degree of consistency in terms of accounting practice would result from their effort. Paton and Littleton largely used the deductive approach as opposed to attempting to determine what was being done in practice.

Other important works of this period included Canning's attempt to relate asset valuation to future cash flows; separate books by Sweeney and MacNeal that were concerned with accounting for, respectively, the chang-

[17]Chatfield (1974, p. 256).
[18]Paton and Littleton (1940).

ing value of monetary unit and the weakness of historical costs; Sanders, Hatfield, and Moore's monograph attempting to derive the principles of accounting from practice; Gilman's book about refining the concept of income; and Littleton's attempt to derive inductively the accounting principles underlying relevant practice.[19]

The concepts discussed here have been identified under many names— as postulates, axioms, assumptions, doctrines, conventions, constraints, principles, and standards. Use of the word "concepts" for these terms probably depicts them quite accurately. A **concept** represents the process of identifying, classifying, and interpreting various phenomena or precepts.[20] They thus arise outside of formal theory formulation but can be used within it—as part of the structure of postulates, or in the conclusions deduced from the postulates, or even as the subject of testing in empirical research. Accounting, of course, is concerned with many elements that fall into the concept category. They are quite rightly considered to be a part of accounting theory. Many have been and will be part of a general theoretical framework for interpreting and presenting financial accounting data as well as being part of the subject matter of individual accounting theories. Indeed several of them will be discussed in Chapter 5 in terms of their place in the emerging conceptual framework of the FASB.

Other attempts besides ARS 1 and ARS 3 and those mentioned in Chapter 1 have been made to set up deductive systems of postulates and principles.[21] Lack of rigor in reasoning, overlapping definitions, and different value judgments make a high degree of consensus extremely difficult. Bearing this in mind, we have organized the material here strictly for teaching purposes. The concepts are broken down as follows:

Postulates are basic assumptions concerning the business environment.

Principles are general approaches utilized in recognition and measurement of accounting events. Principles are, in turn, divided into two main types:

Input-oriented principles are broad rules that guide the accounting function. Input-oriented principles can be divided into two general classifications: general underlying rules of operation and constraining principles. As their names imply, the former are general in nature while the latter are geared to certain specific types of situations.

Output-oriented principles involve certain qualities or characteristics that financial statements should possess if the input-oriented principles are appropriately executed.

---

[19]Canning (1929); Sweeney (1936); MacNeal (1939); Sanders, Hatfield, and Moore (1938); Gilman (1939); and Littleton (1953).
[20]Caws (1965, pp. 24–29).
[21]For example, Study Group at the University of Illinois (1964).

A schema of these various concepts is shown in Exhibit 4-1.

EXHIBIT 4-1.
Basic Concepts Underlying Historical Costing

POSTULATES   **PRINCIPLES**

Going Concern   *Input-Oriented Principles*
Time period   • General Underlying Rules of Operation
Accounting entity   1. Realization
Monetary unit   2. Matching
                               • Constraining Principles
                                  1. Conservatism
                                  2. Disclosure
                                  3. Materiality
                                  4. Objectivity (reclassified as part of measurement
                                     theory)
                               Output-Oriented Principles
                               • Applicable to Users
                                  1. Comparability
                               • Applicable to Preparers
                                  1. Consistency
                                  2. Uniformity

POSTULATES

Going Concern or Continuity

The going-concern postulate simply states that unless there is evidence to the contrary, it is assumed that the firm will continue indefinitely. As a result, liquidation values for assets and equities are in violation of the postulate under ordinary circumstances. However, the continuity assumption is simply too broad to lead to any kind of a choice among valuation systems, including historical cost. The postulate has received extensive criticism from Fremgen and Sterling.[22] Sterling logically demolishes it because the time period of continuity is presumed to be long enough to conclude the firm's present contractual arrangements. However, by the time these affairs are concluded, they will have been replaced by new arrangements. Hence the implication is one of indefinite life. However, we know that over the long run, many firms do conclude their activities. Therefore, continuity is more in the nature of a prediction than an underlying assumption. Suffice it to say that, aside from ordinarily excluding liquidation values, going concern has little to add to accounting theory.

---

[22]Fremgen (1968) and Sterling (1968).

Time Period

Time period concerns the fact that business, as well as virtually every form of human and animal society, operates within fairly rigidly specified periods of time. The time period idea is nevertheless, somewhat artificial because it creates segments out of a continuing process. For operating entities, the time period is the calendar or business year.[23] As a result, of course, annual reports contain statements of financial condition, earnings, and funds flow. Since the year is a relatively short period of time in the life of most enterprises, the time period postulate has led to accrual accounting and to the principles of realization and matching under historical costing.

Furthermore, with the fiscal year as the "standard" time period, user needs have led to financial reporting for less than full year intervals. Interim financial statements have their own problems and sets of rules. In general, however, APB 28 states that accounting methods followed in annual financial statements must likewise be followed in interim reports. Hence estimates of annual amounts must be made.

Accounting Entity

It is well understood that the business entity is separate from its owners when we view it in the accounting context as well as in its corporate legal form. Two important problems arise from the accounting entity perspective.

First is the problem of defining the entity and accounting for the relation between its parts. Involved here is the question of whether entities should be combined as a result of one controlling the other(s). The control question concerns whether to combine accounts or to use a noncombinative method of showing the relationship. If combination is deemed appropriate, the purchase versus pooling question arises with the main issue being whether a new accountability has been created and, if so, how? The whole combination issue is made more complex by the presence of foreign operations. Theoretical aspects of these questions are discussed in Chapters 17 and 18.

The second issue that is related to the question of the accounting entity concerns the relation between the firm and its owners. While the accounting is separate, the point of interface exists in the owners' equity accounts. A number of deductive theories have arisen, purporting to describe this relationship and the role of the owners' equity accounts. These ideas influence our interpretation of whether certain elements should be included in income, the meaning of equities, and other important issues. The equity theories, as they are called, are discussed later in this chapter.

---

[23]For an example holding revenues constant with time as a variable, see Nichols and Grawoig (1968).

Monetary Unit

In nonbarter economies, money serves as the medium of exchange. As a result, money has also become the principal standard of value and is the subject of the measurement process. Thus financial statements are expressed in terms of the monetary unit of their particular nation. The assumption, for accounting purposes, that the monetary unit is stable, became a bulwark supporting the principles and methods. Hence the historical cost principle became enshrined as a virtually unchallengeable tenet of accounting.

While historical cost still serves as the primary accounting method in published financial statements, the severe inflation in the United States and other nations of the Western world has led to the activation of valuation theories and new ways of presenting financial information. In the United States, Statement of Financial Accounting Standards (SFAS) 33 has led to supplementary general purchasing power and current valuation disclosures. Theoretical issues and problems of implementing SFAS 33 are discussed in Chapters 11 and 12.

PRINCIPLES

The word "principles" has not been well defined in ARSs of the AICPA. Neither ARS 1 nor ARS 3 precisely defines the word, though the latter study contains the term "broad accounting principles" in its title. The preface of ARS 7, by Paul Grady, indicates that accounting principles are synonymous with practices.[24] However, some four hundred pages later, Grady identifies principles as postulates derived from "experiences and reason" which have proved useful.[25] Deductively, then, it appears that principles are postulates that have had successful usage in practice, an interpretation that Grady himself would probably tend to reject.

Perhaps the most useful definition of principles stemming from official publications comes from APB Statement 4. **Generally accepted accounting principles** are rooted in "experience, reason, custom, usage, and . . . practical necessity."[26] Furthermore, they ". . . encompass the conventions, rules, and procedures necessary to define accepted accounting practice at a particular time."[27] At this point, there is still overlap with Grady's definition, in which principles are identified with acceptable practice; but principles are seen as distinct from postulates even though they stem from practical necessity and related experiences.[28] However, a subset of generally ac-

---

[24]Grady (1965, p. ix).

[25]Grady (1965, p. 407).

[26]AICPA (1970, p. 9084).

[27]AICPA (1970, p. 9084).

[28]One reason for the overlap is that APB Statement 4 envisions a three-tiered approach to principles. The bottom level, detailed principles, is made up of the actual operating rules themselves, such as the opinions of the APB. AICPA (1970, p. 9084).

cepted accounting principles, **pervasive principles,** is largely synonymous with the way the term is being used here:

> . . . pervasive principles are few in number and fundamental in nature. . . . pervasive principles specify the general approach accountants take to recognition and measurement of events that affect the financial position and results of operations of enterprises.[29]

Notice that both definitions of principles from APB Statement 4 stop short of the virtual permanence given to the word in the scientific sense discussed previously. Pervasive principles overlap with what we refer to here as input-oriented principles.

INPUT-ORIENTED PRINCIPLES

Accounting principles are classified here into two broad types: input-oriented principles and output-oriented principles. The distinctions between these groups are at least somewhat clear. Input-oriented principles are concerned with general approaches or rules for specifying the method of how financial statements are to be prepared, and the content, including any necessary supplementary disclosures. Output-oriented principles are concerned with comparison of financial statements of different firms. Although some of these principles apply to preparers of the statements and others to users, there is a close linkage between them.

General Underlying Rules of Operation

Input-oriented principles are further broken down into two classifications. Principles concerned with general underlying rules of operation are involved with broad approaches to revenue and expense recognition. These principles illustrate the primary orientation of historical cost accounting towards income measurement rather than asset and liability valuation.

Realization. **Revenue** is defined here as the output of the enterprise in terms of its product(s) or service(s). Notice that this definition says nothing about the receipt or inflow of assets arising as a result of revenue performance. Defining revenue in conjunction with what it gives rise to can easily lead to problems in terms of when to recognize revenue as being earned.[30] It is generally conceded that revenues arise in conjunction with all of the operations of a firm.[31] For a manufacturing enterprise, these would include acquisition of raw materials, production, sale, collection of cash or other consideration from customers, and after-sale services such as product warranties and guarantees.

---

[29] AICPA (1970, p, 9084).
[30] For further coverage see Hendriksen (1982, pp. 172–174).
[31] For a classic statement of the idea see Paton and Littleton (1940, pp. 48–49). Of course, this is also Principle A of ARS 3.

Realization concerns the problem of when to recognize revenue. By far the most prevalent revenue recognition point is at the point of sale. Other possibilities may, however, arise. One suggestion is to recognize it in accordance with the firm's "critical event." The critical event is that operating function, as mentioned above, which is the most crucial in terms of the earning process of an enterprise.[32] Revenue recognition points are discussed in Chapter 9. Suffice it to say that the revenue realization principle is the most pervasive principle in the canon of historical cost accounting.

Matching. **Expenses** are defined as costs that expire as a result of generating revenues. Expenses are thus necessary to the production of revenues. If all expenses could be directly identified with either specific revenues or specific time periods, expense measurement would present few problems. Unfortunately, many important expenses cannot be specifically identified with particular revenues, and they also bring benefit to more than one time period.

The various methods used for recognizing cost expiration (expense incurrence) for categories such as depreciation, cost of goods sold, interest, and deferred charges is called **matching**. Matching implies that expenses are being recognized on a fair and equitable basis relative to the realization of revenues. Matching is thus the second aspect, after realization, of the primacy of income measurement over asset and liability valuation in our present system, which is oriented toward historical cost.

Matching is currently under extensive attack on two accounts. First, the historical cost approach often tends to result in expense measurements that are vastly understated relative to the value of expired-asset services. Second, the "systematic and rational" methods employed under generally accepted accounting principles tend to be extremely arbitrary: more than one method for handling a particular problem can be defended. This imprecision is known as the "allocation problem" and is discussed in Chapter 6.

Constraining Principles

The second group of input-oriented principles partially overlap with the "modifying conventions" mentioned in APB Statement 4. They are described in the following fashion:

> Certain widely adopted conventions modify the application of the pervasive measurement principles. These modifying conventions . . . have evolved to deal with some of the most difficult and controversial problem areas in financial accounting.[33]

The constraining principles either impose limitations upon financial statements, as in the case of conservatism, or provide checks on them, as in the case of materiality and disclosure.

---

[32]Myers (1959).
[33]AICPA (1970, p. 9089).

Conservatism. Unquestionably conservatism holds an extremely important place in the ethos of accountants. Indeed it has even been called the dominant principle of accounting.[34] A classic example of conservatism is the lower-of-cost-or-market valuation for inventories and marketable securities.

Conservatism is defined here as the attempt to select "generally accepted" accounting methods that result in any of the following: (1) slower revenue recognition, (2) faster expense recognition, (3) lower asset valuation, (4) higher liability valuation.

However, in some situations there can be a conflict among some of the above criteria. If so, lower income considerations would take precedence over higher asset valuations in determining whether a method or approach is conservative. For example, in the case of current valuation of assets, one approach—called distributable income—does not include real holding gains in the computation of income. As a result, in an inflationary environment, distributable income often results in higher asset valuations and lower income calculations than would occur under the historical cost alternative. Therefore, the distributable income approach to current valuation can be more conservative than historical costing even though, as a general statement, historical cost is assumed to be more conservative.

Several reasons account for the rise of the conservatism notion. Littleton points out that "lower-of-cost-or-market" originated with the purpose of minimizing inventories for property tax valuation purposes.[35] Similarly, accountants have often undoubtedly been in a defensive position relative to clients who may have desired to maximize either asset valuation or income measurement as highly as possible to maximize security prices—as, for example, prior to the stock market crash of 1929.

As the conceptual foundations of accounting change in accordance with new theoretical approaches, it is quite likely that conservatism, as a dominating principle, will decline in importance.

Disclosure. Disclosure was construed as an imperative postulate (C-5) by Moonitz. However, he cast it in a rather negative mold, saying that disclosure pertains to ". . . that which is necessary to make them (accounting reports) not misleading." Moonitz's outlook may arise from the fact that it is virtually impossible to quantify the concept of adequate disclosure for users. Hence it is not surprising, as Most has observed, that the concept has not been adequately defined by either Securities and Exchange Commission or AICPA sources.[36] Nor has FASB defined it, though two important SFASs deal with it: SFAS 14 on segmental disclosures and SFAS 33 on general price-level and current value data. SFAS 14 requires segmental disclosures by product lines, foreign operations, and major customers where

---

[34]Sterling (1967).
[35]Littleton (1941).
[36]Most (1982, p. 182).

any of these is construed to be a major segment in terms of various quantitative criteria set forth in the statement.

Disclosure refers to relevant financial information both inside and outside the main body of the financial statements themselves, including mention of methods employed in financial statements where more than one choice exists or an unusual or innovative selection of methods is used.[37] The principle outside categories include

1. Supplementary financial statement schedules, such as those pertaining to SFAS 14 and SFAS 33.
2. Footnote disclosure of information that cannot be adequately presented in the body of the financial statements themselves.
3. Disclosure of material or major post-statement events in the annual report.
4. Forecasts of operations for the forthcoming year.
5. Management's analysis of operations in the annual report.

Two important considerations lead to the conclusion that disclosure will become even more important in the future. First, as the business environment grows more complex, it becomes more difficult to adequately express important financial and operating information within the confines of the traditional financial statements. Second, a considerable body of evidence indicates that capital markets are able rapidly to absorb and reflect new information within security prices. Hence disclosure per se, as opposed to its particular form, is considered the key factor by many individuals who rely on the market efficiency mechanism. The increased dependency on disclosure in the light of market efficiency requires a more extensive examination in Chapter 7.

Materiality. There are two aspects of materiality in accounting that are related but, nevertheless, distinct from each other. Materiality, as it applies in auditing, is concerned with consistency of judgment by auditors, given a particular level or standard of materiality that is accepted in accounting practice. It is the latter aspect of materiality, the standard or threshold of materiality that should be employed in accounting practice, that we are concerned with here. **Materiality** refers to the degree of importance of an item (or group of items) to users in terms of its relevance to evaluation or decision making. It can thus be viewed as the other side of the disclosure coin because what is disclosed should, of course, be material.

Attention has turned in recent years to attempts to assess quantitative perceptions of materiality. The most ambitious study of this type was done by Pattillo for the Financial Executives Research Foundation.[38] Pattillo's investigation employed twenty-eight cases in which the respondents used

---

[37] APB 22 (1972).
[38] Pattillo (1976).

their own materiality judgments. Six hundred eighty-four individuals participated in the project. They represented preparers of financial statements (financial executives from "Fortune 500" and medium-sized firms), users of accounting information (bankers and financial analysts), auditors, and also academics.

Pattillo's major findings included the following:

1. While many respondents widely use a range of 5% to 10% of net income as the boundary of materiality, no overall single absolute dollar or percentage relationship is applicable to all situations.
2. Perceptions of materiality differ between groups with financial executives having the highest percentage threshold of net income and certified public accountants and financial analysts having the lowest overall percentage.
3. Modifying elements such as the particular characteristics of the firm and the political and economic environment influence the perception of materiality in particular situations.

Another important empirical study was done by Rose, Beaver, Becker, and Sorter, who attempted to relate materiality to the psychological concept of "sensation," which measures the individual's response to a physical stimulus.[39] Their subjects were 121 MBA students. Materiality was viewed in this study as the reaction of investor-type individuals to accounting information. The nature of the test was to present simulated financial data for hypothetical firms on December 31, 1966, and December 31, 1967. The stimulus–response variable was earnings per share. It was always $2.50 for the first year and ranged from $2.00 to $3.00 in the second year at even 10-cent intervals ($2.50 and $2.00, $2.50 and $2.10, etc.). Each of the resulting eleven pairs was presented six times in a randomly selected order. Respondents were asked to identify whether earnings per share were "essentially more, essentially the same, or essentially less" in the second year. Upper and lower materiality bounds for essentially more and essentially less were $2.68 and $2.35 as indicated by 50% of the responses. The test was repeated for some of the subjects using a $5.00 earnings per share figure in the base year in combination with a $4.00 to $6.00 range in the second year. Materiality responses of essentially more or less were very close in percentage terms to the earlier phase of the study. The authors noted that their subjects responded in a "symmetric, regular and predictable manner" consistent with other response patterns relative to sensory stimuli. Moreover, O'Connor and Collins observed in another study that the nature of the Rose study casts materiality in a predictive context—since information from one period is linked to another period.[40] However, the

[39]Rose, Beaver, Becker, and Sorter (1970).
[40]O'Connor and Collins (1974, p. 174).

Rose study is somewhat simplistic because the stimulus is restricted to one variable, perceived changes in earnings per share.[41]

Despite their limitations, these and other empirical studies, using questionnaires and simulated situations, have helped to shed light on the concept of materiality—though it is far from a settled issue. It would appear, however, that along with disclosure, materiality will become an issue of growing importance in the foreseeable future. In light of the increasing importance of materiality, the FASB issued a Discussion Memorandum which took up many of the factors that influence the judgment of materiality.[42]

Objectivity. Objectivity has had several interpretations in the past. Perhaps the most important saw it in terms of the quality of verifiability of evidence underlying transactions that are eventually summarized and organized in the form of financial statements.[43] In this interpretation, quality of evidence is separate from those who carry out the measurement function. However, **objectivity** is now more frequently seen in the statistical sense (discussed in Chapter 1) of the degree of consensus among measurers. As such, it is an integral part of the measurement process rather than being either a postulate or principle. APB Statement 4 adopts this outlook although it is classified as a "qualitative objective" of accounting and is relabeled **verifiability.**[44] It is also in this same newer, statistical sense that verifiability appears in the Conceptual Framework Project of the FASB in Statement of Financial Accounting Concepts 2.

OUTPUT-ORIENTED PRINCIPLES

Output-oriented principles, as mentioned earlier, deal with qualities that financial statements should possess when viewed from the standpoint of both preparers and users. Of necessity, then, there is both some degree of overlap as well as complementariness among these concepts. As viewed here, comparability is a concept that applies to users of financial statements, whereas consistency and uniformity are qualities geared to preparers of financial information.

[41]Hofstedt and Hughes (1977) used three stimuli variables for assessing materiality. Their study involved a hypothetical situation dealing with the write-down of an investment in an unconsolidated subsidiary. Criteria for materiality concerned the size of the write-down relative to (1) the net income, (2) the balance in the parent's investment-in-subsidiaries account, and (3) the write-down size relative to total book value of the subsidiary involved. In addition, Hofstedt and Hughes used a finer measure for their subjects to indicate perceived materiality than did the Rose group. Hofstedt and Hughes used a scale from 0 to 100 for indicating the need for disclosure, whereas Rose used the cruder response of whether changes in earnings per share were "essentially more . . . the same . . . or less than in the previous year." Unfortunately the Hofstedt and Hughes study was restricted to only nineteen second-year MBA students.
[42]FASB (1975).
[43]Paton and Littleton (1940, pp. 18–21).
[44]AICPA (1970, p. 9076). Vatter (1963, p. 190) was an early adherent of the view that objectivity is part of measurement methodology.

Comparability

Comparability has often been described as accounting for like events in a similar manner.[45] This definition is too simplistic to be operational. Also, this definition is geared toward preparers of financial statements. It is viewed here from the user's standpoint. **Comparability** refers to the degree of reliability users should have in financial statements when utilizing them on an interfirm basis for purposes such as evaluating financial condition or the results of operations or predicting income or cash flows.

Obviously, then, comparability is largely subservient to the amount of uniformity attained in recording transactions and preparing financial statements. Despite the secondary role of comparability relative to uniformity, the cost–benefit relation between them should be borne in mind: comparability might be improved by more uniformity, but costs may exceed benefits.

Consistency

Consistency refers to the use of the same accounting methods over consecutive time periods by a given firm. Consistency is necessary if reliability is to be placed upon predictions or evaluations stemming from a firm's financial statements over more than one time period. Should change occur—because of adoption of a more relevant or objective method—full disclosure must be made to users and the auditor's opinion must be appropriately qualified.

Consistency is really an aspect of the broader issue of uniformity. It has been advocated by individuals who believe that differing circumstances among firms, particularly when different industries are involved, make it impossible to attain uniformity of accounting techniques on an interfirm basis.[46] Therefore, consistency on an intrafirm basis, with full disclosure being made where changes occur, would be the best target to attain relative to output-oriented principles.

Uniformity

Two comments can immediately be made relative to **uniformity.** First, it has been and continues to be an important issue in accounting. Second, there are several aspects of uniformity which have not always been perceived, hence discussion of the subject has often been impeded. Interpretations of uniformity have include the following:

1. A uniform set of principles for all firms, with interpretation and application left up to the individual entity.
2. Similar accounting treatment required in broadly similar situations, ignoring possibly different circumstances **(rigid uniformity).**

---

[45]One example is Sprouse (1978, p. 71).
[46]For example see Peloubet (1961, pp. 35–41) and Kemp (1963, pp. 126–132).

3. Similar accounting treatment, which takes into account different economic circumstances **(finite uniformity)**.

The second and third definitions differ from the first because they are concerned with the degree of uniformity entering into interpretation of transactions. The first definition simply prescribes a broad theoretical framework to serve as a basis for interpretation of transactions. The difference between rigid and finite uniformity is best achieved by illustration. SFAS 2 which requires immediate expensing of research and development costs is an example of rigid uniformity. The broad category of research and development is accompanied by different expectations relative to cash flows that will be received from these costs. The treatment is thus uniform even though different underlying circumstances exist relative to the pattern of receipt of benefits. SFAS 13 provides an example of finite uniformity. The statement sets down some rather specific criteria to enable differentiation between capital and operating leases. Hence different circumstances are taken into account in distinguishing between the two types of leases and the resulting accounting (we are not concerned here with the question of agreement in terms of the capitalization criteria themselves).

Rigid and finite uniformity would require different underlying theoretical structures in order to make them operational. These are discussed in Chapter 7. Suffice it to say that, along with materiality and disclosure, uniformity is perceived here as a concept which will take on increasing importance as a conceptual framework of accounting emerges.

EQUITY THEORIES

The pivotal point where the enterprise interfaces with owners is in the owners' equity accounts. Several deductive theories have arisen which attempt to depict the relationship between the firm and those having ownership interests in it. These theories have significance in interpreting rights and interests of a nonlegal variety in the owners' equity accounts as well as in determining certain components of income. Prior to the rise of empirical research in accounting, these normative theories received considerable attention. Today they play a secondary role to newer research approaches. Nevertheless, some important insights can be gleaned from a brief introduction to them.

PROPRIETARY THEORY

The proprietary theory assumes that the owners virtually overlap with the firm itself. The theory goes back at least as far as the early eighteenth century.[47] It is quite descriptive of economies made up largely of small owner-operated firms that existed prior to the Industrial Revolution.

Under proprietary theory the assets belong to the firm's owners and the liabilities are their obligations. Similarly, ownership equities accrue to the owners and the balance sheet equation would be:

$$\sum \text{Assets} - \sum \text{Liabilities} = \text{Owners' Equities} \qquad (4.1)$$

Expenses include deductions for labor costs, taxes, and interest but not for preferred and common dividends. In other words, income represents the owners' increase in both net assets (assets minus liabilities) and owners' equities arising from operations during the period. The essentials of the proprietary approach largely coincide with the components of income measurement as it is presently construed in historical cost based systems, although owners certainly do not exercise the control over owners' equity accounts suggested by proprietary theory. Furthermore, the relation between the firm and its owners has changed markedly since the advent of the giant corporation in technologically advanced societies.

ENTITY THEORY

Dissatisfaction with the orientation of the proprietary theory led to development of the entity theory. Its chief architect was William A. Paton, long-time professor at the University of Michigan.[48]

Under the entity theory, the firm and its owners are separate beings. The assets belong to the firm itself while both liability and equity holders are investors in those assets with different rights and claims against them. The balance sheet equation would be:

$$\sum \text{Assets} = \sum \text{Equities (including liabilities)} \qquad (4.2)$$

Under orthodox entity theory there is a dual nature to both the owners' equity accounts and the question of the primary claim to income. Stockholders have rights relative to receiving dividends when declared, voting at the annual corporate meeting, and sharing in net assets after all other claims have been met. Nevertheless, owners' equity accounts do not represent their interest as owners but simply their claims as equity holders.

The same duality applies to net income. It does not belong to the owners although the amount is credited to the claims of equity holders after all other claims have been satisfied. Income does not belong to capital providers until dividends are declared or interest becomes due. In measuring income, both interest and dividends represent distributions of income to providers of capital. Hence both are treated the same, and *neither* is a deduction from income.

---

[47]Chatfield (1974, p. 220).
[48]Paton (1922, pp. 50–84).

Taking the entity theory to its logical conclusion would probably result in seeing the owners' equity accounts as belonging unequivocally to the firm, despite the presence of stockholder claims. Furthermore, income should belong to the firm itself and interest and dividends, in turn, would both be deductions in calculating it.[49]

While the entity theory provides a good description of the relation between the firm and its owners, its duality relative to income and owners' equity in the traditional form has probably been responsible for the fact that its precepts have not taken a strong hold in committee reports and releases of various accounting bodies.[50]

RESIDUAL EQUITY THEORY

The residual equity theory is a variant of both proprietary and entity theory. The theory has been developed by George Staubus but its roots also lie in the works of William A. Paton.[51] The residual equity holders are that group of equity claimants whose rights are superseded by all other claimants. This would be the common stockholders, though the members of that group can change if an event such as a reorganization occurs. Common stockholders are, of course, the ultimate risk takers within an enterprise. Their interest in the firm serves as a "buffer" or protector for all groups with prior claims on the firm, such as preferred stockholders and bond owners.

This theory's underlying assumption is that appropriate information such as that which is helpful for predicting cash flows must be supplied to the residual equity holders for decision-making purposes. The balance sheet equation under this approach would be:

$$\sum \text{Assets} - \sum \text{Specific Equities (including liabilities}$$
$$\text{and preferred stock)} = \text{Residual Equity} \qquad \textbf{(4.3)}$$

Although the assets are still owned by the firm, they are held in a "trust" type of arrangement, with management's objective being maximization of the value of the residual equity. Income accrues to the residual equity holders after all other claims have been met. Interest and preferred dividends (but not common dividends) would be deductions in arriving at income.

Development of the residual equity approach has been relatively recent. It undoubtedly played a role in contributing to the movement toward defining objectives of income measurement with an emphasis on measures which would aid in predicting future cash flows.

---

[49]Li (1960).

[50]AAA (1957, p. 5) discusses *enterprise net income* in which interest, taxes, and dividends are excluded from the determination of net income; hence a broad entity theory approach is advocated. Enterprise net income, however, is contrasted with *income to shareholders*, which coincides with proprietary theory.

[51]See Staubus (1961, pp. 17–27) for an overview, and Paton (1922, pp. 84–89).

FUND THEORY

The fund theory backs away from both the entity and proprietary theories because of the inherent weaknesses and inconsistencies of both. It was developed by William J. Vatter.[52] A **fund** is simply a group of assets and related obligations devoted to a particular purpose, which may or may not be that of generating income. The balance sheet equation would be:

$$\sum \text{Assets} = \sum \text{Restrictions of Assets} \qquad \textbf{(4.4)}$$

The restrictions on the assets arise from both liabilities and invested capital. The invested capital must be maintained intact unless specific authority for partial or total liquidation has been received. The restriction on assets also pertains to the fact that the assets must be used for the specific purposes mandated by law or contract.

The fund theory is most applicable to the governmental and not-for-profit areas with their prevalence of endowment funds, encumbrances, and special asset groups often devoted to specific and separate purposes.

SUMMARY

Despite APB Statement 4's usage of the word "principles" to describe several concepts, the postulates–principles approach had, in essence, died by 1970.

Several factors underlie the failure of the postulates–principles approach and the rise of objectives and standards. The failure of ARS 1 and ARS 3 and the difficulty of building on a postulate base have already been discussed.

The demise of the APB was certainly one of the inherent factors leading to the end of the postulates and principles orientation to standard setting. It is true that by the late 1960s the APB had abandoned this approach despite the publication of Grady's ARS 7 of 1965. Nevertheless, the APB had become identified with postulates and principles and its decline signalled the obsolescence of this orientation as a theoretical underpinning for the standard-setting process.

Other, more fundamental factors, were also at work. New research and committee reports began taking into account issues such as user needs and diversities which, in turn, led to a focus on the objectives of financial statements, considerations that were barely mentioned in the postulates and principles literature. Indeed the very challenge to income measurement itself posed by the efficient markets hypothesis and the decline in the search

[52]Vatter (1947).

for the one income approach that could be deemed superior to all other—what has sometimes been referred to as "true income"—signalled the need for new outlooks and approaches to income formulation and measurement as well as the broader topic of financial reporting.

The new outlook began stressing the need for objectives and standards. Several of the concepts that have been loosely labelled as principles—disclosure, materiality, and uniformity, for example—will undoubtedly take their place in an objectives-oriented framework. Other concepts, such as going concern, conservatism, and stability of the monetary unit, will tend to diminish in importance.

The rise of objectives and standards has also rendered the equity theories of accounting somewhat obsolete. The equity theories are normative–deductive theories which have grown up around the relationship between the corporation itself and its owners. While these theories can provide interesting insights into some problem areas, their scope is not sufficiently global in perspective to permit their extensive use for solving fundamental accounting problems.

Hence our attention turns next to objectives and standards.[53] In Chapter 5 important conceptual and institutional pronouncements occurring in the wake of the demise of the postulates and principles approach are examined.

APPENDIX 4-A: THE BASIC POSTULATES OF ACCOUNTING (ARS 1)

POSTULATES STEMMING FROM THE ECONOMIC AND POLITICAL ENVIRONMENT

Postulate A-1. Quantification.
  Quantitative data are helpful in making rational economic decisions, i.e., in making choices among alternatives so that actions are correctly related to consequences.
Postulate A-2. Exchange.
  Most of the goods and services that are produced are distributed through exchange, and are not directly consumed by the producers.
Postulate A-3. Entities (including identification of the entity)
  Economic activity is carried on through specific units or entities. Any report on the activity must identify clearly the particular unit or entity involved.

---

[53]Paton and Littleton noted that the word "standards" has less of a flavor of permanence about it than does "principles." Paton and Littleton (1940, p. 4).

Appendices 4-A and 4-B are reprinted by permission of the American Institute of Certified Public Accountants.

Postulate A-4. Time period (including specification of the time period)
Economic activity is carried on during specifiable periods of time. Any report on that activity must identify clearly the period of time involved.

Postulate A-5. Unit of measure (including identification of the monetary unit)
Money is the common denominator in terms of which goods and services, including labor, natural resources, and capital are measured. Any report must clearly indicate which money (e.g., dollars, francs, pounds) is being used.

POSTULATES STEMMING FROM THE FIELD OF ACCOUNTING ITSELF

Postulate B-1. Financial statements. (Related to A-1)
The results of the accounting process are expressed in a set of fundamentally related financial statements which articulate with each other and rest upon the same underlying data.

Postulate B-2. Market prices (Related to A-2)
Accounting data are based on prices generated by past, present or future exchanges which have actually taken place or are expected to.

Postulate B-3. Entities (Related to A-3)
The results of the accounting process are expressed in terms of specific units or entities.

Postulate B-4. Tentativeness (Related to A-4)
The results of operations for relatively short periods of time are tentative whenever allocations between past, present, and future periods are required.

THE IMPERATIVES

Postulate C-1. Continuity (including the correlative concept of limited life)
In the absence of evidence to the contrary, the entity should be viewed as remaining in operation indefinitely. In the presence of evidence that the entity has a limited life, it should not be viewed as remaining in operation indefinitely.

Postulate C-2. Objectivity
Changes in assets and liabilities, and the related effects (if any) on revenues, expenses, retained earnings, and the like, should not be given formal recognition in the accounts earlier than the point of time at which they can be measured in objective terms.

Postulate C-3. Consistency
The procedures used in accounting for a given entity should be appropriate for the measurement of its position and its activities and should be followed consistently from period to period.

Postulate C-4. Stable unit
Accounting reports should be based on a stable measuring unit.

Postulate C-5. Disclosure
Accounting reports should disclose that which is necessary to make them not misleading.

APPENDIX 4-B: A TENTATIVE SET OF BROAD ACCOUNTING PRINCIPLES FOR BUSINESS ENTERPRISES (ARS 3)

The principles summarized below are relevant primarily to formal financial statements made available to third parties as representations by the management of the business enterprise. The "basic postulates of accounting" developed in *Accounting Research Study No. 1* are integral parts of this statement of principles.

Broad principles of accounting should not be formulated mainly for the purpose of validating policies (e.g., financial management, taxation, employee compensation) established in other fields, no matter how sound or desirable those policies may be in and of themselves. Accounting draws its real strength from its neutrality as among the demands of competing special interests. Its proper functions derive from the measurement of the resources of specific entities and of changes in those resources. Its principles should be aimed at the achievement of those functions.

The principles developed in this study are as follows:

A. Profit is attributable to the whole process of business activity. Any rule or procedure, therefore, which assigns profit to a portion of the whole process should be continuously re-examined to determine the extent to which it introduces bias into the reporting of the amount of profit assigned to specific periods of time.

B. Changes in resources should be classified among the amounts attributable to

1. Changes in the dollar (price-level changes) which lead to restatements of capital but not to revenues or expenses.

2. Changes in replacement costs (above or below the effect of price-level changes) which lead to elements of gain or of loss.

3. Sale or other transfer, or recognition of net realizable value, all of which lead to revenue or gain.

4. Other causes, such as accretion or the discovery of previously unknown natural resources.

C. All assets of the enterprise, whether obtained by investments of owners or of creditors, or by other means, should be recorded in the accounts and reported in the financial statements. The existence of an asset is independent of the means by which it was acquired.

D. The problem of measuring (pricing, valuing) an asset is the problem of measuring the future services, and involves at least three steps:

    a. A determination if future services do in fact exist. For example, a building is capable of providing space for manufacturing activity.

    b. An estimate of the quantity of services. For example, a building is estimated to be usable for twenty more years, or for half of its estimated total life.

    c. The choice of a method or basis or formula for pricing (valuing) the quantity of services arrived at under (b) above. In general, the choice of a pricing basis is made from the following three exchange prices:

        (1) A past exchange price, e.g., acquisition cost or other initial basis. When this basis is used, profit or loss, if any, on the asset being priced will not be recognized until sale or other transfer out of the business entity.

        (2) A current exchange price, e.g., replacement cost. When this basis is used, profit or loss on the asset being priced will be recognized in two stages. The first stage will recognize part of the gain or loss in the period or periods from time of acquisition to time of usage or other disposition; the second stage will recognize the remainder of the gain or loss at the time of the sale or other transfer out of the entity, measured by the difference between sale (transfer) price and replacement cost. This method is still a cost method; an asset priced on this basis is being treated as a cost factor awaiting disposition.

        (3) A future exchange price, e.g., anticipated selling price. When this basis is used, profit or loss, if any, has already been recognized in the accounts. Any asset priced on this basis is therefore being treated as though it were a receivable, in that sale or other transfer out of the business (including conversion into cash) will result in no gain or loss, except for any interest (discount) arising from the passage of time.

The proper pricing (valuation) of assets and the allocation of profit to accounting periods are dependent in large part upon estimates of the existence of future benefits, regardless of the bases used to price the assets. The need for estimates is unavoidable and cannot be eliminated by the adoption of any formula as to pricing.

1. All assets in the form of money or claims to money should be shown at their discounted present value or the equivalent. The interest rate to be employed in the discounting process is the market (effective) rate at the date the asset was acquired.

   The discounting process is not necessary in the case of short-term receivables where the force of interest is small. The carrying-value of receivables should be reduced by allowances for uncollectible elements; estimated collection costs should be recorded in the accounts.

   If the claims to money are uncertain as to time or amount of receipt, they should be recorded at their current market value. If the current market value is so uncertain as to be unreliable, these assets should be shown at cost.

2. Inventories which are readily salable at known prices with readily predictable costs of disposal should be recorded at net realizable value, and the related revenue taken up at the same time. Other inventory items should be recorded at their current (replacement) cost, and the related gain or loss separately reported. Accounting for inventories on either basis will result in recording revenues, gains, or losses before they are validated by sale but they are nevertheless components of the net profit (loss) of the period in which they occur.

   Acquisition costs may be used whenever they approximate current (replacement) costs, as would probably be the case when the unit prices of inventory components are reasonably stable and turnover is rapid. In all cases the basis of measurement actually employed should be "subject to verification by another competent investigator."

3. All items of plant and equipment in service, or held in stand-by status, should be recorded at cost of acquisition or construction, with appropriate modification for the effect of the changing dollar either in the primary statements or in supplementary statements. In the external reports, plant and equipment should be restated in terms of current replacement costs whenever some significant event occurs, such as a reorganization of the business entity or its merger with another entity or when it becomes a subsidiary of a parent company. Even in the absence of a significant event, the accounts could be restated at periodic intervals, perhaps every five years. The development of satisfactory indexes of construction costs and of machinery and equipment prices would assist materially in making the calculation of replacement costs feasible, practical, and objective.

4. The investment (cost or other basis) in plant and equipment should be amortized over the estimated service life. The basis for adopting a particular method of amortization for a given asset should be its ability to produce an allocation reasonably consistent with the anticipated flow of benefits from the asset.

5. All "intangibles" such as patents, copyrights, research and de-velopment, and goodwill should be recorded at cost, with ap-propriate modification for the effect of the changing dollar either in the primary statements or in supplementary state-ments. Limited term items should be amortized as expenses over their estimated lives. Unlimited term items should continue to be carried as assets, without amortization.

   If the amount of the investment (cost or other basis) in plant and equipment or in the "intangibles" has been increased or de-creased as the result of appraisal or the use of index-numbers, depreciation or other amortization should be based on the changed amount.

E. All liabilities of the enterprise should be recorded in the accounts and reported in the financial statements. Those liabilities which call for settlement in cash should be measured by the present (dis-counted) value of the future payments or the equivalent. The yield (market, effective) rate of interest at date of incurrence of the liabil-ity is the pertinent rate to use in the discounting process and in the amortization of "discount" and "premium." "Discount" and "pre-mium" are technical devices for relating the issue price to the prin-cipal amount and should therefore be closely associated with prin-cipal amount in financial statements.

F. Those liabilities which call for settlement in goods or services (other than cash) should be measured by their agreed selling price. Profit accrues in these cases as the stipulated services are per-formed or the goods produced or delivered.

G. In a corporation, stockholders' equity should be classified into in-vested capital and retained earnings (earned surplus). Invested cap-ital should, in turn, be classified according to source, that is, ac-cording to the underlying nature of the transactions giving rise to invested capital.

   Retained earnings should include the cumulative amount of net profits and net losses, less dividend declarations, and less amounts transferred to invested capital.

   In an unincorporated business, the same plan may be followed, but the acceptable alternative is more widely followed of reporting the total interest of each owner or group of owners at the balance sheet date.

H. A statement of the results of operations should reveal the compo-nents of profit in sufficient detail to permit comparisons and inter-pretations to be made. To this end, the data should be classified at least into revenues, expenses, gains, and losses.

1. In general, the revenue of an enterprise during an accounting period represents a measurement of the exchange value of the products (goods and services) of that enterprise during that pe-riod. The preceding discussion, under D(2), is also pertinent here. *Current exchg price.*

2. Broadly speaking, expenses measure the costs of the amount of revenue recognized. They may be directly associated with revenue-producing transactions themselves (e.g., so-called "product costs") or with the accounting period in which the revenues appear (e.g., so-called "period costs").

3. Gains include such items as the results of holding inventories through a price rise, the sale of assets (other than stock-in-trade) at more than book value, and the settlement of liabilities at less than book value. Losses include items such as the results of holding inventories through a price decline, the sale of assets (other than stock-in-trade) at less than book value or their retirement, the settlement of liabilities at more than book value, and the imposition of liabilities through a lawsuit.

QUESTIONS

1. Do you think the "broad principles" of ARS 3 are really principles as that term is used in science?

2. "Assuming all other things equal, it is possible that the lower-of-cost-or-market method can result in any given year in *higher* income than would be the case under the same inventory costing method *without* the use of lower-of-cost-or-market. If so, then lower-of-cost-or-market cannot be classified as a conservative method." Do you agree with these statements? Discuss.

3. Why is it the case that postulates stemming from the economic and political climates as well as the customs and viewpoints of the business community would not serve as a good foundation for deducing a set of accounting principles?

4. Why do you think it the case that financial executives appear to have a higher mean for materiality judgments when expressed as a percentage of net income than either certified public accountants or financial analysts?

5. Do you think that the so-called "equity theories" of accounting are really theories in the scientific sense? If so, how would you classify them?

6. Why do you think the equity theories are less important today than they were, say, twenty-five years ago?

7. Four postulates (going concern, time period, accounting entity, and monetary unit) were discussed as part of the basic concepts underlying historical costing. Can any of the principles discussed under the same general category be deduced or logically derived from these postulates?

8. How does agency theory (Chapters 1 and 3) differ from the equity theories discussed in this chapter?

9. Does the entity theory or the proprietary theory provide a better description of the relationship existing between the large modern corporation and its owners?
10. Why has the entity theory fragmented into two separate conceptions?
11. Of the nine so-called principles shown in Exhibit 4-1, which do you think are the most important in terms of establishing a historical costing system?
12. How important are the principles used to answer question 11 relative to establishing a current value accounting system?
13. Postulates are supposed to be "tight" enough to prevent conflicting conclusions being deduced from them. Is this the case with ARS 1?
14. Is it fair to categorize ARS 1 and ARS 3 as "failures"?
15. How do the "imperative" postulates (group C) differ from the other two categories of postulates?

CASES AND PROBLEMS

1. Assume the following for the year 1982 for the Staubus Company:

Revenues		$1,000,000
Operating Expenses		
Cost of Goods Sold	$400,000	
Depreciation	100,000	
Salaries and Wages	200,000	
Bond interest (8% Debentures sold at maturity value of $1,000,000		80,000
Dividends declared on 6% Preferred Stock (par value $500,000)		30,000
Dividends declared of $5 per share on Common Stock (20,000 shares outstanding with a par value of $100 per share)		100,000

(a) Determine the income under each of the following equity theories:
   - Proprietary theory
   - Entity theory (orthodox view)
   - Entity theory (unorthodox view)
   - Residual equity
(b) Would any of your answers change if the preferred stock is convertible at any time at the ratio of 2 preferred shares for 1 share of common stock?

2. This case involves a critique of *A Statement of Basic Accounting Postulates and Principles* by a study group at the University of Illinois (it should be on reserve or otherwise made available to you). Your critique should cover, but not be restricted to, the following points:

   (a) How do the definitions of postulates, concepts, and principles differ?

   (b) Are the examples of postulates, principles, and concepts consistent with their definitions?

   (c) Does this set of postulates, principles, and concepts provide a useful framework for deriving operating rules by a legislative body?

BIBLIOGRAPHY OF REFERENCED WORKS

American Accounting Association (1957). *Accounting and Reporting Standards for Corporate Financial Statements and Preceding Statements and Supplements* (American Accounting Association).

American Institute of Certified Public Accountants (1953). *Accounting Terminology Bulletin No. 1* (American Institute of Certified Public Accountants), pp. 9503–9517.

——— (1970). "Basic Concepts and Accounting Principles Underlying Financial Statements of Business Enterprises," *APB Statement No. 4* (American Institute of Certified Public Accountants), pp. 9057–9106.

Accounting Principles Board (1972). Opinion No. 22, *Disclosure of Accounting Policies* (Accounting Principles Board).

Canning, John B. (1929). *The Economics of Accountancy* (Ronald Press).

Carlson, Marvin L., and James W. Lamb (1981). "Constructing a Theory of Accounting—An Axiomatic Approach," *The Accounting Review* (July 1981), pp. 554–573.

Caws, Peter (1965). *The Philosophy of Science* (D. Van Nostrand Company, Inc.).

Chambers, Raymond J. (1964). "The Moonitz and Sprouse Studies on Postulates and Principles," *Accounting, Finance and Management* (Butterworths), pp. 396–414.

——— (1966), *Accounting, Evaluation and Economic Behavior* (Prentice-Hall).

——— (1970). "Second Thoughts on Continuously Contemporary Accounting," *Abacus* (September 1970), pp. 39–55.

Chatfield, Michael (1974). *A History of Accounting Thought* (The Dryden Press).

"Comments on a Tentative Set of Broad Accounting Principles" (1958). *Journal of Accountancy* (April 1963), pp. 36–48.

Deinzer, Harvey T. (1965). *Development of Accounting Thought* (Holt, Rinehart & Winston).

Financial Accounting Standards Board (1975). *An Analysis of Issues Related to Criteria for Determining Materiality* (Financial Accounting Standards Board).

Fremgen, James (1968). "The Going Concern Assumption: A Critical Appraisal," *The Accounting Review* (October 1968), pp. 49–56.

Gilman, Stephen (1939). *Accounting Concepts of Profit* (Ronald Press).

Grady, Paul (1965). "Inventory of Generally Accepted Accounting Principles." *Accounting Research Study No. 7* (American Institute of Certified Public Accountants).

Hendriksen, Elden S. (1982). *Accounting Theory*, 4th ed. (Richard D. Irwin).

Hofstedt, Thomas R., and G. David Hughes (1977). "An Experimental Study of the Judgment Element in Disclosure Decisions," *The Accounting Review* (April 1977), pp. 379–395.

Ijiri, Yuji (1975). "Theory of Accounting Measurement," *Studies in Accounting Research #10* (American Accounting Association).

Jennings, Alvin R. (1958). "Present-Day Challenges in Financial Reporting," *Journal of Accountancy* (January 1958), pp. 28–34.

Kemp, Patrick (1963). "Controversies on the Construction of Financial Statements," *The Accounting Review* (January 1963), pp. 126–132.

Li, David H. (1960). "The Nature and Treatment of Dividends Under the Entity Concept," *The Accounting Review* (October 1960), pp. 674–679.

Littleton, A. C. (1941). "A Genealogy for 'Cost or Market,'" *The Accounting Review* (June 1941), pp. 161–167.

———— (1953). *Structure of Accounting Theory* (American Accounting Association).

MacNeal, Kenneth (1939). *Truth in Accounting* (Scholars Book Co., reissued 1970).

Mattesich, Richard (1964). *Accounting and Analytical Methods* (Richard D. Irwin).

Mautz, Robert K. (1965). "The Place of Postulates in Accounting," *Journal of Accountancy* (January 1965), pp. 46–49.

Mautz, Robert K., and Hussein A. Sharaf (1961). *The Philosophy of Auditing* (American Accounting Association).

Moonitz, Maurice (1961). "The Basic Postulates of Accounting," *Accounting Research Study #1* (American Institute of Certified Public Accountants).

Morgenstern, Oscar (1963). "Limits to the Use of Mathematics in Economics," *Mathematics and the Social Sciences*, J. C. Charlesworth, editor (American Academy of Political and Social Science), pp. 12–39.

Most, Kenneth S. (1982). *Accounting Theory* (Grid Publishing).

Myers, John H. (1959). "The Critical Event and Recognition of Net Profit," *The Accounting Review* (October 1959), pp. 528–532.

Nichols, Arthur C., and Dennis E. Grawoig (1968). "Accounting Reports With Time as a Variable," *The Accounting Review* (October 1968), pp. 631–639.

O'Connor, Melvin, and Daniel W. Collins (1974). "Toward Establishing User-Oriented Materiality Standards," *Journal of Accountancy* (December 1974), pp. 171–179.

Paton, William A. (1922). *Accounting Theory* (Accounting Studies Press, Limited, reissued 1962).

Paton, William A., and A. S. Littleton (1940). *An Introduction to Corporate Accounting Standards* (American Accounting Association).

Pattillo, James W. (1976). *The Concept of Materiality in Financial Reporting* (Financial Executives Research Foundation).

Peloubet, Maurice (1961). "Is Further Uniformity Desirable or Possible?", *The Journal of Accountancy* (April 1961), pp. 35–41.

Rose, J.; William Beaver; Selwyn Becker; and George Sorter (1970). "Toward an Empirical Measure of Materiality," *Empirical Research in Accounting: Selected Studies, 1970* (Supplement to *Journal of Accounting Research*), pp. 138–153.

Sanders, Thomas H.; Henry Rand Hatfield; and Underhill Moore (1938). *A State-ment of Accounting Principles* (American Accounting Association).

Special Committee on Research Program (1958). "Report to Council of the Special Committee on Research Program," *Journal of Accountancy* (December 1958), pp. 62–68.

Sprouse, Robert T. (1978). "The Importance of Earnings in the Conceptual Frame-work," *The Journal of Accountancy* (January 1978), pp. 64–71.

Sprouse, Robert and Maurice Moonitz (1962). "A Tentative Set of Broad Accounting Principles for Business Enterprises," *Accounting Research Study No. 3* (Amer-ican Institute of Certified Public Accountants).

Staubus, George (1961). *Accounting to Investors* (University of California Press).

Sterling, Robert R. (1967). "Conservatism: The Fundamental Principle of Valuation in Accounting," *Abacus* (December 1967), pp. 109–132.

——— (1968). "The Going Concern: An Examination," *The Accounting Review* (July 1968), pp. 481–502.

Study Group at the University of Illinois (1964). *A Statement of Basic Postulates and Principles* (Center for International Education and Research in Account-ing, University of Illinois).

Sweeney, Henry W. (1936). *Stabilized Accounting* (Holt, Rinehart & Winston).

Vatter, William J. (1947). *The Fund Theory of Accounting and Its Implications for Financial Reports* (University of Chicago Press).

——— (1963). "Postulates and Principles," *Journal of Accounting Research* (Au-tumn 1963), pp. 179–197.

Wright, F. K. (1967). "Capacity for Adaptation and the Asset Measurement Problem," *Abacus* (August 1967), pp. 74–79.

ADDITIONAL READINGS

POSTULATES AND PRINCIPLES

Chambers, Raymond J. (1955). "Blueprint for a Theory of Accounting," *Accounting Research* (January 1955), pp. 17–25.

——— (1957). "Detail for a Blueprint," *The Accounting Review* (April 1957), pp. 206–215.

——— (1963). "Why Bother with Postulates," *Journal of Accounting Research* (Spring 1963), pp. 3–15.

"Comments on the 'Basic Postulates of Accounting.'" (1963). *Journal of Accoun-tancy* (January 1963), pp. 44–55.

Goldberg, Louis (1971). "Varieties of Accounting Theory," *Foundations of Account-ing Theory*, ed. W. E. Stone (University of Florida Press), pp. 31–49.

Lambert, S. J. III. (1974). "Basic Assumptions in Accounting Theory Construction," *The Journal of Accountancy* (February 1974), pp. 41–48.

Metcalf, Richard (1964). "The Basic Postulates in Perspective," *The Accounting Re-view* (January 1964), pp. 16–21.

Moonitz, Maurice (1963). "Why Do We Need 'Postulates' and 'Principles'", *Journal of Accountancy* (December 1963), pp. 42–46.

Popoff, Boris (1972). "Postulates, Principles and Rules," *Accounting and Business Research* (Summer 1972), pp. 182–193.

Tietjen, A. C. (1963). "Accounting Principles, Practices, and Methods," *Journal of Accountancy* (April 1963), pp. 65–68.

Zeff, Stephen A. (1971). "Comments on 'Varieties of Accounting Theory,'" *Foundations of Accounting Theory*, ed. W. E. Stone (University of Florida Press), pp. 50–58.

BASIC CONCEPTS

Ashton, Robert H. (1977). "Objectivity of Accounting Measures: A Multi-rule–Multimeasurer Approach," *The Accounting Review* (July 1977), pp. 567–575.

Barlev, Benzion (1972). "On the Measurement of Materiality," *Accounting and Business Research* (Summer 1972), pp. 194–197.

Bedford, Norton (1973). *Extensions in Accounting Disclosure* (Prentice-Hall).

Bedford, Norton, and Toshio Iino (1968). "Consistency Reexamined," *The Accounting Review* (July 1968), pp. 453–458.

Bernstein, Leopold A. (1967). "The Concept of Materiality," *The Accounting Review* (January 1967), pp. 86–95.

Boatsman, James R., and Jack C. Robertson (1974). *The Accounting Review* (April 1974), pp. 342–352.

Frishkoff, Paul (1970). "An Empirical Investigation of the Concept of Materiality in Accounting," *Empirical Research in Accounting: Selected Studies 1970* (Supplement to *Journal of Accounting Research*), pp. 116–129.

Horngren, Charles T. (1965). "How Should We Interpret the Realization Concept?" *The Accounting Review* (April 1965), pp. 323–333.

Murphy, George (1976). "A Numerical Representation of Some Accounting Conventions," *The Accounting Review* (April 1976), pp. 277–286.

Yu, S. C. (1971). "A Reexamination of the Going Concern Postulate," *International Journal of Accounting, Education and Research* (Spring 1971), pp. 37–58.

EQUITY THEORIES

Bird, Francis A.; Lewis F. Davidson; and Charles H. Smith (1974). "Perceptions of External Accounting Transfers Under Entity and Proprietary Theory," *The Accounting Review* (April 1974), pp. 233–244.

Goldberg, Louis (1965). *An Inquiry into the Nature of Accounting* (American Accounting Association).

Gynther, Reginald S. (1967). "Accounting Concepts and Behavioral Hypotheses," *The Accounting Review* (April 1967), pp. 274–290.

CHAPTER 5

Objectives and Standards

The postulates and principles approach largely ignored the question of user objectives. This issue began to take a more prominent role in both research and important theoretically oriented monographs and pronouncements sponsored by organizations such as the American Accounting Association (AAA), American Institute of Certified Public Accountants (AICPA), Accounting Principles Board (APB), and the Financial Accounting Standards Board (FASB). In fact, user objectives became an important connecting link among these documents, many of which were attempting to forge a solid theoretical underpinning for financial accounting standards.

Therefore our approach will be one of chronologically (with one exception) examining the important committee reports and documents which gave rise to objectives and standards in place of postulates and principles. A good working definition of "standards" is provided by Paton and Littleton:

> Standards should deal . . . with fundamental conceptions and general approaches to the presentation of accounting facts. . . . Although accounting standards are not in themselves procedures they point toward accounting procedures, that is, toward rules which cover the details of specific situations . . . accounting standards should be orderly, systematic, coherent. . . .[1]

[1]Paton and Littleton (1940, pp. 5–6).

Standards, as Paton and Littleton also note, have less of an aura of permanence about them than is implied by the word principles.[2] Our discussion and analysis will include the following works:

Title	Published By	Year
A STATEMENT OF BASIC AC-COUNTING THEORY (ASOBAT)	AAA	1966
BASIC CONCEPTS AND ACCOUNTING PRINCIPLES UNDERLYING FINANCIAL STATEMENTS OF BUSINESS ENTERPRISES (APB Statement 4)	APB	1970
OBJECTIVES OF FINANCIAL STATEMENTS (Trueblood Committee Report)	AICPA	1973
FASB Discussion Memorandum: An Analysis of Issues Related To CONCEPTUAL FRAMEWORK FOR FINANCIAL ACCOUNTING AND REPORTING: ELEMENTS OF FINANCIAL STATEMENTS AND THEIR MEASUREMENT (Conceptual Framework)	FASB	1976
STATEMENT OF ACCOUNTING THEORY AND THEORY ACCEPTANCE (SATTA)	AAA	1977
Statements of Financial Accounting Concepts:		
No. 1 OBJECTIVES OF FINANCIAL REPORTING BY BUSINESS ENTERPRISES (SFAC 1)	FASB	1978
NO. 2 QUALITATIVE CHARACTERISTICS OF ACCOUNTING INFORMATION (SFAC 2)	FASB	1980
NO. 3 ELEMENTS OF FINANCIAL STATEMENTS OF BUSINESS ENTERPRISES (SFAC 3)	FASB	1980
NO. 4 OBJECTIVES OF FINANCIAL REPORTING BY NONBUSINESS ORGANIZATIONS (SFAC 4)	FASB	1980

A general criticism that can be, and has been, leveled at all these works is that they have not broken any new ground. While this criticism is largely

[2]Paton and Littleton (1940, p. 4).

true, it is not the appropriate issue. Neither new research findings nor totally new deductive proposals generally come from committee reports and similar documents. Instead the reports evaluate current positions stemming from either practice or research, or a combination of the two. Therefore, the important question is what positions have been adopted or what is the general outlook of the work. From this standpoint, these reports are highly significant.

It should also be stressed that major financial accounting change is an evolutionary process which will continue to unfold indefinitely. However, the reports covered here will most certainly play a crucial role in the future direction of financial accounting research and rule making.

Two short appendices conclude this chapter. One concerns user objectives and the other discusses who the various users are, by group, of corporate financial reports. The appendices relate very closely to the works reviewed and analyzed in the main body of the chapter.

ASOBAT

ASOBAT represented an important change in the work of the AAA. It made a relatively sharp break from the four previous statements and numerous supplements published between 1936 and 1964. The latter were both descriptive and normative in nature, stating general rules or approaches to recording transactions and to presenting financial statements. The Executive Committee of the AAA in 1964 broke with the previous approach by giving the Committee a charge of developing

> . . . an integrated statement of basic accounting theory which will serve as a guide to educators, practitioners, and others interested in accounting. . . . The committee may want to consider . . . the role, nature, and limitations of accounting.[3]

DEVELOPMENT OF THE USER APPROACH

The Committee's definition of accounting represented a departure from the past at the most basic level. ASOBAT defined accounting as:

> . . . the process of identifying, measuring and communicating economic information *to permit informed judgments and decisions by users of the information* (emphasis added).[4]

---

[3]AAA (1966, p. v).
[4]AAA (1966, p. 1).

Perhaps the most widely disseminated previous definition was developed in 1941 and was used in Accounting Terminology Bulletin No. 1 of 1953, which stated:

> Accounting is the art of recording, classifying, and summarizing in a significant manner and in terms of money, transactions and events which are in part at least of a financial character, and interpreting the results thereof.[5]

The emphasis in this latter definition is on the work and skill of the accountant, with virtually no mention of the user. In further elaborating on the definition and work of the accountant, the Terminology Bulletin stated:

> ... it is more important to emphasize the creative skill and ability with which the accountant applies his knowledge to a given problem. . . . The complexities of modern business have brought to management some problems which only accounting can solve, and on which accounting throws necessary and helpful light.[6]

Hence the accountant is the "grey eminence" who alone is responsible for bringing some semblance of order out of chaos relative to presenting the affairs of business; and it is up to users to accommodate themselves to this highly skilled practitioner. From the sociological standpoint, it very strongly appears that the definition and discussion in the bulletin are attempting to fortify the view of the accountant as a learned professional whose presentation must by accepted by those who do not have his qualifications and credentials.

Emphasis on users and their needs first appears in the literature in the 1950s, an amazingly recent time in light of the ancient heritage of accounting.[7]

ORIENTATION TO THEORY

The Committee defined theory as ". . . a cohesive set of hypothetical, conceptual and pragmatic principles forming a general frame of reference for a field of study."[8] In applying the definition, it sought to carry out the following tasks:

1. To identify the field of accounting so that useful generalizations about it can be made and a theory developed.
2. To establish standards by which accounting information may be judged.
3. To point out possible improvements in accounting practice.

---

[5]AICPA (1953, para. 9).
[6]AICPA (1953, paras. 11 and 13).
[7]AAA (1977b, p. 10).
[8]AAA (1966, p. 1).

4. To present a useful framework for accounting researchers seeking to extend the uses of accounting and the scope of accounting subject matter as needs of society expand.[9]

Notice that ASOBAT's definition of theory is a subset of the definition presented here in Chapter 1. Our definition is broader because it not only encompasses the ideas expressed above but also includes possibilities relative to valuation systems as well as empirical work in financial accounting.

The ASOBAT definition is specifically concerned with setting up a framework for evaluating systematic approaches to recording transactions and presentation of financial statements geared to a user-oriented outlook. Since ASOBAT was concerned with the conceptual apparatus for evaluating specific accounting models and rules, their concern is with a **metatheory** of accounting, the topmost part of the theoretical structure concerned with purposes and goals of accounting information. A metatheory would also be concerned with certain restrictions on published accounting information as well as with delineating criteria or guidelines for selecting among alternatives. Issues relative to the metatheoretical structure of accounting are further discussed in Chapter 7.

OBJECTIVES OF ACCOUNTING

Since accounting is concerned with user needs, a set of objectives relative to user needs stands at the apex of a metatheory. Below the objectives would be a set of standards and supporting guidelines that would enable the objectives to be accomplished. Despite the importance of objectives, they are covered rather briefly in ASOBAT. Therefore, it appears that an assumption underlying ASOBAT is that the evaluative framework of standards and guidelines can be largely independent of the objectives themselves.

Despite the short shrift given to objectives by ASOBAT, they should be briefly discussed. The four objectives are these:

1. Making decisions concerning the use of limited resources (including the identification of crucial decision areas) and determining objectives and goals.
2. Effectively directing and controlling an organization's human and material resources.
3. Maintaining and reporting on the custodianship of resources.
4. Facilitating social functions and controls.[10]

---

[9]AAA (1966, p. 1).
[10]AAA (1966, p. 4).

Making Decisions Concerning Limited Resources

Decision making involves an evaluation of what is expected to happen in the future. These assessments can be done in an informal manner or can involve extremely complex formulations. An example of the latter is the discounted cash flow model used in capital budgeting analysis as a means of selecting among competing capital projects. Payback and nondiscounted cash flow methods are simpler—and, presumably, less effective—tools for appraising the likely future. Whether extremely crude or highly complex and refined, the methods used for assessing what will happen in the future are called **decision models.** The capacity to provide information that is useful in the decision-making process pertaining to the future is called **predictive ability.** Under the user-oriented approach, the most important objective of accounting is to provide information useful for making decisions.

If all decision makers required the same information, the accounting theory problem would be less difficult. Unfortunately, as ASOBAT recognizes, users of accounting reports come from several different groups—such as creditors, investors, customers and suppliers, governmental agencies, and employees with widely diverging backgrounds and abilities. Whether user diversity leads to heterogeneous information needs by the different user groups has become absolutely crucial to the future development of accounting, though it had not reached this point of development when ASOBAT was written.

Predictive ability is discussed in terms of gauging future earnings, financial position, and debt-paying ability. An important point which the report makes, though somewhat briefly, is that accounting reports do not make predictions; rather users must make predictions, employing inputs from accounting reports as data in their decision models.

Directing and Controlling Resources

This objective is directed toward managerial uses of accounting data. ASOBAT saw managerial needs as different from those of external users but subject to the same four standards of reporting, although the standards themselves may be applied differently. Managerial needs and uses of accounting data are beyond the scope of this text so we will not be concerned with this objective. However, it should be mentioned that some individuals do not perceive any differences betwen internal (managerial) and external (financial) uses of accounting data.[11]

Maintaining Custodianship of Resources

The third objective is commonly called "stewardship." A proper accounting for the use of funds by one party (management) that have been entrusted to it by another party (stockholders) is a relationship, in one guise

---

[11]Borst (1981).

or another, which extends back to the Middle Ages. This objective has become much more broadly conceived in modern times under conditions of absentee ownership and easy acquisition and disposition of ownership shares through the medium of securities exchanges. The stewardship association has led to the agency theory view of the firm discussed in Chapters 1 and 3.

Facilitating Social Functions and Controls

The last objective appears to be an extension of the stewardship function to society as a whole. Thus accounting is concerned with areas such as taxation, fraud prevention, governmental regulation and collection of statistics for purposes of measuring economic activity. An issue not addressed by ASOBAT concerns who should bear the costs of producing this additional data.

Though objectives stand at the summit of a metatheory, it is clear that their subject matter was not the main concern of ASOBAT. Subsequent reports, however, began opening up this topic.

STANDARDS FOR ACCOUNTING INFORMATION

The heart of ASOBAT concerns four standards for evaluating accounting. As mentioned previously, these and the subsequent guidelines for communicating accounting information, as well as objectives, could be viewed as part of a metatheory of accounting. The standards, as well as other parts of ASOBAT, appear to be aimed at evaluation of published financial statement information itself. However, usage of the standards by a policy-making body for the purpose of assessing proposed rules would appear to be in line with ASOBAT's intentions. The four standards propounded by the report are relevance, verifiability, freedom from bias, and quantifiability.

Relevance

Relevance pertains to usefulness for the decision at hand. It stems directly from the four objectives concerned with various types of information; hence, it is the primary standard. Since there are different user groups having different backgrounds making decisions in different contexts, relevance can be conceived as the major issue of accounting. The question of further defining relevance, however, was beyond the scope of ASOBAT, save for a few simple and obvious examples.

Verifiability

Verifiability is synonymous with objectivity as defined in Chapter 1. It is thus an aspect of measurement. In Chapter 1 it was stated that it is important to separate theoretical concepts from measurement issues because they involve different domains. Selection of valuation systems in their totality, as well as individual rules for subsets of the system, should be primarily based on questions of relevance. However, measurement aspects must be secondarily considered because valuation systems and methods that have a low consensus (in terms of agreement among measurers) might have to be bypassed in favor of approaches that are less desirable from the standpoint of usefulness.

Hence, selection of methods should not be based on either relevance alone without considering verifiability or the converse. Therefore, it is necessary to have standards of measurement as part of the metatheoretical framework. A last point to reiterate here is that "verifiability" appears to have supplanted "objectivity" as the appropriate term for describing the concept of the degree of statistical consensus among measurers.

Freedom from Bias

This standard is necessary because of the user heterogeneity problem existing in financial accounting as well as the potential adversary relationship that exists between management (which, of course, is responsible for statement presentation) and external users. Biases, of course, may be subtle or flagrant and may be extremely difficult to resolve equitably. Suppose, for example, that in the interests of relevance and disclosure, a firm were required to quantify in financial statements or the notes thereto, amounts of expected judgments against it in legal cases. An enterprise's own best interests—minimizing legal damages—conflicts with standards of relevance and disclosure because the court's judgment could be influenced by the firm's "admission of guilt" as a result of quantifying it in financial statements.

Freedom from bias is complementary to the qualitative characteristic of neutrality of SFAC 2 which will be discussed shortly. Neutrality refers to the orientation of standard-setting agencies, whereas freedom from bias is concerned with the preparation of financial statements.

Quantifiability

Quantifiability appears to be very closely related to the general conception of measurement theory. While it is important to bring measurement and quantification into the metatheoretical structure, it appears that ASOBAT, if anything, goes too far: ". . . it can be said that the primary, if not the total concern of accountants, is with quantification and quantified data."[12] The recent thrust toward disclosure, emanating largely from the efficient markets hypothesis literature, extends beyond the bounds of mere quantification.

A minor problem arises as a result of a standard that refers largely to the general area of measurement. Since verifiability is an aspect of measurement theory, verifiability appears to be a subset of quantifiability.

[12]AAA (1966, p. 12).

A final important point brought up in this section concerns the question of why accounting should be restricted to single numbers in financial statements. ASOBAT suggests the possibility of utilizing ranges and also multiple valuation bases in "side-by-side" columnar arrangements.

These new possibilities are seen both as responses to the increased data and information needs of users and as possible solutions to the problem of heterogeneous user groups. In addition, these possibilities might be a means for getting around the overriding problem of choice among accounting methods faced by a rule-making body. Provision of more information is known as **data expansion.**

The data expansion solution has been criticized on the grounds that it can lead to problems of **information overload** on the part of users.[13] Hence, any attempt to circumvent the problem of choice among valuation systems or methods by simply providing more data is subject to the information-processing constraints of users, a point not discussed in ASOBAT.

GUIDELINES FOR COMMUNICATING ACCOUNTING INFORMATION

In addition to the four standards, five guidelines pertaining to communication of accounting information are presented in ASOBAT:

1. Appropriateness to expected use.
2. Disclosure of significant relationships.
3. Inclusion of environmental information.
4. Uniformity of practice within and among entities.
5. Consistency of practices through time.[14]

The report itself notes that there is overlap between standards and guidelines, though the latter are conceded to be less fundamental.

Appropriateness to Expected Use

The first guideline basically reiterates the relevance standard although timeliness of presentation is also mentioned here.

Disclosure of Significant Relationships

Despite its title, this guideline deals only in a very limited aspect with the broad problem of disclosure discussed in Chapter 4. Rather it deals with

---

[13]Within a given time frame in a "complex environment," such as that provided by financial information, the point is reached where an individual cannot absorb or process additional information. See Revsine (1970b) and Miller (1972). However, disclosure (providing additional information) is seen as an important means for resolving reporting problems because the market uses a broad informational set. See, for example, AAA (1977a, pp. 20–21). Additional research is needed in terms of both individual abilities to process accounting information and the "black box" effect when going from individuals to the aggregated level of the market.
[14]AAA (1966, p. 7).

the problem of "aggregation" of data in which important information may be buried or hidden in the summarization of figures in financial reports. Statement of Financial Accounting Standards (SFAS) 14 on segmental disclosure is an example of one statement that has dealt with this problem.

Inclusion of Environmental Information

As used here *environmental information* refers to the very broad category of conditions under which data were collected and to the preparer's assumptions relative to uses of information, particularly if the information is being employed for specific rather than general purposes. More detail may well be appropriate where specific rather than general usage is intended.

Uniformity of Practices Within and Among Entities and Consistency of Practices Through Time

The last two guidelines have direct reference to uniformity and consistency as discussed in Chapter 4. It appears that the type of uniformity desired by ASOBAT corresponds to finite uniformity as that term was previously defined. Bringing about finite uniformity cannot be accomplished merely by means of setting it forth as a guideline or even a standard. There must be sufficient detail in the theoretical structure, a topic to be further probed in Chapter 7.

CONCLUDING REMARKS ON ASOBAT

ASOBAT can be criticized on numerous grounds. Certainly the guidelines were far too brief to cover the topics adequately. The metatheoretical structure could have been extended and more appropriate terminology used. However, these are carping criticisms. ASOBAT has had an important and beneficial influence on succeeding documents and reports, as will become evident in the remainder of this chapter.

APB STATEMENT 4

APB Statement 4 is a curious document because it was conceived during a transition point in terms of theoretical orientations of rule-making bodies. It appeared when the postulates and principles approach had run its course and objectives and standards were emerging. The statement was published in October 1970, exactly a half year prior to the formation of the Wheat and Trueblood Committees. At that time the APB was under heavy fire for Opinions 16 and 17 on business combinations and goodwill. In addition, it was subject to broader criticisms, such as inadequacy of its research thrust, lack of independence on the part of its members, and lack of sufficient exposure of its work prior to final publication.

The purpose of the document was to develop fundamental aspects of financial reporting to serve as a foundation for the opinions of the APB. This charge came from the Special Committee on Opinions of the APB which appeared in May 1965, a time when it would certainly have been expected that the APB would continue indefinitely despite problems that had already begun to surface.

Moonitz felt that the report should have been issued as an opinion rather than as a statement—since departures from "generally accepted accounting principles" in the latter form need not be disclosed.[15] The point might be raised, however, whether agreement with a theoretical structure—since that was the intended charge to the drafters of the statement—should be forced by fiat. Theory acceptance cannot be easily mandated, as we will see later in this chapter.

DEFINITION ORIENTATION

Definition of Accounting

The statement starts by defining accounting along the newer, user-oriented track that ASOBAT took:

> Accounting is a service activity. Its function is to provide quantitative information, primarily financial in nature, about economic entities that is *intended to be useful in making economic decisions* (emphasis added).[16]

In following through on the definition, the statement also takes cognizance of ASOBAT's very strong emphasis on diversity of users. Users of financial information are classified into two groups: those with direct interests in the enterprise and those with indirect interests. The statement goes further than ASOBAT—which had been silent on this issue—by prescribing that users of financial statements should be knowledgeable and should understand the characteristics and limitations of financial statement usage. Finally, and in agreement with ASOBAT, financial statements are viewed as being general purpose in nature as opposed to being oriented toward a limited group of users.

Other Definitions

Despite its promising start, APB Statement 4 often backslides into useless definitions. Definitions of assets, liabilities, owners' equity, revenues,

---

[15]Moonitz (1971).
[16]APB (1970, para. 9).

and expenses are given as the "basic elements of financial accounting." All these definitions (save owners' equity, which is a residual) state that they are ". . . recognized and measured in conformity with generally accepted accounting principles."[17] However, the statement later states that ". . . generally accepted accounting principles incorporate the consensus at a particular time as to which economic resources and obligations should be recorded as assets and liabilities.. . . ."[18] Hence the most basic definitions of accounting terminology were once again largely defaulted by leaving them open to whatever is being done in practice. Furthermore, since the document is a statement rather than an opinion, thus carrying less enforcement status, the decision not to take a stronger prescriptive position in terms of basic definitions is doubly disappointing.

OTHER FACETS OF APB STATEMENT 4

Despite the shortcomings, there are many good aspects of this document, which indicate that its drafters were cognizant of ASOBAT as well as of recent research developments. For example, the fact that accounting is a measurement discipline is noted in paragraph 67.

The section on objectives is obviously heavily grounded in the work of ASOBAT. The standards and guidelines of that report have been combined and largely overlap with the "qualitative objectives" of APB Statement 4. The statement recognizes the factor of timeliness, which received scant mention in ASOBAT. Furthermore, while APB Statement 4 agrees with ASOBAT on the need for finite uniformity, it acknowledges that such would be a difficult objective to meet. Finally, APB Statement 4 concurs with ASOBAT that there may be conflict among objectives (such as relevance and verifiability) and that the conflict is a very knotty problem which should be resolved in the metatheoretical framework.

Other aspects of APB Statement 4 are more mundane. The "basic features" of financial accounting are largely a rehash of some of the postulates from ARS 1. The pervasive principles and modifying conventions that form the section on generally accepted accounting principles consist of those concepts which constitute the heart of the presently ill defined system of historical costing. The remaining sections of the report, which include statements of the principles of selection and measurement and financial statement presentation, likewise present virtually nothing containing any theoretical innovation.

CONCLUDING REMARKS ON APB STATEMENT NO. 4

APB Statement 4 is a curious work. Large parts of it are restatements of the "conventional wisdom" of the time whereas other parts recognize that

---

[17] APB (1970, paras. 132 and 134).
[18] APB (1970, para. 137).

important evolutionary changes had begun to occur.[19] The former part is relatively concise and complete. The document, in fact, is often quoted in position papers prepared by public accounting firms outlining their positions on various proposals.

Finally, the many parts of the document do not tie together as a whole. For example, it is extremely conjectural that the objectives, which largely stem from ASOBAT, can be implemented by means of the various levels of principles which have come from the existing body of accounting. This problem is further compounded by the loosely—if not circularly—worded set of definitions previously mentioned. Hence the document is, to a large extent, justly accused of being all things to all people. Nevertheless, considering its positive aspects as well as the fact that the APB was under heavy fire during the document's drafting, it has served a useful purpose.

THE TRUEBLOOD REPORT

The Trueblood Committee was formed in April 1971 by the AICPA. It thus came into being at a time of extreme criticism of the APB but also at a point when some degree of quiet progress was being made in terms of reformulating the structure of accounting theory. The committee was charged with using APB Statement 4 as a vehicle for refining the objectives of financial statements as a part of a metatheoretical structure.

A total of twelve objectives of financial accounting were enumerated by the committee:

1. The basic objective of financial statements is to provide information useful for making economic decisions.
2. An objective of financial statements is to serve primarily those users who have limited authority, ability, or resources to obtain information and who rely on financial statements as their principal source of information about an enterprise's economic activities.
3. An objective of financial statements is to provide information useful to investors and creditors for predicting, comparing, and evaluating potential cash flows to them in terms of amount, timing, and related uncertainty.
4. An objective of financial statements is to provide users with information for predicting, comparing, and evaluating enterprise earning power.
5. An objective of financial statements is to supply information useful in judging management's ability to utilize enterprise resources effectively in achieving the primary enterprise goal.

---

[19]Critiques of APB Statement 4 recognized the dual nature of the document. See Ijiri (1971), Schattke (1972), and Staubus (1972).

6. An objective of financial statements is to provide factual and interpretive information about transactions and other events which is useful for predicting, comparing, and evaluating enterprise earning power. Basic underlying assumptions with respect to matters subject to interpretation, evaluation, prediction, or estimation should be disclosed.

7. An objective is to provide a statement of financial position, useful for predicting, comparing, and evaluating enterprise earning power. This statement should provide information concerning enterprise transactions and other events that are part of incomplete earning cycles. Current values should also be reported when they differ significantly from historical costs. Assets and liabilities should be grouped or segregated by the relative uncertainty of the amount and timing of prospective realization or liquidation.

8. An objective is to provide a statement of periodic earnings useful for predicting, comparing, and evaluating enterprise earning power. The net result of completed earnings cycles and enterprise activities resulting in recognizable progress toward completion of incomplete cycles should be reported. Changes in the values reflected in successive statements of financial position should be reported, but separately, since they differ in terms of their certainty of realization.

9. Another objective is to provide a statement of financial activities useful for predicting, comparing, and evaluating enterprise earning power. This statement should report mainly on factual aspects of enterprise transactions having or expected to have significant cash consequences. This statement should report data that require minimal judgment and interpretation by the preparer.

10. An objective of financial statements is to provide information useful for the predictive process. Financial forecasts should be provided when they will enhance the reliability of users' predictions.

11. An objective of financial statements for governmental and not-for-profit organizations is to provide information useful for evaluating the effectiveness of the management of resources in achieving the organization's goals. Performance measures should be quantified in terms of identified goals.

12. An objective of financial statements is to report on those activities of the enterprise that affect society which can be determined and described or measured and which are important to the role of the enterprise in its social environment.[20]

While the committee did not indicate a structural order for these objectives, a study by Anton, and another by Sorter and Gans, arranged them in a hierarchical framework.[21] Sorter and Gans, it should be noted, were the

---

[20]AICPA (1973).
[21]Sorter and Gans (1974, p. 4) and Anton (1976, pp. 4 and 5).

Research Director and the Administrative Director, respectively, of the Staff for the Study Group. Exhibit 5-1 shows the arrangement of Sorter and Gans. The Anton structuring agrees with Sorter and Gans on most major points.

EXHIBIT 5-1.

Hierarchy of Objectives

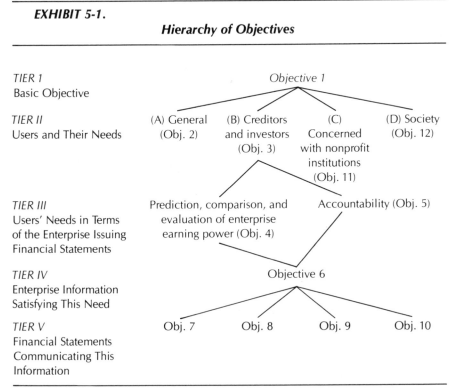

TIER 1 Basic Objective	*Objective 1*
TIER II Users and Their Needs	(A) General (Obj. 2) (B) Creditors and investors (Obj. 3) (C) Concerned with nonprofit institutions (Obj. 11) (D) Society (Obj. 12)
TIER III Users' Needs in Terms of the Enterprise Issuing Financial Statements	Prediction, comparison, and evaluation of enterprise earning power (Obj. 4) Accountability (Obj. 5)
TIER IV Enterprise Information Satisfying This Need	Objective 6
TIER V Financial Statements Communicating This Information	Obj. 7 Obj. 8 Obj. 9 Obj. 10

Source: Sorter and Gans (1974), p. 4

OBJECTIVES OF FINANCIAL STATEMENTS

Objective 1

The topmost objective is in agreement with the user thrust of both ASO-BAT and APB Statement 4. Objective 1 overlaps with the standard of relevance and the guideline of appropriateness to expected use from ASOBAT and the general objectives of APB Statement 4. This objective is not operational. Rather it is a very broad statement of a goal or direction for the standard-setting process.

Objective 2

The second objective delineates the users primarily being served by financial statements. By zeroing in on users with "limited authority, ability, or resources," the Trueblood Committee went beyond its two predecessors. In terms of ability, ASOBAT had nothing to say. To the extent the matter was discussed in APB Statement 4, users were expected to be knowledgeable about financial statements and information. Opting to serve users with the limitations listed may be deemed an unusual choice in light of the efficient markets hypothesis—since that body of research states that naive investors are not penalized in an efficient market setting as long as they are properly diversified. However, Sorter and Gans made a curious disclaimer relative to this point:

> This objective may be the most misunderstood of all objectives. Although it may be interpreted to mean that financial statements should serve those with "limited ability," that was not the study group's intention. . . . Financial statements should not serve special or narrow needs of specific users but rather should serve the general needs of all users. Among the implications of this objective are: 1) that financial statements . . . should provide full disclosure; and 2) that all information should be presented as *simply* as the subject matter allows (emphasis supplied).[22]

"Limited ability," then, may simply be a code word for full disclosure and broad general purpose financial statements.

Furthermore, discussion of the primary user group in the Trueblood Report reveals an extremely important value judgment: while user groups may differ, their economic decisions are essentially similar. This, in turn, leads deductively to similar information needs for the various user groups; hence the justification for general purpose financial statements with disclosure, as noted in the Sorter and Gans quotation above.

Objective 3

The third objective zeroes in on the importance of cash flows. The users mentioned for whom this information is necessary are lenders and investors. While lenders and investors may well be the most important user groups, it is not totally clear why it was necessary to specify them in light of the committee's value judgment that user decisions and information needs have a large degree of homogeneity. Since the cash flows being discussed are future (potential) in nature, they are not susceptible to direct measurement.

Objective 4

Earning power (income) is one of the measures seen as extremely useful in terms of helping to predict, compare, and evaluate cash flow potential as well as being important in its own right. Over the long run, cash flow and earnings have a high correlation. During the short run, earnings may actually be a better predictor of cash-generating potential than cash flows themselves because much of the latter may be either nonoperational in na-

---

[22]Sorter and Gans (1974, p. 6).

ture or plowed back into the enterprise for the purpose of breeding future cash flows and earnings.

Objective 5

The word "accountability" was used in both the Trueblood Report itself and by Sorter and Gans in Exhibit 5-1 to summarize the fifth objective. It extends beyond the ancient concept of stewardship (which is limited to the functions of safekeeping of assets and ensuring that they are used in accordance with investors purposes).[23] Accountability here also includes the ideas of effectively and efficiently utilizing assets in order to carry out the enterprise objective of maximizing future cash flows consistent with a given level of risk. As such, there appears to be a very large degree of overlap between accountability and the word "evaluating" used in Objectives 3 and 4.

Objective 6

The key words in the sixth objective are "factual" and "interpretive." The difference between these two conditions is connected to the concept of the various enterprise cycles. Cycles can be either broad or narrow. The acquisition, usage, and disposition of a fixed asset would be an example of a broad cycle. The broadest of all cycles would comprise the beginning and end of the enterprise itself. A fairly narrow cycle would be this one: cash to inventory to accounts receivable to cash. From the standpoint of cycles, the broader the cycle is, the more interpretive and the less factual the accounting information is liable to be. For a broad cycle such as acquisition, usage, and disposition of fixed assets, current values of fixed assets may be indicative of progress toward completion of the cycle, although these values may be subject to a great deal of uncertainty.

As a general proposition, it is probably the case that the funds flow statement provides more factual and less interpretive information than the income statement which, in turn, has more factual and less interpretive information than the balance sheet. In drawing the distinction between factual and interpretive information, Objective 6 provides the rationale for presenting different types and qualities of information to users.

Objectives 7, 8, and 9

These objectives call for the use of a balance sheet, an earnings (income) statement, and a funds flow type of statement for prediction, comparison, and evaluation of enterprise earning power—without prescribing the format of these statements.

In the statement of financial position (balance sheet), current values are indicative of present value of future cash flows as determined by the market; hence, these values are useful for predicting, comparing, and evaluat-

---

[23]"Accountability" is used in a similar manner, extending well beyond the bounds of stewardship, by Ijiri (1975, pp. ix and 10 and 32–35).

ing enterprise earning power.[24] Outside of cash and to a slightly lesser extent accounts and notes receivable, the great majority of assets held represent the results of incomplete cycles. Hence current valuation, as opposed to historical cost, is a means of presenting information of an interpretive nature where incomplete cycles exist. This does not necessarily mean, however, that all historical cost information is factual in basis.

Earnings statements could largely be restricted to a completed earnings cycle basis by eliminating from them expense measurements pertaining to long-lived assets consumed during the period. However, statements of this type would not be as useful as a more complete model in terms of predicting, comparing, and evaluating enterprise earning power. This objective might be further abetted by using current value measurements of expired assets rather than historical cost approaches. The committee itself was divided on the question of whether the earnings figure should include valuation changes relative to unexpired assets. The report appears to call for a multistep income figure where separate amounts are shown for earnings components having different degrees of certainty relative to the factual basis (completion of cycle) of the figures involved.

The statement of financial activities would supplement the other two statements because there would be much less uncertainty relative to the information presented. The statement could concentrate on highly probable effects on changes in cash (such as revenues and purchases) rather than "narrower"—but even more probable—figures such as cash receipts and cash disbursements. The statement would also show acquisitions and dispositions of fixed assets, changes in long-term debt, and contributions and distributions of capital. In addition, information not shown elsewhere, such as purchase commitments and sales backlog differentials, could also be shown here. All these components would be factual in nature even though some of them (fixed-asset acquisitions, for example) pertain to incomplete cycles.

Objective 10

Financial forecasts are, of course, totally interpretive in nature. As a result, there are dangers in presenting them. Excessive optimism or undue pessimism might arise. Furthermore, it can safely be said that public accounting firms do not show any great enthusiasm for auditing forecasts. At the present time, the SEC encourages—but by no means requires—firms to present them.[25] Their potential usefulness for predicting, comparing, and evaluating enterprise earning power should be readily apparent.

---

[24]Revsine (1970a) shows that current value income using replacement costs is an indirect measurement of "economic income" (the discounted cash flow approach illustrated in Chapter 1) under conditions of perfect competition. However, replacement cost income is a "mere approximation" of economic income under real-world conditions of imperfect competition. For additional coverage see Barton (1974).

[25]Rule 175 of the SEC issued in 1979 provides "safe harbors" from liability provisions of the federal securities laws where forecasts are made.

Objectives 11 and 12

Both these objectives are beyond the general scope of this text so they will not be discussed here. However, this is not to deny the importance of governmental and not-for-profit organizations. The whole area of costs to society that are not borne by business is a fascinating one. There are many activities carried on by business that are not reported on financial statements.

CONCLUDING REMARKS ON THE TRUEBLOOD COMMITTEE REPORT

The Trueblood Report also contains a short chapter on "qualitative characteristics of reporting." The elements here come largely from the standards and guidelines of ASOBAT and the qualitative objectives from APB Statement 4. In addition, there is a brief but useful chapter on the various valuation systems of accounting. The report expresses the belief that different valuation bases are appropriate for different assets and liabilities, a view that ignores the additivity argument.

But it is on the objectives of financial statements that the report must be evaluated. Criticisms have been raised along the line that the objectives are obvious and do not specify operational objectives that could be put into practice.[26] The criticism is true but largely irrelevant. These objectives represent a first step in what must necessarily be a complex web of objectives if a meaningful conceptual framework, one which can gain acceptance by those affected, is to be implemented.

Finally, it is important to reiterate that the Trueblood Report emphasizes the importance of cash flows to users and the relation of earning power measurements to the generation of future cash flows. The earning power orientation to income is grounded in the notion that economic income is the change in the present value of future cash flows discounted at an appropriate rate (the discounted cash flow approach was illustrated in Chapter 1). It is very likely that the earning power touchstone will remain a very strong influence upon the FASB in its future activities.

SATTA

SATTA was commissioned by the Executive Committee of the AAA in 1973. Its overall purpose, similar to that of ASOBAT a decade earlier, was to provide a survey of the current financial accounting literature and a statement of where the profession stood relative to the area of accounting theory.

---

[26]Miller (1974, p. 18).

The report accomplished its objectives admirably. However, the results may not be pleasing to accounting theorists and policy makers.

In order to more fully comprehend SATTA, it is necessary to understand its relationship to ASOBAT. Both documents, of course, are products of AAA committees having similarly broad guidelines. ASOBAT attempted to develop metatheoretical guidelines for evaluation of accounting information and valuation systems. SATTA, on the other hand, viewed the many valuation systems of accounting as well as other theoretical considerations and enumerated the reasons why it was impossible to develop criteria that would enable the profession to unequivocally accept a single valuation system for accounting. In effect, then, SATTA is a very cautionary document relative to the possibility of theory acceptance.

THEORY APPROACHES IN ACCOUNTING

Classical Approaches

SATTA laid its groundwork by concisely and efficiently tracing and categorizing the various valuation systems presented in the literature. Older attempts were classified under the rubric of "classical approaches to theory development."[27] Most of the listings in this group were categorized primarily as normative and deductive in nature. Little attention was given to the decision aspects of users. Instead, it was rationalized that the models developed were superior to competing alternatives for user needs. In some cases, SATTA used what it called an inductive approach. However, "inductive" was used by SATTA in the rather special sense—a gleaning from the accounting literature itself as well as from observations of practice—instead of the usual sense of "inductive," a systematic review and analysis of practice.

Decision-Usefulness Approach

Among the contemporary approaches to accounting theory is the wide body of research that has concentrated on users of accounting reports, their decisions, information needs, and information-processing abilities. Decision usefulness was further dichotomized into two overall areas: one being **decision models** and the other being **decision makers.**

Decision Model Orientation. Metatheoretical frameworks (or parts thereof) that were developed in ASOBAT and the Trueblood Committee Report pertain to the decision model orientation. The systems that fall into this category are united by the following characteristics: (1) they are normative and deductive in nature since the theoretical system must meet, as closely as possible, criteria of a metatheoretical framework; (2) some form

---

[27]Older approaches covered the years 1922 to 1962—with the single exception of a work by Ijiri in 1975, which was a defense of historical cost accounting based on the importance of accountability. Many of the items listed, however, were current valuation methods.

of relevance for particular decisions by a particular user group or groups is stressed; and (3) the relevance criterion is instrumental for measuring the selected attributes with regard to assets, liabilities, and income transactions.

Those approaches grouped under the decision model category often stem from formal investment decision models, such as discounted cash flow approaches.[28] Since decision model approaches are deemed to be appropriate in terms, at least, of communicating extremely relevant information for decisions, a rather unpleasant problem arises if users do not understand or prefer these systems. At least one individual has taken the position in this situation that users must be educated to understand the method, a reasoning consistent with the normative framework of the approach.[29] However, the task of normatively selecting a model and forcing it on users, particularly if they neither prefer nor understand it, is indeed extremely formidable.

Decision Maker Orientation. The main point to make about the decision maker orientation is that it is descriptive rather than normative because the outlook of this school is to attempt to find out what information is actually utilized or desired by users. In turn, the supposition is that the type of information that is desired should be supplied.[30] Hence, in addition to being descriptive, research that falls into the decision maker category is also inductive (empirical) in nature. Much of the behavioral research mentioned in Chapter 1 falls into the decision maker category.

It is important to note that while many important "bits" of information have come from the rather extensive research falling into this category, there has been no coalescence into strong advocacy for particular valuation methods. This is consistent with the descriptive nature of the approach, which is also not "global" in nature. On the other hand, since the decision model approach is normative, advocacy for particular systems has arisen under that orientation.

Information Economics Approach

Information economics as applied to accounting theory does not deal directly with alternate valuation systems. Instead it is concerned with the issue of costs and benefits arising from information production and usage. Hence, accounting information is viewed from the standpoint of being an economic good, an outlook that had not previously been considered in theory formulation. The approach and problems highlighted by information economics are covered in Chapter 6.

---

[28]A good example would be AAA (1969), which utilized a present-value model of gains or losses on long-term debt and equity investments for the ultimate purpose of valuation of elements used in financial reports.

[29]Sterling (1967, p. 106).

[30]Unfortunately the problem of determining user information preferences appears to be almost totally intractable. Abdel-Khalik (1971) developed a stochastic model for measuring preference ordering of users but the model has never been implemented.

DEFICIENCIES OF PRESENT THEORY APPROACHES

The overriding message of SATTA relates to why we cannot arrive at "theory closure"—acceptance of a particular valuation system—at this time. Our analysis of this aspect of SATTA will cover the most important issues raised (when viewed from the accounting theory standpoint).

Perhaps the principal problem brought up by SATTA relative to lack of theory closure involves the problem of diversity of users in terms of their decisions and their possible different information needs. Both ASOBAT and APB Statement 4 recognized the fact that many user groups require information for decision-making purposes. One of ASOBAT's reactions to this problem was the call for multiple measures. However, there are perceived limits to the ability of users to absorb and process additional information, so data expansion does not provide a cure-all for the problem.[31] The Trueblood Report establishes rather early the premise that while there are different user groups, they have a large commonality in terms of similar decisions and information needs. Like ASOBAT, the Trueblood Report is concerned with providing a part of the metatheoretical framework for evaluating theoretical systems and methods from a normative viewpoint. The Trueblood Report is, thus, also closely related to the decision model school.

SATTA is much more pessimistic than the Trueblood Report with regard to decisions and information preferences both among and within user groups. The differences between user homogeneity and user heterogeneity of information needs can be very simply illustrated by means of Venn diagrams (see Exhibit 5-2). The circles represent user groups and their information needs. There is a large degree of overlap in the user homogeneity part of the diagram and very little in the other part.

A condition of heterogeneity of information preferences and needs compounds an already difficult situation. Corporate financial reports and disclosures are a free good. Users do not pay the preparer for the information received and the information is available to virtually anyone who really desires it. Accounting information is, therefore, a public good rather than being a private good. If it were a private good, the required information would be amenable to a market type of solution: it would be determined by supply and demand considerations.

Given user heterogeneity and the public-good character of financial information, an impasse must develop relative to formulation of accounting standards and prescribed methods. Providing one set of accounting information rather than another means that one set of users is being favored to the detriment of other user groups. Moreover, different sets of accounting information lead to different security prices, which again means that some individuals are being favored at the expense of others. Furthermore, if a value judgment is adopted which states that a policy-setting organization should not take actions that make one group better off at the expense of

[31]See Footnote 13.

EXHIBIT 5-2.
Degrees of User Homogeneity of Information Needs

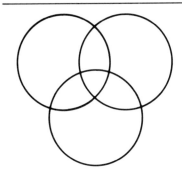

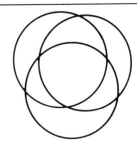

Low User Homogeneity   High User Homogeneity

---

another, then accounting policy formulation becomes totally straitjacketed. Hence, a very bleak result is presented by SATTA in terms of theory closure.

We do not wish to quarrel with SATTA's outcome. It is attempting to state where financial accounting theory stood as of the late 1970s. Nevertheless, a few remarks are in order.

The case for user heterogeneity of information needs is far from proved. The assertions of both homogeneity of information needs and heterogeneity proponents are totally a priori in nature.[32] Empirical research is desperately needed to shed some light on this extremely important question. Miller has stated the case very well:

> Certainly I am in favor of on-going research to discover the needs of statement users. But I would not be surprised if users were to indicate that they expect accounting information questions to be resolved by the experts who know something about the merits and helpfulness of accounting measurements. So I believe it is reasonable to expect users to look to the accountant for guidance. This line of reasoning has led me to believe there is a risk that accountants may have been giving too much weight to the lack of (and the desire for) knowledge about users' needs.[33]

---

[32]One example that leans toward user heterogeneity on an a priori basis is Beaver and Demski (1974). Dopuch and Sunder (1980) see potential heterogeneity among three groups: management, auditors, and users. In turn, the user group is itself heterogeneous. The heterogeneity among the three groups is seen at three different levels: desired information in financial statements, desired accounting principles, and desired objectives. As a result they see an attempt to arrive at objectives as a futile exercise. Therefore, they see FASB's task as one of knowing how to mediate among competing interests.

[33]Miller (1974, pp. 19–20).

Strict adherence to Pareto-optimality is also open to question. In a situation of any social complexity, it will be virtually impossible for any policy-making organization to conform to the very rigid criteria of Pareto-optimality. It is very interesting to note that Pareto himself, a well-known Italian economist, did not see his optimality approach as the sole decision rule.[34] Perhaps what is needed are judiciously applied constraints on policy-setting organizations to control their actions to attain the greatest good for the greatest number of individuals. Unquestionably even this easing of the Paretian reins still leaves organizations such as FASB with a herculean task.

CONCLUDING REMARKS ON SATTA

SATTA is a remarkable synthesis of the theoretical financial accounting literature. While the jury is still out on the question of heterogeneity of information needs and the application of Pareto-optimality, it is difficult to argue with the conclusion of SATTA. We cannot expect accounting theorists to develop a theoretical framework that will be universally satisfactory. In turn, the statements and pronouncements of a rule-making group such as FASB, which are propounded in an incomplete market setting, can be expected to be met with less than full enthusiasm.

Hence, a paradoxical situation has resulted. An important document authored by a distinguished group of academicians took a very pessimistic view of the role and possibilities of accounting theory formulation at exactly the same time that a conceptual framework emanated from a rule-making body that is supposed to pave the way for formally implementing at least part of a metatheoretical structure for guiding statements and pronouncements. We look next at that conceptual framework.

CONCEPTUAL FRAMEWORK

Why is a conceptual framework needed? The project has been likened to a constitution because it is supposed to embody ". . . a coherent system of interrelated objectives and fundamentals that can lead to consistent standards and that prescribes the nature, function, and limits of financial ac-

---

[34]There are two important points that should be borne in mind relative to Pareto-optimality. Firstly, the status quo should not be treated as a unique Pareto-optimum situation. There are many possible Pareto-optimum situations where change in social rules cannot be made without adversely affecting some parties. Secondly, Pareto himself did not see his optimality approach as the sole decision rule. Ethics and cost–benefit analysis, for example, could also be used for judging social change. For further coverage see Samuels (1974, pp. 200–206).

counting and financial statements."[35] So we see that the conceptual framework project is an attempt to provide a metatheoretical structure for financial accounting. To date, four statements of financial accounting concepts (SFACs) have been issued in addition to the discussion memorandum.

DISCUSSION MEMORANDUM

A discussion memorandum is, of course, not the end product of the FASB's deliberations. However, the discussion memorandum for the Conceptual Framework Project is a massive study, perhaps the most extensive ever published by the FASB. In addition, it was widely disseminated and publicized.

The discussion memorandum was accompanied by another document which pertained to tentative conclusions of the Trueblood Report on objectives.[36] This latter report accepted the user orientation and the importance of cash flows stemming from the Trueblood Report but added little more of a substantive nature.

Two new basic issues were brought up in the discussion memorandum: (1) three views of financial accounting and financial statements, and (2) an outline of the various approaches to capital maintenance. The former might be termed orientations to the financial statements. In both these cases the attempt was to show the various alternatives and possibilities open for adoption, without taking any firm position, in order to elicit responses from the profession. In addition, various definitions for basic terms such as assets, liabilities, revenues, expenses, gains, and losses were presented—along with a discussion of qualitative characteristics of financial statements.

The most important new issue brought up in the document is capital maintenance. In Chapter 1 it was noted that this concept is concerned with how earnings are measured in terms of maintaining intact the firm's capital (assets minus liabilities) existing at the beginning of the period. This is a problem of overriding importance that should be given a very prominent place in the normative objectives of a metatheoretical structure. It was not considered extensively, if at all, in any of the other documents considered in this chapter. Capital maintenance will be extensively discussed in Chapter 11. The discussion memorandum also considered qualitative characteristics of financial information. These will be considered in our discussion of SFAC 2.

STATEMENTS OF FINANCIAL ACCOUNTING CONCEPTS

The SFACs constitute the finished portion of the conceptual framework project. These statements are analogous to APB Statement 4 in one respect:

---

[35] FASB (1976b, p. 2).
[36] See FASB (1976a), and FASB (1976c).

like that document, these statements do not establish "generally accepted accounting principles" and are not intended to invoke Rule 203 of the Rules of Conduct of the AICPA (which prohibits departures from generally accepted accounting principles).

While there might be considerable disappointment over this weak status of the statements, there are nonetheless some important benefits to this treatment. First of all, it avoids any possibility of a crisis arising from a failure to comply with the statements. Second, the process of arriving at a workable and utilitarian metatheoretical-type structure must be acknowledged as a slow evolutionary process. Trial and error should certainly be expected to occur, and the tentative nature of the statements may make it easier to change components as the need arises. Unfortunately, there is also the possibility that these statements will have a purely cosmetic effect.

STATEMENT NO. 1

SFAC 1 is concerned with the objectives of financial reporting by business enterprises. As such, it is a direct descendant of the Trueblood Report. In general, the statement conforms to a boiled down version of the Trueblood Report, with some necessary value judgments as well as some redundant statements scattered throughout the narrative.

The statement continues the user-oriented thrust appearing throughout the documents being reviewed here. While heterogeneity of external user groups is acknowledged, a common core characteristic of all outside users is their interest in the prediction of the amounts, timing, and uncertainties of future cash flows. Hence financial statements must be general purpose in nature rather than being geared toward specific needs of a particular user group. The report also takes the position that users of financial statements must be assumed to be knowledgeable about financial information and reporting, an apparent departure from the Trueblood Report's statement assuming "limited ability" of users. (We have already noted the potential qualification of the literal meaning of that phrase.)

The statement also notes the importance of stewardship in terms of assessing how well management has discharged its duties and obligations to owners and other interested groups. The notion of stewardship discussed here is quite brief but goes beyond the narrow interpretation of proper custodianship of the firm's resources.

Several important value judgments are made throughout the report:

1. Information is not costless to provide, so benefits of usage should exceed costs of production.
2. Accounting reports are by no means the only source of information about enterprises.
3. Accrual accounting is extremely useful in assessing and predicting earning power and cash flows of an enterprise.
4. Information provided should be helpful, but users make from it their own predictions and assessments.

Finally, the document does not specify what statements should be used, much less their format. Hence, SFAC 1 is an extremely cautious invocation of the Trueblood Committee objectives.

STATEMENT NO. 2

SFAC 2 deals with qualitative characteristics of accounting information. the term "qualitative characteristics" was used in APB Statement 4, but the concepts discussed here proceed directly from ASOBAT.

The content of SFAC 2 can be best visualized from Exhibit 5-3, which comes from that document. Decision makers stand at the apex of the diagram, a position symbolic of the orientation of the financial accounting function toward the criterion of serving the decision needs of users.

With regard to users, SFAC 1 previously established that financial statements should be aimed at a common core of similar information needs. Users are also presumed to be knowledgeable about financial statements and information; hence, understandability is recognized in Exhibit 5-3 as a "user-specific quality." However, even if users are assumed to be knowledgeable, information itself can have different degrees of comprehensibility. The quality of understandability is a characteristic influenced by both users and preparers of accounting information.

Listed above understandability is the pervasive constraint that benefits of financial information must exceed its costs. The importance of this idea is shown by its place on the diagram.

The specific qualitative characteristics of accounting that SFAC 2 has centered on come under the general heading of decision usefulness, which simply continues the emphasis on decision makers and their needs. The two principal qualities are relevance and reliability.

Relevance

Relevance carries forward from ASOBAT and is rather awkwardly expressed in SFAC 2 as being "capable of making a difference in a decision by helping users to form predictions about the outcomes of past, present, and future events or to confirm or correct expectations."[37] Relevance has two main aspects—predictive value and feedback value—and one minor one, timeliness.

Predictive Value. Predictive value, as in previous documents, is the value of useful inputs for predictions, such as cash flows or earning power, rather than being an actual prediction itself.

Feedback Value. Feedback value refers to "confirming or correcting their (decision makers) earlier expectations."[38] It thus refers to assessing where the firm presently stands and therefore overlaps with how well management has carried out its functions. When viewed broadly, feedback

[37]FASB (1980a, p. 21).
[38]FASB (1980a, p. 22).

EXHIBIT 5-3.

A Hierarchy of Accounting Qualities

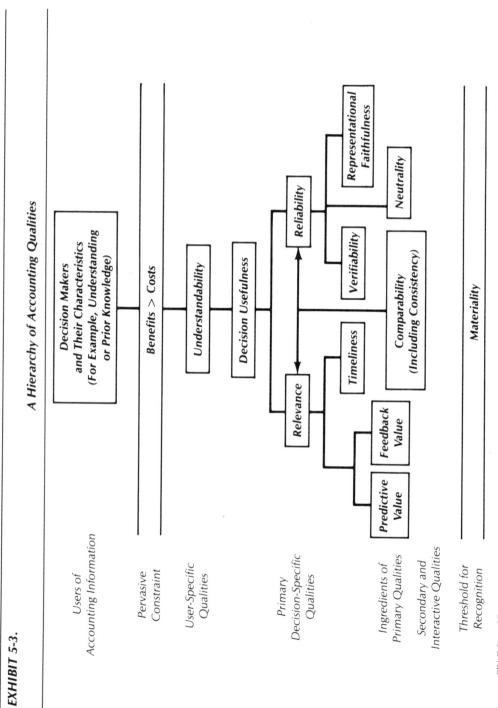

Source: SFAC 2, p. 15.

value is closely related to accountability. It is also noted that information providing this quality must also influence or affect predictive value. Hence there appears to be a dual meaning to the term "feedback value" that is somewhat confusing. However, this confusion does not deny that linkage exists between feedback value and predictive value.

Timeliness. Timeliness is really in the nature of a constraint on both the other aspects of relevance. To be relevant, information must be timely, which means that it must be "available to decision makers before it loses its capacity to influence decisions."[39] There is a conflict between timeliness and the other aspects of relevance because information can be complete and more accurate if the time constraint is relaxed. Hence a trade-off is often present between timeliness and other components of relevance.

Reliability

Reliability is composed of three components: verifiability, representational faithfulness, and neutrality.

Verifiability. Verifiability refers, as in previous documents, to the degree of consensus among measurers. It is thus concerned with measurement theory. Unlike relevance or its parts, there is a quantifiable element to verifiability. However, it is unquestionably difficult to measure, so SFAC 2 stops short of specifying how "high" the degree of verifiability should be.

Representational Faithfulness. Representational faithfulness, likewise, pertains to measurement theory. It refers to the idea that the measurement itself should correspond with the phenomenon it is attempting to measure. For example, valuation of all fixed assets might be measured by employing straight-line depreciation for 20 years with no salvage value. There would be an extremely high degree of verifiability but the resulting values would, in most cases, not be representative of the attribute of "unamortized cost" if this property is supposed to be indicative of the proportion of historical cost which still has economic utility. Individually determined depreciation schedules might represent a better measurement of the attribute of unamortized cost as defined above. Similarly, if replacement cost were selected as the property to be measured, actual market values, if available, would accomplish representational faithfulness whereas the amount the firm could sell the asset for would not.

It is clear, then, that there can easily be a conflict between verifiability and representational faithfulness. Hence a trade-off between these two characteristics of reliability may well arise.

Neutrality. Neutrality refers to the belief that the policy-setting process should be primarily concerned with relevance and reliability rather than the effect a standard or rule might have on a specific user group or the

---

[39]FASB (1980a, p. 25).

enterprise itself. In other words, neutrality is concerned with financial statements "telling it like it is" rather than the way a particular interest group, like management or stockholders, might like it to be.

Trade-off Between Relevance and Reliability

It should be clear that trade-off effects are present not only within components of relevance and reliability, as previously discussed, but also between relevance and reliability as total entities. For example, current value figures might be more relevant for predictive purposes than historical costs. However, historical costs might be more verifiable than current value measures. Whether criteria can ever be developed to guide implementation of the many potential trade-offs is a very speculative question.

Conservatism

Conservatism is not shown in Exhibit 5-3 but, curiously enough, it is discussed in SFAC 2 where it is called a "convention." SFAC 2 is not in favor of deliberate understatements of assets or income or, for that matter, deliberate overstatements of the same type. Deliberate understatement conflicts with representational faithfulness, neutrality, and both main aspects of relevance. Conservatism is associated with the need for "prudent reporting" by means of attempting to inform readers where uncertainties and risks lie. Thus conservatism really appears to pertain to disclosure, an extremely important concept that is not discussed in SFAC 2.

Comparability and Consistency

These qualities are defined essentially the same way that they were defined in Chapter 4. We view these characteristics as being output oriented. Hence comparability and consistency should stem from a viable conceptual framework rather than being part of the theoretical structure itself.

Materiality

Materiality is also discussed in much the same terms used in Chapter 4. The question that must be raised relative to materiality is whether an item is large enough to influence users' decisions. Materiality is recognized as being a quantitative characteristic, though the profession is not yet ready to implement it in this fashion. Materiality is also a relative concept rather than an absolute one, an aspect that most research in this area has stressed.

STATEMENT NO. 3

SFAC 3 provides definitions of ten "elements" of financial statements. This statement is obviously a resolution of the definitions presented in the discussion memorandum of the Conceptual Framework. The statement can, perhaps, be best understood by presenting the definitions themselves:

1. Assets are probable future economic benefits obtained or controlled by a particular entity as a result of past transactions or events.
2. Liabilities are probable future sacrifices of economic benefits arising from present obligations of a particular entity to transfer assets or provide services to other entities in the future as a result of past transactions or events..
3. Equity is the residual interest in the assets of an entity that remains after deducting its liabilities. In a business enterprise, the equity is the ownership interest.
4. Investments by owners are increases in net assets of a particular enterprise resulting from transfers to it from other entities of something of value to obtain or increase ownership interests (or equity) in it. Assets are most commonly received as investments by owners, but that which is received may also include services or satisfaction or conversion of liabilities of the enterprise.
5. Distributions to owners are decreases in net assets of a particular enterprise resulting from transferring assets, rendering services, or incurring liabilities by the enterprise to owners. Distributions to owners decrease ownership interests (or equity) in an enterprise.
6. Comprehensive income is the change in equity (net assets) of an entity during a period from transactions and other events and circumstances from nonowner sources. It includes all changes in equity during a period except those resulting from investments by owners and distributions to owners.
7. Revenues are inflows or other enhancements of assets of an entity or settlements of its liabilities (or a combination of both) during a period from delivering or producing goods, rendering services, or other activities that constitute the entity's ongoing major or central operations.
8. Expenses are outflows or other using up of assets or incurrences of liabilities (or a combination of both) during a period from delivering or producing goods, rendering services, or carrying out other activities that constitute the entity's ongoing major or central operations.
9. Gains are increases in equity (net assets) from peripheral or incidental transactions of an entity and from all other transactions and other events and circumstances affecting the entity during a period except those that result from revenues or investments by owners.
10. Losses are decreases in equity (net assets) from peripheral or incidental transactions of an entity and from all other transactions and other events and circumstances affecting the entity during a period except those that result from expenses or distributions to owners.[40]

---

[40]FASB (1980b, pp. xi–xii).

Several observations are worth making, particularly about what is *not* included in this statement. First of all, the three views of financial accounting which were in the discussion memorandum have all but disappeared. The type of capital maintenance concept to employ has also not been specified in SFAC 3. Likewise matters of recognition (realization) and measurement as well as "display" in financial statements are not addressed here. Thus it seems that these definitions are in the nature of a "first screen" relative to determining content of financial statements. It is clear that much work remains to be done in prescribing the properties of these various elements, not to mention their arrangement in financial statements.

SFAC 3 also reveals a reversal of terminology. Throughout the discussion memorandum and SFAC 1, the word "earnings" had supplanted the more commonly used "income." In SFAC 2 earnings had disappeared and income was used in paragraphs 90 and 94. Finally, SFAC 3 made the reversal official by designating *income* as the term to indicate the comprehensive or total change in net assets occurring during the period as a result of operations. *Earnings* was reserved as a possible component of income, to be specified at a later date.

STATEMENT NO. 4

SFAC 4 is concerned with objectives of financial reporting by nonbusiness organizations. Nonbusiness organizations are characterized by:

1. receipts of significant amounts of resources from providers who do not expect to receive either repayment or economic benefits proportionate to resources provided;
2. operating purposes that are primarily other than to provide goods or services at a profit. . . ;
3. absence of defined ownership interests that can be sold, transferred, or redeemed, or that convey entitlement to a share of residual distribution of resources in the event of liquidation of the organization.[41]

SFAC 4 also notes that nonbusiness organizations do not have a single indicator of the entity's performance comparable to income measurement in the profit sector.[42] Since the emphasis in this text is on the profit sector, SFAC 4 is outside the scope of our interest.

CONCLUDING REMARKS ON STATEMENTS OF FINANCIAL ACCOUNTING CONCEPTS

These statements are a tentative start toward implementation of a conceptual framework. The statements themselves are not to be construed as constituting "generally accepted accounting principles." Furthermore, the

[41]FASB (1980c, p. x).
[42]FASB (1980c, p. xi).

most concrete of the statements, SFAC 3, is not intended to bring about "... upheavals in present practice or at least in the way certain items are viewed."[43]

Of the three statements reviewed here, SFAC 2 appears to have most completely covered the intended ground. Even here the very thorny problem of how to engineer trade-offs must eventually be faced. It can only be repeated that while a start has been made on a conceptual framework, the most difficult issues still lie ahead. These include the question of the attributes or properties of assets and liabilities to be recognized, which must also be coordinated with expense and revenue recognition. The type of capital maintenance to utilize is an important aspect of these recognition problems. Finally, the implementation of the measurement process relative to these qualities or characteristics is of major significance.

There are certainly other possible approaches to a conceptual framework than the one embarked upon by the FASB. Another orientation will be examined in Chapter 7.

SUMMARY

The most common thread running through the various documents, reports, and monographs discussed here is that financial statements should be relevant to users for decision-making purposes. As a result, the orientation of standard-setting bodies turned away from the postulates and principles toward objectives and standards.

ASOBAT was the first document to put forth the new orientation toward user relevance. However, little further detail or explication of user relevance was provided. APB Statement 4 continued the thrust of user relevance. The statement itself is a curious mixture of the old and new approaches. This can be understood in light of the fact that the document appeared at a time of transition. It was clear that the APB would be terminated but the organization of its successor was not apparent.

The first statement to begin extensively addressing the issue of user objectives was the Trueblood Report. While predictive ability and accountability are mentioned, the discussion is still not at an operational level. However, a criticism on this account is unfair because a preliminary statement of the type made by the report can do nothing more than point the way for future efforts.

SATTA was to the 1970s as ASOBAT was to the 1960s. Both are the product of AAA committees that were attempting to summarize the "state of the art" concerning accounting theory. The opinion is expressed in SATTA that choice among accounting theories (valuation systems) could

---

[43]FASB (1980b, p. 50).

not be made at that time owing to diversity of users and their presumably different objectives and information needs.

At approximately the same time as the appearance of SATTA, the FASB's Conceptual Framework Project began to appear. In addition to the discussion memorandum, four statements of financial accounting concepts have been issued to date. SFAC 1 basically reiterates the objectives put forth in the Trueblood Committee Report. Users are assumed to be knowledgeable about financial statement reporting. SFAC 2 has been the most substantial effort to date. The qualitative characteristics center around relevance and reliability. In turn, relevance consists of predictive value and feedback value, both of which are under the constraint of timeliness. Reliability is made up of verifiability and representational faithfulness buttressed by neutrality of the underlying standards concerning the desires of vested interests. Many potential conflicts exist among these qualitative characteristics, including the general one between relevance and reliability. SFAC 3 presents basic definitions of accounting terms which serve as a "first screen" relative to later work in terms of measurement and recognition of these elements on financial statements. SFAC 4 deals with objectives of nonbusiness organizations and is beyond the general scope of this text.

The crucial issues faced in this chapter concern what the objectives of financial statements are, or at least are perceived to be, and the information needs of the very heterogeneous users of financial statements. The major objectives appear to be predictive ability and accountability. The latter is an extension of the more traditional stewardship objective into the areas of effective and efficient usage of enterprise resources by management. Minor objectives appear to be capital maintenance measurement and adaptivity. There is some potential conflict among (and within) these objectives. There are three ways to measure capital maintenance. Adaptability is best determined by exit valuation of assets, which gives a result that has little if any utility for predictive ability or accountability purposes.

All that can be said about user diversity at this time is that, despite the heterogeneity of users by type as well as within groups, it has not been proved that the groups have strongly differentiated information needs.

APPENDIX 5-A: USER OBJECTIVES

The user objectives stated in documents such as the Trueblood Committee Report and SFAC 1 are quite broad and general in nature. Further specificity in terms of objectives may be necessary if policy making is to be appropriately executed. Unfortunately only a very limited amount of accounting research has focused on this issue. Nevertheless, there appear to be two major areas where broad information is applicable to many user groups.

The first of these is referred to as the **predictive ability** objective. The second is an extension of stewardship called **accountability.** Both these objectives can be divided into numerous subcategories. Our discussion, however, is restricted to the principal aspects of each objective.

PREDICTIVE ABILITY

Numerous studies have attempted to use accounting data for prediction of future variables. One group of studies has attempted to predict future income on the basis of present and past income numbers.[44] One of the purposes of these studies was to obtain evidence concerning whether historical cost income, general price-level adjusted income or current value income is a better predictor of itself. These studies indicate that historical cost appears to be at least as good a predictor of itself as the other two methods.

However, Revsine has pointed out that income itself is an "artifact."[45] An artifact, in this sense, refers to a number, the determination of which is based on prescribed rules rather than being representationally faithful to the attribute being measured. Furthermore, because there is sufficient latitude about selecting alternative methods (combined with the potential desire of management to smooth income), it is not surprising that historical income appears to be a better predictor of itself than other income measurement methods which intuitively appear to contain numbers more economically relevant.

Revsine also suggests that since income is an "artificial construct," its predictive importance lies in the ability to anticipate a real event such as future cash flows.[46] Finally, since the real event may itself be quite volatile, the predictor should similarly be volatile whereas the tests in the research previously discussed were really examining the issue of income smoothing.[47]

Many other studies have focused on the predictive ability of two other sets of accounting-generated numbers: quarterly earnings announcements as predictors of annual earnings and financial ratios as predictors of bankruptcy.[48] In both these cases, the accounting data—as might be expected—has been highly useful in the predictive process.

One cautionary note, however, should be added. These studies have employed particular models as part of the predictive ability process. Only insofar as users avail themselves of at least roughly similar methods can

[44]Simmons and Gray (1969) and Frank (1969).

[45]Revsine (1971, pp. 480–481).

[46]Revsine (1971, p. 487).

[47]Barnea, Ronen, and Sadan (1975) suggest the segregation of recurring income components from the transitory elements in order to facilitate the prediction of cash flows by users. Excluded from recurring income would be extraordinary (nonrecurring and nonoperating) items designated in APB 30, as well as nonrecurring operating factors.

[48]For predictive aspects of quarterly data see Coates (1972), Brown and Kennelly (1972), and Foster (1977). For financial ratios as predictors see Beaver (1966) and Elam (1975). For a critical look at the predictive ability objective see Greenball (1971).

predictive ability tests be relied upon.[49] The alternative, of course, involves attempting to educate users about what are presumed to be the best predictive models—a task, as noted previously, which could be quite difficult to implement. Another point to keep in mind is that valuation and income methods that are presumed to be best for an objective such as predictive ability may have less utility for other objectives.

ACCOUNTABILITY

We use the word "accountability" in a broader sense than the more narrowly restrictive stewardship concept, which is mainly concerned with safeguarding of assets. The meaning here follows the usage of accountability by Ijiri to indicate the responsibility of management to report on achieving goals relating to the effective and efficient utilization of enterprise resources.[50] Measurements that stem from the accountability objective would include earnings per share and return on investment and its components (capital turnover and profit margin). The question of the valuation system that provides what is deemed to be the best input for these and other accountability-oriented measurements must be specified in a lower part of the theoretical structure.

Predictive ability and accountability are separate objectives. One is concerned with data that will be useful in terms of assessing future prospects, whereas the other is concerned with evaluating enterprise performance. Between these two objectives, there is, of course, a linkage of a feed-forward nature. How well a firm is presently doing can certainly be an important input for predictive purposes. Nevertheless, whether the information needed for these objectives differs has never really been determined. Obviously the problem would be more acute if different valuation systems were preferable in terms of providing information for these objectives. Much work of an empirical nature needs to be done to gather evidence to help answer the question.

SECONDARY OBJECTIVES

We see two other possible user objectives for which accounting information can be extremely useful. They are much narrower in conception than predictive ability and accountability. One is a measure of capital maintenance, which gives information relative to how much dividends can be paid during a period without returning capital to the stockholders. This is covered in detail in Chapter 11.

Another possible objective would be that of adaptability. This objective is concerned with measuring total liquidity available to the firm. By defi-

---

[49]The seminal article on predictive ability and its limitations is Beaver, Kennelly, and Voss (1968).
[50]Ijiri (1975, pp. ix–x).

nition this is determined by measuring the net realizable value of the firm's assets minus its liabilities. Both would be measured in exit-value terms as illustrated in Appendix 1-A. An income statement under the exit-value approach measures the change in liquidity occurring during the period as a result of operations.[51] Chambers has been the principal proponent of this system and also of this objective, though Sterling has also advocated it.[52]

While a measure of total liquidity available to a firm certainly has some relevance, we consider adaptability far less important than predictive ability and accountability. Firms that are successful going concerns will probably draw upon only a very small portion of the total available liquidity during relatively short time periods. Adaptability measures would probably be most important to the owners of small closely held firms and possibly short-term creditors. Consequently, the adaptive approach appears to be more closely oriented to the proprietary theory than to the entity theory.

Exit-value approaches appear to have limited usefulness for predictive ability and accountability purposes. Indeed Chambers stoutly denies that accounting figures can have any relevance for predictive purposes.[53]

These four objectives have been discussed in fairly broad terms. Further specification of issues, such as attributes to be measured and valuation systems to be employed, should appear in lower levels of the theoretical structure. A broad statement of objectives should be the topmost level of a metatheoretical framework, which would be concerned with implementing finite uniformity. Certainly the development of objectives in SFAC 1 and qualitative characteristics of financial statements in SFAC 2 indicates a hierarchical ordering in a prescriptive type of metatheoretical framework. Since implementing a set of user objectives implies a fairly high degree of information needs on the part of users, user diversity is examined in Appendix 5-B.

APPENDIX 5-B: USER DIVERSITY

Unquestionably there are a large number of diverse users of published financial statements.[54] What is not clear, however, is whether their information needs for the various types of objectives discussed in Appendix 5-A can be satisfied by general purpose statements prepared under conditions

---

[51]It is quite unlikely that an exit-value income statement would be particularly useful for either predictive ability or accountability purposes. The sizable declines in exit values for many fixed assets in the early years of usage occur because of market imperfections. These lowered exit values result in excessive depreciation charges, which make the exit-value income statement unrepresentative.

[52]Chambers (1967) and Sterling (1981, p. 119), for example.

[53]Chambers (1968, p. 246).

[54]A good short summary of users and their needs is provided in Stamp (1980, pp. 39–51).

of neutrality. The list of possible user groups is indeed lengthy. It would include

1. shareholders,
2. creditors,
3. financial analysts and advisors,
4. employees,
5. labor unions,
6. customers,
7. suppliers,
8. industry trade associations,
9. governmental agencies,
10. public-interest groups,
11. researchers and standard setters.

Furthermore, even within these groups there is extensive diversity. Shareholders include diversified versus undiversified, those using professional financial advisers and those who do not, those knowledgeable about financial statements versus those uninformed, and actual versus potential owners of securities. Creditors can be segregated into short-term and long-term types. Public-interest groups would include, among others, consumer and environmental groups. Researchers and standard setters include academic accountants, members of the SEC and FASB, and economists. Governmental agencies (such as the Internal Revenue Service, Interstate Commerce Commission, and Federal Trade Commission) are often able to acquire by mandate the information that they desire.

Some of the information needs of different user groups may be complementary. For example, short-term creditors may be concerned with liquidity measurements such as the current or quick ratios, whereas long-term creditors may have greater interest in the composition of capital structures. Serious problems do not appear to exist where complementary needs exist. Perhaps the most serious conflict lies between actual and potential security holders. The former would probably desire information that would maximize security values, whereas the latter would prefer information that would minimize security values (interests of potential security owners would change if they acquire shares). However, at present, it is not clear which types of information are most consistent with the two objectives. Furthermore, the above-stated objectives conflict with the neutrality criterion of SFAC 2. Hence the information that should be supplied to the diverse user groups should still be aimed at being useful for the type of objectives stated in Appendix 5-A.

Certainly it may be the case that the diverse user groups have different information needs for their perceived objectives. However, at this time the possibility of diverse user needs is simply an untested proposition. Until the hypothesis becomes validated through empirical testing, the aim of standard-setting organizations should be to produce general purpose financial statements where rules are determined in a neutral setting with adequate disclosure for knowledgeable users.

QUESTIONS

1. How do objectives differ from postulates?
2. Do you think it is the case that the funds flow statement is more "factual" and less "interpretative" than the income statement and balance sheet?
3. Do you think that the "standards" mentioned in ASOBAT are really standards?
4. Of what importance in a conceptual framework or metatheory are definitions of basic terms such as assets, liabilities, revenues, and expenses?
5. Are feedback value and predictive value independent of each other or is there some degree of overlap?
6. Why is the problem of heterogeneous users so critical in the development of accounting theory?
7. What is "Pareto optimality" and why is it a very restrictive concept from the standpoint of policy makers?
8. How do the research orientations of accounting in Chapter 1 compare with SATTA's organization of research?
9. What is the relationship between economic consequences of accounting standards discussed in Chapter 3 and the quality of neutrality presented in SFAC 2?
10. Why must objectives be at the topmost level of a conceptual framework of accounting?
11. Among the four objectives discussed in Appendix 5-A, what conflicts are present?
12. How does "freedom from bias" mentioned in ASOBAT compare to the quality of neutrality mentioned in SFAC No. 2?
13. The statement of Herbert Miller (footnote 33) is closest to which theory approach delineated in SATTA?
14. How has the definition of "accounting" been modified in recent years?
15. What potential conflicts are present in terms of different user needs?

CASES AND PROBLEMS

1. Discuss as many of the potential trade-offs among the qualities mentioned in SFAC 2 as you can, and give either a general or concrete example of each.

2. The crucial question brought up in this chapter concerns the issue of whether the admittedly heterogeneous users of financial statements have highly diverse information needs in terms of their underlying ob-

jectives. State as carefully as you can (1) the case as to why the user groups have largely diverse information needs, and (2) the case as to why the user groups may have relatively similar information needs.

BIBLIOGRAPHY OF REFERENCED WORKS

Abdel-Khalik, A. Rashad (1971). "User Preference Ordering Value: A Model," *The Accounting Review* (July 1971), pp. 437–471.

American Accounting Association (1966). *A Statement of Basic Accounting Theory* (AAA).

———— (1969). "An Evaluation of External Reporting Practices: A Report of the 1966–68 Committee on External Reporting," *Accounting Review Supplement* (AAA), pp. 79–123.

———— (1977a). *Responses to the Financial Accounting Standards Board's "Tentative Conclusions on Objectives of Financial Statements of Business Enterprises" and "Conceptual Framework for Financial Accounting and Reporting: Elements of Financial Statements and Their Measurement"* (AAA).

———— (1977b). *Statement on Accounting Theory and Theory Acceptance* (AAA).

American Institute of Certified Public Accountants (1953). *Accounting Terminology Bulletin No. 1* (AICPA, 1973).

———— (1970). "Basic Concepts and Accounting Principles Underlying Financial Statements of Business Enterprises," *APB Statement No. 4* (AICPA), pp. 9057–9106.

———— (1973). *Objectives of Financial Statements* (AICPA).

Anton, Hector (1976). "Objectives of Financial Accounting: Review and Analysis," *The Journal of Accountancy* (January 1976), pp. 40–51.

Barnea, Amir; Joshua Ronen; and Simcha Sadan (1975). "The Implementation of Accounting Objectives: An Application to Extraordinary Items," *The Accounting Review* (January 1975), pp. 58–68.

Barton, A. D. (1974). "Expectations and Achievements in Income Theory," *The Accounting Review* (October 1974), pp. 664–681.

Beaver, William H. (1966). "Financial Ratios as Predictors of Failure," *Empirical Research in Accounting: Selected Studies 1966* (Supplement to *Journal of Accounting Research*), pp. 71–111.

Beaver, William H., and Joel S. Demski (1974). "The Nature of Financial Accounting Objectives: A Summary and Synthesis," *Studies on Financial Accounting Objectives* (Supplement to *Journal of Accounting Research*), pp. 170–185.

Beaver, William H.; John W. Kennelly; and William M. Voss (1968). "Predictive Ability as a Criterion for the Evaluation of Accounting Data," *The Accounting Review* (October 1968), pp. 675–683.

Borst, Duane (1981). "Accounting vs. Reality: How Wide is the 'GAAP'," *Financial Executive* (July 1981), pp. 12–15.

Brown, Philip, and John W. Kennelly (1972). "The Information Content of Quarterly Earnings—An Extension and Some Further Evidence," *Journal of Business* (July 1972), pp. 403–415.

Chambers, Raymond J. (1967). "Continuously Contemporary Accounting—Additivity and Action," *The Accounting Review* (October 1967), pp. 751–757.

——— (1968). "Measures and Values: A Reply to Professor Staubus," *The Accounting Review* (April 1968), pp. 239–247.

Coates, Robert (1973). "The Predictive Content of Interim Reports: A Time Series Analysis," *Empirical Research in Accounting: Selected Studies, 1973* (Supplement to *Journal of Accounting Research*), pp. 132–144.

Dopuch, Nicholas, and Shyam Sunder (1980). "FASB's Statements on Objectives and Elements of Financial Accounting: A Review," *The Accounting Review* (January 1980), pp. 1–21.

Elam, Rick (1975). "The Effect of Lease Data on the Predictive Ability of Financial Ratios," *The Accounting Review* (January 1975), pp. 25–43.

Financial Accounting Standards Board (1976a). *FASB Discussion Memorandum: Conceptual Framework for Financial Accounting and Reporting: Elements of Financial Statements and Their Measurement* (FASB).

——— (1976b). *Scope and Implications of the Conceptual Framework Project* (FASB).

——— (1976c). *Tentative Conclusions on Objectives of Financial Statements of Business Enterprises* (FASB).

——— (1978). "Objectives of Financial Reporting by Business Enterprises," *Statement of Financial Accounting Concepts No. 1* (FASB).

——— (1980a). "Qualitative Characteristics of Accounting Information," *Statement of Financial Accounting Concepts No. 2* (FASB).

——— (1980b). "Elements of Financial Statements of Business Enterprises," *Statement of Financial Accounting Concepts No. 3* (FASB).

——— (1980c). "Objectives of Financial Reporting by Nonbusiness Organizations," *Statement of Financial Accounting Concepts No. 4* (FASB).

Foster, George (1977). "Quarterly Accounting Data: Time-Series Properties and Predictive-Ability Results," *The Accounting Review* (January 1977), pp. 1–21.

Frank, Werner (1969). "A Study of the Predictive Significance of Two Income Statements," *Journal of Accounting Research* (Spring 1969), pp. 123–136.

Greenball, Melvin N. (1971). "The Predictive-Ability Criterion: Its Relevance in Evaluating Accounting Data," *Abacus* (June 1971), p. 1–7.

Ijiri, Yuji (1971). "Critique of the APB Fundamentals Statement," *Journal of Accountancy* (November 1971), pp. 43–50.

——— (1975). "Theory of Accounting Measurement," *Studies in Accounting Research #10* (American Accounting Association).

Miller, Henry (1972). "Environmental Complexity and Financial Reports," *The Accounting Review* (January 1972), pp. 31–37.

Miller, Herbert E. (1974). "Discussion of Opportunities and Implications of the Report on Objectives of Financial Statements," *Studies on Financial Accounting Objectives: 1974* (supplement to *Journal of Accounting Research*) pp. 18–20.

Moonitz, Maurice (1971). "The Accounting Principles Board Revisited," *New York Certified Public Accountant* (May 1971), pp. 341–345.

Paton, William A., and A. C. Littleton (1940). *An Introduction to Corporate Accounting Standards* (American Accounting Association, 1957).

Revsine, Lawrence (1970a). "On the Correspondence Between Replacement Cost Income and Economic Income," *The Accounting Review* (July 1970), pp. 513–523.

——— (1970b). "Data Expansion and Conceptual Structure," *The Accounting Review* (October 1970), pp. 704–711.

—— (1971). "Predictive Ability, Market Prices, and Operating Flows," *The Accounting Review* (July 1971), pp. 480–489.

Samuels, Warren (1974). *Pareto on Policy* (Elsevier Scientific Publishing Company).

Schattke, R. W. (1972). "An Analysis of APB Statement No. 4," *The Accounting Review* (April 1972), pp. 233–244.

Simmons, Jóhn K., and Jack Gray (1969). "An Investigation of the Effect of Differing Accounting Frameworks on the Prediction of Net Income," *The Accounting Review* (October, 1969), pp. 757–776.

Sorter, George H., and Martin S. Gans (1974). "Opportunities and Implications of the Report on the Objectives of Financial Statements," *Studies on Financial Accounting Objectives: 1974* (supplement to *Journal of Accounting Research*), pp. 1–12.

Stamp, Edward (1980). *Corporate Reporting: Its Future Evolution* (Canadian Institute of Chartered Accountants).

Staubus, George (1972). "An Analysis of APB Statement No. 4," *Journal of Accountancy* (February 1972), pp. 36–43.

Sterling, Robert R. (1967). "A Statement of Basic Accounting Theory: A Review Article," *Journal of Accounting Research* (Spring 1967), pp. 94–112.

—— (1981). "Costs (Historical Versus Current) Versus Exit Values," *Abacus* (December 1981), pp. 93–129.

ADDITIONAL READINGS

CONCEPTUAL FRAMEWORK

Arthur Young & Company (1977). *Conceptual Framework for Financial Accounting and Reporting* (Arthur Young & Company).

Burton, John C. (1978). "A Symposium on the Conceptual Framework," *Journal of Accountancy* (January 1978), pp. 53–58.

Coe, Teddy L., and George H. Sorter (1978). "The FASB has Been Using an Implicit Conceptual Framework," *Accounting Journal* (Winter 1977–78), pp. 152–159.

Ernst & Ernst (1977). *Conceptual Framework—Our Analysis and Response* (Ernst & Ernst).

Sprouse, Robert T. (1978). "The Importance of Earnings in the Conceptual Framework," *Journal of Accountancy* (January 1978), pp. 64–71.

Storey, Reed K. (1981). "Conditions Necessary for Developing a Conceptual Framework," *Financial Analysts Journal* (May–June 1981), pp. 51–58.

OBJECTIVES OF FINANCIAL STATEMENTS

Bedford, Norton (1974). "Discussion of Opportunities and Implications of the Report on Objectives of Financial Statements," *Studies on Financial Accounting Objectives: 1974* (Supplement to *Journal of Accounting Research*), pp. 13–17.

Cyert, Richard M., and Yuji Ijiri (1974). "Problems of Implementing the Trueblood Objectives Report," *Studies on Financial Accounting Objectives: 1974* (Supplement to *Journal of Accounting Research*), pp. 29–42.

Kripke, Homer (1972). "The Objectives of Financial Accounting Should Be to Provide Information for the Serious Investor," *Corporate Financial Reporting: the Issues, the Objectives and Some New Proposals*, ed. A. Rappaport and L. Revsine (Commerce Clearing House), pp. 94–119.

Most, Kenneth, and A. L. Winters (1976). "Focus on Standard Setting: From Trueblood to the FASB," *Journal of Accountancy* (February 1977), pp. 67–75.

Ronen, Joshua (1974). "A User Oriented Development of Accounting Information Requirements," *Objectives of Financial Statements* Vol. 2, ed. J. J. Cramer, Jr., and G. H. Sorter (American Institute of Certified Public Accountants), pp. 80–103.

CHAPTER 6

The Usefulness of Accounting Information

Much of the accounting theory literature before the 1970s was little more than a debate as to which income number produced under alternative global accounting models was correct. In retrospect it was simplistic to think that a single basis of measurement was "correct" and could capture all relevant financial information about a firm. This point was recognized in *A Statement of Basic Accounting Theory*, which suggested the possibility of multicolumn reporting, with each column representing a different basis of measurement.[1] Finally, the *Statement of Accounting Theory and Theory Acceptance* stated that there is no conclusive way of determining the best valuation system.[2] This dilemma is due to user heterogeneity in decision making, and diverse information needs relative to making these decisions. In other words, different sets of information produced under alternative systems may be best for different users. Although user diversity presents an obstacle to the development of a single basis of measurement, it may be, as pointed out in Chapter 5, that the user diversity problem is exaggerated.

[1] American Accounting Association (1966).
[2] American Accounting Association (1977, Chapters 4 and 5).

The impasse in normative and deductively oriented theory development was partially responsible for a change in direction by the Financial Accounting Standards Board (FASB). Emphasis is now placed on decision usefulness as the criterion which guides the formulation of accounting policy. One consequence of this new orientation is the need to study the usefulness of accounting information in order to evaluate the economic consequences and benefits of financial reporting.

In this chapter we review a wide range of research that has examined the usefulness of accounting information to decision makers. Many approaches have been taken. The research reviewed is classified into four categories: (1) information economics, (2) capital market research, (3) studies of individual decision making, using experimental settings, and (4) surveys of the usefulness of financial reports. The first area, information economics, is deductive research while all of the other three are inductive.

The chapter commences with information economics. It provides a general model of how information has value to decision makers. Empirical research into the value of accounting information is then examined from the several perspectives mentioned above. The chapter concludes with an assessment of the usefulness of accounting allocations.

INFORMATION ECONOMICS

The economic market model assumes information is perfect (complete) and available to every one at no cost. Perfect and costless information is the instrument by which equilibrium market prices are established. Because perfect information has been assumed to exist, the process of information production, dissemination, and use has not been studied until recently.

In more recent literature, models have been developed in which economic decisions are assumed to be made in a world characterized by uncertainty and imperfect information. Uncertainty exists because the future cannot be known in advance. It follows that information will always be incomplete and subjective. Analysis of economic decision making under uncertainty has focused attention on the critical role of information in the decision-making process. Information is a key variable. As a result, information is now considered to be a commodity in its own right, separate and distinct from decisions which may be based on the information. In other words, information can be studied in an economic framework of supply and demand. For this reason, the name **information economics** is used to describe the research. However, the research originated in statistics where it was called *statistical decision theory*.

Information economics is a general framework for determining the value of information. It does not deal specifically with accounting infor-

mation. However, information economics has been used to study accounting information and is illustrated here with examples based on accounting
information.

MODEL FOR INFORMATION EVALUATION

The decision theory model for determining the value of information to
a decision maker is illustrated with the following example. Assume a decision maker is faced with a choice between two actions (a_j):

a_1 = lend $1 million to XYZ for one year at 15%.

a_2 = invest $1 million in government bonds for one year at 12%.

For simplicity, only two alternative future outcomes or scenarios are assumed to be possible. These outcomes are called **states** (s_i):

s_1 = XYZ repays the loan plus interest.

s_2 = XYZ defaults on the loan, and $200,000 of costs are incurred to
recover the loan and interest in full.

Based on existing information or knowledge, the subjective probability (ϕ)
of each state occurring is considered by the decision maker to be:

$$\phi(s_1) = .8$$
$$\phi(s_2) = .2$$

Note that the subjective probability of both states must total 1.0.
The decision problem is summarized by expressing the future value of
each action/state combination in the payoff matrix in Exhibit 6-1.

EXHIBIT 6-1.

Payoff Matrix

a_j \ s_i	s_1 XYZ Does Not Default	s_2 XYZ Defaults
a_1 Lend to XYZ	$1,150,000	$ 950,000
a_2 Invest in Government Bonds	$1,120,000	$1,120,000

Utility is determined by the expected monetary value of each action (a_j) using Bayesian statistics. Letting $E(U|a_j)$ be the utility of each action we have:

$$E(U|a_j) = \sum_{i=1}^{s} U(s_i,a_j) \cdot \phi(s_i) \tag{6.1}$$

$$= U(s_1,a_j) \times \phi(s_1) + U(s_2,a_j) \times \phi(s_2).$$

The expected monetary values of actions a_1 and a_2 are:

$$E(U|a_1) = \$(1,150,000 \times .8) + (950,000 \times .2) = \$1,110,000. \tag{6.1a}$$

$$E(U|a_2) = \$(1,120,000 \times .8) + (1,120,000 \times .2) = \$1,120,000. \tag{6.1b}$$

Given the present information known by the decision maker, action a_2 would be taken since it has a higher utility than action a_1.

VALUE OF PERFECT INFORMATION

The next question to consider is the value of what is called **perfect information.** In the preceding example, perfect information means that we would know with certainty which future state, s_1 or s_2, is going to occur. If s_1 occurs (XYZ does not default), the utility maximizing action is a_1, lending $1 million to XYZ. If s_2 occurs (XYZ defaults), utility would be maximized by action a_2, investing in the government bonds. The values of these alternative optimal acts, given the two alternative outcomes, are $1,150,000 (given s_1) and $1,120,000 (given s_2).

The utility of knowing in advance what state is going to occur is defined as:

$$E(U|\text{advance state revelation}) = \sum_{i=1}^{s} \{\max_{a \in A} U(s_i,a)\} \cdot \phi(s_i) \tag{6.2}$$

$$= (\$1,150,000 \times .8) + (\$1,120,000 \times .2)$$

$$= \$1,144,000.$$

This formula takes the value of the two optimal acts if s_1 and s_2 were to occur, and derives the utility of knowing in advance which state occurs. This is done by multiplying these amounts by the subjective probability estimates of s_1 and s_2 based on existing information. The utility of having perfect information is the expected value of the optimal acts, given the original subjective probability of each state occurring. This is computed as $1,144,000. The value of perfect information is the difference between the utility as computed above ($1,144,000) and the utility of $1,120,000 given action a_2 in the original analysis. This amount, $24,000, is the maximum the decision maker would be willing to pay for additional information that reveals the state that will occur.

VALUE OF LESS THAN PERFECT INFORMATION

In reality one could not buy perfect information because future outcomes cannot be known in advance. But new information can cause a revision in the decision maker's subjective probability estimation of each state's occurring. The value of new but less than perfect information can also be calculated using Bayesian statistics.

Continuing the previous example, assume a new piece of information can be purchased that is relevant to assessing the probability of default by XYZ. The decision maker believes the predicted ratio of expense to sales for the next year is a good indicator of XYZ's likelihood of defaulting. This predicted information can be extrapolated from historical trends. The new information or signal is designated Y_k, and it comes from an information system called η. For simplicity the new signal (Y_k) can have one of two values:

$$Y_1 = \text{expense to sales ratio} \leq 1.$$

$$Y_2 = \text{expense to sales ratio} > 1.$$

Given that XYZ does not default, the decision maker believes the probability of receiving signal Y_1 would be .9. This is also defined as $\phi(Y_1 \mid s_1)$, the probability of receiving signal Y_1, given state s_1. The probability of receiving signal Y_2, given state s_1, is of course .1 ($1.0 - .9$).

The decision maker also believes the probability of signal Y_2, given state s_2, to be .7. In other words, the signal Y_2 is *bad news*, and would be expected to be associated with default, while signal Y_1 is *good news* and is more likely to be associated with not defaulting. Finally, to complete the analysis, the probability of signal Y_1, given s_2, would be .3 ($1.0 - .7$). These four probabilities are summarized in Exhibit 6-2.

EXHIBIT 6-2.

New Signal Probabilities

Y_k \ s_i	s_1 No Default	s_2 Default	$\phi y i$
Y_1 Ratio ≤ 1	.9 0.72	.3 0.0	0.78
Y_2 Ratio > 1	.1 .08	.7 0.0	0.22

(column heads: 0.8 and 0.2 handwritten above s_1 and s_2)

The probability of actually receiving the signals Y_1 and Y_2 is computed from the formula:

$$\phi(Y_k) = \sum_{i=1}^{s} \phi(Y_k \mid s_i) \cdot \phi(s_i) \tag{6.3}$$

$$\begin{aligned}
\phi(Y_1) &= \phi(Y_1 \mid s_1) \cdot \phi(s_1) + \phi(Y_1 \mid s_2) \cdot \phi(s_2) \\
&= (.9 \times .8) + (.3 \times .2) \\
&= .78
\end{aligned} \tag{6.3a}$$

$$\begin{aligned}
\phi(Y_2) &= \phi(Y_2 \mid s_1) \cdot \phi(s_1) + \phi(Y_2 \mid s_2) \cdot \phi(s_2) \\
&= (.1 \times .8) + (.7 \times .2) \\
&= .22.
\end{aligned} \tag{6.3b}$$

It is now possible to compute the revised probabilities of each state, given the new signals Y_1 or Y_2. These revisions are based on Bayes Theorem:

$$\phi(s_i \mid Y_k) = \frac{\phi(Y_k \mid s_i) \cdot \phi(s_i)}{\phi(Y_k)} \tag{6.4}$$

$$\phi(s_1 \mid Y_1) = \frac{.9 \times .8}{.78} = .92 \tag{6.4a}$$

$$\phi(s_2 \mid Y_1) = \frac{.3 \times .2}{.78} = .08 \tag{6.4b}$$

$$\phi(s_1 \mid Y_2) = \frac{.1 \times .8}{.22} = .36 \tag{6.4c}$$

$$\phi(s_2 \mid Y_2) = \frac{.7 \times .2}{.22} = .64 \tag{6.4d}$$

These are revised probabilities of states s_1 and s_2, given the receipt of signals Y_1 or Y_2 from information system η.

The final step is to recompute the utility of each action a_1 and a_2, given the revised state probabilities. If signal Y_1 (expense to sales ratio ≤ 1) is received, the utility of each act is:

$$\begin{aligned}
E(U \mid a_1, Y_1) &= (\$1,150,000 \times .92) + (\$950,000 \times .08) \\
&= \$1,134,000
\end{aligned}$$

$$\begin{aligned}
E(U \mid a_2, Y_1) &= (\$1,120,000 \times .92) + (\$1,120,000 \times .08) \\
&= \$1,120,000.
\end{aligned}$$

Action a_1, the loan to XYZ, is the optimal act if signal Y_1 is received.

If signal Y_2 (expense to sales ratio >1) is received, the utility of each act is:

$$E(U \mid a_1,Y_2) = (\$1,150,000 \times .36) + (\$950,000 \times .64)$$
$$= \$1,022,000$$

$$E(U \mid a_2,Y_2) = (\$1,120,000 \times .36) + (\$1,120,000 \times .64)$$
$$= \$1,120,000$$

Action a_2, investment in the government bonds, is the optimal act if signal Y_2 is received.

The value of new information from the information system η is derived from the utility of each of the above two optimal acts, given the probabilities of receiving each signal. The formula is:

$$E(U \mid \eta) = \sum_{k=1}^{Y} (U \mid a^*{}_{Y_k},\eta) \cdot \phi(Y_k \mid \eta) \qquad (6.5)$$

$$= (\$1,134,000 \times .78) + (\$1,120,000 \times .22)$$

$$= \$1,130,920.$$

where $a^*{}_{Y_k}$ is the optimal action given the signal Y_k.

In the original case, given existing knowledge, the expected utility of the decision was $1,120,000. The expected utility of the decision, given new information Y_k, is $1,130,920. Therefore the decision maker would be prepared to spend up to $1,130,920 minus $1,120,000, or $10,920, for the signal Y_k from information system η. This amount would be the point at which the marginal cost of the new information equals the marginal benefit.

SUMMARY OF INFORMATION ECONOMICS AT THE INDIVIDUAL DECISION-MAKER LEVEL

Information economics, or decision theory, does not provide answers to normative questions, such as what sets of accounting information are optimal. The analysis can determine only the value of specific information for a narrowly defined decision. Therefore, the question of which are the optimal sets of policies could be analyzed only after calculating the value of each alternative set of policies and then comparing them. This approach would be tedious because there are virtually limitless accounting and disclosure policies that could be prescribed. However, such an approach could be used to assess the net benefits of specific proposals. One other contribution of the information economics model is that it has increased our understanding of how accounting information has value in the decision-making process.

A limitation of information economics is that real-world decision makers face more complex decisions (having many more actions and states) than can be illustrated in the model. Human bounds on the ability to process information limit the formal application of decision theory. Thus, real decision-making behavior has been described as "satisficing" rather than maximizing utility. Another limitation of information economics concerns its generality: unless one assumes that decision makers behave homogeneously, it is impossible to generalize to all decision makers from the analysis of individuals. User diversity is the critical issue in this limitation.

MARKET-LEVEL ANALYSIS USING INFORMATION ECONOMICS

Information has also been deductively analyzed in a multiuser setting. This entails a market-level analysis of information supply and demand in which information is treated as an economic good. This type of research is very abstract and is based on narrowly defined sets of assumptions concerning economic markets. Information is also treated in a nondescript manner—that is, the analyses are of information markets rather than of specific types of information; for this reason, the conclusions are of a very general nature. These types of deductive analyses try to evaluate market incentives for information production and consumption, as well as the effects on aggregate social welfare or optimality of resource allocation. The effect of regulation on information markets is also examined in these studies, but again in a very generalized manner.

Since these studies are based on narrow sets of assumptions about economic markets, the conclusions are necessarily restricted and heavily qualified. For example, one line of reasoning suggests that the search for new information about securities is a waste of social resources.[3] The argument is that new information will benefit one investor only to the detriment of another. This will result in wealth transfers between investors. However, society as a whole is no better off, and has actually been made worse off because otherwise-productive resources have been allocated to information search. Other analyses have determined there are market conditions in which there are positive social benefits to the search for new information.[4]

Because of the abstractness and generality of these analyses, the multiuser setting of information economics has not yielded specific conclusions concerning the value of accounting information. Commenting on this, the *Statement of Accounting Theory and Theory Acceptance* said

> In summary, the information economics approach offers an explicit individual-demand-based analysis of accounting policy questions. . . . The power of the approach is in isolating general relationships and effects of alternative scenarios. At present, however, the approach is still too general to provide definitive answers. . . .[5]

---

[3]Hirschleifer (1971).
[4]Ohlson and Buckman (1981), Gonedes (1980), and Hakansson (1977).
[5]American Accounting Association (1977, p. 25).

CAPITAL MARKET RESEARCH

A large body of research has attempted to determine the response of security prices to accounting information. This type of research helps evaluate the usefulness of accounting information in setting security prices. The analysis is made at the market level; but by studying aggregate price effects, it is possible to infer that information has value to individual investors. Because the Securities and Exchange Commission was created to regulate the securities market, and because accounting regulation is justified on these same grounds, it is an important body of research.

The value of information in the pricing of securities is to assist investors in assessing risk and return of individual stocks and portfolios. Expected returns are analagous to monetary values of *actions* in decision theory. These values were given in the decision theory exercise. In reality, assessments of the values of alternative actions change all the time with new information. Information is also considered useful in assessing investment risk. **Investment risk** is a very abstract concept: theoretically, it is defined as the variance of expected returns. Risk is comparable to *states* in decision theory—that is, it deals with the likelihood of realizing certain outcomes.

The link between risk and return assessments by individual decision makers and security prices is a "black box." It remains unknown how subjective assessments are translated into market prices. What we do know, though, is that market prices represent aggregate consequences of individual investor assessments.

The theoretical foundation of capital market research comes from **portfolio theory**, which is a theory of rational investment choice and utility maximization: simply stated, risk can be reduced by holding a portfolio of investments. Risk that can be eliminated in this manner is called **unsystematic (diversifiable) risk,** while the remaining portfolio risk is called **systematic (nondiversifiable) risk.**

An extension of portfolio theory has been the development, given the assumption of diversified portfolios, of models for pricing individual securities. These models are called capital asset pricing models. They have been used in much of the capital market research since the early 1970s. The models are used to calculate predicted stock prices, which are then compared to actual prices. Using this technique, newly released information can be evaluated to determine if it abnormally affects security prices. A more detailed explanation of portfolio theory and capital asset pricing models is presented in Appendix 6-A.

Much of the capital market research falls under the label of efficient markets studies. It is based on the efficient markets hypothesis which refers to the speed with which securities in the capital market respond to new information announcements. The classic definition of market efficiency is that (1) the market fully reflects available information, and (2) by implication, market prices react instantaneously to new information.[6] The efficient markets hypothesis, if true, means that when new information has usefulness in revising risk and return assessments, new equilibrium prices will be quickly established. In other words, new information is quickly impounded in the price of the security. If the hypothesis is correct, an item of information has value to investors only if there is evidence of a price response to the new information. When this occurs the item of information is said to have **information content.**

There are three forms of the efficient markets hypothesis. The weak form says that securities prices reflect all past information, the semistrong form says that prices reflect all past and current information that is publicly available, and the strong form which says that prices reflect all information (both public and private). Most testing has been of the semistrong form, which deals with publicly available information. In order to test for information content it is necessary to have some control over the choice of information tested. Information tested must have a clearly identifiable public release date. Because of this requirement, much of the information tested has been of an accounting nature—for example, financial statements and earnings announcements.

Before reviewing the empirical findings, a few observations should be made regarding the difficulties in doing this type of research.[7] The study of price movements and the pricing mechanism in any market is an imposing task. Cause and effect between information and security prices is especially difficult because new information is continuously causing price movements. Since the set of information affecting security prices is large, it is extremely difficult to isolate the effects of one piece of information. This difficulty means that the tests are going to be somewhat crude rather than precise. The research should be interpreted with this in mind. Failure to find evidence of information content should be interpreted cautiously. The methodology is not always capable of detecting information content. For this reason, the stronger evidence from efficient markets research exists where there is information content rather than where there is none.

Another weakness of efficient markets research is that it contains a tautology: the hypothesis concerns information efficiency. This is only a hypothesis for which empirical support is sought, not a proven fact. Yet the absence of price responses is usually interpreted to mean that the information tested has no information content. This interpretation is correct only if the market is efficient. But what if the market is inefficient? If the market is inefficient, there is no way of determining what the absence of a price response means. This is another reason why the research findings are much stronger when there is evidence of information content.

[6]Fama (1970).
[7]For detailed critiques of the research methodology, see Roll (1977) and Foster (1980).

THE INFORMATION CONTENT OF ACCOUNTING INCOME NUMBERS

The strongest evidence from capital market research concerns the information content of accounting earnings. The seminal study was published in 1968, showing that the direction of change in reported accounting earnings (from the prior year) was positively correlated with security price movements.[8] The study also found that the price movements anticipated the earnings results, and that there was virtually no abnormal price movement one month after the earnings were announced. This is consistent with the semistrong form of the efficient markets hypothesis. Other studies have refined the research methodology and have reached the same conclusions.[9] Quarterly earnings announcements have also shown the same results.[10]

These results are not surprising. Accounting income could be expected to be part of the information used by investors in assessing risk and return. Capital market research has confirmed an almost self-evident proposition. The findings are important, though, as part of the growing body of research linking accounting information with investment decisions.

ALTERNATIVE ACCOUNTING POLICIES

A more complex type of securities price research has examined the effect of alternative accounting policies on security prices. The underlying purpose of these tests is to investigate the so-called "naive-investor" hypothesis. Earlier research found that security prices respond to accounting income numbers. Alternative accounting policies can affect reported income numbers; for example, flexibility in the choice of depreciation and inventory methods. While these types of differences affect reported accounting income, there is no apparent impact on company cash flows. These types of accounting alternatives simply represent different patterns of expense recognition.

The question of interest to researchers is whether alternative accounting policies have an effect on security prices. If security prices do respond to different income levels that are attributable solely to alternative accounting methods, then there is support for the naive-investor hypothesis. On the other hand, if security prices do not respond to such artificial book-income differences, then there is evidence that investors in the market are sophisticated and able to see through such superficial bookkeeping differences. Virtually all the initial research was interpreted as rejecting the naive-investor hypothesis. However, recent research findings have challenged some of the earlier conclusions and reopened what was once considered a

---

[8]Ball and Brown (1968).
[9]Beaver (1968) and Beaver, Clarke, and Wright (1979).
[10]Brown and Kennelly (1972) and Foster (1977a).

closed issue in accounting research. The naive-investor hypothesis is still being tested and the evidence is less conclusive today—given new findings such as the LIFO situation (discussed later in the chapter).

Alternatives with No Known Cash Flow Consequences

Numerous studies have compared companies which use different accounting methods. One of the earliest studies compared companies using accelerated and straight-line depreciation methods.[11] The two groups of companies had different accounting income numbers because they used alternative depreciation methods. There were differences in income between the two groups of companies based solely on the use of alternative accounting policies. There were also differences in price-earnings multiples between the two groups. Companies using accelerated methods had lower earnings but higher price-earnings multiples than companies using straight line. However, when earnings of companies using accelerated methods were adjusted to a straight-line depreciation basis, the price-earnings multiple between the two groups of companies was not significantly different.

The market assessments did not appear to be affected by arbitrary and alternative accounting income numbers. This finding is often expressed by saying that the market is not "fooled" by accounting differences. Other similar research has supported this conclusion. Additional areas tested include purchase versus pooling accounting, expensing versus capitalizing research and development costs, and recognition versus deferral of unrealized holding gains on marketable securities.[12]

A related area of investigation concerns security price responses to a reported change in accounting policy by a company. Changes in depreciation policy have been researched, and there is no evidence that the change per se affects security prices.[13] Another area tested has been a change from the deferral to flow-through method of accounting for the investment credit.[14] Again no price effects were found. While changes in accounting policies may cause the income number to change (solely because of the policy change), these research studies have not found that security prices respond to the changes. Higher accounting income achieved solely from a change in accounting policy with no apparent real changes in underlying cash flows does not fool the market.

The evidence from the type of research discussed in the preceding paragraphs supports the claim that there is no information content in accounting policy changes, at least where there are no apparent underlying changes in cash flows. This finding has also been interpreted as rejecting the naive-investor hypothesis. Investors appear to adjust accounting income between firms for artificial bookkeeping differences with no real sub-

---

[11]Beaver and Dukes (1973).
[12]Ball (1972), Hong, Kaplan, and Mandelker (1978), and Foster (1977b).
[13]Archibald (1972).
[14]Cassidy (1976).

stance. Investors do not appear to respond mechanistically and naively to reported accounting income.[15]

Alternatives with Known Cash Flow Consequences

One type of change in accounting policy which has evidenced a security price response is a change from FIFO to LIFO inventory accounting. Changes to LIFO have been associated with a positive security price movement, even though LIFO lowers accounting income in a period of rising inventory prices.[16] Given the apparent sophistication of investors in other areas of accounting policy differences, what can be the logical explanation for the existence of price responses? The suggested reason for the price response is that LIFO must be adopted for both book and tax purposes. In a period of rising prices, tax expense will be lower for companies that use LIFO, in which case there are real cash flow consequences due to the change in accounting policy. Even though book income is lowered by the use of LIFO, cash flows are higher because the taxable income is lower. Positive security price responses are therefore consistent with an increase in the value of the firm.

Two recent studies have challenged the earlier analysis of LIFO changes.[17] One study found no evidence of price response and the other found evidence of a negative price response. Either result is contrary to the earlier finding of positive price responses. Both the recent studies suggest the earlier research failed to isolate the real effect of the LIFO change because of a self-selection bias. (This means that companies changing to LIFO had other things occurring simultaneously which confounded the results and may have caused the positive price response.) These newer studies claim to have better isolated the price response that is due solely to the LIFO change. If the newer studies are correct, then there may be some support for the naive-investor hypothesis. There are positive tax benefits associated with the LIFO change which should increase the value of the firm. Yet security price responses were not positive. Since LIFO will lower accounting book income, a negative price response could be interpreted as a mechanistic response to a lower accounting number, a response made without considering the positive cash flow consequences due to lower taxes.

As discussed at the beginning of this section, security price research is extremely difficult to conduct and interpret, but it can be said that the research methods have improved over time. For this reason, recent evidence is likely to be more reliable than earlier evidence. The early LIFO research rejected the naive-investor hypothesis. Recent research on the LIFO question reopens what was once thought to be a closed issue. Either the theory concerning LIFO cash flow consequences is wrong, or there is evidence that the market is naive.

---

[15]Foster (1978, p. 357).
[16]Sunder (1973).
[17]Brown (1980) and Ricks (1982).

Alternatives with Indirect Cash Consequences

The most recent security price research has been probing more subtle areas referred to as indirect consequences. An **indirect consequence** occurs when an accounting policy change affects the value of the firm through an indirect effect on owners, rather than a direct effect on company cash flows. One such study was motivated by an attempt to explain why securities prices of certain oil and gas companies responded negatively to a mandatory change in accounting policy.[18] The required change from full costing to successful efforts was regarded as simply a change in how exploration costs are allocated to the income statement. Therefore, it was expected that no security price response would be evident since there was no direct cash flow consequence on the companies.

Security price responses were found to exist and since previous research has predominantly rejected the naive-investor hypothesis, a search was made for the existence of some indirect cash flow consequences to explain the price response. The study found that a change to successful efforts accounting for oil and gas exploration costs lowered firms' ability to pay dividends in the short term, because of debt covenants. Therefore, even though the change in accounting policy appeared to affect only book income on the surface, there were indirect cash flow consequences to investors, which might explain the negative price response. This explanation derives from agency theory. When accounting numbers are used to monitor agency contracts, there can be indirect consequences on the firm's owners (stockholders and bondholders) from changes in accounting policies. In the case of debt covenants restricting dividend payments, accounting numbers are used to protect the security of bondholders at the expense of stockholders. If accounting policy changes lower accounting income (as could occur in a change to successful efforts), stockholder returns could be lowered, thus causing a negative price response.

A similar type of study found negative security price responses for firms using pooling accounting when pooling was restricted by the Accounting Principles Board in favor of purchase accounting for combinations.[19] Differences between purchase and pooling accounting were thought to affect only book income, with no real cash effects. However, the reduced use of pooling accounting could affect dividend distribution because of debt covenants. Income would normally be lower under purchase accounting than pooling, and the same type of dividend restrictions found in the oil and gas study were found in the purchase/pooling study. Another research study along these newer lines examined the requirement to capitalize leases that had previously been reported as operating leases.[20] There was some evidence of negative price responses for certain companies. The study found support that this situation could have been due to the existence

---

[18]Collins, Rozeff, and Dhaliwal (1981).
[19]Leftwich (1981).
[20]Pfeiffer (1980).

of debt covenants, along with the adverse effect lease capitalization would have on firms' future borrowing capacity.

Capital market research is discussed in this chapter mainly in the context of the value of accounting information. While recent research is still addressing information content and the naive-investor hypothesis, there is a shift in emphasis in some of the studies. Some capital market research is now examining the question of why companies choose the accounting policies they do, particularly where choice (flexibility) is permitted. Since earlier research on accounting policy differences did not reveal any security price responses, researchers became interested in why companies select the policies they do. This interest, coupled with evidence that some seemingly innocuous policy differences do affect security prices (for example, oil and gas accounting, which is examined in detail in Chapter 14), has led to this new research approach. Agency theory arguments underlie this research, and the attempt is to identify indirect consequences to either owners or managers—consequences that might motivate the selection of particular accounting policies or explain market reactions to proposed or implemented changes in accounting policies.

SUPPLEMENTAL DISCLOSURES

Another area of security price research concerns the value of supplemental financial statement disclosures. Three areas have been studied: segmental disclosure, general price-level adjusted financial statements, and supplemental replacement cost data. Of the three studies examining segmental disclosure, two found evidence that the inclusion of segment information affected the market risk measure, beta (see Appendix 6-A for a discussion of beta).[21] This finding suggests that new information is revealed through the disaggregation of information via segmental disclosure, and that this information causes a revision in the market's perception of risk.

The other two areas of supplemental disclosure concern inflation accounting. One study found that in inflationary periods, general price-level income was more highly correlated with market risk (beta) than was historical accounting income.[22] Studies of supplemental replacement cost disclosure have failed to show any information content[23] (see Chapter 12).

ACCOUNTING INFORMATION AND RISK ASSESSMENT

Capital market research has also investigated the usefulness of accounting numbers for assessing the risk of securities and portfolios. Some of these studies were mentioned in the previous section. Other studies have

[21]Collins (1975), Collins and Simmonds (1979), Ajinkya (1980), and Horwitz and Kolodny (1977).
[22]Baran, Lakonishok, and Ofer (1980).
[23]Gheyara and Boatsman (1980), Beaver, Christie, and Griffin (1980), and Ro (1980).

found high correlations between the variability of accounting earnings and beta, the market risk measure.[24] The high correlations imply that accounting data may be useful for assessing risk. Some other research has tried to determine if alternative accounting policies have any affect on risk. The purpose of this type of research is to identify how alternative accounting policies or disclosures may affect the usefulness of accounting numbers for assessing risk. For example, one study tried to determine if unfunded pension benefits (reported in footnotes at present) affected beta.[25] There was no significant impact. From this evidence, it might be concluded that pension information is not useful for risk assessments, even though it has been argued that pension obligations should be reported as an accounting liability.

Some studies have also tested the association of financial ratios with beta.[26] Some of the ratios and computations tested include dividend payout ratio, leverage, growth rates, asset size, liquidity, and pretax interest coverage, as well as earnings and earnings variability. In general these tests indicate a strong association between accounting-based risk measures and the market measure of risk, beta.

PREDICTIVE VALUE OF ACCOUNTING INFORMATION

In Statement of Financial Accounting Concepts 2, one of the criteria which contributes to the relevance of accounting information is predictive value.[27] A number of capital market studies have explored this area. Some of the research has analyzed the usefulness of accounting income in predicting future period income. The evidence is mixed with findings of both high and low predictability.[28] Usefulness of this type of research has been questioned on the grounds that investors are more interested in predicting future cash flows or stock prices than accounting income. One study found that cash flows and accounting income are both correlated with stock prices.[29] Another study found that the quarterly earnings that differed significantly from time-series income projections were also correlated with security price changes.[30]

Another area of prediction has also been studied—the usefulness of financial ratios derived from accounting reports in predicting bankruptcy. Although these are not capital market studies (in the sense that they are not

---

[24]Beaver, Kettler, and Scholes (1970), Bildersee (1975), Thompson (1976), Eskew (1979), and Elgers (1980). For a review of the methodological problems in this type of research see Elgers and Murray (1982).

[25]Stone (1981).

[26]For example Beaver, Kettler, and Scholes (1970), Bildersee (1975), and Thompson (1976).

[27]FASB (1980).

[28]Watts and Leftwich (1977) and Albrecht, Lookabill, and McKeown (1977) found low predictability using time-series analysis of annual income. However Foster (1977a) was able to fit a good regression equation to quarterly time-series earnings data using a seasonal adjustment factor.

[29]Staubus (1965).

[30]Foster (1977).

concerned with security prices), they are still concerned with the usefulness of accounting numbers to investors. The studies are in agreement that financial ratios can successfully categorize a sample of companies into those which will fail and those which will not.[31] The ratios differed significantly between companies that failed and companies which survived. Predictability up to five years prior to bankruptcy has been found to exist. These findings do not mean that companies with "bad" ratios will automatically go bankrupt in the future. It simply means that bankrupt companies tend to have financial ratios prior to bankruptcy that differ from non-bankrupt companies. The existence of "bad" ratios does not mean bankruptcy will occur, just that it is more probable.

SUMMARY OF CAPITAL MARKET RESEARCH

Empirical evidence from capital market research supports these statements: (1) accounting earnings have information content and affect security prices; (2) alternative accounting policies with no apparent direct or indirect cash flow consequences to the firm do not seem to affect security prices; (3) alternative accounting policies which have direct or indirect cash flow consequences to the firm (or its owners) do affect security prices; (4) there are incentives to choose certain accounting policies where choice exists, owing to indirect cash consequences to the firm or its owners; (5) accounting-based risk measures correlate with market risk measures, suggesting that accounting numbers are useful for risk assessment; and (6) accounting numbers and financial ratios have predictive value with respect to bankruptcy. Overall, then, the research supports that accounting numbers are useful to investors. Just how useful or valuable, however, cannot be determined from capital market research, particularly in the context of optimal policies as discussed in Chapter 3.

In the early 1970s, it was argued that capital market research could be used as a basis for (1) choosing the best accounting policies, and (2) evaluating the economic consequences of alternative accounting policies on security prices.[32] Accounting policies that most affected security prices were thought to be most useful. In other words, such policies would have had the most information content. The argument had intuitive appeal, particularly since deductively based research had proved unable to resolve the accounting theory debate. However, the early advocates of security price research now recognize the limitations of this research for such a use.[33]

---

[31]Beaver (1967), Altman (1971), and Elam (1975).

[32]Gonedes (1972), and Beaver and Dukes (1972).

[33]Gonedes and Dopuch (1974) argue that the free-rider problem makes it impossible to use capital market research to identify optimal accounting policies. The reason is that production costs cannot be internalized on users because accounting information has characteristics of a public good. See the discussion in Chapter 3. So, even though mandatory information may have information content, there is no way of determining if users would really demand the information in a free-market situation.

Reasons for these limitations are the public-good nature of accounting information, the existence of free riders, and the resultant market failure in terms of optimal resource allocation.

In spite of its inability to resolve accounting theory and policy questions, capital market research will continue to be useful in empirically evaluating economic consequences of accounting policies on security prices and usefulness of accounting numbers for risk and return assessments. Perhaps more than anything else, though, the contribution of capital market research is that it brought a fresh perspective to accounting theory and policy at a time when the emphasis was primarily on deductively-based theory.

STUDIES OF INDIVIDUAL DECISION MAKING USING EXPERIMENTAL SETTINGS

Behavioral research using laboratory experiments has been conducted to determine how investment decisions are made, and how accounting information is used in making decisions. While capital market studies examine the aggregate effect of investor decision making, experimental research attempts to discover more about the "black box" of how individual decisions are made and the role of information in the decision process.

An early study explored the usefulness of alternative income numbers based on historical cost and replacement cost systems.[34] There was no evidence to support the hypothesis that a current value system produces information decision makers prefer over historical cost information. More recent experiments have been influenced by an area of psychology called human information processing. Some of the investment decisions studied are predictions of bankruptcies, stock prices, and bond ratings.[35]

The usefulness of accounting information emerges in this body of research only in an indirect way. The more direct questions being examined are the decision models used by subjects, and the consistency of judgments between subjects. Generally, it can be said from the research that accounting income numbers and financial ratios are used by decision makers to discriminate between companies. But the research has been more concerned with describing the decision process and evaluating judgment consistency between decision makers. For these reasons, the research has not yielded insight comparable to that produced by capital market research about the value and usefulness of accounting information. If user decision models do come to be more fully understood from this type of research, it may be possible for policy-making bodies to mandate policies that produce more useful sets of information through an understanding of how decisions

---

[34]McIntire (1973).
[35]Libby (1975), Wright (1977), and Kessler and Ashton (1981).

are made and what information is used. Such an approach to policy has been called the decision maker approach (and was discussed in Chapter 5).

The limitation that applies to information economics is also applicable to experimental research: it is very hard to generalize to all decision makers from small samples of individuals. Once again, the potential problem of user diversity may limit the generality of individual-based research.

SURVEYS OF INVESTORS

Another way of determining the usefulness of accounting information is to ask investors if they read annual reports. Surveys of investors have been undertaken in several countries and generally have shown a rather low readership of accounting information.[36] Approximately one half of the surveyed investors have indicated they read financial statements. Institutional investors have shown a much higher level of readership.[37] These surveys, particularly of individual investors, should be interpreted cautiously, however. Investors may rely on investment analysts to process accounting information. It would be simplistic to assume accounting information has no usefulness to investors merely because many individual stockholders do not read annual reports in detail.

Another type of survey research has been to ask investors to weight the importance of different types of investment information, including accounting information. Several studies of this type have been reported.[38] Accounting information ranks fairly highly in importance in these surveys, though not at the top. This status seems to be attributable to the historical nature of accounting information and the reporting lag effect. More timely accounting information from company press reports, and nonaccounting information such as economic conditions and company announcements on products and markets, rank ahead of annual reports in perceived importance.

Survey-type research is notoriously unreliable because respondents frequently do not consciously know what they believe or even how they act. With accounting information, the danger is that investors may not consciously know exactly how they value and use the information. This possibility is supported by findings of the experimental studies into decision making. Of all the types of empirical research, surveys are probably the least reliable. However, they do complement other research methods and they are broadly consistent with other research findings that accounting information has value to investors.

[36]Epstein (1975) and Lee and Tweedie (1975).
[37]Anderson (1981) and Chang and Most (1977).
[38]Baker and Haslem (1973) and Chenhall and Juchau (1977). See Hines (1982) for a concise summary of the major investor surveys.

THE USEFULNESS OF ACCOUNTING ALLOCATIONS

At present the historical cost accounting model remains the basic framework for financial reporting. Central to this model are revenue recognition rules and the matching of costs to revenues. Many costs are recognized over multiple accounting periods. Some examples include depreciation, organizational startup costs, goodwill amortization, and bond premium/discount amortization. The recognition of these types of costs over multiple periods is referred to as **accounting allocation**.[39] Allocations have been criticized on the grounds that they are "incorrigible." By this it is meant that there is no obviously correct way to allocate the costs because no single allocation method can be proved superior to another. For example, it cannot be proved that straight-line depreciation is any more appropriate than accelerated depreciation methods.

Another way of describing this dilemma is to say that no allocation is completely defensible against other methods. For this reason it has been concluded that all accounting allocations are, in the end, arbitrary. Conceptually, this is a very disturbing idea and strikes at the logical core of historical cost accounting. Because of the arbitrariness of accounting allocations, allocation-free financial statements have been advocated as a better way of reporting useful information. Allocation-free accounting can be accomplished by using cash flow statements, exit-price systems (as discussed in Appendix 1-A of Chapter 1), and certain types of replacement cost systems (also discussed in Appendix 1-A of Chapter 1).

However, the fact that accounting allocations are arbitrary does not prove that accounting information is useless. The allocation argument is deductive and examines the logic of historical cost accounting. Usefulness is an empirical question, not a matter of deductive logic. There is no evidence to support the contention that allocation-based financial statements are useless. In fact, there is a great deal of evidence from capital market research which supports that accounting income numbers do have information content.

Capital market research in the area of alternative accounting policies does support the argument that accounting allocations are arbitrary. Alternative policies with no known cash flow consequences have no effect on security prices. This finding supports the argument that allocations are arbitrary and convey no information to users. However, the research findings also support the fact that investors are not naive, and that they are capable of adjusting accounting numbers in order to achieve comparability between companies. In spite of allocations, income numbers are useful and investors appear able to achieve comparability by informally adjusting for the effects of arbitrary allocations.

---

[39]The pioneering allocation research was done by Thomas (1969).

It must also be remembered that allocations represent only a part of the total accounting information in financial statements. Much accounting information contains no allocations. Even if the allocation criticism is valid, usefulnes may still be high. It has also been suggested that the historical cost, allocation-based approach may be the most cost effective method of reporting financial information about firms.

A policy implication of the allocation research is that the FASB should not try to resolve problems by resorting to a search for the "best" allocation. On the other hand, the FASB should not necessarily avoid allocations. They may be the most cost-effective means of producing financial statements. But the convenience of allocation-type policies should be carefully weighed against allocation-free approaches, which may be less ambiguous and easier to understand. It can also be argued that the FASB should reduce flexibility in accounting allocations. Given evidence from capital market research, there is no compelling reason to permit arbitrary flexibility. Rigid uniformity would be easier to apply and would eliminate some arbitrary differences between companies. It will be recalled that security prices adjust for such arbitrary differences in accounting allocations. In the case of accounting allocations with no real cash flow consequences, a strong case exists for rigid uniformity.

SUMMARY

The value of accounting information has been researched using many different approaches. Information economics provides a general framework for understanding how accounting information has value to decision makers. The range of empirical research reviewed in this chapter is complementary and supports the finding that accounting information is useful to users.

From a policy viewpoint, the research reviewed here helps in assessing economic consequences of existing accounting regulation. The research allows us to evaluate the benefits of information production. Objectives of financial reporting have broadened as a result of the FASB's decision-usefulness orientation. Continuing research into the value of accounting information, as well as economic consequences in a more general sense, are essential ingredients of the new orientation.

In conclusion, the research reviewed does support that accounting information is useful. However, from a normative perspective, the type of research reviewed here cannot be used to determine if existing accounting policies are optimal, or even if regulation is producing a net benefit to society. The evidence is that accounting information has value, but just how much value has not been determined. Furthermore, the net benefits of existing or proposed accounting policies can be evaluated only after one considers production costs to preparers. Whether or not there is a net benefit to society from financial reporting and accounting regulation remains an important but unanswered question.

APPENDIX 6-A: PORTFOLIO THEORY AND THE CAPITAL ASSET PRICING MODEL

Portfolio theory was developed as a scientific basis for selecting stocks. In very general terms the theory states that investment return can be maximized for a given level of risk by holding a mix of investments. This process is known as **portfolio diversification**. Investors are assumed to be **risk averse**, which means they require a premium in the form of higher expected returns as an inducement to hold higher risk portfolios.

In portfolio theory, risk is defined as either the variance or the standard deviation of expected investment returns. We conveniently think of expected return as a single number, but in reality it is a probability distribution of possible returns. The larger the variance around the mean of expected returns, the greater the risk associated with the investment. This variance may be quite high in individual stocks, but when evaluated for a portfolio as a whole, it is much lower. The reason for this situation is that variances of individual securities are offset when combined in a portfolio. In this way it is possible to select a stock portfolio that minimizes risk for a given rate of return. This is called an **efficient portfolio** and is explained in the following manner:

> A portfolio is not efficient if there is another portfolio with a higher expected value of return and lower standard deviation, a higher expected value and the same standard deviation, or the same expected value but a lower standard deviation.[40]

It is not possible to diversify all variance. What remains after eliminating all the risk possible is called nondiversifiable or systematic risk of the portfolio. And that risk which has been eliminated through diversification is called diversifiable or unsystematic risk. An investor will rationally select a portfolio with a risk-return parameter that meets the investor's own utility preferences. The theoretical choice of portfolios is graphically presented in Exhibit 6-3.

The capital market line represents alternative efficient portfolios for increasing levels of systematic risk. Since investors are risk averse, the expected portfolio return increases as risk increases. The capital market line

---

[40]Van Horne (1980, p. 55).

EXHIBIT 6-3.

Capital Market Line

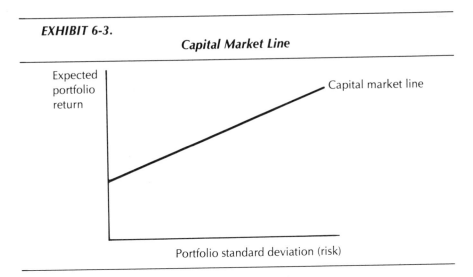

EXHIBIT 6-4.

is linear only under restrictive conditions, but whether linear or curvilinear, a direct relationship exists between the levels of risk and expected returns.

Portfolio theory is the foundation for a related development in finance—the pricing of individual stocks given the concept of efficient portfolios. A model called the **capital asset pricing model** has been developed for the theoretical pricing of individual stocks. Its first step is to determine the risk of an individual security relative to the market as a whole. The market is assumed to be an efficient portfolio. A correlation is made between the returns on individual stocks and market returns for the same periods of time, usually sixty observations. This process produces a scattergram and is illustrated in Exhibit 6-4.

EXHIBIT 6-4.
Scattergram of Security Returns Against Market Returns

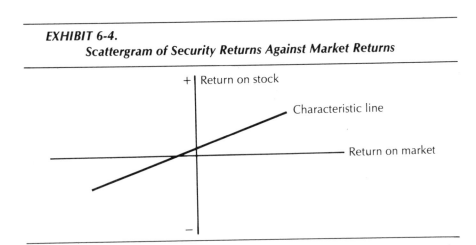

Regression analysis is used to fit a line to the scattergram. The slope of the characteristic line is called **beta** and represents a market-based measure of the risk of an individual security relative to the average risk in the market as a whole. If beta equals one, the returns are perfectly correlated and the risks are equal. If beta exceeds one, the returns on the individual stock are greater than the market. In other words, if the rate of return on an individual security is greater than the market average, systematic risk of the security must also be greater because of the direct relationship between risk levels and expected returns. Higher returns must be accompanied by higher risks. This point was illustrated in Exhibit 6-3. The reverse relationship is true if beta of the individual security is less than one; lower returns must also mean lower systematic risk.

The assumption of the capital asset pricing model is that individual securities are priced solely on systematic risk. Given the assumption of diversified portfolios, it is argued that no one would pay for unsystematic risk. Beta measures are used to represent systematic risk of individual securities and to predict the risk-based price of securities. A standard two-parameter version of the capital asset pricing model defines the rate of return for an individual security as follows:

$$R_j = i + (\bar{R}_m - i)B_j \tag{6.6}$$

where

$$R_j = \text{return on security } j;$$

$$i = \text{risk-free rate of return;}$$

$$\bar{R}_m = \text{expected return on the market portfolio;}$$

$$B_j = \text{beta coefficient for security } j.$$

The beta term was explained in the preceding discussion, but it can also be defined statistically as follows:

$$B_j = (Y_{jm}\delta_j\delta_m)/\delta_m^2 \tag{6.7}$$

where

$$Y_{jm}\delta_j\delta_m = \text{covariance of individual security } j, \text{ and the market-level portfolio;}$$

$$\delta_m^2 = \text{variance on the market-level portfolio returns.}$$

The capital asset pricing model calculates the return of an individual security as the risk-free rate plus a risk premium for the relative level of systematic risk of the security. There is a direct relationship between the return on the security and the level of systematic risk. The capital asset pricing model is used to predict stock prices in capital market studies. By comparing actual returns to predicted returns for a large sample of companies, it is possible to determine if there are consistent differences. If the residuals (the difference between actual and predicted returns) are significantly different from zero, then there is evidence of abnormal returns. These abnormal returns or residuals are interpreted to be the result of the new information being tested in the research study.

In recent years capital asset pricing models have come in for heavy criticism for their underlying theory (or lack thereof), as well as for the difficulty in measuring the parameters. One problem is that there is no single correct method for determining the market rate of return. This means that beta measurements vary and could affect the statistical significance of the results. Another well-documented problem concerns the instability of individual betas over time. The implication of beta instability is that historical beta measurement may not be a correct measure of current beta. There is also the problem of specifying the risk-free rate of return, and again there are choices available which may influence the statistical results. The result of all this criticism has been to temper the interpretations of the strength of the past research, to search for better asset pricing models using additional parameters, and to examine the sensitivity of the results to the choices of parameters used. There is also another approach used to study for information content, called the **market model**.[41] By eliminating the risk-free rate, this approach avoids one problem inherent in asset pricing models. In other words, it is a one-parameter model rather than two.

QUESTIONS

1. How does information have value, given a setting of economic decision making under uncertainty?
2. What is the role of information in security analysis, and how is it analagous to the value of information using an information economics framework?
3. In the multiuser analysis of information, it has been argued that information produced solely for the use of investment trading is a waste of resources. Evaluate this proposition.
4. What is the efficient markets hypothesis?
5. What is meant by information content? How does capital market research determine the information content of accounting numbers? What difficulties exist in this type of research?
6. It was suggested in the chapter that there is a tautology in the efficient markets hypothesis. What is it, and how does it affect the interpretation of capital market research?

---

[41]See Griffin (1982, pp. 50–52) for a concise explanation of the difference between capital asset pricing models and the market model.

7. Describe the general findings from capital market research concerning the information content of accounting numbers and effects of alternative accounting policies.

8. Why may there be indirect incentives for companies in which flexibility exists to choose certain accounting policies? Why may alternative accounting policies affect stockholder wealth, as reflected in security prices? How are these arguments related to agency theory?

9. Why does the public-good nature of accounting information prevent the use of capital market research for determining optimal accounting policies? See footnote 33.

10. What insight has been gained from behavioral research of decision making and the usefulness of accounting information? What major limitations apply to this type of research?

11. What has been revealed from stockholder surveys? Why is this research unreliable?

12. Explain why accounting allocations are incorrigible. What does this mean regarding the usefulness of allocation-based accounting reports?

13. In what ways does capital market research both support and refute the arguments concerning the usefulness of accounting information in terms of allocations?

14. Discuss the policy implications of the allocation argument.

15. How does the research reviewed in this chapter help to evaluate economic consequences of accounting policies and accounting regulation? Why is it insufficient to evaluate the net benefits of regulation or the optimality of accounting policies?

CASES AND PROBLEMS

1. An investor is considering two $100,000 investments: (1) ABC Company bonds maturing in one year and paying 12% interest at maturity, and (2) U.S. Treasury Notes also maturing in one year and paying 7% interest at maturity. The investor believes there is a .10 probability that ABC Company will default. If default were to occur, it is estimated that the investor would receive eighty cents on the dollar.

Required:

(a) Determine the expected utility of each investment.

(b) What is the value of perfect information?

(c) Assume the investor can privately contract to obtain ABC Company's profit forecast for the next year. If default were not to occur, there is an estimated probability of .8 that the profit forecast would be positive, and a .2 probability it would be negative. If default were to occur, the probability of a positive forecast is .4, while the probability is .6 that the profit forecast would be negative. Calculate the utility of each investment based on the new information.

(d) What is the maximum price an investor would be willing to pay for the new information?

(e) What are some reasons why this type of private contracting may not occur?

(f) Why is this type of analysis difficult to apply to real-world situations? What limitations apply to using this type of approach for studying economic consequences of alternative accounting policies?

2. A retail company begins operations late in 19X0 by purchasing $600,000 of merchandise. There are no sales in 19X0. During 19X1 additional merchandise of $3,000,000 is purchased. Operating expenses (excluding management bonuses) are $400,000, and sales are $6,000,000. The management compensation agreement provides for incentive bonuses totalling 1% of after-tax income (before the bonuses). Taxes are 25%, and accounting and taxable will be the same.

The company is undecided about the selection of the LIFO or FIFO inventory methods. For the year ended 19X1, ending inventory would be $700,000 and $1,000,000, respectively, under LIFO and FIFO.

Required:

(a) How are accounting numbers used to monitor this agency contract between owners and managers?

(b) Evaluate management incentives to choose FIFO.

(c) Evaluate management incentives to choose LIFO.

(d) Assuming an efficient capital market, what effect should the alternative policies have on security prices and shareholder wealth?

(e) Why is the management compensation agreement counter-productive as an agency monitoring mechanism?

(f) Devise an alternative bonus system to avoid the problem of the existing plan.

BIBLIOGRAPHY OF REFERENCED WORKS

Ajinkya, Bipin B. (1980). "An Empirical Evaluation of Line-of-Business Reporting," *Journal of Accounting Research* (Autumn 1980), pp. 343–361.

Albrecht, W. Steve; Larry L. Lookabill; and James C. McKeown (1977). "The Time-Series Properties of Annual Earnings," *Journal of Accounting Research* (Autumn 1977), pp. 226–244.

Altman, Edward I. (1971). *Corporate Bankruptcy in America* (Heath).

American Accounting Association (1966). *A Statement of Basic Accounting Theory* (AAA).

———— (1977). *Statement of Accounting Theory and Theory Acceptance* (AAA).

Anderson, Ray (1981). "The Usefulness of Accounting and Other Information Disclosures in Corporate Annual Reports to Institutional Investors in Australia," *Accounting and Business Research* (Autumn 1981), pp. 259–265.

Archibald, T. Ross (1972). "Stock Market Reaction to Depreciation Switch-Back," *The Accounting Review* (January 1972), pp. 22–30.

Baker, H. Kent, and John A. Haslem (1973). "Information Needs of Individual Investors," *Journal of Accountancy* (November 1973), pp. 64–69.

Ball, Ray (1972). "Changes in Accounting Techniques and Stock Prices," *Empirical Research in Accounting: Selected Studies 1972* (Supplement to *Journal of Accounting Research*), pp. 1–38.

Ball, Ray, and Philip Brown (1968). "An Empirical Evaluation of Accounting Income Numbers," *Journal of Accounting Research* (Autumn 1968), pp. 159–177.

Baran, A.; J. Lakonishok; and A. Ofer (1980). "The Information Content of Adjusted Accounting Earnings: Some Empirical Evidence," *The Accounting Review* (January 1980), pp. 22–35.

Beaver, William H. (1967). "Financial Ratios as Predictors of Failure," *Empirical Research in Accounting: Selected Studies, 1967* (Supplement to *Journal of Accounting Research*), pp. 71–111.

———— (1968). "The Information Content of Annual Earnings Announcements," *Empirical Research in Accounting: Selected Studies, 1968* (Supplement to *Journal of Accounting Research*), pp. 67–92.

Beaver, William H.; Andrew A. Christie; and Paul A. Griffin (1980). "The Information Content of SEC Accounting Series Release No. 190," *Journal of Accounting and Economics* (August 1980), pp. 127–157.

Beaver, William H.; Roger Clarke; and William F. Wright (1979). "The Association Between Unsystematic Security Returns and the Magnitude of Earnings Forecast Errors," *Journal of Accounting Research* (Autumn 1979), pp. 316–340.

Beaver, William H., and Roland E. Dukes (1972). "Interperiod Tax Allocation, Earnings Expectations, and the Behavior of Security Prices," *The Accounting Review* (April 1972), pp. 320–332.

Beaver, William H., Paul Kettler; and Myron Scholes (1970). "The Association Between Market-Determined and Accounting-Determined Risk Measures," *The Accounting Review* (October 1970), pp. 654–682.

Bildersee, John S. (1975). "Market-Determined and Alternative Measures of Risk," *The Accounting Review* (January 1975), pp. 81–98.

Brown, Robert Moren (1980). "Short-Range Market Reactions to Changes to LIFO Accounting Using Preliminary Earnings Announcements," *Journal of Accounting Research* (Spring 1980), pp. 38–62.

Brown, Philip, and John W. Kennelly (1972). "The Information Content of Quarterly Earnings," *Journal of Business* (July 1972), pp. 403–421.

Cassidy, D. (1976). "Investor Evaluation of Accounting Information: Some Additional Evidence," *Journal of Accounting Research* (Autumn 1976), pp. 212–229.

Chang, Lucia, and Kenneth S. Most (1977). "Investor Uses of Financial Statements: An Empirical Study," *Singapore Accountant* (1977), pp. 83–91.

Chenhall, Robert H., and Roger Juchau (1977). "Investor Information Needs: An Australian Survey," *Accounting and Business Research* (Spring 1977), pp. 111–119.

Collins, Daniel W. (1975). "SEC Product-Line Reporting and Market Efficiency," *Journal of Financial Economics* (June 1975), pp. 125–164.

Collins, Daniel W., and Richard R. Simmonds (1979). "SEC Line-of-Business Disclosures and Market Risk Adjustments," *Journal of Accounting Research* (Autumn 1979), pp. 352–383.

Collins, Daniel W.; Michael S. Rozeff; and Dan S. Dhaliwal (1981). "The Economic Determinants of the Market Reaction to Proposed Mandatory Accounting Changes in the Oil and Gas Industry," *Journal of Accounting and Economics* (March 1981), pp. 37–71.

Elam, Rick (1975). "The Effect of Lease Data on the Predictive Ability of Financial Ratios," *The Accounting Review* (January 1975), pp. 25–43.

Elgers, Pieter T. (1980). "Accounting-Based Risk Measures: A Re-Examination," *The Accounting Review* (July 1980), pp. 389–408.

Elgers, Pieter T., and Dennis Murray (1982). "The Impact of the Choice of Market Index on the Empirical Evaluation of Accounting Risk Measures," *The Accounting Review* (April 1982), pp. 358–375.

Epstein, Mark (1975). *The Usefulness of Annual Reports to Corporate Stockholders* (California State University, Los Angeles, Bureau of Business and Economic Research).

Eskew, Robert K. (1979). "The Forecasting Ability of Accounting Risk Measures: Some Additional Evidence," *The Accounting Review* (January 1979), pp. 107–118.

Fama, Eugene F. (1970). "Efficient Capital Markets: A Review of Theory and Empirical Work," *Journal of Finance* (May 1970), pp. 383–417.

Financial Accounting Standards Board (1980). "Qualitative Characteristics of Accounting Information," *Statement of Financial Accounting Concepts No. 2* (Financial Accounting Standards Board).

Foster, George (1977a). "Quarterly Earnings Data: Time Series Properties and Predictive Ability Results," *The Accounting Review* (January 1977), pp. 1–21.

——— (1977b). "Valuation Parameters of Property-Liability Companies," *Journal of Finance* (June 1977), pp. 823–836.

——— (1978). *Financial Statement Analysis* (Prentice-Hall).

——— (1980). "Accounting Policy Decisions and Capital Market Research," *Journal of Accounting and Economics* (March 1980), pp. 26–62.

Gheyara, Kelly, and James R. Boatsman (1980). "Market Reactions to the 1976 Replacement Cost Disclosures," *Journal of Accounting and Economics* (August 1980), pp. 107–125.

Gonedes, Nicholas J. (1972). "Efficient Capital Markets and External Accounting," *The Accounting Review* (January 1972), pp. 11–21.

——— (1980). "Public Disclosure Rules, Private Information-Production Decisions, and Capital Market Equilibrium," *Journal of Accounting Research* (Autumn 1980), pp. 441–476.

Griffin, Paul A. (1982). *Usefulness to Investors and Creditors of Information Provided by Financial Reporting: A Review of Empirical Accounting Research* (Financial Accounting Standards Board).

Hakansson, Nils H. (1977). "Interim Disclosure and Public Forecasts: An Economic Analysis and Framework for Choice," *The Accounting Review* (April 1977), pp. 396–416.

Hines, R. D. (1982). "The Usefulness of Annual Reports: the Anomaly Between the

Efficient Markets Hypothesis and Shareholder Surveys," *Accounting and Business Research* (Autumn 1982), pp. 296–309.

Hirshleifer, Jack (1971). "The Private and Social Value of Information and the Reward to Inventive Activity," *The American Economic Review* (September 1971), pp. 561–573.

Hong, Hai; Robert S. Kaplan; and Gershon Mandelker (1978). "Pooling vs. Purchase: The Effects of Accounting for Mergers on Stock Prices," *The Accounting Review* (January 1978), pp. 31–47.

Horwitz, Bertrand, and Richard Kolodny (1977). "Line of Business Reporting and Security Prices: An Analysis of an SEC Disclosure Rule," *Bell Journal of Economics* (Spring 1977), pp. 234–249.

Kessler, L., and Robert H. Ashton (1981). "Feedback and Prediction Achievement in Financial Analysis," *Journal of Accounting Research* (Spring 1981), pp. 146–162.

Lee, T. A., and D. P. Tweedie (1975). "Accounting Information: An Investigation of Private Shareholder Usage," *Accounting and Business Research* (Autumn 1975), pp. 280–291.

Leftwich, Richard W. (1981). "Evidence on the Impact of Mandatory Changes in Accounting Principles on Corporate Loan Agreements," *Journal of Accounting and Economics* (March 1981), pp. 3–36.

Libby, Robert (1975). "Accounting Ratios and the Prediction of Failure: Some Behavioral Evidence," *Journal of Accounting Research* (Spring 1975), pp. 150–161.

McIntire, Edward V. (1973). "Current-Cost Financial Statements and Common Stock Investment Decisions," *The Accounting Review* (July 1973), pp. 575–585.

Ohlson, James A., and A. G. Buckman (1981). "Toward a Theory of Financial Accounting: Welfare and Public Information," *Journal of Accounting Research* (Autumn 1981), pp. 399–433.

Pfeiffer, G. (1980). "The Economic Effects of Accounting Policy Regulation; Evidence on the Lease Accounting Issue" (Ph.D. diss., Cornell University).

Ricks, William E. (1982). "The Market's Response to the 1974 LIFO Adoptions," *Journal of Accounting Research* (Autumn 1982), pp. 367–387.

Ro, Byung T. (1980). "The Adjustment of Security Returns to the Disclosures of Replacement Cost Accounting Information," *Journal of Accounting and Economics* (August 1980), pp. 159–189.

Roll, Richard (1977). "A Critique of the Asset Pricing Theory's Tests: Part 1: On Past and Potential Testability of the Theory," *Journal of Financial Economics* (March 1977), pp. 129–176.

Staubus, George J. (1965). "The Association of Accounting Variables with Common Stock Values," *The Accounting Review* (January 1965), pp. 119–134.

Stone, Mary S. (1981). "An Examination of the Effect of Disclosures Concerning Unfunded Pension Benefits on Market Risk Measures" (Ph.D. diss., University of Illinois).

Sunder, Shyam (1973). "Relationship Between Accounting Changes and Stock Prices: Problems of Measurement and Some Empirical Evidence," *Empirical Research in Accounting: Selected Studies, 1973* (Supplement to *Journal of Accounting Research*), pp. 1–45.

Thomas, Arthur L. (1969). "The Allocation Problem in Financial Accounting Theory," *Studies in Accounting Research #3* (American Accounting Association).

Thompson, Donald J. (1976). "Sources of Systematic Risk in Common Stock," *Journal of Business* (April 1976), pp. 173–188.

Van Horne, James C. (1980). *Financial Management and Policy,* 5th ed. (Prentice-Hall).

Watts, Ross L., and Richard W. Leftwich (1977). "The Time Series of Annual Accounting Earnings," *Journal of Accounting Research* (Autumn 1977), pp. 253–271.

Wright, William F. (1977). "Financial Information Processing Models: An Empirical Study," *The Accounting Review* (July 1977), pp. 676–689.

ADDITIONAL READINGS

INFORMATION ECONOMICS

Demski, Joel S., and Gerald A. Feltham (1976). *Cost Determination: A Conceptual Approach* (Iowa State University Press).

Feltham, Gerald A. (1972). "Information Evaluation," *Studies in Accounting Research #4* (AAA).

Raiffa, H., and R. Schlaifer (1961). *Applied Statistical Decision Theory* (MIT Press).

Stiglitz, J. (1975). "Information and Economic Analysis," in *Current Economic Problems,* ed. M. Parkin and A. Nobay (Cambridge University Press), pp. 27–52.

CAPITAL MARKET RESEARCH

Beaver, William H. (1981). *Financial Reporting: An Accounting Revolution* (Prentice-Hall).

Dyckman, Thomas R.; David Downs; and Robert P. Magee (1975). *Efficient Capital Markets and Accounting: A Critical Analysis* (Prentice-Hall).

Gonedes, Nicholas J. (1976). "The Capital Market, the Market for Information, and External Accounting," *Journal of Finance* (May 1976), pp. 611–630.

Kaplan, Robert S. (1978). "The Information Content of Financial Accounting Numbers: A Survey of Empirical Evidence," in *Impact of Accounting Research on Practice and Disclosure,* ed. A. Abdel-Khalik and T. Keller (Duke University Press).

Ricks, William E. (1982). "Market Assessment of Alternative Accounting Methods: A Review of the Empirical Evidence," *Journal of Accounting Literature* (Spring 1982), pp. 59–99.

Ronen, Joshua (1974). "The Need for Accounting Objectives in an Efficient Market," in *Objectives of Financial Statements—Volume 2, Selected Papers* (American Institute of Certified Public Accountants).

Wyatt, Arthur R. (1983). "Efficient Market Theory: Its Impact on Accounting," *Journal of Accountancy* (February 1983), pp. 56–65.

HUMAN INFORMATION PROCESSING

Ashton, Robert H. (1982). "Human Information Processing in Accounting," *Studies in Accounting Research #17* (American Accounting Association).

Libby, Robert (1981). *Accounting and Human Information Processing: Theory and Applications* (Prentice-Hall).

Libby, Robert, and B. L. Lewis (1977). "Human Information Processing Research in Accounting: The State of the Art," *Accounting, Organizations and Society*, Vol. 2, No. 3: 245–268.

———— (1982). "Human Information Processing Research in Accounting: The State of the Art in 1982," *Accounting, Organizations and Society* Vol. 7, No. 3: 231–286.

ACCOUNTING ALLOCATIONS

Eckel, Leonard G. (1976). "Arbitrary and Incorrigible Allocations," *The Accounting Review* (October 1976), pp. 764–777.

Thomas, Arthur L. (1974). "The Allocation Problem: Part Two," *Studies in Accounting Research #9* (American Accounting Association).

———— (1975). "The FASB and the Allocation Fallacy," *Journal of Accountancy* (November 1975), pp. 65–68.

CHAPTER 7

Uniformity and Disclosure: Some Policy-Making Directions

We have seen in Chapter 5 that an emerging metatheoretical structure of accounting is being developed by the Financial Accounting Standards Board (FASB). Many new concepts and hypotheses, stemming largely from economics and finance, that have potentially important influences upon a metatheory were discussed in Chapter 6. Uniformity and disclosure and their place in such a structure is the subject matter of this chapter.

A conceptual framework is a normative structure because both the objectives and standards are the result of choice. After the conceptual framework is in place it should provide a guide for standard setting. A deductive relationship thus exists between a metatheoretical structure and rule making. While theoretical work should obviously be allowed to influence a conceptual framework as it emerges, as well as the rule-making process itself, theory and policy making lie in separate domains. However, Ijiri points out that theory and policy appear to be more intertwined in accounting than in other fields.[1] We have already seen that attempting to combine

[1]Ijiri (1975, pp. 9–11).

these functions led to disaster for the APB. Certainly FASB has been and will continue to be under pressure from outside bodies and groups over the issue of both the conceptual framework and its actual standard-setting activities. Consequently, the issues and concepts which concern a meta-theoretical structure must be as clear and complete as possible in order to minimize the slippage between the structure and subsequent policy making. In other words, conceptual clarity and completeness are necessary if the resulting standards are to be consistent with the metatheoretical structure.

In this chapter we examine two extremely important conceptual issues that must play an important role in determining the structure and components of a metatheoretical framework: uniformity and disclosure. Whether or not the presently evolving conceptual framework of FASB takes in the near future any of the possible shapes discussed here, it should be remembered that a metatheoretical structure in a discipline such as accounting will always be an evolving instrument, changing in response to new needs and new research findings.

We commence with an analysis of uniformity. It is a topic extensively discussed in the accounting literature but it has not been precisely formulated. The type of uniformity desired should influence the structure of the metatheoretical framework. Information economics (cost–benefit considerations) obviously play a key role in this determination.

An appropriate starting point for understanding uniformity comes, we believe, from an analysis of event types. Events are economic occurrences that require accounting entries. They can be classified as simple or complex. Complex events are broadly similar in nature where "effect of circumstances" exist which might justify different accounting treatments. Effect of circumstances or relevant circumstances are thus economically significant variables that should be identified and categorized.

After defining relevant circumstances, we are in a better position to analyze the uniformity question. In our opinion, there are two concepts of uniformity—finite and rigid uniformity—that have been evolving in the accounting literature. These concepts were briefly mentioned in Chapter 4.

With the concepts of finite and rigid uniformity in place, we next need an analysis of the types of metatheoretical frameworks necessary to underlie these approaches. Issues such as efficient markets, the allocation problem, and costs and benefits of information are brought into the context of the uniformity discussion.

Given the different transaction types and the two approaches to uniformity, we will attempt to discover why the presently existing body of rules are basically inconsistent. This topic is something of a digression from the main objectives of the chapter, but it is extremely worthy of examination because it relates theory to standard setting.

Finally, the concept of disclosure is brought into closer focus. Of particular importance is its potential interaction with the uniformity question.

The chapter closes with an assessment of some of the directions FASB might take relative to the issues discussed in the chapter.

UNIFORMITY

Uniformity has been extensively discussed in both the accounting literature and statements and pronouncements of policy-making organizations. It also appears to overlap with comparability in the accounting literature. For example, Sprouse has stated:

> Finally, because comparing alternative investment and lending opportunities is an essential part of most investor and creditor decisions, the quest for comparability is central. The term comparability is used here to mean accounting for similar transactions similarly and for different circumstances differently. A conceptual framework should foster consistent treatment of like things, provide the means for identifying unlike things, and leave open for judgment the estimates inherent in the accounting process.[2]

Sprouse sees comparability as both a process (accounting for circumstances in accordance with similarities or differences) and an end result of this process (comparing alternatives in order to make a decision). We view **comparability** here only in the latter context, while **uniformity** is seen as the concept which influences comparability. Because comparability is linked to uniformity, the degree of comparability that users can rely on is directly dependent on the level of uniformity present in financial statements.

The relationship between uniformity and comparability espoused here is quite close to the position taken in Statement of Financial Accounting Concepts No. 2 (SFAC 2). Comparability is not an inherent quality of accounting numbers in the sense pertaining to relevance and reliability but instead deals with the relationship between accounting numbers; "The purpose of comparison is to explain similarities and differences."[3] However, SFAC 2 also states that:

> Comparability should not be confused with identity, and sometimes more can be learned from differences than from similarities if the differences can be explained.[4]

Though uniformity and comparability are usually discussed in terms of the necessity to account for similar events in a similar manner, no extensive formal attempt has been made to specify the bounds of similarity and

[2]Sprouse (1978, p. 71).
[3]FASB (1980a, p. 45).
[4]FASB (1980a, p. 48).

difference among events. Consequently, a fruitful starting point for examining the uniformity issue lies in the area of analyzing events.

THE NATURE AND COMPLEXITY OF EVENTS

Transactions are economic or financial events that are recorded in the firm's accounts. An **event** has been defined in SFAC 3 as "a happening of consequence to an entity."[5] Transactions arise between entities, between a firm and its employees, and between a firm and investors or lenders. Transactions are thus external events pertaining to an enterprise. Events that are internal to the firm also require entries in the firm's accounts. Examples would include recognition of depreciation and completion of work-in-process inventories. It is up to the rules of accounting to specify the necessary criteria for event recognition. Rules of realization are concerned with the question of when to recognize revenues as being earned, for example.

Another aspect of events that particularly concerns us here is their degree of simplicity or complexity. In a complicated and involved business environment, events are often accompanied by a complex set of restrictions, contingencies, and conditions. For example, in the case of long-term leases, these would be some of the factors:

1. A clause in the lease providing for cancellation by either party.
2. The proportion of the asset's life the lease a period is expected to cover.
3. The possible existence of favorable renewal privileges (either for purchase or rental) at the end of the original lease period.

Some other examples of event complexity would involve situations such as these:

1. Acquisition of common stock for control purposes where the percentage of stock owned may vary.
2. Expected usage or benefit patterns of depreciable fixed assets and intangibles may differ.
3. Deferred tax credits arising from income tax allocation situations can either grow indefinitely or decrease during the planning horizon.

Before we examine the nature of complex events further, it should be mentioned that there are many events that do not have any significant economic variables capable of leading to essentially different recording. We denote these as **simple events.** Examples would include asset acquisitions, liability payments, and sales of assets.

Simple events of the same general type may have some differences, but they are not economically significant differences. For example, when assets

---

[5]FASB (1980b, p. 37).

are acquired, either the buyer or the vendor may pay the transportation charges. If the buyer pays, the situation is easily handled by means of the "cost rule," which charges all costs necessary for acquisition and installation to the asset rather than directly to expense. If the seller pays, transportation costs are charged to a freight-out type account. These situations are similar enough to result in highly uniform recording of events. **Complex events,** however, may have different economic circumstances, which can lead to significantly different cash flows. The term "effect of circumstances" has been used in the literature to describe these situations but we prefer the less cumbersome "relevant circumstances."

RELEVANT CIRCUMSTANCES

With regard to the complex events mentioned above, we can say that, while the variables mentioned represent potential economic differences between relatively similar events, there are some subtle differences as well. In the case of leases, all the elements considered would be stipulated in the contract hence they would be known at the inception of the lease. Similarly, the percentage of common stock owned is a condition that would be known at the time of the transaction. On the other hand, expected usage or benefit patterns of depreciable assets and the question of the drawdown or reversal of deferred tax credits pertain to future events.

The Terminology of Relevance

Relevant circumstances, then, can be defined as the presence of diverse economic factors, leading to different potential cash flows, in broadly similar event situations. As the preceding examples suggest, they can be categorized into two general types. Those conditions known at the time of the event will be referred to as **present magnitudes.** Factors that can be known only at a later date shall be called **future contingencies.** Relevant circumstances pertain directly to the event being accounted for and not to the accounting method selected to represent that event. For example, LIFO has different tax implications than FIFO, but its selection would not be the result of a relevant circumstance.

A case can certainly be made that one of the principal tasks of a rule-making body should be that of attempting to identify appropriate relevant circumstances and setting up criteria about how they should govern the recording of events or the format of financial statements. This has been done in a rather unsystematic fashion by rule-making bodies in areas such as lease capitalization (SFAS 13); purchase versus pooling (APB Opinion 16); and choice among full consolidation, equity, and cost methods where common stock in another firm is held for control purposes (ARB 51 and SFAS 18).

Identifying relevant circumstances, not to mention setting criteria to govern choice among accounting methods or format of financial statements, is indeed a formidable task. Whether a conceptual framework can be useful is an important question that will be addressed later in this chapter. However, there are some considerations concerning future contingencies that should be carefully noted. The two cases mentioned previously, usage or benefit patterns of fixed assets and the question of reversal of deferred tax credits, have some important qualitative differences.

In the case of depreciation, we are dealing with an allocation. There are several other future contingency-type relevant circumstances that are allocations. These include amortization of intangibles, such as goodwill, research and development costs, and depletion of natural resources. One method of avoiding the allocation problem for at least some future contingency problems is by means of current valuations. Hence depreciation and depletion, at least, could be computed as the difference between market values of their respective assets at the beginning and end of the period.

However, in the situation of the prospective reversal of deferred tax credits arising from an excess of accelerated depreciation for tax purposes over straight-line depreciation for book purposes, the reversal is not an allocation problem but rather a prediction question based on factors such as the pattern of future capital acquisitions and their tax and book depreciation schedules. At present, the prospective reversal of deferred tax credits is a relevant circumstance in the United Kingdom but is not in the United States. The whole tax allocation problem is discussed in depth in Chapter 13.

Future contingencies that are allocations are likely to have limited information content, whereas those which attempt to predict relevant future variables—such as payments of deferred taxes—may have significant information content for users. However, an important element becomes the degree of verifiability of predictive variables that might be selected as factors governing accounting methods.

The Role of Management in Relevant Circumstances

Given that relevant circumstances are an extremely important aspect of the uniformity issue, the question arises as to whether management should have the choice of determining them. Weldon Powell, the former managing partner of a Big Eight firm, saw managerial influence as an important consideration in terms of allowing different methods.[6] For example, if two firms acquired the same type of fixed asset but one intended to use it intensively in the early years whereas the other anticipated relatively even usage throughout its life, then, from Powell's viewpoint, the first firm would be justified in using an accelerated depreciation method and the second could go for straight-line depreciation.

While these choices might be merited, the problem is that selection of accounting methods might be guided by different motives than the pre-

[6]Powell (1965, pp. 680–681).

sumed relevant circumstances. These ulterior motives would include the following:

1. Maximizing short-run reported income if managerial compensation is based on it.
2. Minimizing short-run reported income if there is fear of governmental intervention on antitrust grounds.
3. Smoothing income (minimizing deviations in income from year to year) if it is believed that stockholders perceive the firm has a lower amount of risk than would be the case if greater fluctuations of earnings were present.[7]

Because management is potentially capable of distorting income measurement, Cadenhead favors limiting relevant circumstances to elements beyond managerial control, elements he refers to as "environmental conditions."[8] Environmental conditions must differ between firms and lead to problems of either excessive cost of measurement or a low degree of verifiability relative to the preferred accounting method.[9] If environmental conditions possess either of these two qualities, they are designated as "circumstantial variables" by Cadenhead. For example, if valuation of inventories were to be based on the specific identification method, cost of record keeping would be exorbitant for retail firms having extensive inventories with a low unit value. As an example of the second type, if net realizable value of inventories were required, costs of completion and disposal might be extremely difficult to estimate in some industries, leading to a low degree of verifiability. Only in cases of circumstantial variables would Cadenhead allow departure from rigidly prescribed accounting methods.

Despite the importance of relevant circumstances in allowing different accounting treatments in generally similar transactions, little research has been done on the topic. This inattention has led, by default, to two concepts of uniformity that have evolved in both the accounting literature and the standards propounded by rule-making bodies.

FINITE AND RIGID UNIFORMITY

Finite uniformity attempts to equate prescribed accounting methods with the relevant circumstances in generally similar situations. The word "finite" was selected in accordance with the Random House Dictionary definition of "having bounds or limits; not too great or too small to be mea-

---

[7]A very extensive literature in the area of income smoothing developed during the 1970s. For an excellent summary, see Ronen and Sadan (1981).

[8]See Cadenhead (1970).

[9]The use of LIFO would not be an environmental condition because those electing to use it for tax purposes must use it for financial reporting purposes. Hence its use for financial reporting purposes is beyond managerial control and is applicable to *all* firms electing it for tax purposes.

surable." Statement of Financial Accounting Standards (SFAS) 13 on long-term leases provides a good example of finite uniformity. If a lessee has a long-term noncancellable lease for 75% or more of the estimated economic life of an asset, capitalization is required. However, if the lease period is for less than 75% of the estimated economic life of the asset, the lease is not capitalized.[10] This lease provision is one of four set down in the standard, any of which is sufficient to require capitalization on the grounds that the lease contract ". . . transfers substantially all of the benefits and risks incident to the ownership of the property . . ." to the lessee. In discussing the 75% lease period, the Board further elaborated:

> Although the lease term may represent only 75 percent of the economic life of the property in terms of years, the lessee can normally expect to receive significantly more than 75 percent of the total economic benefits to be derived from the use of the property over its life span. This is due to the fact that new equipment, reflecting later technology and in prime condition, can be assumed to be more efficient, and hence yield proportionately more use benefit, than old equipment which has been subject to obsolescence and the wearing-out process. Moreover, that portion of use benefit remaining in the equipment after the lease term, in terms of the dollar value that may be estimated for it, when discounted to present worth, would represent a still smaller percentage of the value of the property at inception.[11]

An obvious difficulty with the 75% lease period provision is the fact that it attempts to draw a line in terms of determining relevant circumstances where a continuum exists. Would 70% or even 60% have been a better "break-point" between capital and operating leases? The point is very debatable and can never be totally resolved. Furthermore, the door is open for managerial manipulation if noncapitalization is desired merely by extending, within reasonable bounds, the estimated economic life of the asset.

SFAC 2 appears to accept implicitly the idea of finite uniformity, as the following example reveals:

> For example, to find whether a man is overweight, one compares his weight with that of other men—not women—of the same height. . . . Clearly, valid comparison is possible only if the measurements used—quantities or ratios—reliably represent the characteristic that is the subject of comparison.[12]

The Need for an Alternative to Finite Uniformity

Since establishment of appropriate criteria for relevant circumstances is difficult and often somewhat arbitrary, an alternative type of uniformity has been implicitly formulated. Rigid uniformity means prescribing one

---

[10]Provided none of the other conditions held and there is no bargain lease renewal present. SFAS 13 (1976, para. 7).
[11]SFAS 13 (1976, para. 75).
[12]FASB (1980a, p. 46).

method for generally similar transactions, even though relevant circumstances may be present. For example, SFAS 2 requires that research and development costs must be expensed even though future benefits may be present. Accounting Principles Board Opinion (APB) 11 requires that income tax allocation must be used even if there is no anticipated reversal of deferred tax credits during the foreseeable future.

SFAC 2 also implicitly mentions rigid uniformity. It is seen in the context of attempting to improve comparability (by using the same accounting method) in situations where representational faithfulness is not strived for. However, "improving" comparability may, in reality, be counterproductive:

> Improving comparability may destroy or weaken relevance or reliability if, to secure comparability between two measures, one of them has to be obtained by a method yielding less relevant or reliable information. Historically, extreme examples . . . have been provided . . . in which the use of standardized charts of accounts has been made mandatory in the interest of interfirm comparability but at the expense of relevance and often reliability as well. That kind of uniformity may even adversely affect comparability of information if it conceals real differences between enterprises.[13]

An analogy may help to explain the difference between finite and rigid uniformity as well as the greater utility of the former. Suppose that one is an American diplomat in Europe. In dealing with individuals it is important to know their country of origin but it is not "correct" to ask. Diplomat A can only tell if individuals are European or non-European. Diplomat B is able to tell by the spoken accent of individuals whether they are (a) Slavic, (b) Scandinavian, or (c) from the rest of Europe. Diplomat C is able to tell by a combination of accent and name the particular country of origin of each individual. The situation faced by Diplomat A is equivalent to rigid uniformity while Diplomat C has achieved finite uniformity, with B being in between. The analogies to general event similarity and relevant circumstances are the general European origin and particular country (or region, in the case of B) of birth respectively. In accounting we presume that if finite uniformity can be attained it is superior to rigid uniformity from the standpoint of usefulness in decision making or performance evaluation. However, meaningful finite uniformity could be obtained only at a greater cost than rigid uniformity, so the advantage is merely relative and depends on marginal benefits and costs.

Finite and Rigid Uniformity Compared

Finite and rigid uniformity are both based on an underlying rationale. Finite uniformity is based on the belief that accounting methods should attempt to follow economically meaningful circumstances. Consequently, pertinent measures of performance and relevant measures of assets and liabilities should result. Therefore, objectives of a conceptual framework,

---

[13]FASB (1980a, p. 47).

such as prediction of cash flows and evaluation of managerial effectiveness, should be enhanced. In addition, a relatively high degree of comparability between financial statements of different firms should occur.[14] As a result, finite uniformity should help to improve resource allocation because security prices would better reflect risk-adjusted present value of the firm's cash flows.[15]

Rigid uniformity has a more restricted outlook because it simply attempts to eliminate alternatives in broadly similar situations. Its immediate linkage to an objective of accounting would appear to be stewardship in the context of custodianship of the enterprise's resources and their appropriate usage.

Proponents of rigid uniformity might say that the complexity of major business enterprises tends to make comparability of financial statements among firms extremely difficult, if not impossible. Hence the costs of finite uniformity would far exceed its benefits. Rigid uniformity, on the other hand, would not require as extensive a metatheoretical framework (as will be shortly discussed) so it could be implemented less expensively. There are several areas where finite and rigid uniformity can be further compared.

Current Value Accounting.   Current value accounting is more attuned to finite uniformity while historical costs and general price-level adjustments would be more applicable to rigid uniformity. Since current value accounting attempts to measure economically relevant properties of assets and liabilities, it dovetails quite closely with finite uniformity, which is concerned with the relevance of different economic circumstances.

Rigid uniformity, however, is more concerned with limiting alternative accounting treatments in broadly similar transactions. Consequently, the application of current values in situations where relevant circumstances are ignored would not appear to have a high priority.

Conversely, while finite uniformity could be attempted in conjunction with historical costing, it does not appear to be highly beneficial to attempt to differentiate among circumstances if current economic values are to be ignored. Indeed changing prices can be interpreted as an extremely important relevant circumstance.

Users of Financial Statements.   The focusing of financial accounting theory upon the needs and capabilities of users was extensively discussed in Chapter 5. How might finite and rigid uniformity be related to this important consideration?

Finite uniformity could be correlated with the viewpoint that normative models must be developed for implementing various objectives of accounting, such as cash flow prediction, and assessing managerial effective-

---

[14]As well as comparability of financial statements over time for the same firm.
[15]For more on the role of security prices relative to resource allocation, see Ronen (1974, pp. 82–86).

ness in carrying out enterprise goals. Thus it might be necessary to educate users in their role as decision makers about how to understand these models.

On the other hand, rigid uniformity would be more attuned to the view that sees heterogeneous users and user groups with different decision needs and capabilities. Decision models cannot be determined for such users, or they may be so diverse that they cannot be classified. Given these problems, any attempt to institute finite uniformity would ultimately fail. Therefore the thrust of a standard-setting body should be to eliminate alternative accounting treatments.

Reliability and Relevance. As defined in SFAC 2 and discussed in Chapter 5, reliability consists of two characteristics: verifiability and representational faithfulness. Verifiability is represented by the degree of statistical consensus relative to measurements of financial and economic phenomena reached by accountants. Clearly finite uniformity would be less verifiable than rigid uniformity because more judgment would have to be applied in terms of interpreting what relevant circumstance is appropriate to a given situation.

Representational faithfulness refers to whether the attribute actually being measured is really what it purports to be. Thus if replacement cost of an asset were estimated by a net realizable value measurement, there would be a low degree of representational faithfulness. Rigid uniformity would be more representationally faithful if, and only if, users understand that a number representing a quality (such as "unamortized cost") means that quality and nothing more. Therefore, on the grounds of the verifiability issue (which is much more clear-cut than the question of representational faithfulness) rigid uniformity would have a greater degree of reliability than finite uniformity would have.

In terms of relevance, finite uniformity—since it does attempt to come to grips with different circumstances—should be more relevant than rigid uniformity is—with regard to uses such as prediction of cash flows and assessment of managerial effectiveness. Therefore, a trade-off exists: finite uniformity is more relevant but rigid is more reliable.

Effect on the Audit Function. If finite uniformity were to become a reality, the auditor's role would expand significantly, hence costs to the firm would increase. The auditor would be concerned not only with the reliability of financial data and its presentation in accordance with a conceptual framework but also with the interpretation of underlying circumstances that gave rise to the data. The auditor must substantiate what circumstances apply to various transactions and whether those circumstances were correctly interpreted by management in terms of accounting methods selected. Thus the independent auditor must substantiate monetary amounts and internal controls; but equally important, he or she must audit circumstances surrounding major transactions.

Relation to the Efficient Markets Hypothesis. Clearly, the principal question that arises about any attempt to institute a system of finite uniformity is the question of costs and benefits. Obviously costs would be higher with finite, so the question might be raised as to whether finite uniformity is needed given that securities markets are presumably efficient. As discussed in Chapter 6, the efficient markets hypothesis is supported by a considerable body of evidence that indicates that all publicly available information is rapidly impounded in market prices of securities. Furthermore, many studies have revealed that the market is able to distinguish between real events and accounting changes that are nothing more than allocations devoid of economic content. Therefore, assuming that investors are appropriately diversified, the possibility of their making abnormal returns relative to the risk undertaken is relatively small. So, the possibility is raised that the principal task of an organization such as FASB should be in the area of increasing disclosure rather than refining income measurements and asset and liability valuations.[16] Perhaps, then, the presence of efficient securities markets may preclude the necessity to develop an extensive finite uniformity system.

The opposing argument is that market efficiency alone does not guarantee optimal resource allocation. To state it in slightly different terms—alternative accounting information (finite versus rigid) can lead to different security prices, which affect important matters such as corporate cost of capital and distribution of wealth among security holders. Finite uniformity should result in security prices providing a more economically valid relationship between risk and expected return.[17] Thus the quality of information is an important issue. Consequently, finite uniformity could increase the quality or fidelity of information provided. Finally, it should be remembered that although other means are available for providing information, the accounting process might well provide the most economical means for disseminating this information.[18] The final answer, of course, still comes down to the crucial issue of costs versus benefits.

The Role of a Metatheoretical Framework. A metatheoretical framework would play a much more limited role under rigid as opposed to finite uniformity. The main functions of a policy-making body under rigid uniformity would be eliminating alternatives for generally similar transaction types and perhaps increasing disclosure. In addition, standards could be promulgated for specifying how financial statements should be presented in terms of how account balances should be listed and grouped.

Under finite uniformity it is necessary to have a metatheoretical structure to serve as a guide for developing both standards geared toward common objectives and consistent valuation methods that take into account

[16] See Beaver (1973) for additional coverage.
[17] Ronen (1974, pp. 82–86).
[18] Ronen and Sorter (1972), p. 259.

relevant circumstances. Hence it would have to provide a framework for an extensive classification system that attempts to provide criteria for determination of factors affecting economic substance of transactions. A summary comparison of finite and rigid uniformity is shown in Exhibit 7-1. We next take a closer look at the possible components of a metatheoretical framework that would be necessary to support either finite or rigid uniformity.

UNIFORMITY AND A METATHEORETICAL FRAMEWORK

Obviously, determining objectives of users is the appropriate starting point in a metatheoretical structure. Indeed SFAC 1 and its predecessor, the Trueblood Committee Report, discussed in Chapter 5, have been the starting point for FASB's Conceptual Framework. It is assumed here that most users have relatively similar objectives from which a broad set of information needs can eventually be determined. If diverse information needs of various user groups prevail, then a chaotic situation exists, which may be beyond the aid of a metatheoretical framework. This issue is, of course, the "user heterogeneity" debate discussed previously. Another assumption made here is that users have a basic understanding of financial statements. This accords with one of the tenets of the efficient markets hypothesis which states that naive investors are not at a disadvantage in the market as long as they are appropriately diversified. In order to get a better perspective of what a metatheoretical structure should contain, we need to take a closer look at a metatheoretical framework below the level of objectives.

EXHIBIT 7-1.

Comparison of Finite and Rigid Uniformity

Type	Value System Most Applicable	Possible Objectives	Position Relative to Users	Reliability and Relevance	Audit Function	Efficient Markets Hypothesis	Metatheoretical Framework
Finite	Current value	Prediction of cash flows; assessment of managerial performance	Best normative models should be developed; if necessary educate users	Lower reliability and higher relevance than rigid	Expanded and more costly	Better quality of information	Extensive
Rigid	Historical Cost	Stewardship	Users are heterogeneous in terms of abilities and needs	Higher reliability and lower relevance than finite	Less costly	Goal of FASB should be toward more disclosures	Limited

Constitutional Standards

A possible model for a metatheoretical structure containing several levels of standards below the user objectives was provided by Cyert and Ijiri.[19] Their system provides some insights about conceptual issues below the level of user objectives which forms the apex of their system (as well as the FASB's conceptual framework).

Constitutional standards, as set forth by Cyert and Ijiri, are concerned with determining qualifications or restrictions relative to carrying out the topmost level, user objectives. For example, limitations on disclosure requirements would come under this category.[20] Segmental disclosure is illustrative: the issue is that information about product lines and territories is useful to prospective investors but it can also be beneficial to a firm's competitors.

Another issue that would come under constitutional standards concerns criteria for handling trade-offs among the various elements of relevance and reliability that were discussed in Chapter 5. Perhaps the only empirical work done in this area was a survey by Stanga.[21] His questionnaire went to a sample of 500 chartered financial analysts and 500 chief commercial lending officers, with a response of 20.2% and 22.6%, respectively. The questionnaire had thirty items in the areas of segmental reporting, financial forecasting, interim reporting, and replacement cost versus historical cost. Beside each question were two scales that respondents were asked to use in terms of evaluating the degree of relevance and reliability for various types of information in the four areas mentioned. Interestingly enough, his findings were that a modest positive correlation appears to exist between relevance and reliability rather than the presumed trade-off. However, Stanga himself is cautious in terms of interpreting his findings. His questions cover only a limited number of financial reporting issues; and responses are, of course, based only on user perceptions rather than harder forms of evidence. Nevertheless, the results are indeed interesting if not surprising.

In addition to being concerned with balancing potentially conflicting issues among the firm, the present and potential investors and creditors, and the competition, constitutional standards have two other potentially important functions. First, to whatever extent possible, to set general guidelines for determining relevant circumstances (if the intent is to implement a finite uniformity system). Second, cost–benefit issues should be taken into account.

Constitutional standards are probably the most difficult and persistent of all metatheoretical issues. While these problems must be appropriately resolved under both finite and rigid uniformity, the former would be more

---

[19]Cyert and Ijiri (1974). We use "standards" here rather than "objectives."
[20]Cyert and Ijiri (1974, p. 32).
[21]Stanga (1980).

difficult and costly to resolve because of the finer nature of the information required.

The Cyert–Ijiri system does not specifically provide for the qualitative characteristics of relevance and reliability and of their sub-categories covered in SFAC 2. Since these are below the level of objectives, and constitutional standards are concerned with resolving trade-offs among qualitative characteristics, placement of them must be between user objectives and constitutional standards.

Operating Standards

The concerns at this level are more mundane than at the constitutional level. Issues arising here would include the form and content of financial statements.[22] Content would cover matters such as what kinds of information should be provided in financial statements based on user objectives and subject to limitations of disclosure delineated in the constitutional objectives. Included under form of financial statements would be the issue of understandability. Both finite and rigid uniformity systems would have to address the issues falling under the category of operating standards, though the former would place more emphasis on the content of financial statements based on user objectives.

Basic definitions of the elements of financial statements could form part of this level of the metatheoretical framework. One reason definitions are needed is for the broad purpose of maintaining consistency among the various financial statement components. To whatever extent possible, the definitions should be consistent with the objectives and the constitutional standards previously determined.

Below the level of operating standards, the theoretical structure becomes more concrete in terms of specification of accounting methods. Consequently, the metatheoretical structure or conceptual framework ends at this level.

Prescriptive Standards

Prescriptive standards form the bottom level of the Cyert–Ijiri system. The name indicates their normative nature. They are viewed as "dicta used to indicate which alternatives should be selected."[23] Thus, included here would be selection of the valuation system to be employed.[24]

Cyert and Ijiri saw prescriptive standards as being involved with both policy and procedural issues. This would be consistent with rigid uniformity and would form the bottom level of standards for this type of system. However, under a system of finite uniformity, prescriptive standards should

[22]Cyert and Ijiri (1974, p. 33).
[23]Cyert and Ijiri (1974, p. 34).
[24]Cyert and Ijiri (1974, p. 34).

be restricted to policy issues, though they would be quite precise in terms of zeroing in on specific approaches to be employed in financial statements. In addition, finite uniformity would require an additional level of standards below the prescriptive level called procedural standards where operational issues concerning relevant circumstances would be determined.

Procedural Standards

Below prescriptive standards would be an enumeration of the particular accounting applicable to major relevant circumstances. Additional allowances for secondary or minor relevant circumstances (including specialized industry problems now handled by the Accounting Standards Executive Committee of the AICPA) might appear as a subset of the main listing of procedural standards. Two hypothetical examples showing possible prescriptive and procedural standards are shown in Exhibit 7-2.

The subsystem of prescriptive and procedural standards should be derived from the metatheoretical structure though not necessarily by means of deductive logic. Empirical testing among methods in light of prescriptive standards might be useful as a means of choosing among methods. For example, lease capitalization might be a better predictor of failure than noncapitalization.

EXHIBIT 7-2.

Hypothetical Example of Prescriptive Standards, Procedural Standards and Relevant Circumstances

Prescriptive Standards	Ownership interests in other corporations should reflect the degree of control therein.	Operating assets should be shown at their value in use to the firm.
Procedural Standards (including major relevant circumstances)	0–20% ownership use cost; 20–49% use equity; 50% or more use full consolidation.	If a firm intends to keep an asset because discounted cash flow exceeds exit value and/or replacement cost, use replacement cost. If exit value exceeds discounted cash flow and/or replacement cost, use exit value.
Other possible relevant circumstances	a. Must use equity if control is demonstrated below 20% ownership; b. Use equity if control is above 50% but firms are in dissimilar industries.	

There may, however, be many areas in which absolutely conclusive criteria cannot be derived. For example, where common stock of other firms has been acquired for purposes of control, an appropriate circumstance allowing usage of different methods might be the percentage of stock owned. Since differences in percentage of shares owned are totally divisible, relevant circumstances may well be logical but will, nevertheless, be somewhat arbitrary. Possible exceptions to major circumstantial differences would still require the use of judgment, though adequate justification and disclosure should be required.

It would also be the case that relevant circumstances, prescriptive standards, and procedural standards would change over time as new research, changing economic conditions, and other information shed light on various problem areas of financial accounting. While no part of the entire theoretical structure would be expected to stand permanently, change would certainly be more frequent at the lower levels of the system.

This examination of possible metatheoretical frameworks and lower levels of the policy-making construct, as well as the comparison of finite and rigid uniformity, should make it clear that the former would be more expensive than the latter. Whether the presumed additional benefits would outweigh the incremental costs is the key question. Finite uniformity, in and of itself, is by no means a panacea for the present problems faced by the profession. It would be very difficult to implement a meaningful finite uniformity system. Relevant circumstances arising from present magnitudes are often somewhat arbitrary (the 75% lease period rule, for example). Similarly, relevant circumstances stemming from future contingencies will virtually always present problems of measurement and verifiability (reversal of deferred tax credits).

A diagram comparing possible theoretical structures for implementing finite and rigid uniformity is shown in Exhibit 7-3. Now that this survey of a possible system of finite uniformity is concluded, let us examine the present state of uniformity in terms of some applications of finite and rigid uniformity.

THE PRESENT STATE OF UNIFORMITY

Finite and rigid uniformity represent, to a certain extent, ideal types. At the present time, a mixed system exists, in which some standards attempt to take into account relevant circumstances whereas others are clearly examples of rigid uniformity. A brief survey of extant accounting standards is therefore useful in terms of illustrating the present state of accounting relative to the uniformity question. However, several qualifications must be made clear.

First, the fact that a standard is an example of finite uniformity should not necessarily be construed to mean that the standard cannot be improved or even that the factor selected as the relevant circumstance is appropriate.

EXHIBIT 7-3.
Possible Theoretical Structures
for Implementing Uniformity

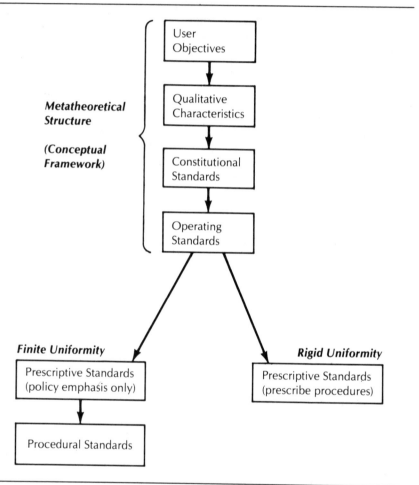

Second, where rigid uniformity is in effect, the underlying reasons may be attributable to one or more of the following factors: (1) a desire for conservatism, (2) an inability of the standard-setting organization to prescribe meaningful relevant circumstances, (3) an attempt to increase verifiability of the measurement, (4) the recognition of the fact that an allocation is involved, (5) the perception that, given adequate disclosure and an efficient securities market, costs of implementing relevant circumstances exceed the resulting benefits. Third, another approach to the uniformity problem, usually called flexibility, exists in many accounting rules.

Flexibility applies to situations in which there are no discernible relevant circumstances but more than one possible accounting method exists, any of which may be selected at the firm's behest.[25] The investment credit provides a good example of flexibility. Holding aside the carryforward problem, which is relatively rare, no relevant circumstance appears to be present. However, APB 4 allows enterprises to take all benefits immediately in the year of acquisition, or they may be spread over the useful life of the asset. Either alternative is acceptable.

Some examples of each of the three approaches to uniformity will be given. These examples are intended to be illustrative only and do not cover the entire range of policies comprising generally accepted accounting principles. The cases given will highlight relevant circumstances and allowable alternatives. Intermediate or advanced accounting texts should be consulted for in-depth discussion of the various methods and other details.

Rigid Uniformity

There are numerous examples of rigid uniformity in official pronouncements of standard-setting bodies. Comprehensive income tax allocation is required by APB 11 whether or not deferred tax credits actually reverse. In the case of research and development costs, despite the presumed presence of future benefits arising from an important proportion of these costs, SFAS 2 requires that they be immediately expensed. SFAS 19 attempted to eliminate "full costing" and allow only "successful efforts" amortization of drilling and exploration costs in the oil and gas industry. More will be said about oil and gas accounting in Chapter 14.

Finite Uniformity

Examples of finite uniformity include long-term leases and ownership of common stock of another firm for control purposes. In the former case, any one of four conditions is sufficient to warrant capitalization, whereas the absence of all four results in an operating lease. In the second situation, ownership of various percentage ranges of common stock results in either full consolidation, equity, or cost methods of handling the investment.

These two illustrations of finite uniformity concern situations of present magnitudes. A case of finite uniformity where future contingencies are involved is the question of reversal of deferred tax credits. Reversal is seen as a viable circumstance in the United Kingdom, where partial tax allocation must be used, but it is not accepted at present in the United States.

Another case of finite uniformity involving a future contingency involves loss contingencies. SFAS 5 sets up two conditions under which a contingent loss must be charged against income of the current year: (1) an adverse future event, such as an expropriation of assets by a foreign govern-

---

[25]Flexibility is sometimes called "diversity." See Grady (1965, p. 33) for one example.

ment, is likely to occur; and (2) the amount of the loss can be reasonably estimated. If either or both of these conditions are not met, disclosure of the loss contingency (presumably in the footnotes) should be made if there is at least a "reasonable possibility" of a loss occurring. SFAS 5 can also be interpreted as an example of conservatism because gain contingencies are not mentioned except to state that Accounting Research Bulletin (ARB) 50 is still in effect relative to them. That pronouncement states that gain contingencies are not reflected in income prior to realization. However, adequate disclosure is to be made, though care must be exercised in order "to avoid misleading implications as to the likelihood of realization."[26]

Flexibility

Flexibility is very prevalent in terms of generally accepted accounting principles. The investment credit has already been mentioned. Inventory and cost of goods sold accounting provides another illustration of flexibility. The actual physical flow of inventory to cost of goods sold does not fall within the definition of relevant circumstances presented here. Nevertheless firms may choose among FIFO, LIFO, and weighted average methods as they see fit.[27] If FIFO or weighted average are used, the lower-of-cost-or-market modification is required. Lower-of-cost-or-market itself is simply a valuation procedure that has been tacked onto FIFO and weighted average methods for purposes of conservatism.

Depreciation accounting provides a special example of flexibility. The estimated usage pattern of the asset provides a potential relevant circumstance. However, choice among the many acceptable methods such as straight-line, accelerated methods, and the annuity method is again at the user's behest and need not be related to the estimated pattern of usage.

Another example of flexibility is provided by treasury stock which is acquired for later reissuance. Among the reasons for acquisition are: (1) issuance to employees under stock option plans, (2) usage for acquiring stock of another corporation in a business combination, and (3) for temporary investment purposes. The three reasons for acquisition are not a future contingency type of relevant circumstance because they are not a direct result of the event being accounted for. Nevertheless there are two methods for handling treasury stock acquisitions: the par value and the cost methods. Once again either method can be used at the firm's option.

Overview of Practice

The situation presently existing in financial accounting can, perhaps, best be understood by means of a diagram. In Exhibit 7-4 a two-by-two matrix is shown, with one illustration in each cell. Column I represents

[26] ARB 50 (1958, para. 5).
[27] Powell, (1965, pp. 680–681).

EXHIBIT 7-4.

Uniformity and Relevant Circumstances
in Practice

Policy Employed	Relevant Circumstances	
	Yes	No
Finite	IA SFAS 13 Leases *appropriate*	IIA APB 16 Purchase Versus Pooling *not appropriate*
Rigid	IB SFAS 2 *inappropriate* Research and Development Costs	IIB SFAS 19 *appropriate* Oil and Gas Accounting

situations where relevant circumstances are present. Column II represents situations where relevant circumstances are not present. Row A depicts transactions in which a policy-setting body has treated the situation as if it were finite. Similarly, Row B represents transactions in which a policy-setting body has treated the situation as one of rigid uniformity.

The cells where policy matches the complexity of the situation are IA and IIB. In IA a relevant circumstance is present and the policy-making body has given it recognition. In IIB no relevant circumstance is present and the rule making organization has attempted to treat the situation in a rigid uniformity fashion.

The cells where suboptimization is present are IIA and IB. In IIA no relevant circumstances are present but the policy-setting group has set up criteria as if relevant circumstances existed. The result is two different methods of treatment which do not appear to have any real substantiation in fact. In IB relevant circumstances are present but the policy-making group has not been able to implement them, resulting in a situation of rigid uniformity.

Situation IIA is more serious than IB. In the former, the standard-setting group has expended resources and taken actions that were not required and indeed led to extremely serious problems in the case of purchase versus pooling. In IB the board restricted alternate treatments because the different circumstances were simply not verifiable.

Finally, it should once again be stressed that even though cell IA provides a "match" between the standard-setting body's action and the complexity of the situation, it is not necessarily the case that relevant circumstances have been optimally defined and applied or even if they have, that benefits of the standard exceed its costs.

DISCLOSURE

Broadly interpreted, disclosure is concerned with information presented in both the financial statements themselves and supplementary means of communications—including footnotes, post-statement events, management's analysis of operations for the forthcoming year, financial and operating forecasts, and additional financial statements covering segmental disclosure and extensions beyond historical costs. The term **financial reporting** is often used as an umbrella to cover both financial statements themselves and the additional types of information mentioned above. For purposes of our discussion, **disclosure** refers to the whole area of financial reporting and not simply to the financial statements.

DISCLOSURE FUNCTION OF THE SEC

It has always been implicitly recognized that disclosure under SEC stewardship has two aspects.[28] One of these might be termed **protective disclosure** since one of the concerns of the SEC has been protecting unsophisticated investors from unfair treatment. The other aspect is **informative disclosure,** the scope of which is to provide useful information for investment analysis purposes. Obviously there is some degree of overlap between these functions of disclosure.

In its earlier history, the SEC stressed protective rather than informative disclosure. The Securities Act of 1933 required the filing of a registration statement with the SEC prior to the sale of a new issue of securities. Included in the registration statement and the prospectus given to the purchaser is extensive information pertaining to the business of the issuer, provisions relative to the securities being sold, and identity and relevant financial interests of those distributing the securities. In addition, extensive information about the underwriter's compensation and dealings between the corporation and its officers, directors, and principal shareholders must be provided in the registration statement. Much of this information is protective in nature, though there is certainly informative material in the registration statement and the prospectus. The Securities Exchange Act of 1934 extended most of these rules for new issues of securities to sales of

---

[28]Much of the information on the SEC and the disclosure process was obtained from Anderson (1974).

existing issues. In effect, then, the intention was to keep the information on the initial registration current.

Several restrictions were put into effect when a firm filed a registration statement: a 20-day waiting period; delivery of the prospectus to purchasers; and the potential imposition of rather heavy civil liability damages upon the issuer, its officers, directors, and underwriters for filing inadequate or misleading information. It was thought that this package of restrictions would be a strong deterrent against blatant attempts to defraud investors. The SEC also had the authority to invalidate a registration or suspend it if it had already become effective if the information was either incomplete or inaccurate in any material respect.

THE SHIFT TOWARD INFORMATIVE DISCLOSURE

While the protective and informative aspects of disclosure tended to overlap, the SEC shied away from requiring disclosure of "soft information." However, since approximately the early 1970s, a shift in emphasis toward informative disclosure appears to have taken place. For example, the Commission had always shunned inflation accounting proposals, very likely on the grounds that the data were not highly verifiable and the average investor would probably not understand the numbers—despite the presumed importance for informative purposes. However, after the FASB exposure draft on general price-level statements was outstanding, the SEC in Accounting Series Release 190 boldly put forth requirements for supplementary disclosures for most major firms mandating replacement cost information for depreciation expense, fixed-asset valuation, cost of goods sold, and inventories. It is very likely that the movement toward informative disclosure has occurred as a result of the efficient markets hypothesis and its conclusion that naive investors are not at a disadvantage in the market as long as they are properly diversified.

The thrust of the SEC toward informative disclosure was continued by the Advisory Committee on Corporate Disclosure to the SEC. The committee prepared a voluminous report in 1977 summarizing the present state of disclosure and making further recommendations about disclosure. It endorsed the thrust away from hard information (as signified by objectively verifiable historical data) toward the soft information area embodied in opinions, forecasts, and analyses.

Among their informative-disclosure suggestions were earnings forecasts with a "safe harbors" provision which would protect management from the liability provisions of the federal securities laws provided projections are reasonable and made in good faith.[29] Other forward looking informative data recommended by the Committee include planned capital expenditures and their financing, management plans and objectives, divi-

---

[29]SEC (1977, pp. 344–65).

dend policies, and policies relative to enterprise capital structure.[30] In addition, other informative disclosures recommended by the committee include standard product line classifications for segmental reporting, determined on an industry-by-industry basis, and disclosure of social and environmental information if it is expected to affect future financial performance, such as a constant violation of the law.[31]

The SEC acted on the recommendations of the committee by adopting Rule 175 in 1979 which provided safe harbor from the liability provisions of the federal securities laws for projections that are reasonably based and made in good faith.[32]

IMPERFECTIONS OF THE DISCLOSURE PROCESS

While the thrust toward informative disclosure should improve the evaluation of risk and return of enterprises, there are several important qualifications to bear in mind. An important channel of disclosure communication comes from the corporation by means of financial analysts representing brokerage firms and investment consultants.[33] Several aspects of this type of arrangement were discussed in Chapter 3. Since financial analysts do not pay for this information, it is liable to be overproduced in relation to the information that would have been acquired if it were supplied on a market-oriented basis. Furthermore, although the financial intermediaries, in turn, sell this information to their clients, usage cannot be restricted to those who pay for it because it is a public good.

An adverse complementary factor relative to overproduction of disclosure information is the possibility of information overload: the inability of users to process and intelligently utilize all the information provided in financial reports.

Still another problem relative to disclosure, mentioned previously in this chapter, is that of competitive disadvantage. For example, in an area such as segmental disclosure, firms may be somewhat reluctant to reveal

---

[30]SEC (1977, pp. 365–379). There has been a growing trend starting in the late 1970s toward inclusion of a voluntary management report in the annual report, focusing on management's assessment of the internal accounting control system. For further details see Golub (1981).

[31]U.S. Government Printing Office (1977, pp. 380–398).

[32]SEC (1979, p. 19).

[33]The system of disclosure largely in effect today is called "differential disclosure." The 10-K and 10-Q reports filed annually and quarterly by management with the SEC are basically aimed toward professional financial analysts. They are more detailed and technical than the annual report going to shareholders. The analysts act as intermediaries by interpreting the SEC filings for the investing public. Beaver (1978, p. 50) believes that the thrust toward more disclosure in the annual report will downgrade the importance of the differential disclosure approach. Differential disclosure should be distinguished from "selective disclosure." The latter indicates more information available to some individuals. This constitutes insider information and raises the possibility that those in possession of the insider information may be able to earn an abnormal return.

information about product lines because they might give vital information to competitors, eroding their own favorable market situations. Hence there may be a situation of inequity since some individuals will tend to be unfavorably affected, such as present owners of securities of enterprises whose competitive advantage is revealed. A situation of this type would be an economic consequence of an accounting standard. In this particular situation, as long as there were no bias relative to firms (in terms of the information being reported), neutrality (SFAC 2) should govern the disclosure: as long as the information required is relevant and reliable, the effect on a particular interest should not be considered.

An additional point that has been mentioned in the disclosure literature is that adequate diversification by the investor may cut down his need for information at the firm-specific level.[34] The investor's concerns, it is argued, are with firm-specific information only insofar as it effects the portfolio. However, it appears virtually impossible to separate firm-specific information into categories of that which has no effect on the portfolio and that which is useful in terms of portfolio assessment.

A complementary argument involves the undiversified investor.[35] Since unsystematic risk can be virtually eliminated by proper diversification, the question arises as to the responsibilities that should be undertaken specifically for this group in terms of disclosure, since the costs must be borne largely by others (costs passed on to customers of the firm or lower dividends for all stockholders, for example). However, it is difficult to separate information provided specifically for undiversified portfolios and that which is also useful for diversified portfolios. Furthermore, we would raise the point that many individuals are undiversified because they do not have the financial resources to enable them to diversify. In a democratic society, an argument can be made that this group should be encouraged to invest in securities. Hence we likewise reject any argument tending to cut down disclosure on the basis that specific information applicable to this group can be segregated.

Despite these problems of the disclosure process, our value judgment is that, on balance, operations of securities markets and investors, as a totality, will benefit by expanding the disclosure process.

DIRECTIONS OF THE STANDARD-SETTING PROCESS

The desirability of improving comparability of financial statements, by means of increasing both the degree of uniformity among them and the

---

[34]Beaver (1978, pp. 46–47).

[35]Beaver (1978, p. 47).

extent of disclosure, raises several issues in terms of possible directions that can be taken by the accounting profession. These matters bear discussion in terms of both theoretical and institutional considerations.

Finite and rigid uniformity, as was previously mentioned, are ideal types. A standard-setting body would not attempt to impose totally, in one enormous swoop, an entire system of either form. Such an undertaking would be virtually impossible in an economic and political context of a capitalistic and democratic orientation.

However, a preliminary assessment of the influence of increasing disclosure relative to finite and rigid uniformity is definitely in order. Given market efficiency, increasing the amount of disclosure should increase the utility of both finite and rigid uniformity as well as of any prevailing mixed system. However, it is our presumption that increasing the amount of disclosure will tend to give a comparative advantage to rigid uniformity relative to finite uniformity. To state the case slightly differently, we think that increasing disclosure will lower the cost–benefit differential of finite uniformity compared to the cost–benefit differential of rigid uniformity.

OPTIMAL ACCOUNTING SYSTEMS

Somewhat related to issues such as metatheoretical structures and finite and rigid uniformity are optimal accounting systems or optimal information systems. An **optimal accounting system** is "one for which the expected payoff to a user employing an optimal decision strategy is greater than or equal to the corresponding payoff for any alternative system . . ."[36] In other words, user utility cannot be improved by alternative financial statement presentations based on any other set of accounting rules.

Most, if not all, of the parties engaged in the debate agree that an optimal system is not attainable.[37] This would apply even if there were no user heterogeneity problem. The utility of the virtually limitless number of systems of accounting standards would be almost impossible to measure. However, we believe the issue should be addressed somewhat differently. With or without a metatheoretical framework, the development of accounting standards is an evolutionary process. It proceeds on a step-by-step basis. The presence of a conceptual framework or metatheoretical structure is intended to guide the standard-setting process in terms of deriving relevant goals of users consistent with qualitative characteristics and constitutional-type standards. Therefore, the relevant question about proceeding concerns whether a new position of existing standards is better than its immediate predecessor (in terms of whether resulting securities prices better reflect

---

[36]Marshall (1972, p. 286).
[37]For example Demski (1973), Cushing (1977), Bromwich (1980), Benston (1980).

the relationship of risk to return).[38] In other words, accounting information should facilitate the prediction of prospective risk-adjusted cash flows.[39]

The process of setting standards will always be extremely difficult to evaluate. Whether securities prices that result after new standards are imposed will better equate risk with return is an extremely difficult question to answer. Standard setting should also occur within a framework in which benefits exceed costs, another extremely difficult question. Of course a program of finite uniformity must have a fairly large degree of homogeneity in terms of information needs of the various user groups, or else failure will surely result.

Adding to these difficulties are the workings of the standard-setting group itself. Compromises among board members and the possibility of succumbing to political pressures of outside groups are but two of the dangers faced.

MUDDLING THROUGH

All these difficulties and constraints indicate that a standard-setting body is much more likely to satisfice or just plain muddle through than to attempt to find the presumed holy grail of optimal accounting standards. Even "optimal accounting standards," if such a concept exists other than in the minds of accounting researchers, must be constantly changing as new business conditions and problems emerge. However, muddling through is often the stuff of which good and reasonable progress is made. It is this interaction between the policy-setting process and research (both inductive and deductive) which offers us at least a modest amount of hope that financial reporting will continue to improve.

It is not certain whether there will be an eventual push toward finite or rigid uniformity in conjunction with a meaningful disclosure system. The main consideration here is the question of benefits versus costs. Part of the cost entails extensive research into determining where relevant circumstances lie in the various valuation areas of accounting. Nevertheless, no matter which way, if either, the profession goes and despite the many qualifications and shortcomings surrounding the development of a conceptual framework, a strong case can be made that the effort is worthwhile. Obviously the FASB thinks so too, since its project is well under way. It is possible, of course, that the Conceptual Framework Project is simply intended as a form of window dressing intended to do nothing more than

---

[38]Even a step-by-step basis is fraught with difficulties. The problem lies in the interdependence among standards. As a new—and presumably better—standard is promulgated, it must not decrease the utility of previously enacted standards. See Bromwich (1980) for further analysis. Of course a conceptual framework should reduce the interdependency problem by making standards consistent in terms of user needs and objectives, but it is no outright guarantee.

[39]See Ronen (1974, pp. 82–86).

fend off the pressures of critics.[40] We do not, however, hold such a jaundiced view. Time will tell whether this optimism is warranted.

SUMMARY

Under finite uniformity, policy-making organizations attempt to take into account relevant circumstances in broadly similar event situations. Policy-making bodies do not attempt to cope with relevant circumstances under rigid uniformity. The main attempt under rigid uniformity is to limit alternatives which, in turn, would lead to greater verifiability but less relevance. Relevant circumstances are different economic factors leading to potentially different patterns of cash flows in broadly similar types of event situations.

While finite uniformity should lead to greater relevance because rule making attempts to take into account appropriate circumstances, it is not at all clear that the resulting additional benefits would exceed the incremental costs of implementation. Certainly a more extensive metatheoretical framework would be needed to delineate the accounting required for relevant circumstances. In addition, extensive empirical research would have to be focused on the search for relevant circumstances.

Finite and rigid uniformity are ideal types. It is unlikely that either could ever be totally and consistently applied. At present, examples of both rigid and finite uniformity can be found in various pronouncements of rule-making bodies. One step that might be taken is to eliminate alternatives in event situations where it doees not appear that relevant circumstances exist.

The increasing complexity of economic and financial events, along with the rise of the efficient markets hypothesis, has led to the increasing importance of disclosure in financial reporting. Two examples would be SFAS 14 on segment reporting and SFAS 33 on changing prices. Since approximately 1970 the SEC appears to have changed its primary focus from the area of protective disclosure—which had been its primary emphasis since its inception—to informative disclosure. The increasing emphasis on informative disclosure will probably work to the benefit of rigid uniformity as opposed to finite uniformity—from the cost–benefit standpoint.

An optimal accounting system will never be obtained. While criticism can easily be made of efforts to construct a conceptual or metatheoretical

---

[40]The views of both Peasnell (1982) and Dopuch and Sunder (1980) appear to fall in this category. The latter (p. 17) state that "... a body like the FASB needs a conceptual framework simply to boost its public standing." Much of the Dopuch and Sunder argument against the conceptual framework centers around the presumption of heterogeneous user information needs.

framework, we believe that these efforts will improve the process of financial reporting.

QUESTIONS

1. Is Cadenhead's conception of circumstantial variables as the only allowed departure from prescribed accounting methods closer to finite or rigid uniformity? Discuss.
2. Do you think managerial policies should be acceptable as potential relevant circumstances? Discuss.
3. How do present magnitudes differ from future contingencies?
4. Are simple transactions really examples of rigid uniformity? Discuss.
5. Finite and rigid uniformity would result in different information being received by users of financial statements. What difference would this make in terms of resource allocation when viewed from a macroeconomic standpoint?
6. If the efficient markets hypothesis is accepted, why does additional disclosure work to the advantage of rigid uniformity rather than finite uniformity?
7. How do protective and informative disclosure differ?
8. Under previous disclosure requirements of the SEC, dividends paid during the past two years in the annual report to shareholders must be stated. This requirement has been broadened: (1) There must be disclosure of any restrictions on the firm's present or future dividend-paying ability. (2) If the firm has not paid dividends in the past despite the availability of cash, and the corporate intention is to continue to forego paying dividends in the foreseeable future, disclosure of this policy is encouraged. (3) If dividends have been paid in the past, the enterprise is encouraged to disclose whether this condition is expected to continue in the future. Do you think that this broadening of disclosure of dividend policy is primarily protective or informative? Discuss.
9. Accounting Series Release No. 242 of the SEC states that, relative to payments made to foreign governmental and political officials, ". . . registrants have a continuing obligation to disclose all material information and all information necessary to prevent other disclosures made from being misleading with respect to such transactions." This ASR appeared shortly after the passage of the Foreign Corrupt Practices Act. Do you think this type of disclosure is primarily protective or informative in nature? Discuss.
10. If "uniformity" means eliminating alternative accounting treatments, then surely comparability of financial statements of different enterprises should be improved. Do you agree with this statement? Comment.

11. What are "optimal accounting systems" and why are they totally unattainable?

12. If constitutional and operating standards are not part of the FASB's conceptual framework, how are these issues resolved?

13. SFAC 3 defines *circumstances* as follows:

> Circumstances are a condition or set of conditions that develop from an event or series of events, which may occur almost imperceptibly and may converge in random or unexpected ways to create situations that might otherwise not have occurred and might not have been anticipated. To see the circumstance may be fairly easy, but to discern specifically when the event or events that caused it occurred may be difficult or impossible. For example, a debtor's going bankrupt or a thief's stealing gasoline may be an event, but a creditor's facing the situation that its debtor is bankrupt or a warehouse's facing the fact that its tank is empty may be a circumstance.

How does this definition of circumstances relate to the definition of relevant circumstances presented in the chapter?

14. SFAS 13, in effect, sees a lease period of 75% or more as a relevant circumstance in terms of distinguishing between capital and operating leases. What economic (cash flow differentials) underline this policy choice?

CASES AND PROBLEMS

1. Refer to either a current intermediate accounting text or a guide of current "generally accepted accounting principles." Give at least one example for each of the four cells of Exhibit 7-4 (your instructor may desire to modify this problem).

2. Using the article by Cyert and Ijiri as background (in *Objectives of Financial Statements*, Vol. 2, AICPA, 1974, pp. 30–35), list as many issues as you can that fall under the category of (1) constitutional standards, (2) operating standards.

BIBLIOGRAPHY OF REFERENCED WORKS

American Institute of Certified Public Accountants (1958). "Contingencies," *Accounting Research Bulletin No. 50* (AICPA).

Anderson, Alison Grey (1974). "The Disclosure Process in Federal Securities Regulation: A Brief Review," *The Hastings Law Journal* (January 1974), pp. 311–354.

Beaver, William (1973). "What Should Be the FASB's Objectives?," *Journal of Accountancy* (August 1973), pp. 49–56.

——— (1978). "Future Disclosure Requirements May Give Greater Recognition to the Professional Community," *Journal of Accountancy* (January 1978), pp. 44–52.

Benston, George J. (1980). "The Establishment and Enforcement of Accounting Standards: Methods, Benefits and Costs," *Accounting and Business Research* (Winter 1980), pp. 51–60.

Bromwich, Michael (1980). "The Possibility of Partial Accounting Standards," *The Accounting Review* (April 1980), pp. 288–300.

Cadenhead, Gary (1970). "'Differences in Circumstances': Fact or Fantasy?" *Abacus* (September 1970), pp. 71–80.

Cushing, Barry (1977). "On the Possibility of Optimal Accounting Principles," *The Accounting Review* (April 1977), pp. 308–321.

Cyert, Richard, and Yuji Ijiri (1974). "A Framework for Developing the Objectives of Financial Statements," *Objectives of Financial Statements*, Vol. 2 (American Institute of Certified Public Accountants), pp. 30–35.

Demski, Joel (1973). "The General Impossibility of Normative Accounting Standards," *The Accounting Review* (October 1973), pp. 718–723.

Dopuch, Nicholas, and Shyam Sunder (1980). "FASB's Statements on Objectives and Elements of Financial Accounting: A Review," *The Accounting Review* (January 1980), pp. 1–21.

Financial Accounting Standards Board (1976). "Accounting for Leases," *Statement of Financial Accounting Standards No. 13* (FASB).

——— (1980a). "Qualitative Characteristics of Accounting Information," *Statement of Financial Accounting Concepts No.2* (FASB).

——— (1980b). "Elements of Financial Statements of Business Enterprises," *Statements of Financial Accounting Concepts No. 3* (FASB).

Golub, Steven J. (1981). "Management Reports: Growing Acceptance," *Financial Executive* (December 1981), pp. 26–29.

Grady, Paul (1965). "Inventory of Generally Accepted Accounting Principles for Business Enterprises," *Accounting Research Study No. 7* (American Institute of Certified Public Accountants).

Ijiri, Yuji (1975). "Theory of Accounting Measurement," *Studies in Accounting Research #10* (American Accounting Association, 1975).

Marshall, Ronald (1972). "Determining an Optimal Accounting Information System for an Unidentified User," *Journal of Accounting Research* (Autumn 1972), pp. 286–307.

Peasnell, K.V. (1982). "The Function of a Conceptual Framework for Corporate Financial Reporting," *Accounting and Business Research* (Autumn 1982), pp. 243–256.

Powell, Weldon (1965). "Putting Uniformity in Financial Accounting into Perspective," *Law and Contemporary Problems* (Autumn 1965), pp. 674–690.

Ronen, Joshua (1974). "A User Oriented Development of Accounting Information Requirements," *Objectives of Financial Statments*, Vol. 2 (American Institute of Certified Public Accountants, 1974), pp. 80–104.

Ronen, Joshua, and George Sorter (1972). "Relevant Accounting," *Journal of Business* (April 1972), pp. 252–280.

Securities and Exchange Commission (1979). *Annual Report* (SEC).

Sprouse, Robert (1978). "The Importance of Earnings in the Conceptual Framework," *Journal of Accountancy* (January 1978), pp. 64–71.

Stanga, Keith G. (1980). "The Relationship Between Relevance and Reliability: Some Empirical Results," *Accounting and Business Research* (Winter 1980), pp. 29–39.

U.S. Government Printing Office (1977). *Report of the Advisory Committee on Corporate Disclosure to the Securities and Exchange Commission* (U.S. G.P.O.).

ADDITIONAL READINGS

UNIFORMITY AND COMPARABILITY

Graham, Willard (1965). "Some Observations on the Nature of Income, Generally Accepted Accounting Principles, and Financial Reporting," *Law and Contemporary Problems* (Autumn 1965), pp. 652–673.

Hendriksen, Eldon (1967). "Toward Greater Comparability Through Uniformity of Accounting Principles," *New York Certified Public Accountant* (February 1967), pp. 105–115.

Keller, Thomas (1965). "Uniformity Versus Flexibility: A Review of the Rhetoric," *Law and Contemporary Problems* (Autumn 1965), pp. 637–651.

Langenderfer, Harold (1967). "A Problem of Communication," *Journal of Accountancy* (January 1967), pp. 33–40.

Mautz, R. K. (1972). *Effect of Circumstances on the Application of Accounting Principles* (Financial Executives Research Foundation).

Merino, Barbara, and Teddy Coe (1978). "Uniformity in Accounting: A Historical Perspective," *Journal of Accountancy* (August 1978), pp. 62–69.

Miller, Paul (1978). "A New View of Comparability," *Journal of Accountancy* (August 1978), pp. 70–77.

Olson, Wallace (1977). "Financial Reporting—Fact or Fiction?" *Journal of Accountancy* (July 1977), pp. 68–71.

Revsine, Lawrence (1975). "Toward Greater Comparability in Accounting Reports," *Financial Analysts' Journal* (January–February 1975), pp. 45–51.

OPTIMAL ACCOUNTING SYSTEMS

Bejan, Mary (1981). "On the Application of Rational Choice Theory to Financial Reporting Controversies: A Comment on Cushing," *The Accounting Review* (July 1981), pp. 704–712.

Chambers, Raymond J. (1976). "The Possibility of a Normative Accounting Standard," *The Accounting Review* (July 1976), pp. 646–652.

Cushing, Barry (1981). "On the Possibility of Optimal Accounting Principles: A Restatement," *The Accounting Review* (July 1981), pp. 713–718.

Demski, Joel (1974). "Choice Among Financial Reporting Alternatives," *The Accounting Review* (April 1974), pp. 221–232.

——— (1976). "An Economic Analysis of the Chambers' Normative Standard," *The Accounting Review* (April 1976), pp. 653–656.

DISCLOSURE

Bedford, Norton (1973). *Extensions in Accounting Disclosure* (Prentice-Hall).

Buzby, Stephen (1974). "Nature of Adequate Disclosure," *Journal of Accountancy* (April 1974), pp. 38–47.

———— (1974). "Selected Items of Information and Their Disclosure in Annual Reports," *The Accounting Review* (July 1974), pp. 423–435.

Chandra, Gyan (1974). "Study of the Consensus on Disclosure Among Public Accountants and Security Analysts," *The Accounting Review* (October 1974), pp. 733–742.

Mautz, Robert, and William May (1978). *Financial Disclosure in a Competitive Economy* (Financial Executives Research Foundation).

Singhvi, Surendra (1972). "Corporate Management's Inclination to Disclose Financial Information," *Financial Analysts Journal* (July–August 1972), pp. 66–73.

Singhvi, Surendra, and Harsha Desai (1971). "Empirical Analysis of the Quality of Corporate Financial Disclosure," *The Accounting Review* (January 1971), pp. 129–138.

PART II

Contemporary Issues and Accounting Theory

The second part of this text attempts to assess important contemporary accounting problems. Institutional developments including the evolution of standards are reviewed and—wherever possible—the relation of theoretical concepts, definitions, and issues pertaining to these problems are discussed.

The first three chapters are the most general in nature because they are concerned with the present state of the three principal financial statements. Chapter 8 reviews the statement of financial position. The main concern is with the development of working definitions of the three main balance sheet elements: assets, liabilities, and owners' equity. The three orientations to the relationship between the balance sheet and income statement discussed in the Conceptual Framework Discussion Memorandum (asset-liability, revenue-expense, and nonarticulated) are used as a reference point for the development of the three definitions. Chapter 9 continues the thrust of Chapter 8 by examining the development of definitions of the principal income statement categories: revenues and gains, and expenses and losses. The income statement is also examined within the framework of the current operating approach versus the all-inclusive approach. The movement toward the all-inclusive approach has guided the evolution of categories such as extraordinary items, prior period adjustments, discontinued operations, and accounting changes. Other income statement topics such as earnings per share and income smoothing are also briefly discussed as well as several specialized income statement problems. The statement of changes in financial position is covered in Chapter 10. Emphasis is placed on the broadening of coverage of types of transactions reported in the statement. Also of importance is the question of how "funds" should be defined. In addition, the usefulness of the statement of changes in financial position is discussed.

One of the principal theoretical problems that has faced policy-making agencies concerns financial reporting in light of inflation and changing prices. The basic models were presented in Appendix 1-A. Chapter 11 provides an extensive theoretical overview of the main issues including choices between entry and exit values, meaning and computation of purchasing power gains and losses, and holding gains and losses. Various income measurement systems, including general price level adjustment, are then examined and evaluated. One of the key issues concerning current value (cost) systems concerns the disposition of real holding gains and losses and how the measurement of capital maintenance is affected. How capital maintenance pertains to general price level adjustment is also illustrated. And two specialized problems of current valuation systems are discussed: measuring current value depreciation when newer technology comes on the market and whether purchasing power gains on long-term debt during inflation are illusory. Chapter 12 is concerned with how inflation accounting has been implemented by standard-setting agencies in light of the many possibilities and theoretical problems presented in Chapter 11. The main topic of the chapter is a critique of Statement of Financial

Accounting Standards 33. An assessment of empirical research in accounting for inflation and changing prices is also presented. The chapter concludes with a discussion of inflation accounting standards in selected English-speaking countries.

Chapter 13 is concerned with problems arising in accounting as a result of income taxes. The principal area discussed is income tax allocation. The underlying reasons that led to income tax allocation are discussed along with an analysis of the various positions on the question. The latter are developed within the context of the most important application of income tax allocation: accelerated depreciation for tax purposes and straight-line for financial reporting. Another important tax allocation problem examined here arises from net operating loss carryforwards, including the particularly tricky situation when deferred tax credits are on the books. The second main topic of the chapter is the investment credit. While the investment credit has some similarities to tax allocation, it is a separate and distinct issue. The 1981 and 1982 tax acts are also examined here in terms of their significance for income tax allocation and the investment credit.

Oil and gas accounting is discussed in Chapter 14. Though the subject matter pertains to a specialized—though highly important—industry, virtually all facets of accounting theory have some bearing on this unique problem. These include economic consequences, the allocation problem, present valuation and verifiability, uniformity and relevant circumstances, and the politics of standard-setting.

Pension accounting is examined in Chapter 15. Perhaps more progress has been made in this area than in any other major problem area of accounting. Pensions have gone from a pure cash basis to the requirement that pension expense must be recognized in accordance with an acceptable actuarial funding plan (whether or not actually financed by that particular type of actuarial funding plan) as determined by Accounting Principles Board Opinion 8. Statement of Financial Accounting Standards 35 extends regulation to the assets and obligations of the pension plan itself as opposed to the sponsoring company. Standards in the pension area have largely been promulgated from the revenue-expense viewpoint. Pensions are also examined from the liability standpoint in the chapter. Definitions of key terms in the extremely complex area of pensions are presented. The key aspects of the Employee Retirement Income Security Act of 1974 (ERISA) insofar as they impinge upon pension accounting, are likewise mentioned.

Lease accounting is covered in Chapter 16. Leases are a good example of an economic condition that influenced standard-setting. After World War II, leasing became a popular means of financing the usage, if not acquisition, of fixed assets. One advantage of leasing was "off-the-balance-sheet-financing." The major part of the chapter is concerned with the evolution of lease capitalization beginning with Accounting Research Bulletin 38 as standard-setting agencies have attempted to make purchase and lease accounting more comparable. There has been an extension of leases subject to capitalization, though the present rules are perhaps not as comprehensive as they might be. Both the lessee and the lessor are covered in the discussion. Sale and leaseback and the leveraged lease are two particular leasing formats that are also covered. The chapter concludes with a discussion of the economic consequences of lease capitalization.

The last two chapters of the book are concerned with the entire spectrum of investment by one firm in the equity securities of other firms, including a brief discussion of "marketable securities" type equity investments. Chapter 17 discusses the cost and equity methods of accounting for investments of less than 50 percent in equity securities of other enterprises. The two methods are examined and critiqued with the presumed difference in terms of "degree of control" between the two situations being, in effect, a relevant circumstance. A theoretical analysis of consolidated financial statements is undertaken next with emphasis upon possible treatments of minority interests and goodwill. Entity and proprietary theories are brought into this discussion. The presumed usefulness of consolidated financial statements is also examined. The chapter concludes with the problem of foreign currency translation when foreign operations are consolidated. Included here is a discussion of the economic consequences caused by translation under Statement of Financial Accounting Standards 8 and the changes brought about in Statement of Financial Accounting Standards 52. Chapter 18 is concerned with business combinations. Purchase versus pooling accounting is closely examined, including the question of whether relevant circumstances separate the two treatments. The evolution of standards pertaining to business combinations are also surveyed here. Finally, research on purchase and pooling accounting is evaluated.

CHAPTER 8

The Statement of Financial Position

The next three chapters examine the balance sheet, income statement, and statement of changes in financial position, respectively. The purpose of this examination is to review the theoretical foundation of current financial reporting practices. Emphasis is on the definitions of accounting elements, principles of recognition, and rules of measurement applicable to each financial statement. It is not the intent to cover all extant accounting standards pertaining to accounting measurement: such an approach is taken in intermediate accounting textbooks. Rather, the intent here is to gain an appreciation of the fundamental principles of accounting measurement embodied in the three basic financial statements.

The balance sheet, also called the statement of financial position, is examined in this chapter. In the first section the relationship betwen the balance sheet and income statement is reviewed. There are two basic approaches which may be taken: **articulated,** which means the two are mathematically linked, and **nonarticulated,** which means the two statements are independently defined. The basic accounting elements—assets, liabilities, owners' equity, revenues, gains, expenses and losses—are also introduced in the first section.

The remainder of the chapter reviews the three balance sheet elements of assets, liabilities, and owners' equity. Definitions and their evolution are considered first, then principles of recognition, and finally rules of measurement for specific types of assets, liabilities, and owners' equity. Classification of accounting elements in the balance sheet is considered in the final section of the chapter.

RELATIONSHIP BETWEEN THE BALANCE SHEET AND INCOME STATEMENT

Two approaches have been advocated for defining accounting elements and the relationship between the balance sheet and income statement.[1] These are the articulated and nonarticulated concepts. Articulation means that the two statements are mathematically defined in such a way that net income is equal to the change in owners' equity for a period, assuming no capital transactions or prior period adjustments. The nonarticulated approach severs the mathematical relationship between the balance sheet and income statement: each statement is defined and measured independently of the other.

ARTICULATION

Accounting elements identified in Statement of Financial Accounting Concepts (SFAC) 3 are these: assets, liabilities, owners' equity, revenues, gains, expenses, and losses.[2] Income is calculated from revenues, gains, expenses, and losses. Under articulation, income is a subclassification of owners' equity. The articulated accounting model and classification system is illustrated in Exhibit 8-1. For ease of presentation, we take a proprietary approach, in which the net assets are equal to owners' equity.

Under the articulated concept all accounting transactions can be classified by the model in Exhibit 8-1. There are three subclassifications of owners' equity: contributed capital, retained earnings and unrealized capital adjustments. Contributed capital is subclassified into legal capital (par value) and other sources of contributed capital (e.g., premiums and donated assets). Retained earnings has three subclassifications: income statement accounts, prior period adjustments, and dividends. Because income is a subclassification of retained earnings, the income statement and balance sheet articulate. There are further subclassifications within the income

[1]FASB (1976).
[2]FASB (1980).

statement itself: the distinctions between revenues and gains, and expenses and losses, and the classification of gains and losses as ordinary or extraordinary. These topics are all addressed in Chapter 9. Also, some accounting transactions bypass the income statement altogether because they are considered to be adjustments of previous years' income. These adjustments are made directly to retained earnings. Dividends represent a distribution of income. The third subclassification of owners' equity, unrealized capital adjustments, arises from a few specific accounting rules. It is discussed later in the chapter.

The accounting classification system is rather simple. This simplicity causes some difficulty because complex transactions cannot always be neatly categorized into one of the classifications in Exhibit 8-1. New types of business transactions challenge the limits of the basic accounting model. An example of this is mandatory redeemable preferred stock. Because it is stock, it has definite ownership characteristics; but because it must be redeemed it also resembles bonds. The Securities and Exchange Commission (SEC) prevents its inclusion in owners' equity. However, an equally strong case could be made for classification as owners' equity.[3] Complex transactions such as mandatory redeemable preferred stock go beyond the limits of the accounting classification system. It is remarkable that the categoric framework used to classify accounting transactions is virtually unchanged since Paciolli's time. It may be that supplemental disclosure is the only way to deal with such complexities—short of developing an entirely new accounting classification system.[4]

Within the articulated approach are two alternative orientations to defining accounting elements. One approach, called **revenue–expense,** focuses on defining the income statement elements. It places primacy on the income statement, principles of income recognition, and rules of income measurement. Assets and liabilities are defined, recognized, and measured as a byproduct of revenues and expense. The other approach is called **asset–liability.** It is the antithesis of the revenue-expense approach. Emphasis is placed on the definition, recognition, and measurement of assets and liabilities. Income is defined, recognized, and measured as a byproduct of asset and liability measurement.

Revenue–Expense Approach

Since the 1930s accounting policy has been mainly concerned with the definition, recognition, and measurement of income. Income is derived by matching costs (including arbitrary allocations such as depreciation) to recognized revenues. Revenue recognition and matching are examined in detail in Chapter 9. For now, though, it is important to understand that both

[3]SEC (1979).
[4]For an example of an extended classification system see Ijiri (1982).

the income statement and balance sheet are primarily governed by accounting rules of revenue recognition and cost matching, and that these rules represent a revenue–expense orientation.

One consequence of the revenue–expense approach is to burden the balance sheet with byproducts of income measurement rules. As a result, the balance sheet contains not only assets and liabilities (defined later), but ambiguous debits and credits called deferred charges and deferred credits. These items do not conform to current definitions of assets and liabilities, yet are included in the balance sheet because of deferred recognition in the income statement. An example of a deferred charge is organizational start-up costs. These costs are allocated to the income statement over a number of years rather than expensed immediately. Once incurred, organizational costs are a sunk cost and cannot be recovered. Therefore, it is questionable if such costs should be carried forward in the balance sheet. The same is true of some deferred credits. Many of these types of credit balances are not really liabilities; they are simply future income statement credits arising from present transactions that are deferred to future income statements. An example of this type of deferred credit is deferred taxes. Deferred taxes do not represent a legal liability, rather, they simply arise from income statement rules of tax expense accrual.

There are many examples of accounting standards which emphasize the income statement effects of transactions somewhat to the exclusion of the balance sheet impact. For example, pension accounting under Accounting Principles Board (APB) 8 is mainly concerned with income statement recognition of pension expense.[5] Virtually no consideration is given to the question of whether a pension liability exists. The recognition and amortization of intangible assets under APB 17 introduces a dubious debit into the balance sheet (arising from the purchase method of accounting for business combinations) and arbitrarily amortizes it over a maximum of forty years.[6] The question of whether an intangible asset (goodwill) really exists is not addressed.

Asset–Liability Approach

An asset–liability approach is directly concerned with measuring and reporting assets and liabilities. Income is regarded as nothing more than a way of classifying and reporting certain changes that have occurred in the firm's net assets. Because assets and liabilities are the real things that exist, it seems logical that measurement should focus on them. The owners' equity account is merely an invention to make possible the double-entry accounting system. Income and its components (revenues, gains, expenses, and losses) are regarded as secondary concepts that are simply a way of reporting changes in assets and liabilities.

---

[5] APB (1966a).
[6] APB (1970b).

The asset–liability approach focuses on the measurement of net assets. This approach is logical and arguably superior to a revenue–expense approach because assets and liabilities are the real things that exist. It is the increase in the value of net assets that gives rise to what we call income, not vice versa. The revenue–expense approach turns things around the other way and implies that changes in net assets are the consequences of "income" measurement. The current value models presented in Appendix 1-A of Chapter 1 are examples of the asset–liability approach.

While the revenue–expense approach is the basic orientation of current financial reporting practices, some of the specific accounting standards reflect an asset–liability emphasis. For example, Statement of Financial Accounting Standards (SFAS) 2 requires the expensing of research and development costs rather than capitalization because the existence of an intangible asset is considered to be subjective and uncertain.[7] SFAS 7 proscribes loss capitalization for companies that are in the development stage.[8] Previous practice had been to capitalize losses while in the development stage, and to write off the losses against future income. The requirement under SFAS 7 keeps a deferred charge out of the balance sheet. Of course it can be said in both of these examples that a better income statement is also produced in addition to a better balance sheet.

NONARTICULATED APPROACH

The possibility of nonarticulated financial statements has not been widely discussed in accounting literature. However, the idea appears to have some merit. At present there is a great deal of polarization between proponents of the traditional revenue–expense approach and those of the asset–liability approach. This occurs because revenue–expense proponents are primarily concerned with stabilizing the fluctuating effect of transactions on the income statement and are prepared to introduce deferred charges and deferred credits in order to smooth income measurement. On the other hand, asset–liability advocates are mainly concerned with reporting changes in the value of net assets, and they are prepared to tolerate a fluctuating income statement which may include unrealized holding gains and losses.

It is evident that the two groups are polarized partly because the balance sheet and income statement are mathematically articulated. Since articulation exists only by custom, the two statements could be severed and both groups might be satisfied with a revenue–expense-based income statement and an asset–liability-based balance sheet. A reconciliation between the two nonarticulated statements might also be included as supplemental disclosure.

[7]FASB (1974).
[8]FASB (1975c).

While nonarticulation does not exist, per se, there are some specific accounting standards that represent the essence of nonarticulation wherein changes in net asset values are recorded in the balance sheet—but are not recognized in the income statement. SFAS 52 requires the translation of foreign assets and liabilities using end of period exchange rates; but gains or losses on the translation arising from exchange rate changes are not charged to the income statement.[9] Any gains or losses are recorded directly in owners' equity as an unrealized capital adjustment and are recognized in the income statement only if the foreign operations are sold. There is no articulation with the income statement. A similar result occurs when the lower of cost or market rule is applied to noncurrent investments under SFAS 12.[10] Temporary losses are not charged to income, they are classified as an unrealized capital adjustment. The losses are recognized in the income statement only if the investments are sold, or if the losses are deemed permanent rather than temporary.

In both of these examples, changes have occurred in the measurement of net assets, yet the gains or losses are classified as unrealized and recorded directly in owners' equity. The treatment of unrealized capital adjustments in SFASs 12 and 52 has been criticized because the income statement is bypassed. Articulation does prevent the bypassing of the income statement in accounting for net assets. An argument favoring articulation is that it maintains the integrity of the income statement by reporting all changes in net assets in the income statement. On the other hand, there is no self-evident reason why net assets need to be measured the same way for both the balance sheet and the income statement. For example, replacement costs might be most useful for the income statement and exit prices most useful for the balance sheet. Nonarticulation is a concept that deserves more serious consideration than it has received, particularly in terms of relevance and decision usefulness.

ASSETS

Each of the three elements in the balance sheet will now be discussed. The same approach is taken for assets, liabilities, and owners' equity. Evolution of definitions is presented first, because definitions are necessary to classify business transactions into the appropriate elements (as illustrated in Exhibit 8-1). The next stage of accounting measurement is to define the point in time when elements are recognized in the balance sheet; this is called

[9]FASB (1982).
[10]FASB (1975d).

EXHIBIT 8-1.
Accounting Classification System

Assets − Liabilities =   Owners' Equity

```
                        ┌──────────────────┬──────────────────┐
                  Contributed          Retained           Unrealized
                    Capital            Earnings             Capital
                       │                   │              Adjustments
            ┌──────────┴──────────┐        │
      Legal Capital          Other         │
                           Contributed     │
                             Capital       │
                                           │
            ┌──────────────────────────────┼──────────────────────────┐
      Income Statement              Prior Period                  Dividends
          Accounts                   Adjustments
              │
      ┌───────┴───────────────────────┐
    Debits                          Credits
      │                               │
  ┌───┴────┐                     ┌────┴─────┐
Expenses  Losses             Revenues     Gains
            │                               │
     ┌──────┴──────┐                 ┌──────┴──────┐
  Ordinary   Extraordinary        Ordinary   Extraordinary
```

---

recognition. Finally, the attributes to be measured are reviewed for specific types of assets, liabilities, and owners' equity.

DEFINITION OF ASSETS

The definition of assets is important because it establishes what types of economic events will appear in the balance sheet. It identifies the **assets**—the elements to be recognized, measured, and reported in the balance sheet. A good definition of assets should be solely concerned with the criteria for classifying accounting transactions as assets. As indicated in Chapter 1, the attribute to be measured should be stated independently of the object to be measured. Many definitions of assets can be found in accounting literature. However, the accounting profession in the United States has made only three formal attempts to define assets:

Accounting Terminology Bulletin 1

Something represented by a debit balance that is or would be properly carried forward upon a closing of books of account according to the rules or principles of accounting (provided such debit balance is not in effect a negative balance applicable to a liability), on the basis that it represents either a property right or value acquired, or an expenditure made which has created a property or is properly applicable to the future. Thus, plant, accounts receivable, inventory, and a deferred charge are all assets in balance-sheet classification.[11]

APB Statement 4

Economic resources of an enterprise that are recognized and measured in conformity with generally accepted accounting principles. Assets also include certain deferred charges that are not resources but that are recognized and measured in conformity with generally accepted accounting principles.[12]

SFAC 3

Assets are probable future economic benefits obtained or controlled by a particular entity as a result of past transactions or events.[13]

The first asset definition emphasizes legal property, but also includes deferred charges on the basis that they are "properly" included with assets. A distinction is made between assets and deferred charges but both are considered to be assets. The justification is that deferred charges relate to future period income statements. They are included with assets solely because of income statement rules which defer the recognition of these costs as expenses until future periods. This aspect of the definition represents a revenue–expense approach.

The second definition emphasizes that assets are economic resources. These are defined as "the scarce means available . . . for the carrying out of economic activity."[14] Assets are perceived to be more than legal property. Anything having future economic value is an asset. For example, a lease agreement which grants the lessee property use rights (though not ownership rights) would satisfy this broader asset definition. Deferred charges are separately identified in this definition but are still grouped with assets.

The third definition is a further evolution of the concept that assets are economic resources. Key characteristics of an asset are its capacity to provide future economic benefits, control of the asset by the firm, and the occurrence of the transaction giving rise to control and the economic benefits.

---

[11]Committee on Terminology (1953, para. 26).
[12]APB (1970a, para. 132).
[13]FASB (1980, para. 19).
[14]APB (1970a, para. 57).

The capacity to provide economic benefits has also been called future service potential. It means that an asset is something that will produce positive net cash flows in the future. These cash flows may occur in one of two ways: in a direct market exchange for another asset, or through conversion in a manufacturing operation to finished goods (which are then exchanged for another asset in a market exchange). SFAC 3 also attempts to reconcile this definition with certain types of deferred charges. Some deferred charges, it is argued, do benefit the cash flows of future periods. For example, prepaid costs are deferred charges that will reduce future period outflows of cash. However, other deferred charges are sunk costs and do not have any impact on future cash flows. One example mentioned earlier in the chapter is organization costs.

The "economic resources" approach represents a broader asset concept than legal property and is consistent with the economic notion that an asset has value because of a future income (cash) stream. The genesis of this broader definition can be found in both economic and accounting literature. It represents an emphasis on control of assets rather than legal ownership.

Because the concept of economic resources is broad, a wide variation exists as to (1) how the future benefits will be realized and (2) the probability of realizing future benefits. Under the asset grouping there will be considerable diversity concerning benefits and the probability of realization. The only subclassification reported within the asset group is the current–noncurrent distinction. This tells very little, though, about how the benefits are to be realized and the probability of realizing the benefits. Classification of assets is discussed further in the final section of the chapter.

Broadness of the economic resources concept has led some accountants to prefer a narrower asset concept based on the notions of exchangeability and severability.[15] According to this narrower viewpoint, an accounting asset should represent only those economic resources which can be severed from the firm and sold. This narrower asset definition would reduce variation in the asset group concerning the realization of future benefits—because having value only from productive use would be excluded by this narrower definition. Assets held for use can be argued to have a higher risk of realizing future benefits than assets held directly for sale. It follows that a balance sheet that excludes such assets would have less uncertainty regarding the realization of future benefits.

The severability–exchangeability approach does highlight a weakness in economic value theory. Economic value is often reduced to the one dimension of market exchange prices. An asset may have value in use to its owner but there may not be an external market due to the nature of the asset. For example, the relocation or installation costs of secondhand manufacturing equipment may preclude a market for such goods. But assets held for use still have the potential to generate future cash flows even though they are not directly saleable. The severability–exchangeability ap-

---

[15]Chambers (1966) and Arthur Andersen and Co. (1974).

proach seems to restrict unnecessarily what is included in the balance sheet as an asset.

Asset definitions have evolved from a narrow legal orientation to a broader concept of economic resources. As the definition has broadened, the boundary around what is and what is not an asset has become hazy and ambiguous. It might seem that accountants have not been very successful at defining one of the basic accounting elements. However, the legal profession has also had difficulty in defining assets. In law the following terms have similar but distinctly different meanings: property, property rights, ownership, title, and possession. There is no clear, unambiguous asset concept in law. The opinion was expressed in a Financial Accounting Standards Board (FASB) discussion memorandum that legal definitions and concepts are not helpful in formulating accounting definitions of assets.[16]

EXECUTORY CONTRACTS

A longstanding problem in accounting has been the question of how to account for mutually unperformed executory contracts.[17] A mutually unperformed **executory contract** is a contract unperformed by both parties. The traditional accounting view is that no recognition is required in financial statements because a binding exchange has not yet occurred. The contract is prospective. Two examples of such contracts are employment contracts and long-term purchase agreements. In both cases neither an asset nor a liability is recorded under present practices. However, it can be argued in the case of an employment contract that the employer incurs a liability to pay future wages and receives a benefit in the form of securing future employee services. Similarly, a long-term purchase agreement could be considered a liability for future payments, and an asset for future purchases made under the agreement. However, conventional accounting wisdom regards such contracts as too uncertain and contingent for accounting recognition.

There is nothing in the asset definitions presented above which would exclude recognition of executory contracts. The exclusion is by custom and seems to rest on the belief that a binding transaction has not yet occurred. There has been some argument in favor of recognizing executory contracts as part of general accounting pratice.[18] The suggestion deserves more attention than it has received.

RECOGNITION AND MEASUREMENT OF ASSETS

The following "pervasive principle" has been stated about the initial recognition and measurement of both assets and liabilities:

[16]FASB (1976, para. 122).
[17]Executory contracts were discussed in accounting literature as early as Canning (1929).
[18]See Hughes (1978), Ijiri (1975, Chapter 8), and Ijiri (1980).

> Assets and liabilities generally are initially recorded on the basis of events in which the enterprise acquires resources from other entities or incurs obligations to other entities. The assets and liabilities are measured by the exchange prices at which the transfers take place.[19]

Hence assets are initially recognized when the transaction transferring control occurs. At this point in time, a potential exists for future economic benefits. Assets are measured at the market value (exchange price) of the consideration exchanged or sacrificed to acquire the assets and place them in operating condition. This is called historical acquisition cost. However, in no case should an asset be recorded in excess of its cash equivalent purchase price. When the consideration is nonmonetary, the market value of the asset received may provide a more reliable basis for measuring acquisition cost. This reflects a primary concern for measurement reliability.

The remainder of this section reviews how specific types of assets are measured in periods subsequent to acquisition. As will be seen, numerous attributes are measured such as original acquisition cost (historical cost), historical cost less cumulative charges to income (book value), replacement cost, selling prices, net realizable value (selling price less disposal costs), and net realizable value less normal markups. This eclectic approach to accounting measurement violates the additivity principle of measurement theory. The resultant balance sheet may convey relevant information to users, but from a pure measurement theory viewpoint it can be criticized for a lack of additivity. One often suggested solution to the additivity problem is multicolumn reporting, with each column representing a different attribute of measurement.[20] However, there is a possibility that expanded reporting might confuse users, on account of information overload.

Receivables

Receivables are carried at historical cost, adjusted by the estimate of uncollectible amounts. The attribute being measured is an approximation of net realizable value. However, a true measure of net realizable value would be the selling price of receivables through factoring—less any estimated liability for recourse due to nonpayment by the debtors. Since factoring involves present value discounting, the accounting approximation of net realizable value is overstated by the amount of interest implicit in factoring.

Investments Not Subject to Equity Accounting

SFAS 12 requires that marketable equity securities must be carried at the lower of historical cost or current market value. Marketable securities are grouped into two portfolios representing current and noncurrent investments. The cost or market rule is applied to each portfolio as a whole. Any writedown to market value is recorded as a charge to income for the

[19] APB (1970a, para. 145).
[20] American Accounting Association (1966) and Stamp (1980).

current portfolio, and charged to owners' equity as an unrealized capital adjustment for the noncurrent portfolio. If a writedown is considered permanent, however, the loss is recognized in the income statement even for the noncurrent portfolio. Other investments (besides marketable equity securities) are also accounted for by the lower of cost or market rule. However, each investment is evaluated on an individual rather than a portfolio basis.

Investment portfolios of financial institutions such as insurance companies and mutual funds are subject to specialized industry practices.[21] Current market prices are used to measure the value of securities, and the resultant gains or losses are reported in the income statement.

Investments Subject to Equity Accounting

Equity securities in an amount of 20% to 50% of the outstanding voting stock are normally accounted for using the equity method under the requirements of APB 18.[22] When equity accounting is used the investment no longer represents a real attribute of measurement. It is best described as adjusted historical cost, with the adjustment determined by the rules of equity accounting. The investment is increased for the equity share of investee income after eliminating any profit arising from investor–investee transactions, and is reduced for amortization of any purchase differential and dividends paid by the investee company.

It can be argued that an investment accounted for by equity accounting may approximate the current selling price of the securities. However, there is no compelling reason to believe this to be true. The attribute being measured is a unique accounting concept. There is no direct measurement of the attribute by reference to a market price. The attribute does not exist in the real world; it can be derived only by applying the rules of APB 18. This peculiar effect on the balance sheet represents another example of the revenue–expense approach to accounting policy. The main emphasis of equity accounting is on the income statement, with less concern given to the introduction of a dubious measurement in the balance sheet.

Investments in excess of 50% are reported through consolidation with the investor's (parent company's) own accounts. This topic is examined further in Chapter 17.

Inventories

Ending inventory is measured by first determining the quantity on hand, then multiplying this quantity times the unit acquisition cost. A choice must be arbitrarily made as to the assumed unit cost, and this depends on the flow assumption made. Major alternative flow assumptions

---

[21]Industry-specific accounting policies are recommended in industry accounting and audit guides and *Statements of Position* issued by the AICPA. The FASB is in the process of reissuing *Statements of Position* as formal accounting standards.
[22]APB (1971a).

are FIFO, LIFO, and weighted average. The attribute being measured is historical cost in all methods. However, the result is arbitrary because unit prices will differ depending on the flow assumption. A FIFO pricing of inventory will price the cost of goods sold assuming the oldest stock is sold first. Ending inventory is priced at the most recent unit cost. The reverse is true with LIFO. Goods are assumed sold from the most recent purchases, leaving ending inventory as the oldest units on hand. It is not necessary that goods actually flow in the manner assumed by the inventory pricing system and this is why the methods are arbitrary. Other inventory pricing systems exist in specialized industries; for example, dollar-value LIFO, retail inventory, process costing and job order costing.

Accounting Research Bulletin (ARB) 43 requires a lower of cost or market rule to be used in inventory measurement.[23] Market value is defined as replacement cost, but a range is established in which replacement cost must fall. The upper limit is net realizable value and the lower limit is net realizable value less a normal markup. The upper and lower limits are used only if replacement cost falls outside the range. These upper and lower limits reduce fluctuations in accounting income between periods when inventory is written down. This policy reflects a concern for the income statement effect of inventory writedowns.

In summary, inventory is carried out at the lower of historical cost or market (replacement cost). Historical cost is an arbitrary amount owing to the required assumption concerning the flow of goods. If replacement cost is lower than historical cost, the actual measurement may be one of replacement cost, net realizable value, or net realizable value less a normal markup. This variety exists because there are upper and lower limits on the value of replacement cost which may be used in applying the lower of cost or market rule.

Self-Constructed Assets and Manufactured Inventories

The measurement problem with regard to self-constructed assets concerns the identification of costs incurred to create the asset. The problem of cost identification applies to any type of asset which is self-constructed or manufactured rather than purchased. However, two specific problem areas are discussed—inventory production and the treatment of interest costs.

A controversy surrounds the measurement of manufactured inventory. The controversy concerns the treatment of certain costs. Two methods are discussed in accounting literature: variable costing and full absorption costing.[24] Only variable production costs are charged to inventory under variable costing. All fixed costs, such as overhead allocations and supervisory salaries, are expensed as period costs. Full absorption costing attempts to assign all costs to the production of inventory, both fixed and variable.

---

[23]Committee on Accounting Procedure (1953).
[24]See Sorter and Horngren (1962) for a good summary of these issues.

This necessitates the development of arbitrary overhead rates based on assumed production levels.

ARB 43 requires the use of full absorption costing. It is argued that a better estimate of the total production cost is achieved with full absorption costing. From a measurement viewpoint, however, the attribute being measured under full absorption costing is not clear. Since some fixed costs are incurred over a wide range of production it is questionable if fixed costs are part of the direct, unavoidable sacrifice required to produce inventory. This accounting debate is not resolved by the asset definition presented in SFAC 3.

SFAS 34 requires an amount representing interest costs on borrowed funds to be added to the acquisition cost of self-constructed assets if the amount is significant.[25] The requirement applies to assets constructed for use or sale, but not to routine inventory production. This policy is justified on the grounds that interest on borrowed funds is part of the total sacrifice required to acquire the asset. Similar practices apply to the capitalization of property taxes and insurance costs on land and buildings which are being readied for production. However, one of the major criticisms of SFAS 34 is that it imputes an interest cost regardless of whether any specific debt has been incurred to finance the asset construction. In such cases the interest cost is only a *notional charge*, or *opportunity cost*, rather than an actual incurred cost. Another criticism is that interest is not added to the acquisition cost of other assets. Interest is usually treated as a period expense and is classified as a financing cost. Therefore, SFAS 34 is inconsistent with general accounting policies for interest expense recognition.

Assets Subject to Depreciation or Depletion

The historical acquisition cost of assets which are depreciated or depleted is allocated over estimated useful life. Depreciation allocation is achieved by any of several arbitrary methods: straight-line, sum of the years' digits, declining balance, and units-of-production. There are no relevant circumstances which dictate that any one method must be used in a particular situation. The policy choice is subject only to the constraint of consistency from year to year.

Specialized depreciation systems are used in certain situations. These systems include group and composite depreciation, the replacement and retirement methods, and the inventory depreciation system. All these systems are simpler to apply than regular methods and are acceptable only on the grounds that the results do not vary materially from conventional depreciation methods.

Costs of natural resources are depleted rather than depreciated. Depletion costs are allocated over useful life in the same manner as depreciable assets. The units-of-production method is used, in which an estimate must

---

[25] FASB (1979).

be made of the total expected production. Yearly depletion cost is based on the pro rata amount of production. These depletion costs are charged to inventory and become expensed when the inventory is sold.

The balance sheet carrying value for assets subject to depreciation and depletion is historical cost less cumulative allocations of cost to the income statement. This amount is called **book value.** Book values do not represent real attributes and therefore cannot be directly measured. They can only be calculated by applying the rules specified in the depreciation or depletion method being used. This is another example of a unique accounting attribute.

Nonmonetary Exchanges of Similar Assets

APB 29 establishes a unique rule to account for nonmonetary exchanges of similar assets. The rule is contrary to the general principle of using the value of the sacrifice to measure the transaction.[26] In a nonmonetary exchange the sacrifice to obtain a new asset consists of a traded-in asset and possibly some cash. Under APB 29, the new asset is recorded at the book value of the traded-in asset (rather than market value), plus any additional cash consideration. As with other asset acquisitions the cash equivalent purchase price sets an upper limit on the recorded value. The rationale for this policy is that an exchange of similar assets represents a continuation of the earning process. It is as though the former asset is embodied in the new asset, thus justifying no recognition of a gain or loss on the old asset disposal. Any implied gain or loss is recognized indirectly through subsequent depreciation. This accounting policy is at variance with general accounting practices. One reason for its existence may be that a similar (though not identical) procedure exists under Internal Revenue Service regulations.

Intangible Assets

Assets can be classified into tangible and intangible assets. Physical substance is the distinguishing criterion. It is not a good characteristic, however, because some assets (such as accounts receivable, investments, and capitalized lease rights) are legally intangible in nature, yet are not regarded as such by accountants. Assets more commonly thought of as intangible are copyrights, patents, and trademarks. Also considered to be intangible assets are purchased franchise rights and purchased goodwill.

All intangible assets are initially recorded at the sacrifice incurred to acquire the assets. APB 17 brought some order to intangibles by requiring straight-line amortization of costs over a period not exceeding forty years. If a shorter period of economic benefit exists, it should be used. Copyrights, patents, and franchise agreements all have finite legal lives which can be used to determine a more specific period of future economic benefit. In

[26] APB (1973).

these circumstances a specific amortization period can be determined which reflects useful economic life.

It can be argued that amortization of intangibles (such as trademarks and purchased goodwill) is not necessary because they have an unlimited life. APB 17 rejected this notion in favor of compulsory amortization. Prior to APB 17 it was common not to amortize goodwill. APB 17 can best be understood as an attempt to bring rigid uniformity to a subjective area of practice, one where flexibility was producing poor comparability.

Like assets subject to depreciation and depletion, intangible assets are measured at historical cost less cumulative charges to income. As stated before, book value is a unique accounting attribute of measurement.

Until SFAS 2, research and development costs were capitalized and classified as an intangible asset. The justification was that future benefits existed in the form of probable future patents or products having economic value. However, uncertainty surrounding the likelihood of realizing these benefits led to the uniform policy in SFAS 2 of expensing all research and development costs as incurred. This is another example of a situation where the concern about measurement reliability led to rigid uniformity in the form of expensing all research and development costs. Obviously, some research and development expenditures would satisfy the asset definition in SFAC 3. The FASB's policy in SFAS 2 can be seen as emphasizing measurement reliability rather than representational faithfulness or relevance.

Deferred Charges

There are two distinct types of deferred charges. One type represents prepaid costs which provide a future benefit in the form of reduced future cash outflows for services; for example, prepaid insurance. Prepayments are normally allocated to the income statement on a straight-line basis over the period of future benefit. The other type of deferred charge represents a cost which is being deferred from expense recognition solely because of income measurement rules. This latter type includes organizational startup costs, tax liability in excess of accounting-based tax expense, pension fund contributions in excess of accrued pension expenses (discussed in Chapter 15), and deferred losses on sale–leasebacks (discussed in Chapter 16). Most deferred charges are amortized in the same manner as intangible assets except where specific requirements apply.

SUMMARY OF ASSET MEASUREMENT

This review is by no means comprehensive of all assets. Some topics were omitted, because they are covered in later chapters; for example, deferred tax charges, leased assets, and capitalization of oil and gas exploration costs. Individual assets in the balance sheet may represent one of many attributes, some of which are unique accounting concepts and have no real-world meaning. Book values of depreciable assets and investments accounted for under equity accounting are two examples of unique accounting attributes. Such a situation is uncomfortable, at least in terms of measurement theory. However, as stated at the outset of this section, an eclectic balance sheet may still convey relevant information to users. A summary of asset measurement is presented in Exhibit 8-2.

There are three distinct types of assets which appear in balance sheets: those held for sale, those which have economic value through use in production, and deferred charges. The benefits of these assets are derived differently and represent differing degrees of certainty and measurement reliability. Assets held for sale and measured at net realizable value (such as receivables) represent a high degree of certainty as to realization as well as measurement reliability. Assets held for production represent more uncertainty as to the realization of future economic benefits due to the inherent uncertainty of manufacturing. Furthermore, historical cost gives little indication of the productive value of such assets. Finally, certain types of deferred charges do not have any impact on future cash flows.

Because of the wide variation in asset realization and measurement, it is very difficult to interpret assets in the aggregate. In terms of additivity, it

---

EXHIBIT 8-2.

Summary of Asset Measurement

Asset	Attribute(s)
Receivables	Approximation of net realizable value.
Investments (not subject to APB 18)	Cost, lower of cost or market, or market, depending on the type of investment and the reporting entity.
Investments (subject to APB 18)	Unique accounting attribute (equity accounting).
Inventories	Cost, replacement cost, net realizable value, or net realizable value less normal markup.
Self-constructed assets	Full absorption costing for inventory, and capitalization of interest for noninventory assets.
Assets subject to depreciation or depletion	Unique accounting attribute (book value).
Nonmonetary exchanges of similar assets	Book value of old asset plus cash.
Intangible assets	Unique accounting attribute (book value).
Deferred charges	Unique accounting attribute (book value).

is questionable if a balance sheet can really be added. It is added, of course, and used for ratio analysis. However, relevance or usefulness may be impaired because of the additivity problem.

LIABILITIES

DEFINITION OF ACCOUNTING LIABILITIES

Definitions of accounting liabilities have evolved over time in a manner similar to that of asset definitions. The three major statements on liabilities are:

Accounting Terminology Bulletin 1

Something represented by a credit balance that is or would be properly carried forward upon a closing of books of account according to the rules or principles of accounting, provided such credit balance is not in effect a negative balance applicable to an asset. Thus the word is used broadly to comprise not only items which constitute liabilities in the popular sense of debts or obligations (including provision for those that are unascertained), but also credit balances to be accounted for which do not involve a debtor and creditor relation. For example, capital stock and related or similar elements of proprietorship are balance sheet liabilities in that they represent balances to be accounted for, though these are not liabilities in the ordinary sense of debts owed to legal creditors.[27]

APB Statement 4

Economic obligations of an enterprise that are recognized and measured in conformity with generally accepted accounting principles. Liabilities also include certain deferred credits that are not obligations but that are recognized and measured in conformity with generally accepted accounting principles.[28]

SFAC 3

Liabilities are probable future sacrifices of economic benefits arising from present obligations of a particular entity to transfer assets or provide services to other entities in the future as a result of past transactions or events.[29]

An entity theory view of the firm is implied in the first definition. No distinction is made between owners' equity and liabilities. The entity theory views the firm as a self-sufficient enterprise, and both liabilities and

---

[27]Committee on Terminology (1953, para. 27).
[28]APB (1970a, para. 132).
[29]FASB (1980, para. 28).

owners' equity are sources of external capital for which the firm is account-able. In the other two liability definitions no mention is made of owners' equity, which seems to imply a proprietary view of the firm in which own-ers' equity represents owners' residual interest in the net assets.

The liability portion of the first definition emphasizes legal debts. In the second definition, the liability concept is broadened to mean economic obligations. APB Statement 4 defines economic obligations as the respon-sibility to transfer economic resources or provide services to another entity in the future. This parallels the change in the asset definition. In addition, deferred credits are identified separately but are still considered to be a part of liabilities.

The third definition continues the emphasis on economic obligations rather than legal debt. It is also interesting to note that deferred credits have been dropped from the most recent definition. The same thing occurred with deferred charges in the asset definition. SFAC 3 elaborates on the def-inition by listing three essential characteristics of an accounting liability:

1. A duty exists.
2. The duty is virtually unavoidable.
3. The event obligating the enterprise has occurred.

Most liabilities are contractual in nature. **Contractual liabilities** result from events in which a liability arises that is either expressly or implicitly contractual in the legal sense of the term. SFAC 3 indicates that a duty can also arise from constructive and equitable obligations as well as legal con-tracts. A **constructive obligation** is one which is implied rather than ex-pressly written. SFAC 3 specifically mentions the accruals of noncontrac-tual vacation pay and bonuses. An employer duty may exist if such payments have been made in the past even if there is no written agreement to pay them in the future. **Equitable obligations** are an ambiguous, gray area of common law in which a duty is not contractually present, but which may nevertheless exist due to ethical principles of fairness (called equity). The example given in SFAC 3 concerns the responsibility of a monopoly supplier to deliver goods or services to dependent customers. In spite of their mention in SFAC 3, equitable obligations are not presently recognized in balance sheets.

Contingent liabilities are a subset of accounting liabilities. SFAS 5 de-fines these as "An existing situation, or set of circumstances involving un-certainty as to possible gain or loss to an enterprise that will ultimately be resolved when one or more future events will occur or fail to occur."[30] Only losses are recognized, owing to conservatism. A loss contingency (contin-gent liability) is accrued if (1) it is probable that a liability has occurred, or an asset has been impaired, and (2) it can be reliably measured. Examples of contingent liabilities given in SFAS 5 are product warranties and pend-

---

[30]FASB (1975b).

ing or threatened litigation. The definition of a contingent liability is consistent with the SFAC 3 definition, with the additional proviso concerning feasibility and reliability of measurement.

Finally, there are **deferred credits.** While not specifically mentioned in the most recent definition, they continue to be part of the liability section in the balance sheet under present practices. There are two different types of deferred credits. One type represents prepaid revenues; for example, magazine or newspaper subscriptions. When this occurs there is a contractual duty to provide a future good or service. A liability clearly exists in such a situation. The other type of deferred credit is more ambiguous and arises from income rules which defer income statement recognition of the item. Some examples of this second type of deferred credit include investment tax credits (APB 2), deferred gains on sale–leaseback transactions (SFAS 13),and deferred tax credits (APB 11).[31] These types of items impose no obligations on the firm to transfer assets in the future. Rather, they are simply past transactions being deferred from the income statement until future periods.

In summary, accounting liabilities include five distinctly different types of liabilities: contractual liabilities, constructive obligations, equitable obligations, contingent liabilities, and deferred credits. As with assets there are considerable differences within the liability group. However, there does not appear to be the extreme variation which occurs with assets. This is because the core of liabilities is legal in nature. Of the remaining nonlegal liabilities, contingent liabilities are disclosed separately, and deferred credits are identifiable in the balance sheet. As a result, there is a natural subclassification of liabilities which can easily be inferred from the balance sheet. This is not the case with assets.

RECOGNITION AND MEASUREMENT OF LIABILITIES

APB Statement 4 indicates that liabilities are measured at amounts established in the transaction, usually amounts to be paid in the future, sometimes discounted.[32] The general principle is that liabilities are measured at the amount established in the exchange. For current liabilities such as accounts payable this represents the face value of the obligation to be settled in the future. For noncurrent obligations the measurement represents a present value calculation based on current interest rates. An example is bonds, which are recorded at the net proceeds received. The net proceeds represent the stream of interest payments and principle repayment discounted at the current market rate of interest. If the stated interest rate on the bonds is at the current rate, the present value, net proceeds, and face value are all equal at the time of issuance. If the stated interest rate differs from market rates, a premium or discount will occur. The nondiscounting

---

[31]APB (1962), FASB (1975d), and APB (1967a).
[32]APB (1970a, para. 181).

of current liabilities is justified on the grounds of immateriality, that is, the present value is not materially different from the nondiscounted future value.

Notes Payable with Below-Market Rates of Interest

Notes payable with below-market interest rates must be discounted under APB 21.[33] The purpose of the discounting is to adjust the note to an equivalent note having the market rate of interest. The discount is then amortized over the life of the note in order to adjust periodic interest expense to a market rate. By this procedure the real economic value of the transaction is measured at market prices and is consistent with the general principle of discounting noncurrent liabilities at the market rate of interest. An identical procedure is required for notes receivable with below-market interest rates.

Bonds

As noted previously, bonds are initially recorded at the net proceeds of the transaction. The net proceeds are equal to the present value of future interest payments and principle repayment, discounted at the market rate of interest, less any bond issue costs. It is necessary to create a bond premium or discount account if the stated interest rate differs from the market rate. The carrying value of bonds in subsequent balance sheets represents the face value of the bonds plus unamortized premiums or minus unamortized discounts. This is the book value of bonds and is analogous to book value of depreciable assets. Book value of bonds payable is another example of a unique accounting attribute. The book value of bonds must be calculated instead of measured directly. A direct measurement of bonds is not made after they are initially recorded.

Premiums and discounts are amortized to income over the term of the bonds by the effective interest method (APB 21). This has the effect of adjusting interest expense to the market rate that existed at the time of issue. Straight-line amortization is also permitted if the results are not materially different from the effective interest method.

Convertible Bonds

Bonds may have a feature which permits an exchange of bonds for common stock. It is typical for convertible bonds to have a lower coupon interest rate than conventional bonds. The reason for this is that investors are willing to pay a price for the conversion option and the price is paid in the form of lower interest rates. For this reason convertible bonds have elements of both debt and owners' equity. The foregone interest can be thought of as capital donated to the firm in exchange for this privilege.

---

[33] APB (1971c).

Two policies have been used to account for convertible bonds. One approach is to treat convertible debt as conventional debt until conversion. This is the method required under APB 14.[34] The other approach is to segregate an amount of the debt as the price paid for the conversion privilege, and to add this amount to contributed capital. Interest on the face amount of the debt is imputed, using the market rate for nonconvertible debt which existed at the time of issue. This more complex approach was adopted in APB 10, suspended almost immediately in APB 12, and superseded in APB 14.[35] The reason for suspension was the perception of measurement difficulties. There was subjectivity concerning the choice of market interest rate, and, so long as a subjective evaluation could be made, the results were of questionable reliability. Because of the perceived measurement problems, APB 14 established a simpler method of accounting by treating convertible debt as regular bonds.

Convertible debt highlights the limitations of the accounting classification system (see Exhibit 8-1). The balance sheet is incapable of subtle distinctions such as those implied by convertible versus conventional bonds. However, APB 15 requires recognition of the conversion feature in earnings per share (EPS) calculations.[36] Bonds meeting the cash yield test are treated "as if" they are converted for primary EPS calculations, if the effect is dilutive. Bonds not meeting the cash yield test are treated "as if" they are converted for fully diluted EPS, if the effect is dilutive. Limitations of accounting classification are more easily overcome with EPS rules, however, because EPS is supplemental disclosure rather than part of the financial statements.

When convertible debt is converted, a gain or loss is not normally recognized. The rationale for not recognizing a gain or loss is that, since the security has both debt and equity characteristics, the conversion represents only a reclassification of the security from debt to equity. This procedure is inconsistent with SFAS 4, which deals with accounting for early retirement of debt.[37] Because convertible debt is initially accounted for as conventional debt, it would be logical to recognize a gain or loss on conversion. Conversion represents the equivalent of early debt retirement. In other words, two separate transactions are implied by APB 14. The first is the recording as conventional debt, then there is the equivalent of early retirement and the issue of common stock in exchange for debt retirement. Since no initial recognition is given to the conversion feature prior to conversion, it is inconsistent to ignore gains and losses on the grounds that the conversion merely represents a reclassification from debt to equity. APB 14 is therefore inconsistent.

---

[34] APB (1969a).
[35] APB (1966b), APB (1967b), and APB (1969a).
[36] APB (1969b).
[37] FASB (1975a).

Debt with Stock Warrants

APB 14 requires that a value be assigned to detachable stock warrants which may accompany the issue of debt. This policy is inconsistent with the treatment of convertible debt. The reason for the two different policies is that a convertible bond is argued to be either debt or equity at any one time; it cannot be both simultaneously. Detachable warrants, however, permit the holder to own simultaneously both debt and equity (if the warrant is exercised). Therefore, part of the proceeds can be thought of as a direct payment for the right to buy stock. And since a market price is readily determinable for stock warrants, there is not the measurement problem encountered with convertible debt.

In theory, there is little distinction between convertible debt and debt with detachable stock warrants. In both cases an amount of money is being paid in the transaction for the right to acquire stock. The money paid for this privilege is clearly identifiable in the case of detachable warrants traded in the market. It is a more subjective calculation in the case of convertible debt. Hence, measurement reliability considerations have led to two different accounting policies for two similar areas of accounting.

SUMMARY OF LIABILITY MEASUREMENT

Like assets, liabilities are recognized when the transaction giving rise to the obligation occurs. There are many different types of accounting liabilities just as there are many different types of assets. Unlike assets, however, the different types of accounting liabilities are more easily recognized in the balance sheet. The different types of accounting liabilities represent differing degrees of obligations to the firm. For example, not all accounting liabilities represent legal debt, so in the case of bankruptcy some accounting liabilities would be ignored. The certainty of differing types of obligations also differs, as well as the reliability of measurement. Legal debt has a high probability of being paid and has a high degree of measurement reliability as well. Certain types of deferred credits, on the other hand, do not represent future cash flows at all. Contingent liabilities often represent a lower degree of measurement reliability than other accounting liabilities. All these characteristics must be considered in evaluating accounting liabilities. As with assets, it is difficult to interpret liabilities in the aggregate because of these differences.

Liabilities are initially measured at face value of the future obligation in the case of current liabilities. There is no present value adjustment. Noncurrent liabilities are initially measured at the present value of future interest and principal repayments. The current market rate of interest is used as the discount rate. This is not a subjective measurement because market values of debt are established in exactly the same manner—the discounting of a stream of payments at the market rate of interest. There may exist a premium or discount which is amortized to the income statement over the term of the debt. Book value of debt is used in subsequent balance sheets. This is a unique accounting attribute representing face value of debt adjusted for any unamortized premiums or discounts.

OWNERS' EQUITY

DEFINITION OF OWNERS' EQUITY

Owners' equity is defined as the stockholders' residual interest in the net assets of the firm. This definition represents the proprietary theory of the firm in which stockholders are perceived to be owners. It will be recalled from the liability definition in Accounting Terminology Bulletin No. 1 that no clear distinction was made between liabilities and owners' equity. However, APB Statement 4 and SFAC 3 do make a distinction between the two: APB Statement 4 offers a passive definition of owners' equity as the excess of the firm's assets over its liabilities. The same approach is also taken in SFAC 3. Both definitions imply a proprietary ownership of the firm by the stockholders.

In a sole proprietorship, owners' equity can be represented by a single owner's equity account. The corporate form of ownership form gives rise to a legal distinction between contributed capital and earned capital (retained earnings). Dividends can legally be paid only from the latter. So a typical breakdown of total owners' equity will include contributed capital and retained earnings. Contributed capital may be subclassified into legal capital and other capital. Legal capital represents the limited liability of stockholders. If shares are fully paid up there is no additional stockholder liability. Legal capital is measured at par value, or at the issue price if the stock is no par. Other contributed capital includes stock premiums, donated capital, capital from the reissue of treasury stock, and capital from the issue of stock options and warrants.

A third component of owners' equity (see Exhibit 8-1) represents unrealized gains or losses. As indicated previously in this chapter, certain changes in net asset values are recognized in the balance sheet; but instead of these amounts being charged to the income statement, they are classified as capital adjustments. The sources of these adjustments are unrealized portfolio losses for noncurrent marketable securities (SFAS 12) and unrealized foreign exchange gains or losses from the translation of foreign net assets into dollars (SFAS 52).

RECOGNITION AND MEASUREMENT OF OWNERS' EQUITY

Owners' equity transactions can be of two types—capital transactions or income-related transactions. Capital transactions represent the direct contributions or withdrawals of assets by owners. Income-related transactions represent income statement transactions and prior period adjustments which pertain to income of previous periods. This chapter deals only with capital transactions. The next chapter addresses income-related transactions. The general principle of measurement for all capital transactions is the same as for assets and liabilities: the market value at the time of the transaction. These values are then carried forward unchanged in subsequent balance sheets.

Contributed capital is measured by the value of assets contributed to the firm by stockholders. It is possible to contribute services rather than assets, in which case the value of the services is used to measure contributed capital. If the value of contributed assets or services exceeds the legal capital of issued stock, the excess is recorded as a premium. Other sources of contributed capital include conversions of convertible debt and the issue of detachable stock warrants with debt. These two sources of contributed capital were discussed earlier in the liability section of the chapter. Two other sources of contributed capital are the reissue of treasury stock and the issue of employee stock options. The measurement of these capital transactions is discussed below.

Retained earnings is equal to the cumulative income or loss of the firm as measured by the rules of income determination, less distributions of earnings as cash dividends. Prior period adjustments will also affect the retained earnings balance. Income determination and prior period adjustments are examined in the next chapter. Stock dividends also affect the balance of retained earnings and are discussed in the section that follows.

Stock Options

Employee stock option plans (ESOPs) are considered a form of deferred compensation to employees if there is a bargain purchase price established in the plan. If a bargain purchase does exist, the accounting recognition and measurement focuses on the value of the bargain purchase option. The value represents additional compensation and a corresponding amount is credited to other contributed capital. Employee services are deemed to be exchanged for the right to buy stock below market price. Measurement at four different points in time has been discussed in the literature. The four dates are the grant date, receipt date by the employee, the first exercisable date, and the actual exercise date. The actual value to the employee is known with certainty only on the exercise date. If measurement occurs any earlier, it must be based on the estimated value of the option to the employee.

APB 25 requires the bargain amount of stock options to be allocated as a periodic expense from the grant date through the period of service required to receive the benefits.[38] The bargain amount is measured by the difference between market price and the stock option exercise price on the measurement date. The measurement date is defined as the point in time when both the number of options and the exercise price are known. Usually the grant date and measurement date are one and the same, in which case the measurement is straightforward. A deferred compensation expense account is debited and contributed capital is credited for the total bargain purchase. The deferred compensation expense is amortized over the number of periods required to exercise the options. The debit is a contra-capital account.

If either the number of shares or exercise price is unknown at grant date, a yearly estimate must be made of both. In such a situation it is also necessary to estimate the market price of the stock at the future measurement date. Having made these necessary estimates, one must make a yearly accrual of the estimated additional compensation expense arising from the options. This results in a debit to expense and a credit to contributed capital, just for an estimate of the current period cost. The entire bargain purchase is not recognized because it is not yet determinable. However, an estimate is made of the bargain purchase and the pro rata effect on yearly compensation expense. At measurement date (the point when both number of shares and exercise price is known) the actual compensation cost is measured by subtracting the option price from the market price on that date. The actual bargain value of the ESOP at measurement date, less previous yearly expense recognition based on estimates, is debited to deferred compensation expense and amortized over the remaining service period required to exercise the options. A corresponding amount is credited to contributed capital. This procedure represents a change in accounting estimate and any adjustment is made prospectively as required under APB 20.[39]

Contributed capital is credited for the bargain purchase element in an ESOP. The rationale for this policy is that employee services are being exchanged for the opportunity to buy stock below market price. This amount is considered to be part of the consideration given by these shareholders for the right to buy stock under an ESOP.

Treasury Stock

United States corporations are permitted to trade in their own securities. However, state laws and accounting policies prohibit companies from recognizing income on such transactions. This prohibition is intended to discourage stock price manipulations. Reacquired stock is classified as a contra-account to outstanding stock. The stock is still legally issued, but is not considered to be outstanding.

---

[38] APB (1972).
[39] APB (1971b).

Two methods may be used to account for treasury stock, the cost and par value methods. The methods differ only in terms of the accounts used, but the net effect on owners' equity is the same. This is an example of flexibility since there is unconditional choice in the selection of the accounting policy. However, it makes very little difference since the only effect is on subclassifications within owners' equity. When treasury stock is reissued, the difference between reissue price and carrying value of the treasury stock is recorded as contributed capital.

Stock Dividends

ARB 43 requires two separate accounting policies for stock dividends, depending on the size of the dividend.[40] Large stock dividends are defined as those over 25% and are accounted for by reclassifying retained earnings to contributed capital based on the par value of the stock issued. Small stock dividends are defined as those less than 20%. The accounting policy is to reclassify retained earnings to contributed capital, on the basis of the market value of the stock and using predividend market prices to value the dividend. A gray area exists from 20% to 25% in which either method may be used.

An attempt has been made in the area of stock dividends to use the size of the dividend to define relevant circumstances. However, little defense can be made for using the predividend market price per share to value the transaction because total market value of outstanding stock should not change on account of stock dividends. All that has occurred is an increase in the total number of shares. The market price per share should decline exactly in proportion to the dilutive effect of the new shares. If the price is not diluted, it is due to the existence of other new information which causes investors to revise their assessment of the stock.[41]

Using the par value to measure a stock dividend makes more sense given that the total market value of outstanding stock should be unchanged. It can even be argued that a stock dividend is no different in principle from a stock split in which no change is recorded in owners' equity. This is unacceptable for stock dividends, though, because the dollar amount of legal capital has increased. So, reclassification of retained earnings to contributed capital is necessary because there has been an increase in legally issued capital.

It is difficult to justify finite uniformity that is based on size of the dividend. This does not appear to be a relevant circumstance justifying two accounting methods. For both large and small dividends, market price per share should fall in accordance with the dilutive effect of the stock dividend. Therefore, use of predividend market prices is a hard policy to defend.

[40]Committee on Accounting Procedure (1953).
[41]Capital market reserach supports the argument there is no theoretical change in the value of the firm. See Foster (1978) for a review of this research.

CLASSIFICATION IN THE STATEMENT OF FINANCIAL POSITION

ARB 43 requires classification of assets and liabilities based on liquidity. Two classifications are used—current and noncurrent. Current is defined as the firm's operating cycle or one year, whichever is longer. The operating cycle is the time required to go from materials acquisition to cash collection from revenues. Operating cycles will differ from firm to firm and industry to industry. A liquidity ranking within the current and noncurrent groups is also normally made, though it is not required by any specific accounting standard.

The current–noncurrent approach gives only a crude indication of a firm's liquidity. Current assets cannot be used to assess critical cash flow capacity because the operating cycle may be a year or even longer. In addition, the current asset grouping contains some assets which do not affect current cash flows at all; for example, deferred charges and credits. Other classifications might be better for liquidity assessment. For example, a monetary–nonmonetary classification system combined with a current–noncurrent classification would give a better understanding of future cash flows. The problems of liquidity measurement are considered further in Chapter 10 when discussing the statement of changes in financial position.

Another way of subclassifying assets would be those held for exchange (sale), those held for use, and those representing deferred charges. This would provide some additional information about how economic benefits will be realized and the uncertainty surrounding realization. As indicated earlier in the chapter, considerable variation exists in the asset group. As a general rule, the realization of future benefits will be more uncertain from production than from exchange. A classification system based on this approach would communicate relevant information about how the benefits will be realized and give some awareness of the relative risks concerning the realization of the benefits. A case could also be made that the most relevant information to report would be net realizable values for assets held for sale, and replacement costs for assets held for production (assuming replacement would in fact occur).

More detailed reporting could also be made of liabilities. There are five distinctly different types of accounting liabilities: contractual, constructive, equitable, contingent, and deferred charges. Separate classifications by type would assist in evaluating the nature of the different types of obligations. As mentioned earlier in the chapter, it is relatively easy to group liabilities into these classifications. It would also aid the reader of balance sheets to know which liabilities are legally enforceable in the event of bankruptcy and which ones are not. As with assets, liabilities also have differing degrees of certainty concerning realization.

Finally, from a pure measurement viewpoint, classifying assets by the attribute being measured might aid in understanding the eclectic nature of measurement in the balance sheet. There are numerous asset attributes being measured and reported in a balance sheet. It is not always clear from reading a balance sheet just how much variation there is in asset measurement. By custom, a balance sheet is added. In terms of measurement theory, the accounting elements in a balance sheet are not additive because of the different attributes being measured. This does not mean that balance sheets or financial ratios lack relevance, but the additivity question does raise an important issue concerning usefulness.

SUMMARY

Definitions of accounting elements determine the types of economic events which are recognized as accounting transactions and how they are classified in the accounting classification system illustrated in Exhibit 8-1. Yet it is apparent that the definitions are of a general nature and that the transactions we recognize in accounting are derived as much from tradition as from the definitions of elements themselves. This may be inevitable. However, the value of good definitions from a policy-making perspective is that they enable policy-makers to categorize and understand new types of transactions. Definitions should also aid in identifying those areas of existing practice which are inconsistent. In any science, classification is fundamental to understanding the nature of the discipline. The same is true of accounting classification and the understanding of economic events being reported in the financial statements.

Historical cost is considered to be the basis of measurement in accounting. While the historical cost model is the basic system which is used, it is very clear that many other types of measurement are embodied in current practices. The many attributes of asset measurement were summarized in Exhibit 8-2. Liability measurement is less eclectic than asset measurement, but it too has variation. Face amount of debt is measured for current liabilities, and noncurrent debt is initially measured at discounted present values. Capital transactions in owners' equity basically represent the historical amounts of the transactions. However, as was evident, there are different ways of determining the values of some capital transactions, for example treasury stock transactions and stock dividends.

This chapter should make it clear that accounting policy and practice are pragmatic. There is no single global accounting model on which accounting policy is based. Departures from historical costs are frequently made. There are many reasons for the departures. The lower of cost or market rule represents balance sheet conservatism. Some accounting practices exist because of measurement reliability problems—for example, the treatment of convertible debt. Other departures exist because more relevant information may be conveyed by the reporting of current values—for example, the use of current exchange rates to translate foreign operations. As stated throughout this chapter, the balance sheet violates the concept of additivity. However, it must be remembered that accounting policies are the result of a political process and inevitable compromises. In addition, measurement purity per se does not insure that accounting information will be useful or relevant.

QUESTIONS

1. What are the characteristics of assets, liabilities, and owners' equity? How have they evolved over time?
2. Why is it difficult to define accounting elements?
3. Why are asset and liability definitions important to the theoretical structure of accounting? Why are definitions important to policy-setting bodies?
4. Numerous attributes are measured in the statement of financial position. What are the different attributes? Why is this practice criticized?
5. What do aggregated balance sheet totals represent? This data is used for ratio analysis. How useful do you think ratio analysis is?
6. Three approaches have been advocated concerning the definition of accounting elements and the relationship between the balance sheet and income statement. What are the three approaches and how do they differ?
7. What is the meaning of "owners' equity" in the balance sheet? Why are certain unrealized gains or losses included in owners' equity?
8. What are deferred charges and deferred credits, how do they come about, and do they conform to asset and liability definitions?
9. Why have mutually unperformed executory contracts traditionally been excluded from financial statements? Can this practice be justified in terms of asset and liability definitions? How relevant is this approach for professional sports franchises?
10. What is the purpose of balance sheet classification? How useful is the information produced from a classified balance sheet? What are some alternative classification systems which could be used?
11. As a potential investor, what do you feel would be the most useful attribute of measurement for each of the following: inventories held for sale, inventories held for production, and long-term debt? Would your answer differ if you were a potential lender? What if you were a man-

ager of a company? What measurement problems are illustrated in this question?

12. Why is it difficult to determine the historical acquisition cost of self-constructed assets? Do definitions of accounting elements and general principles of recognition and measurement resolve the controversy over full absorption costing and variable costing of manufactured inventory?

13. Throughout the chapter reference was made to the limitation of the accounting classification system depicted in Exhibit 8-1. What is meant by this? Give some examples. Why is the accounting classification system the foundation of the accounting discipline?

14. Employee stock option plans represent a classic accounting measurement problem involving the trade-off between relevance and reliability. Explain why this is so. Does relevance or reliability seem to dominate in the accounting requirements of APB 25?

15. Based on your reading of this chapter, plus your general knowledge of accounting standards, identify as many examples as you can of measurement flexibility in the statement of financial position.

CASES AND PROBLEMS

1. SFAS 5, paragraph 5, defines a contingent liability as ". . . an existing condition, situation, or set of circumstances involving uncertainty as to . . . possible loss . . . to an enterprise that will ultimately be resolved when one or more future events occur or fail to occur." Paragraph 8 indicates that a contingent liability should be recognized (1) if the contingency exists at balance date, (2) if it is probable that future events will confirm the existence of the loss, and (3) if the loss can be reasonably estimated. Evaluate this definition of a contingent liability. Include in your assessment a comparison with the liability definition in SFAC 3. Are recognition and measurement considerations clearly separated from the definition? What trade-offs seem to be implied between relevance and reliability?

2. Review a recent annual report. Identify all attributes of measurement which are explicitly identified in the balance sheet and accompanying notes. Notice which items are not specified. Group the accounting elements by attribute. How thorough is the explanation of measurement in the balance sheet? Identify any unusual assets or liabilities. How useful is the current–noncurrent distinction for assessing liquidity? Based on your review, what level of user sophistication do you think is

necessary to understand how the balance sheet numbers have been derived? How useful do you think the balance sheet is? What are its limitations, and how might it be improved, especially from a communication viewpoint?

3. In 1983, a number of computer software companies reported use of an accounting procedure which was investigated by the SEC. The accounting policy is to capitalize the cost of developing computer software and amortize it over the life of the software (usually three to five years). This procedure is used by large and small companies, but the impact is more pronounced on smaller, new companies, in which a greater portion of their activity is devoted to software development.

An article in *The Wall Street Journal,* April 8, 1983, page 4, noted:

> . . . the procedure has a bigger effect on small companies that specialize in software, such as Comserv. Comserv's president, Richard Daly, said the company's deferred expenses totaled $11.3 million last year with the method. Its net income in the period was $2.5 million, and its assets (including the software costs) $53 million, he said.
>
> The issue, while somewhat arcane to non-accountants, is important to the software industry, which produces computer programs and related equipment. For the past few months, some computer software concerns and their trade group, the Association of Data-Processing Service Organizations, have been negotiating the issue with SEC aides. Mr. Daly of Comserv, defending the practice, said small companies wouldn't be able to invest as much cash in their own growth if they couldn't use the method.
>
> "The costs of developing these (software) products have gone up tremendously" in recent years, Mr. Daly said. His company's products include computerized systems to help manage inventory and ordering at auto and other manufacturing plants. If companies charged the development costs to their income, they would be under greater pressure to keep the costs down so they can show a decent profit, he said.

The SEC's concern is whether this accounting policy is consistent with SFAS 2 concerning the expensing of research and development costs as incurred.

Required:
(a) Evaluate the software capitalization argument with reference to SFAS 2. Should this practice be permitted?
(b) Why is the choice of accounting policies (expensing vs. capitalization) more likely to affect smaller companies?
(c) Comment on the assertion that small companies "wouldn't be able to invest as much cash in their own growth if they couldn't use [capitalization]." Is this a real economic consequence?
(d) If you were an FASB member, how would you vote on this issue? Why?

BIBLIOGRAPHY OF REFERENCED WORKS

Accounting Principles Board (1962). "Accounting for the Investment Credit," *APB Opinion No. 2* (AICPA).
—— (1966a). "Accounting for the Cost of Pension Plans," *APB Opinion No. 8* (AICPA).
—— (1966b). "Omnibus Opinion—1966," *APB Opinion No. 10* (AICPA).
—— (1967a). "Accounting for Income Taxes," *APB Opinion No. 11* (AICPA).
—— (1967b). "Omnibus Opinion—1967," *APB Opinion No. 12* (AICPA).
—— (1969a). "Accounting for Convertible Debt and Debt Issued with Stock Purchase Warrants," *APB Opinion No. 14* (AICPA).
—— (1969b). "Earnings Per Share," *APB Opinion No. 15* (AICPA).
—— (1970a). "Basic Concepts and Accounting Principles Underlying Financial Statements of Business Enterprises," *APB Statement No. 4* (AICPA).
—— (1970b). "Intangible Assets," *APB Opinion No. 17* (AICPA).
—— (1971a). "The Equity Method of Accounting for Investments in Common Stock," *APB Opinion No. 18* (AICPA).
—— (1971b). "Accounting Changes," *APB Opinion No. 20* (AICPA).
—— (1971c). "Interest on Receivables and Payables," *APB Opinion No. 21* (AICPA).
—— (1972). "Accounting for Stock Issued to Employees," *APB Opinion No. 25* (AICPA).
—— (1973). "Accounting for Nonmonetary Transactions," *APB Opinion No. 29* (AICPA).
American Accounting Association (1966). *A Statement of Basic Accounting Theory* (AAA).
Arthur Andersen and Co. (1974). *Accounting Standards for Business Enterprises Throughout the World* (Arthur Andersen and Co.).
Canning, John B. (1929). *The Economics of Accountancy* (Ronald Press).
Chambers, Raymond J. (1966). *Accounting, Evaluation and Economic Behavior* (Prentice-Hall).
Committee on Accounting Procedure (1953). "Restatement and Revision of Accounting Research Bulletins," *ARB No. 43* (AICPA).
Committee on Terminology (1953). "Review and Resume," *Accounting Terminology Bulletin No. 1* (AICPA).
Financial Accounting Standards Board (1974). "Accounting for Research and Development Costs," *Statement of Financial Accounting Standards No. 2* (FASB).
—— (1975a). "Reporting Gains and Losses from Extinguishment of Debt," *Statement of Financial Accounting Standards No. 4* (FASB).
—— (1975b). "Accounting for Contingencies," *Statement of Financial Accounting Standards No. 5* (FASB).
—— (1975c). "Accounting and Reporting by Development Stage Enterprises," *Statement of Financial Accounting Standards No. 7* (FASB).
—— (1975d). "Accounting for Certain Marketable Securities," *Statement of Financial Accounting Standards No. 12* (FASB).
—— (1976). *FASB Discussion Memorandum: An Analysis of Issues Related to Conceptual Framework for Financial Reporting: Elements of Financial Statements and Their Measurement* (FASB).

————— (1979). "Capitalization of Interest Cost," *Statement of Financial Accounting Standards No. 34* (FASB).

————— (1980). "Elements of Financial Statements of Business Enterprises," *Statement of Financial Accounting Concepts No. 3* (FASB).

————— (1982). "Foreign Currency Translation," *Statement of Financial Accounting Standards No. 52* (FASB).

Foster, George (1978). *Financial Statement Analysis* (Prentice-Hall).

Hughes, John S. (1978). "Toward a Contract Basis of Valuation in Accounting," *The Accounting Review* (October 1978), pp. 882–894.

Ijiri, Yuji (1975). "Theory of Accounting Measurement," *Studies in Accounting Research 10* (American Accounting Association).

————— (1980). *Recognition of Contractual Rights and Obligations: An Exploratory Study of Conceptual Issues* (FASB).

————— (1982). "Triple-Entry Bookkeeping and Income Momentum," *Studies in Accounting Research 18* (American Accounting Association).

Securities and Exchange Commission (1979). "Presentation in the Financial Statements of Redeemable Preferred Stocks," *Accounting Series Release No. 268* (SEC).

Sorter, George H., and Charles T. Horngren (1962). "Asset Recognition and Economic Attributes—The Relevant Costing Approach," *The Accounting Review* (July 1962), pp. 391–399.

Stamp, Edward (1980), *Corporate Reporting: Its Future Evolution* (Canadian Institute of Chartered Accountants).

ADDITIONAL READINGS

MEASUREMENT OF ASSETS AND LIABILITIES IN GENERAL

American Accounting Association (1972). "Report of the Committee on Accounting Valuation Bases," *The Accounting Review* (Supplement to Volume 47), pp. 535–573.

Henderson, M. Scott (1974). "Nature of Liabilities," *The Australian Accountant* (July 1974), pp. 329–334.

Kulkarni, Deepak (1980). "The Valuation of Liabilities," *Accounting and Business Research* (Summer 1980), pp. 291–297.

Ma, Ronald, and Malcolm C. Miller (1978). "Conceptualizing the Liability," *Accounting and Business Research* (Autumn 1978), pp. 258–265.

Moonitz, Maurice (1960). "The Changing Concept of Liabilities," *Journal of Accountancy* (May 1960), pp. 41–46.

Sprouse, Robert T. (1971). "Balance Sheet—Embodiment of the Most Fundamental Elements of Accounting Theory," in *Foundations of Accounting Theory*, Willard E. Stone, ed. (University of Florida Press), pp. 90–104.

Staubus, George J. (1973). "Measurement of Assets and Liabilities," *Accounting and Business Research* (Autumn 1973), pp. 243–262.

Sterling, Robert R., ed. (1971). *Asset Valuation and Income Determination* (Scholars Book Company).

Walker, Robert G. (1974). "Asset Classification and Asset Valuation," *Accounting and Business Research* (Autumn 1974), pp. 286–296.

Warrell, C. J. (1974). "The Enterprise Value Concept of Asset Valuation," *Accounting and Business Research* (Summer 1974), pp. 220–226.

MEASUREMENT OF SPECIFIC ASSETS AND LIABILITIES

Anthony, Robert N. (1975). *Accounting for the Cost of Interest* (Lexington Books).

Barden, Horace G. (1973). "The Accounting Basis of Inventories," *Accounting Research Study No. 13* (AICPA).

Beidelman, Carl R. (1973). "Valuation of Used Capital Assets," *Studies in Accounting Research 7* (American Accounting Association).

Chasteen, Lanny G. (1973). "Economic Circumstances and Inventory Method Selection," *Abacus* (June 1973), pp. 22–27.

Clancy, Donald K. (1978). "What is a Convertible Debenture? A Review of the Literature in the U.S.A." *Abacus* (December 1978), pp. 171–179.

Coughlan, J. D., and W. K. Strand (1969). *Depreciation; Accounting, Taxes and Business Decisions* (Ronald Press).

Gellein, Oscar S., and Maurice S. Newman (1973). "Accounting for Research and Development Expenditures," *Accounting Research Study No. 14* (AICPA).

O'Connor, Melvin C., and James C. Hamre (1972). "Alternative Methods of Accounting for Long-Term Nonsubsidiary Intercorporate Investments in Common Stock," *The Accounting Review* (April 1972), pp. 308–319.

Storey, Reed K., and Maurice Moonitz (1976). "Market Value Methods for Intercorporate Investments in Stock," *Accounting Research Monograph No. 1* (AICPA).

MEASUREMENT OF OWNERS' EQUITY

American Accounting Association (1965). "The Entity Concept—Report of the 1964 Concepts and Standards Research Committee," *The Accounting Review* (April 1965), pp. 358–369.

Boudreaux, Kenneth J., and Stephen A. Zeff (1976). "A Note on the Measure of Compensation Implicit in Employee Stock Options," *Journal of Accounting Research* (Spring 1976), pp. 158–162.

Melcher, Beatrice (1973). "Stockholders' Equity," *Accounting Research Study No. 15* (AICPA).

Scott, Richard A. (1979). "Owners' Equity, the Anachronistic Element," *The Accounting Review* (October 1979), pp. 750–763.

Smith, Ralph E., and Leroy F. Imdieke (1974). "Accounting for Stock Issued to Employees," *Journal of Accountancy* (November 1974), pp. 68–75.

CHAPTER 9

The Income Statement

Standard setting, to the extent that it is influenced by theory, will, of course lag behind theory. That is simply inevitable. Furthermore, it will be affected by the political process—both in the sense mentioned in Chapter 3 and in the narrower context of the Financial Accounting Standards Board (FASB) pronouncements, which are set by a committee and therefore are the result of compromise. However, a viable conceptual framework would allow standards to close the gap relative to theory. Throughout this chapter, reference will be made to underlying theoretical issues discussed in the first part of the book.

One concern, however, must be voiced immediately. As we saw earlier, the rise in importance of the efficient markets hypothesis, combined with the dilemma posed by changing prices (see Chapters 11 and 12), has led to the increasing importance of disclosure and the broader topic of financial reporting as opposed to the more narrow topic of accounting numbers reported in traditional financial statements. Nevertheless, it is highly probable that the traditional historical cost income statement will continue to play a very significant role during the foreseeable future because it has been found to have information content and is relatively well understood.

The chapter starts with reviews of the general state of revenue and expense recognition standards. Next we turn to the controversy over current operating versus all-inclusive income. This argument has been quite instrumental in leading to the present extended format of the income statement. Single-step versus multiple-step formats are then quickly examined. Classifications comprising the extended format of the income statement—extraordinary items, accounting changes, discontinued operations, and prior period adjustments (for completeness)—are discussed. The chapter continues with enumeration of important areas where recent standards affect the income statement. While the balance sheet is also affected by those pronouncements, primary emphasis appears to have been focused on income statement effects. Accounting standards where the balance sheet aspect appears to predominate were discussed in Chapter 8; hence, these two chapters are complementary in nature.

Two other topics are discussed here. Earnings per share is an important "summary indicator" of enterprise performance. Its development and future are briefly discussed. Since the chapter is largely concerned with income measurement rules prescribed by standard-setting agencies, the chapter closes with a review of income-smoothing research.

INCOME CONCEPTS

There are at least two approaches to the determination of and definition of accounting income. The approach generally used in accounting practice today is the revenue–expense approach. Under this approach, measurement and recognition standards are centered on revenues and expenses and net income or loss is the difference between the two. The other approach, the asset–liability approach, is more balance sheet oriented. Measurement and recognition standards under this approach are centered on assets and liabilities and net income or loss is the net change for the period in net assets excluding capital transactions.

Accounting income has been formally defined in the following ways:

> Income and profit . . . refer to amounts resulting from the deduction from revenues, or from operating revenues, of cost of goods sold, other expenses, and losses. . . .[1]
> Net income (net loss)—the excess (deficit) of revenue over expenses for an accounting period. . . .[2]
> Comprehensive income is the change in equity (net assets) of an entity during a period of transactions and other events and circumstances from nonowner sources.[3]

---

[1]Committee on Terminology (1955, para. 8).
[2]APB (1970, para. 134).
[3]FASB (1980, para. 56).

The first two definitions from Accounting Terminology Bulletin (ATB) 2 and Accounting Principles Board (APB) Statement 4, clearly represent the revenue–expense approach. When the primary emphasis is on revenue and expense measurement, it is necessary to have standards that define those elements and specify their recognition and measurement. The third definition, Statement of Financial Accounting Concepts (SFAC) 3, represents a clear change in direction to the asset–liability approach. This appears to be the direction to be taken by the FASB in the future. The impact on the income statement of the apparent change in direction cannot be foreseen; however, its impact, if any, probably will be slight for at least several years because the income statement is largely a legacy of fifty years of accounting standards based on the revenue–expense approach.

REVENUE AND GAINS

Revenues have been defined in the following ways:

Revenue results from the sale of goods and rendering of services and is measured by the charge made to customers, clients, or tenants for goods and services furnished to them.[4]

Revenue—gross increases in assets and gross decreases in liabilities measured in conformity with generally accepted accounting principles that result from those types of profit-directed activities. . . .[5]

Revenues are the inflows or other enhancements of assets of an entity or settlements of its liabilities (or a combination of both) during a period from delivering or producing goods, rendering services, or other activities that constitute the entity's ongoing major or central operations.[6]

The first definition, from ATB 2, reflects a revenue–expense approach and emphasizes the direct identification of revenue-producing activities. A difference can be detected in the second definition, which is from APB Statement 4. Revenues are defined as an increase in net assets arising from income-producing activities. At first glance, this appears to represent a change to the asset–liability orientation; however, measurement is said to be based on generally accepted accounting principles, which implies the revenue–expense orientation. Finally, the third definition, from SFAC 3, does clearly define revenue as an increase in net assets. This implies an asset–liability approach, and is consistent with the SFAC 3 definition of

[4]Committee on Terminology (1955, para. 5).
[5]APB (1970, para. 134).
[6]FASB (1980, para. 63).

comprehensive income. Again, the impact on the income statement of this change in definition cannot be foreseen.

The definition from ATB 2 is similar to the presentation of revenues in Chapter 4, in which revenues were defined as the output of the enterprise in terms of its product or service. However, all three of these definitions, by introducing the issue of how to measure revenues, interject the issue of realization into the definition. How to measure an element should conceptually be kept separate from the definition since questions of recognition and measurement may well supersede the issue of what is being measured. Realization is examined in more detail shortly.

Gains and revenues typically have been defined and displayed separately on the financial statements. Gains have been defined in the following manner:

> ... revenues ... from other than sales of products, merchandise, or services. ...[7]

> Gains are increases in equity (net assets) from peripheral or incidental transactions ... except those that result from revenues or investments by owners.[8]

The distinction between a revenue and gain once was a subject of considerable controversy. One school of thought believed that only revenues should be reported on income statements. The secondary or peripheral nature of gains means that they did not represent recurring income from the entity's main area of income-producing activities, and, therefore, should be excluded from the income statement. This school of thought has been called the current operating income concept. The competing position was called the all-inclusive income concept. Its proponents believed that all revenues and gains, regardless of source, should be included in the income statement. There has been an evolution through accounting standards away from the current operating concept to the all-inconclusive concept, thus, somewhat defusing the controversy. This evolution is reviewed later in the chapter.

THE REALIZATION CONCEPT

When is a revenue a revenue? From a theoretical point of view, the answer to this question is clear:

> [Revenues] should be identified with the period during which the major economic activities necessary to the creation and disposition of goods and services has been accomplished.[9]

---

[7]APB (1970, para. 198).

[8]FASB (1980, para. 167).

[9]Sprouse and Moonitz (1962, p. 177).

The practical problem with the preceding definition, however, is one of being able to make an objective measurement of the results of those economic activities. Until a verifiable measurement can be made, no revenue can be recognized. Unfortunately the accomplishment of the "major economic activities necessary to the creation and disposition of goods and services" and the ability to measure those accomplishments objectively frequently occur at different times and in different reporting periods. To deal with this difficulty, four points in time for recognizing revenue are discussed in the accounting literature and used in accounting practice:

1. during production,
2. at the completion of production,
3. at the time of sale,
4. when cash is collected.

Revenue is recognized during production for certain long-term contracts (see Accounting Research Bulletin (ARB) 45 and Statement of Position (SOP) 81-1); it is recognized at the completion of production for certain agricultural and mining operations (see ARB 43, Chapter 4, paragraphs 15–16); and it is recognized at the time of cash collection when the installment method is used for sales of real estate (see Statement of Financial Accounting Standards (SFAS) 66).

Although the topic of revenue recognition has been lively and provocative,[10] the fact remains that revenues generally are recognized at the point of sale when legal title is transferred. This standard is clearly expressed in Chapter 1 of ARB 43:

> Profit (revenue) is deemed to be realized when a sale in the ordinary course
> of a business is effected, unless the circumstances are such that collection
> of the sales price is not reasonably assumed.[11]

This rule was one of the six originally adopted by the American Institute of Certified Public Accountants (AICPA) in 1934 (see discussion in Chapter 2). Exceptions are sanctioned in the accounting rules, as mentioned above, but the general principle is that revenues are recognized at the time of sale.

SOME EXCEPTIONS TO THE GENERAL RULES OF REVENUE RECOGNITION

The vast majority of exceptions to recognizing revenue at the point of sale have evolved because "new" transactions have emerged that do not fit the mold of "traditional" transactions. In many instances, but not all, these transactions are peculiar to specific industries. As noted in Chapter 2, the

---

[10]See complete discussion of revenue recognition concepts in AAA (1965a).
[11]Committee on Accounting Procedure (1953, Chapter 1, para. 1).

AICPA has been the primary source of the development of accounting standards, particularly revenue recognition standards, as new transactions emerge. Its Accounting Standards Division periodically issues accounting guides (Guides) and SOPs. These documents, however, are not mandatory and do not have to be followed in practice as do FASB Standards and Interpretations. Perhaps because of that fact, Jaenicke found the accounting practices for revenue recognition that have evolved for these "new" transactions are inconsistent in rationale; consequently, they result in inconsistent outcomes.[12]

Recently the FASB (see Chapter 2) embarked on a program of extracting standards from the Guides and SOPs; modifying them, if necessary, to be internally consistent with FASB Standards and Concepts; and issuing them as SFASs. To date, twelve SFASs on specialized standards have been issued: franchise fee revenue (No. 45), revenue recognition when right of return exists (No. 48), product financing arrangements (No. 49), the record and music industry (No. 50), cable television companies (No. 51), motion pictures (No. 53), insurance enterprises (No. 60), title plant (No. 61), broadcasters (No. 63), mortgage banking (No. 65), sales of real estate (No. 66), and costs and initial rental operations of real estate projects (No. 67).

We will next review some of these new SFASs that are of limited scope. The purpose of the review is to illustrate how the AICPA originally established the standard, how the FASB's extraction process works and the problems it encounters, and the shortcomings in certain circumstances of the process.

Revenue Recognition When Right of Return Exists

Revenue recognition when the right of return exists provides a good example of the establishment of accounting standards for a specialized or narrow-scope subject. In fact, it is perhaps the best example of how the FASB's extraction process should ideally be expected to work because the SOP on the subject generally was followed in practice with little controversy. Prior to the issuance of SOP 75-1, the following alternative accounting practices were being used to recognize revenue: (a) no sale was recognized until the product was unconditionally accepted, (b) a sale was recognized and an allowance for estimated returns was provided, and (c) a sale was recognized without providing an allowance for returns. Hence, a system of flexibility prevailed because there was no consideration of the underlying relevant circumstance of the transaction. In 1975 the AICPA established criteria for recognizing revenue when the right of return exists. In order to recognize revenue in these situations, all the following conditions had to be met:

1. The price is substantially fixed or determinable at the date of sale.
2. The buyer has paid the seller or is obligated to pay the seller and payment is not contingent on resale of the product.

[12]Jaenicke (1981, pp. 6–10).

3. The buyer bears risk of loss from theft, destruction, and physical damage to the product.
4. The buyer acquiring the product for resale has economic substance apart from that provided by the seller.
5. The seller has no significant obligations for future performance to bring about resale of the product.
6. Future returns can be reasonably estimated.[13]

Although the preceding criteria are clear, the problem was that no one had to follow them because SOPs are not mandatory accounting practices. The FASB, in June 1981, issued significant portions of the SOP as SFAS 48. The accounting for recognition of revenue when the right of return exists finally is consistent from enterprise to enterprise, resulting in a form of finite uniformity.

Motion Picture Producers and Broadcasters

The evolution of accounting standards for motion picture producers and for broadcasters provides an interesting example of how specialized industry standards frequently are inconsistent. Moreover, it shows that the FASB's extraction process doesn't always work ideally.

Prior to the issuance of the Guide, "Accounting for Motion Picture Films," in 1973, the timing of revenue recognition from films licensed to television broadcasters was accomplished at several different times. Those times varied from the date the license agreement was signed to apportioning the revenue over the license period. The Guide narrowed the choices by recommending that revenue be recognized when the license period began (and the film was available to the licensee)—when, in effect, the licensor and licensee were contractually obligated. The principles in APB 21, "Interest on Receivables and Payables," applied and, accordingly, the revenue and corresponding receivable were recorded net of interest with interest income imputed throughout the payment period.[14] This practice, although not mandatory, generally was followed in the industry. As a result, SFAS 53 is for the most part a direct extraction from the Guide.

Licensee accounting does not represent an example of revenue recognition problems, but it does reflect clearly how inconsistent accounting practices may and do evolve in different industries for similar events. Licensee accounting does not parallel licensor accounting. SOP 75-5, "Accounting Practices in the Broadcasting Industry," was issued with the hope of narrowing existing practices and bringing those practices into conformity with licensor accounting. Prior to SOP 75-5, a variety of practices regarding the recognition of license agreements existed:

1. The agreements were considered to be commitments, not liabilities, and neither the film rights nor related fees were reported on balance sheets.

---

[13]Accounting Standards Executive Committee (1975a, para. 11).
[14]Committee on the Entertainment Industries (1973, pp. 6–8).

2. Assets and liabilities were recorded for all license agreements. Some broadcasters discounted the amounts while others reported them at gross.
3. Assets and liabilities were recorded only for license agreements where the films were currently available for showing. Some broadcasters discounted the amounts while others reported them at gross.[15]

SOP 75-5 recommended that licensee accounting should parallel licensor accounting and established criteria similar to the motion picture Guide. Moreover, amounts recorded were to be recorded at net after discounting. The FASB found, however, that SOP 75-5 was not followed in practice. It found that some broadcasters did not report an asset or liability for license agreements and those that did generally did not discount the amounts reported. Thus, the practical effect prior to SFAS 63 was that motion picture producers were recognizing sales and receivables while the majority of broadcasters were not recognizing corresponding purchases and payables. Even for the broadcasters that did recognize a purchase and payable simultaneously with the recognition of receivables and revenues by motion picture producers, the amounts recognized were different.

Unfortunately, the FASB did not require symmetry in accounting. SFAS 53 requires motion picture producers to recognize a receivable and corresponding revenue when certain conditions are met. The amount recognized is the discounted amount. SFAS 63 does require broadcasters to recognize a purchase and liability at the same time the motion picture producer recognizes the receivable/revenue; however, the amounts do not have to be the same. The broadcaster may recognize either the gross or discounted amount. The state of the art today, then, is that motion picture producers and broadcasters may report different amounts on their financial statements for the same underlying event and that two broadcasters could report different amounts for identical transactions.

Why has this inconsistency (and others) occurred and why did the FASB allow it to continue? One problem is that standard setting for specialized industries typically has been by committees consisting of representatives of those industries. Those representatives have their own vested interests at heart and naturally establish standards that are biased toward those interests. For example, motion picture producers want to recognize revenue as soon as possible while broadcasters would prefer to delay, if not avoid entirely, recognizing liabilities for the purchase of film rights. Prior to the FASB, no group was able to oversee all industry practices to ensure consistent accounting treatment for similar events.

Although the FASB had a chance to close the gap with respect to motion picture/broadcasters, it chose not to do so. The reason it acted that way makes sense: political pressure on an issue that has limited practical effect.

[15] Accounting Standards Executive Committee (1975b, paras. 9–11).

In other words, it was not worth the fight on a problem of such narrow scope. However, one dissenting Board member stated the opposing case very cogently:

> Requiring the seller's receivable and revenue to be reported at the present value of the future license payments and permitting the purchaser's asset and payable to be reported at either the gross amount or present value of those future cash payments can only serve to detract from the credibility and usefulness of financial reporting.[16]

Transfer of Receivables with Recourse

Accounting for the transfer of receivables with recourse is a problem of identifying whether the transaction is a sale or a financing thereof. If a sale occurs, gain or loss should be recognized immediately; however, if the transaction is a financing, gain recognition (presumably a loss would be recognized immediately on the ground of conservatism) would be deferred and realized over the life of the receivables as interest income. Both methods of accounting were prevalent prior to SOP 74-6.

In SOP 74-6, "Recognition of Profit on Sales of Receivables with Recourse," the AICPA reached the conclusion that most transfer-with-recourse transactions are financings. Therefore, gain recognition should be deferred and realized over time.[17] The conclusion was based on the theory that the transfer, or in this case lack of transfer, of risk must occur in order for a sale to have occurred. Because the transfer is with recourse, the transferor is still at risk and a sale has not occurred.

When the FASB undertook the project, SFAC 3 was in place. That SFAC defines an asset as

> probable future economic benefits obtained or *controlled* by a particular entity as a result of past transactions or events (emphasis added).[18]

In applying that definition, the FASB tentatively decided in an exposure draft (ED) that if control over the receivables is transferred by the transaction (which it usually is), an asset no longer exists for the transferor and a gain should be recognized immediately (asset–liability approach to determination of income).

While we do not find fault with the FASB's logic, it did not apply that logic consistently. Basically the FASB applied the concept of control to an entire receivable and did not recognize that receivables have at least two components that can be separated, and transferred individually.

Coupon bonds provide a good example of the type of transfer transaction that the FASB apparently did not foresee. A coupon bond has two components: the right to receive an amount of money at a future date, i.e.,

---

[16]FASB (1982).
[17]Accounting Standards Executive Committee (1974, para. 41).
[18]FASB (1980, para. 19).

principal; and the right to receive periodically a series of cash payments, i.e., interest. It is possible to sell one component and retain the other. The sale of the principal amount separately is referred to as a "bond strip," and the sale of the coupons separately is referred to as a "coupon strip." When either the principal or the coupons is sold separately, the amortized cost of the bond should be allocated between the bond's two components to determine gain or loss on the transferred component. The allocation between principal and interest should be based on the present values of the future cash flows of each component using as the discount rate the yield at which the bond was purchased.

Transferring part of a receivable provides a good example of the patchwork nature of current standards and of the fact that the game of catch-up relative to new issues and new theory contributions continuously takes place. Unless the FASB clarifies its concept of control in the final SFAS on transfer of receivables, confusion and inconsistency will remain in accounting practices.

SUMMARY ON REVENUE RECOGNITION

Exceptions to the general rule of recognizing revenue at the point of sale have been sanctioned by the professional literature. Revenue recognized on a production basis may be used for long-term construction contracts if reliable estimates of the extent of progress and of the cost to complete can be made and if reasonable assurance of collectibility exists. If immediate marketability at a quoted price exists for a product whose units are interchangeable, revenue may be recognized at the completion of production. Recognizing revenue on a cash basis, either installment or cost recovery, is allowed if no reasonable basis exists for estimating collectibility.

Two additional bases for recognizing revenue have been suggested by many but are not permitted by authoritative literature. Some support recognizing revenue on an accretion basis where product marketability at known prices exists and it is desirable to recognize changes in assets, such as growing timber.[19] Regarding material resources, particularly natural gas and petroleum, many support a view of recognizing revenue on a discovery basis because of the significance of discovery on the earnings process (see discussion in Chapter 14).

While the standard for revenue recognition is the point of sale, the primary criterion applied in practice for revenue recognition is the completion of the earnings process. In other words, revenue should be recognized when the transaction or event that culminates the earnings process has occurred. Measurement problems must be resolved, however, before revenue is recognized. Attributes that must be measurable are (1) sales price, (2) cash collections, and (3) future costs. If all three can be measured with

[19]Philips (1963).

reasonable accuracy, then revenue is recognized when the earning process is complete; otherwise recognition must be delayed until reasonable measurements can be made.

Although, there is no question that inconsistent revenue recognition practices exist today and probably will continue as new industries and transactions emerge, the hope is that once the FASB's conceptual framework project is complete, the inconsistencies will be minimized.

EXPENSES AND LOSSES

Expenses have been defined in the following ways:

> Expense in the broadest sense includes all expired costs which are deductible from revenues. . . .[20]

> Expenses—gross decreases in assets or gross increases in liabilities recognized and measured in conformity with generally accepted accounting principles that result from those types of profit-directed activities of an enterprise. . . .[21]

> Expenses are outflows or other using up of assets or incurrences of liabilities (or a combination of both) during a period from delivering or producing goods, rendering services, or carrying out other activities that constitute the entity's major or central operations.[22]

The first definition, from ATB 4, represents the traditional revenue–expense orientation. In the second definition, APB Statement 4, a relationship is established between expense and net assets. However, measurement is still based on rules of the revenue–expense orientation. The third definition, SFAC 3, represents a strong asset–liability approach. Again, the FASB may be looking forward in applying this definition. Expense recognition continues to be guided by a strong revenue–expense orthodoxy, however.

Losses are defined in APB Statement 4, and in SFAC 3, in a parallel manner to gains. Losses represent a reduction in net assets, but not from expenses or capital transactions. As with gains, the distinction between expenses and losses is not important under the all-inclusive income concept. At one time, however, this was a major issue in accounting.

A good review of the matching concept literature may be found in a 1964 American Accounting Association (AAA) Committee report.[23] Like

---

[20]Committee on Terminology (1957, para. 3).
[21]APB (1970, para. 134).
[22]FASB (1980, para. 65).
[23]AAA (1965b).

the companion report on revenue recognition, this literature is largely passé—given the current emphasis on asset valuation and the concept of asset–liability measurement. A summary of current expense recognition rules is found in APB Statement 4. Expenses are classified into three categories:[24]

1. Costs directly associated with the revenue of the period.
2. Costs associated with the period on some basis other than a direct relationship with revenue.
3. Costs that cannot, as a practical matter, be associated with any other period.

A hierarchy exists and this is the principle of the matching concept. If possible, costs should be matched against the revenues directly produced. If a direct cause and effect relationship does not exist, costs should be matched in a rational and systematic manner to revenue. Finally, if there is not even an indirect cause and effect relationship, the costs are recognized as period expenses when incurred.

Typically the third category is the only one that does not give accountants significant recognition problems. Costs incurred in the current period that provide no discernible future benefit as well as costs incurred in past periods that no longer provide discernible future benefits are expensed immediately. The relevant event generally is recognizable: no future benefit. For example, when a building is destroyed by fire, there is no future benefit; thus, an expense (loss) is recognized immediately.

The first and second categories provide recognition problems. The first category is basically the application of the matching concept. That is, match costs against revenues that they helped to generate. Some items, such as direct material and labor are relatively free of problems. Others, however, such as overhead items, require allocation on some basis to the products manufactured. In the absence of a direct means of associating expenses with revenues (cause and effect), costs must be associated with accounting periods on the basis of a "systematic and rational allocation" (category two). The major expense recognition problem, then, concerns those costs that are clearly not expired in the period incurred and are clearly not associated with the revenues of a particular period.[25]

The standard of expense recognition through allocation does not provide guidance to events triggering accounting recognition as does the standard of revenue recognition. Revenue recognition standards specify not only the amount of revenue to recognize (sales price) but also the period for which the revenue should be recognized (period of sale). Expense recognition standards aid in determining the amount of expense to be allocated over future years, the cost to be amortized. Those standards, however,

---

[24]APB (1970, para. 155).
[25]Jaenicke (1981, pp. 117–118).

prescribe neither how the assets provide their benefit nor when the benefit is provided; thus, they give little practical guidance.[26] Moreover, the APB Statement 4 classification system provides no practical benefit whatsoever and, in fact, the distinctions it makes frequently are not applicable to real-life situations. It is a shame the APB did not spend more time with this issue. Inability to resolve this issue underlies the absorption costing versus direct costing controversy.

The need for systematic and rational allocation cannot be avoided in the existing accounting model. The model based on historical cost rather than one based on measuring value must allocate the costs incurred. In fact many accountants share the view that the method of allocation used is nothing more than an arbitrary decision. After extensive study of the subject, Thomas concluded (as discussed in Chapter 6) that selection of a particular allocation method over alternative methods is meaningless because the superiority of an allocation method can be neither verified nor refuted.[27]

A decision not to allocate would require major changes in our existing accounting model. As Sterling has suggested, the decision to define depreciation as an allocation rather than valuation has created a problem that is unresolvable.[28] In order to avoid allocation, Meyers makes this suggestion:

> It would be necessary either to adopt a concept of income measurement that does not depend on matching, such as a strict market value approach, or to settle on a reporting philosophy, such as a pure disclosure approach that does not require income measurement.[29]

Although this is not a judgment on the merits of Meyers statement, we believe that the existing accounting model based on historical costs (with all its inherent problems) will be around for the foreseeable future.

CURRENT OPERATING VS. ALL-INCLUSIVE INCOME

Until relatively recently (1968), there was a controversy regarding whether certain components of comprehensive income should be displayed in the income statement or retained earnings statement. This controversy surrounded the display of unusual (nonoperating) and infrequently occurring gains and losses. One school of thought, **current operating**, held that the income statement should contain normal operating items while nonoperating items should be reported in the retained earnings statement. The

---

[26]Jaenicke (1981, p. 119).
[27]Thomas (1969) and (1974).
[28]Sterling (1975).
[29]Meyers (1976, p. 54).

other school of thought, **all-inclusive,** maintained that all components of comprehensive income should be in the income statement. As a corollary, the retained earnings statement would reflect only total earnings as reported in the income statement and dividend distributions in addition to beginning and ending balances.

Advocates of the current operating concept contended that the income statement is more useful in assessing management's performance and predicting future years' performance if items extraneous to current management decisions are excluded. They believed that most financial statement users look only to reported net income to assess current performance and to make predictions regarding subsequent years' performance. If material, extraneous, nonoperating, infrequently occurring items are reported in the income statement, financial statement users would be seriously misled and might make incorrect decisions as a result.

Those favoring the all-inclusive concept cited several reasons for their position. First, current operating lends itself to easy manipulation by management because they make the decision on whether or not an item is extraordinary. Second, financial statement users may be misled because they may not realize substantial gains or losses have been "hidden" in the retained earnings statement. Third, the summation of all income displayed on the income statement for a period of years should reflect the reporting entity's net income for that period. Finally, they pointed out that proper classification within the income statement allows both normal recurring items and unusual infrequently occurring items to be displayed separately within the same statement.

Historically the American Accounting Association (AAA) favored the all-inclusive concept. In 1936 the AAA's *A Tentative Statement of Accounting Principles Underlying Corporate Financial Statements,* contained the following statement:

> The income statement for any given period should reflect all revenues properly given accounting recognition and all costs written off during the period, regardless of whether or not they are the results of operations in that period. . . .[30]

Conversely, the AICPA consistently favored the current operating concept until APB 9. For example, in ARB 43, the Committee on Accounting Procedure indicated that all extraordinary items should be carried directly to the surplus account.[31] However, in December 1966, the APB took a position that leaned strongly in favor of the all-inclusive concept. APB 9 as amended requires that all nonoperating, infrequently occurring items except for prior period adjustments be included in the computation of net income and reported separately on the income statement.[32] The specific

[30]AAA (1936, section 8).
[31]Committee on Accounting Procedure (1953, Chapter 8, para. 13).
[32]APB (1966, para. 16).

financial statement display of nonoperating, infrequently occurring items and prior period adjustments will be reviewed in the following section.

OPERATING SECTION FORMAT

Specific guidelines exist in the professional literature regarding the income statement format for displaying nonoperating items (extraordinary gains and losses, discontinued operations, and changes in accounting principle). On the contrary, however, specific format guidelines do not exist for the operating section. As a result, at least two formats have evolved and are used in the United States today—single-step and multiple-step. These formats represent a good example of "operating standards" as discussed in Chapter 7.

The single-step income statement focuses on two broad categories, revenues and expenses. All revenues and gains that are not included in one of the nonoperating sections are displayed together and summed for total revenues. This category includes revenues from both primary and secondary operations and gains not meeting the criteria for being extraordinary. Similarly, all costs, expenses, and losses not included in a nonoperating section are displayed together and totaled. Total expenses are subtracted from total revenues to derive net income (loss) before extraordinary items.

The multiple-step statement provides several intermediate steps in arriving at net income before extraordinary items. Net primary revenues are shown first, followed by cost of goods sold, which is subtracted from net revenue to derive gross margin. Operating expenses are then listed and subtracted from gross margin to give income (loss) from primary operations. Other revenues and expenses are then added to or subtracted from income (loss) from primary operations. This classification includes revenues and expenses from secondary sources as well as gains and losses not qualifying as extraordinary. The resulting computation is income (loss) before income tax and nonoperating items. Income taxes on operating income are then deducted to arrive at income (loss) from normal operations.

The single-step format allows more flexibility in reporting than the multiple-step due to the broader classifications. Many believe, however, the multiple-step is preferred because it provides relevant intermediate subtotals, such as gross margin. Use of the single-step format is predominant in practice today, but the multiple-step is gaining in popularity.[33] Assuming market efficiency, however, it is not at all clear that the multiple-step format discloses anything that is not readily available to financial statements users

---

[33]The frequency of use of the multiple-step format has increased from 38% of enterprises in 1978 to 45% in 1981. AICPA (1982, p. 218).

in the single-step format. Nevertheless the multiple-step approach may reveal additional information for a class of users who are not adept at making the transformations themselves and who do not rely on financial intermediaries. Regardless, it appears the information production costs of the multiple-step approach are extremely small.

NONOPERATING SECTIONS

The nonoperating section of the income statement has grown tremendously over the past ten years in both size and complexity. It now includes at least three subdivisions: (1) extraordinary items, (2) accounting principle changes, and (3) discontinued operations. Furthermore, a fourth item, prior period adjustments, is reported in the retained earnings statement. This, of course, represents the continuing dilemma between the current operating versus all-inclusive concepts.

EXTRAORDINARY ITEMS

Reporting extraordinary items has been a subject of controversy for many years. It represents a good example of movement away from finite uniformity to rigid uniformity in accounting standards. As we will see, this shift was necessitated because the concept of finite uniformity was thought to be abused in accounting practice; to circumvent that abuse, rigid uniformity became the rule.

The basis of the controversy is the impact that extraordinary items may have on financial statement users' perceptions of the results of operations and projections of future operations for the reporting entity. Evaluating the results of current and past operations and projecting future operations relies heavily on an ability to separate normal recurring components of comprehensive income from those that are not recurring.

Prior to APB 9, the prevailing standard covering extraordinary items was Chapter 8 of ARB 43, which was a reprint of ARB 32 issued in 1947. The ARBs were vague, as the following quote illustrates:

> [There] should be a general presumption that all items of profit and loss recognized during the period are to be used in determining the figure reported as net income. The only possible exception to this presumption relates to items which in the aggregate are material in relation to the company's net income and are clearly not identifiable with or do not result from the usual or typical business operations of the period.[34]

---

[34]Committee on Accounting Procedure (1953, Chapter 8, para. 11).

Needless to say, with no more guidance than the above for nineteen years prior to APB 9, accounting practice for extraordinary items was in disarray. APB 9 attempted to bring order out of disarray. It required display of all extraordinary items in a specifically designated section of the income statement—as opposed to leaving the decision up to the reporting entity. Also it provided a new definition of "extraordinary items:"

> ... events and transactions of material effect which would not be expected to recur frequently and which would not be considered as recurring factors in any evaluation of the ordinary operating processes of the business.[35]

Unfortunately, the definition proved to be unworkable in practice. As a result, the APB restudied the problem in 1973 and issued APB 30. This Opinion resorted to rigid uniformity and virtually eliminated the existence of extraordinary items because the definition of and criteria for an extraordinary item were so restrictive. In fact, the APB expressly stated that extraordinary items should occur in only rare situations.[36] For an item to qualify as extraordinary it must be both unusual in nature *and* infrequent in occurrence. The APB defined these terms as follows:

> *Unusual nature*—The underlying event or transaction should possess a high degree of abnormality and be of a type clearly unrelated to, or only incidentally related to, the ordinary and typical activities of the entity, taking into account the environment in which the entity operates.
>
> *Infrequency of occurrence*—The underlying event or transaction should be of a type that would not reasonably be expected to recur in the foreseeable future, taking into account the environment in which the entity operates.[37]

The environment in which the entity operates is often the controlling factor in applying the two criteria. For example, frost damage to a citrus grower's crop in North or Central Florida would not qualify as extraordinary because frost damage there is normally experienced every three or four years. Conversely, similar damage to a citrus grower's crop in South Florida or Southern California probably would qualify as extraordinary because frost damage there is not experienced on a recurring basis. As a result of APB 30, extraordinary items, other than those specifically legislated (gains and losses from early extinguishment of debt and tax benefits of loss carryforwards), have practically disappeared from the scene.

The display of an extraordinary item, should one occur, in the income statement is in a specified section entitled "extraordinary items." This section is below net operating income and above net income. All items are shown net of tax.

Events or transactions that are unusual or infrequent but not both must be displayed with normal recurring revenues, costs, and expenses. If these

---

[35] APB (1966, para. 21).
[36] APB (1973, para. 23).
[37] APB (1973, paras. 19–20).

items are not material in amount, they are not shown separately from other items. If they are material in amount they are exhibited separately above the caption "income (loss) before extraordinary items." They may not be displayed net of tax. However, normal disclosure practices require footnote explanation of the item.

ACCOUNTING CHANGES

Changes in accounting methods employed by a reporting entity may affect significantly both the financial statements of the current reporting period and any trends reflected in comparative financial statements and historical summaries of the reporting entity. Accounting changes are classified in three broad categories:

1. Change in accounting principle—Results from adoption of a generally accepted accounting principle different from a generally accepted accounting principle previously used for reporting purposes. A characteristic of a change in accounting principle is that the change is from one generally accepted that *has been used previously* to another that *is also* generally accepted—for example, changing from straight-line depreciation to sum-of-the-years digits depreciation.
2. Change in accounting estimate—Results when a change in a previously estimated item occurs because, through the passage of time, more information for making the estimate is known—for example, the change in estimated life of a depreciable asset where previous depreciation was based on a ten-year life, and after five years it is estimated the asset will be used only an additional two years.
3. Change in Reporting Entity—Results when there has been a material change in the reporting entity since the last financial statements were compiled—for example, when the specific group of subsidiaries comprising the reporting entity is significantly different from the specific group reported on the previous reporting period.

Prior to APB 20, there was no comprehensive, consistent standard dealing with accounting changes. That document established standards to be followed for accounting changes.

For all changes in accounting principle, except those specifically excluded by APB 20 and subsequent APB Opinions and FASB Statements, the cumulative effect of changing to a new accounting principle as of the beginning of the period of change is included in comprehensive income on the income statement of the period of change.

The amount is displayed in a separate section entitled "accounting changes." This section is below net operating income and above net income. All items are shown net of tax. Prior financial statements are not restated. However, income before extraordinary items and net income computed on a pro forma basis is shown for all periods presented as if the newly adopted principle was applied in those previous years. Furthermore, the effect of adopting the new accounting principle on income before extraordinary items and on net income of the period of change is disclosed.[38]

A change in accounting estimate is not reported separately, as is a change in accounting principle. However, the effects of the change are accounted for in the period of change if that is the only period affected, or in the period of change and future periods if the change affects both. Typically, no separate amount is exhibited by the reporting entity. For example, assume a ten-year life has been used to depreciate an asset, and in the sixth year the life is adjusted to eight years. Depreciation expense for the sixth through eighth years is simply the undepreciated cost at the beginning of the sixth year spread over the remaining three years. In essence, an overstatement of depreciation for the last three years will offset the understatement of the first five years.[39]

For a change in reporting entity, APB 20 requires that financial statements of all prior periods be restated in order to show financial information for the new reporting entity for all periods. The financial statements of the period of change should describe the nature of and reasons for the change. Furthermore, the effect of the change on income before extraordinary items, net income, and corresponding per share amounts is disclosed for all periods.[40]

Accounting for accounting changes is straightforward with clear definitions and reporting requirements. This example of rigid uniformity appears to be working well in accounting practice. The FASB, however, increasingly appears to favor retroactive restatement for accounting principle changes it promulgates in new SFASs. In a majority of its major SFASs, the FASB has either required or encouraged retroactive restatement rather than the method of accounting required by APB 20 for a change in accounting principle.

DISCONTINUED OPERATIONS

A special type of extraordinary item requiring specific accounting treatment was recognized by APB 30: discontinued operations. Specifically, the Opinion requires special accounting treatment for gains and losses on the disposal of a segment of a business. The term "segment of a business" refers to a component of an entity whose activities entail a separate major line of business or class of customer. The distinguishing characteristic of a segment of a business is that its activities clearly can be separated physically, operationally, and for financial reporting purposes from the other assets, results of operations, and activities of the reporting entity.[41]

---

[38] APB (1971, paras. 18–22).
[39] APB (1971, paras. 31–32).
[40] APB (1971, paras. 34–35).
[41] APB (1973, para. 13).

Two dates are of utmost importance in accounting for the disposal of a
segment—measurement date and disposal date. The **measurement date** is
the date that management commits itself to a formal plan to dispose of the
segment. The plan of disposal includes identification of the segment,
method of disposal, expected time required to accomplish disposal, the
estimated results of operations of the segment until disposal, and the estimated proceeds to be received on disposal. The **disposal date** is the date of
closing the sale of the segment or the date operations cease if disposal is by
abandonment.[42]

If a loss is expected on disposal, the estimated loss is recognized in the
financial statements of the reporting entity as of the measurement date. On
the other hand, if a gain is expected, recognition is deferred until realization, another example of conservatism. The determination of whether a
gain or loss is expected is made on the measurement date and includes
these two factors:

1. Net realizable value of the segment after giving effect to any estimated costs directly associated with the disposal.
2. Any estimated income or loss from operations of the segment from
   measurement date until disposal date.

The above two items are combined and if a loss results, it is reported
net of tax as a separate component of comprehensive income displayed
before extraordinary items on the income statement. In addition to the reported loss, the current year's income statement must display (as a separate
component of income before extraordinary items) the results of operations
net of tax for the segment being eliminated for the current reporting period
prior to the measurement date. Likewise, financial statements of prior years
are restated to reflect operations net of tax of the segment being discontinued as a separate component of income before extraordinary items. Errors
in estimate of the loss on disposal between the measurement date and disposal date are treated as changes in accounting estimate in the income
statement for the period of disposal. Additional disclosures in the financial
statements for the period that includes the measurement date are the identity of the segment, the expected disposal date, the manner of disposal, a
description of the segment's assets and liabilities, and the income or loss
for the segment from measurement date to financial statement date. Similar
disclosures are required in subsequent financial statements covering the
period in which disposal occurs.[43]

Accounting for the disposal of a segment provides some practice problems in identifying whether a particular part of an enterprise qualifies as a
segment. These problems, however, are minimal and, in general, rigid uniformity has worked well here. The most serious criticism of accounting for

[42]APB (1973, para. 14).
[43]APB (1973, para. 18).

the disposal of a segment involves the complexity of the accounting. Many small enterprises believe that they should be exempt from the requirements of accounting for the disposal of a segment because of its complexity (as they are exempt from reporting earnings per share and segment reporting).[44]

PRIOR PERIOD ADJUSTMENTS

Accounting for (and the display of) prior period adjustments is quite straightforward. The amount of prior period adjustments is charged or credited to the beginning retained earnings balance. They are exhibited net of tax in the retained earnings statement, thereby being excluded from the determination of net income for the current period.

APB 9 first dealt with prior period adjustments and was fairly restrictive. To be classified as a prior period adjustment under APB 9, an event or transaction had to be (a) identified specifically with particular prior periods, not attributable to economic events occurring subsequent to the prior period; (b) primarily determined by persons other than management; and (c) not susceptible to estimation prior to determination.[45] The criteria were definitive and in an efficient accounting system, the number of prior period adjustments would be very limited. However, the Securities and Exchange Commission's (SEC) staff increasingly began to question the application of APB 9. In SEC staff administrative interpretations of APB 9 and later in *Staff Accounting Bulletin No. 8*, it excluded charges or credits resulting from litigation from being treated as prior period adjustments. But this item was illustrated in APB 9 as a specific example of a prior period adjustment. As a result of this and other problems, the FASB reconsidered the concept of prior period adjustments.

SFAS 16 is the result of the FASB's reconsideration. It limits prior period adjustments to the following:

1. Correction of an error in the financial statements of a prior period.
2. Adjustments that result from realization of income tax benefits of preacquisition operating loss carryforwards of purchased subsidiaries.[46]

. SFAS 16 does not affect the manner of reporting certain accounting changes that are treated, for accounting purposes, like prior period adjustments. This treatment is required for a few specified changes in accounting principle, including changes from LIFO to another inventory method, changes in accounting for long-term construction contracts, and changes to

---

[44]Technical Issues Committee (1982, p. 9).
[45]APB (1966, para. 23).
[46]FASB (1977, para. 11).

or from the "full-cost" method used in the oil and gas industry. As mentioned earlier, frequently the FASB requires or permits changes in accounting principle that result from adoption of a new SFAS to be treated like prior period adjustments. Examples of these include SFAS 2, research and development cost; SFAS 4, early extinguishment of debt; SFASs 5 and 11, contingencies; SFAS 7, development stage enterprises; SFAS 12, marketable securities; SFAS 19, oil and gas; SFAS 35, reporting by defined benefit pension plans; SFAS 43, compensated absences; SFAS 45, franchise fee revenue; SFAS 48, revenue recognition when right of return exists; SFAS 50, records and music; SFAS 52, foreign currency; SFAS 53, motion pictures; SFAS 60, insurance; SFAS 61, title plant; SFAS 63, broadcasters; and SFAS 65, mortgage banking activities. Furthermore, several existing EDs call for retroactive restatement; however, the eventual resolution of those issues by the FASB cannot be predicted at this time.

EARNINGS PER SHARE

The term "summary indicator" was coined by the FASB in its 1979 Discussion Memorandum entitled *Reporting Earnings*.[47] It exists when information is summarized in such a way that a single item, the **summary indicator,** can communicate considerable information about an enterprise's performance or financial position. Examples of summary indicators include earnings per share (EPS), return on investment, and the debt-to-equity ratio. Undoubtedly the most used summary indicator to date, and the one that has received the most attention from accounting policy-making bodies, is EPS.

Reporting EPS has been commonplace for many years. However, the decision to report it, the manner in which it was calculated, and where it was reported were entirely at management's discretion prior to APB 9. This Opinion strongly recommended, but did not require, that EPS be calculated and reported in the income statement. It also suggested how hybrid securities, such as convertible debentures, should be handled in the calculation. However, without specific rules, EPS calculations can be manipulated, with the result of misleading users. Because of the potential for manipulation and the apparent reliance on reported EPS, the APB restudied the subject and, in 1969, issued APB 15.

APB 15 is a set of rigid rules that accountants must follow to calculate and report EPS. Those rules are designed to result in an EPS number that reflects the underlying economic substance of the capital structure of the

---

[47]FASB (1979).

reporting enterprise rather than its legal form. Needless to say, the calculations are complex and necessitated the APB's publishing an interpretative booklet of 116 pages. Subsequently the FASB, in SFAS 21, suspended APB 15 for nonpublic enterprises.

The usefulness of summary indicators in general and EPS specifically (because it is the most published and researched summary indicator) was the subject of an FASB research report entitled *Reporting of Summary Indicators: An Investigation of Research and Practice.*[48] The report found that summary indicators are used to evaluate past performance and predict future performance and financial position. Although EPS remains the most used single summary indicator, both return on investment and cash flow per share are gaining in popularity. The report concludes that the FASB need not be concerned at this time in establishing additional standards regarding summary indicators, but that it should attempt to educate users away from reliance on a single summary indicator, such as EPS. However, the continuing trend toward complexity in financial reporting and the information overload complaint of many will undoubtedly eventually require that the FASB add to its agenda a project on summary indicators.

SPECIALIZED SUBJECTS CONCERNING INCOME MEASUREMENT

Numerous accounting standards affecting income statements today exist. Earlier in the chapter, many of those standards, both of a generalized nature, such as APB 30, and of a narrow scope, such as SFASs 53 and 63, were examined. Another type of SFAS, "specialized subjects," provides important examples of the evolution and development of a consensus in accounting standards. As will be seen, this evolutionary process frequently takes several years and may have a significant impact on reported earnings. Moreover, these examples will reflect how the lack of a consistent accounting theory framework hinders the establishment of accounting practice standards.

DEVELOPMENT STAGE ENTERPRISES

A development stage enterprise is any enterprise that "is devoting substantially all of its efforts to establishing a new business" and either principal operations have not commenced or, if principal operations have com-

---

[48]Frishkoff (1981, particularly pp. 17–45).

menced, no significant revenues have been generated as yet.[49] A theoretical question exists as to whether certain costs incurred in the development stage should be properly expensed or deferred.

Theoretical justification can be made for deferring certain costs incurred in the development stage because these costs (1) have not generated revenue and (2) provide a future benefit such as the very existence of the enterprise and its ability to operate. Cost incurred in the development stage typically will be in connection with financial planning, exploring for natural resources, developing products and channels of distribution, and establishing sources of supply for raw material. Prior to January 1, 1976, costs of the nature described generally were deferred by enterprises in the development stage, while operating enterprises expensed most costs of a similar nature. Thus, a dual set of accounting standards existed—one for development stage enterprises and another for operating enterprises—even though there is no relevant circumstance separating the two.

SFAS 7 requires that costs of a similar nature be accounted for similarly, regardless of the stage of development of the entity incurring the cost. In other words, the FASB said the nature of the cost, not the nature of the enterprise, determines the appropriate accounting.

Cost incurred by development stage enterprises provides an interesting example of a setting in which multiple accounting theories, although all perhaps are equally supportable, can lead to different answers. The FASB certainly made a wise choice in terms of the issue here. This is particularly true because the FASB (1) required complete disclosure by the development stage enterprise to enable financial statement users not to be misled by heavy initial losses, while at the same time they (2) achieved uniformity on the basis of the nature of the transaction or event that has occurred rather than the nature of the enterprise experiencing the transaction or event. It is interesting to note, however, that this problem is yet another allocation problem. The FASB obviously opted for rigid uniformity in selecting a solution as opposed to finite uniformity, where relevant circumstance might be viewed as the development stage of the enterprise.

TROUBLED DEBT RESTRUCTURING

A **troubled debt restructuring** occurs whenever ". . . the creditor for economic or legal reasons related to the debtor's financial difficulties grants a concession to the debtor that it would not otherwise consider."[50] A troubled debt restructuring can have a significant impact on both the creditor's and debtor's income statements. The calculation of the impact (gain or loss) is not obvious, however. It is measured by both the debtor and creditor as the difference between the carrying amount of the obligation immediately

---

[49]FASB (1975b, para. 11).
[50]FASB (1977, para. 1).

prior to restructuring and the undiscounted total future cash flows after restructuring. Since APB 21 required discounting, the concept of present value is commonly accepted and used in accounting. However, it does not apply to the restructuring of debt.

If property or an equity interest is exchanged in satisfaction of the debt, the accounting is straightforward. The creditor recognizes a loss for the difference in fair market value of the asset or equity interest received and the carrying amount of the debt. The loss would probably not be extraordinary. The creditor recognizes a gain or loss (not extraordinary) for the difference between fair market value and book value of any property given up. In addition, the creditor recognizes an extraordinary gain equal to the difference in the fair market value of the asset given up and the carrying amount of the debt.

When the terms of the debt are modified, but it continues as an obligation (such as a reduction in interest rate, extension of maturity date, reduction in face amount, or similar modifications), the FASB concluded no transaction or event occurred as long as the total undiscounted future cash flows are equal to or greater than the carrying amount of the obligation. Thus, in this situation no gain or loss is recorded by either party. If total undiscounted future cash flow is less than the carrying amount of the debt, the obligation is reduced to the cash flow amount. The creditor records a loss for the reduction (not extraordinary) while the debtor records an extraordinary gain for the reduction. This again represents an example of rigid uniformity, one that does not appear to be based on any logical economic analysis.

EARLY EXTINGUISHMENT OF DEBT

The early extinguishment of debt provides an interesting example of changing standards and their effect on the income statement. Prior to APB 26, there were three acceptable methods of accounting for the gain or loss on early extinguishment: (1) amortize over the remaining life of the original issue, (2) amortize over the life of the new issue, or (3) recognize currently on the income statement. The APB opted for the third alternative and stated that criteria of APB 9 apply in determining whether the gain or loss is extraordinary.

The consensus of the accounting profession was that the gain or loss met the requirements to be classified as extraordinary. Nine months after APB 26 was issued, APB 30 was issued. This Opinion altered the criteria for extraordinary status established in APB 9. Under APB 30, the gain or loss from early extinguishment of debt definitely was not considered extraordinary. Thus, in the short period of nine months an item that typically was not given immediate income statement recognition became a mandatory extraordinary item and then a mandatory operating item. The amount involved is frequently very significant in relation to comprehensive income for a given period.

Finally the FASB settled the issue. In SFAS 4, they declared that gains and losses from the early extinguishment of debt, if material, are reported like, and along with, extraordinary items net of the applicable tax effects.[51] The reporting of a gain or loss from early extinguishment of debt provides a good example of where the standard-setting agency gave in to its constituency on a single-line financial statement item, but did not change the overall standard (of what qualifies as extraordinary). Obviously, the reason for the concession is the magnitude of the numbers involved.

INCOME SMOOTHING

A significant amount of empirical research in accounting has been directed toward the study of income smoothing. In particular, a hypothesis that has been tested is that income trends can be smoothed by discretionary management choices of accounting policies. A large body of research confirms the existence of income smoothing.[52]

Smoothing may come about in several ways. One way is simply the timing of transactions between two periods. Another way is a change in accounting policy; this method, however, cannot be used capriciously because of APB 20 requirements—and because of the likelihood of receiving a qualified audit report. Another area is the selection of one method (and its use on a consistent basis) where choice among methods exists. There is evidence that choice of alternative methods can smooth income. All three of these areas are, however, quite legitimate decisions for management to make.

A final area is classificatory smoothing—that is, smoothing operating income by classifying certain items as extraordinary. This type of smoothing could be regarded as manipulative, and beyond the legitimate choice of management. As the review in the earlier section indicates, it was very possible to manipulate income prior to APB 9, and was still possible afterward but to a lesser extent. APB 30 has virtually closed the opportunities for classificatory smoothing. Research evidence supports the existence of classificatory smoothing prior to APB 30.[53] Again, based on the earlier review of APBs 9 and 30, this is not a surprising finding. It does, however, help to understand why standard setters opted for rigid rather than finite uniformity. The circumstances which might justify classifying a transaction as extraordinary could not be specified narrowly enough to prevent abuses.

---

[51]FASB (1975a, para. 8).

[52]For a comprehensive literature review, see Ronen and Sadan (1981).

[53]See Ronen and Sadan (1981, Chapter 4) and Barnea, Ronen, and Sadan (1976).

It is interesting to consider the smoothing research findings in the light of efficient markets research. The efficient markets hypothesis would suggest that smoothing via mere accounting manipulations does not fool the market. As indicated in Chapter 6, this hypothesis has been strongly supported. As a result it has been said (with tongue only slightly in cheek) that accounting manipulation may be fun, but there is no money in it. If this is true, what explains the apparent existence of income smoothing behavior? There are two possible answers. One is that the research methodology has a built-in bias which has incorrectly identified smoothing behavior. This possibility has been suggested in a critique of smoothing research.[54] The other possibility is that internal reasons exist for income smoothing. Internal reasons would relate to managers maximizing their own utility. For example, smoothed income could be related to job security (meeting income targets), or incentive compensation arrangements. These are, of course, agency theory issues.

SUMMARY

The income statement based on the historical cost model will be with us for many years to come. That does not mean, however, that it will not change both conceptually and practically. Many changes in the income statement that have occurred in the past ten years provide a hint as to what might be expected in the future. It is safe to say that if abuses occur regarding the recognition of revenue, where a form of finite uniformity exists today, the FASB may edge more toward rigid uniformity. Likewise, in expense recognition which is largely based on a system of arbitrary allocation, it would not be surprising to see the FASB move toward rigid uniformity. Rigid uniformity has proved that it works satisfactorily in the nonoperating sections of the income statement and, therefore, reasonably may be assumed by the FASB to work in the operating sections.

For the past fifty years, the income statement has been viewed by users of financial statements, as well as by standard setters, as the predominant financial statement. A review of past ARBs and APBs clearly indicates that more time and effort was placed on refining the income statement at the sacrifice of the balance sheet. Since the inception of the FASB, however, there appears to have been a shift to "clean up" the balance sheet. The second SFAS on research and development cost was the first appearance of this shift as well as SFAS 19 on oil and gas and provides clear evidence of the FASB's thought.

---

[54]Ronen and Sadan (1981, Chapter 2).

QUESTIONS AND EXERCISES

1. The revenue recognition standard is approximately fifty years old. Is it applicable today? Is it applied consistently in all industries? Is it applied consistently to all similar transactions and events? Do you believe it should be changed? If so, what do you propose?

2. The recognition of expense frequently is dependent on the basis of a systematic and rational allocation. Is there any logical basis for selecting one allocation method over another? Discuss.

3. Is there any way the necessity of allocating costs can be eliminated from accounting? Discuss.

4. Is there any discernible trend in recent SFASs regarding transition? That is, does the FASB favor retroactive or cumulative effect when a new standard is applied initially?

5. APB 30 requires special accounting treatment for discontinued operations. Why is this special treatment required?

6. Why are prior period adjustments reported in the retained earnings statement instead of the income statement?

7. Evidence seems to indicate that even though the FASB applies extensive due process procedures prior to issuing an SFAS, the SFAS, once it has been issued, frequently does not completely clear up the controversy. As a result, the FASB must either reconsider the subject altogether (e.g., foreign currency) or issue several amendments and interpretations (e.g., leases). Why is this the case?

8. How have definitions of income, revenues, and expenses changed over time? Is a trend evident?

9. Why are there exceptions to the general principle of revenue recognition?

10. There has been a trend toward some rigid uniformity in the format of the income statement. Explain how and why this has occurred.

11. Why are the concepts of revenue realization and cost matching related to a revenue–expense approach rather than an asset–liability approach to the financial statements?

12. What does the efficient markets hypothesis (and research evidence) contribute to the analysis of gains and losses in the income statement, and of the possible alternative classifications reviewed in this chapter?

13. It was suggested in the chapter that extensive research and debate of the concepts of realization and matching are passé. What do you think was meant by this statement, and why is it probably true?

14. Review the accounting standards issued by the FASB which were discussed in the chapter. Classify each one as supporting the revenue–expense or asset–liability approaches. Is there any pattern evident?

15. A major problem facing the FASB today is not enough time to resolve all issues it faces. Do you believe the FASB should have undertaken the massive project of promulgating standards for specialized industries? Why? Why not?

CASES AND PROBLEMS

1. The JJT Corporation is a large manufacturer located in Kansas. Its operating data for the past three years are provided below.

	1985	1986	1987
Sales	$10,000,000	$12,000,000	$14,000,000
Cost of sales	6,000,000	7,000,000	8,200,000
Operating expenses	2,000,000	2,800,000	3,500,000
Interest expense	100,000	100,000	100,000
Uninsured loss from earthquake	—	—	500,000
Gain on sale of plant assets (not separate segment)	—	200,000	—
Estimated loss on sale of a segment	500,000	—	—
Realized loss on sale of segment (estimated above at 500,000)	—	650,000	—
Cumulative credit adjustment from change in accounting principle	—	—	200,000
Debit adjustment from correction of error made in prior years	300,000	—	—

Additional information:
1. The tax rate on all components of income is 32%.
2. The only tax/accounting timing differences relate to depreciation. In 1985 tax depreciation exceeded accounting depreciation by $100,000; in 1986, by $50,000; and in 1987, accounting depreciation exceeded tax depreciation by $40,000.
3. In 1987 JJT was sued in a patent infringement case. The suit is for $1,000,000, and lawyers estimate that approximately $200,000 actually may be lost. No accounting entry for this has been made.
4. Stock options were issued to key executives in 1987. They allow the purchase of 10,000 shares at $35 each. When granted, the shares

were selling for $38 per share, but the current price is $34 per share. No options have been exercised and no accounting entries recorded.

Required:
(a) Prepare an income statement in accordance with generally accepted accounting principles for each of the three years for which data are available.
(b) Discuss your classification of all items on the income statement and cite various authoritative standards in support of your position.

2. Bryco Incorporated (BI) has agreed to sell one of its subsidiaries to Flinto Corporation. The net assets of the subsidiary are $1,200,000—for which BI will receive 25,000 shares of $100 par value and 7% of newly issued nonconvertible preferred stock. The preferred stock carries a mandatory redemption feature (at par) in equal amounts of 5,000 shares over each of the next five years (5,000 shares 1 year from transaction date, 5,000 shares 2 years from transaction date, etc.). The preferred stock is nontransferable; therefore, BI cannot sell the stock nor does a market exist for it. An investment banker estimates that similar stock selling today probably would yield the buyer 10%. There is no collectibility question regarding the redemption of the preferred stock.

Required:
(a) Should revenue be recognized in the period in which the transaction is consummated, or should it be recognized as the preferred stock is redeemed?
(b) At what amount should the revenue or deferred revenue be recorded by BI?

3. Micro Tect Incorporated (MTI) is a high technology firm located in Weston, Connecticut. MTI has consistently followed a practice of expensing all costs incurred in its research and development department; however, certain other costs, called "preproduction and start-up costs," have been deferred and amortized on a unit of production basis over a 2- to 3-year period. That period is used because that is the average useful life of most MTI's products. According to MTI, the deferred costs are costs incurred in placing a developed product into production—including costs of material, labor, and overhead for the initial units produced and special equipment and tooling, special engineering tests, and excess material labor, as well as the overhead of the preproduction run because of the effect of the learning curve.

Required: Should any, or all, of the preproduction and start-up costs be deferred? Defend your analysis with reference to appropriate accounting standards.

4. Barbo Corporation (BC) makes electronic optical scanners. In the past (and currently) it has used a printed circuit board, but now is converting to a chip. BC contracted with an outsider to develop the mask for

making the chips. The contract with the outsider calls for three payments. The first payment is for designing the mask, the second for buying the design, and the third for a minimum purchase of chips.

Required: The basic question is whether the first payment should be expensed as outside research or deferred as tool design. Discuss the issues of expense vs. deferral, citing the appropriate authoritative standards. Which alternative do your favor? Why?

BIBLIOGRAPHY OF REFERENCED WORKS

Accounting Principles Board (1966). "Reporting the Results of Operations," *APB Opinion No. 9* (AICPA).
———— (1970). "Basic Concepts and Accounting Principles Underlying Financial Statements of Business Enterprises," *APB Statment No. 4* (AICPA).
———— (1971). "Accounting Changes," *APB Opinion No. 20* (AICPA).
———— (1973). "Reporting the Results of Operations," *APB Opinion No. 30* (AICPA).
Accounting Standards Executive Committee (1974). "Recognition of Profit on Sales of Receivables with Recourse," *SOP 74-6* (AICPA).
———— (1975a). "Accounting Practices in the Broadcasting Industry," *SOP 75-5* (AICPA).
———— (1975b). "Revenue Recognition When Right of Return Exists," *SOP 75-1* (AICPA).
American Accounting Association (1936). *A Tentative Statement of Accounting Principles Underlying Corporate Financial Statements* (AAA).
———— (1965a). "The Matching Concept," *The Accounting Review* (April 1965), pp. 368–372.
———— (1965b). "The Realization Concept," *The Accounting Review* (April 1965), pp. 312–322.
American Institute of Certified Public Accountants (1982). *Accounting Trends and Techniques* (AICPA).
Barnea, Amir; Joshua Ronen; and Simcha Sadan (1976). "Classificatory Smoothing of Income with Extraordinary Items," *The Accounting Review* (January 1976), pp. 110–122.
Committee on Accounting Procedure (1953). "Restatement and Revision of Accounting Research Bulletins," *ARB No. 43* (AICPA).
Committee on the Entertainment Industries (1973). "Accounting for Motion Picture Films," *Industry Accounting Guide* (AICPA).
Committee on Terminology (1955). "Proceeds, Revenue, Income, Profit, and Earnings," *Accounting Terminology Bulletin No. 2* (AICPA).
———— (1957). "Cost, Expense and Loss," *Accounting Terminology Bulletin No. 4* (AICPA).
Financial Accounting Standards Board (1975a). "Reporting Gains and Losses from Extinguishment of Debt," *Statement of Financial Accounting Standards No. 4* (FASB).

———— (1975b). "Accounting and Reporting by Development Stage Enterprises," *Statement of Financial Accounting Standards No. 7* (FASB).

———— (1977a). "Accounting By Debtors and Creditors for Troubled Debt Restructuring," *Statement of Financial Accounting Standards No. 15* (FASB).

———— (1977b). "Prior Period Adjustments," *Statement of Financial Accounting Standards No. 16* (FASB).

———— (1979). *Reporting Earnings* (FASB).

———— (1980). "Elements of Financial Statements of Business Enterprises," *Statement of Financial Accounting Concepts No. 3* (FASB).

———— (1982). "Financial Reporting by Broadcasters," *Statement of Financial Accounting Standards No. 63* (FASB).

Frishkoff, Paul (1981). *Reporting of Summary Indicators: An Investigation of Research and Practice* (FASB).

Jaenicke, Henry R. (1981). *Survey of Present Practices in Recognizing Revenues, Expenses, Gains, and Losses* (FASB).

Meyers, Stephen L. (1976). "A Proposal for Coping with the Allocation Problem," *Journal of Accountancy* (April 1976), pp. 52–56.

Philips, G. Edward (1963). "The Accretion Concept of Income," *The Accounting Review* (January 1963), pp. 14–25.

Ronen, Joshua, and Simcha Sadan (1981). *Smoothing Income Numbers: Objectives, Means, and Implications* (Addison-Wesley).

Sprouse, Robert T., and Maurice Moonitz (1962). "A Tentative Set of Broad Accounting Principles for Business Enterprises," *Accounting Research Study No. 3* (AICPA).

Sterling, Robert R. (1975). "Toward a Science of Accounting," *Financial Analysts Journal* (September–October 1975), pp. 28–36.

Technical Issues Committee (1982). *Sunset Review of Accounting Principles* (AICPA).

Thomas, Arthur L. (1969). "The Allocation Problem," *Studies in Accounting Research #3* (American Accounting Association).

———— (1974). "The Allocation Problem: Part Two," *Studies in Accounting Research #9* (American Accounting Association).

ADDITIONAL READINGS

REVENUE RECOGNITION

Horngren, Charles T. (1965). "How Should We Interpret the Realization Concept?" *The Accounting Review* (April 1965), pp. 323–33.

Mobley, Sybil C. (1966). "The Concept of Realization: A Useful Device," *The Accounting Review* (April 1966), pp. 292–296.

Myers, John H. (1959). "The Critical Event and Recognition of Net Profit," *The Accounting Review* (October 1959), pp. 528–532.

Storey, Reed K. (1959). "Revenue Realization, Going Concern and Measurement of Income," *The Accounting Review* (April 1959), pp. 232–238.

Thomas, Arthur L. (1966). "Revenue Recognition," *Michigan Business Reports No. 49* (Bureau of Business Research, Graduate School of Business Administration, University of Michigan).

Windal, Floyd (1961). "The Accounting Concept of Realization," *Occasional Paper No. 5* (Bureau of Business and Economic Research, Michigan State University).

MATCHING

Carroll, Thomas J. (1974). "The Accountants' Extraordinary Dilemma," *World* (Summer 1974), pp. 14–19.

Most, Kenneth S. (1974). "A Proposal for the Abolition of 'Extraordinary Events' and Transactions," *Singapore Accountant* (1974), pp. 23–29.

Snaveley, Howard J., and Allan H. Savage (1970). "Clean Surplus vs. Current Operating Performance—Gaps in APB Opinion No. 9," *New York Certified Public Accountant* (February 1970), pp. 124–129.

CHAPTER 10

Statement of Changes in Financial Position

The statement of changes in financial position (SCFP) reports on changes in assets, liabilities, and owners' equity account balances. Inclusion of a SCFP in the annual report was recommended by Accounting Principles Board (APB) 3 in 1963; however, it was not required.[1] The Securities and Exchange Commission (SEC) made it mandatory for statutory filings beginning in 1971.[2] In response to the SEC action, APB 19 was issued in 1971. It superseded APB 3 and made the statement mandatory for financial reporting.[3] An early name for this financial statement was the *funds flow statement*. APB 3 recommended the name *statement of source and application of funds*. The preferred name in APB 19, however, is *statement of changes in financial position*.

The name adopted in APB 19 is consistent with the information reported in the statement. The SCFP summarizes and classifies changes in all balance sheet accounts. Because the income statement is a subclassification of retained earnings in the balance sheet, both balance sheet and income

[1]APB (1963).
[2]SEC (1970).
[3]APB (1971).

statement transactions are included. Therefore, the SCFP is simply another way of classifying, summarizing, and reporting accounting transactions for a period.

APB 19 states that the reporting objectives of the SCFP are to (1) complete the disclosure of changes in financial position, (2) summarize financing and investment activity, and (3) report funds flow from operations. These three items of information cannot be directly obtained from an income statement and comparative balance sheets because of the manner in which data is aggregated in these two financial statements. Therefore, new information is reported in a SCFP, even though it summarizes the same transactions reported in an income statement and comparative balance sheets.

The logic and structure of the SCFP are examined in the first section of the chapter. Reporting requirements of APB 19 make up the next section, including an assessment of alternative formats and alternative definitions of funds. Usefulness of information reported in the SCFP is evaluated in the concluding section of the chapter. This section includes a review of empirical research that has investigated the value of information contained in the SCFP.

STRUCTURE OF THE STATEMENT OF CHANGES IN FINANCIAL POSITION

A statement of changes in financial position is a different way of classifying and reporting accounting transactions than occurs in a balance sheet and income statement. However, it relies on definitions and measurement of accounting elements from the other two financial statements, and for this reason it may be described as a derivative financial statement. The underlying logic can be summarized as follows:

$$\text{TRANSACTION CREDITS} = \text{TRANSACTION DEBITS} \quad (10.1)$$

There are two balancing sections in the statement of changes in financial position. These are called **sources of resources** and **uses of resources,** respectively. Sources of resources are defined as transaction credits. Transaction credits arise from increases in liabilities and owners' equity, and decreases in assets. Increases in liabilities and owners' equity represent new capital available to the firm from external sources such as debt and stock issues, and internal sources such as net income. Proceeds from the disposal of assets (asset decreases) also generate internal sources of resources available to the firm.

Uses of resources are defined as transaction debits. Transaction debits arise from decreases in liabilities and owners' equity, and increases in assets. Decreases in liabilities and owners' equity represent a reduction in the firm's capital. These types of transactions include debt retirement, capital reductions from many sources including treasury stock purchases, dividend payments, and of course net losses. Asset increases represent new investment, which is also a use of the firm's resources. In all cases, the firm's available resources decrease as a result of debit transactions.

The basic structure outlined in Equation 10.1 forms the logic of the SCFP. However, the SCFP is successor to an earlier financial statement called the funds flow statement. In a funds flow statement, certain balance sheet accounts are defined as comprising what is called the fund balance. The purpose of the statement was to show how the "fund balance" accounts increased from income and other sources, and how the "fund balance" accounts decreased from losses and other uses. The funds flow concept was emphasized because it represented the liquid, useable, and available resources of the firm. As such, it was an operating statement closer to cash flow accounting than accrual accounting. It was common for "fund balance" accounts to be defined as working capital accounts.

The funds flow statement has affected the structure of the SCFP. In both the sources and uses sections of the SCFP, transactions are subclassified into those affecting the fund balance and those affecting other accounts. The effect of net income on the fund balance is also reported separately. This complex structure of the SCFP is illustrated in Exhibit 10-1. It must be emphasized, though, that the basic logic is still as defined in Equation 10.1. The more complex format in Exhibit 10-1 is only a more detailed way of

---

EXHIBIT 10-1.

Standard Format of the Statement of Changes in Financial Position

Sources of Resources
(transaction credits)

1. Increases to the "fund balance" accounts.
    a. From net income.
    b. From other sources.
2. Other sources of resources.
3. Decrease, if any, in the fund balance for the period.

Uses of Resources
(transaction debits)

1. Decreases to the "fund balance" accounts.
    a. From net losses.
    b. From other sources.
2. Other uses of resources.
3. Increase, if any, in the fund balance for the period.

classifying transaction debits and credits; and it incorporates a funds flow statement within the SCFP.

Evolution from the funds flow statement to the SCFP represents an expansion of reported information. The funds flow statement included only the transactions listed under points 1a and 1b in Exhibit 10-1. Transactions not affecting fund accounts were excluded. The result was a report on the change in fund balance and how this change came about. The emphasis in funds flow reporting focused much more narrowly on liquidity.

By adding the transactions listed under point 2 in Exhibit 10-1, a comprehensive summary is made of all changes in financial position, not just those pertaining to "fund balance" accounts. This approach is referred to as either the all-inclusive or all-resources SCFP. The types of transactions listed under point 2 will pertain to investment and financing activities not affecting fund accounts. Examples include the conversion of convertible debt to common stock, stock issued for nonmonetary assets, dividends paid in property rather than cash, and nonmonetary exchanges of assets. APB 19 has opted for the all-inclusive approach rather than the narrower funds flow statement. However, it is apparent that a funds flow statement is still contained within the SCFP.

Preparation of the SCFP requires four distinct steps. The initial step is to define those balance sheet accounts making up the "fund balance" accounts. APB 19 permits any one of four definitions: cash, cash plus near cash (short-term marketable securities and other temporary investments), quick assets, and working capital. A discussion of these alternative definitions is presented later in the chapter.

The next step is to determine the effect of income statement transactions on the fund balance. Income (or loss) must be carefully analyzed and adjusted for any items not affecting the fund balance. For example, if funds are defined as working capital, all income statement debits and credits that have no corresponding credits and debits to current assets and current liabilities are excluded. Depreciation expense is an example. The credit to accumulated depreciation is to a nonfund account. After adjustments have been made to income, the adjusted number is classified as a source of resources if the amount is a credit balance (adjusted net income), and as a use of resources if the amount is a debit balance (adjusted net loss). This classification corresponds to point 1a in Exhibit 10-1.

The third step is to analyze all nonincome statement transactions in nonfund accounts. There are two possible types: transactions involving one fund account and one nonfund account, and transactions involving two nonfund accounts. When a transaction involves a fund and nonfund account, the transaction classification corresponds to point 1b in Exhibit 10-1. If a fund account is debited and a nonfund account is credited, the credit to the nonfund account would be classified as a source of resources because it is a transaction credit. An example would be a debit to cash and a credit to bonds payable for the issue of new debt. If a fund account is credited and a nonfund account is debited, the transaction would be classified as a use of resources because there is a debit to a nonfund account. An example would be a debit to assets and a credit to cash for the purchase of assets. These types of transactions represent investment and financing activity.

Transactions in which both the debit and credit affect nonfund accounts are classified as both sources and uses of resources. The debit represents a use of resources and the credit is classified as a source of resources. An example of this type of transaction is the conversion of convertible debt. The accounting transaction would be recorded as a debit to bonds payable and a credit to contributed capital. The debit is classified as a use of resources and the credit is classified as a source of resources. These types of transactions correspond to point 2 in Exhibit 10-1. They represent investment and financing transactions, but differ from the types in point 1b because there is no effect on fund accounts.

Finally, the balancing item in the SCFP is the change in the fund balance itself. The change is classified as a source or use of resources, depending on whether the balance has decreased or increased, respectively. The fund balance represents the equivalent of an asset account, so the change is reported in the same manner as a change in any other asset. A credit (decrease) represents a source of resources, and a debit (increase) represents a use of resources. This item corresponds with point 3 in Exhibit 10-1.

PRESENTATION OF THE STATEMENT OF CHANGES IN FINANCIAL POSITION

REQUIREMENTS OF APB 19

As indicated earlier in the chapter, APB 19 requires an all-inclusive SCFP. However, the definition of **funds** is a matter of choice. Working capital is the most widely used definition according to annual report surveys.[4] It is easy to understand why the working capital definition of funds dominates accounting practice. This definition of funds requires the fewest adjustments in converting the income number to funds flow from operations. In other words, working capital minimizes the cost of producing a statement of changes in financial position. As the definition of funds narrows to cash, more adjustments to net income will be required. This requires an extended analysis of income statement transactions.

Some of the major adjustments to income when funds are defined as working capital are shown in Exhibit 10-2. All adjustments represent in-

[4]American Institute of Certified Public Accountants (1982). Funds are defined as working capital for 78% of the 600 companies surveyed for the 1981 reporting year. There has been a shift to a cash definition, but working capital continues to dominate. For example, in 1978, 93% of the 600 companies defined funds as working capital.

come statement debits/credits which have no corresponding credits/debits to working capital accounts. The items in Exhibit 10-2 arise as a consequence of noncash accruals, deferrals, and allocations in the measurement of income.

Regardless of which definition of funds is chosen, all transactions in nonfund accounts are to be included in the statement of changes in financial position. This is true even if the transactions have no direct effect on fund accounts. When funds are defined as working capital, nonfund transactions are restricted to nonmonetary transactions, such as nonmonetary exchanges of assets and the conversion of convertible debt to common stock. Of course when funds are defined as cash, there are many additional accounting transactions that do not affect cash. Therefore, the narrower the definition of funds, the greater the number of nonfund transactions to be reported separately. This is the reason why a working capital definition of funds minimizes the cost of producing a SCFP.

APB 19 does not specify format beyond (1) the source and use classification, and (2) a requirement that the increase or decrease to funds from

---

EXHIBIT 10-2.
Examples of Nonfund Adjustments to Income when Funds Are Defined as Working Capital

---

Elimination of Income Statement Credits

1. All book gains (both ordinary and extraordinary) arising from asset disposals, debt retirement, and debt restructuring.
2. Amortization of premiums on debt.
3. Amortization of discounts on investments.
4. Extraordinary gains arising from a change in accounting principle.
5. Equity accounting investment income in excess of cash dividends.
6. Amortization of deferred investment tax credits.
7. Amortization of deferred gains from sales–leaseback transactions.
8. Tax expense in excess of taxes payable due to deferred taxes.

Elimination of Income Statement Debits

1. All book losses (both ordinary and extraordinary) arising from asset disposals, debt retirement, and debt restructuring.
2. Amortization of discounts on debt.
3. Amortization of premiums on investments.
4. Depreciation, depletion, and leasehold amortization.
5. Amortization of intangible assets and deferred charges.
6. Tax expense reductions relating to reversals of deferred taxes.
7. Extraordinary losses arising from a change in accounting principle.
8. Equity accounting investment losses (less cash dividends).
9. Amortization of deferred losses from sale–leaseback transactions.
10. Compensation expense due to the issue of employee stock options.

income-producing operations be disclosed separately. This latter requirement can be met in one of two ways: the indirect method, which entails an
adjustment to accounting income as described above in Exhibit 10-2; and
the direct method, which reports individual revenues and expenses adjusted for nonfund effects. Fund increases or decreases from income-producing operations must be presented before extraordinary items, with extraordinary items being disclosed separately. When funds are defined as
working capital, a separate schedule must also be presented showing
changes in each of the working capital account balances.

The following specific disclosures are also required:

1. Outlays for long-term assets.
2. Proceeds from sale of long-term assets.
3. Conversion of long-term debt or preferred stock to common stock.
4. Issuance, redemption, and repayment of long-term debt.
5. Issuance, redemption, or repurchase of capital stock.
6. Distributions of assets to stockholders (excluding stock dividends
   and stock splits).

The information contained in the first five disclosures pertains to investment and financing transactions. These types of transactions will be classified under items 1b or 2 in the basic format illustrated in Exhibit 10-1. By
specifying these five items of disclosure, APB 19 is simply assuring that
detailed information regarding investment and financing transactions is reported in the SCFP.

Item 6 in the list specifies the only transactions not reported in the
SCFP: stock dividends and stock splits. The rationale for excluding these is
that they represent nothing more than a reclassification within owners' equity accounts. A stock dividend results in a debit to retained earnings and
a credit to contributed capital, while a stock split entails nothing more than
a memorandum denoting the change in par value and number of shares
issued. By excluding these two transactions, APB 19 is saying there is no
real change affecting the firm on account of stock splits or stock divdends.

A criticism sometimes made of APB 19 is that too much information is
reported in a SCFP. There is liquidity information concerning the effect of
operations and other transactions on fund accounts, and there is investment
and financing information. However, the problem is not that too much information is being reported. The problem is that the simple use and source
classification system is not the best way to summarize these three distinct
types of information. Alternative formats are considered later in the
chapter.

ALTERNATIVE DEFINITIONS OF FUNDS

Given that there are four alternative concepts of funds, which definition
(if any) should be required in an accounting standard? APB 19 did not

address this issue and permits any of the four to be used. A FASB discussion memorandum suggests the following criterion in choosing the most relevant definition:

> The definition of funds adopted should be the one that provides the most information to users for making their assessment of future cash flows.[5]

The question, then, is which definition of funds is the best *predictor* of future cash flows from operations. Current cash flows from operations are not necessarily a good predictor. Cash flows from operations are erratic from period to period, owing to inventory increases or decreases and to unevenness in the collection of accounts receivable. Therefore, the most direct measure of past cash flows is also the most volatile from period to period. This same criticism would also hold for funds defined as cash plus near cash.

Another definition of funds is **quick assets** which are defined as cash, near cash, and accounts receivable. Quick assets would be less volatile from period to period than either cash, or cash plus near cash, because of the inclusion of accounts receivable in the funds definition. Yearly variations in the collection of accounts receivable would not be reflected in the fund measurement if fund accounts include accounts receivable. Working capital would be the least volatile measure of funds because inventory and current liabilities are included. Changes in inventory would normally be accompanied by changes in either cash or accounts payable. The net effect of inventory changes on the fund balance would be zero if funds are defined as working capital.

In terms of the yearly volatility of funds flow from operations, working capital is the lowest; and as the definition of funds moves closer to cash, greater yearly volatility could be expected to occur. This single criterion, however, does not necessarily make working capital flows a better predictor of future cash flows. The existence of yearly volatility simply makes it difficult to develop a predictive model for predicting future cash flows from current funds flow.

On the other hand, less volatility in working capital flows from operations does not guarantee that a good model can be developed to predict future cash flows. Working capital from operations may be very stable from year to year, but the figures may have no relevance for predicting future cash flows. In order to be a good predictor, working capital flows need to have some identifiable relationship with future cash flows. The mere fact that working capital is less volatile does not ensure usefulness for predictive purposes. At this point in time, we do not know which definition of funds is most relevant for predicting future cash flows. It may be that this is why APB 19 permits flexibility.

Funds flow from operations also provide an *assessment* of a firm's current results. At issue here, then, is which definition of funds is most rele-

---

[5]FASB (1980).

vant for assessing past operations. Funds flow reporting is intended to report on how the firm's liquid resources have changed as a result of income activity and other transactions. When funds are defined as cash, it is quite clear what the measurement of funds flow represents. It represents the net cash effect from income-producing activities and other transactions. As the definition of funds moves away from cash, it is less clear what is being measured. For example, working capital is not a good measure of liquidity because current assets and current liabilities contain deferred charges and credits which are noncash items. In addition, conversion of current assets to cash could take up to a year or even longer if the firm's operating cycle exceeds one year. Quick assets provide a better measure of liquidity because all the assets could be converted to cash readily (assuming accounts receivable can be factored). Cash and cash plus near cash are obviously faithful measures of liquidity.

Rigid uniformity will be achieved only if all companies use the same definition of funds. However, this may not necessarily produce the most useful information for all companies. It is possible that different definitions of funds would be better for some firms or industries. From a policy viewpoint it is necessary to determine if flexibility is needed in order to report relevant information in the SCFP. If there is evidence to support the need for different definitions of funds, then finite uniformity could be prescribed to recognize the relevant circumstances. However, the current system of unconditional choice is hard to justify.

CLASSIFICATION, PRESENTATION, AND FORMAT

Classification and presentation formats are defined only in broad terms by APB 19. In general the information is to be presented as illustrated in Exhibit 10-1. Funds flow from operations are included as a separate subsection and may be presented by either the direct or indirect methods. The **direct method** discloses how funds are derived from operations in terms of individual revenue and expense accounts. It is an income statement recast in terms of funds flow. The **indirect method** adjusts the aggregate income number for those items in the income statement which have no effect on funds. The difference between these two formats is the level of detail reported. More detail is presented with the direct method and less with the indirect method. Present accounting practice is dominated by the indirect method.[6] Holding aside the problems of production cost and possible information overload, more detail is preferable to less. Therefore, the direct method would be the preferable approach. Examples of the two formats are presented in Exhibit 10-3.

The same question of detail versus aggregation applies to the overall classification format. The source-and-use format uses two classifications.

---

[6]American Institute of Certified Public Accountants (1982). The indirect method was used by 578 of the 600 companies surveyed for the 1981 reporting year.

EXHIBIT 10-3.

Format Alternatives

Report of Working Capital Provided by Operations
for the Year Ended December 31, 1979

Sales		$13,517,550
Interest income		54,950
Dividends received from affiliate		25,200
		13,597,700
Cost of goods sold		9,238,950
		4,358,750
Selling, general, and administrative expenses (including amortization of prepaid expenses—$13,600)	$2,102,550	
Interest expense	379,100	
Income taxes payable	510,100	
		(2,991,750)
Working capital provided by operations		$ 1,367,000
Net income		$ 814,000
Items not affecting working capital:		
Depreciation		404,600
Amortization		38,500
Deferred taxes		183,300
Gain on sale of land and building		(19,800)
Increase in undistributed equity of affiliate		(53,600)
Working capital provided by operations		$ 1,367,000

Source: FASB (1980, pp. 48–49).

An expanded system could use three classifications: (1) funds flow from operations, (2) investment transactions, and (3) financing transactions; both increases and decreases would be included in the last two classifications. Investments would include increases to resources due to disposals (disinvestments) and decreases to resources due to new investment. Financing activities would be classified as increases to resources from borrowings and stockholder investments; and decreases would be resources to retire debt, pay stockholder dividends, purchase treasury stock and other capital reductions. A three-way classification system would more clearly report the three separate items of the information which are reported in a SCFP.

More detailed classification systems are possible. One format that has been suggested is the following: (1) funds provided from operations before interest and taxes (further subdivided into funds available for taxes, suppliers of debt capital, and stockholders); (2) investment transactions, subdivided into sources and uses; and (3) financing transactions, subdivided into sources and uses.[7] This system is an extension of the three-way classification system discussed above.

USEFULNESS OF THE STATEMENT OF CHANGES IN FINANCIAL POSITION

Statement of Financial Accounting Concepts (SFAC) 1 lists three general objectives of financial reporting. The first of these is very broad and simply states: "Financial reporting should provide information that is useful to present and potential investors and creditors and other users in making rational investment, credit, and similar decisions."[8] Two additional objectives can be thought of as specific ways of meeting the first objective. These are (1) reporting information about the firm's net resources and changes in those resources and (2) reporting information useful in assessing future cash flows. These two reporting goals are now considered with respect to the SCFP.

REPORTING CHANGES IN RESOURCES

A great deal can be inferred about the changes in a firm's resources from an income statement and comparative balance sheets. However, there is a loss in detail because the changes are reported in aggregate and represent "net" changes arising from both increases and decreases to the accounts. For example, a depreciable asset balance changes from investment and disinvestment, as well as from depreciation charges. The SCFP can supplement an income statement and comparative balance sheets by providing detail of the change, that is, details of both increases and decreases rather than the net effect. This is true regardless of how funds are defined. Although, as indicated earlier in the chapter, more new information is contained in the SCFP when funds are defined as cash. The reason for this is that more transactions will involve nonfund accounts and will be reported in the SCFP. At the very minimum, then, one useful purpose of the SCFP is to supplement the other two financial statements by providing detail lost in the aggregation process.

[7]FASB (1980).
[8]FASB (1978, para. 34).

FUNDS FLOW FROM OPERATIONS

Assessment of past cash flows and prediction of future cash flows from operations are important uses of accounting reports as identified in SFAC 1. The cash flow orientation was first stated in the Trueblood Report (discussed in Chapter 5). Historical reporting of funds flow data can be useful for making these cash flow assessments and predictions. A Financial Accounting Standards Board (FASB) discussion memorandum identified six reasons why funds flow data are a useful supplemental disclosure for this purpose.[9] The data

1. provide feedback on actual cash flows,
2. help to identify the relationship between accounting income and cash flows,
3. provide information about the quality of income,
4. improve comparability of information in financial reports,
5. aid in assessing flexibility and liquidity, and
6. assist in predicting future cash flows.

In one way or another all the above points deal with limitations of the income statement. This is not to say that income is useless, but rather, that funds flow data can supplement other information. Many types of information are useful and all useful information cannot be captured in the income statement.

Since funds flow is closer to actual cash flow than to accrual income (indeed they are the same when funds are defined as cash), it is obvious that funds flow is useful in assessing past cash flows (point 1). It follows that funds flow is also useful in understanding the actual cash flow being generated from operations (point 2)—that is, the relationship between accounting income and cash flows. The third point also relates to the cash flow component of accounting income. **Quality of income** is a term used by financial analysts to describe this relationship. The higher the correlation between accounting income and cash flows, the better the quality of earnings. The quality of earnings concept reflects an awareness that accounting income comprises many noncash accruals and deferrals, and that it does not give a good indication of liquidity.

The fourth point deals with the uniformity problem. Owing to flexibility in the choice of some accounting policies, comparability between companies may not be achieved. Comparability is achieved when the same events and circumstances are accounted for in the same way by all companies. As indicated in Chapter 7, many areas of accounting fail to achieve uniformity. Funds flow from operations is a simpler measurement and is less subject to arbitrary choices of accounting policy. For this reason, funds flow measurement is more uniform than income measurement and results in a higher level of comparability. If funds are defined as cash, cash plus

[9]FASB (1980).

near cash, or quick assets, the measurement of funds flow is virtually un-affected by arbitrary accounting policy choices exercised by management. This is less true if funds are defined as working capital because of the in-clusion of deferred charges and credits, as well as the arbitrary measure-ment of inventory.

Cash flow statements have been advocated as an alternative to account-ing income statements by those people concerned with the arbitrariness of income measurement.[10] There is an appealing simplicity to funds flow when contrasted with the abstractness and complexity of accounting in-come. However, as indicated in Chapter 6, the usefulness of accounting income is supported by research evidence. Accounting income is not use-less and is not likely to be replaced by the funds flow statement.

Accounting income will continue to be important, but new information will also be demanded. A few years ago when inflation was high, there was a demand for inflation-adjusted accounting income. At present there is con-siderable emphasis being put on cash flow data. An often-heard sentiment is that investors want earnings per share in good times and cash flows per share in bad times. Right now cash flow data is in demand because of what is perceived to be very high financial risk facing companies. It is also this concern that has emphasized the quality of earnings concept—in other words, identification of the "hard" cash flow items in income as distinct from the noncash accruals and arbitrary allocations.

The fifth point concerns the use of funds flow data to assist in assessing a firm's financial flexibility and liquidity. **Flexibility** is the ability of the firm to adapt to new situations and opportunities. **Liquidity** is the capabil-ity for quick conversion of assets to cash. Funds being generated internally from operations give one indication of both liquidity and flexibility. Funds flow represents internal resources available for debt servicing and repay-ment, new investment, and distributions to stockholders. This was the orig-inal reason for reporting a funds flow statement.

Liquidity information is also contained in the balance sheet. As noted in Chapter 8, however, the current–noncurrent classification system is a poor guide to liquidity; this is because some current items are deferred charges or credits that have no impact on future cash flows. Other assets such as inventory may not be readily converted into cash. Within the cur-rent group of assets, very few are actually convertible to cash within a short period of time. And since the attribute of measurement reported in the bal-ance sheet is normally something other than net realizable value, it is not possible to determine how much cash will be generated from assets. A bal-ance sheet presents nothing more than a crude ranking of liquidity. As a consequence, the balance sheet in its present form reveals very little about liquidity and flexibility. A funds flow statement, on the other hand, gives insight into the cash-generating potential of operations.

---

[10]This is due to arbitrary allocations in the determination of accounting income. See Thomas (1969).

The exit-price accounting system illustrated in Appendix 1-A to Chapter 1 is intended to measure flexibility of the firm in terms of the amount of cash which could be realized from nonforced liquidation of assets.[11] However, even exit-price measurement is only a crude indicator of liquidity and flexibility. While such a measurement system might provide an estimate of the cash conversion value of a firm's resources, it is the speed of conversion that ultimately determines both liquidity and flexibility. It is therefore questionable how useful exit-price accounting is for assessing a firm's flexibility. In addition, a firm is more likely to raise capital incrementally rather than by selling all its assets. In a normal situation a firm would not sell its productive assets to raise new capital needed for new investment opportunities. A firm is more likely to use either new capital or cash realized from assets being held for sale, such as inventories.

Flexibility and liquidity are not central features of present accounting. It is important to recognize the limits of what the financial statements can do. If flexibility and liquidity are important, it will be necessary to supplement the three financial statements. In recognition of this limitation, supplemental disclosure has been suggested in the areas of flexibility and liquidity. One recent proposal, for example, is the disclosure of a firm's lines of credit and other access to financing.[12]

The sixth and final point suggests that funds flow data is useful for predicting future cash flows. This question was addressed earlier when we reviewed alternative definitions of funds. It makes some sense that both cash flow and funds flow would be useful for predicting future cash flows. However, it is really not known if cash flow, funds flow, or accounting income are better predictors of future cash flows. The expanded disclosure philosophy would maintain that all potentially useful information should be disclosed, holding aside the question of costs. In the case of a SCFP, there is minimal cost in presenting the information since it is nothing more than a different way of summarizing and classifying accounting transactions for the period.

THE FASB'S RECENT INTEREST IN CASH FLOW REPORTING

In 1981 the FASB issued an exposure draft of a proposed concepts statement.[13] The exposure draft is an outgrowth of the 1980 FASB discussion memorandum on funds flow reporting. Cash flow data from operations are stated to be a useful supplement to the income statement and balance sheet. The justification for this viewpoint is based on the points discussed in the previous section.

The exposure draft states that cash flow data is useful in five areas: assessing income and its components, risk, financial flexibility, liquidity,

[11]Chambers (1966) used the term "adaptability," but it means the same thing as flexibility.
[12]FASB (1980).
[13]FASB (1981). Further work on the exposure draft is being held up, pending work on the recognition and measurement phases of the conceptual framework project.

and operating capability. The cash flow component of current income aids in understanding the nature of income, particularly where income is determined by complex rules, as now occurs. Cash flow data also aid in assessing financial risk, financial flexibility, and liquidity. Cash flows may help in evaluating the ability of operations to cover debt, which is one key aspect of financial risk and liquidity. Cash flow data also give some insight into the amount of internally generated funds for new investment and the replacement of capacity used in earning income.

There is strong interest by the FASB in funds flow reporting, but the emphasis is on supplementing information contained in balance sheets and income statements. It is also interesting to note that funds are assumed to mean cash in the exposure draft. If the draft concepts statement were adopted, APB 19 would probably be amended to define funds as cash. Such a change is consistent with the discussion throughout this chapter. A cash definition of funds yields the most new information about the firm's transactions for the period not available in an income statement or comparative balance sheets.

RESEARCH ON THE USEFULNESS OF FUNDS FLOW INFORMATION

There has been only limited research concerning the usefulness of funds flow information to decision makers. The findings have consistently shown that investors and analysts use funds flow information for securities analysis.[14] In one study, the ratio of fund flows from operations (the working capital definition) to debt was found to be one of the best predictors of business failures.[15] A survey commissioned by the Financial Accounting Foundation found that 67% of the analysts surveyed believe funds flow information is highly important.[16] The study also indicated a decline in the perceived importance of the accounting income number.

A few capital market studies have investigated the effect of funds flow information on security prices. One study found that funds flow measures were more highly correlated with security prices than was accounting income.[17] Another study found that funds flow had no *information content* when funds were defined as working capital. However, when funds were defined as cash, new information content was evidenced.[18] This last finding is consistent with the discussion throughout this chapter—that the most new information in a SCFP will occur when funds are defined as cash.

While the research has been limited, it does support that funds flow information has relevance and is useful to decision makers. This especially

---

[14] For example, see Clarkson (1962), Hawkins and Campbell (1978), and Backer and Gosman (1978).

[15] Beaver (1968).

[16] Louis Harris and Associates, Inc. (1980), cited in FASB (1980, p. 31).

[17] Staubus (1965).

[18] Gombola and Ketz (1980), cited in FASB (1980, p. 31).

seems to be the case when funds are defined as cash. The information content of investment and financing information reported in a SCFP has not been researched. However, since this type of investment and financing information is not contained in the other two financial statements, it would also seem to be a very important disclosure.

SUMMARY

The statement of changes in financial position is a derivative statement. It relies on definitions of accounting elements and rules of recognition and measurement from the balance sheet and income statement. Therefore, the SCFP is an alternative way of summarizing, classifying, and reporting accounting transactions for a period. But because of the way transactions are aggregated and reported in the balance sheet and income statement, there is new information contained in a SCFP. The new information falls into three categories: investment transactions, financing transactions, and funds flow from operations.

Choice in the definition of funds does not appear to be justified. The most new information is reported in a SCFP when funds are defined as cash. In addition the simple source and use classification system does not clearly present the three separate types of information being reported in the SCFP. A three-way classification system which identifies separately funds flow from operations, investment, and financing transactions would be an improvement on the simple two-way system required by APB 19.

Recent activity by the FASB indicates a renewed interest in funds flow reporting. The FASB views funds flow data in a supplemental role to the balance sheet and income statement. The emphasis by the FASB is on cash flow reporting, in other words, a cash definition of funds. This is consistent with research findings that the most new information is reported when funds are defined as cash.

QUESTIONS

1. Why does a statement of changes in financial position contain new and useful information not reported in a balance sheet or income statement?
2. Explain how funds flow data complements the income statement and balance sheet.

3. How does the statement of changes in financial position articulate to the balance sheet and income statement?
4. What is the "quality of earnings" concept, and how does funds flow reporting relate to it?
5. Why is cash flow reporting advocated as an alternative to accounting income by critics of accounting allocations such as Thomas (1969)?
6. What attribute is being measured in the statement of changes in financial position, and how well is representational faithfulness achieved with each of the different measures of funds flow from operations?
7. What are the arguments supporting the different definitions of funds? Can flexibility as permitted by APB 19 be justified?
8. Why is there more new information in a SCFP when funds are defined as cash?
9. How could the format requirements of APB 19 be improved?
10. What criticisms can be made of APB 19 in terms of uniformity, representational faithfulness, and relevance of the statement of changes in financial position?
11. Explain why the adjustments summarized in Exhibit 10-2 are necessary to derive funds flow from operations. Give additional examples of your own. What would be some additional adjustments required if funds are defined as cash?
12. What is the purpose of reporting changes in all resources, in addition to the change in fund balance from operations and other sources?
13. Why is the statement of changes in financial position called a derivative statement?
14. It was suggested in the chapter that liquidity and flexibility data do not compose a central feature of financial reporting. Explain why this is so.
15. What do research findings indicate concerning the usefulness of the SCFP? Why is "information content" of the SCFP difficult to measure using the methodology discussed in Appendix 6-A of Chapter 6?

CASES AND PROBLEMS

1. **a** Give five examples of income adjustments required to derive funds flow from operations. The five examples should be adjustments that are required if funds are defined as cash (but not required if funds are defined as working capital). For example, the accrual of uncollectible accounts expense would require adjusting if funds are cash, but not if funds are working capital. Why is more new information reported about the components of income if funds are defined as cash?

   b Refer to Exhibit 10-1. Give five examples of transactions that would be classified under category 1b if funds are defined as working capital,

---

EXHIBIT FOR CASE 2

W. T. Grant Company Net Income, Working Capital and Cash Flow From Operations
For Fiscal Years Ending January 31, 1966 to 1975.

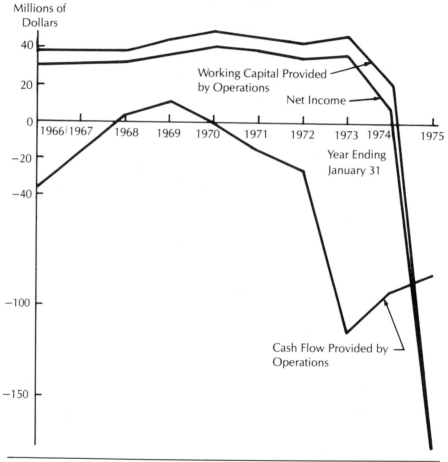

Source: Largay and Stickney (1980).

but which would be classified under category 2 if funds are defined as cash. For example, a five-year interest-bearing note issued in exchange for an account payable balance would be classified under 1b if funds are working capital, but under category 2 if funds are cash. For these types of transactions does the definition of funds affect the amount of information reported?

c Refer again to Exhibit 10-1. Give five examples of transactions that would affect fund accounts only if funds are defined as working capital, but which would be reported under categories 1b or 2 if funds are defined as cash. For example, collections of prior period accounts receivable (Dr. cash, Cr. accounts receivable) affect only working capital accounts; but if funds are defined as cash, the transaction would be reported under category 1b. How does the definition of funds affect the amount of information reported in the SCFP for these types of transactions?

d What overall conclusion do you reach regarding the relationship between the definition of funds and the amount of information reported in the SCFP?

2. Presented in the Exhibit for Case 2 is a graph of accounting income, cash flows from operations, and working capital flows from operations for W. T. Grant Company, a retailer which filed for bankruptcy in 1976. As late as 1973, the company's stock was selling for twenty times earnings. What does the chart indicate concerning the usefulness of income and funds flow? What could explain the significant differences between working capital flows and cash flows?

BIBLIOGRAPHY OF REFERENCED WORKS

Accounting Principles Board (1963). "The Application and Source of Funds," *APB Opinion No. 3* (AICPA).
———— (1971). "Reporting Changes in Financial Position," *APB Opinion No. 19* (AICPA).
American Institute of Certified Public Accountants (1982). *Accounting Trends and Techniques—1982* (AICPA, 1980).
Backer, Morton, and Martin L. Gossman (1978). *Financial Reporting and Business Liquidity* (National Association of Accountants).
Beaver, William H. (1968). "Alternative Accounting Measures as Predictors of Failure," *The Accounting Review* (January 1968), pp. 113–122.
Chambers, Raymond J. (1966). *Accounting, Evaluation and Economic Behavior* (Prentice-Hall).
Clarkson, Geoffrey P. E. (1962). *Portfolio Selection: A Simulation of Trust Investment* (Prentice-Hall).
Financial Accounting Standards Board (1978). "Objectives of Financial Reporting by Business Enterprises," *Statement of Financial Accounting Concepts No. 1* (FASB).
———— (1980). *FASB Discussion Memorandum: An Analysis of Issues Related to Reporting Funds Flows, Liquidity, and Flexibility* (FASB).
———— (1981). *Reporting Income, Cash Flows, and Financial Position of Business Enterprises* (Exposure Draft) (FASB).
Gombola, Michael J., and J. Edward Ketz (1980). "Similarities Among Asset Flow Measures" (Unpublished Paper, University of Connecticut).
Hawkins, David F., and Walter J. Cambell (1978). *Equity Valuation: Models, Analysis and Implications* (Financial Executives Research Foundation).

Largay, James A. and Clyde P. Stickney (1980). "Cash Flows, Ratio Analysis and the W.T. Grant Company Bankruptcy," *Financial Analysts Journal* (July–August 1980), pp. 51–54.

Louis Harris and Associates, Inc. (1980). "A Study of the Attitudes Toward and an Assessment of the Financial Accounting Standards Board," (Louis Harris and Associates, Inc.).

Securities and Exchange Commission (1970). "Adoption of Article 11A of Regulation S-X," *Accounting Series Release No. 117* (SEC).

Staubus, George J. (1965). "The Association of Financial Accounting Variables with Common Stock Values," *The Accounting Review* (January 1965), pp. 119–134.

Thomas, Arthur L. (1969). "The Allocation Problem," *Studies in Accounting Research #3* (American Accounting Association).

ADDITIONAL READINGS

Anton, Hector R. (1962). *Accounting for the Flow of Funds* (Houghton Mifflin, 1968).

Buzby, Stephen L., and Haim Falk (1974). "A New Approach to the Funds Statement," *Journal of Accountancy* (January 1974), pp. 55–61.

Coleman, Almand R. (1979). "Restructuring the Statement of Changes in Financial Position," *Financial Executive* (January 1979), pp. 34–42.

Giese, J. W., and T. P. Klammer (1974). "Achieving the Objectives of APB Opinion No. 19," *Journal of Accountancy* (March 1974), pp. 54–61.

Gonedes, Nicholas J. (1969). "The Significance of Selected Accounting Procedures: A Statistical Test," *Empirical Research in Accounting: Selected Studies, 1969* (Supplement to *Journal of Accounting Research*,) pp. 90–123.

Goodman, Hortense, and Leonard Lorensen (1974). *Illustrations of the Statement of Changes in Financial Position: A Survey of Reporting Under APB 19* (AICPA).

Heath, Loyd C. (1978a). "Financial Reporting and the Evaluation of Solvency," *Accounting Research Monograph No. 3* (AICPA).

——— (1978b). "Let's Scrap the Funds' Statement," *Journal of Accountancy* (October 1978), pp. 94–103.

Jaedicke, Robert K., and Robert T. Sprouse (1965). *Accounting Flows: Income, Funds and Cash* (Prentice-Hall).

Johnson, Orace (1970). "Towards an 'Events' Theory of Accounting," *The Accounting Review* (October 1970), pp. 641–653.

Kafer, Karl, and V. K. Zimmerman (1967). "Notes on the Evolution of the Source and Application of Funds," *International Journal of Accounting Education and Research* (Spring 1967), pp. 89–121.

Largay, James A.; Edward P. Swanson; and Max Block (1979). "The Funds' Statement: Should it be Scrapped, Retained or Revitalized? *Journal of Accountancy* (December 1979), pp. 88–97.

Lawson, G. H. (1978). "The Rationale of Cash Flow Accounting," in *Trends in Managerial and Financial Accounting*, ed. C. van Dam (Leiden), pp. 85–104.

Lee, T. A. (1972). "A Case for Cash Flow Reporting," *Journal of Business Finance and Accounting* (Summer 1972), pp. 27–36.

Mason, Perry (1961). "Cash Flow Analysis and the Funds Statement," *Accounting Research Study No. 2* (AICPA).

Moonitz, Maurice (1956). "Reporting on the Flow of Funds," *The Accounting Review* (July 1956), pp. 378–385.

Nurnberg, Hugo (1972). "APB Opinion No. 19—Pro and Con," *Financial Executive* (December 1972), pp. 58–70.

Rayman, R. A. (1969). "An Extension of the System of Accounts: The Segregation of Funds and Value," *Journal of Accounting Research* (Spring 1969), pp. 53–89.

Rosen, L. S., and Don T. DeCoster. "Funds' Statements: A Historical Perspective," *The Accounting Review* (January 1969), pp. 124–136.

Sorter, George H. (1969). "An 'Events' Approach to Basic Accounting Theory," *The Accounting Review* (January 1969), pp. 12–19.

——— (1982). "The Emphasis on Cash and Its Impact on the Funds Statement—Sense and Nonsense," *Journal of Accounting, Auditing and Finance* (Spring 1982), pp. 188–194.

Sorter, George; Martin S. Gans; Paul Rosenfield; R. M. Shannon; and Robert G. Streit (1974). "Earning Power and Cash Generating Ability," *Objectives of Financial Statements, Vol. 2, Selected Papers* (AICPA).

Spiller, Earl A., and Robert L. Virgil (1974). "Effectiveness of APB Opinion No. 19 in Improving Funds Reporting," *Journal of Accounting Research* (Spring 1974), pp. 112–133.

Thomas, Barbara S. (1983). "Deregulation and Cash Flow Reporting: One Viewpoint," *Financial Executive* (January 1983), pp. 20–24.

Yu, S. C. (1969). "A Flow of Resources Statement for Business Enterprises," *The Accounting Review* (July 1969), pp. 571–582.

CHAPTER 11

Conceptual Issues in Accounting for Inflation and Changing Prices

Inflation can be defined very simply as the rise in the average price level for all goods and services produced in an economy. We are all, of course, painfully aware of this phenomenon. It has wracked the United States fairly continually since the end of World War II though it really increased substantially in 1973 in the wake of the Arab oil boycott. Prices finally began moderating in late 1981 and 1982. Nevertheless, it is fairly safe to say that inflation has posed the single greatest problem that we face in accounting theory. Finally, it should also be added that, even in the absence of inflation, individual prices are always changing because of shifts in supply and demand for individual products and services.

Under a historical cost based system of accounting, inflation leads to two basic problems. First, many of the historical numbers appearing on financial statements are not economically relevant because prices have changed since they were incurred. This is, of course, the problem of representational faithfulness discussed in Statement of Financial Accounting Concepts 2 as an element of the primary quality of reliability. Second, since the numbers on financial statements represent dollars expended at different points of time and, in turn, embodying different amounts of purchasing power, they are simply not additive. Hence adding cash of $10,000 held on December 31, 1982 with $10,000 representing the cost of land acquired in 1955 (when the price level was significantly lower) is a dubious operation because of the significantly different amount of purchasing power represented by the two numbers.

Because of these two underlying problems, several aspects of the relevance quality are badly impaired under historical costing. It is quite likely that predictive value is restricted as a result of utilizing and combining dollars of different purchasing power. Uses of financial reporting for accountability are similarly inhibited owing to the basic shortcomings of historical costing. The same also applies to comparability among financial statements of different firms. Perhaps the principal deficiency resulting from the fundamental weaknesses of historical costs lies in the area of capital maintenance. Under historical costing, income is usually overstated relative to amounts that can be distributed to stockholders without reducing the beginning balance of the enterprise's net assets. Thus many "dividends" are really liquidating in nature, rather than stemming from earnings (as they appear to be under historical costing).

The purpose of this chapter is to examine some of the principal financial reporting responses to inflation and changing prices. A better appreciation of the complexities of inflation accounting can be gained as a result of seeing how price indexes are devised. Consequently, the chapter commences by illustrating how price indexes are constructed, using a very simple example. An in-depth examination of the various accounting responses to inflation and changing prices comes next. Included in this section is an explanation of basic terms that arise in this subject area, such as holding gains and purchasing power gains. With the various approaches to inflation in place, the third section presents a related series of simple examples showing the principle theoretical approaches to the problem. Of central importance here will be capital maintenance proofs, which underlie several of the methods. The concluding section of the chapter discusses two particularly difficult problem areas: (1) determining current value depreciation, and (2) a closer look at purchasing power gains on long-term debt during inflation.

CONSTRUCTING PRICE INDEXES

In order to measure the change in the level of prices occurring during a particular time period, a price index must be constructed. A **price index** is

EXHIBIT 11-1.

PRICES AND QUANTITIES OF X AND Y
SOLD DURING THREE TIME PERIODS

Time Period	Commodity X		Commodity Y	
	Price	Quantity	Price	Quantity
P_0	2.00	100	1.00	100
P_1	2.20	95	1.05	105
P_2	2.42	90	1.10	115

a weighted average of the current prices of goods and services; these averages are related to prices in a base period, and their purpose is to determine how much change has occurred.

Price indexes may be narrowly constructed to determine the changing level of prices in a particular segment of the economy, such as capital equipment used in the steel industry, or broadly constructed for ascertaining the change in prices for all goods and services of an economy. The first type is called a specific price index and the second a general price index. For both types of indexes considerable statistical sampling must be done because the number of goods and services involved, as well as the number of transactions occurring, may be very large. Hence sampling error may easily occur, particularly if the weighting of certain transaction types is not representative of their actual occurrence during the period.

A simple example of price index construction is useful in terms of understanding the accounting process of price translation used in inflation accounting. Assume an economy in which only two goods, X and Y, are produced and consumed. The prices and quantities of X and Y sold during three periods are shown in Exhibit 11-1.

Our illustration will comprise two of the types of indexes that are widely used. The **Laspeyres index** is computed from the following formula.

$$I_n = 100 \cdot \frac{\sum_i P_{ni} \cdot Q_{oi}}{\sum_i P_{oi} \cdot Q_{oi}} \qquad (11.1)$$

where

$\quad I_n \quad$ = Index number for year n;

$\quad P_{ni}$ = Price at period n of commodity i;

$\quad P_{oi}$ = Price at period o (the base period) of commodity i;

$\quad Q_{oi}$ = Quantity sold in period o of commodity i;

$\quad \sum_i \quad$ = Sum over all items.

Substituting in the formula the transactions for commodities X and Y and using P_o as the base period, the indexes for P_1 and P_2 are:

$$P_1 = 100 \cdot \frac{(2.20 \cdot 100) + (1.05 \cdot 100)}{(2.00 \cdot 100) + (1.00 \cdot 100)} = 108.33 \qquad \textbf{(11.1a)}$$

$$P_2 = 100 \cdot \frac{(2.42 \cdot 100) + (1.10 \cdot 100)}{(2.00 \cdot 100) + (1.00 \cdot 100)} = 117.333 \qquad \textbf{(11.1b)}$$

The index tells us that prices in P_1 are 8.33% higher than in the base year and 17.33% higher in P_2 relative to the base year. In P_2 prices rose 9% relative to P_o (117.33 − 108.33). Prices rose 8.3% in P_2 relative to P_1 $\left[\frac{117.33}{108.33} - 1\right]$. The latter calculation, in effect, substitutes P_1 as the base year.

Another frequently used price index is the **Paasche index.** It is computed by means of the following formula:

$$I_n = 100 \cdot \frac{\sum_i P_{ni} \cdot Q_{ni}}{\sum_i P_{oi} \cdot Q_{ni}} \qquad \textbf{(11.2)}$$

where

Q_{ni} = Quantity sold in period n of commodity i.

Again substituting in the formula the transactions from Exhibit 11-1 and using P_o as the base period, the indexes for P_1 and P_2 are:

$$P_1 = 100 \cdot \frac{(2.20 \cdot 95) + (1.05 \cdot 105)}{(2.00 \cdot 95) + (1.00 \cdot 105)} = 108.22 \qquad \textbf{(11.2a)}$$

$$P_2 = 100 \cdot \frac{(2.42 \cdot 90) + (1.00 \cdot 115)}{(2.00 \cdot 90) + (1.00 \cdot 115)} = 116.71 \qquad \textbf{(11.2b)}$$

Paasche index calculations state that prices in P_1 are 8.22% higher than in the base year and 16.71% higher in P_2 relative to the base year. Relative to P_1, the price rise in P_2 is 7.84% $\left[\frac{116.71}{108.22} - 1\right]$. P_1 is used as the base year in the latter calculation.

As can be seen from this example, Laspeyres indexes use base year quantities only whereas Paasche indexes employ current year quantities. Whereas Laspeyres calculations may be somewhat "purer" because they employ base year quantities throughout, Paasche calculations take into account movement into goods and commodities that have become relatively cheaper, as can be seen even in this very simple illustration. As a result, Paasche indexes may be more cognizant of technological change since lower costs should result from using improved technology. On the other hand, because changes in quantities are largely ignored, Laspeyres indexes are less costly to construct.[1] The Wholesale Price Index (of the Department of Commerce) and the Consumer Price Index (prepared by the Department of Labor) are both Laspeyres-type indexes. The latter is required for general price-level adjustment by SFAS 33.

Price index calculations are obviously extremely complex. In addition to the far more important problem of possible sampling error, the fact that several index possibilities exist indicates that a conceptual problem of measurement is also present. Nevertheless, it appears to be far better to attempt to measure the results of inflation, no matter how crudely accomplished, instead of ignoring the problem.

AN OVERVIEW OF INFLATION ACCOUNTING

In discussing responses to inflation, one distinction must immediately be stressed: that between general purchasing power adjustment and current valuation. The difference in purpose and approach was briefly discussed in Chapter 1. General price-level adjustment is concerned with the change in purchasing power of the monetary unit over time relative to all goods and services produced by the economy. Adjustment is accomplished by taking the historical cost of an item and multiplying it by a fraction consisting of the general price index for the current period in the numerator divided by the general price index existing at the time of acquisition. Hence if land acquired for $10,000 in 1954, when the price index was 80, were being restated into 1979 dollars, when the index was 220, the calculation would be:

$$\$10,000 \times \frac{220}{80} = \$27,500.[2]$$

The $27,500 does not in any sense, except by pure coincidence, represent the "value" of the land in 1979. The cost has simply been "translated" into the number of 1979 dollars having purchasing power equivalent to the number of dollars originally expended in 1954. Of course our examination of price index construction in the previous section shows that this is no easy measurement task.

Current valuation—also called current cost—represents an attempt to derive the specific value or worth for a particular point or period in time of

---

[1]For more on these points, see Weil (1976, pp. 101–104).

[2]If the land was restated in 1978 to $26,250 when the index was 210, the $27,500 can also be

determined by taking $26,250 \times \dfrac{220}{210}$.

assets, liabilities, expenses, and revenues. The two types of current valuation, referred to in Chapter 1, are called entry and exit values.[3] **Entry value**
refers to replacement cost in markets in which the asset, liability, or expense is ordinarily acquired by the enterprise. **Exit valuation** refers to the
net realizable value or disposal value of the firm's assets and liabilities in
what has been termed a system of "orderly liquidation."[4] Both measures are
examples of opportunity costs and both are certainly relevant in some decision situations, such as capital budgeting. The underlying arguments,
both pro and con, for these measurements require a closer examination.

ENTRY VALUES

One of the principal arguments of entry value adherents is that in most
cases, value in use to the firm is best represented by replacement cost. In
order to understand the meaning of "value in use" for assets, three valuations must be compared: present value of future cash flows attributable to
the asset (PV), entry value or replacement cost (EV), and exit or net realizable value (NRV).[5]

Possible Ordering Combinations

With three value types, six possible ordering combinations can occur:

1. NRV>PV>EV
2. NRV>EV>PV
3. PV>EV>NRV
4. PV>NRV>EV
5. EV>PV>NRV
6. EV>NRV>PV

All three measures would be totally identical for cash. PV and EV
would appear to be virtually identical for accounts and notes receivable net

---

[3]The terms appear to have first been used by Edwards and Bell in their classic work. Both
terms were used by them with regard to three different time dimensions: past, current, and
future. See Edwards and Bell (1961, pp. 74–80). Today the terms *entry value* and *exit value*
used alone are understood to be referring to the present time dimension.

[4]Edwards and Bell (1961, p. 76) denote exit value as being net of removal costs and transport
and installation costs that the seller might have to bear. For major fixed-asset installations,
these costs might be considerable. Sterling (1979, p. 220, footnote 1), in his conception of exit
value, would not deduct these and similar costs. Chambers does not even appear to treat the
issue in his major work. However, his definition of "current cash equivalent" does not appear
to take these reductions into account. See Chambers (1966, pp. 201–202, 208–209, and 218),
for example. For exit values to be representationally faithful to the concept of measuring the
total funds available to the firm, selling price net of costs of disposition appears to be the most
appropriate measure. Of course these costs would fall heaviest in the first year of an asset's
usage.

[5]There has been an extensive discussion and analysis of "value in use" and the relation of these
concepts in the literature. See, for example, Solomons (1966, pp. 122–125), Bell (1971, pp.
26–31), and Parker and Harcourt (1969, pp. 15–20).

of allowance for doubtful accounts. NRV would be lower, as evidenced by factoring of accounts receivable and discounting of notes receivable. EV is higher than NRV for marketable securities, due to the effect of commissions. The crucial assets—because of their materiality—are inventories held for resale, productive fixed assets, and possibly intangibles. Our analysis, therefore, concentrates on inventories and fixed assets.

An asset should be held for use as long as PV>NRV. If, on the other hand, NRV>PV, the asset should be sold. Consequently, in situations 3, 4, and 5 assets will be held for use whereas in 1, 2, and 6 they should be sold. Situations 3, 4, and 5 would definitely appear to be applicable to the majority of fixed and intangible assets. Assets should continue to be used and replaced as long as situations 3 and 4 prevail because productive usage (represented by PV) predominates. Situation 3, in fact, would be expected to be the single most predominant circumstance for productive fixed assets. Situation 4 would be highly unusual. Since NRV is greater than EV, the asset should be sold as well as being used, though primary use would continue to be productive because PV>NRV. In situation 5 the asset should continue to be used productively but should not be replaced.

In cases 3, 4, and 5, PV represents value in use to the firm. However, since PV is based on estimating and discounting future values, it will assuredly be less verifiable than either EV or NRV. Given the choice between EV and NRV as a proxy for PV, it should be borne in mind that the latter will almost always be lower than the former for three reasons: (1) NRV includes the effects of "tearing out" costs and other disposal-related elements; (2) since the enterprise is only a sporadic seller of productive fixed assets, it may be able to communicate with only a limited number of potential buyers of the asset; (3) since the firm does not ordinarily deal in the productive asset, perceptions of its quality may be more negative than is warranted. The difference between EV and NRV is thus brought about by special considerations that are totally unrelated to productive usage represented by PV. Therefore EV appears to be a better indicator of economic value than NRV for productive fixed assets and intangibles. For these assets EV would thus appear to have greater utility for purposes such as predictive ability and accountability.

Situations 1, 2, and 6 where resale is appropriate would be applicable to inventories. Case 6 indicates that the item should be sold but not replaced. NRV represents selling price of inventories less costs of completion and selling. The main difference between NRV and EV is the unrealized income element, even though both are a form of current value. A case might therefore be made for NRV for inventories resulting in multivaluation bases for assets; but this treatment leads to the additivity problem.[6] Consequently, on the basis of analysis of value in use for inventories and fixed assets, if one valuation base is to be selected, an extremely strong case can be made for EV.

---

[6]Indeed, Sprouse and Moonitz (1962, p. 57) opted for net realizable value of inventories in their broad principles study.

Measurement Problems

There are numerous estimation difficulties in terms of determining current entry valuations. Direct measurements are preferable to indirect ones because they are more representationally faithful, more verifiable, and usually less expensive to produce.

Direct measurement for inventories would be determined by obtaining the current selling price in the market where goods are normally acquired by the firm—or the current manufacturing cost if the firm usually produces them. There should be no problem for commonly acquired items, but manufactured goods present a more complex situation. Current costs of raw materials, direct labor, and variable overhead are relatively easy to find out. Fixed overhead costs, particularly depreciation, are more difficult. Consequently, indirect measurement of the fixed overhead element of manufactured inventories may have to be resorted to by means of specific index adjustment.

In the case of fixed assets, direct measurement would be determined by finding the selling price in the used-asset market of the same type of asset in the same condition as that being valued. Appropriate secondhand valuation is possible only for a relatively small proportion of fixed assets. Replacement cost of the majority of fixed assets would have to be indirectly measured, by means of appropriate specific index adjustment.

EXIT VALUES

The underlying rationale of exit valuation totally differs from the entry value orientation. Exit value adherents see the firm in a constant state of flux. Over a long enough period of time, a firm will indeed turn over the majority of its productive assets. Exit value balance sheets provide a measure of the firm's adaptability: the capacity to switch out of its present asset structure into new opportunities. **Exit valuation** denotes the selling price that can be received from the firm's assets when sold through a process of orderly liquidation. **Orderly liquidation** refers to a situation in which the firm continues operations—as opposed to the larger discounts arising in forced liquidation circumstances.[7]

Under exit valuation, the balance sheet becomes the principal financial statement. The income statement shows the increase in the firm's adaptive ability resulting from operations during the period. However, the income statement under exit valuation is likely to have severe limitations for predictive ability and accountability objectives because of disproportionate declines from purchase price to exit valuation that arise immediately after an

---

[7]Orderly liquidation refers to disposal of assets in the usual course of business operations where the firm is not forced to accept heavily discounted prices. See Chambers (1966, p. 204). Of course, it would be impossible, by definition, to have an orderly liquidation of an enterprise's entire stock of nonmonetary assets.

asset is acquired, as discussed above. Indeed exit value partisans deny that accounting numbers can have significance for predictive ability purposes.[8]

Exit values are a form of opportunity cost. They represent the sacrifice to the enterprise of holding its existing package of assets. Unquestionably exit values also provide numbers which are additive. On balance, however, despite a small but vocal number of supporters, the preponderance of opinion among both researchers and members of standard-setting bodies is strongly disposed toward replacement costs. The advantage of entry values is comparative, rather than absolute. Both numbers have relevance based on the particular needs at hand. Capital budgeting analyses, for example, require the exit values of currently owned assets that may be disposed of and the entry values of assets that may be acquired. Both measures can be criticized on grounds of what can be termed "inapplicability." What is the significance of replacement cost if the asset is already owned? It is a matter, perhaps, of avoided sacrifice. Similarly, how meaningful is exit valuation if the present intention is to keep the asset? In this case it is a matter of opportunities foregone.

Both measures unquestionably have relevance. Our value judgment is in accordance with the majority. While exit values have importance, the great majority of an enterprise's assets will virtually never be converted into cash during any given short-run period. Furthermore, the weakness of the income statement in terms of user objectives other than adaptive ability has already been discussed. Conversely, the value-in-use analysis, particularly as it applies to productive fixed assets, is indeed persuasive. Consequently, the balance of our current value discussion will concentrate on the entry value alternative.

PURCHASING POWER GAINS AND LOSSES

Purchasing power gains and losses arise as a result of holding net monetary assets or liabilities during a period when the price level changes. **Monetary assets and liabilities** include cash itself and other assets and liabilities that are receivable or payable in a fixed number of dollars. These include accounts and notes receivable and payable and also long-term liabilities.[9]

Purchasing power gains and losses arise because monetary items, which are fixed in terms of the number of dollars to be received or paid, gain or lose purchasing power as the price level changes. The potential for

---

[8]Sterling (1979, pp. 125–136) contrasts measurements concerned with objective assessments of existing attributes of assets with forecasts of future phenomena, which are subjective and personal in nature. Chambers (1968, pp. 245–246) is far more vehement in his views. He strongly contrasts measurement of existing phenomena and any goal of predictive ability, which he sees as being tied to the process of "valuation."

[9]For an excellent discussion and analysis of the monetary versus nonmonetary distinction, see Heath (1972).

EXHIBIT 11-2.

PURCHASING POWER GAINS AND LOSSES

	State of the Economy	
State of the Enterprise	Inflation	Deflation
Net Monetary Asset Position	Purchasing Power Loss	Purchasing Power Gain
Net Monetary Liability Position	Purchasing Power Gain	Purchasing Power Loss

gains and losses is summarized in Exhibit 11-2 where "net monetary assets" refers to total monetary assets exceeding monetary liabilities and the converse is true for "net monetary liabilities."

Purchasing power gains and losses are determined by calculating the purchasing power of the monetary items available to a firm and comparing it with the actual amount of the net monetary accounts. A simple example should clarify the method of calculation. Assume a firm's activity in its monetary elements is summarized in the T-account that follows:

Net Monetary Assets

Beginning balance	$10,000		
1st quarter net inflows	8,000	2nd quarter net outflows	12,000
3rd quarter net inflows	13,000		
4th quarter net inflows	6,000		
	37,000		12,000
Ending balance	$25,000		

The general price index shows the following for the year:

Beginning index	180
1st quarter	192
2nd quarter	197
3rd quarter	205
4th quarter	210

To measure the purchasing power gain or loss for the year stated in terms of the purchasing power of the dollar during the 4th quarter, the beginning balance and the subsequent changes in net monetary items are restated in terms of their purchasing power measured in 4th quarter terms. This is done by multiplying these elements by a fraction consisting of the 4th quarter index in the numerator, divided by the index at the time the net change occurred or when the item was on hand (in the case of the beginning balance). This is shown in the following T-account:

Net Monetary Assets (in terms of 4th quarter purchasing power)

$$\$10,000 \times \frac{210}{180} = \$11,667$$

$$8,000 \times \frac{210}{192} = 8,750 \qquad\qquad 12,000 \times \frac{210}{197} \qquad\qquad \$12,792$$

$$13,000 \times \frac{210}{205} = 13,317$$

$$6,000 \times \frac{210}{210} = \underline{6,000} \qquad\qquad\qquad\qquad\qquad\qquad \underline{}$$

$$\underline{39,734} \qquad\qquad\qquad\qquad\qquad\qquad\qquad \underline{12,792}$$

$$\underline{\$26,942}$$

The ending balance in the price-level adjusted T-account shows the monetary purchasing power available to the firm measured in 4th quarter dollars. Since this is more than the actual amount of net monetary assets at the end of the year, the firm has lost purchasing power by holding net monetary assets during a period when the value of the dollar was declining.

All systems of both general purchasing power adjusted income and current value income include purchasing power gains and losses as an element of income. The measurement itself, however, may be in either general or specific purchasing power terms.[10] Classification would be as a nonoperating component of income.

HOLDING GAINS AND LOSSES

Just as monetary items are subject to a gain or loss as the price level changes, nonmonetary assets (which we will call **real assets**) are subject to a gain or loss as a result of change in their value. **Holding gains and losses** on real assets can be divided into two parts: (1) monetary holding gains and losses, which arise purely because of the change in the general price level during the period; and (2) real holding gains and losses, which are the difference between general price-level adjusted amounts and current values.

Monetary holding gains and losses are capital adjustments only. They are not a component of income. The disposition of real holding gains and losses is an important theoretical issue affecting the determination of income; we will examine that issue shortly.

Holding gains and losses can also be classified from the standpoint of being realized or unrealized in the conventional accounting sense.[11] A simple example should aid in clarifying these relationships. Assume that a piece of land was acquired for $5,000 on January 2, 1980, when the general

---

[10]For a discussion of the choice, see Gynther (1966, pp. 155–158).

[11]A good example is shown by Edwards (1954).

price index was 100. One-tenth of the land was sold on December 31, 1980, for $575. The entire parcel of land was valued at $5,750 on December 31, 1980. The total real and monetary holding gains are computed in the following manner:

Current value on December 31, 1980		$5,750
General price level adjusted historical cost on Dec. 31, 1980	($5,000 × $\frac{110}{100}$)	5,500
Total real holding gain		$ 250
General price level adjusted historical cost on Dec. 31, 1980		$5,500
Historical cost		5,000
Total monetary holding gain		$ 500

The total holding gain comprises the algebraic sum of the real and monetary holding gains or losses. Hence if all the facts were the same except that the current value of the land was $5,400 on December 31, 1980; there would have been a total real holding loss of $100.

Holding gains and losses are realized by the process of selling the asset or using it up over time in the case of a depreciable asset.[12] The division of the holding gains in the example is summarized in Exhibit 11-3.

With the concepts of holding gains and purchasing power gains and losses in place, we now take up an examination of income measurement systems that attempt to cope with the inflation problem and their underlying rationale.

EXHIBIT 11-3.

ANALYSIS OF HOLDING GAINS

	Holding Gain Type		
State	Real	Monetary	Total
Realized	$ 25	$ 50	$ 75
Unrealized	$225	$450	$675
Total	$250	$500	$750

---

[12]See Edwards and Bell (1961, pp. 112–114) for further details.

INCOME MEASUREMENT SYSTEMS

Both income statements and balance sheets using different theoretical approaches to the inflation problem will be illustrated, using a relatively simple example, in this section. Our principle focus, however, will be on the income statement because it poses many significant theoretical issues.

GENERAL PRICE LEVEL ADJUSTMENT (GPLA)

The one additional point that should be added to the discussion of GPLA in Chapter 1 concerns the type of capital maintenance provided by this measure of income. Historical costs provide capital maintenance in terms of unadjusted dollars. GPLA goes one step further. Capital maintenance is provided in terms of general price-level adjusted dollars.[13]

CURRENT VALUE APPROACHES

The three approaches to current value discussed here are oriented to entry valuation methods. All will show current operating income (revenues minus expenses computed on a replacement cost basis). Therefore, current operating income should have user relevance from the standpoint of accountability and, quite possibly, predictive ability. The methods differ in terms of disposition of real holding gains and the resulting type of capital maintenance measure.

Distributable Income (DI)

Under DI, real capital gains are considered to be capital adjustments.[14] The resulting capital maintenance is in physical capital terms because income is equal to the excess of revenues over expenses measured in replacement cost terms. The purchasing power gain or loss is computed by using a Paasche type of index to measure the change in the replacement costs of the operating assets used by the enterprise.

---

[13]Hendriksen (1982, pp. 224–225) suggests that price-level adjustment of real accounts can be achieved by use of specific indexes as well as by a general price-level index. He suggests three possible specific indexes: (1) investment goods in general, (2) capital goods generally acquired by the industry of which the enterprise is a member, and (3) goods similar to those that the firm itself has been investing in during past periods. The resulting capital maintenance measures would be entity-theory oriented.

[14]Revsine (1973, pp. 34–35 and 128–129) uses the term "distributable operating flows" but it is the same as "distributable income" as used here. The same concept has also been called "disposable income" by Zeff (1962, pp. 617–621).

Realized Income (RI)

As the name implies, realized components of real holding gains are routed through income.[15] The resulting capital maintenance measure is generally quite similar to that provided under GPLA even though the statements are totally different in other respects. The reason is that replacement cost measures of expense, by definition, exceed historical costs by realized portions of monetary and real holding gains. When realized real holding gains are run through income, the result is generally similar to income determination under GPLA.

Earning Power Income (EPI)

All real holding gains arising during the period, whether or not realized, are components of income under EPI.[16] This method has been advocated on the grounds that real holding gains are an indicator or "signal" to users that real future earnings of the firm in the future are expected to increase.[17] Future income is expected to rise on the presumption that real holding gains indicate an increasing demand for goods and services provided by the particular enterprise. EPI is thus recommended on predictive ability grounds.

Unfortunately, the rationale underlying EPI has several drawbacks. If productive assets and resources are utilized by several industries, increasing demand for final product in some industries may drive up the cost of inputs for all firms—including those where no such increase in demand for final product is present. Therefore, the real holding gain may be quite illusory for many firms in terms of signaling future increases in income. Another possibility is that real holding gains may be stemming from supply-side conditions rather than the demand aspect. A good example is the OPEC cartel's control over petroleum prices, particularly during the 1970s.

There is no direct capital maintenance measurement stemming from EPI. The reason for this lies in the fact that unrealized capital gains cannot be counted as income when measuring capital maintenance because beginning-of-period net assets are restated in terms of end-of-year real values.[18] Unrealized holding gains are thus "wiped out." The illustration in the next section should highlight capital maintenance and other features of these methods.

---

[15]Edwards and Bell (1961, pp. 117–119) use the term "realized profit" similarly to the way "realized income" is used here.

[16]"Earning power income" was used by Zeff (1962, p. 617). It is more descriptive than the term "business profit" used by Edwards and Bell (1961, pp. 119–122).

[17]For an interesting critique, see Revsine (1981a, pp. 347–348).

[18]Of course capital maintenance could also be definitionally measured as the unadjusted difference between beginning and ending owners' equity before capital transactions. However, the meaning of this measure in terms of capital maintenance is not clear.

EXHIBIT 11-4.

W-F-T COMPANY BALANCE SHEET
December 31, 1981

Assets

Cash		$15,000
Merchandise Inventory		15,000
Fixed Assets	$28,000	
Less: Accumulated Depreciation	8,000	20,000
Total Assets		$50,000

Liabilities and Owners' Equities

5% Bonds Payable	$10,000
Capital Stock	20,000
Retained Earnings	20,000
Total Liabilities and Owners' Equities	$50,000

AN ILLUSTRATION

Assume that W-F-T Company had the historical cost balance sheet on December 31, 1981, shown in Exhibit 11-4.

The fixed assets were acquired on January 2, 1980. They are expected to have a seven-year productive life with no salvage value. The merchandise inventory was acquired during 1981. The historical cost income statement for 1982 is shown in Exhibit 11-5.

Revenues resulted from cash sales. No other transactions occurred during 1982 except for those indicated by the income statement.

EXHIBIT 11-5.

W-F-T COMPANY INCOME STATEMENT

For the Year Ending December 31, 1982

Revenues		$15,000
Operating Expenses		
Cost of Goods Sold	$ 6,000	
Depreciation	4,000	10,000
Operating Income		5,000
Bond Interest Expense		500
Net Income		$ 4,500

EXHIBIT 11-6.

GENERAL AND SPECIFIC PRICE INDEXES

Index Type	Year		
	1980	1981	1982
General price index	100	105	110
Specific price index applicable to firm's merchandise inventory	100	110	120
Specific price index applicable to firm's fixed assets	100	102	105

For purposes of replacement cost valuation, the firm is using appropriate specific price indexes for inventories and fixed assets in lieu of direct measurements of replacement cost. One of the hallmarks of current value accounting is that measurements of asset values and expenses are expected to be realistic approximations of the economic values they are intended to portray. In other words, they are expected to have a high degree of representational faithfulness. We assume in this illustration that specific index adjustment of straight-line historical cost depreciation provides a measure of current value depreciation that is representationally faithful. More will be said shortly relative to measuring current values.

General and specific price indexes are shown in Exhibit 11-6. For simplicity in this example we assume that prices change once and for all in 1981 and 1982 on January 1. Further complications relative to price movements within a year are discussed in Chapter 12.

General Price Level Adjustment

The GPLA income statement for 1982 with the translations from historical cost to GPLA is shown in Exhibit 11-7. The purchasing power loss is computed by taking the net monetary assets on December 31, 1981, of $5,000 (cash of $15,000 less bonds payable of $10,000) and multiplying it by $\frac{110 - 105}{105}$ which equals $238. The numerator represents the change in general purchasing power in 1982 relative to 1981.

A capital maintenance proof is shown in Exhibit 11-8. Since the beginning and ending balance sheets under historical costing are not expressed in units of the same general purchasing power, a common unit of measurement must be used. Because GPLA income for 1982 was stated in terms of the general purchasing power of the dollar in 1982, the two encompassing balance sheets are likewise stated in the same way. Monetary assets and liabilities in the opening balance sheet must be restated to cost them in units of 1982 purchasing power. No restatement, however, of monetary items in the ending balance sheet is made because they are, by definition, expressed in terms of purchasing power in 1982.

EXHIBIT 11-7.

GENERAL PRICE-LEVEL ADJUSTED
INCOME STATEMENT

For the Year Ended December 31, 1982

	Historical Cost	Conversion Factor	GPLA
Revenues	$15,000	—	$15,000
Operating Expenses			
Cost of Goods Sold	6,000	$\dfrac{110}{105}$	6,285
Depreciation	4,000	$\dfrac{110}{100}$	4,400
Total Expenses	10,000		10,685
Operating Income	5,000		4,315
Other Expenses			
Bond Interest	500		500
Purchasing Power Loss on Net Monetary Assets	—		238[a]
Total	—		738
Net Income	$ 4,500		$ 3,577

[a] $\dfrac{110 - 105}{105}$ ($15,000 − $10,000)

EXHIBIT 11-8.

CAPITAL MAINTENANCE UNDER GENERAL PRICE-LEVEL ADJUSTMENT

	(1) 12/31/81	(2) Conversion Factor	(3) Restated in 1982 Dollars	(4) 12/31/82	(5) Conversion Factor	(6) Restated in 1982 Dollars	(7) Net Change in 1982 Dollars[a]
Cash	$15,000	110/105	$15,714	$29,500	—	$29,500	$13,786
Merchandise Inventory	15,000	110/105	15,714	9,000	110/105	9,429	(6,285)
Fixed Assets	28,000	110/100	30,800	28,000	110/100	30,800	—
Less: Accumulated Depreciation	(8,000)	110/100	(8,800)	(12,000)	110/100	(13,200)	(4,400)
Total Assets	50,000		53,428	54,500		56,529	3,101
5% Bonds Payable	(10,000)	110/105	(10,476)	(10,000)	—	(10,000)	476
Owners' Equity (Net Assets)	$40,000		$42,952	$44,500		$46,529	$ 3,577

[a] Column 6 minus Column 3

Notice that the difference between opening and closing net assets is equal to the income for the year computed under GPLA. Hence, GPLA income is the maximum that can be distributed as dividends and still leave the enterprise as well off (in terms of GPLA adjusted owners' equities) at the end of the year as it was at the beginning of the year.

GPLA adjustment brings additivity to both the balance sheet and income statement because dollars in terms of the same general purchasing power are used throughout. It should also be mentioned that GPLA adjustment can be construed as adhering to the proprietary theory approach mentioned in Chapter 4. The reason underlying the proprietary thrust is that general purchasing power would be more representative of the orientation of the owners of the enterprise than would specialized asset indexes.

Distributable Income

DI is a replacement cost approach that attempts to measure the maximum dividend that can be paid to stockholders without impairing the level of future operations. This is accomplished, as mentioned previously, by deducting from revenues the current value (replacement cost) of expenses incurred during the period. Holding gains must be treated as capital adjustments. Hence, there is no distinction between monetary and real holding gains. The DI statement for 1982 is shown in Exhibit 11-9.

The purchasing power loss on net monetary assets was determined by utilizing a Paasche type of specific index geared to the firm's mix of real assets:

$$I_2 - I_1 = \frac{\sum_i (P_{ni} \cdot Q_{ni})}{\sum_i (P_{oi} \cdot Q_{ni})} - \frac{\sum_i (P_{n-1i} \cdot Q_{ni})}{\sum_i (P_{oi} \cdot Q_{ni})} \tag{11.3}$$

where

$I_2 - I_1$ = change in the firm's weighted average of its specific asset holdings from last year to this year;

P_{n-1i} = price of the ith commodity in the previous year (I_1).

Substituting from our example, we have:

$$\frac{(\$20,000 \cdot \frac{105}{100}) + (\$15,000 \cdot \frac{120}{110})}{\$20,000 + (\$15,000 \cdot \frac{100}{110})} -$$

$$\frac{(\$20,000 \cdot \frac{102}{100}) + (\$15,000 \cdot \frac{110}{110})}{\$20,000 + (\$15,000 \cdot \frac{100}{110})} = 5.84\% \tag{11.3a}$$

The denominators of the two terms are expressed in base year prices (1980) for the composition of real assets held at the end of 1981. The two terms in

---

EXHIBIT 11-9.

DISTRIBUTABLE INCOME STATEMENT

For the Year Ended December 31, 1982

	Historical Cost	Specific Index Conversion Factor	Current Value
Revenues	$15,000	—	$15,000
Operating Expenses			
Cost of Goods Sold	6,000	$\frac{120}{110}$	6,545
Depreciation	4,000	$\frac{105}{100}$	4,200
Total Expenses	10,000		10,745
Operating Income	5,000		4,255
Other Expenses			
Bond Interest	500		500
Purchasing Power Loss on Net Monetary Assets	—		292
	—		792
Net Income (Distributable)	$ 4,500		$ 3,463

---

the numerator are stated in 1982 and 1981 prices, respectively. The resulting 5.84% rise in the firm's weighted average of real assets is multiplied by the $5,000 of net monetary assets shown on the December 31, 1981, balance to arrive at the specific purchasing power loss of $292.[19]

A capital maintenance proof in the specific purchasing power of the enterprise is shown in Exhibit 11-10. The beginning and ending balance sheets are shown in terms of 1982 replacement costs. Beginning-of-period monetary items are adjusted by the firm-specific index to make them comparable in specific purchasing power to the ending monetary items. Once again the net asset differential equals income.

The firm-specific measure of capital maintenance shown in Exhibit 11-10 becomes less relevant as the probability increases that the enterprise will invest in assets outside the perimeter of its present industry. DI is a measure oriented toward entity theory because it is geared to the enterprise maintaining its productive capacity (in real terms).

---

[19]For an extensive discussion of specific price index construction see Tritschler (1969, pp. 99–124).

EXHIBIT 11-10.

DISTRIBUTABLE INCOME CAPITAL MAINTENANCE

	(1) 12/31/81	(2) Specific Conversion Factor	(3) Restated in 1982 Dollars	(4) 12/31/82	(5) Specific Conversion Factor	(6) Restated in 1982 Dollars	(7) Net Specific Change[a]
Cash	$15,000	1.0584	$15,876	$29,500	—	$29,500	$13,624
Merchandise Inventory	15,000	$\frac{120}{110}$	16,364	9,000	$\frac{120}{110}$	9,818	(6,545)
Fixed Assets	28,000	$\frac{105}{100}$	29,400	28,000	$\frac{105}{100}$	29,400	—
Less: Accumulated Depreciation	(8,000)	$\frac{105}{100}$	(8,400)	(12,000)	$\frac{105}{100}$	(12,600)	(4,200)
Total Assets	50,000		53,240	54,500		56,118	2,879
5% Bonds Payable	10,000	1.0584	10,584	10,000	—	10,000	584
Owners' Eq- uity (Net Assets)	$40,000		$42,656	$44,500		$46,118	$ 3,463

[a]Column 6 minus Column 3

Realized Income

In the last two methods to be illustrated, general price-level adjustment and replacement costs are both employed with holding gains segregated into monetary and real portions. Under RI, the realized portion of real holding gains is added back to income. If a general price-level index is used to determine purchasing power gains or losses on monetary items, the resulting "bottom line" is quite consistent with GPLA adjustment even though the income statement organization is totally different.

The reason is that the adding back of the realized real holding gain component of cost of goods sold and depreciation in effect leaves only the GPLA component of these expenses that are beyond historical cost. It should be understood that the change in the general purchasing power of the dollar is reflected in specific price indexes. Therefore, the real holding gain element can be determined by taking the general price level component out of the specific index. This is done in the footnote of the RI income statement shown in Exhibit 11-11.[20]

---

[20]The monetary and real holding gains shown in Exhibit 11-11 are based on changes from the preceding year, except for the fixed assets which were purchased during 1980. The real change was related to the 1980 acquisition date for the fixed assets. The realized real holding loss is also equal to the excess of general price-level adjusted depreciation of $4,400 shown in Exhibit 11-7 and current value depreciation of $4,200. No capital maintenance proof is shown because net income is exactly the same as GPLA adjusted income.

EXHIBIT 11-11.

REALIZED INCOME STATEMENT

For the Year Ended December 31, 1982

	Historical Cost	Conversion Factor	Current Value
Revenues	$15,000	—	$15,000
Operating Expenses			
Cost of Goods Sold	6,000	$\dfrac{120}{110}$	6,545
Depreciation	4,000	$\dfrac{105}{100}$	4,200
Total Expenses	10,000		10,745
Operating Income	5,000		4,255
Other Income and Expenses			
Bond Interest	500		500
Purchasing Power Loss on Net Monetary Assets	—		238
Realized Real Holding Gains and Losses			
Cost of Goods Sold			(260)[a]
Fixed Assets			200[b]
Total			678
Net Income	$ 4,500		$ 3,577

---

[a]Specific index change for 1982 relative to 1981 minus the general index change for 1982 relative to 1981: $\dfrac{120 - 110}{110} - \dfrac{110 - 105}{105} = 4.34\%$

The 4.34% is multiplied by the historical cost of goods sold of $6,000 to arrive at $260.

[b]Same procedure for fixed assets as for cost of goods sold: $\dfrac{5}{100} - \dfrac{10}{100} = -5\%$, which is multiplied by depreciation of $4,000 to arrive at $-$200. Notice that this is also the difference between current value depreciation of $4,200 and GPLA adjusted depreciation of $4,400.

Earning Power Income

EPI includes in income all real holding gains arising during the year. The concept does not appear to be strongly rooted to either entity or proprietary theories. It might be loosely related to the residual equity theory because of the presumed predictive usefulness of the real holding gains arising during the year. However, it should be noted that these are not severable for dividend purposes and a capital maintenance proof cannot be

EXHIBIT 11-12.

EARNING POWER INCOME STATEMENT

For the Year Ended December 31, 1982

	Historical Cost	Conversion Factor	Current Value
Revenues	$15,000	—	$15,000
Operating Expenses			
Cost of Goods Sold	6,000	$\dfrac{120}{110}$	6,545
Depreciation	4,000	$\dfrac{105}{100}$	4,200
Total Expenses	10,000		10,745
Operating Income	5,000		4,255
Other Income and Expenses			
Bond Interest	500		500
Purchasing Power Loss on Net Monetary Assets	—		238
Real Holding Gains			
Inventories			(651)[a]
Fixed Assets			400[b]
Total			487
Net Income	$ 4,500		$ 3,768

[a]The entire inventory of $15,000 is now multiplied by 4.34% computed in Exhibit 11-11.

[b]Realizable holding gain is determined in three steps:

(1) Compute the holding gain for a two-year-old asset:

Estimated replacement cost of a similar two-year-old asset *after* the price rise ($28,000 × 1.05 × 5/7)	$21,000
Estimated replacement cost of a similar two-year-old asset *before* the price rise ($28,000 × 1.02 × 5/7)	20,400
Total holding gain	$ 600

(2) Break the $600 into its real and monetary components:
Since specific prices have increased by 3% (105 − 102) and general prices have risen by 5% (110 − 105), the real price rise from 1981 to 1982 is −2%.

(3) The holding gains are:

Monetary ($20,000 × .05)	$ 1,000
Real ($20,000 × −.02)	− 400
Total	$ 600

The division of the holding gain shown above determined the specific and general price-level changes relative to the base year 1980. The splits could also have been based on the change in price levels from the previous year, 1981. The computation would have been:

Total holding gain (from the specific index)		Monetary holding gain		Specific or real holding gain
$(\frac{105 - 102}{102}) = .0294$	$-$	$(\frac{110 - 105}{105}) = .0476$	$=$	$- .0182$
$20,400		$20,400		$20,400
× .0294		× .0476		× −.0182
$ 600		$ 971		$ −371

The $20,400 is the estimated replacement cost at the beginning of 1982 *before* the price rise. The presence of two possible methods is yet another example of the allocation problem.

given.[21] If purchasing power gain or loss on monetary items is computed, we lean toward use of the general price-level index in the measurement; but theory is still inconclusive on this question. The EPI statement is shown in Exhibit 11-12.

SPECIAL PROBLEMS IN MEASUREMENT AND VALUATION

The state of our knowledge and techniques relative to price changes and inflation accounting procedures is still quite primitive. In this section we examine two problems: (1) current valuation of fixed assets that are partially obsolete and (2) inclusion of long-term debt in the measurement of purchasing power gains and losses.

DEPRECIATION AND PARTIAL TECHNOLOGICAL OBSOLESCENCE

Current valuation of fixed assets and depreciation become particularly difficult when technological obsolescence arises. **Technological obsolescence** is defined as a situation that arises when new machinery and equip-

---

[21]The unrealized portion of the real holding gain is included as part of the asset balance of both beginning and ending balance sheets because both are stated in current value terms for the year. As a result, unrealized holding gains cannot be included in income from the capital maintenance standpoint (see footnote 18).

ment come on the market providing productive services similar to those of existing assets at a lower total cost of production. Typically we would expect discounted cash flow analyses to occur with some firms opting for the newer technology and other firms maintaining their existing assets. In the latter case, the assets held are partially obsolete.

In terms of depreciation expense, there has been a debate as to whether replacement cost depreciation should be measured in terms of the best available technology on the market or the technology that is actually utilized by the firm.[22] The appearance of new technology on the market generally depresses the price of older machinery and equipment. In fact, in an efficiently operating market where a new asset and an old asset provide similar output services, such as passenger miles for airplanes, the market would depress the cost of old technology so that cost per unit of output for old and new technology—including cost of the asset—would be equal.[23]

A simple example will show how the obsolescence writedown might be determined in the absence of actual market values. Assume that an enterprise owns a cement plant. A technological improvement occurs in which variable costs per unit decrease. The facts of the case are summarized in Exhibit 11-13. Assume that the appropriate cost of capital is 10%. For simplicity we ignore income taxes and assume that all production occurs at the end of the year.

EXHIBIT 11-13.

PARTIAL TECHNOLOGICAL OBSOLESCENCE

	Old Asset	New Asset
Original Cost	$1,400,000	$2,000,000
Replacement cost prior to appearance of new technology	$1,050,000	
Estimated total life	10 years	10 years
Present Age	5 years	
Annual productivity	200,000 bbl.	200,000 bbl.
Variable cost	$.90 per bbl.	$.50 per bbl.

---

[22]Wright (1965, pp. 167–181) favors basing depreciation on the best available alternative on the grounds that it will ". . . indicate what the firm can expect to earn in the long run if it continues to follow its present general policies" (p. 175). There is thus an element of predictive ability underlying Wright's reasoning. Wright is critical of Edwards and Bell, who favor computing depreciation related to the actual fixed assets owned. Edwards and Bell (1961, p. 271), however, have a more limited accountability objective with regard to evaluating past business decisions.
[23]See Solomons (1962, pp. 28–42) and Revsine (1979, pp. 306–322) for extensive discussion. Backer (1973, pp. 205–206) and Weil (1976, pp. 89–104) suggest valuation methods grounded on the equalized cost per unit of output approach.

The first step is to translate into equal annual cost terms the purchase price of the new technology. This is done by dividing the $2,000,000 cost by the present value of an ordinary 10-year annuity at 10% per period. The result is $325,491 ($2,000,000 ÷ 6.14457). Because the firm's present technology is less efficient, we deduct the excess variable costs of production of $.40 per barrel ($.90 − $.50) and multiply by the annual production of 200,000, to yield an amount of $80,000, which is deducted from the $325,491 to arrive at a value equivalent of the old equipment relative to the new. Because there are only 5 years left in the old machinery, the $245,491 is multiplied by the present value of a 5-year annuity at 10% (3.79079) to arrive at an estimated replacement cost of $930,605. The obsolescence writedown is thus $119,395 ($1,050,000 − $930,605). Obsolescence write-downs are a type of real holding loss.

The new estimated market value of $930,605 represents, in essence, a breakeven value of the old technology to the firm. If the exit value the firm could receive exceeds this figure, the new technology should be acquired because the time-adjusted rate of return determined by capital budgeting calculations would exceed the 10% cost of capital. Similarly, if the exit value is less than $930,605, the old technology should be retained because the time-adjusted rate of return would be less than 10%.

An obvious question of verifiability must be raised about the determination of the estimated replacement cost and obsolescence writedown. Annual productivity and years of life are predictions. Thus, they may not be highly verifiable. The trade-off between relevance and reliability is obviously a key factor in terms of replacement cost measurements. Furthermore, the method illustrated here can apply only to fixed assets that are homogeneous in terms of the output of their productivity. The determination of current value depreciation is even more dubious from the standpoint of verifiability in the absence of market value quotations. Further discussion of current value depreciation appears in Appendix 11-A of this chapter.

PURCHASING POWER GAINS ON LONG-TERM DEBT

The usual assumption that the firm makes a "gain" on its long-term debt during inflation because bondholders will be repaid with cheaper dollars is being seriously questioned.[24] Bondholders surely understand that if inflation continues, the repayment of principal to them will have less purchasing power than the dollars originally lent to the enterprise.

Consequently, the interest rate is made up of two components: (1) the required return, which consists of the risk-free rate plus a risk premium based on the issuer's credit standing; and (2) an additional element equated to the expected rate of inflation during the period of the debt. As a result,

[24]See Kaplan (1977, pp. 369–378), Bourn (1976, pp. 167–182), and Revsine (1981b, pp. 20–29).

EXHIBIT 11-14.

CURRENT VALUE INCOME STATEMENTS
For the Year Ending December 31, 1980 and 1981

	1980	1981
Revenues	$3,000	$3,000
Expenses		
Depreciation	1,100[a]	1,210[b]
Bond interest	155	155
Total expenses	1,255	1,365
Net income	$1,745	$1,635

[a]Replacement cost of $2,200 ÷ 2 years = $1,100. Replacement cost is $2,000 × 1.1.
[b]Replacement cost of $2,420 ÷ 2 years = $1,210. Replacement cost is $2,200 × 1.1.

it is posited that there will be a "gain" only if the actual rate of inflation is greater than the anticipated rate. Conversely, there will be a loss if the actual rate is less than the anticipated rate. The nature of this gain and loss and the implications for capital maintenance measurement require a closer look by means of an illustration.[25]

Assume that an enterprise is formed on December 31, 1979. It purchases one asset costing $2,000 with a life of two years and no salvage value. The asset was acquired by issuing $1,000 of common stock and selling one bond, also at $1,000. The bond carries interest of 15½% as a result of a 5% basic interest rate and an anticipated inflation rate of 10% (1.05 × 1.10 = 1.15½). Revenues of $3,000 are earned each year. The only expenses are depreciation and bond interest. All income is distributed to stockholders as a dividend. For simplicity, income taxes are ignored. Finally, we assume that the actual rate of inflation is 10% per year (beginning in early 1982) and that replacement cost for the fixed asset likewise increases by 10% a year. Current value statements for 1980 and 1981 are shown in Exhibit 11-14.

Notice that distributable income has been used without recognizing the purchasing power gain on the bonds. A capital maintenance proof is shown in Exhibit 11-15. In line with the changed conception of purchasing power gains on long-term debt, the beginning balance of bonds payable is not restated in end-of-year dollars. A similar capital maintenance proof could likewise be provided for 1981.

That the exclusion of bonded debt from the purchasing power gain is correct rests upon one additional assumption: the $1,100 of cash equal to the depreciation of 1980 is invested in a separate fund, which earns a return equal to the anticipated rate of inflation (10%), which is not made available

[25]This illustration was adapted from Revsine (1981b).

EXHIBIT 11-15.

CAPITAL MAINTENANCE SCHEDULE

	(1) 12/31/79	(2) Specific Conversion Factor	(3) Restated in 1980 Dollars	(4) 12/31/80	(5) Specific Conversion Factor	(6) Restated in 1980 Dollars	(7) Net Specific Change[b]
Cash	—			$ 2,845[a]	—	$ 2,845	$ 2,845
Fixed Asset	$ 2,000	$\frac{110}{100}$	$ 2,200	2,000	$\frac{110}{100}$	2,200	—
Less: Accumulated Depreciation	—		—	(1,000)	$\frac{110}{100}$	(1,100)	(1,100)
Total Assets	2,000		2,200	3,845		3,945	1,745
15½% Bonds Payable	1,000		1,000	1,000	—	1,000	—
Owners' Equity	$ 1,000		$ 1,200	$ 2,845	—	$ 2,945	$ 1,745

[a]Before payment of dividends
[b]Column 6 minus Column 3

---

for dividends.[26] As a result, the cash accumulated exactly equals the replacement cost of $2,420 of the fixed asset at the end of 1981 [($1,100 × 1.1) + $1,210 = $2,420].

As shall be seen in Chapter 12, the purchasing power computation required in SFAS 33 requires the inclusion of long-term debt. On the basis of this analysis, we would recommend its exclusion.

When there is a change in the expected rate of inflation, the market adjusts by raising or lowering the market value of the bonds. From the physical capital maintenance aspect, these gains and losses are irrelevant in terms of their effect on income. This viewpoint is geared to the entity theory. From the standpoint of financial capital maintenance, redistribution between bondholders and stockholders occurs if the expected rate of inflation is greater than the actual rate, and the price of the bonds increases— with a gain to that group and an offsetting loss by stockholders. The converse also applies. Notice that the gain or loss is the change in market value of the bonds rather than a purchasing power gain or loss. The financial capital maintenance approach represents an application of proprietary theory.

In actual practice, however, it would be virtually impossible to distinguish between anticipated and unanticipated rates of inflation. Furthermore, changes in perceived risk relative to the individual firm also bring

---

[26]This problem is discussed in Vancil and Weil (1976, pp. 38–45) and in Nichols (1982, pp. 68–73).

about changes in the market value of the bonds. Therefore, any attempt to apply the proprietary approach would be hopelessly mired in extremely difficult measurement problems.

However, as a matter of consistent valuation and the presentation of additional information to users, long-term debt could be shown at market value where current values are being employed. The difference between current value and unamortized historical cost would appear as an element of owners' equity and would not go through income under an approach that is entity-theory oriented (such as distributable income).

SUMMARY

Coping with inflation and changing prices has presented an extremely serious challenge to accounting theory. Numerous methods of grappling with these problems have been extensively presented and discussed in the literature.

General price-level adjustment is largely an extension of historical costing. Under this method, unamortized costs of nonmonetary assets and liabilities are adjusted for the change in the general level of prices that has arisen since incurrence of these costs. The results in both balance sheet and income statement would be additive because they are stated in terms of the current general price level. Capital maintenance is likewise measured in terms of the general level of prices. The results, however, should not be confused with "current valuation." It is merely a matter of restatement of historical costs in terms of the change in the general level of prices.

Current valuation can be expressed in terms of either entry or exit values. The latter type of measure appears to be most useful in terms of measuring the adaptability of the firm to move into new asset holdings because existing assets (and liabilities) are measured in terms of their disposal value. From the standpoint of user information needs, exit values appear to be relatively limited. Entry values seem to have more value in use than their exit value counterparts.

Under entry value approaches, the main point of difference concerns disposition of real holding gains. Disposable income recognizes no real holding gains as income. The resulting capital maintenance measure is in physical capital terms, an approach oriented toward entity theory. Realized income, as the name implies, recognizes realized real holding gains as income elements. The results are frequently quite close to general price-level adjusted measurements of income but the orientation of the statement is totally different. Earning power income runs all real holding gains through income in the period when they arise. The intention is that users would receive a "signal" relative to higher (or lower) future income. Unfortunately holding gains may result from either supply-side problems, causing price rises above the average, or price rises may be generated by increasing demand for resources in a limited number of industries only.

Two special problems were discussed in the chapter. One issue that has concerned theorists is whether current value depreciation should be equated to presently owned fixed assets or the most efficient technology of the type under consideration. In an efficiently operating used-asset market, the price of older technology would be depressed to the point where operating costs per unit of output of old and new technology would tend to be equated. However, the measurement of holding losses due to partial obsolescence as well as current value depreciation is still very difficult.

The other issue concerns whether purchasing power gains should be picked up on long-term debt during inflationary periods. Holders of long-term debt obviously understand that during inflationary periods they will receive dollars having less purchasing power than those that were lent. Consequently, long-term debt includes an interest element compensating holders for the expected purchasing power decline that they will suffer. As a result, the firm would have a purchasing power gain if the actual rate of inflation exceeds the expected rate. However, the measurement problems are, once again, exceedingly difficult to overcome. A possible substitute might be to show long-term debt at market value rather than unamortized historical cost with the difference being an element of owners' equity.

APPENDIX 11-A: CURRENT VALUE DEPRECIATION

Valuation of fixed assets in the absence of direct market quotations when improved technology comes on the market was discussed in the body of this chapter. Determining current value depreciation is an even stickier problem because depreciation is, of course, an allocation which makes it difficult to justify one measure over another.

EFFICIENT MARKET VALUATION

A possibility, however, would be to equate the total cost of production per unit of output—including interest and depreciation—of old equipment with the best available technology. There would be a tendency toward this condition in an efficient market: all relevant cost and production figures relative to both new and used assets would be available to all participants in the market.

An example can be seen by using the information presented in Exhibit 11-13 and the resulting new determination of theoretical replacement cost of $930,605 of the old asset. The total annual cost of the new technology is

---

EXHIBIT 11-16.

ANNUAL COST OF PRODUCTION OF BEST
AVAILABLE TECHNOLOGY

Cost of new asset	$2,000,000
Present value of all production costs associated with new asset (200,000 units per year × $.50 × 6.14457)	614,457
Total present value of all costs	2,614,457
Divide by present value of a 10-year annuity at 10%	÷ 6.14457
Total annualized cost	$ 425,491[a]

---

[a] Annual costs can be determined by taking the annual cost of the asset of $325,491 ($2,000,000 ÷ 6.14457) and adding it to the annual variable costs of $100,000.

shown in Exhibit 11-16. The present value of all costs is divided by the present value of a 10-year annuity at 10% to arrive at the equalized annual total cost of $425,491 including interest.

Exhibit 11-17 now takes the total annual cost of the best technology of $425,491 and applies it to the old asset.

The resulting "present value" depreciation is a variant of the present valuation approach discussed in Chapter 1. To the variable costs are added interest at 10% on the beginning balance of the fixed asset and depreciation is "forced" to make the total equal to $425,491. It should come as no surprise that the total accumulated depreciation equals the original simulated market value of $930,605 because this was "equated" with the price of the new technology. The resulting annual carrying values of the fixed asset are likewise simulated market values.

COMPLEXITIES OF PRESENT VALUE DEPRECIATION AS A
SURROGATE FOR REPLACEMENT COST DEPRECIATION

Unfortunately too many drawbacks surround present value depreciation, drastically limiting its potential usefulness.

In addition to the troublesome problem of being an allocation, present value depreciation can become exceedingly complex when factors such as uneven annual production, changing production costs as the asset ages, and various tax considerations (including the investment credit) are considered.

These complications also lead to the question of the degree of verifiability that would exist—since several estimations must be made about the future in order to measure depreciation of the current period. The same criticism applies, of course, to many present value types of calculations.

Since the measurement is supposed to give an estimation of replacement cost, the question might be raised as to whether the market actually does behave in this manner—as opposed to whether it should behave this

---

EXHIBIT 11-17.

ANNUAL COST OF PRODUCTION OF
PRESENTLY OWNED TECHNOLOGY

Year	1	2	3	4	5
Total costs of best technology (from Exhibit 11-16)	$425,491	$425,491	$425,491	$425,491	$425,491
Variable costs	$180,000	$180,000	$180,000	$180,000	$180,000
Interest at 10% on beginning asset balance	93,061	77,818	61,050	42,606	22,318
Depreciation (by deduction)	152,430	167,673	184,441	202,885	223,173[a]
Total costs of presently owned equipment	$425,491	$425,491	$425,491	$425,491	$425,491
Beginning-of-period asset balance	$930,605	$778,175[b]	$610,502	$426,061	$223,176

---

[a]$3 rounding error.

[b]($930,605 − $152,430). Succeeding years are calculated the same way.

way. This question concerns descriptive versus normative behavior. The issue here is basically an empirical one and can be answered only by study of the market behavior of fixed asset prices.[27]

Another problem arises in the event of frequent improvements in technology. Recalculations of both obsolescence and present value depreciation must be made—which may be expensive.

Still another question arises about the appropriate interest rate to use. The firm's cost of capital was used here; but perhaps the rate of interest used by the market in arriving at asset values is appropriate—because market efficiency has been assumed in these examples.[28]

Finally, all of the aforementioned difficulties logically led to two other major enigmas. First, the question of users and their objectives must be raised: the issues here are whether present value depreciation would have

---

[27]Beidleman (1973) attempted to use statistical models for determining the elements underlying the valuation of used capital assets.

[28]See Boatsman and Baskin (1981, pp. 38–53) for application of the capital asset pricing model to valuation of used assets.

more information content than presumably cruder methods, such as straight-line depreciation of current values; also, one must ask whether users even understand present value concepts. Second, as a result of these qualifications, the question of benefits versus costs of current value depreciation must be given very careful consideration.

All these issues raise very grave doubts about the utility of present value depreciation at this time as a substitute for direct market measurement of value declines in fixed assets.

QUESTIONS

1. Why do Paasche-type indexes tend to take into account technological changes, whereas Laspeyres indexes do not?
2. Do you believe that exit-value measurements should or should not deduct "tearing out" and other disposal costs from the selling price of assets?
3. Why are exit values generally considered to be less useful than entry values?
4. Why are the "bottom line" income statement results quite similar between GPLA and RI type income statements?
5. What is the major purpose of EPI and why is it likely that the objective will often not be achieved?
6. Why is GPLA oriented to the proprietary theory?
7. Why is DI primarily entity theory oriented?
8. Why are beginning balance sheets restated in capital maintenance proofs?
9. What type of capital maintenance proof can be applied to EPI measurements?
10. A firm has a net monetary liability balance of $10,000 on January 1, 1984. During the first third of the year the balance decreased to $7,500. During the second third of the year the balance increased to $12,500. During the last third of the year the balance increased to $20,000. The general price index was 100 during the first third of the year, 110 during the second third, and 106 during the last third.

   Required: Compute the purchasing power gain or loss for the year.
11. A plot of land costing $200,000 was acquired on January 1, 1982. The price level was 120 on that date. One quarter of the land was sold on December 31, 1982, for $60,000 when the general price level was 180.

   Required: Compute the following gains:
   (a) Realized real holding gain.
   (b) Unrealized real holding gain.
   (c) Realized monetary holding gain.
   (d) Unrealized monetary holding gain.

12. What is the argument against including bonds payable as a monetary liability in the purchasing power gain or loss computation?

13. Price-level adjustment may be accomplished by using specific price indexes as well as a general price-level index. One possibility is to use a weighted average price index for the firm's own mix of assets. What dangers does this present?

14. What is "present value" depreciation and why is the prospect of its eventual adoption by a policy-making organization extremely doubtful?

15. Why, in an efficient market, should partially obsolescent technology and new technology providing the same services have equalized total annual costs of production for the same quantity of output?

CASES AND PROBLEMS

1. Using the balance sheet and income statement shown in Exhibits 11-4 and 11-5, construct the following types of income statements for 1982:

(a) GPLA
(b) DI
(c) RI
(d) EPI

Use the following general and specific indexes:

	1980	1981	1982
General price index	100	110	106
Specific price index applicable to the firm's merchandise inventory	100	103	97
Specific price index applicable to the firm's fixed assets	100	115	125

2. An asset is acquired at a cost of $10,000 with a 5-year life and no anticipated salvage value. Straight-line depreciation is considered appropriate. The asset was acquired on January 1, 1980. Price indexes for the 5 years are:

	1980	1981	1982	1983	1984
Fixed asset index	100	95	108	120	125
General price index	100	110	115	112	125

Required:
(a) Compute the current value depreciation for each year.
(b) What is the realized real holding gain for the years 1981–1984?
(c) What would the holding gain be under EPI for the years 1981–1984?

BIBLIOGRAPHY OF REFERENCED WORKS

Backer, Morton (1973). Current Value Accounting (Financial Executives Research Foundation).

Beidleman, Carl (1973). "Valuation of Used Capital Assets," Studies in Accounting Research #7 (American Accounting Association).

Bell, Philip (1971). "On Current Replacement Costs and Business Income," in Asset Valuation, ed. Robert Sterling (Scholars Book Co.), pp. 19–32.

Boatsman, James, and Elba Baskin (1981). "Asset Valuation with Incomplete Markets," The Accounting Review (January 1981), pp. 38–53.

Bourn, Michael (1976). "The 'Gain' on Borrowing," Journal of Business Finance and Accounting (Spring 1976), pp. 167–182.

Chambers, Raymond J. (1966). Accounting, Evaluation and Economic Behavior (Prentice-Hall).

————— (1968). "Measures and Values," The Accounting Review (April 1968), pp. 239–247.

Edwards, Edgar (1954). "Depreciation Policy Under Changing Price Levels," The Accounting Review (April 1954), pp. 267–280.

Edwards, Edgar, and Philip Bell (1961). The Theory and Measurement of Business Income (University of California Press).

Gynther, R. S. (1966). Accounting for Price-Level Changes: Theory and Procedures (Pergamon Press).

Heath, Loyd (1972). "Distinguishing Between Monetary and Nonmonetary Assets and Liabilities in General Price-Level Accounting," The Accounting Review (July 1972), pp. 458–468.

Hendriksen, Elden (1982). Accounting Theory, 4th ed. (Richard D. Irwin).

Kaplan, Robert (1977). "Purchasing Power Gains on Debt: The Effect of Expected and Unexpected Inflation," The Accounting Review (April 1977), pp. 369–378.

Nichols, Donald (1982). "Operating Income and Distributable Income Under Replacement Cost Accounting: The Long-Life Asset Replacement Problem," Financial Analysts Journal (January–February 1982), pp. 68–73.

Parker, R. H., and G. C. Harcourt (1969). "Introduction, " in Readings in the Concept and Measurement of Income, ed. R. H. Parker and G. C. Harcourt (Cambridge University Press), pp. 1–30.

Revsine, Lawrence (1973). Replacement Cost Accounting (Prentice-Hall).

————— (1979). "Technological Changes and Replacement Costs: A Beginning," The Accounting Review (April 1979), pp. 306–322.

————— (1981a). " 'The Theory and Measurement of Business Income:' A Review Article," The Accounting Review (April 1981), pp. 342–354.

————— (1981b). "Inflation Accounting for Debt," Financial Analysts Journal (May–June 1981), pp. 20–29.

Solomons, David (1966). "The Determination of Asset Values," Journal of Business (January 1962), pp. 28–42.

————— (1966). "Economic and Accounting Concepts of Cost and Value," in Modern Accounting Theory, ed. Morton Backer (Prentice-Hall), pp. 117–140.

Sprouse, Robert, and Maurice Moonitz (1962). "A Tentative Set of Broad Accounting Principles for Business Enterprises," Accounting Research Study No. 3 (AICPA).

Sterling, Robert (1979). *Toward a Science of Accounting* (Scholars Book Co., 1979).

Tritschler, Charles (1969). "Statistical Criteria for Asset Valuation by Specific Index," *The Accounting Review* (January 1969), pp. 99–124.

Vancil, Richard, and Roman Weil (1976). "Current Replacement Cost Accounting, Depreciable Assets, and Distributable Income," *Financial Analysts Journal* (July–August 1976), pp. 38–45.

Weil, Roman (1976). "Implementation of Replacement Cost Accounting: the Theory and Use of Functional Pricing," in *Replacement Cost Accounting: Readings on Concepts, Uses & Methods,* ed. Richard Vancil and Roman Weil (Thomas Horton and Daughters), pp. 89–104.

Wright, F. K. (1965). "Depreciation and Obsolescence in Current Value Accounting," *Journal of Accounting Research* (Autumn 1965), pp. 167–181.

Zeff, Stephen (1962). "Replacement Cost: Member of the Family, Welcome Guest, or Intruder?" *The Accounting Review* (October 1962), pp. 611–625.

ADDITIONAL READINGS

INFLATION AND CHANGING PRICES

Beaver, William (1979). "Accounting for Inflation in an Efficient Market," in *The Impact of Inflation on Accounting: A Global View,* ed. K. Zimmerman (Center for International Education and Research in Accounting, University of Illinois), pp. 21–42.

Bierman, Harold (1981). *Financial Management and Inflation* (Free Press).

Brinkman, Donald (1977). "Replacement Cost/Current Value Accounting," in *Handbook of Modern Accounting,* 2nd ed., ed. S. Davidson and R. Weil (McGraw-Hill), pp. 46-1 to 46-49.

Bruns, William, Jr., and Richard Vancil (1976). *A Primer on Cost Replacement Accounting* (Thomas Horton and Daughters).

Chambers, Raymond J. (1975). *Accounting for Inflation: Methods and Problems* (Department of Accounting of the University of Sydney).

Largay, James, III, and John Leslie Livingstone (1976). *Accounting for Changing Prices* (Wiley/Hamilton).

Lee, T. A. (1975). *Income and Value Measurement: Theory and Practice* (University Park Press).

Moonitz, Maurice (1974). *Changing Prices and Financial Reporting* (Stipes Publishing Company).

Revsine, Lawrence (1974). "Replacement Cost Accounting: A Theoretical Foundation," in *Objectives of Financial Statement Vol. 2: Selected Papers,* ed. Joe Cramer and George Sorter (AICPA), pp. 178–198.

Revsine, Lawrence, and Jerry Weygandt (1974). "Accounting for Inflation: the Controversy," *Journal of Accountancy* (October 1974), pp. 72–78.

Sterling, Robert (1975). "Relevant Financial Reporting in an Age of Price Changes," *Journal of Accountancy* (February 1975), pp. 42–51.

Summers, Edward, and James Deskins (1970). "A Classification Schema of Methods for Reporting Effects of Resource Price Changes (with Technical Appendix)," *International Journal of Accounting* (Fall 1970), pp. 101–120.

Vancil, Richard (1976). "Inflation Accounting—The Great Controversy," *Harvard Business Review* (March–April 1976), pp. 58–67.

Zimmerman, V. K., ed. (1979). *The Impact of Inflation on Accounting: A Global View* (Center for International Education and Research in Accounting, University of Illinois).

GENERAL PRICE-LEVEL ADJUSTMENT

Davidson, Sidney; Clyde Stickney; and Roman Weil (1976). *Inflation Accounting* (McGraw-Hill).

HOLDING GAINS AND LOSSES

Prakash, Prem, and Shyam Sunder (1979). "The Case Against Separation of Currrent Operating Profit and Holding Gains," *The Accounting Review* (January 1979), pp. 1–22.

Samuelson, Richard (1980). "Should Replacement Cost Changes Be Included in Income," *The Accounting Review* (April 1980), pp. 254–287.

PURCHASING POWER GAINS AND LOSSES

Bradford, William (1974). "Price-Level Restated Accounting and the Measurement of Inflation Gains and Losses," *The Accounting Review* (April 1974), pp. 296–305.

Gringyer, John (1978). "Holding Gains on Long-Term Liabilities—An Alternative Analysis," *Accounting and Business Research* (Spring 1978), pp. 130–148.

CAPITAL MAINTENANCE

Edwards, Edgar (1961). "Depreciation and the Maintenance of Real Capital," in *Depreciation and Replacement Policy*, ed. J. L. Meij (North-Holland), pp. 46–136.

Revsine, Lawrence (1981). "Let's Stop Eating Our Seed Corn," *Harvard Business Review* (January–February 1981), pp. 128–134.

CURRENT VALUE DEPRECIATION

Lewis, W. Arthur (1977). "Depreciation and Obsolescence as Factors in Costing," in *Studies in Accounting*, 3rd ed., ed. W. T. Baxter and S. Davidson (Institute of Chartered Accountants in England and Wales), pp. 210–233.

Lowe, Howard (1963). "The Essentials of a General Theory of Depreciation," *The Accounting Review* (April 1963), pp. 293–301.

Wright, F. K. (1964). "Towards a General Theory of Depreciation," *Journal of Accounting Research* (Spring 1964), pp. 80–90.

CHAPTER 12

Implementing Inflation Accounting

Most of the inflation accounting alternatives discussed in Chapter 11 received considerable attention in academic journals for several decades. However, their practical implementation was not taken seriously until relatively recent years. This is not surprising because the historical cost model has served relatively well until recent years.

Reviewing price trends over the last 180 years in the United States, one can see clearly why the historical cost model was not challenged seriously. The United States Consumer Price Index (1967=100) was 46 in 1810 and 42 in 1940.[1] Certainly, the Consumer Price Index (CPI) changed during this 130-year period, but the changes were not nearly as rapid as in recent years. The highest CPI between 1810 and 1940 was 63 in 1914, and the lowest was 25 in 1900. The average annual rate of change in the CPI by decade in the twentieth century reflects clearly why accounting for the effects of changing prices has come to the forefront in the past ten years as a practical problem rather than simply a theoretical one. Exhibit 12-1 shows this clearly.

[1]Griffin (1979, p. 4).

EXHIBIT 12-1.

AVERAGE ANNUAL RATE OF CHANGE IN THE CONSUMER PRICE INDEX

Decade	Percentage Rate
1900–1910	1.1
1910–1920	7.9
1920–1930	−1.8
1930–1940	−1.7
1940–1950	5.5
1950–1960	2.1
1960–1970	2.7
1970–1980	7.9

(The rate of change refers to the change within the decade itself as opposed to a base period.)

Sources: *Historical Statistics of the United States* (Bureau of the Census, 1975), pp. 210–211; and *International Financial Statistics, 1982 Yearbook* (International Monetary Fund, 1982), p. 467.

The fact that the general price level remained relatively flat, at least by 1980 standards, for the 160 years preceding 1970 undoubtedly had a significant impact on the development of accounting in the United States. Over the long run, if price levels are stable, the difference between income flows, as measured by the traditional historical cost model, and cash flows is relatively small. In inflationary conditions, especially double- or near-double-digit inflation, however, the weaknesses of the traditional model are magnified. Income flows become distorted and are not a good predictor of cash flows. Thus, practical implementation of methods to account for the effects of changing prices has become a major issue in the United States and throughout the Western World.

This chapter will trace the development of accounting for the effects of changing prices in the United States; review the provisions of Statements of Financial Accounting Standards (SFASs) 33, 39, 40, 41, 46, and 54; provide an example of the disclosures required by them; and examine methods of accounting for the effects of changing prices in selected other English-speaking countries.

HISTORY OF ACCOUNTING FOR THE EFFECTS OF CHANGING PRICES IN THE UNITED STATES PRIOR TO SFAS 33

It is naive to state that accountants were not warned about the fallacy of measuring business transactions in terms of historical cost. Economists have warned us for decades about the problem of assuming the monetary unit is stable and that the measurement of historical cost income and capital is correct. Even if the general price level remains fairly stable, considerable price movement occurs as a result of changes in supply and demand.

Accountants in the United States have realized for over fifty years the potential impact on reported accounting numbers of the effects of changing prices, whether specific or general in nature. In fact some corporations restated their primary financial statements for the effects of changes in specific prices during the 1920s.

Perhaps W. A. Paton summed up in 1932 the unsettled nature of accounting for the effects of changing prices that existed fifty years ago:

> It is evident that this whole problem is an unsettled one, with much to be said on both sides. It is a question to be determined on its own merits with particular reference to the sound needs of business management and not on the basis of tradition. The accountant in general will do well to concentrate his attention on the development of methods of bringing revaluations and their subsequent effects onto the books in a manner which will not impair the integrity of original cost figures, nor lead to misinterpretation of financial reports, rather than take the position that the effects of revaluation are outlawed as far as accounting records are concerned.[2]

Accounting organizations, such as the American Accounting Association (AAA) and the American Institute of Certified Public Accountants (AICPA) have discussed accounting for the effects of changing prices in their publications for nearly a half century. Both organizations strongly supported the historical cost model in the mid-thirties. The AAA made this statement:

> Accounting is . . . not essentially a process of valuation, but the allocation of historical costs and revenues to the current and succeeding periods.[3]

The AICPA adopted as one of its first six rules:

> Profit is deemed to be realized when a sale in the ordinary course of business is effected, unless the circumstances are such that the collection of the sale price is not reasonably assured.[4]

By the early fifties, however, both organizations began to modify their positions. In 1951 the AAA issued *Supplementary Statement No. 2*, "Price Level Changes and Financial Statements." The statement recommended that financial statements should be stated in units of general purchasing power rather than units of money.[5]

In 1952 the AICPA sponsored a study on changing concepts of income. Its report stated:

> Corporations whose ownership is widely distributed should be encouraged to furnish information that will facilitate the determination of income

[2]Paton (1932, p. 6).
[3]AAA (1936).
[4]Special Committee on Development of Accounting Principles (1951).
[5]Committee on Concepts and Standards Underlying Corporate Financial Statements (1951).

measured in units of approximately equal purchasing power, and to provide such information wherever it is practicable to do so as part of the material upon which the independent accountant expresses his opinion.[6]

The AAA continued to support price-level restated financial statements in their 1957 and 1966 reports. Likewise, the AICPA in *Accounting Research Study No. 6* in 1961 and *Accounting Principles Board Statement No. 3* supported general price-level adjusted statements. The Trueblood Committee reaffirmed the need to recognize changing prices in financial statements without making any commitments to either general price-level or current value concepts.[7]

Shortly after its inception, the Financial Accounting Standards Board (FASB) issued an Exposure Draft (ED) entitled "Financial Reporting in Units of General Purchasing Power." The ED proposed to require the presentation, as supplementary information to the primary financial statements, information in units of general purchasing power of key financial statement items, such as fixed assets and depreciation expense. The FASB deferred action on its ED because the Securities and Exchange Commission (SEC) issued Accounting Series Release (ASR) 190. ASR 190 reversed the SEC's long-standing position of forbidding the presentation of information other than historical cost.

ASR 190 required certain registrants (approximately the nation's 1000 largest enterprises) to disclose as supplementary information in their form 10-K:

> ... the estimated current replacement cost of inventories and productive capacity at the end of each fiscal year for which a balance sheet is required and the approximate amount of cost of sales and depreciation based on replacement cost for the two most recent full fiscal years.[8]

The replacement cost disclosures required by ASR 190 differed from the requirements of SFAS 33. In general the SEC required that replacement cost information reflect the probable effect of replacement by new, more efficient, productive assets. For example, if replacement of current equipment would probably result in lower labor costs, those anticipated lower labor costs should be reflected in the supplementary disclosures. The FASB specifically prohibits reflecting possible operating economies resulting from the assumed replacement of existing equipment.

While a case can be made that the necessity to consider the effects of changing prices on financial reports has followed a rather evolutionary development, the opposite is true. For nearly forty years the majority of the literature on the subject dealt with the possibility of restating historical cost financial statements for changes in general price levels, not the adoption of

[6]Study Group on Business Income (p. 105).
[7]Study Group on the Objectives of Financial Statements (1973, p. 14).
[8]SEC (1976, General Statement).

a new measurement system. Price-level restated financial statements continue to use historical cost as the measurement system but alter how historical cost is reported—i.e., units of constant dollars rather than units of nominal dollars. A current cost approach, however, changes the basic measurement system to one of current values rather than historical values.

Accountants in general and accounting organizations, such as the AAA, AICPA, and FASB, tended to favor price-level restated historical cost until the SEC's rather dramatic action of issuing ASR 190. Why the accounting profession tended to favor price-level restated historical cost over current cost is purely conjecture, but several possible reasons exist. The methodology of restating historical cost for changes in units of currency is generally easier than remeasurement to current cost. It involves merely obtaining an externally derived index, such as the CPI, and multiplying that index by the historical cost. If agreement can be made regarding the appropriate index to use, auditing the result is simple and any third-party liability resulting from the audit is minimal.

The SEC's action, however, changed the evolution of accounting for changing prices in the United States. ASR 190 resulted in the FASB immediately reconsidering its position (price-level restatement at that time) and led to the dual approach adopted in the SFAS 33. This development (ASR 190) significantly moved forward the development of accounting for changing prices. It was not an evolutionary step but rather more a reflection of the thinking of the then-chief accountant of the SEC, John C. Burton. Burton's background was in academe and he firmly believed that if any changes in financial reporting were needed because of changing prices, those changes should be made to the measurement system itself in order to permit the system to report more useful information to the users of financial reports. The following quotation best exemplifies Burton's thinking:

> [Inflation] creates greater distortions when the historical monetary unit approach to measurement is used. It is obvious that matching historical monetary costs against current revenues will not give a good approximation of the long-run average net cash inflow at current activity levels under conditions of rapidly changing costs. . . .[9]

This seems to argue strongly for a measurement system using current economic costs. Under such an approach, expenses would be based on the current cost of replacement of particular assets sold or used. In this way, the matching process would show a long-run average cash flow figure based on current costs at the times transactions occur.

While the ease in application cannot be denied (general price-level adjustments), since no new economic measurements must be made, there are serious doubts as to whether any significant benefit will be achieved from such a system, according to Burton.

[9]Burton (1975, p. 69).

Certainly the impact on accounting for changing prices by Burton's position cannot be overemphasized. It is quite possible that the FASB probably would not have considered current cost had Burton not been the SEC's chief accountant.

THE SIGNIFICANCE OF SFAS 33

In SFAS 33, the FASB decided to keep nonrestated historical costs in the primary financial statements. SFAS 33 specifies that reporting the effects of changing prices should be presented as supplementary information in annual reports. As discussed in Chapter 11, there are several approaches to account for the effects of changing prices. The FASB realized that a consensus could not be obtained on which method of accounting should be adopted. The proponents of a constant dollar approach as well as those of a current cost approach both hold quite strong views about the usefulness of one to the exclusion of the other. As a result, the FASB concluded that enterprises should report supplementary information under both of these fundamentally different measurement approaches.

Not all enterprises must comply with SFAS 33. It applies to these:

... public enterprises that prepare their primary financial statements in U.S. dollars and in accordance with U.S. generally accepted accounting principles and that have, at the beginning of the fiscal year for which financial statements are being presented either:

a. Inventories and property, plant, and equipment [excluding goodwill or other intangible assets] (before deducting accumulated depreciation, depletion, and amortization) amounting in aggregate to more than $125 million; or

b. Total assets amounting to more than $1 billion (after deducting accumulated depreciation).[10]

SFAS 33 defines a "public enterprise" as one:

... (a) whose debt or equity securities are traded in a public market on a domestic stock exchange or in the domestic over-the-counter market (including securities quoted only locally or regionally) or (b) that is required to file financial statements with the Securities and Exchange Commission.[11]

Approximately 1200 enterprises are affected directly by SFAS 33, however, the FASB encouraged those not affected to experiment with disclosing changing price information.

---

[10]FASB (1979, para. 23).
[11]FASB (1979, para. 22).

For constant dollar reporting, the SFAS requires disclosure of

a. Information on income from continuing operations for the current fiscal year on a historical cost/constant dollar basis . . .
b. The purchasing power gain or loss on net monetary items for the current fiscal year. . . .

The purchasing power gain or loss on net monetary items shall *not* be included in income from continuing operations.[12]

Regarding current cost, the following must be disclosed:

a. Information on income from continuing operations for the current fiscal year on a current cost basis . . .
b. The current cost amounts of inventory and property, plant, and equipment at the end of the current fiscal year . . .
c. Increases or decreases for the current fiscal year in the current cost amounts of inventory and property, plant, and equipment, net of inflation. . . .[13]

The increases or decreases in current cost amounts are *not* to be included in income from continuing operations which indicates primarily a distributable income orientation, though one without purchasing power gains or losses.[14]

Constant dollar revenue and expense calculations are computed by the method indicated in Chapter 11. Restatements, however, are in terms of the average price index prevailing during the year rather than the end-of-year index.

CONSTANT DOLLAR DISCLOSURES

SFAS 33 does not require a comprehensive application of constant dollar accounting to each element of income from continuing operations. Instead, the FASB requires application to those elements of income from continuing operations most significantly affected by inflation—cost of goods sold and depreciation, depletion, and amortization. Revenues and other expenses are assumed to already reflect average current-year dollars; thus, no restatement is necessary. Illustrative constant dollar disclosures are provided later in this chapter. To simplify the calculations for some enterprises, those that use LIFO inventory procedures in their primary financial statements need not restate cost of goods sold, because LIFO should approximate average current-year dollars, assuming no liquidation of prior years' LIFO layers.

The purchasing power gain or loss on net monetary items is determined by restating to constant dollars the beginning and ending balances

[12]FASB (1979, para. 29).
[13]FASB (1979, paras. 29 and 30).
[14]FASB (1979, para. 30).

of net monetary items as well as restating transactions in monetary items that occurred during the year. Again, the FASB requires restatement by using the average CPI for the current fiscal year. Exhibit 12-2 illustrates a method of calculating the purchasing power gain or loss under the provisions of SFAS 33. The FASB did not specify exactly how the purchasing power gain or loss should be calculated, but Exhibit 12-2 is based on examples provided in Appendix E of SFAS 33.

Because the firm in Exhibit 12-2 is a net monetary debtholder, it has a purchasing power gain during inflation. The beginning balance of net liabilities is "rolled forward" to $41,600 when restated into constant purchasing power using the average price index for the year. The net change of a $10,000 increase in net monetary assets is assumed to have occurred evenly during the year, thus, no restatement is required. Since the average index for the year is the basis of the calculation, the ending balance is "pulled back" to $28,889 in order to restate it in constant dollars again using the average index for the year. Since the beginning balance of monetary liabilities minus the decrease exceeds the ending balance, all in restated constant dollars for the year, there is a "gain" of $2,711. This method of calculation is the same as that illustrated in Chapter 11, except that in Chapter 11 all items were restated in end-of-year dollars rather than average-for-the-year dollars. The backward restatement of ending balance that is used in SFAS 33 is conceptually difficult to justify.

Constant dollar disclosures for consolidated foreign subsidiaries proved to be a subject the FASB had difficulty resolving. Initially it opted

---

EXHIBIT 12-2.

ILLUSTRATION OF CALCULATING PURCHASING POWER
GAIN OR LOSS UNDER SFAS 33

Net Monetary Liability Position:

January 1	$40,000
December 31	30,000

CPI:

January 1	250
December 31	270
Average for the Year	260

	Nominal Dollars	Conversion Factor	Constant Dollars
January 1	$40,000	260/250	$41,600
Net change during year	(10,000)	*	(10,000)
December 31	30,000	260/270	(28,889)
Gain			$ 2,711

---

*Assumed to be in average constant dollars.

for the so-called translate–restate approach as opposed to the restate–translate approach. Under the translate–restate approach, the foreign financial statements are translated first into U.S. dollars and then restated using the U.S. CPI. The restate–translate approach is the opposite: the foreign financial statements are restated first using the foreign CPI (or equivalent) and then translated into U.S. dollars. Because of the change in the objective of translating foreign operations from SFAS 8 to SFAS 52 (see Chapter 17), the FASB proposed, in an ED, that the restate–translate approach be used.[15] That proposal, however, was not well received. Finally, the FASB decided that there were no easy solutions to constant dollar disclosures for foreign operations and ultimately exempted those operations from SFAS 33 constant dollar disclosures. SFAS 70 states:

> An enterprise that measures a significant part of its operations in functional (foreign) currencies other than the U.S. dollar is exempted from Statement 33's requirements to present historical cost information measured in units of constant purchasing power.[16]

CURRENT COST DISCLOSURES

The current cost disclosures focus on specific price changes for individual assets, rather than price changes caused by general inflation. Current cost measurements typically are made for assets presently owned and used by the enterprise, and not for technologically improved assets that might replace existing assets. In an efficiently operating used–asset market, user costs per unit of output for old and new assets should be reasonably close.

As with constant dollar disclosures, SFAS 33 does not require a comprehensive application of current cost to each element of income from continuing operations. Only cost of goods sold and depreciation, depletion and amortization need be restated at current cost. Illustrative current cost disclosures are provided later in this chapter.

The FASB allowed considerable flexibility in how an enterprise could determine current cost amounts. It provided examples of the types of information an enterprise may want to use, but indicated that "enterprises are expected to select types of information appropriate to their particular circumstances . . ."[17] Examples included in SFAS 33 are:

a. Indexation
  (1) Externally generated price indexes for the class of goods or services being measured.
  (2) Internally generated price indexes for the class of goods or services being measured.

---

[15]FASB (1982a).
[16]FASB (1982b, Summary).
[17]FASB (1979, para. 60).

b. Direct pricing
  (1) Current invoice prices.
  (2) Vendors' price lists or other quotations or estimates.
  (3) Standard manufacturing costs that reflect current costs.[18]

Again like constant dollar disclosures, an enterprise using LIFO inventory procedures can assume cost of goods sold reported in the primary financial statements represents a good approximation of current cost. Although using the same amounts for constant dollar and current cost may appear inconsistent, the Board's reasoning was that both represent the average dollars for the year and historical cost and current cost are identical at the time of purchase.

For consolidated foreign subsidiaries that use functional currencies other than the U.S. dollar, current cost amounts and increases or decreases therein should be measured in the functional currency. Adjustments to current cost information to reflect the effects of general inflation, however, may be based on either the U.S. CPI or functional currency CPI.[19] The FASB, in allowing use of either the U.S. CPI or the functional currency CPI, recognized that use of the functional currency CPI is more theoretically correct. However, it also is much more costly when several functional currencies are used by the same reporting entity. Therefore, it permitted use of the U.S. CPI.

An initial review of annual reports prepared in compliance with SFAS 33 indicates that the use of indexes to determine current cost amounts is predominant. Arthur Young found that 49% of the enterprises in their survey used indexes exclusively, 47% used both indexes and direct pricing, and only 4% used direct pricing exclusively. Of those enterprises employing indexing techniques to determine current cost amounts, 56% relied exclusively on externally generated indexes, 3% used exclusively an internally generated index, and 20% used both external and internal indexes (the remaining enterprises did not report what method they used.)[20] The most frequently used external indexes were those published by the U.S. Department of Labor, such as Producer Price Indexes. The use of external indexes undoubtedly minimizes information production costs. The question of how much representational faithfulness is sacrificed by not using internal indexes or direct pricing is an important question which cannot be answered at this time.

The technique of determining current cost by using an index is the same as that illustrated for constant dollar restatements, except that a specific price index for a particular type or group of assets is used rather than the CPI.

[18]FASB (1979, para. 60).
[19]FASB (1982b, Summary).
[20]Arthur Young & Co. (1980, p. 25).

EXHIBIT 12-3.

CALCULATION OF CHANGE IN CURRENT COST AMOUNTS
NET OF INFLATION

Current Cost Amount:*
January 1	$100,000
December 31	120,000

CPI:
January 1	250
December 31	270
Average for the Year	260

	Current Cost	Conversion Factor	Average Dollars
January 1	$100,000	260/250	$104,000
December 31	120,000	260/270	115,556
Net Increase	$ 20,000		$ 11,556
Increase in current cost (nominal dollars)			$ 20,000
Increase in current cost (constant dollars)			11,556
Inflation Component			$ 8,444

*Assume no physical change in the asset during the year, i.e., no increase or decrease.

The steps to calculate the increases or decreases for the current fiscal year in the current cost amounts of inventory and property, plant, and equipment, net of inflation are as follows:

1. Determine the current cost amounts at the beginning and end of the year.
2. Convert those amounts to average dollars for the current year.
3. The change in current cost amounts determined in (1) less the change in current cost average dollar amounts determined in (2) represents the inflation component of the increase in current cost amounts.

Exhibit 12-3 provides an illustration of calculating the increases or decreases in current cost amounts net of inflation.

The holding gain shown in Exhibit 12-3 of $11,556 is the real holding gain arising during the current year. If it were combined with adjusted current cost income from continuing operations, the result would be earning power income (excluding purchasing power gains or losses on net monetary items).

FIVE-YEAR SUMMARY

In addition to the basic constant dollar and current cost disclosures just discussed, enterprises are required to present a five-year summary of selected financial data to aid users in assessing trends. This summary must include the following information:

a. Net Sales and Other Operating Revenues
b. Historical Cost/Constant Dollar Information
   (1) Income from continuing operations
   (2) Income per common share from continuing operations
   (3) Net assets at fiscal year end
c. Current Cost Information . . .
   (1) Income from continuing operations
   (2) Income per common share from continuing operations
   (3) Net assets at fiscal year-end
   (4) Increases or decreases in the current cost amounts of inventory and property, plant, and equipment, net of inflation
d. Other information
   (1) Purchasing power gain or loss on net monetary items
   (2) Cash dividends per common share
   (3) Market price per common share at fiscal year-end.[21]

All the information disclosed in the five-year summary must be presented in constant dollars. Enterprises, however, have a choice between using current-year dollars or base-period dollars, i.e., 1967 dollars. Those enterprises that elect to use current-year dollars must restate or roll forward prior years' data in the summary each year. Although using base-year dollars avoids the rollforward problem, it does result in a confusing presentation. Current-year constant dollar and current cost disclosures will be different numerical amounts from the same figures in the five-year summary.

SPECIALIZED INDUSTRY PROVISIONS

Pending further study, the FASB exempted certain specialized industries from the current cost provisions of SFAS 33 because of the difficulty in determining current cost amounts and the lack of usefulness of such amounts for those industries. The industries exempted were forest products, mining, oil and gas producers, and real estate.

Subsequently, the FASB issued SFASs 39, 40, and 41 regarding current cost disclosures for these industries. SFAS 39 requires the application of SFAS 33 current cost provisions to mining and oil and gas producers. However, SFAS 69 (see Chapter 14 for discussion) reversed SFAS 39's current cost provisions for oil and gas producers. These producers do not need to disclose current costs unless they have significant inventory and property,

[21]FASB (1979, para. 35).

plant, and equipment apart from oil and gas operations.[22] SFAS 40 continues the exemption provisions of SFAS 33 for the forest products industry. SFAS 41 requires real estate enterprises to apply SFAS 33 current cost provisions.

Motion picture producers complained that determining the current cost of completed films in inventory was impossible. After considerable deliberation the FASB agreed and issued SFAS 46 which exempts motion picture producers from the current cost provisions of SFAS 33.

The investment industry also complained to the FASB about the current cost provisions of SFAS 33. Its complaint was that the calculations were confusing and the results misleading. As a result, the FASB issued SFAS 54 that exempts investment companies from the current cost provisions of SFAS 33.

EXAMPLE OF SFAS 33 CALCULATIONS AND DISCLOSURES

The disclosure requirements of SFAS 33 are provided by means of an illustration. Assume the information shown in Exhibit 12-4. The constant dollar calculations for the information are shown in Exhibit 12-5, and the current cost calculations are shown in Exhibit 12-6. There are two alternatives for disclosing the constant dollar and current cost information (excluding the five-year summary): the statement format and the reconciliation format. These are shown in Exhibit 12-7.

EXHIBIT 12-4.

ABC COMPANY
Balance Sheet
January 1, 1981

Assets			Liabilities		
Cash		$ 1,000	Accounts Payable	$ 2,000	
Accounts Receivable		2,000	Long-term Debt	10,000	$12,000
Inventory		5,000	*Stockholders' Equity*		
Equipment	$20,000		Common Stock	$10,000	
Accumulated Depr.	5,000	15,000	Retained Earnings	1,000	11,000
			Total Liabilities &		
Total Assets		$23,000	Stockholders Equity		$23,000

---

[22]FASB (1982c).

EXHIBIT 12-4. *(Continued)*

Income Statement
For the Year of 1981

Sales	$20,000	
Cost of Goods Sold	12,000	
Gross Profit		$8,000
Operating Expenses excluding		
Depreciation	5,000	
Depreciation Expense	2,000	7,000
Net Income from Continuing		
Operations		$1,000

Balance Sheet
December 31, 1981

Assets			Liabilities		
Cash		$ 5,500	Accounts Payable	$ 1,000	
Accounts			Long-term Debt	15,000	$16,000
Receivable		1,000			
Inventory		8,000	*Stockholder's Equity*		
Equipment	$20,000		Common Stock	$10,000	
Accumulated			Retained		
Depr.	7,000	13,000	Earnings	1,500	11,500
			Total Liabilities &		
Total Assets		$27,500	Stockholders Equity		$27,500

Additional Information:

(a) Dividends paid on July 1, 1981 .... $ 500

(b) Inventory is accounted for on a FIFO basis and turns over
four times per year (12,000 units sold in 1981).

(c) Current cost of inventory:

January 1, 1981 ($1.00 per unit)	5,200
December 31, 1981 ($1.25 per unit)	8,300

(d) Current Cost of Equipment:

	Current Cost	Current Cost Accum. Depr.	Net Current Cost
January 1, 1981			
Equipment X (30% depreciated)	$13,000	$3,900	$ 9,100
Equipment Y (20% depreciated)	7,000	1,400	5,600
Equipment Z (10% depreciated)	3,000	300	2,700
Total	$23,000	$5,600	$17,400
December 31, 1981			
Equipment X (40% depreciated)	$15,000	$6,000	$ 9,000
Equipment Y (30% depreciated)	9,000	2,700	6,300
Equipment Z (20% depreciated)	4,000	800	3,200
Total	$28,000	$9,500	$18,500

EXHIBIT 12-4.   (Continued)

(e) Depreciation is 10% per year
(f) Index information (CPI):

January 1, 1981	250
December 31, 1981	270
Average for 1981	260
When equipment X purchased	200
When equipment Y purchased	225
When equipment Z purchased	240
Fourth quarter 1980	245
Fourth quarter 1981	265

EXHIBIT 12-5.

CONSTANT DOLLAR CALCULATIONS

Cost of Goods Sold:

January 1, 1981	$ 5,000 ×	$\dfrac{260 \text{ average } 1981}{245 \text{ 4th qtr } 1980}$ =	c $ 5,306
Purchases	$15,000 ×	$\dfrac{260 \text{ average } 1981}{260 \text{ average } 1981}$ =	15,000
December 31, 1981	$ 8,000 ×	$\dfrac{260 \text{ average } 1981}{265 \text{ 4th qtr } 1981}$ =	(7,849)
			c $12,457

Depreciation Expense:

Equipment X	$12,000 ×	$\dfrac{260 \text{ average } 1981}{200 \text{ when purch.}}$ =	c $15,600
Equipment Y	$ 6,000 ×	$\dfrac{260 \text{ average } 1981}{225 \text{ when purch.}}$ =	$ 6,933
Equipment Z	$ 2,000 ×	$\dfrac{260 \text{ average } 1981}{240 \text{ when purch.}}$ =	$ 2,167
Total			c $24,700

Depreciation expense at 10% (c$24,700 × 10%)   c $ 2,470

Purchasing Power Gain (Net Monetary Liability):

January 1, 1981	$ 9,000 ×	$\dfrac{260 \text{ average } 1981}{250 \text{ Jan. 1, } 1981}$ =	c $ 9,360
Net Change	$ 500 ×	$\dfrac{260 \text{ average } 1981}{260 \text{ average } 1981}$ =	$ 500
December 31, 1981	$ 9,500 ×	$\dfrac{260 \text{ average } 1981}{270 \text{ Dec. 31, } 1981}$ =	$ 9,148
Total Gain			c $ 712

---

c = Constant dollars in this and succeeding exhibits

EXHIBIT 12-6.

CURRENT COST CALCULATIONS

Cost of Goods Sold:

Current cost per unit January 1, 1981	$ 1.00
Current cost per unit December 31, 1981	$ 1.25
	$ 2.25
Average current cost for 1981: $2.25 ÷ 2 =	$ 1.125
Units sold in 1981	× 12,000
	$13,500

Depreciation Expense:

Total current cost of equipment January 1, 1981	$23,000
Total current cost of equipment December 31, 1981	28,000
	$51,000
Average current cost for 1981: $51,000 ÷ 2 =	$25,500
Depreciation expense at 10%	$ 2,550

Current Cost of Inventory and Equipment:

Inventory (amount given)	8,300

Equipment:

	Current Cost	Percent Depreciated	Accumulated Depreciation
X	$15,000	40%	$ 6,000
Y	9,000	30%	2,700
Z	4,000	20%	800
	$28,000		$ 9,500

Current cost	$28,000
Amount depreciated	9,500
Net	$18,500

Increase in current costs amounts, net of inflation:

Inventory:

	Historical cost	Current Cost			Current Cost Constant Dollar
Beg January 1, 1981	5000	$ 5,200 ×	$\frac{260 \text{ average } 1981}{250 \text{ Jan. 1, } 1981}$	=	c $ 5,408
Purchases	15000	$15,000 ×	$\frac{260 \text{ average } 1981}{260 \text{ average } 1981}$	=	15,000
Cost of sales	(12000)	(13,500) ×	$\frac{260 \text{ average } 1981}{260 \text{ average } 1981}$	=	(13,500)
December 31, 1981	8000	$(8,300) ×	$\frac{260 \text{ average } 1981}{270 \text{ Dec. 31, } 1981}$	=	(7,993)
	∅	(1,600) *holding gain*			($ 1,085)

Inflation component: $1600 − c$1,085 → c $ 515

EXHIBIT 12-6. *(Continued)*

		Current Cost		*Current Cost Constant Dollar*
Equipment:				
January 1, 1981	$17,400 ×	$\dfrac{260 \text{ average } 1981}{250 \text{ Jan. 1, 1981}}$	=	c $18,096
Depreciation	(2,550) ×	$\dfrac{260 \text{ average } 1981}{260 \text{ average } 1981}$	=	(2,550)
December 31, 1981	(18,500) ×	$\dfrac{260 \text{ average } 1981}{270 \text{ Dec. 31, 1981}}$	=	(17,815)
	$(3,650)			($ 2,269)

Inflation component: $3,650 − c$2,269	=	c $ 1,381
Total Holding Gain (1,600 + 3,650)	=	5,250
Unrealized Holding Gain (1,085 + 2,269) *Real Holding gains.*	=	3,354
Inflation Component (515 + 1,381)		1,896

EXHIBIT 12-7.

DISCLOSURE FORMAT
Statement Format

	Primary Statement	*Constant Dollar*	*Current Cost*
Sales	$20,000	c $20,000	c $20,000
Cost of sales	(12,000)	(12,457)	(13,500)
Depreciation	(2,000)	(2,470)	(2,550)
Operating expenses	(5,000)	(5,000)	(5,000)
Net income from continuing operations	$ 1,000	c $ 73	c $(1,050)
Purchasing Power Gain		c $ 712	c $ 712
Increase in current cost			
Inventory			$ 1,600
Equipment			3,650
Total Holding Gain			$ 5,250
Effect of increase from general inflation			1,896
Increase in current cost, net of inflation (unrealized holding gain)			$ 3,354
Current cost of inventory			$ 8,300
Current cost of equipment			$18,500

EXHIBIT 12-7. (Continued)

Reconciliation Format

Net income from continuing operations		$ 1,000
Adjustment to restate costs for inflation:		
Cost of sales	457	
Depreciation	470	c$ (927)
Net income from continuing operations adjusted for inflation		c $ 73
Adjustment to restate for current costs		
Cost of sales	1043	
Depreciation	80	$ (1,123)
Net income from continuing operations adjusted for current costs		c$ (1,050)
Purchasing Power gain		c $ 712
Increase in current cost		
Inventory		$ 1,600
Equipment		3,650
Total Holding Gain		$ 5,250
Effect of increase from inflation		$ 1,896
Increase in current cost, net of inflation (unrealized holding gain)		$ 3,354
Current cost of inventory		$ 8,300
Current cost of equipment		$18,500

OVERVIEW OF SFAS 33

The experimental nature of SFAS 33 cannot be overemphasized. The FASB did not specify the methods to use to calculate the various disclosures required. It stated:

> [The FASB] encourages experimentation within the guidelines of this Statement and the development of new techniques that fit the particular circumstances of the enterprise. This Statement has been written to provide more flexibility than is customary in Board Statements in the belief that those involved will help to develop techniques that will further the understanding of the effects of price changes on the enterprise.[23]

Moreover, the FASB is committed to review the usefulness of the information produced by SFAS 33 and must decide whether to continue it as is, modify it, or eliminate it entirely. It stated:

> The requirements of this Statement will be reviewed on an ongoing basis and the Board will amend or withdraw requirements whenever that course

[23]FASB (1979, para. 14).

is justified by the evidence. This Statement will be reviewed comprehensively after a period of not more than five years.[24]

Obviously the FASB is, perhaps for the first time ever for a standard-setting body, performing a massive laboratory experiment within the financial statements.

The overall format adopted in SFAS 33 of disaggregation rather than aggregation of information is significant. It reflects that the Board itself has not decided whether real holding gains and losses and purchasing power gains and losses are part of income from continuing operations. Also, it points out the Board's confidence in relying on the disclosure mechanism, possibly utilizing market efficiency as opposed to dictating a particular aggregation of information. It leaves the problem of aggregating information to the user. For example, realized income may be estimated by taking the difference between the current cost and price-level adjusted depreciation and cost of goods sold and adding these estimates of realized real holding gains to income from continuing operations.

While SFAS 33 clearly does represent an experiment which will undoubtedly be modified, some of the decisions made by the Board appear to be suboptimal. The choice of the CPI as a measure of general inflation is not a good decision on theoretical grounds. Its selection implies a strong proprietary theory orientation. Both APB Statement 3 and the 1974 FASB ED recommended use of the gross national product implicit price deflator (GNP deflator), which is an index of changes in prices of all producer and consumer goods and services. Certainly the GNP deflator would provide a better index of the impact of changing prices on American businesses than the CPI. Both indexes tend to move in the same direction and presumably the FASB chose the CPI because it is calculated and published more frequently than the GNP deflator.

A problem encountered in the real world is the fact that the prices change daily throughout the year (in Chapter 11 all price changes for a year were assumed to occur on the first day of the year). The FASB attacked the problem by requiring restatement into average-for-the-year dollars. The benefits of using the average index for the year is that transactions occurring during the year do not have to be restated and an estimation of the index at the end of the year does not have to be made. Hence using average prices for the year may be less costly and more timely. Of course, if transactions occurring during the year are not representative of average prices for the year, the measurement will not have representational faithfulness. Moreover, its use produces results that may be slightly confusing and also probably less useful than using end-of-the-year prices. A strong case can still be made for end-of-year prices rather than average prices. And SFAS 33 does permit use of year-end prices if comprehensive financial statements are prepared rather than minimal disclosures.

---

[24]FASB (1979, para. 15).

For SFAS 33 purposes, long-term debt is considered a monetary liability in calculating the purchasing power gain or loss. As was pointed out in Chapter 11, the appropriateness of its inclusion is questionable because of the inflation effect built into the determination of interest rates. Moreover, many enterprises are beginning to issue long-term debt with "inflation-proof features." An example is Sunshine Mining's silver-indexed bonds. These bonds provide that the principal repayment is tied to the price of silver. The repayment for each $1000 face value bond is the greater of $1000 or the current market price of 50 ounces of silver. Bond holders may receive silver in lieu of cash at maturity.[25] The FASB undoubtedly will have to rethink its position on automatically including all long-term debt as monetary liabilities for purposes of the calculation of purchasing power gains or losses when it reconsiders the SFAS 33 experiment.

According to most definitions of monetary/nonmonetary assets and liabilities, such items as claims to and obligations in foreign money and deferred income taxes are nonmonetary. SFAS 33, however, treats them as monetary items. Referring specifically to deferred income taxes, the FASB stated

> ... classification of this item as nonmonetary may be technically preferable, however the monetary classification provides a more practical solution for the purposes of constant dollar accounting.[26]

It is hard to follow the Board's logic. Deferred income taxes, as applied under APB 11, are acknowledged not to be liabilities and certainly they do not meet the definition of a liability in Statement of Financial Accounting Concepts 3. Experience has shown that those amounts typically are not reduced significantly but rather continue to grow. The effect of the Board's decision is to create purchasing power gains or significantly reduce purchasing power losses for most major U.S. enterprises.

The current cost disclosures, as illustrated in Exhibit 12-6, produce results that defy definition. The disclosure includes a mixture of beginning-of-the-year current cost, depreciation for the year based on average-for-the-year current cost, and end-of-the-year current cost. These amounts are combined and restated in average-for-the-year dollars. The net result is difficult, if not impossible, to interpret.

EMPIRICAL RESEARCH IN ACCOUNTING FOR INFLATION AND CHANGING PRICES

While empirical work has been quite extensive in terms of assessing the usefulness of providing general price-level and current value information, the results are far from conclusive and are also somewhat contradictory. In general, the findings of the various studies appear to lean to the

---

[25] Swieringa (1981, p. 166).
[26] FASB (1979, para. 208).

negative side relative to the issue of information content. As a result, a paradox appears to exist. On a deductive basis, researchers have long advocated the need to cope with inflation and changing prices. Empirical studies, however, raise the question as to the usefulness of this type of information. Of course it may merely be a matter of users being unfamiliar with general price-level and current value types of data.

Empirical studies can be classified into three general types: (1) surveys of users relative to the usefulness of information on changing prices, (2) studies concerning the significance of differences between historical cost and general price-level adjusted income measurements, and (3) affect of general price-level and current value information on security prices. The studies discussed here are illustrative of the three categories of empirical research in nonhistorical financial reporting measurements.

User Surveys

Perhaps the most interesting and extensive user survey was conducted by Benston and Krasney.[27] Their survey comprised sixty-two of the largest firms in the life insurance industry. Each firm received two questionnaires, one for decision makers involved with direct placement of bonds of business and industrial issuers and the other for decision makers concerned with the insurance firm's common stock portfolio. The response rate was 94%, virtually eliminating the problem of nonrespondent bias: 89% of direct placement officers chose historical costing under present rules as the single preferred basis of evaluation while 9% chose replacement cost and 2% opted for general price-level adjusted statements. The preference for historical costing was not quite as strong among the common stock investment officers: 66% preferred historical costing, 31% preferred some form of current values, and 2% were for general price-level adjustment.

Several criticisms of the Benston and Krasney study were made. One was that even this sophisticated group of users might not be sufficiently familiar with nonhistorical cost methods. Also the issue of bias on the part of respondents was raised—owing to the "bad press" received by ASR 190.[28] In addition, the question was raised as to whether the population surveyed was representative of a broader group of sophisticated equity investors and long-term lenders, not to mention short-term creditor groups.[29]

Income Differences

Several studies have been made concerning differences between historical cost income and general price-level adjusted income. Parker's study, unlike other work concerned with this problem, attempted to use FASB-

---

[27] Benston and Krasney (1978).
[28] Adkerson (1978, pp. 32–33).
[29] Buzby and Falk (1978).

sanctioned adjustment methods.[30] Both balance sheets and income statements were developed for the years 1972, 1973, and 1974 for 1,050 American industrial corporations. This represented approximately one-third of
the firms appearing on the Compustat data files. The firms not included
were omitted because of various deficiencies in the data appearing on the
tapes. Hence the 1,050 firms Parker used did not constitute a "sample" of
all firms on the tape but were more in the nature of a separate and specific
population. The study developed ratios showing the relationship between
various general price-level adjusted numbers and historical cost figures on
an aggregated basis.

Parker's findings showed that, for all the firms in the study, general
price-level adjusted income was 83.5% of historical income in 1972, 91.3%
of income in 1973, and 102.8% in 1974. However, even in 1974 where the
aggregate relationship between the two numbers was extremely close, differences for many firms on an individual basis was extensive.

Most of the other studies, in agreement with Parker, found significant
differences between historical cost numbers and general price-level transformations.[31] This is not surprising during a decade which had an 8% average annual rate of inflation. Whether inflation-adjusted information is
useful for decision-making purposes, however, cannot be answered by this
type of research.

Effect of General Price-Level and Current Value Information on Security Prices

One way to attempt to come to grips with the problem of information
content is to assess the impact on security prices of nonhistorical cost information. Several studies found no unusual stock price movements resulting from the disclosure of current cost information from ASR 190.[32] It was
therefore concluded that ASR 190 had no information content. However,
that finding is qualified because of (1) problems of sample selection, (2) the
timing of the various tests in terms of attempting to measure any possible
effects of information, and (3) the usual problem of a possible inability to
hold constant other events which could influence security prices.

Lustgarten, on the other hand, did find a statistically significant relationship when he examined, by means of multiple regression analysis, the
relation between abnormal security returns and estimated replacement
costs as evidenced by the difference between accumulated depreciation on
a current value basis and on a historical cost basis.[33] His sample consisted

---

[30]Parker (1977). Parker attempted to implement the FASB exposure draft of December 31, 1974,
which was later withdrawn.

[31]See Peterson (1973) and Staubus (1976), for example.

[32]See Beaver, Christie, and Griffin (1980), Gheyara and Boatsman (1980), and Ro (1980). In
addition, Ketz (1983) found virtually no information content provided by constant dollar income measurements as long as the annual level of inflation remained stable.

[33]Lustgarten (1983).

of 623 firms which were included in the holdings of several financial data providing services. They provided current value information for fiscal years ending in 1977.

He found a negative correlation (lower security prices and higher current value accumulated depreciation), which might be expected because this would indicate higher replacement costs without saying anything about the influence of changing prices upon revenues. This finding of the Lustgarten study is in philosophic agreement with the rejection of earning power income on the grounds that market imperfections (such as pure supply-side considerations) prevent holding gains from being a signal about future earnings.

Lustgarten appropriately qualified his findings by noting that the effect on security prices that he found, which preceded the appearance of ASR-mandated data by several months, may have been caused by the fact that this was privately produced information or by a variable not included in his study, as well as by the possibility of information leakage from the ASR 190 data prior to its issuance.

Studies of this type, which attempt to determine information content through the effect on security prices, must be viewed cautiously because of the difficulty of isolating influences upon security prices that are, in turn, presumed to be indicative of information content. Therein lies both the strength and weakness of these studies. Much more evidence appears to be necessary before conclusions relative to the usefulness of nonhistorical cost data can be solidly formed.

ACCOUNTING FOR CHANGING PRICES IN OTHER COUNTRIES

Inflation is an economic phenomenon that is not limited to the United States. Indeed the majority of the countries in the world are experiencing inflation, many at higher rates and for a longer period of time than in the United States.

The International Accounting Standards Committee (IASC) recently issued International Accounting Standard (IAS) 15, "Information Reflecting the Effects of Changing Prices." The IASC recognizes that there is not an international consensus on the methods for reflecting the effects of changing prices, but it believes that evaluation of the subject would be assisted if enterprises that present primary financial statements on the historical cost basis also provided supplementary information reflecting the effects of price changes. As a result the IASC does not desire one method to the exclusion of others but allows each enterprise to select the method it chooses to reflect the effect of changing prices.

IAS 15 calls for disclosure on either a constant dollar basis or current cost basis. It recommends the following information:

1. The amount of the adjustment to or the adjusted amount of depreciation of property, plant, and equipment.
2. The amount of the adjustment to or the adjusted amount of cost of sales.
3. The adjustments relating to monetary items, the effect of borrowing, or equity interests, purchasing power gain or loss when such adjustments have been taken into account in determining income under the accounting method adopted.
4. The overall effect on results of the adjustments described in (1) and (2) and, where appropriate, (3), as well as any other items reflecting the effects of changing prices that are reported under the accounting method adopted.[34]

IAS 15 is effective for periods beginning on or after January 1, 1983. Its experimental nature, like that of SFAS 33, can be clearly detected.

Standards on accounting for the effects of changing prices are being implemented in many countries. In this section, we will briefly review some of those requirements for selected English-speaking countries. The countries selected are those countries that have been experiencing inflation at or close to the level experienced in the United States and that have a standard-setting process similar to ours.

A common thread can be detected in the standard-setting process regarding changing prices in all countries reviewed: the process is a lengthy one that in most cases, as in the United States, started with constant dollar restatement of historical cost financial statements and concluded with current cost financial statements.

UNITED KINGDOM

The United Kingdom experience is similar to that of the United States but it has progressed further. In 1973 and 1974 an ED and proposed standard called for constant dollar restated historical cost financial statements. This approach was debated extensively and eventually discarded in favor of a current cost approach. A final standard was issued in March, 1980.

As in the United States, the United Kingdom Standard does not cover all enterprises but rather only the largest ones, estimated to be no more than one percent of all enterprises.[35] Unlike the United States, however, the United Kingdom Standard requires a comprehensive current cost income statement and balance sheet, in addition to the historical cost financial statements. Either the historical cost or current cost statements may be the primary financial statements with the others as supplementary disclosures.

---

[34]International Accounting Standards Committee (1981, para. 24).
[35]International Accounting and Financial Report (1980, p. 5).

The significant adjustments to the historical cost income statement required to prepare the current cost statement are these:

1. depreciation expense on a current cost basis,
2. cost of sales on a current cost basis,
3. a monetary working capital adjustment (similar to purchasing power gains and losses).

The current cost balance sheet should reflect the current cost of property, plant, equipment, investments (both those accounted for on the equity basis and those on the cost basis), and intangible assets other than goodwill. Reserves for revaluation would be displayed in stockholders' equity.

CANADA

Canada's experience also is similar to our own, but constant dollar restated historical cost financial statements are not required. Its discussion started in 1974 with a guideline for preparation of constant dollar restated historical cost financial statements. It ended in 1983 with a standard that is a five-year experiment like ours, which likewise does not require comprehensive remeasurement of financial statements but rather selected supplemental disclosures. Only about 400 enterprises must prepare the required disclosures. The specific rules require these disclosures:

1. The current cost of goods sold, and depreciation, depletion and amortization, or the current cost adjustments for these items.
2. Income on a current cost basis—income before extraordinary items adjusted for the above charges, with income tax on an historical cost basis.
3. The amount of the changes during the reporting period in the current cost amounts of inventory and property, plant, and equipment.
4. The carrying values of inventory and property, plant, and equipment on a current cost basis at the end of the reporting period.
5. Net assets after these current cost changes attributable to general inflation.
6. The gain or loss in general purchasing power from holding net monetary items.[36]

AUSTRALIA

In Australia constant dollar restated historical cost financial statements were extensively discussed but not put forth as an ED. Rather, drawing from the experience of the United Kingdom, Canada, and the United States, current cost disclosures were more seriously considered. A provisional standard (similar to an ED) was issued, calling for supplemental disclosure of

[36]World Accounting Report (1982, p. 4).

current cost information. The current cost disclosures are very similar to SFAS 33; however, purchasing power gains and losses are separated into current, which includes normal trading monetary items, and noncurrent, which relates to long-term nonoperating items. This is an attempt to acknowledge that long-term debt is not the same as short-term debt because inflation automatically is factored by way of interest rates (see Chapter 11).

The standard-setting bodies were unable to reach agreement on a final standard, however, and abandoned plans to make current cost disclosures mandatory. A special practice statement was issued to provide guidelines for those who choose to disclose current cost information, but no enterprise is required to disclose anything regarding changing prices.[37]

SUMMARY

The problem of accounting for the effects of changing prices has been with us for over fifty years, but only in the last ten to fifteen years has it been seriously considered by standard-setting bodies. Typically these agencies initially approached the problem by considering constant dollar restated historical cost financial statements. Actions by the SEC in the United States and experience with constant dollars in the United Kingdom led to an abrupt change in accounting for the effects of changing prices. Today, most standard-setting bodies in English-speaking countries believe that some form of current cost accounting is the correct solution.

The FASB, in SFAS 33, refused to abandon constant dollar restated historical cost financial statements. As a result, it adopted a dual disclosure requirement—constant dollar and current cost. While it is easy to find fault with various aspects of SFAS 33, one cannot lose sight of the fact that it is only an experiment. The objective of the experiment is to determine the most useful manner of reporting the effects of changing prices and to develop new techniques for calculating those effects.

Some recent actions in the United States may indicate that the SFAS 33 experiment has at least resulted in the realization by standard-setting bodies that constant dollar restated historical cost financial statements are of limited use. The FASB exempted reporting entities with significant foreign operations from the constant dollar disclosures but continued to require current cost disclosures. Moreover, the Accounting Standards Executive Committee of the AICPA required, in Statement of Position 82-1, current cost financial statements as the primary financial statements for individuals.[38]

---

[37]World Accounting Report (1983, p. 14).
[38]Accounting Standards Executive Committee (1982).

Empirical research does not appear to be conclusive, at this time, in terms of indicating whether accounting for inflation and changing prices is useful. The majority of studies appear to lean toward the negative side of the question. If this is the case, there would be a strong disagreement between deductive and inductive approaches to the user relevance issue pertaining to inflation accounting.

QUESTIONS

1. Accounting for the effects of changing prices has not been considered seriously in accounting practice until relatively recent times. Why?
2. Explain the relationship between (1) reported earnings determined by use of historical cost and (2) cash flows in times of stable prices versus times of changing prices.
3. ASR 190 and SFAS 33 differ significantly in required current cost disclosures. How do they differ (discuss the conceptual differences)? Which pronouncement do you believe is the better regarding current cost?
4. Why did the FASB require disaggregation of changing price disclosures rather than a comprehensive restatement of the primary financial statements? Do you believe that one format is better than the other? Which? Why?
5. Using the CPI as opposed to a company-specific index for restatements has some disadvantages. What are the disadvantages? In your opinion, why did the Board select the CPI?
6. Do you believe that the disclosures required by SFAS 33 are useful? Is historical cost/constant dollar more useful than current cost, or vice versa? Do you believe that both historical cost/constant dollar and current cost disclosures should be required?
7. Describe the method(s) of determining the historical cost/constant dollar disclosures required by SFAS 33.
8. Describe the method(s) of determining the current cost disclosures required by SFAS 33.
9. For SFAS 33 purposes, deferred income taxes are classified as monetary items. What is a monetary item? Does "deferred income taxes" meet the definition of a monetary item? What is the practical result of classifying deferred income taxes as monetary items?
10. When prices are changing rapidly, why are financial statements that are prepared using nonrestated historical cost less useful than they would be when prices are not changing rapidly?
11. At the beginning of a year, a company purchased inventory for $100,000. During the year, it sold half the inventory for $90,000 when

the current cost of the inventory sold was $70,000. At the end of the year, the remaining inventory had a current cost of $95,000. Compute the current cost income from continuing operations, the realized holding gain, the unrealized holding gain, and the current cost net income.

12. Why do you believe the FASB required a dual disclosure approach?

13. What are the major arguments in favor of and in opposition to constant dollar restated historical cost financial statements?

14. What are the major arguments in favor of and in opposition to current cost financial statements?

15. The FASB required use of average-for-the-year dollars for SFAS 33 disclosures. Why did it make this choice? Was it a good choice? Why? What other alternatives are available and what are their advantages and disadvantages?

CASES AND PROBLEMS

1. Weston Credit Corporation (Weston) owns two international banking subsidiaries that are shown on its financial statements on an unconsolidated equity basis. In effect, these banking subsidiaries are wholly owned subsidiaries of Weston.

   Required: For SFAS 33 constant dollar reporting, should the investment in the two international banking subsidiaries be treated as a nonmonetary or monetary asset? Discuss the pros and cons of each classification.

2. Redding Credit Corporation (Redding) is a diversified finance company with a large leveraged lease portfolio. Consequently, deferred investment tax credits (deferred ITCs) and unguaranteed residual values arise as a result of its leveraged leasing activities. Redding is in the process of complying with the provisions of SFAS 33 and has two questions.

   Required:

   (a) Should Redding disaggregate deferred ITCs and unguaranteed residual values from lease receivables for purposes of calculating the purchasing power gain or loss? Discuss.

   (b) Are deferred ITCs and unguaranteed residual values monetary or nonmonetary items? Discuss.

3. The financial statements of a business entity could be prepared by using cost or current value as a basis. In addition, the basis could be stated in terms of unadjusted dollars or dollars restated for changes in purchasing power. The various permutations of these two separate and distinct areas are shown in the following matrix:

	Unadjusted Dollars	Dollars Restated for Changes in Purchasing Power
Historical Cost	1	2
Current Value	3	4

Block number 1 of the matrix represents the traditional method of accounting for transactions in accounting today, wherein the absolute (unadjusted) amount of dollars given up or received is recorded for the asset or liability obtained (this is called the **relationship between resources**). Amounts recorded in the method described in block number 1 reflect the original cost of the asset or liability and do not give effect to any change in value in the unit of measure (that is, there is no **standard of comparison**). This method assumes the validity of the accounting concepts of going concern and stable monetary unit. Any gain or loss (including holding and purchasing power gains and losses) resulting from the sale or satisfaction of amounts recorded under this method is deferred in its entirety until sale or satisfaction.

Required: For each of the remaining matrix blocks (2, 3 and 4) respond to the following questions. Limit your discussion to nonmonetary assets only.

(a) How will the method of recording assets affect the relationship between resources and the standard of comparison?

(b) What is the theoretical justification for using each method?

(c) How will each method of asset valuation affect the recognition of gain or loss during the life of the asset and ultimately from the sale or abandonment of the asset? Your response should include a discussion of the timing and magnitude of the gain or loss and conceptual reasons for any difference from the gain or loss computed using the traditional method. (AICPA adapted.)

BIBLIOGRAPHY OF REFERENCED WORKS

Accounting Standards Executive Committee (1982). "Accounting and Financial Reporting for Personal Financial Statements," *Statement of Position 82-1* (AICPA).

Adkerson, Richard C. (1978). "Discussion of DAAM: The Demand for Alternative Accounting Measurements," *Studies on Accounting for Changes in General and Specific Prices: Empirical Research and Public Policy, 1978* (Supplement to *Journal of Accounting Research*), pp. 31–36.

Arthur Young & Company (1980). *Financial Reporting and Changing Prices* (Arthur Young & Company).

Beaver, William H.; Andrew A. Christie; and Paul A. Griffin (1980). "The Information Content of Accounting Series Release No. 190," *Journal of Accounting and Economics* (August 1980), pp. 127–157.

Benston, George J., and Melvin A. Krasney (1978). "DAAM: The Demand for Alternative Accounting Measurements," *Studies on Accounting for Changes in General and Specific Prices: Empirical Research and Public Policy, 1978* (Supplement to *Journal of Accounting Research*), pp. 1–30.

Burton, John C. (1975). "Financial Reporting in an Age of Inflation," *Journal of Accountancy* (February 1975), pp. 68–71.

Buzby, Stephen L., and Haim Falk (1978). "Discussion of DAAM: The Demand for Alternative Accounting Measurements," *Studies on Accounting for Changes in General and Specific Prices: Empirical Research and Public Policy, 1978* (Supplement to *Journal of Accounting Research*), pp. 37–45.

Committee on Concepts and Standards Underlying Corporate Financial Statements (1951). "Price Level Changes and Financial Statements," *Supplementary Statement No. 2* (AAA).

Financial Accounting Standards Board (1979). "Financial Reporting and Changing Prices," *Statement of Financial Accounting Standards No. 33* (FASB).

———— (1982a). "Financial Reporting and Changing Prices: Foreign Currency Translation," *Exposure Draft* (FASB).

————(1982b). "Disclosures about Oil and Gas Producing Activities," *Statement of Financial Accounting Standards No. 69* (FASB).

———— (1982c). "Financial Reporting and Changing Prices: Foreign Currency Translation," *Statement of Financial Accounting Standards No. 70* (FASB).

Gheyara, Kelly, and James Boatman (1980). "Market Reaction to the 1976 Replacement Cost Disclosures," *Journal of Accounting and Economics* (August 1980), pp. 107–125.

Griffin, Paul A., ed. (1979). *Financial Reporting and Changing Prices: The Conference* (FASB).

International Accounting and Financial Report (1980). (Institute for International Research Ltd., April 28, 1980).

International Accounting Standards Committee (1981). "Information Reflecting the Effects of Changing Prices," *International Accounting Standard No. 15* (The Committee).

Parker, James E. (1977). "Impact of Price-Level Accounting," *The Accounting Review* (January 1977), pp. 69–96.

Paton, W. A., ed. (1932). *Accountants' Handbook*, 2d ed. (Ronald Press).

Petersen, Russell J. (1973). "Interindustry Estimation of General Price-level Impact on Financial Information," *The Accounting Review* (January 1973), pp. 34–43.

Report of Special Committee on Development of Accounting Principles (1934). *Bulletin of the American Institute of Accountants* (American Institute of Accountants).

Ro, Byung T. (1980). "The Adjustment of Security Returns to the Disclosure of Replacement Cost Accounting Information," *Journal of Accounting and Economics* (August 1980), pp. 159–189.

Securities and Exchange Commission (1976). "Disclosure of Certain Replacement Cost Data," *Accounting Series Release No. 190* (The Commission).

Staubus, George J. (1976). "The Effects of Price-Level Restatements on Earnings, *The Accounting Review* (July 1976), pp. 574–589.

Study Group on Business Income (1952). *Changing Concepts of Business Income* (American Institute of Accountants).

Study Group on the Objectives of Financial Statements (1973). *Objectives of Financial Statements* (AICPA).

Swieringa, Robert J. (1981). "The Silver-Lined Bonds of Sunshine Mining," *The Accounting Review* (January 1981), pp. 166–177.

World Accounting Report (1982). (*The Financial Times*, November 1982), pp. 3–5.

—— (1983). (*The Financial Times*, March 1983), pp. 14–15.

ADDITIONAL READINGS

GENERAL PRICE-LEVEL RESTATEMENTS

Baran, Arie; Josef Lakanishok; and Aharon Ofer (1980). "The Information Content of General Price Level Adjusted Earnings: Some Empirical Evidence," *The Accounting Review* (January 1980), pp. 22–35.

Davidson, Sidney; Clyde P. Stickney; and Roman L. Weil (1976). *Inflation Accounting* (McGraw-Hill).

Gynther, R. S. (1966). *Accounting for Price-Level Changes: Theory and Procedures* (Pergamon Press).

Hillison, William A. (1979). "Empirical Investigation of General Purchasing Power Adjustments on Earnings Per Share and the Movement of Security Prices," *Journal of Accounting Research* (Spring 1979), pp. 60–73.

Ijiri, Yuji (1976). "The Price-Level Restatement and its Dual Interpretation," *The Accounting Review* (April 1976), pp. 227–243.

Ketz, J. Edward (1978). "The Effect of General Price-Level Adjustments on the Predictive Ability of Financial Ratios," *Studies on Accounting for Changes in General and Specific Prices: Empirical Research and Public Policy* (Supplement to *Journal of Accounting Research*, 1978), pp. 273–284.

Vickrey, Don W. (1976). "General Price-Level Adjusted Historical Cost Statements and the Ratio-Scale View," *The Accounting Review* (January 1976), pp. 31–40.

CURRENT VALUE ACCOUNTING

Abdel-Khalik, A. Rashad, and James C. McKeown (1978). "Disclosure of Estimates of Holding Gains and the Assessment of Systematic Risk," *Studies on Accounting for Changes in General and Specific Prices: Empirical Research and Public Policy*, (Supplement to *Journal of Accounting Research*, 1978), pp. 46–77.

Arnold, Donald F., and Ronald J. Huefner (1977). "Measuring and Evaluating Replacement Costs: An Application," *Journal of Accounting Research* (Autumn 1977), pp. 245–252.

Backer, Morton (1973). *Current Value Accounting* (Financial Executives Research Foundation, 1973).

Bromwich, Michael (1977). "The General Validity of Certain 'Current' Value Asset Valuation Bases," *Accounting and Business Research* (Autumn 1977), pp. 242–249.

Friedman, Lawrence A. (1978). "An Exit-Price Income Statement," *The Accounting Review* (January 1978), pp. 18–30.

Rosenfield, Paul (1975). "Current Replacement Value Accounting—A Dead End," *Journal of Accountancy* (September 1975), pp. 63–73.

Samuelson, Richard A. (1980). "Should Replacement Cost Changes Be Included in Income?" *The Accounting Review* (April 1980), pp. 254–287.

CHAPTER 13

Income Taxes and Financial Accounting

Accounting has become far more complex as a result of the federal government's attempt to influence macroeconomic factors such as corporate investment by means of the income taxation process. In this chapter, two financial accounting problems arising from income taxes are examined. Income tax allocation is the most important of the problems discussed here. The investment credit is narrower in scope but creates somewhat similar problems.

The creation of the income tax law in 1913 has resulted in many items being recognized in different time periods for tax and book purposes. While the efforts to "synchronize" tax and book accounting go back to the 1930s, Accounting Research Bulletins (ARBs) 43 and 44 (revised), which came out in 1953 and 1958, respectively, firmly established income tax allocation as a canon of financial accounting. The major part of the discussion in this chapter centers on income tax allocation. After examining the basic elements of tax allocation, we consider an extensive analysis of the principal timing difference: use of accelerated depreciation for tax purposes and straight-line depreciation for published financial reporting. Tax loss carry-backs and carryforwards are also examined because important theoretical questions and policy issues arise as a result of the carryforward situation.

The section closes with a careful scrutiny of the allocation process relative to tax loss carrybacks and carryforwards.

The remaining parts of the chapter are concerned with the investment tax credit and tax leases. Tax leases are only briefly mentioned since they expired on December 31, 1983. As with the area of tax allocation, current provisions of the 1981 and 1982 tax laws applicable to the investment credit as well as the various theoretical aspects are analyzed.

INCOME TAX ALLOCATION

The allocation of corporate income taxes is one of the most controversial issues that has ever arisen in financial accounting theory. It was enacted in Accounting Research Bulletin (ARB) 43 in words that today have an almost archaic-sounding innocence when viewed with the hindsight of thirty years of heated debate:

> Income taxes are an expense that should be allocated, when necessary and practicable, to income and other accounts, as other expenses are allocated. What the income statement should reflect under this head . . . is the expense properly allocable to the income included in the income statement for the year.[1]

Tax allocation occurs as a result of timing differences arising when a revenue or expense item reaches the published financial statements as opposed to when it appears on the tax return. In these situations, tax expense is based on the published before-tax income figure. The difference between the tax expense and tax liability also appears on the balance sheet. However, it is not always clear what, if anything, the number represents.

Accounting Principles Board Opinion (APB) 11 continued the thrust of ARBs 43 and 44 (revised). As long as timing differences arise, tax allocation must take place, despite the possibility of potential relevant circumstantial differences. This requirement is known as **comprehensive allocation.**

Permanent differences between published statements and tax returns are not subject to the allocation process. In the case of a nontaxable item such as municipal bond interest, for example, no effect occurs relative to either tax expense or tax liability.

Another aspect of the tax picture is called **intrastatement** or **intraperiod tax allocation.** Where prior period adjustments, extraordinary items, or operations of discontinued segments of a firm have tax effects, these items are shown net of the tax effect. The balance of the total tax expense figure then appears below net income before income taxes and extraordi-

---

[1]AICPA (1953, p. 88).

nary items. Intrastatement allocation is relatively easy to employ and probably has relevance for users. Hence, the benefits appear to outweigh the costs. Nothing else of a theoretical nature is involved relative to intrastatement tax allocation.

There are numerous examples of timing differences. The tax liability will be greater than tax expense where either revenues are recognized for tax purposes earlier than for published reporting purposes or expenses are recognized more rapidly on the financial statements than on the tax return. Examples include the following:

1. Receipt of cash for rent or subscriptions prior to the period in which services are performed.
2. Warranties recognized for financial accounting purposes when goods are sold and for tax purposes when work is performed.
3. Pension expenses recognized prior to cash payment.

Conversely, tax expense is greater than tax liability when either revenues are recognized more slowly or expenses more rapidly for tax purposes than for book purposes. These would include:

1. Income from long-term construction contracts using percentage-of-completion for financial accounting and the completed contract approach for income taxes.
2. Installment sale income recognized for financial purposes at time of sale and the collection point for taxes.
3. Accelerated depreciation for taxes and straight-line depreciation for financial accounting.
4. Intangible drilling and development costs deducted when incurred for taxes and capitalized for financial accounting.

THE RATIONALE OF INCOME TAX ALLOCATION

As the name explicitly states, income tax allocation is indeed an allocation. Thomas, in fact, has characterized it in very pithy terms:

> . . . tax allocation embodies the allocation problem in one of its most pathological forms. . . . tax allocation may be perceived as an attempt to make allocation consistent, and its allocation problems are the consequences of other allocations.[2]

While the language of ARB 43 is not explicit, it appears that income tax allocation is grounded in the matching concept. However, matching, as it is employed in tax allocation, differs from all other applications of matching. In the usual situation, expenses are matched against revenues. The result is expected to at least roughly portray efforts (expenses) that have given rise to accomplishments (revenues). However, the matching that oc-

[2]Thomas (1974, pp. 146–147).

curs under income tax allocation attempts to normalize income tax expense with pretax accounting income. Hence, after-tax income is also correlated with pretax income. The matching brought about by tax allocation literally occurs at a lower point on the income statement than occurs with any other expense.

Income tax allocation may smooth income but, because its use is mandatory where timing differences exist, it cannot be construed as a smoothing instrument—since management does not have any options relative to its usage under APB 11. Comprehensive allocation is thus an example of rigid uniformity. While it might be conceived of as useful for predicting cash flows, there have been no empirical studies attempting to portray the relationship between income using tax allocation in comparison with other income measurement methods and future cash flows.

However, another aspect of prediction was examined in two articles by Beaver and Dukes.[3] Their studies concern the effect on security prices of allocation versus nonallocation. They assumed that because of market efficiency, security price behavior would indicate which method the market perceives to be most appropriate in terms of setting equilibrium prices. In their first study, they found that the use of tax allocation had the highest degree of association with security price behavior, while income without tax allocation was second, and cash flows were last. They thus concluded that employment of income tax allocation is a correct procedure. Their second study also found that income tax deferred earnings had a higher association with security prices than income without allocation. However, they amended their earlier conclusion and suggested that the net-of-tax method (to be discussed shortly) using a tax rate significantly higher than current rates gave a higher association with security prices than tax allocation using existing rates.

The general weakness of studies of the type done by Beaver and Dukes—where an attempt to measure the association of an accounting method with security prices is made—lies in the imperfection of the market for accounting information, namely the "free-rider" problem discussed in Chapter 3. Hence these studies provide descriptive information but they cannot be relied on for the normative purpose of choosing among competing accounting alternatives.[4]

Viewed from the perspective of the 1980s, matching provides a weak rationale for income tax allocation. However, within the framework of the historical cost approach, and in an era when the arbitrariness of the allocation process was not questioned, a strong case might be made for income tax allocation. Nevertheless, a great deal of controversy has surrounded in-

---

[3]Beaver and Dukes (1972 and 1973).
[4]Gonedes and Dopuch (1974, pp. 115–16) suggest that where several alternative methods are possible, the one which can be converted to other methods at the least cost may be optimal. In the case of income tax expense, it would be easier for users to transform allocation figures to cash flow than vice versa.

come tax allocation in its most important application since the late 1950s: use of accelerated depreciation for tax purposes and straight-line depreciation for the financial statements.

TAX ALLOCATION AND ACCELERATED DEPRECIATION

In the early years of the income tax allocation debate, the case favoring allocation was often made by using what was, in effect, a single-asset type of example.[5] For example, assume that an asset with a five-year life and a cost of $15,000 and no salvage, is depreciated by the sum-of-the-years' digits for tax purposes and by straight-line depreciation for financial accounting with a 40% tax rate. The results are shown in Exhibit 13-1.

The fifth column shows an increase in deferred taxes in the first and second years and reversal and elimination in the fourth and fifth years. If this model were representative of real circumstances, the tax allocation situation would present few problems. The extra tax benefits above those stemming from straight-line depreciation received in the early years of the asset's life are paid back in the later years.

Another situation is depicted in Exhibit 13-2 where a new asset acquisition is made each year until the firm reaches a stable point. It is assumed that beyond Year 6, the pattern of acquiring a new asset each year and the disposal of an old one continues as before. Cost and depreciation methods are the same as in the first example. Beyond Year 5 total accelerated and straight-line depreciation are equal—so the tax benefits occurring in Years 1–3 become permanent when viewed in the aggregate sense. Of course, if

EXHIBIT 13-1.
Tax Deferral with a Single Asset

(1) Year	(2) Sum-of-the- Years-Digits Depreciation	(3) Straight-line Depreciation	(4) Excess Tax Depreciation	(5) Deferral of Taxes (40% Tax Rate Times Column 4)
1	$ 5,000	$ 3,000	$2,000	$800
2	4,000	3,000	1,000	400
3	3,000	3,000	0	0
4	2,000	3,000	(1,000)	(400)
5	1,000	3,000	(2,000)	(800)
	$15,000	$15,000	0	0

[5] For example, Moonitz (1957, p. 177).

EXHIBIT 13-2.

Tax Deferral in a Multiasset Situation

Sum-of-the-Years'-Digits Depreciation

	Year 1	Year 2	Year 3	Year 4	Year 5	Year 6
Asset A	$5,000	$4,000	$3,000	$2,000	$1,000	
Asset B		5,000	4,000	3,000	2,000	$1,000
Asset C			5,000	4,000	3,000	2,000
Asset D				5,000	4,000	3,000
Asset E					5,000	4,000
Asset F						5,000
Total	5,000	9,000	12,000	14,000	15,000	15,000

Straight-line Depreciation

	Year 1	Year 2	Year 3	Year 4	Year 5	Year 6
Asset A	3,000	3,000	3,000	3,000	3,000	
Asset B		3,000	3,000	3,000	3,000	3,000
Asset C			3,000	3,000	3,000	3,000
Asset D				3,000	3,000	3,000
Asset E					3,000	3,000
Asset F						3,000
Total	3,000	6,000	9,000	12,000	15,000	15,000
Excess of sum-of-the-years'-digits over straight-line depreciation	2,000	3,000	3,000	2,000	0	0
Deferral (excess times 40% tax rate)	$ 800	$1,200	$1,200	$ 800	$ 0	$ 0

the firm continues to expand or if costs of new assets increase, the amount of deferred taxes will continue to increase.[6] In fact, the great bulk of empirical evidence appears to indicate that the deferred tax account does indeed increase over time.[7]

The situation of virtually permanent deferral has presented an enigma to accounting standard setters and theoreticians in terms of both interpreting the credit and even questioning the whole process of tax allocation in situations of potential permanent deferral.

---

[6] The classic article discussing the multiasset case and its ramifications is by Davidson (1958).
[7] See Livingstone (1967a, 1967b, and 1969) and Price Waterhouse & Co. (1967). For an opposing view, see Herring and Jacobs (1976). For a refutation of Herring and Jacobs, see Davidson, Skelton, and Weil (1977).

Interpreting Deferred Tax Credits

Unquestionably there is no legal liability arising as a result of using accelerated depreciation for income tax purposes. The federal government's desire in allowing accelerated depreciation as well as shorter guideline lives (the so-called Asset Depreciation Range system prescribing the number of years of tax life for the various classes of assets) has been to stimulate economic growth and modernize the nation's productive capacity by raising the internal rate of return on capital investment projects. Nothing is owed the government as a result of "excess" depreciation allowances taken for tax purposes. Moreover, the problem simply disappears if the enterprise uses accelerated depreciation for both tax and book purposes. The legal liability definition, however, is too narrow for accounting purposes, which are, of course, concerned with portraying economic reality in accordance with user objectives and needs.

Another way of looking at the problem is to view each asset individually rather than looking at the aggregate balance of the deferred tax credit account. This is often referred to as the **rollover** method.[8] From the individual asset standpoint, the "liability" is paid off, even though a new "loan" is received when a new asset is acquired, thereby offsetting the payback on the older asset as its tax depreciation diminishes. Thus, rollover proponents might say that there is no move not to recognize accounts payable even though accounts that are paid off may be replaced with new payables. However, the rollover view has been strongly criticized because the payoff of each loan on older assets cannot be compared to the accounts payable situation because the debts are paid off individually, which, of course, is not the case with income taxes.[9]

Comprehensive tax allocation with deferred taxes interpreted as liabilities was weakened, though not totally demolished, by the argument that deferred taxes are not the same as accounts payable. Because of this indeterminate status, deferred taxes were viewed as "deferred credits" in APB 11. As a result, the income statement, under the mantle of the matching concept, took precedence over the balance sheet (which now contained deferred charges that might not be assets and deferred credits that might not be liabilities). The deferred credit approach differs from the liability interpretation under comprehensive allocation in terms of the fact that the deferred credit account is not adjusted if tax rates change, whereas it is adjusted under the liability method if tax rates change. This is in addition to the interpretation of the account itself.

Orientations to Income Tax Allocation

There are several possible policy positions that may be taken on the income tax allocation issue. One possibility is that allocation is not appro-

[8]For a discussion see Black (1966, pp. 69–72).
[9]See the comments of Davidson in Black (1966, pp. 117–19).

priate. In other words, tax expense equals tax liability. Some theoretical justification for advocating no allocation has been derived from the interpretation that income tax payments are a distribution of income rather than being an expense.[10] However, this has not been a popular position and cannot be strongly defended.

Somewhat related to the idea that income taxes are a distribution of profits rather than an element deducted in arriving at profits is the "new form of equities" position of Graul and Lemke.[11] Under their interpretation, the credit arising under income tax allocation represents a subordinated equity investment in the firm by the federal government. The reason the government makes this "investment" in the enterprise is for the purpose of stimulating business investment. Deferred tax credits would be listed as an element of invested capital in the owners' equities section of the balance sheet.

While there is indeed some logic underlying this position, it is simply one possible interpretation and nothing more. The fact that macroeconomic policy has led to certain tax benefits for business does not make government an "investor" in the firm except in the most limited sense.

Another possibility is the **net-of-tax** method. Under this approach, income tax expense is equal to the tax liability. However, the book depreciation is increased (or reduced) in any year by the excess tax benefits received above (or below) those that would have been derived from straight-line depreciation according to the following formula:

$$D_t = S + r (A_t - S) \tag{13.1}$$

where

D_t = net of tax depreciation for period t;
S = straight-line depreciation;
r = tax rate;
A_t = accelerated depreciation for period t.

Hence, if accelerated depreciation were $500 for a particular year and straight-line were $400 with a 40% tax rate, net-of-tax depreciation would be $440, determined by

$$\$440 = \$400 + .40 (\$500 - \$400). \tag{13.1a}$$

Net-of-tax depreciation gives the same "bottom line" net income effect as comprehensive allocation but moves the deferred credit over to the asset side as an additional element of accumulated depreciation. Certainly it would eliminate a large stumbling block present under comprehensive allocation—the question of interpreting deferred tax credits.

---

[10]Suojanen (1954, p. 393). For a broad discussion of this question, see Wheeler and Galliart (1974, pp. 51–56).
[11]Graul and Lemke (1976). For a somewhat similar argument, see Watson (1979).

Moreover, there is some theoretical justification for net-of-tax depreciation in a historical cost context. Assume that amortization should concur with benefits received. Now in the case of fixed assets, it can be postulated that they have two benefits: (1) revenue-producing or cost-avoidance potential from productive utilization, and (2) tax reduction benefits. Therefore, if an asset renders relatively even service over its life and accelerated depreciation benefits are taken, there is certainly some justification for net-of-tax depreciation. However, it is still an allocation and not a method of valuation. Along the same line, it cannot be transformed or related to any current value measurements. It might, however, be transformed into general price-level adjusted depreciation numbers.

Still another possible orientation to the timing difference problem is called partial allocation. Under **partial allocation,** only those deferred credits that can reasonably be expected to be paid off in the foreseeable future on an aggregate basis are recorded on the books. Thus, income tax expense for a given year is defined as the total tax costs attributable to the given year's operations, costs that will be levied against the firm, both in the current and future years, on a gross or aggregate basis. Hence, the deferred tax credit is clearly definable as a liability. The balance of the deferred tax liability account represents the amount expected to be paid in the future, attributable to the current and past years' operations on a gross basis.

An example should clarify the partial allocation approach. Assume that a firm's income before depreciation is $20,000 each year and the tax rate is 40%. Depreciation is the only timing difference between tax and book figures. The planning horizon is a five-year period. Depreciation figures are shown in Exhibit 13-3 (assets are designated $A_1 \ldots A_n$). All predictions are assumed to be accurate. For comparison and completeness the numbers are also shown for comprehensive allocation. Beyond Year 5 tax depreciation is expected to exceed book depreciation.

Notice that the liability in Year 1 under partial allocation results from the fact that tax depreciation in Years 3 and 4 is less than book depreciation. This results in an anticipated obligation because tax payments in those

---

EXHIBIT 13-3.
Partial and Comprehensive Income Tax Allocation

	Tax	Depreciation		Book	Depreciation		Comprehensive Allocation	Partial Allocation
Year	A_1	A_2	A_3	A_1	A_2	A_3	40%(TD−BD)	
1	$8,000			$5,000			$1,200	$1,120
2	6,000			$5,000			400	
3	4,000	$2,400		5,000	$1,500		(40)	
4	2,000	1,800		5,000	1,500		(1,080)	
5		1,200	$8,000		1,500	$5,000	1,080	
6		600	7,000		1,500	5,000	440	

years would be greater than the anticipated "normal" amount based on book depreciation. This liability resulting under partial allocation is consistent with the definition of liabilities in Statement of Financial Accounting Concepts (SFAC) 3, which defines them as ". . . probable future sacrifices of economic benefits arising from present obligations of a particular entity to transfer assets . . . as a result of past transactions or events."[12] Whether deferred tax credits arising under comprehensive allocation are liabilities consistent with the above definition is not entirely clear.[13] Partial allocation is, of course, an example of finite uniformity. The relevant circumstance is whether tax depreciation will be less than book depreciation in any given year. Allocation occurs if, and only if, this condition is expected to exist over the period of the planning horizon.

Entries for the first four years that would arise under partial allocation in accordance with the previous example are shown in Exhibit 13-4 along with entries under comprehensive allocation.

The obvious question that must be raised about partial allocation concerns the issue of verifiability since the method is concerned with predicting a cash flow variable. Some progress has been made in this area by Buckley.[14] He has developed a predictive model embracing the appropriate variables, which include anticipated capital investment over the planning horizon, tax and book depreciation differentials, including different lives, and expected changes in the tax rate. After setting up matrices for these variables, matrix algebra is used to solve for the predicted annual change in the deferred tax liability account. The model was tested by five firms in the Los Angeles area. The results had a high degree of predictive accuracy; not surprisingly, the enterprises found the results of the model useful for cash budgeting and planning.

Partial allocation has received some support in the recent literature.[15] An added impetus to its possible adoption in the United States is the fact that the United Kingdom has essentially adopted it for years beginning after January 1, 1979.

One more question remains to be answered under the orientations of partial allocation and comprehensive liability. Since the resulting credits are interpreted as liabilities that mature beyond a year, is discounting of these values appropriate?

Discounting Deferred Tax Liabilities. Long-term liabilities, such as bonds payable and noncancellable leases are carried at their present values. This is accomplished by discounting future payments by the effective or

---

[12]FASB (1980, p. 12).

[13]Nair and Weygandt (1981, p. 100) do not think that deferred tax liabilities arising under comprehensive allocation are consistent with the liability definition of SFAC 3. However, the statement itself appears to admit the possibility that the comprehensive liability approach is consistent with the liability definition presented there. See FASB (1980, p. 71). It appears that both partial allocation and the comprehensive liability approaches may result in the credits qualifying as liabilities according to SFAC 3.

[14]Buckley (1972, pp. 71–101).

[15]See Nair and Weygandt (1981, p. 100).

EXHIBIT 13-4.
Entries Under Partial and Comprehensive Tax Allocation

Partial Allocation				Comprehensive Allocation		
Year 1				**Year 1**		
Income Tax Expense	5,920			Income Tax Expense	6,000	
				Deferred Tax Credit or		
Deferred Tax Liability		1,120		Liability		1,200
Income Tax Liability		4,800		Income Tax Liability		4,800
Tax liability is						
.4(20,000 − $8,000)						
Year 2				**Year 2**		
Income Tax Expense	5,600			Income Tax Expense	6,000	
				Deferred Tax Credit or		
Income Tax Liability		5,600		Liability		400
.4($20,000 − $6,000)				Income Tax Liability		5,600
Year 3				**Year 3**		
Income Tax Expense	5,400			Income Tax Expense	5,400	
				Deferred Tax Credit or		
Deferred Tax Liability		40		Liability		40
Income Tax Liability		5,440		Income Tax Liability		5,440
.4($20,000 − $6,400)						
Year 4				**Year 4**		
Income Tax Expense	5,400			Income Tax Expense	5,400	
				Deferred Tax Credit or		
Deferred Tax Liability		1,080		Liability		1,080
Income Tax Liability		6,480		Income Tax Liability		6,480
.4($20,000 − $3,800)						

implicit interest rate. Similarly, APB 21 requires that noninterest-bearing notes receivable must be discounted at their implicit interest rate. Consistency would, therefore, appear to dictate that tax liabilities (not deferred credits, however) under either the comprehensive or partial approaches should likewise be discounted.

In reality, the tax liabilities under either of the two interpretations are interest-free loans. However, the opportunity cost doctrine from economics has been advocated as a justification for discounting by the implicit interest rate: if the funds were not received from the government in the form of lower income taxes through higher depreciation allowances, borrowing from another source would have been necessary.[16] The interest rate on the funds from the next best source would be their **opportunity cost.**

The opportunity cost doctrine is by no means absent from financial accounting. If an asset is donated to a firm, it should be booked at its fair

[16] See Nurnberg (1972, pp. 657–658).

market value with a credit to donated capital. Therefore, from the economic standpoint, it appears to be quite reasonable that deferred tax liabilities should be shown at their present value using the interest rate for a loan of similar duration, repayment schedule, and risk borne by the lender. While there is still debate in terms of exactly how to measure the implicit interest rate, we will assume that it is 10%.[17] Entries for discounting deferred tax liabilities under partial and comprehensive allocation are shown in Exhibit 13-5.

Under comprehensive allocation, the tax expense consists of current tax liabilities and the present value of future obligations using an individual-asset rollover interpretation. Where partial allocation is employed, the tax expense includes the present value of future obligations where an actual payment above the future years' liabilities is involved because book depreciation of presently owned assets is expected to exceed tax depreciation without a "shielding" effect from assets to be acquired in the future. This would, of course, be in addition to the current year's tax liability.

EXHIBIT 13-5.

Entries for Discounting Deferred Tax Liabilities

Partial Allocation			Comprehensive Allocation		
Year 1			*Year 1*		
Income Tax Expense	5,644		Income Tax Expense	5,731	
Deferred Tax Liability		844	Deferred Tax Liability		931
Income Tax Liability		4,800	Income Tax Liability		4,800
As shown in Exhibit 13-3, reversal occurs in years 3 and 4 which are 2 and 3 years after year 1:			As shown in Exhibit 13-3, reversal occurs for asset A_1 in years 3 and 4 which are 2 and 3 years after year 1:		
$.826 \times \$40 =$	\$ 33		$.826 \times .40 \times \$1,000 = \$330$		
$.751 \times 1,080 =$	811		$.751 \times .40 \times \$2,000 = $	601	
	\$844			\$931	
Year 2			*Year 2*		
Income Tax Expense	5,600		Income Tax Expense	5,930	
Interest on Deferred Tax Liability		84	Interest on Deferred Tax Liability		93
Deferred Tax Liability		84	Deferred Tax Liability		423
Income Tax Liability		5,600	Income Tax Liability		5,600

---

[17]For more background on the appropriate rate, see Nurnberg (1972, pp. 659–665), Williams and Findlay (1974), Wolk and Tearney (1980, pp. 126–127), and Findlay and Williams (1981).

EXHIBIT 13-5. *(Continued)*

Interest at 10% on the
balance of the
deferred tax liability is
(.10 × $844)

Interest at 10% on the
balance of the
deferred tax liability is
(.10 × $934). The
current liability on A₁
reverses in 2 years in
year 4:
.826 × .40 × $1,000 = $330

	Year 3				Year 3	
Income Tax Expense	5,400			Income Tax Expense	5,319	
Interest on Deferred Tax				Interest on Deferred Tax		
Liability	93			Liability	135	
Deferred Tax Liability		53		Deferred Tax Liability		14
Income Tax Liability		5,440		Income Tax Liability		5,440

Interest at 10% on the
balance of the
deferred tax liability is
(.10 × $1354). The
reversal on A₁ is $400.
Present value of
additional liabilities on
A₂ which reverses in
years 5 and 6 is:
.826 × .40 × $300 = $ 99
.751 × .40 × 600 = 180
                      $279

Deferred tax liability is
credited for interest
(.10 × $928) and
debited for the $40
reversal.

	Year 4				Year 4	
Income Tax Expense	5,400			Income Tax Expense	5,379	
Interest on Deferred Tax				Interest on Deferred Tax		
Liability	98			Liability	137	
Deferred Tax Liability	982			Deferred Tax Liability	964	
Income Tax Liability		6,480		Income Tax Liability		6,480

Deferred tax liability is
debited for the $1,080
reversal and credited
for interest
(.10 × $981). The
account has a zero
balance except for the
$1 rounding error.

Interest at 10% on the
balance of the
deferred tax liability is
(.10 × $1368). The
reversal on A₁ is
$1,200. Present value
of additional liabilities
on A₂ which reverse in
year 6 is:
(.826 × .40 × $300).

EXHIBIT 13-6.

Summary of Tax Allocation Positions

Major Position	No Allocation	Comprehensive Allocation					Partial Allocation	
Principal Variations	Not Applicable	New Form of Equities	Net of Tax	Deferred	Liability		Liability	
Discounting of Liability	Not Applicable	Not Applicable	Not Applicable	Not Applicable	Yes	No	Yes	No

---

Summary of Orientations to Income Tax Allocation. In this section a possibly bewildering number of approaches to the income tax allocation question has been reviewed and analyzed. The various positions are shown in Exhibit 13-6.

The tax allocation debate can be resolved only in terms of criteria such as consistency with other areas of valuation, relevance to users, and verifiability of measurements. Pure deductive logic alone cannot resolve this very perplexing issue.

Present Value Depreciation and Income Tax Allocation

Another theoretical facet of tax allocation concerns present value depreciation, which was discussed in Chapter 11. Usage of this depreciation is intended to bring about a constant return on investment throughout the life of an asset. However, income tax allocation is essentially inconsistent with the constant rate of return approach.[18] The key point is that present value depreciation evens return on an *after*-tax basis. Thus, any attempt at income tax allocation would destroy the equalized rate of return that is built into the depreciation schedule.

Several attempts have been made to make present value depreciation and income tax allocation consistent in terms of utilizing both and maintaining a constant rate of return.[19] While these attempts have been tactically successful, too many other problems remain. First, the necessity to unite depreciation theory and capital budgeting analysis is something of a quixotic venture. The latter is a planning method which looks forward for at least several years while the former is a profit-reporting technique that

---

[18]Drake (1961).

[19]For example Bierman and Dyckman (1974), Meyers (1973), and Bullock (1974). Meyers' approach, in particular, is successful. He would discount the pretax cash flows back to the cost of the asset to determine its internal rate of return. Annual depreciation would then be equal to the change in the present value of the asset's remaining pretax cash flows, using the internal rate of return as the discount rate. Income tax allocation would then be employed by taking the tax rate times the difference between accelerated and present value depreciation, which would then be added to the tax expense.

looks backward for one-year periods. Thus, one is ex-post and the other is ex-ante. Their contexts are completely different. Second, the present value method is somewhat artificial because it is designed to bring about a predetermined rate of return. To put it slightly differently, depreciation becomes a causal agent in the determination of income rather than a residual effect.[20] Closely related to the artificial nature of the write-off is the fact that the increasing charge structure that ordinarily results with present value depreciation is inconsistent with the pattern of benefits ordinarily received from many assets: greatest benefits in the earliest years. Third, the jointness problem among productive assets makes it virtually impossible to pinpoint cash flow generation, a drawback that would make the present value method extremely difficult to implement on a practical basis. This is, of course, the allocation problem once again.

The Economic Recovery Tax Act of 1981

At the present time, corporate balance sheets in the United States are encumbered by hundreds of billions of dollars of deferred tax credits under the comprehensive deferral approach required by APB 11. Whatever its economic merits might be, the deferred tax credit situation will become further aggravated under the 1981 tax act because the period of tax recovery has been further shortened.

The new system, called ACRS (Accelerated Cost Recovery System), eliminates the concept of useful depreciable life. Instead it substitutes five classes of capital assets with prescribed lives. Furthermore, salvage values are not considered. As a result, controversies over useful life between the IRS and corporations have been eliminated. The classes of capital assets are the following:

3-year class: automobiles, light trucks, machinery, and equipment used in research and development activities, and assets having a midpoint guideline life under the previous Asset Depreciation Range (ADR) system of 4 years or less;

5-year class: the great bulk of machinery and equipment and some special equipment such as petroleum storage facilities, agricultural structures, and certain public utility property (midpoint guideline lives between 4.5 and 18 years);

10-year class: most public utility property (midpoint guideline lives between 18.5 and 25 years);

15-year class: most depreciable real estate.

The new shortened depreciation lives under ACRS are being phased in between 1981 and 1985. Depreciation schedules for the various classes are shown in Exhibit 13-7.

---

[20]This point is discussed in Vatter (1966).

EXHIBIT 13-7.

ACRS Allowances Under the 1981 Tax Act

Property Placed in Service after December 31, 1980 and before January 1, 1985					Property Placed in Service in 1985					Property Placed in Service after December 31, 1985				
	Class of Investment					Class of Investment					Class of Investment			
Ownership Year	3-Year	5-Year	10-Year	15-Year	Ownership Year	3-Year	5-Year	10-Year	15-Year	Ownership Year	3-Year	5-Year	10-Year	15-Year
	%	%	%	%		%	%	%	%		%	%	%	%
1	25	15	8	5	1	29	18	9	6	1	33	20	10	7
2	38	22	14	10	2	47	33	19	12	2	45	32	18	12
3	37	21	12	9	3	24	25	16	12	3	22	24	16	12
4		21	10	8	4		16	14	11	4		16	14	11
5		21	10	7	5		8	12	10	5		8	12	10
6			10	7	6			10	9	6			10	9
7			9	6	7			8	8	7			8	8
8			9	6	8			6	7	8			6	7
9			9	6	9			4	6	9			4	6
10			9	6	10			2	6	10			2	5
11				6	11				4	11				4
12				6	12				4	12				3
13				6	13				3	13				3
14				6	14				2	14				2
15				6	15				1	15				1
	100	100	100	100		100	100	100	100		100	100	100	100

NET OPERATING LOSSES AND INCOME TAX ALLOCATION

A net operating loss arises if deductions exceed gross income for a taxable year. Congress recognized in the 1954 Internal Revenue Code that it was unfair to tax firms in profitable years without allowing any benefits in loss years. Consequently, the 1954 Code included provisions for carryback and carryforward of net operating losses. The carryback has been maintained for a 3-year period. The carryforward, however, was extended to 15 years by The Economic Recovery Tax Act of 1981.

Net operating losses raise the problem of income tax allocation relative to affected years. There is no controversy relative to carrybacks. Amounts due on refunds for the three prior years would be booked as a tax benefit receivable with a corresponding income tax credit applicable to the loss year. The receivable arises in the loss year as a result of the loss; hence there are no theoretical issues with regard to carrybacks. However, the carryforward situation is not quite as simple. APB 11 opposes booking the carryforward in the loss year except where virtual certainty of realization beyond any reasonable doubt exists when the carryforward arises. Thus, in the usual situation (nonbooking until realization occurs), carryforward benefits would be booked when received rather than in the loss year when they arose. Tax allocation and its basis in matching takes a back seat to conservatism and realization. Furthermore, APB 11 sees "virtual certainty of realization" as a relevant circumstance that would enable booking of the carryforward in the loss year but gives no further criteria for determining when this situation arises.

An Example

An example should clarify the accounting for net operating losses. Assume that a firm has a tax loss of $100,000 in 1983. Taxable income was $25,000 in 1980; $18,000 in 1981; $17,000 in 1982; and $20,000 in 1984. The tax rate is 40%. Taxable income equals book income in all affected years. Entries are shown in Exhibit 13-8, where virtual certainty of realization exists, along with the more usual conservative handling of the carryforward.

Virtual certainty of realization is nothing more than full accrual accounting. Since tax carryforward benefits have up to 15 years to be realized, they should be classified as a noncurrent asset. Income tax credit would appear below "net loss before income tax credit" exactly analogous to income tax expense when profits exist.

Whether conservatism is warranted as a justification for nonbooking of the carryforward benefits is a debatable issue. Very frequently a firm that

---

EXHIBIT 13-8.
Entries for Loss Carrybacks and Carryforwards

Virtual Certainty of Realization			*Nonbooking of the Loss Carryforward*		
1983			*1983*		
Tax Benefits Receivable	24,000		Tax Benefits Receivable	24,000	
Tax Carryforward Benefits	16,000				
Income Tax Credit		40,000	Income Tax Credit		24,000
1984			*1984*		
Income Tax Expense	8,000		No Entry		
Tax Carryforward Benefits		8,000			

has carryforward benefits that it cannot realize through profitable operations will sell out. As a result, loss carryforwards are often realized either by profitable operations or by merging the firm with another enterprise which can take advantage of the carryforward benefits.

Prior to 1954, in the event of an unprofitable firm being acquired by a profitable one, the Internal Revenue Service was required to prove that "tax avoidance" was the primary purpose of the acquisition in order to disallow transference of the carryforward benefit to the acquiring firm. Section 382 of the 1954 Internal Revenue Code attempted to supply more objective criteria. Disallowance of carryforward benefits occurs only where *both* of the following limitations apply:

1. The acquired corporation's ten largest stockholders own fifty percentage points more of the acquiring corporation's outstanding stock after the acquisition than they had owned prior to the change in ownership (based on total fair market value of the acquiring firm's common stock), and

2. The acquired corporation has not continued to carry on a trade or business substantially the same as that conducted before any change in the percentage ownership of such stock.[21]

While there has been considerable litigation relative to the question of whether the acquired firm has continued in the same business, from the acquiree's standpoint there appears to be a very high degree of probability that carryforward benefits will be received in one form or the other. Therefore, the conservatism of not booking carryforward benefits does not appear to be warranted. Likewise, the presumed relevant circumstance of virtual certainty of realization of carryforward benefits does not appear to stand up well.

Tax Carryforward Benefits and Deferred Tax Credits

A further complicating factor relative to unbooked tax carryforward benefits arises when deferred tax credits are on the books. This is a basically inequitable situation because the deferred tax credits, of course, created income tax expense which exceeded the incurred tax liabilities. It appears to be patently unfair as well as inaccurate to invoke conservatism relative to not booking tax carryforward benefits (and the offsetting income tax credits) when income tax expense has exceeded tax liabilities in previous years. As a result, paragraph 48 of APB 11 states:

> Net deferred credits arising from timing differences may exist at the time loss carryforwards arise. In the usual case when the tax effect of a loss carryforward is not recognized in the loss period, adjustments of the existing net deferred tax credits may be necessary in that period or in subsequent periods. In this situation net deferred tax credits should be elimi-

---

[21]See Sharp (1977, pp. 981–982).

nated to the extent of the lower of (a) the tax effect of the loss carryforward or (b) the amortization of the net deferred tax credits that would otherwise have occurred during the carryforward period.[22]

The intention of paragraph 48 is to allow premature reversal of deferred tax credits and an offsetting increase to income tax credit. Thus, premature reversal of deferred tax credits is a substitute for booking the carryforward benefits.

Unfortunately, paragraph 48 presents an extraordinarily tangled grammatical web of possible meanings, which is very difficult to interpret.[23] While complete allocation concerning carryforward benefits is preferable in terms of both simplicity and user relevance, conservatism could be maintained by allowing a more liberal policy concerning premature reversal of deferred tax credits.[24] However, this is at best very much a stopgap solution to the broader problem of the weakness of the comprehensive deferral approach.

THE INVESTMENT TAX CREDIT

The investment tax credit (ITC) was first enacted in 1962. Since that time the provisions of the law have changed several times. As a tool of macroeconomic policy the ITC is seen as a means of stimulating investment and, thus, fighting recession in the short run and combatting inflation over the long run. In the latter capacity the investment is seen as the avenue to eventually increasing supplies of scarce resources such as energy—and thus contributing to holding prices in check.

CURRENT PROVISIONS OF THE ITC

The ITC provides a reduction of income tax liability of up to 10% of the cost of eligible capital acquisitions (6% for property with a 3-year amortization period under ACRS). Liability reduction is restricted to the first $25,000 of tax liability plus, for 1982 and thereafter, 85% of the excess above the first $25,000 of tax liability. Unused current benefits of the ITC can be carried back for 3 years and forward for 15 years.

It is applicable to depreciable tangible property not including buildings (except as they are construed to be an integral part of the manufacturing

---

[22]AICPA (1967, para. 48).
[23]For one possible interpretation, see Bevis and Perry (1969, pp. 20–30).
[24]Wolk and Tearney (1973).

process). Up to $125,000 of used capital acquisitions are eligible for the ITC, up from $100,000 prior to 1981.

The recapture provisions regarding the ITC were changed by the Economic Recovery Tax Act of 1981 in order to align them with ACRS. As a result, 3-year property under ACRS receives a 6% ITC, and 5-year and other property a 10% ITC. If the property is held for less than the 3- and 5-year periods, respectively, the firm keeps 2% for each full year held and must refund the differential.

The Tax Equity and Fiscal Responsibility Act of 1982 (TEFRA) brought one important additional change with regard to the ITC. For assets acquired after December 31, 1982, cost recovery for ACRS purposes must be reduced by 50% of the allowable ITC taken on the asset. Instead of reducing the tax basis of the asset by 50%, the firm may elect to reduce the allowable investment credit by 2%. Hence, assets with 3-year ACRS lives would have the ITC reduced to 4% and all other assets would be lowered to 8%. Cash flow can generally be maximized by adopting the first alternative: taking the maximum allowable ITC.[25] As will be seen shortly, this presents some thorny conceptual problems.

INTERPRETING THE ITC

The fiasco of APBs 2 and 4 relative to prescribing an appropriate accounting for the ITC has already been discussed in Chapter 2. There have been at least four interpretations of the transaction:

1. Reduction of the cost of the asset.
2. Allocation by means of a deferred investment credit account.
3. Capital donated by the government.
4. Flow through (immediate recognition of all benefits taken in the year of acquisition).

The first two methods are allocations, while the last two are not.

Reduction of Asset Cost

The apparent intention of the government concerning the ITC was to reduce the cost of capital acquisitions which, in turn, increases the internal rate of return or net present value of potential capital acquisitions, thus stimulating investment in new plant and equipment. Therefore a possible treatment is to leave tax expense unaffected by the ITC and reduce the cost of the affected assets by these amounts. The method is somewhat analogous to the net-of-tax approach to income tax allocation.

The method would result in the benefits being taken over the lives of eligible assets in the form of lower depreciation. Of course depreciation expense under historical cost is an allocation, and the effect of the ITC

[25]Levy (1982, p. 74).

reduction relative to user relevance is not clear. Under current value approaches in situations in which depreciation is theoretically equal to the change in the market value of the asset between the beginning and end of the period, the ITC reduction to cost is simply not applicable.

Acceptance or rejection of the asset reduction approach largely hinges on the definition of "cost." Indeed SFAC 3 has interpreted the ITC as an asset reduction.[26] Let us examine what this interpretation implies in terms of the meaning of cost. It has linked together two totally separate transactions: (1) the net cash cost of the asset, and (2) the amount of the ITC which is attributable to the particular asset. While there are numerous other examples that link somewhat separate transactions—interest during construction of buildings in SFAS 34 for one—no other linkage is as "wide" as this one. The cost of the asset is literally dependent upon the firm's making a profit in order for income taxes to be reduced by the ITC. A similar problem occurs in the event of an ITC carryforward because the assignment of the ITC taken during the current year to particular assets is arbitrary (another allocation problem). However, if an allocation solution is desired, the balance sheet treatment of the credits as asset reductions does appear to be superior to the deferred investment credit method.

Deferred Investment Credit

This allocation method sets up a deferred investment credit account and writes it off over the life of affected assets by means of reducing (crediting) income tax expense. This account is neither a liability nor an owners' equity account. It is another example of a deferred credit class of account. However, it differs from deferred tax credits arising under income tax allocation. Deferred credits per se are ruled out by SFAC 3. In the case of tax allocation the deferred credit can be interpreted as a liability (the rollover view). The deferred credit under the ITC, however, has no liability elements that pertain to it. While the income result is the same as under the asset reduction method—assuming the amortization methods are the same—the deferred credit nature of the balance sheet account makes it much less desirable than that method.

Donated Capital View

The donated capital view would be instituted by setting income tax expense at the amount it would have been without the investment credit with an offset to donated capital. As with the "new form of equities" interpretation of income tax allocation, there is some plausibility to the argument but it is not really convincing. Macroeconomic policy that results in tax reduction does not persuasively lead to an outcome of "investment" in the firm by the government.

---

[26]FASB (1980, pp. 72–73).

Flow Through

A reasonable case can at least be made for flow through of ITC benefits. The strongest argument against it is that the benefits should be associated with usage rather than purchase. This is, of course, the matching argument which underlies the reduction of asset cost and deferred investment credit methods—which unfortunately leads to allocation problems and some questionable definitions. While the government's intention may have been to reduce capital investment costs, it accomplished this by means of tax reduction, and the flow-through interpretation reflects exactly that.

Non-flow-through treatment leads to allocation problems. Assuming efficient markets, it is simply not clear whether these methods lead to additional information in the form of better cash flow predictions, for example. In the absence of this evidence, flow through has the advantage of being less costly to produce than the allocation methods and its benefits in terms of user relevance appear to be at least on a par with those methods.

ACCOUNTING FOR THE ITC

The provision in TEFRA for reducing an asset's tax base by one half of the ITC taken leads to some serious results. Assume that the ITC on an asset costing $100,000 is taken in full in the year of acquisition. For financial statement purposes, the asset has a 10-year life and no salvage value. Straight-line depreciation is to be employed. The asset will be written off over five years by means of ACRS for tax purposes. Financial depreciation and the application of ACRS are shown in Exhibit 13-9.

Notice that there is both a timing difference and a permanent difference in the expense amounts shown in Exhibit 13-9. Technically speaking, we are faced with an allocation problem. However, this problem can be most simply handled, given comprehensive income tax allocation, by recognizing the timing differences first for income tax allocation purposes and not recognizing the permanent difference till the tenth year. Recognition of the permanent difference first, however, may obviate any need to allocate income taxes. This may be a pleasing prospect because of the swollen size of the deferred tax credit account on the books of many American corporations.

TEFRA has led to even more basic problems for accounting for the ITC as a result of decreasing the tax base of the asset by one half of the ITC taken in the year of acquisition. If flow through is used, should the reduction of the tax expense be for the gross amount of the tax reduction? Or should this tax expense be reduced by the amount of the depreciation shield lost as a result of the lowering of the tax base? The latter may be more useful in terms of indicating future cash flows but cannot be accomplished without using accruals; hence it is a modified cash flow approach to the problem.

If accrual (deferral) of ITC benefits is desired, three possibilities present themselves: (1) credit of the entire liability deduction to a deferred invest-

EXHIBIT 13-9.
ACRS and Financial Depreciation with Different Lives

Year	ACRS	Straight-line Depreciation
1	$14,250[a]	$ 10,000
2	20,900[b]	10,000
3	19,950[c]	10,000
4	19,950	10,000
5	19,950	10,000
6		10,000
7		10,000
8		10,000
9		10,000
10		10,000
	$95,000	$100,000

[a]15% × $95,000
[b]22% × $95,000
[c]21% × $95,000

ment credit account, (2) reduction of the fixed asset by the entire liability deduction, and (3) splitting of the liability deduction betwen the fixed asset and a deferred credit account.

None of these solutions is entirely acceptable. The deferred investment credit account does not qualify as a liability, a revenue, or a gain under SFAC 3. If the entire credit is to the fixed-asset account, then book and tax bases of assets will differ, as will depreciable lives and depreciation methods. Nevertheless, it still appears to be the most palatable of the deferral approaches. The various solutions to the ITC problem are examined in Problem 1 of this chapter.

Theory has thus far provided us with no definitive criteria for unraveling the ITC problem. The definitional screen for both deferred investment credits and deferred tax credits provided in SFAC 3 provides a useful first step for coping with the dilemma. The broader context of relevance to users is thus far largely unexamined. Whether research can provide insights on the question of user relevance appears to be very doubtful at this time.

THE PRESENT STATE OF THE ITC

As a result of the politics of the ITC, either allocation or flow through is allowable, or even a combination of the two (as a result of the complexities brought about by TEFRA). It was noted in Chapter 7 that there does not appear to be a relevant circumstance that differentiates among investment credit transactions.[27] Hence it would appear to be a viable candidate for rigid uniformity treatment. A reasonable choice, as discussed above, would be flow through. Of course that would present an interesting situation of two problems having some similar facets—income tax allocation and the ITC—handled on two entirely different bases. Eventually the Conceptual Framework should prove helpful in terms of clarifying elements and providing consistent solutions to problems, taking into account qualitative factors such as user relevance, verifiability, and cost to produce information.

TAX LEASES

The further liberalizing of depreciation allowances under ACRS was previously described. Firms having net operating losses, carryovers of the ITC, or unused foreign tax credits would have fewer benefits from ACRS than profitable enterprises. The Congress therefore decided that marginal corporations should also get their share of benefits. The wisdom, or lack thereof, of providing investment incentives for marginal firms is beyond the scope of this text.

The means by which benefits were provided to marginal enterprises was literally by a sale of either—or both—the ACRS benefits and the ITC to firms capable of using them. Transactions of these types are clothed in the legal form of sale and leaseback, though the asset itself is not subject to this arrangement.

Perhaps the kindest thing that can be said about tax lease transactions is that they lapsed on December 31, 1983. They were, at best, a very questionable macroeconomic tool. The FASB issued an exposure draft on the subject and then revised it. Neither draft was able to cope in a meaningful and sensible manner with the elusive nature of the transaction. However, under the circumstances, one can only sympathize with the FASB. The influence of government, as the earlier part of the chapter certainly reveals, has added significant complexities to accounting. Tax leases will not be missed, at least by accounting theorists and standard-setting organizations.

[27]The only time that relevant circumstances arise would be in the case of carryforwards. APB 2's position on ITC carryforwards is somewhat similar to the treatment of loss carryforwards in APB 11—that it ". . . should ordinarily be reflected only in the year in which the amount becomes 'allowable,' in which case the unused amount would not appear as an asset." See AICPA (1962, para. 16). As a result of running ITC carryforwards through income when realized, the carryforwards might reach income faster than through capitalization in the year of acquisition. However, this is still less of a problem than the possibility of constantly revising asset costs whenever ITC carryforwards are realized.

SUMMARY

Income tax allocation appears to be grounded in the matching concept. Relevance to users of the allocation process is, however, open to serious question. Comprehensive allocation using the deferred method of presentation is required by APB 11. Comprehensive allocation is a form of rigid uniformity because the question of "loan repayment," a potentially important relevant circumstance, is ignored. The deferral approach simply begs the question of balance sheet interpretation and has been rejected as an appropriate classification in SFAC 3.

Perhaps the principle problem of comprehensive allocation is the growth of the balance sheet credit when accelerated depreciation is used for tax purposes and straight-line for financial reporting purposes. A possible defense of the liability approach is the rollover view, which employs an individual-asset interpretation concerning tax liabilities. This outlook has been criticized on the grounds that tax liabilities are not like accounts payable. The latter are paid off on an individual basis, whereas the former are not.

Consequently, another view of the situation, partial allocation, has arisen. In this situation allocation is employed only if it is foreseen that there will be a real payback of "loans" received as a result of total book depreciation exceeding total tax depreciation in specific future years. Hence, partial allocation is really a form of finite uniformity. The main problem of partial allocation is the question of verifiability since estimates of future tax and book depreciation as well as the tax rate must be made.

Another allocation problem stems from the tax carryback and carryforward provisions of the law. Carrybacks present no problems. They are booked as income tax credits in the loss year. Carryforwards are more controversial. APB 11 has taken a conservative position by not allowing booking in the loss year unless there is "virtual certainty" of realization. However, it is quite likely that the firm will receive the carryforward benefits either through operations or by sale of the firm in order to capitalize on the carryforward benefits. Hence, conservatism is particularly questionable in this area.

Conservatism relative to loss carryforward recognition becomes particularly confusing when deferred tax credits are on the books. APB 11 allows a premature reversal of some of the deferred tax credits in place of recognition of the carryforward benefits.

The investment tax credit is another major problem area created by macroeconomic policy considerations. Four possible interpretations have arisen. If deferral is desired, asset reduction appears to be preferable to the deferred investment credit approach, even though complications were brought about by the 1982 tax law that requires reduction of the tax base of assets by one half of the investment tax credit taken in the acquisition year.

It is not clear, though, whether flow through or deferral is preferable from the standpoint of user relevance.

The investment tax credit and income tax allocation have enough similarities to warrant discussion of the problems together. This does not mean, however, that accounting for them should be the same.

QUESTIONS

1. As a type of allocation, why is income tax allocation unique?
2. Relative to depreciation, why is comprehensive allocation an example of rigid uniformity and partial allocation an example of finite uniformity?
3. Although net-of-tax depreciation gives the same "bottom line" result as comprehensive allocation, are there any financial ratios that would be affected by the choice between these methods?
4. How do the deferral and liability methods of implementing comprehensive allocation differ?
5. What is the "rollover" defense of the liability interpretation of deferred taxes, and how has it been attacked?
6. What is the justification for discounting deferred tax liabilities under either comprehensive or partial allocation?
7. What is the interpretation of income tax expenses under partial allocation?
8. Do you think that loss carryforwards should or should not be booked as assets in the loss year?
9. Why do you think that the Accounting Principles Board opted for premature reversal of deferred tax credits when loss carryforwards are not booked?
10. Using the asset illustrated in Exhibit 13-9, assume that the appropriate interest rate is 10% and the tax rate is 46%. Is the enterprise better off by taking the full investment tax credit and reducing the asset's tax base by one half of the ITC taken or should it take 8% on the ITC without the tax basis reduction? Assume that ITC benefits are received immediately and depreciation tax shield benefits occur at year end.
11. Relative to the investment tax credit, why does TEFRA create both a permanent difference and a timing difference relative to depreciation?
12. TEFRA's requirement is that the depreciable tax basis of an asset must be reduced by half the investment tax credit taken. Why does this create problems if a deferral method of accounting for the investment tax credit is desired?
13. How do deferred investment credits differ from deferred tax credits under comprehensive allocation?

14. How consistent should the accounting for income tax allocation and the ITC be?

15. Do you perceive any problems about booking ITC carryforwards in the acquisition year as opposed to when they are realized?

CASES AND PROBLEMS

1. Assume an asset is acquired at a cost of $100,000 with a 10-year life and no salvage value. It will be amortized over a 5-year period for ACRS purposes. The full investment credit is taken. Income before taxes and depreciation is $150,000 (assume that this asset is the only depreciable asset involved). The tax rate is 46%. Make all entries for income tax expense, tax liability, and related accounts for the year of acquisition under each of the following investment tax credit assumptions:
   (a) Full flow through.
   (b) Modified flow through.
   (c) Deferral using the deferred investment credit account.
   (d) Deferral with one half of the investment tax credit going to the fixed asset and the remainder to the deferred investment credit.
   (e) Deferral with the entire investment credit going to reduction of the fixed asset.

2. Certain financial statement data for Lockheed for the year ended December 30, 1973 were restated in 1974. These data are shown below (000,000 omitted in all figures):

	1973	1974
Inventories	1,291.8	834.6
Future tax benefit (long-term portion)	—	104.3
Deferred income taxes	77.3	4.3
Retained Earnings	192.8	(87.1)

In addition, the financial statements contained the following notes:

1973: There is an operating tax loss carryforward available to offset taxable income of future years, but it is exceeded by the future taxable income that will result from reversals of book-tax differences. Hence, none of the tax loss carryforward is available to offset any book income that may be recorded in future years.

Based upon currently anticipated operations, it is expected that cash outlays for income taxes (principally state and foreign) will not exceed income tax expense in any of the three succeeding years.

Income tax expense for the year 1973, excluding the amount applicable to the extraordinary gain, was less than the amount of tax computed by applying the U.S. federal income tax rate of 48% to earnings before income taxes and extraordinary gain. A reconciliation of such amounts follows:

		($ in thousands)
Computed "expected" tax expense		$9,420
Increases (reductions) in taxes resulting from:		
Investment tax credits		(2,060)
Domestic International Sales		
Corporation exemption		(2,110)
Other	290	290
Total tax expense		$5,540

Unused investment tax credits of approximately $23,000,000 are available for reduction of future taxes, of which $7,900,000 in 1969 and $2,060,000 in 1973 were recorded as a reduction of deferred taxes and $13,040,000 will be reflected in income only when realized in future years. The realization of these credits is dependent upon future taxable income. They expire in varying amounts from 1978 to 1980.

1974: There is a $492 million operating loss carryforward available to offset taxable income of future years, which expires as follows: $81 million in 1975, $107 million in 1976, $22 million in 1977, $224 million in 1978, and $58 million in 1979. The Company anticipates that in 1975 and 1976 significant amounts of earnings will be realized from sales (which are substantially covered by firm backlog) on non-TriStar programs on which the Company has had favorable historical experience. In addition, anticipated earnings during this two year period will be favorably affected by the reduced interest rate on borrowings under the amended 1971 Credit Agreement. Because of these anticipated earnings, the Company believes that realization of the tax benefit attributable to $217 million of this carryforward is assured beyond any reasonable doubt within the next two years and therefore, in connection with the losses prior to 1973 resulting from the change in accounting discussed in Note 2, $104 million was retroactively recorded as a future tax benefit. The tax effect ($36 million) of approximately $74 million of carryforwards has not been recorded and is available to reduce the provisions for income taxes in future years. In 1973 and 1974 deferred taxes aggregating $11 million were provided. The accumulated difference between book and tax income at the end of 1974 amounted to about $223 million, primarily differences arising on the TriStar program.

Because of the operating loss carryforward, it is not expected that cash outlays for federal income taxes will be required in any of the succeeding three years.

Unused investment tax credits of approximately $24 million are available for reduction of future taxes, of which $7 million in 1974 and

$4 million in 1973 were recorded as a reduction of deferred taxes on the flowthrough method and the remainder will be reflected in earnings as a reduction of income taxes to be provided in future years. Realization of these credits is dependent upon future taxable income. The credits expire in varying amounts from 1978 to 1981.

Required:

(a) What entry was evidently made as part of the restatement of Lockheed's financial statements?

(b) Comment on the information quality of the footnotes accompanying these statements.

BIBLIOGRAPHY OF REFERENCED WORKS

Accounting Principles Board (1962). "Accounting for the 'Investment Credit'," *Accounting Principles Board Opinion No. 2* (APB).

——— (1967). "Accounting for Income Taxes," *Accounting Prinicples Board Opinion No. 11* (AICPA).

Beaver, William, and Roland Dukes (1972). "Interperiod Tax Allocation, Earnings Expectations, and the Behavior of Security Prices," *The Accounting Review* (April 1972), pp. 320–332.

——— (1973). "Interperiod Tax Allocation and δ-Depreciation Methods: Some Empirical Results," *The Accounting Review* (July 1973), pp. 549–559.

Bevis, Donald, and Raymond E. Perry (1969). *Accounting for Income Taxes* (AICPA).

Bierman, Harold, and Thomas Dyckman (1974). "New Look at Deferred Taxes," *Financial Executive* (January 1974), pp. 40–49.

Black, Homer (1966). "Interperiod Allocation of Corporate Income Taxes," *Accounting Research Study No. 9* (AICPA).

Buckley, John (1972). *Income Tax Allocation: An Inquiry into Problems of Methodology and Estimation* (Financial Executives Research Foundation).

Bullock, Clayton (1974). "Reconciling Economic Depreciation with Tax Allocation," *The Accounting Review* (January 1974), pp. 98–103.

Committee on Accounting Procedure (1953). "Restatement and Revision of Accounting Research Bulletins," *Accounting Research Bulletin No. 43* (CAP).

Davidson, Sidney (1958). "Accelerated Depreciation and the Allocation of Income Taxes," *The Accounting Review* (April 1958), pp. 173–180.

——— (1966). "Comments," in H. Black, "Interperiod Allocation of Corporate Income Taxes," *Accounting Research Study No. 9* (AICPA), pp. 117–119.

Davidson, Sidney; Lisa Skelton; and Roman Weil (1977). "A Controversy over the Expected Behavior of Deferred Tax Credits," *Journal of Accountancy* (April 1977), pp. 53–56.

Drake, David (1962). "The Service Potential Concept and Interperiod Tax Allocation," *The Accounting Review* (October 1962), pp. 677–684.

Financial Accounting Standards Board (1980). "Elements of Financial Statements of Business Enterprises," *Statement of Financial Accounting Concepts No. 3* (FASB).

Findlay, M. Chapman, III, and E. E. Williams (1981). "Discounting Deferred Tax Liabilities: A Reply," *Journal of Business Finance and Accounting* (Winter 1981), pp. 593–597.

Gonedes, Nicholas, and Nicholas Dopuch (1974). "Capital Market Equilibrium, Information Production, and Selected Accounting Techniques: Theoretical Framework and Review of Empirical Work," *Studies on Financial Accounting Objectives: 1974* (Supplement to the *Journal of Accounting Research*), pp. 48–129.

Graul, Paul, and Kenneth Lemke (1976). "On the Economic Substance of Deferred Taxes," *Abacus* (June 1976), pp. 14–33.

Herring, Hartwell, and Fred Jacobs (1976). "The Expected Behavior of Deferred Tax Credits," *Journal of Accountancy* (August 1976), pp. 52–56.

Levy, Gregory M. (1982). "TEFRA": Its Accounting Implications," *Journal of Accountancy* (November 1982), pp. 74–82.

Livingstone, John L. (1967a). "Accelerated Depreciation and Deferred Taxes: An Empirical Study of Fluctuating Asset Expenditures," *Empirical Research in Accounting: Selected Studies, 1967* (Supplement to the *Journal of Accounting Research*), pp. 93–105.

——— (1967b). "A Behavioral Study of Tax Allocation in Electric Utility Regulation," *The Accounting Review* (July 1967), pp. 544–552.

——— (1969). "Accelerated Depreciation, Tax Allocation, and Cyclical Asset Expenditures of Large Manufacturing Firms," *Journal of Accounting Research* (Autumn 1969), pp. 245–256.

Meyers, Stephen L. (1973). "An Examination of the Relationship Between Interperiod Tax Allocation and Present Value Depreciation," *The Accounting Review* (January 1973), pp. 44–49.

Moonitz, Maurice (1957). "Income Taxes in Financial Statements," *The Accounting Review* (April 1957), pp. 175–183.

Nair, R. D., and Jerry J. Weygandt (1981). "Let's Fix Deferred Taxes," *Journal of Accountancy* (November 1981), pp. 87–102.

Nurnberg, Hugo (1972). "Discounting Deferred Tax Liabilities," *The Accounting Review* (October 1972), pp. 655–665.

Price Waterhouse & Co. (1967). *Is Generally Accepted Accounting for Income Taxes Possibly Misleading Investors?* (Price Waterhouse & Co.).

Sharp, William M. (1977). "An Analysis of Corporate Transactions Involving Net Operating Loss Benefits," *Indiana Law Review*, No. 5, pp. 981–1007.

Suojanen, Waino (1954). "Accounting Theory and the Large Corporation," *The Accounting Review* (July 1954), pp. 391–398.

Thomas, Arthur (1974). "The Allocation Problem: Part Two," *Studies in Accounting Research #9* (AAA).

Watson, Peter L. (1979). "Accounting for Deferred Tax on Depreciable Assets," *Accounting and Business Research* (Autumn 1979), pp. 338–347.

Wheeler, James, and Wilfred Galliart (1974). *An Appraisal of Interperiod Income Tax Allocation* (Financial Executives Research Foundation).

Williams, E. E., and M. Chapman Findlay III (1975). "Discounting Deferred Tax Liabilities," *Journal of Business Finance and Accounting* (Spring 1975), pp. 121–133.

✗ ✗ Wolk, Harry I., and Michael G. Tearney (1973). "Income Tax Allocation and Loss Carryforwards: Exploring Uncharted Ground," *The Accounting Review* (April 1973), pp. 292–299.

——— (1980). "Discounting Deferred Tax Liabilities: Review and Analysis," *Journal of Business Finance and Accounting* (Spring 1980), pp. 119–133.

ADDITIONAL READINGS

TAX ALLOCATION

Barton, Alan (1970). "Comparing Income Tax and Interperiod Allocation," *Abacus* (September 1970), pp. 3–24.

Beresford, Dennis (1982). "Deferred Tax Accounting Should Be Changed," *The CPA Journal* (June 1982), pp. 16–23.

Dewhirst, John (1975). "The Tax Allocation Question Answered," *CA Magazine* (November 1975), pp. 43–50.

Drummond, C., and S. Wigle (1981). "Let's Stop Taking Comprehensive Allocation for Granted," *CA Magazine* (October 1981), pp. 56–61.

Greenball, Melvin (1969). "Appraising Alternative Methods of Accounting for Accelerated Tax Depreciation: A Relative Accuracy Approach," *Empirical Research in Accounting: Selected Studies, 1969*, pp. 262–289.

Hope, Tony, and John Briggs (1982). "Accounting Policy Making—Some Lessons from the Deferred Taxation Debate," *Accounting and Business Research* (Spring 1982), pp. 83–96.

Laibstain, Samuel (1971). "A New Look at Accounting for Operating Loss Carryforwards," *The Accounting Review* (April 1971), pp. 342–351.

Lemke, Kenneth, and Paul Graul (1981). "Deferred Taxes—An 'Explicit Cost' Solution to the Discounting Problem," *Accounting and Business Research* (Autumn 1981), pp. 309–315.

Nurnberg, Hugo (1968). "Present Value Depreciation and Income Tax Allocation," *The Accounting Review* (October 1968), pp. 719–730.

——— (1971). *Cash Movements Analysis of the Accounting for Corporate Income Taxes* (Michigan State University).

Rosenfield, Paul, and William C. Dent (1983). "No More Deferred Taxes," *Journal of Accountancy* (February 1983), pp. 44–55.

Subcommittee of the American Accounting Association's Committee on Financial Accounting Standards (1978). *Response to Exposure Draft Number 13 of the International Accounting Standards Committee Entitled "Accounting for Taxes on Income"* (AAA).

Voss, William (1968). "Accelerated Depreciation and Deferred Tax Allocation," *Journal of Accounting Research* (Autumn 1968), pp. 262–269.

INVESTMENT CREDIT

Moonitz, Maurice (1966). "Some Reflections on the Investment Credit Experience," *Journal of Accounting Research* (Spring 1966), pp. 47–61.

Stamp, Edward (1967). "Some Further Reflections on the Investment Credit," *Journal of Accounting Research* (Spring 1967), pp. 124–128.

Throckmorton, J. (1970). "Theoretical Concepts for Interpreting the Investment Credit," *Journal of Accountancy* (April 1970), pp. 45–52.

TAX LEASES

Financial Accounting Standards Board (1982). *Accounting for the Sale or Purchase of Tax Benefits through Tax Leases*, Revised Exposure Draft (FASB).

Peller, Philip R.; John E. Steward; and Benjamin S. Neuhausen (1982). "The 1981 Tax Act: Accounting for Leases," *Financial Executive* (January 1982), pp. 16–26.

CHAPTER 14

Oil and Gas Accounting

Oil and gas accounting is an important though specialized area, one which demonstrates many theoretical problems of the type discussed in this book. It is a subject that has plagued standard setters for nearly two decades. Moreover, several of the decisions rendered by standard-setting agencies have been extremely dubious. From a theoretical point of view, financial accounting and reporting in the oil and gas industry illustrates very well a situation in which information produced by the historical cost model generally is considered to be much less relevant for decision makers than information produced by some form of current valuation. Because of this factor and the politicization of the oil and gas accounting controversy, we have seen more empirical research using security price movements to ascertain the economic impact of an accounting standard than in any other single area of accounting.

First in this chapter, we look at an example of the impact on financial statements of full cost (FC) versus successful efforts (SE) accounting (the two broad methods of applying historical cost). Then we take up a discussion of the conceptual differences betwen the two methods regarding the application of historical costing; we also review an examination of standard setting on the subject, a review of the various empirical studies, a comparison of oil and gas accounting to the conceptual framework, and an examination of the current value approach proposed by the Securities and Exchange Commission (SEC)—that is, their proposed revenue recognition accounting (RRA). Last, we take up the current status of financial accounting and reporting in the oil and gas industry.

In practice there are slight variations in the application of both FC and SE because of such factors as the definition of a cost center (to be discussed later). However, in this chapter, the two methods will be examined in their broadest sense. The basic difference between the two is their treatment of incurred exploration costs that do not result in the discovery of oil or gas reserves. Under FC, all the costs of exploration are capitalized, regardless of whether those costs lead to a specific discovery of reserves. The reason underlying FC is the probabilistic nature of exploration: it may require, on average, that numerous exploratory wells be dug in order to find one producing well. Therefore, costs of all exploration are included in the cost of the one "hit." Under SE, only the exploration costs that result in a producing well are capitalized and those that result in "dry holes" are expensed immediately. If four exploratory wells are dug and three are dry holes, the costs of those three will not provide future benefits and therefore, should be expensed in the view of SE adherents.

The following example will illustrate the possible impact on financial statements of applying FC versus SE for a relatively young enterprise. XYZ Corporation was formed three years ago and has dug four exploratory wells per year with a success rate of 25%. Depletion expense is 20% of beginning-of-year oil properties (i.e., XYZ produces 20% of its proven reserves each year) and depreciation expense is 10% of beginning-of-year other assets. Production cost is 8% of revenues. In the current year 100,000 barrels of oil were sold at $32 per barrel. Four exploration wells were dug at an average cost of $525,000. One well was successful. Exhibit 14-1 presents the beginning-of-year balance sheets, 14-2 the current-year income statements, and 14-3 the end-of-year balance sheets under both the FC and SE methods.

Although the illustration is admittedly hypothetical, it does point out that the two methods may have a significant impact on financial statements, particularly for a relatively new or developing enterprise. In this illustration assets differ by $4.5 million, or approximately 54% (FC as base). The difference is even more pronounced in Stockholder's Equity, where SE's stockholders' equity is only 24% of FC's. Net income varied by $843,000, or 45%.

These results appear unusually large; however, the amounts were substantiated by several studies of the financial statements of operating enterprises. For example, in a study of 28 enterprises, Klingstedt's data revealed that earnings may increase from 10% to several hundred percent by merely switching from the SE method to the FC method.[1] Touche Ross & Company found in a study of thirty-six enterprises that net income would be reduced by 20%, assets by 30%, and stockholders' equity by 16% if the enterprises

---

[1]Klingstedt (1970, pp. 79–86).

EXHIBIT 14-1.

XYZ CORPORATION
Balance Sheets, Beginning of Year

	FC	SE
Assets		
Current Assets	$ 800,000	$ 800,000
Oil Properties	4,880,000	1,220,000
Other Assets	1,000,000	1,000,000
Total	$6,680,000	$3,020,000
Liabilities and Stockholders' Equity		
Current Liabilities	$ 600,000	$ 600,000
Long-Term Liabilities	2,000,000	2,000,000
Common Stock	2,000,000	2,000,000
Retained Earnings (Deficit)	2,080,000	(1,580,000)
Total	$6,680,000	$3,020,000

EXHIBIT 14-2.

XYZ CORPORATION
Income Statements, Current Year

	FC	SE
Revenues (100,000 barrels at $32)	$3,200,000	$3,200,000
Expenses:		
Production Costs	$ 256,000	$ 256,000
Depletion	976,000	244,000
Depreciation	100,000	100,000
Exploration Costs	—	1,575,000
	$1,332,000·	$2,175,000
Net Income	$1,868,000	$1,025,000

were required to switch from FC to SE.[2] Similarly, the First Boston Corporation's analysis showed net income reductions as high as 55% as a result of switching from FC to SE.[3] The Financial Accounting Standards Board (FASB) staff found similar but smaller variations in its study.[4]

[2]Touche Ross & Co. (1977).
[3]First Boston Corporation (1978).
[4]FASB (1978).

EXHIBIT 14-3.

XYZ CORPORATION
Balance Sheets, End of Year

	FC	SE
Assets		
Current Assets	$1,445,000	$1,445,000
Oil Properties	6,004,000	1,501,000
Other Assets	900,000	900,000
Total	$8,349,000	$3,846,000
Liabilities and Stockholders' Equity		
Current Liabilities	$ 401,000	$ 401,000
Long-Term Liabilities	2,000,000	2,000,000
Common Stock	2,000,000	2,000,000
Retained Earnings (Deficit)	3,948,000	(555,000)
Total	$8,349,000	$3,846,000

CONCEPTUAL DIFFERENCES BETWEEN FC AND SE

Both FC and SE methods of accounting in the oil and gas industry conform to generally accepted accounting principles as we know them today. That is, both methods represent variations of applying the historical cost model. The fundamental difference between FC and SE is the size of the cost center used in the capitalize/expense decision for exploration costs. Under FC, the largest possible cost center is the entire enterprise, and all costs of finding oil and gas reserves would be capitalized regardless of whether a specific local effort is successful. Under SE, the smallest possible cost center is the individual well and all costs of that well would be expensed unless oil and gas reserves are found. Establishing a direct cause-and-effect relationship between costs incurred and reserves discovered is not relevant to recording the costs as assets under FC while such a cause-and-effect relationship must exist to record the costs as assets under SE. Both methods eventually will produce the same accounting results because the same costs are incurred and the same discoveries made. The timing of those results, however, may vary significantly.

SE accounting was the only method used prior to the late 1950s and early 1960s. At that time FC came into use and became widely used by the late 1960s. Problems with the application of the historical cost model have been suggested as a reason for the rise in the use of the FC method.[5] The problem is that in the oil and gas industry, amounts spent on exploration

[5]Arthur Young (1977, p. 5).

have no predictable relationship to the value of oil and gas discovered. For example, a large amount may be spent to find nothing, but in another geographical area a small amount spent could result in a large discovery. The argument favoring FC was that it came into existence because of frustration with a historical cost concept that penalizes enterprises for exploration efforts that result in no discoveries and does not reward those efforts that result in discoveries with recognition of the value discovered. Although FC does not accomplish the latter goal, it does accomplish the former by capitalizing all exploration costs as long as discovery values exceed costs on a company-wide, or at least very broad, basis.

Regardless of the theoretical reason(s) for the rise in the FC method, it does have a desirable impact on reported income, not to mention net assets. FC results in a smoothing of reported income because costs that are written off in the current period under the SE method are capitalized and amortized against revenues of a number of future periods.

The impact of income smoothing rather than the theoretical shortcoming of the historical cost model was the primary reason underlying the rise of the FC method. Evidence of the number of enterprises that use FC contrasted to the quantity of oil and gas produced by those enterprises substantiates this viewpoint. Generally the larger, more mature and fully integrated enterprises in the oil and gas industry use SE, while the smaller, less integrated enterprises use FC. In using FC, the larger enterprises, simply because of their size and the extent of their operations, receive a relatively smaller smoothing impact than the smaller enterprises. A 1973 survey of approximately 300 enterprises found that nearly one half used FC.[6] However, a 1972 survey found that SE enterprises produced 87 percent of the oil and gas produced in the U.S.[7] A later survey, in 1977, found that only 6 percent of the oil and gas produced in the U.S. and Canada was produced by enterprises using the FC method.[8]

While the argument that failure of the historical cost model led to the FC method cannot be accepted, its inappropriateness undoubtedly contributed to a reassessment of oil and gas accounting. According to Statement of Financial Accounting Concepts (SFAC) 1, the primary purpose of financial reporting is to provide useful information to users of those financial reports. Yet, even the FASB realized the failure of the historical cost model to produce useful information in the oil and gas industry:

> Neither full costing nor successful efforts costing reflects success at the time of discovery. Under both methods, success is reported at the time of sale. It might be said, therefore, that both methods tend to obscure, or at least delay, the reporting of success, but that is the consequence of the historical cost basis of accounting, and its adherence to the realization concept.[9]

[6]Ginsburg, Feldman, and Bress (1973, p. 31).
[7]Porter (1972, p. 6).
[8]Arthur Young (1977, p. 4).
[9]FASB (1977, para. 152).

Not only does the realization concept in terms of revenue recognition result in a lack of useful information, but the use of acquisition cost as a measure of economic value does not apply to the oil and gas industry. Under the historical cost model, at the time an asset is purchased, the value to the purchaser is normally assumed to be measured by the cost. Both SE and FC, although they differ significantly in their treatment of costs, present as assets only the costs incurred in exploration and development. Those costs typically do not have any relationship whatsoever to the economic resources acquired. Because of these problems and the political concern in the U.S. regarding the compilation of meaningful information on domestic oil and gas reserves, standard-setting bodies have struggled with oil and gas accounting for nearly two decades.

STANDARD SETTING FOR OIL AND GAS ACCOUNTING

Financial accounting and reporting for the oil and gas industry has been studied by standard setters for a long time. Ijiri put the issue into perspective when he stated that

> ...never in the history of accounting has the choice of an accounting method attracted so much attention as the controversy over full versus successful efforts costing.[10]

The dimensions of the standard-setting process for oil and gas accounting are all encompassing. It is one of the best examples of interaction between accounting researchers and accounting standard setters. Many of the issues are closely related to the FASB's conceptual framework project. Furthermore, the political pressure exerted resulted in a breakdown of the standard-setting process in the private sector. After a brief historical review of oil and gas accounting standard setting, we examine these three broad subjects in this section of the chapter.

HISTORY OF STANDARD SETTING FOR OIL AND GAS ACCOUNTING

In 1964 the American Institute of Certified Public Accountants (AICPA) commissioned an Accounting Research Study (ARS) to study various accounting practices used in the extractive industries and to make recommendations to the APB. This project represented the first ARS commissioned

---

[10]Ijiri (1979, p. 20).

on an industry-related accounting practice as opposed to general accounting practices applicable to all industries. The general recommendation of ARS 11 was that the SE method rather than the FC method should be used.[11]

Following the publication of ARS 11 in 1969, the APB asked its Committee on Extractive Industries to review the ARS 11 recommendations and draft a proposed APB Opinion that would narrow the acceptable accounting practices in the extractive industries. The Committee's paper, "Accounting and Reporting Practices in the Petroleum Industry," was published in 1971. Again, the principal recommendation favored the SE method. The APB scheduled a public hearing on the paper for late November 1971. Just prior to the public hearing, however, the Federal Power Commission (FPC) issued Order No. 440, which required the FC method for mineral leases acquired after October 6, 1969.[12]

Because of Order No. 440 and mixed reactions to the SE method at the public hearings, the Committee on Extractive Industries was unable to finalize its paper for the APB. Subsequently, the AICPA supported formation of the FASB and as a result the APB dropped certain long-term projects from its agenda, including accounting in the extractive industries. In the meantime, the SEC entered the scene. In December 1972, it proposed that those enterprises that do not follow SE should disclose what net income would have been under that method.[13] Later, however, the SEC retreated from its proposal, but it is obvious that the SEC favored the use of SE rather than FC.

Although financial accounting and reporting in the extractive industries, in particular the oil and gas industry, was proposed as a subject the FASB should add to its original agenda, the FASB decided not to do so.

The foreign oil embargo of 1973 had a significant impact on accounting in the oil and gas industry in the United States. During that period, public policy was concerned with attaining self-sufficiency in energy supplies. While pursuing that goal, United States oil and gas producers reported substantial increases in income, an outcome that resulted in arousing opposition to the industry and generally caused their reporting practices to be viewed with skepticism. In December 1975, President Ford signed Public Law 94-163, "The Energy Policy and Conservation Act" (the Act). The thrust of the Act was that the SEC do one of two things, either

> prescribe rules applicable to persons engaged in the production of crude oil or natural gas, or make effective by recognition, or by other appropriate means indicating a determination to rely on, accounting practices developed by the Financial Accounting Standards Board, if the Securities and Exchange Commission is assured that such practice will be observed by persons engaged in the production of crude oil or natural gas to the same

[11]Field (1969, pp. 150–151).
[12]Federal Power Commission (1971, 36 F.R. 21963).
[13]SEC (1972, 38 F.R. 1747).

extent as would result if the Securities and Exchange Commission had
prescribed such practices by rule.[14]

The FASB had added to its agenda a project to promulgate accounting
standards for oil and gas enterprises two months prior to the Act. It worked
closely with the SEC and issued a Discussion Memorandum (DM) in December 1976 and held a public hearing in the spring of 1977.

The FASB issued an Exposure Draft (ED) in July 1977. The ED required
the SE method of accounting. Prior to that issuance, the FASB had begun
several empirical research studies. Although the results of the studies were
not conclusive, they did indicate that

... the method of accounting would not affect their loan officers' investment and credit decisions regarding oil and gas producing companies.[15]

The SEC apparently agreed with the conclusion reached in the ED. On August 31, 1977, it issued "Securities Act Release No. 5861" that proposed to
amend regulations to incorporate the accounting standards set forth in the
ED in the event a Statement of Financial Accounting Standards (SFAS) was
not issued by December 22, 1977 (the mandatory date established by the
Act).

Subsequently, the FASB issued SFAS 19. SFAS 19 required SE and eliminated FC. However, bending to political pressure, the SEC effectively circumvented SFAS 19 in Accounting Series Release (ASR) 253, which permitted either FC or SE. As a result, SFAS 25, which suspended the
mandatory SE provisions of SFAS 19, was issued.

EMPIRICAL STUDIES ON OIL AND GAS ACCOUNTING

There have been numerous empirical research studies regarding oil
and gas accounting. Several of these studies were sponsored by the FASB,
representing a major attempt to work with accounting researchers in the
standard-setting process.

FASB Sponsored Studies

Prior to issuance of the ED but after issuance of the discussion memorandum, the FASB sponsored one research study and conducted another
itself. In the former the purpose was to determine how investment and
credit decisions regarding oil and gas enterprises are made and, in particular, whether the method of accounting, FC or SE, had an impact on those
decisions. Interviews were conducted by academic consultants with various individuals making investment and credit decisions in the oil and gas
industry. Interviewees included loan officers of large and small banks making loans to all sizes of oil and gas enterprises, bank trust department offi-

[14]Energy Policy and Conservation Act (1975, SEC 503(b)(2)).
[15]FASB (1977, para. 90).

cers, institutional securities underwriters, and security analysts. In general a wide spectrum of individuals involved in the everyday investment and credit decisions for oil and gas enterprises, but not employees of those enterprises, were interviewed. A total of only twenty-four individuals were interviewed, thus somewhat limiting the conclusiveness of the results. The interviewees indicated that the method of accounting, FC or SE, did not affect the investment and credit decision. To the contrary, most interviewees relied on such factors as their own valuations of oil and gas reserves and cash flow data rather than on reported earnings.[16]

The second study, conducted by the FASB's staff, concerned the application of SFAS 9, "Accounting for Income Taxes—Oil and Gas Producing Companies." SFAS 9 allowed two alternative approaches to tax allocation for certain timing differences. The purpose of the study was to determine whether the approach adopted by an enterprise was correlated to either the method of accounting it used, FC or SE, or its size. The results showed that a correlation did not exist with regard to either variable.[17]

After the ED was issued, the FASB commissioned two additional studies. Both studies were directed toward determining the economic consequences of proscribing the FC method of accounting. An argument frequently given in opposition to the ED was that if FC enterprises were forced to follow SE accounting, their ability to raise capital would be materially hampered and, as a result, their exploration activities would have to be curtailed drastically or eliminated.

Dyckman conducted security price research designed to determine whether the release of the ED had a negative impact on the security prices of SE enterprises. If FC enterprises' security prices were negatively affected, the impact might be considered as strengthening the argument that those enterprises would have difficulty in raising capital because of the switch to SE accounting. Obviously, it also would imply that the capital markets are naive rather than sophisticated regarding accounting methods because, of course, the enterprise is not different in any way other than its accounting method.

Two research designs were employed by Dyckman. In one, the sample enterprises derived more than 50 percent of their revenue from exploration and production activities. In that study the market prices for 22 FC and 22 SE enterprises were studied for the 11-week period prior to issuance of the ED and the 11-week period after issuance. Testing the differences in security returns, Dyckman found that FC enterprises were somewhat negatively affected around the time the ED was issued, but that negative impact was short term; and for the 22-week period there was no statistically significant difference between FC and SE enterprises.[18] This would be in line with the allocation nature of the differences between the methods.

---

[16]FASB (1977, para. 90).
[17]FASB (1977, para. 90).
[18]Dyckman (1979, p. 24).

The other approach used different statistical tests and was not limited to enterprises engaged primarily in exploration and production. The sample included 65 FC and 40 SE enterprises. The time period studied was 21 weeks, 10 prior to and 11 after the issuance of the ED. Although the differences in the security returns of FC and SE enterprises generally were statistically significant at the 10% level of probability, they were not at the 5% level.[19]

Incidentally, Dyckman conducted a similar study after the issuance of SFAS 19. The methodology was identical to his second one and covered 17 weeks, 8 prior to and 9 after issuance of SFAS 19. The results indicated that differences between security returns of FC and SE enterprises were not statistically significant at the 10% level of probability.[20]

The second study commissioned by the FASB was a telephone interview survey. The survey was of 27 senior executive officers of relatively small and medium-sized SE enterprises. The purpose was to determine whether those executive officers believed that the use of SE had any negative impact on their enterprises' ability to raise capital. None of the executive officers surveyed indicated that the company's use of successful-efforts accounting had hindered its ability to raise capital.[21]

Although the results of the FASB-sponsored research indicated that few, if any, economic consequences would result from proscribing FC accounting, the results of other studies did not all reach the same conclusion.

Other Research Studies

The majority of non-FASB-sponsored research regarding oil and gas accounting centered on two hypotheses: (1) characteristics of the enterprise determine whether FC or SE is used; and (2) proscribing FC would have a negative indirect economic impact on enterprises that use that method. The first hypothesis is concerned with the possibility of relevant circumstances and the second with economic consequences of accounting standards.

Many FC enterprises argued that there were significant differences between them and SE enterprises and that those differences would justify continued use of the FC method. The U.S. Department of Justice agreed with them:

> [Uniformity] as a goal can only claim superiority where like entities are being compared. If two entities or groups of entities were significantly dissimilar, attempts to draw simple accounting comparisons would only confuse the analysis.[22]

Deakin studied 53 "nonmajor" oil and gas enterprises. Nonmajor enterprises were chosen because most major oil and gas enterprises use SE and, moreover, the method of accounting has relatively little impact on major

[19]Dyckman (1979, pp. 31–37).
[20]Dyckman (1979, pp. 43–44).
[21]FASB (1977, para. 93).
[22]U.S. Department of Justice (1978, p. 18).

enterprises. The results of the study were that it would be difficult to distinguish enterprises on the basis of the accounting method used and the aggressiveness of the enterprise in exploration efforts. Although some distinguishing characteristics may exist, such as the age of the enterprise (FC enterprises tend to be younger), Deakin concluded that it would be difficult to promulgate accounting methods based on the characteristics of the enterprises using those methods.[23]

Four other studies, in addition to the FASBs, were made of the economic consequences of proscribing FC accounting. The results are mixed. The Directorate of Economic and Policy Research of the SEC conducted a study of security returns of FC versus SE enterprises. The sample consisted of 35 FC and 37 SE enterprises, including both large and small enterprises. Security prices were studied over a period of 30 days following issuance of the ED. The finding was that initially upon issuance the security returns of FC enterprises were negatively affected; however, the impact was short-lived and generally recovered within thirty days.[24]

Smith used a "reversal method" to study the economic impact of SFAS 19 on FC enterprises. The study was of security prices of FC versus SE enterprises *after* the SEC reinstated FC accounting. The hypothesis was that FC enterprises' securities would be favorably affected by the reinstatement if proscribing FC would have a negative impact. The result was this:

> No evidence . . . is provided of "extreme" price effects of the proposed elimination or retention of full cost accounting. The magnitude of the "unexpected" return observations of the reversal test casts serious doubt that there were extreme "information effects" of the accounting change(s) on individual sample full cost firms.[25]

Collins and Dent conducted a study similar to Dyckman's with two major exceptions: (1) Canadian enterprises were excluded by them, and (2) the period studied was extended to one year. Their finding was directly opposite to the earlier study. The results showed

> . . . that over the three, six and eight month periods following the issuance of the ED, the average risk-adjusted return of the full cost firms was significantly less than that of the successful efforts firms.[26]

Lev's study differed from the others in that he used daily stock prices rather than weekly prices. Lev's belief is that a week between price observations is too long to identify the impact of a single event such as the issuance of the ED. Only seven days were used, two prior and five after issuance of the ED. The sample comprised 49 FC and 34 SE enterprises. He found that the issuance of the ED had a moderate negative impact on the stock prices of FC as compared to SE enterprises.[27]

---

[23]Deakin (1979, pp. 730–733).
[24]Haworth, Matthews, and Tuck (1978).
[25]Smith (1981, p. 207).
[26]Collins and Dent (1979, p. 24).
[27]Lev (1979, p. 500).

Two additional studies were made in connection with the FC versus SE controversy, although neither was directed toward the impact of the accounting method. Dhaliwal examined 72 FC enterprises and 41 SE enterprises. The objective of his study was to determine the impact of an enterprise's capital structure on management's attitude toward accounting standards. He found that FC enterprises generally were more highly leveraged than SE enterprises and that their managements opposed SFAS 19 more than did the managements of the lower leveraged SE enterprises.[28] Collins, Rozeff, and Dhaliwal used agency theory to explain the observed decline in stock prices associated with the ED eliminating FC accounting. The results seem to indicate that stock price declines were associated with an anticipated increase in the cost of supplying information using SE as opposed to FC and with an anticipated negative impact on important financial contracts, such as debt covenants.[29]

RELATIONSHIP TO THE CONCEPTUAL FRAMEWORK

SFAS 19 was issued prior to the issuance of any SFACs; however, concepts discussed in SFACs 1 and 2 were well formulated in the minds of FASB members and served as background for the decisions reached in SFAS 19. The overall criterion of decision usefulness as discussed in SFAC 1 was clearly the objective of the FASB in promulgating SFAS 19.

Information about enterprises is much more useful if it is comparable between enterprises than if not. For example, if similar enterprises use dissimilar accounting procedures, although the inputs (i.e., transactions and events) into the respective systems may be the same, the outputs (i.e., financial statements) will be different and not comparable. Thus, to enhance the usefulness of information reported by oil and gas enterprises, the FASB decided that all enterprises should use the same accounting procedures.

SFAC 2 provides two broad concepts that make accounting information useful—reliability and relevance. To be reliable, information must be faithful to what it purports to represent and it must be verifiable. These two concepts of reliability—representational faithfulness and verifiability—were discussed at length in SFAC 2. Relevant information must affect a decision made by decision makers in order for it to have the quality of relevance. Thus, it must have feedback value and predictive value as well as being timely. Both of the broad concepts—reliability and relevance—weighed heavily on the FASB during its deliberations leading up to SFAS 19.

In the oil and gas industry, most generally agree that the critical event for success is the discovery of reserves. As a result, the FASB considered, but rejected, a method of accounting that would have focused on the discovery of reserves. The method, discovery value accounting, is very similar

---

[28]Dhaliwal (1980, pp. 78–84).
[29]Collins, Rozeff, and Dhaliwal (1981, pp. 37–73).

to an SEC proposal called reserve recognition accounting (RRA) which will be discussed shortly. Although many variations of discovery value accounting exist, the primary thrust of it is that oil and gas reserves would be recorded at their estimated value when discovered. The discovery value would be recorded as revenue from exploration activities and as inventory for future production activities. The inventory would then be charged to the income statement as the reserves are sold.

The FASB rejected discovery value accounting primarily because of the lack of reliability in the measurement process. The measurement process involves estimates of the quantity of reserves, the amount and timing of costs to develop reserves, the timing of production of reserves, the production costs and income taxes, the selling prices, and the discount factor. The Board concluded:

> The uncertainties inherent in those estimates and predictions tend to make estimates of reserve values highly subjective and relatively unreliable for the purpose of providing the basis on which to prepare financial statements of an oil and gas producing company.[30]

The Board, therefore, was left with the choice between FC and SE. It opted for SE and rejected FC primarily because it believed that SE resulted in more relevant information being reported than did FC. In making decisions about enterprises, investors and creditors are concerned with the relative risk of each enterprise for which a decision must be made. Therefore, financial reports should report information about the relative risk of enterprises. The FASB concluded:

> Because it capitalizes the costs of unsuccessful property acquisitions and unsuccessful activities as part of the costs of successful acquisitions and activities, full costing tends to obscure failure and risk. Successful efforts accounting, on the other hand, highlights failures and the risks involved in the search for oil and gas reserves by charging to expense costs that are known not to have resulted in identifiable future benefits.[31]

Another aspect of relevance of information that is discussed in SFAC 2 and was considered by the Board in its deliberations on SFAS 19 is neutrality. Neutrality in the context of accounting information means that economic activity should be reported as faithfully as possible without attempting to alter what is being communicated in order to influence behavior in a particular direction. In other words, it is not the purpose of accounting information to influence behavior in any direction other than the direction indicated by the economic activity being reported. Neutrality has a more obvious impact on standard setters than on those preparing accounting information. The standard setters must establish accounting standards that result in the reporting of reliable and relevant information in accordance with the underlying economic activities being reported, and must not be

[30]FASB (1977, para. 133).
[31]FASB (1977, para. 15b).

influenced by various special-interest groups, including the federal government, whose policies have their own purposes.

There were many, both inside and outside government, who felt that requiring SE and proscribing FC was contrary to national economic policy in the oil and gas industry. The policy was (and is) to encourage the exploration for and development of oil and gas reserves. The argument was that prohibiting FC would be anticompetitive and thus would result in less exploration and development of reserves. The Board rejected this argument because, notwithstanding the fact that it did not accept the economic consequences argument, national policy is best served by limiting acceptable alternatives and promulgating standards that do not obscure economic facts.

POLITICAL PRESSURE

The FC/SE controversy acquired political overtones to a far greater extent than any accounting subject either before or after. Indeed the ultimate outcome could have seriously harmed the credibility of the FASB to set accounting standards; however, such a drastic impact does not appear to have occurred. As noted earlier, the Act empowered the SEC to:

> ... take such steps as may be necessary to assure the development and observance of accounting practices to be followed in the preparation of accounts by persons engaged ... in the production of crude oil or natural gas in the United States.[32]

The SEC elected to rely on the FASB, and both groups interpreted the Act's charge to mean that a single uniform system of accounting should evolve. With knowledge of the recommendation several years earlier by the AICPA Task Force (favoring SE), oil and gas industry representatives pursued their viewpoints by various high-profile methods. They lobbied Congress, sponsored and published studies conducted by the American Petroleum Institute, made their views known in the press, and lobbied government agencies in Washington.

This pressure initially appeared to be of no use because the FASB issued its ED favoring SE, and the SEC announced its intention to incorporate the ED in the regulations in the event the FASB was unable to act fast enough. The FASB, however, did act and issued SFAS 19 promptly. The political pressure did begin to mount shortly after SFAS 19 was issued. The oil and gas industry was under attack for high profiteering and little competition. Many blamed the FASB. Shortly after the issuing of SFAS 19, the Department of Energy was holding hearings to consider the impact of SFAS 19 on competition; also the antitrust division of the Department of Justice registered its concern about SFAS 19; and the Federal Trade Commission

---

[32]Energy Policy and Conservation Act (1975, Sec. 503(a)).

urged the SEC to reject SFAS 19; even the SEC decided to hold hearings on FC versus SE.

The SEC reversed its position, and in ASR 253 indicated that it would accept the FC method and planned to develop some form of a discovery value method. Subsequently, in ASRs 257 and 258, the SEC permitted a method of FC as an acceptable alternative to SE and indicated its future intention to require reserve recognition accounting (RRA). To avoid harm to the FASB's credibility, the SEC reaffirmed its basic policy of looking to the FASB for the leadership in developing and promulgating accounting standards.

The FASB subsequently issued SFAS 25 which suspended the mandatory use of SE. In issuing SFAS 25, the FASB bent to the political pressure that was brought to bear. From a practical point of view, it had no other choice.

RESERVE RECOGNITION ACCOUNTING

A survey of all financial analysts involved with the oil and gas industry was conducted primarily to determine whether analysts favored FC or SE. Over 40% responded, and they overwhelmingly favored the SE method. A secondary finding, however, is perhaps more enlightening. The vast majority of the analysts (83%) thought that the value of recoverable reserves should be disclosed in financial reports.[33] This indicates that, for the oil and gas industry at least, the historical cost model simply does not provide adequate information to decision makers. The perceived failure of the historical cost method led the SEC to develop RRA.

The SEC cited three primary reasons for favoring the development of RRA: (1) historical cost accounting fails to provide sufficient information on financial position and operating results for oil and gas producers; (2) additional information, outside the basic financial statements, is required to permit assessments of the financial position and operating results of an enterprise in the oil and gas industry and allow comparisons between it and other enterprises; and (3) an accounting method based on valuation of oil and gas reserves is needed to provide sufficiently useful information.[34] Hence the SEC was concerned with providing informative disclosure in terms of oil and gas accounting.

In August 1978, the SEC issued Release 33-5969 which ushered in RRA on an experimental basis for three years. If successful, the SEC's plan was

---

[33]Naggar (1978, pp. 72–77).
[34]SEC Docket (1978).

to require RRA in the primary financial statements. The valuation method required for RRA was as follows:

1. Estimate the timing of future production of proven reserves, based on current (i.e., balance sheet date) economic conditions.
2. Estimate future revenue by using the estimate from (1) and applying current prices for oil and gas, adjusted only for fixed contractual escalations.
3. Estimate future net revenue by deducting from the estimate in (2) the costs to develop and produce the proven reserves—on the basis of current cost levels.
4. Determine the present value of future net revenue by discounting the estimate in (3) at 10%.

Exhibit 14-4 illustrates the format for displaying earnings under RRA suggested by the SEC.

EXHIBIT 14-4.

Earnings Summary of Oil- and Gas-Producing Activities

Year Ended December 31, 19XX

Revenues from Oil and Gas:		
Sales to outsiders	$XXXX	
Transfers	XXXX	$XXXX
Costs of Production:		
Lifting costs	$XXXX	
Amortization of proved properties	XXXX	(XXXX)
Income from Producing Activities		$XXXX
Current Additions to Proved Properties		XXXX
Costs of Additions to Proved Properties		
Exploration Costs	$XXXX	
Development Costs	XXXX	(XXXX)
Income from Current Exploration and Development Activities		XXXX
Revisions to Previous Additions to Proved Properties:		
Changes in estimated quantities of proved reserves		XXXX
Changes in rate of production		XXXX
Changes to reflect current prices and costs		XXXX
Holding gains from passage of time		XXXX
Total Revisions		XXXX
Profit before Income Taxes		XXXX
Provision for Income Taxes		(XXXX)
Profit After Income Taxes		$XXXX

As might be expected, RRA received significant criticism from the oil and gas industry. Most of the criticism was based on concepts discussed in SFACs 1 and 2 which, although not in place at that time, had been disseminated for public comment. Some questioned the relevance of the information because it represented a relatively objective and uniform approach but did not produce fair market value of an enterprise's oil and gas properties. RRA considered only proven reserves rather than total reserves; therefore, significant quantities could be ignored. Moreover, it did not anticipate future price and cost changes and by doing so assumed that changes in costs would result in similar changes in prices. This assumption is not necessarily true for oil and gas operations where the price of oil and gas is significantly influenced by the actions of the Organization of Petroleum Exporting Countries and supply and demand, while costs are influenced more by local inflationary conditions. The selection of a discount rate of 10% was nothing more than an arbitrary decision to force rigid uniformity and did not consider any of the enterprise-specific factors, such as risk, that enter into the determination of an appropriate discount rate.

The reliability of the information was the subject of numerous research studies. A massive study undertaken by Stanley P. Porter was designed to determine the accuracy of annual estimates of proven reserves. It included 27 different enterprises that together accounted for 54% of crude oil and natural gas liquid production and 50% of the oil production in the United States in 1978. Participating enterprises were asked to supply information involving the impact of changes in existing reserves on an annual basis. The results reflect the impreciseness of reserve quantity estimates:

1. In 64% of the years studied, reserve revisions were more than 20% of additions and, hence, income was affected by more than 20%; in 46% of the years, the impact was greater than 40%; and in 23% of the years, it was over 100%. . . ;

2. All companies that reported for the entire ten-year period had at least one year in which the impact of judgement would be in excess of 60% of income on an RRA basis.[35]

Price Waterhouse conducted a study of nine oil and gas enterprises. The purpose was an extensive study of RRA to determine the impact on reported earnings of the various estimates that must be made. Some findings were these:

1. Reserve estimates made in the year of discovery were inaccurate by at least ±50%.

2. Generally RRA income is changed percentage-wise by at least as much as the percentage change in reserve estimate.

3. Income from reserve revisions, ignoring price changes, greatly exceeded income from discoveries.

[35]Porter (1980, pp. 36–37).

4. Income from price changes greatly exceeded income from discoveries.[36]

Needless to say RRA's perceived relevance was more than offset by its lack of reliability. As a result the SEC decided not to require it in primary financial statements. The FASB subsequently added a project to its agenda to develop a comprehensive set of disclosures for oil and gas enterprises.

CURRENT STATUS OF ACCOUNTING IN THE OIL AND GAS INDUSTRY

The FASB, working together with oil and gas representatives and the SEC, moved fairly rapidly in developing a set of required disclosures. The SEC issued ASR 289 on February 26, 1981. It stated that the SEC did not consider RRA as a potential method of accounting in primary financial statements. The FASB added its project on oil and gas disclosure to the agenda on March 4, 1981. By May 15, 1981 it had issued an Invitation to Comment. Public hearings were held in August 1981; an ED was issued in April 1982; and SFAS 69, "Disclosures about Oil and Gas Producing Activities," was issued in November 1982, to be effective for fiscal years beginning on or after December 15, 1982.

SFAS 69 is significant for at least two reasons. First, it represents an attempt by the FASB to combat the *standards-overload* problem. SFAS 69 is not applicable to enterprises that are not publicly traded, nor to publicly traded enterprises that do not have significant oil- and gas-producing activities. The reason for exempting those enterprises is "that the costs of providing that information exceed the benefits."[37] Moreover, SFAS 69 represents a significant reduction in total disclosures required under previous SFASs and SEC requirements. Second, SFAS 69 represents another expansion of the concept of financial reporting. It requires the disclosure of financial information outside the basic financial statements or notes thereto. The reason given by the FASB for this requirement is that the information is not historical cost (the basis of the primary financial statements) and its reliability is not such as to make it comparable with the primary financial statements.[38]

The basic information required to be disclosed by oil and gas enterprises covered by SFAS 69 includes disclosures about these items:

1. Proven oil and gas reserve quantities.
2. Capitalized costs relating to oil- and gas-producing activities.

[36]Price Waterhouse & Co. (1979, pp. 15–21).
[37]FASB (1982, para. 113).
[38]FASB (1982, para. 116).

3. Costs incurred in oil and gas property acquisition, exploration, and development activities.
4. Results of operations for oil- and gas-producing activities.
5. A standardized measure of discounted future net cash flows relating to proven oil and gas reserves. The discount rate to use is 10%.[39]

The standardized measure of discounted future net cash flows is calculated by estimating future cash inflow from proven reserves at current prices less estimated future development and production costs and income taxes relating to the cash inflows, both to be computed using current costs and rates. The amount derived is then discounted at 10%. The aggregate change in the discounted future net cash flow during the year must also be disclosed and the sources of that change, if significant, also disclosed. Some likely reasons for a change in the discounted future net cash flow from one year to the next include changes in estimated future sales prices, development and production costs and income taxes relating to future production as well as revisions of reserve quantity estimates and discoveries.[40] As can be seen, this calculation is very similar to the calculation of income from exploration and development under the SEC's RRA. The FASB stopped short of the SEC, however, because an earnings statement based on the various estimates is not required. Presumably the reason is the lack of reliability of the information and the resultant misinterpretation by financial statement users.

Regarding the basic financial statements, either the SE method as defined in SFAS 19 or the FC method as defined in ASR 253 may be used.

SUMMARY

Financial reporting in the oil and gas industry has been the subject of considerable controversy. At the center of that controversy is the shortcomings of the historical cost model to provide adequate information for users of financial reports. The most significant event for an oil and gas enterprise is the discovery of oil and gas reserves, not the revenues derived from oil and gas sales. The historical cost model, however, does not measure or report oil and gas reserves until those reserves have been developed, produced, and sold. A related problem is that the cost incurred to discover oil and gas reserves bear little, if any, relationship to the value of the reserves.

As a result of these shortcomings in the historical cost model, and as an attempt to smooth income, at least two applications of that model evolved (FC and SE). In many cases, the financial statement impact of FC

[39]FASB (1982, paras. 10–38).
[40]FASB (1982, paras. 30–33).

versus SE is dramatic, and it results in financial statements that are not comparable between enterprises. The FASB attempted to solve the uniformity and comparability problem by requiring that all enterprises use SE. Its efforts, however, were undermined by political pressure in general and SEC actions specifically. As a result, both FC and SE accounting continue to be acceptable today.

The SEC attempted to overcome the shortcomings in the historical cost model by eliminating its use in the oil and gas industry. In its place, a form of discovery value accounting (RRA) was to be used. Unfortunately, measurements made under RRA proved to be too unreliable to be used for the basic financial statements. The FASB subsequently issued SFAS 69, which requires the disclosure, outside of the basic financial statements and notes thereto, of information similar to the SEC's RRA information.

The oil and gas controversy has two important ramifications on the standard-setting mechanism today. First, it demonstrates that standard setting is a political process. Second, academic researchers, working together with standard setters, can have a significant impact on the standard-setting process.

QUESTIONS

1. Both FC and SE represent applications of historical cost. How do the two methods differ conceptually?
2. Many believe that the historical cost model is inappropriate for the oil and gas industry. What is the difference between the oil and gas industry and other industries that leads to the perceived inadequacy of the historical cost model?
3. Why did FC come into use and why was it allowed to evolve?
4. What is the general objective of security price research? How was it applied to the oil and gas industry?
5. Economic consequences may be interpreted in at least two ways: (a) the cost to apply a particular standard exceeds the benefits derived from its use; and (b) the application of a particular standard will result in a negative economic impact on certain enterprises. Should the FASB be concerned with either interpretation? In your own opinion, does the FASB consider economic consequences? Provide examples of FASB action in support of your opinion.
6. The FASB readily admitted that historical cost based accounting systems in the oil and gas industry do not meet the overall objective of financial accounting and reporting as stated in SFAC 1. Why, then, did the FASB reject the use of a discovery value method?

7. Many believe that SE unduly penalizes enterprises for unsuccessful exploration efforts and does not appropriately reward enterprises for successful exploration efforts. Discuss the meaning of penalty and reward as used in this context.
8. The FASB was determined to narrow acceptable practices. Why do you think it opted for SE rather than FC?
9. Define neutrality as the term is used in accounting.
10. Should neutrality be a goal of standard setters, even if it results in accounting practices contrary to public policy?
11. The FASB eventually gave in to pressure, which may have undermined its authority to set standards. Did any similar harm to the FASB's credibility occur as a result of the issuance of SFAS 25? Should the FASB have issued SFAS 25?
12. SFAS 69 requires all enterprises to use a 10% discount rate to calculate standardized net future cash flow. Discuss the pros and cons of requiring all enterprises to use the same discount rate.
13. Oil and gas disclosures are not considered part of the basic financial statements or notes thereto and do not require auditor participation. Why did the FASB adopt this approach?
14. Accounting standards in the oil and gas industry are the result of considerable input from several interested groups. Do you believe the best possible standards evolved from this process? Why or why not?
15. The oil and gas industry represents an example of how long the FASB's due process procedures can take to get accounting standards in place. Do you believe the FASB should shorten its process in order to get standards issued on a more timely basis? Why or why not?

CASES AND PROBLEMS

1. Consider the following case: The XYZ Corporation was formed and commenced operations last year. It began with $5,000,000 capitalization (cash/capital stock). Oil properties costing $2,000,000 were acquired by issuing long-term debt. Other assets costing $600,000 cash were acquired. Three exploratory wells costing $500,000 cash each were dug, and one was successful. No production occurred and, therefore, no depreciation or depletion was recorded. In the current year, 19XX, three more exploratory wells costing $525,000 cash each were dug and one was successful. 100,000 barrels, representing 20% of beginning-of-the-year reserves, were produced and sold at $30 per barrel (cash). Production costs average 10% of revenues (cash) and depreciation is 12% of property and other assets. Ignore income taxes.

Required:
(a) Prepare a balance sheet at end of year 19XX and an income statement for year 19XX under:
(1) FC method of accounting,
(2) SE method of accounting.
(b) Discuss the advantages and disadvantages of both methods.

2. Determine the standardized net cash flow required to be disclosed by SFAS 69 using the following information.
   (a) Proven reserves are 1,000,000 barrels.
   (b) Estimated production is 20% per year of proven reserves.
   (c) Current selling prices are $35 per barrel.
   (d) Costs to develop and produce proven reserves are approximately 40% of selling prices.
   (e) Depreciation and depletion averages 75% of development and production costs.
   (f) Income taxes generally are 38% of income before taxes.

3. The Gas Drilling Company (GDC) has asked your opinion as to the appropriate accounting for the following transaction. GDC uses the SE method of accounting.
   GDC is participating in the drilling of an exploratory gas well.
   The drilling arrangement provides that GDC must drill to 20,000 feet in order to earn an interest in any gas found at the drill site.
   During drilling, a producing zone was found at 15,000 feet. However, GDC continued drilling to 25,000 feet. There was no definitive determination of gas reserves below 15,000 feet and GDC has no specific plans to continue exploration.
   The decision has been made to plug back the well to 15,000 feet and operate it as a producing well.
   Total costs of drilling the well were $12,000,000 of which $4,000,000 were incurred between 15,000 feet and 20,000 feet, and $5,000,000 were incurred between 20,000 feet and 25,000 feet.
   (a) What do you believe should be the appropriate accounting (capitalize versus expense) for the costs incurred below 15,000 feet?
   (b) What is the appropriate accounting for the costs incurred beyond 15,000 feet under SFAS 19?

BIBLIOGRAPHY OF REFERENCED WORKS

Arthur Young (1977). *Successful Efforts' Accounting: Why It Is Needed in the Extractive Industries* (Arthur Young).

Collins, Daniel W., and Warren T. Dent (1979). "The Proposed Elimination of Full Cost Accounting in the Extractive Petroleum Industry: An Empirical Assessment of the Market Consequences," *Journal of Accounting and Economics* (March 1979), pp. 3–44.

Collins, Daniel W.; Michael S. Rozeff; and Dan S. Dhaliwal (1981). "The Economic Determinants of the Market Reaction to Proposed Mandatory Accounting Changes in the Oil and Gas Industry: A Cross-Sectional Analysis," *Journal of Accounting and Economics* (March 1981), pp. 37–71.

Deakin, Edward B., III (1979). "An Analysis of Differences Between Non-Major Oil Firms Using Successful Efforts and Full Cost Methods," *The Accounting Review* (October 1979), pp. 722–734.

Dhaliwal, Dan S. (1980). "The Effect of the Firm's Capital Structure on the Choice of Accounting Methods," *The Accounting Review* (January 1980), pp. 78–84.

Dyckman, Thomas R. (1979). *The Effects of the Issuance of the Exposure Draft and FASB Statement No. 19 on the Security Returns of Oil and Gas Producing Companies* (FASB).

Energy Policy and Conservation Act (1975). Public Law 94-163, 94th Congress, S. 622 (December 22, 1975).

Federal Power Commission (1971). Order No. 440, 36 F.R. 21963 (November 5, 1971).

Field, Robert E. (1969). "Financial Reporting in the Extractive Industries," *Accounting Research Study No. 11* (AICPA).

Financial Accounting Standards Board (1977). "Financial Accounting and Reporting by Oil and Gas Producing Companies," *Statement of Financial Accounting Standards No. 19* (FASB).

——— (1978). *Appendices to the Additional Comments of the Financial Accounting Standards Board to the Securities and Exchange Commission, Accounting Practices—Oil and Gas Producers* (SEC File 57-715, May 31, 1978).

——— (1982). "Disclosures about Oil and Gas Producing Activities," *Statement of Financial Accounting Standards No. 69* (FASB).

First Boston Corporation (1978). Statement at the Department of Energy Inquiry (February 21, 1978).

Ginsburg, Feldman, and Bress (1973). Attorneys for the Ad Hoc Committee (Petroleum Companies), *Comments of the Ad Hoc Committee (Petroleum Companies)* (SEC File No. 57-464, March 14, 1973).

Haworth, H.; J. Matthews; and C. Tuck (1978). *Full Cost vs. Successful Efforts: A Study of a Proposed Accounting Changes' Competitive Impact* (SEC Directorate of Economic and Policy Research, February 1978).

Ijiri, Yuji (1979). "Oil and Gas Accounting—Turbulence in Financial Reporting," *Financial Executive* (August 1979), pp. 18–26.

Klingstedt, John (1970). "Effects of Full Costing in the Petroleum Industry," *Financial Analysts Journal* (September–October 1979), pp. 79–86.

Lev, Baruch (1979). "The Impact of Accounting Regulation on the Stock Market: The Case of Oil and Gas Companies," *The Accounting Review* (July 1979), pp. 485–503.

Naggar, Ali (1978). "Oil and Gas Accounting: Where Wall Street Stands," *Journal of Accountancy* (September 1978), pp. 72–77.

Porter, Stanley P. (1972). *"Full Cost" Accounting: The Problem it Poses for the Extractive Industries* (Arthur Young & Co.).

—— (1980). *A Study of the Subjectivity of Reserve Estimates and its Relation to Financial Reporting* (Stanley P. Porter).

Price Waterhouse & Co. (1979). *Reserve Recognition Accounting* (Price Waterhouse & Co., 1979).

SEC Docket (1978). (Volume 15, No. 12—Part III, September 10, 1978).

Securities and Exchange Commission (1972). "Proposed Amendment to Regulation S–X to provide for Disclosure of Significant Accounting Policies," *Securities Act Release 5343, Exchange Act Release 9914* (38 F.R. 1747, December 18, 1972).

Smith, Abbie (1981). "The SEC 'Reversal' of FASB Statement No. 19: An Investigation of Information Effects," *Studies on Standardization of Accounting Practices: An Assessment of Alternative Institutional Arrangements* (1981 Supplement to *Journal of Accounting Research*), pp. 174–211.

Touche Ross & Co. (1977). Letter to the Ad Hoc Committee on Full Cost Accounting (March 29, 1977).

United States Department of Justice (1978). "Comments on Accounting Practices—Oil and Gas Producers—Financial Accounting Standards," Before the Securities and Exchange Commission (February 28, 1978).

ADDITIONAL READINGS

FULL COST AND SUCCESSFUL EFFORTS

Bierman, Harold; Roland Dukes; and Thomas Dyckman (1974). "Financial Accounting in the Petroleum Industry," *Journal of Accountancy* (October 1974), pp. 58–64.

Collins, Daniel W.; Warren T. Dent; and Melvin C. O'Connor (1978). "Market Effects of the Elimination of Full Cost Accounting in the Oil and Gas Industry," *Financial Analysts Journal* (November–December 1978), pp. 48–56.

Committee on Extractive Industries of the Accounting Principles Board (1973). *Accounting and Reporting Practices in the Oil and Gas Industry* (AICPA).

Dyckman, Thomas (1979). "Market Effects of the Elimination of Full Cost Accounting in the Oil and Gas Industry: Another View," *Financial Analysts Journal* (May–June 1979), pp. 75–80.

Dyckman, Thomas, and Abbie Smith (1979). "Financial Accounting and Reporting by Oil and Gas Producing Companies—A Study of Information Effects," *Journal of Accounting and Economics* (March 1979), pp. 45–75.

Financial Accounting Standards Board (1976). *Discussion Memorandum: Financial Accounting and Reporting in the Extractive Industries* (FASB).

Myers, John H. (1974). *Full Cost vs. Successful Efforts in Petroleum Accounting: An Empirical Approach* (John H. Myers).

Patz, Dennis H., and James R. Boatsman (1972). "Accounting Principle Formulation in an Efficient Markets Environment," *Journal of Accounting Research* (Autumn, 1972), pp. 392–403.

Sunder, Shyam (1976). "Properties of Accounting Numbers Under Full Costing and Successful Efforts Costing in the Petroleum Industry," *The Accounting Review* (January 1976), pp. 1–18.

RESERVE RECOGNITION ACCOUNTING

Adkerson, Richard C. (1979). "Can Reserve Recognition Accounting Work?", *Journal of Accountancy* (September 1979), pp. 72–81.

Connor, Joseph E. (1975). "Discovery Value—The Oil Industry's Untried Method," *Journal of Accountancy* (May 1975), pp. 54–63.

——— (1979). "Reserve Recognition Accounting: Fact or Fiction?" *Journal of Accountancy* (September 1979), pp. 92–99.

Cooper, Kerry; Steven Flory; Steven Grossman; and John Groth (1979). "Reserve Recognition Accounting: A Proposed Disclosure Framework," *Journal of Accountancy* (September 1979), pp. 82–91.

Most, Kenneth S. (1979). "A New Method of Accounting for Oil and Gas Producers," *Management Accounting* (May 1979), pp. 53–58.

Peat, Marwick, Mitchell & Co. (1979a). *Financial Accounting for Oil and Gas Reserves* (Peat, Marwick, Mitchell & Co.).

——— (1979b). *1979 Survey by Peat, Marwick, Mitchell & Co. of Petroleum Investment Analysts* (Peat, Marwick, Mitchell & Co.).

Porter, Stanley P. (1980). *Highlights of a Study of the Subjectivity of Reserve Estimates and its Relation to Financial Reporting* (Stanley P. Porter).

Reed, Joel L. (1978). "Exploring for Information on Oil and Gas Companies," *Financial Analysts Journal* (November–December 1978), pp. 42–46.

Touche Ross & Co. (1980). *Oil and Gas Accounting.* (Touche Ross & Co.).

Walendowski, George (1980). "RRA—Will It Work," *Management Accounting* (March 1980), pp. 21–25.

Welsch, Glenn A., and Edward B. Deakin (1977). *A Research Study: Measuring and Reporting the 'Replacement' Cost of Oil and Gas Reserves* (Glenn A. Welsch and Edward B. Deakin).

CHAPTER 15

Pensions

This chapter is concerned with accounting for the effects of pension plan sponsorship. The central accounting questions regard the recognition and measurement of pension expenses and liabilities for the sponsoring company. Pension accounting provides an excellent illustration of the revenue–expense and asset–liability orientations to the financial statements. Present accounting standards are based on a revenue–expense approach, which emphasizes the recognition and measurement of annual pension expense. A liability is recognized only as a byproduct of expense recognition and measurement rules. More recently, there has been interest in the pension liability question.

The chapter is organized in the following manner. A comprehensive review of the nature of pension plans is presented in the first section. Pension plans are complex, so the review is meant to provide the necessary background for analysis of pension accounting. The second section examines the development of accounting standards. Pension accounting standards have had a predominantly revenue–expense orientation. An alternative approach based on the asset–liability orientation is presented in the third section. Economic consequences of pension accounting standards are the subject of the next section, and the relevance of supplemental pension disclosures are discussed in the final section.

OVERVIEW OF PENSION PLANS

A pension plan is an arrangement between an employer and employee for the payment of postemployment income, hereafter called pension benefits.[1] There are many characteristics of pension plan design and funding, some of which are very complex. It is not feasible to review all of them, but significant areas which bear on pension accounting are briefly discussed.

DEFINED CONTRIBUTION AND DEFINED BENEFIT PLANS

An important feature of pension plans concerns the benefit formula and specification of contributions. There are two broad types of plans which differ as to how benefits are specified and funded. **Defined contribution** plans are those in which the benefit is defined as the future value of pension fund contributions made on an employee's behalf. The exact value is unknown prior to retirement because it depends on future earnings of pension fund investments. Benefits are solely a function of accumulated contributions and for this reason the plans are called "defined contribution." The value of benefits is variable. It is dependent on contribution levels and earnings made on invested contributions.

Contribution rates for defined contribution plans are normally stated as a percentage of wages or salaries. Plans may be either noncontributory, in which all contributions are made by the employer, or contributory, where funding is shared by the employer and employee. Mandatory contributions must be made to a pension fund for most plans.[2] This means that assets are set aside for the sole purpose of paying pension benefits. The technical arrangements for accomplishing this are through either the establishment of a formal pension plan trust fund or the purchase of insured annuity contracts from insurance companies on behalf of employees. The term **pension fund** will be used to refer to both situations.

The other type of pension plan is called **defined benefit.** In defined benefit plans, the pension benefit is defined either as a specific dollar amount or by a general formula based on salary. Benefits may be expressed as a specific dollar amount, normally multiplied by years of membership in the plan (hereafter called years of service) to determine the value of the benefit. When benefits are defined by a general formula, two alternatives exist. Benefits can be based on career average salary: in this type of plan,

---

[1]There are other benefits in a pension plan; for example, death and disability. These are normally paid for through group insurance contracts. Therefore, pension funding is assumed to refer just to the funding of retirement benefits.

[2]Funding requirements established by the Internal Revenue Service and the Employee Retirement Income Security Act would be applicable to most pension plans.

pension benefits are based on career average salary multiplied by years of service. Another type of plan is referred to as *final pay*: pension benefits are based on final salary (usually the average of regular compensation a few years prior to retirement) multiplied by years of service. In all types of defined benefit plans, the value of pension benefits is directly related to the employee's years of service.[3]

Benefits in a defined benefit plan may be paid in one of two ways. The benefit may be paid as a single lump sum amount at retirement date. Alternatively, the benefit may be paid as a life annuity.[4] Some plans permit the employee to elect either form of payment. When the benefit is lump sum, the payment represents a multiple of the defined base; for example, final regular salary averaged over five years, multiplied by 15% for each year of service. An employee with forty years of service would receive forty times .15 (which is six times final average salary). When benefits are defined as life annuity, the same principle is used. However, the benefit is paid each regular pay period and represents a fraction of the final average salary. For example, a rate of 1.5% per year of service and forty years of service would create a lifetime monthly pension equal to 60% of final average monthly salary.

VESTING

Vesting refers to a qualifying period of pension plan membership which must be met before pension benefits legally exist. Pension benefits do not come into legal existence before vesting requirements are satisfied. Once benefits vest, there is a formal obligation between the plan and employees as set out in the terms of the plan.

Vested benefits are calculated as follows. The salary base, as defined in the benefit formula, is multiplied by the credited years of plan membership. For example, in a final pay plan, the salary base would be the most recent average salary, rather than final average salary. Because the benefits are not payable until retirement, actuaries compute the present value of vested benefits by discounting them at the assumed rate of interest earned on pension fund investments. Since pension benefits increase with each year of service, the value of vested benefits also increases with each additional year of service after becoming vested. At retirement date, the value of vested benefits will of course be equal to retirement benefits. If an employee withdraws from a plan prior to retirement, statutory requirements dictate that benefits must be "frozen" in the fund and paid when the employee retires.

---

[3]Service credit is normally weighted evenly per year of service, though some plans do weight later years more heavily in order to reward long service. The Employee Retirement Income Security Act sets a limit on the weighting of later years. Backloading is the technical term for uneven weighting.

[4]A life annuity may be one of three forms: single, single with a refund provision, or joint with survivorship. See McGill (1979, p. 122).

A permissible alternative is to transfer assets equal to the actuarial present value of vested benefits into the employee's new pension plan.

SINGLE AND MULTIEMPLOYER PLANS

Another characteristic of pension plans is that they can be either single-employer or multiemployer plans. A multiemployer pension plan is one that is subject to collective bargaining agreements in which two or more employers are plan sponsors. Under statutory requirements, one employer can contribute no more than 50% of initial contributions, and no more than 75% thereafter. There are regulatory differences between the two types of sponsorship, and this does have some accounting implications which are raised later.

ACTUARIAL FUNDING OF DEFINED BENEFIT PLANS

When benefits in a defined benefit plan are based on either career average or final average salary, it becomes something of a guess as to the value of future benefits. Actuaries are consulted to determine annual contribution levels. The principle of actuarial funding is to derive a time series of annual pension fund contributions that will accumulate to produce a projected pension fund balance sufficient to meet the cost of projected pension benefits. There is no single correct way of doing this. Many different actuarial funding models exist and each one derives a different funding pattern over time. However, given the same set of plan conditions and actuarial assumptions, each method builds up a pension fund to the same future balance needed to meet expected retirement benefits. The extreme opposite of actuarial funding is called **terminal funding.** With terminal funding, the sponsor funds benefits only at the time of retirement. It is easy to see how yearly cash flows could be very erratic under terminal funding. Actuarial funding achieves a more even cash flow. The methods developed by actuaries to determine contribution levels are referred to as either **actuarial funding methods** or **actuarial cost methods.** The term *actuarial funding method* will be used for the remainder of the chapter.

Actuarial funding methods are analogous to depreciation methods. A depreciation method allocates a given amount over a specified period of years. Each depreciation method produces a different time series of depreciation expense, but they all sum to the same amount (asset cost less estimated salvage). In a slightly more complicated way, the same thing happens with actuarial funding. Each actuarial funding method produces a time series of future contributions which compound to the same future amount. The mathematical differences between actuarial funding methods are in how benefits are assumed to accumulate (increase) with each year of employee service. It is important to emphasize that this is an arbitrary assumption made solely for the purpose of orderly pension funding. Pension benefits do not legally accumulate or increase in value with each year until vesting requirements are met. For funding purposes, however, benefits are assumed to accumulate each year, even prior to vesting. Actuarial terminology refers to the increase in accumulated benefits each period as **normal cost**; and the accumulated benefits to date, as **actuarial liability.** A very important point to reiterate, though, is that the actuarial calculation of both yearly normal cost and actuarial liability is arbitrary, and that each actuarial method produces different amounts.

Funding becomes more complex in three situations: (1) when a plan is started and past service credit is given to employees; (2) when plan amendments are made which alter benefit levels, and the amendments are made retroactive for past years of service credits; or (3) when actuarial assumptions differ from the subsequent experience of the plan (a situation giving rise to actuarial gains and losses). In all three cases, accumulated benefits will exist (as calculated by the actuarial funding method in use), but are not fully funded. Each of the three is explained below.

When a pension plan commences, credit is often granted to employees for past years of service. From an actuarial funding viewpoint, accumulated benefits exist for past service, but no funding has occurred. This gives rise to what is called **unfunded past service cost.** It is also called **unfunded benefits,** and **unfunded actuarial liability.** The identical situation is encountered when benefit improvements are made. For example, the rate of benefit accumulation per year of service might be increased. If the increased rate is applied to past service as well as future service, accumulated benefits will exist that have not been funded. In both cases, accumulated benefits exceed the existing pension fund balance.

Actuaries deal with the problem of unfunded accumulated benefits in one of two ways. One way is to assume that pension funding dates from the earliest past service credit granted, and to continue calculating future contributions (future normal costs) as though this were true. When this is done, however, a supplemental contribution is necessary because future normal costs will be insufficient to fund expected retirement benefits. The total contribution, therefore, will be normal cost plus a yearly supplement (until the deficiency is fully funded). The other solution is to compute a new time series of yearly contributions (normal costs) over the remaining service life—in order to accumulate a pension fund sufficient to meet expected retirement benefits. Supplemental contributions are not necessary because future normal costs are recalculated to make up the deficiency.

Actuarial gains and losses present a similar problem. In applying actuarial funding methods, actuaries must make assumptions about (1) future withdrawals from the plan, (2) the effects of future salary levels on the value of expected retirement benefits (though this is not always done), and (3) the rate of interest to be earned on pension fund investments. If the pension plan experience differs from these assumptions, the pension fund will be either too high or too low. This difference is an actuarial loss if the fund is less than needed, and an actuarial gain if the fund is greater. Actuarial gains and losses are treated in the same general way as other unfunded accumulated benefits. For example, if an actuarial loss exists, owing to lower than expected earnings on fund investments, a supplemental annual contribution could be made over an arbitrary period of years to make up the deficiency. Alternatively, the loss could be funded implicitly by the calculation of a new time series of future contributions which will fully fund the expected retirement benefits.

Actuarial funding methods are summarized in Exhibit 15-1. This is not an exhaustive list, but it includes the major methods.[5] There are two broad types of actuarial funding methods: **accrued benefit** and **projected benefit.** The FASB refers to these two types as **benefits approach** and the **cost approach,** respectively.[6]

EXHIBIT 15-1.

Actuarial Funding Methods

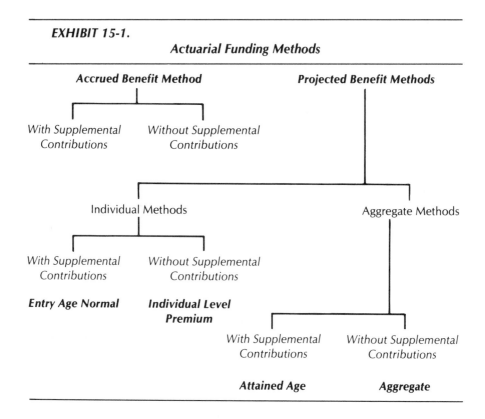

---

[5]Other funding methods also exist. For example, the **frozen initial liability** method is acceptable for ERISA. Frozen initial liability is a projected benefit method, with supplemental funding of unfunded accumulated benefits. It is similar to attained age. Theoretically, an infinite number of actuarial funding methods exist; that is, there are a limitless number of ways that estimated pension costs could be allocated over time.
[6]FASB (1981, para. 211).

The accrued benefit method can be used in either of the two ways discussed to deal with unfunded accumulated benefits: a separate contribution may be calculated to supplement normal cost, or normal cost can be recalculated in such a way that the deficiency is implicitly funded as part of future normal costs. The accrued benefit method is so named because the accumulation of benefits is measured using current salary levels and years of service to value current benefits. This approach is a literal measurement of the value of current accumulated benefits based on the benefit formula in a plan. The method has been criticized for not incorporating future salary increases into the calculations. Eventual benefits will be based on future rather than current salaries. However, one variation of the method does use projected future salaries to calculate accumulated benefits and normal costs.

Projected benefit funding methods are more complex. Each one represents an alternative way of spreading the cost of projected benefits over time. It is for this reason that the projected benefits method is called the cost approach by the FASB. Within this group of methods, the first distinction is between individual and aggregate methods. Individual methods develop contribution rates for individuals, which are then summed to derive the total contribution for the plan. Aggregate methods make funding calculations for the plan as a whole. The other distinction concerns the manner in which unfunded accumulated benefits are funded. Different names have been given to projected benefit methods, depending on whether a supplemental contribution is required to deal with unfunded accumulated benefits. **Entry age normal** and **attained age** both require a supplement to normal cost. **Individual level premium** and **aggregate** do not require a supplement because normal cost is always recalculated to fund implicitly any unfunded accumulated benefits over future periods.

The mathematics of accrued benefit and projected benefit funding methods are defined and illustrated in Appendix 15-A at the end of the chapter. It has been emphasized that actuarial funding is arbitrary and is nothing more than a technique for smoothing a sponsor's pension fund contribution. Differences between the accrued benefit and projected benefit methods are illustrated in Appendix 15-A. The exhibits should be reviewed, though the formulae are not essential. In general, the accrued benefit method assigns more cost to later years of employment and a smaller amount to earlier years, compared to projected benefit methods. There is a more even distribution of contribution levels with projected benefit methods. Differences between the two are less pronounced for stable, mature pension plans because the mixture of young and old employees tends to even out the results. But the differences become pronounced for very young pension plans, or very old pension plans. For very young plans, the accrued benefit method would fund substantially less each year than projected benefit methods, and the reverse would be true for very old plans. Because of the faster pace of funding, it might be inferred that projected benefit methods are better or superior. This is not really true, however. All that can really be said is that the accrued benefit method produces a different time series of future normal costs. The alleged superiority of projected benefit methods stems from a misunderstanding about the arbitrary nature of actuarially-based pension funding.

EMPLOYEE RETIREMENT INCOME SECURITY ACT OF 1974 (ERISA)

ERISA was a landmark in the area of social legislation.[7] Most pension plans are subject to ERISA regulations. Its purpose was to improve the security of pension benefits. The legislation affected four areas: (1) membership eligibility and vesting requirements, (2) mandatory funding requirements, (3) investment diversification requirements, and (4) the guarantee of certain vested benefits in the event of plan terminations. The first area was intended to increase participation levels and to improve the probability of receiving benefits. This was achieved by setting maximum time periods on qualifying years of employment—first to join the plan, and then to qualify for pension benefits. Membership eligibility cannot require a higher minimum age than 25 and a longer term of service than three years.

Vesting must follow one of three alternative formulae: (1) 100% vested after ten years of membership. (2) Graded vesting, in which benefits are 25% vested after five years, increasing 5% for the next five years, and increasing 10% thereafter—so that 100% vesting occurs in fifteen years. (3) The "rule of 45," in which benefits of an employee with five or more years of membership must be 50% vested when the sum of age and years of membership are forty-five, with 10% additional vesting for each year of service (subject to a requirement that vesting be 50% after ten years, and 100% after fifteen years).

The objective in the second area was to override discretionary funding clauses in pension plans. ERISA requires that annual funding must occur and be based on an acceptable actuarial funding method. In addition, unfunded accumulated benefits must be funded over a maximum of forty years for single-employer plans in existence January 1, 1974; thirty years for plans established after that date; and forty years for multiemployer plans. Unfunded accumulated benefits due to actuarial losses must be funded over a maximum of fifteen years.

The third area concerns portfolio diversification. ERISA states that pension fund managers should be concerned with diversification of investments. However, the only specific requirement is to limit investments in the sponsoring company to 10% of the total pension fund. This rule is designed to make a plan financially independent of the sponsor. If a sponsoring company fails, accumulated benefits of the company's pension plan should not be in jeopardy. In a general way, diversification also reduces

[7]United States Public Law 93-406.

investment risk and increases the security of assets held in the pension fund.

Finally, the Pension Benefit Guaranty Corporation (PBGC) was created as a national insurer of pension plans, empowered to collect premiums from plans to pay for guaranteed termination benefits. Vested benefits of participants are partially guaranteed by the PBGC if a plan is terminated. There are different guarantees for single-employer and multiemployer plans.[8] If a pension fund cannot meet guaranteed vested benefits, any shortfall is paid by the PBGC. The PBGC, then, has a statutory lien against the sponsor for this shortfall up to a maximum of 30% of the sponsor's net worth. Premiums collected by the PBGC are intended to cover termination benefits that are not recouped from the sponsors of terminated plans.

Much of the pension controversy centers on whether ERISA has had any effect on the nature of pension plans and the appropriate accounting for pension plans by sponsoring companies. The impetus for review of pension accounting by the Financial Accounting Standards Board (FASB) came in response to the passage of ERISA.

LEGAL RELATIONSHIPS IN DEFINED BENEFIT PLANS

The parties to a defined benefit pension plan are the sponsoring employer, a pension fund, plan participants (the sponsor's present and past employees or their beneficiaries), and the PBGC for plans subject to ERISA. Pension plans are governed by a formal document that sets out the rights and obligations of the employer and employee. Plans have clauses obligating the sponsor to make annual pension fund contributions. The typical requirement is that funding must be based on the advice of actuaries. However, exculpatory clauses usually exist that give the sponsor the right to determine its own contribution levels, to suspend contributions altogether, and to even terminate the plan with no obligation for further contributions. The effect of these clauses is to shelter the sponsor from a legal pension liability.

Pension plans also state that the payment of benefits is to be made solely from pension fund assets, not from the sponsor's assets. This is one

---

[8]Guaranteed benefits are different for single- and multiemployer plans. The guarantee for single-employer plans was set at $750 a month in 1974, to be adjusted upward annually by a ratio based on the social security income base. In 1983, the guarantee level was a monthly pension of $1517.05. For multiemployer plans, the guarantee is $5 of monthly pension benefit per year of service, with the next $15 of monthly pension benefit only partially guaranteed. For strong funds, the guarantee level is 75%, and 65% for weak funds. Funding strength is based on compliance with the annual funding standard. Benefits granted within the last five years are only partially guaranteed (20% per year) for single-employer plans, and are not guaranteed at all for multiemployer plans. In 1983, the PBGC charged an insurance premium of $2.60 and $1.40 per employee, for single- and multiemployer plans, respectively. The charge is intended to cover operating costs and guaranteed benefits from plan terminations. Significant rate increases were being proposed in Congress during 1983.

reason for establishing a pension fund. Exculpatory clauses limit the payment of pension benefits to the existing assets of the pension fund, regardless of how much may be earned according to a plan's benefit formula. These clauses also shelter the sponsor from a legal pension liability. ERISA has not changed this basic relationship between sponsors and employees. Sponsors still have a right to terminate plans. Exculpatory clauses still shelter the sponsor from a direct legal liability to employees for pension benefits. However, there is now a direct annual funding obligation and an indirect obligation to pay vested benefits that are guaranteed by the PBGC.

The PBGC is a fourth party to the plan, guaranteeing certain vested benefits upon termination and having a claim against the plan's sponsor for reimbursement if there is a shortfall in the pension fund at termination. For continuing plans, a funding obligation also exists because of the PBGC guarantee. If the plan continues, unfunded vested benefits will eventually become funded through statutory annual contributions. Either way, then, guaranteed vested benefits must be funded. The significance of this is that the sponsor has an unavoidable funding obligation for vested benefits guaranteed by the PBGC.

There is a pension contract between the employer and employee. The agreement is a mutually unperformed executory contract. An employer is agreeing to make annual pension fund contributions in accordance with the plan in exchange for service from the employee. The employee is exchanging service to the sponsor for benefits available under the terms of the plan. The contract is performed on an annual basis, as the employee completes each year of employment and the employer makes the required pension fund contribution. If pension benefits have not vested, employees receive nothing from the pension plan when leaving the sponsor's employment, other than their own contributions (usually with interest). Once vesting requirements are met, a pension benefit legally exists. At that point, potential benefits are no longer dependent on future performance arising from an unperformed executory contract. However, even if benefits have vested, the sponsor still has no direct obligation to pay benefits to employees because payment of benefits is restricted to pension fund assets. A sponsor's only direct obligation is to make annual pension fund contributions, and to reimburse the PBGC for any deficits if a plan is terminated.[9]

A pension contract, then, is a very weak agreement between a company and employees. The sponsoring company is making a promise to provide future pension benefits (via the pension fund) if employees meet vesting requirements. ERISA has not changed the basic pension contract between the sponsor and employee. But it has superimposed a mandatory annual funding requirement which overrides discretionary funding clauses in pension plans. ERISA has also created an obligation to fund vested benefits guaranteed by the PBGC. These are two significant changes that have a direct impact on the question of an accounting liability.

---

[9]While there is no direct obligation to employees, the PBGC does superimpose an obligation to make up the difference if fund assets are deficient at termination.

There has been some research undertaken to determine the effect of ERISA on companies sponsoring pension plans, specifically, the impact of unfunded accumulated benefits on stock prices and market-based risk measures.[10] No relationship has been found between unfunded accumulated benefits and market-based risk measures. However, some research does indicate that stock prices are reduced in the presence of unfunded accumulated benefits. This seems to indicate that the capital market responds negatively to unfunded accumulated benefits, and that there are direct economic consequences on the value of a company's securities. This research lends support to the argument that unfunded accumulated benefits are a liability of the sponsoring company, at least as perceived by the capital market.

ACCOUNTING ISSUES RELATING TO DEFINED BENEFIT PENSION PLANS

Defined contribution plans do not present difficult accounting problems. An expense is recognized for the sponsor's contribution made in accordance with the terms of the plan. No further obligation exists because pension benefits attributable to employee service to date are restricted to the accumulation of past contributions. In other words, accumulated benefits are fully funded by the sponsor as long as each year's required contribution is made. An expense and liability should be accrued for the current year's required contribution and the liability is discharged when the contribution is made. A cash basis of accounting effectively exists.

The major accounting question that emerges in a defined benefit pension plan is this: when the benefits are defined independently of contribution levels, does the sponsor have an obligation (either contractual or implied) to meet the projected cost of pension benefits arising from employee service to date? The implication is that existing contributions (pension fund assets) may be less than accumulated benefits relating to years of service worked to date. If the sponsor is assumed to be a going entity, any underfunding of accumulated benefits will have to be made up for in future periods in order for the fund to have sufficient assets to meet expected retirement benefits. It can be argued, then, that unfunded accumulated benefits give rise to an accounting liability that should be recognized. This proposition holds aside the difficult question of actually measuring the value of accumulated benefits.

Another accounting question concerns the recognition and measurement of yearly pension expense: is it simply the cash contributed to the pension fund, or is it a more complex accrual based on the yearly increase in accumulated benefits? If a complex accrual is to be made, the problem is one of defining how pension benefits are assumed to accumulate in each period.

---

[10]See Stone (1982) for a review of empirical studies which have been conducted.

The recognition and measurement of pension expenses and liabilities as specified in accounting standards are examined in the next section. This coverage provides a historical perspective on the development of pension accounting. Another interpretation of the pension accounting problem is then presented in the following section. It is based on a liability approach to pension accounting, rather than an expense approach.

DEVELOPMENT OF PENSION ACCOUNTING STANDARDS

ARB 36 (Codified as ARB 43, Chapter 13, Section A)

Prior to any accounting standards, a cash basis of pension accounting existed. Pension expense was equated with cash contributions to pension funds. The first pension accounting standard was Accounting Research Bulletin (ARB) 36 issued in 1948. It was later codified as ARB 43, Chapter 13, Section A.[11] ARB 36 was concerned with recognition of unfunded accumulated benefits (arising from plan startups) in the financial statements. There are three possible methods that might have been used to account for unfunded accumulated benefits. One was to make a prior period adjustment—the reason being that the accumulated benefits were related to service given in the past. An alternative followed the same basic argument, but the adjustment was charged to current income and classified as an extraordinary item. These two methods represent the current operating and all-inclusive income concepts, respectively. ARB 36 adopted a third approach, which allocated unfunded accumulated benefits over current and future periods.

The argument in ARB 36 was that the cost of providing pension benefits should be spread over the remaining service life of employees. If unfunded accumulated benefits exist on account of a plan startup, the employer's cost of meeting these benefits should be matched against future revenues to be generated from employees' labor. The matching concept is the underlying principle of ARB 36 and all subsequent pension accounting standards up to the present. Since the employer's future costs will increase because of future funding of unfunded accumulated benefits, future sales revenue will have a markup based on these higher pension contributions. The fact that service giving rise to the benefits occurred in the past is unimportant. It is future contributions and revenues which will be affected by the decision of the firm to incur unfunded accumulated benefits.

ARB 36 would not necessarily have changed the cash basis of accounting. If firms were expensing the amount of pension fund contributions and

[11]Committee on Accounting Procedure (1948).

if the cash contribution included an element for unfunded accumulated benefits, a cash basis of accounting would still have existed. All ARB 36 did was to reduce flexibility in how the cost relating to unfunded accumulated benefits was dealt with in the income statement.

ARB 47

A pension liability concept was introduced for the first time in ARB 47.[12] The standard recommended that the balance sheet report unfunded vested benefits. It also implied that the income statement report the increase in unfunded vested benefits as the minimum pension expense for the period. In spite of the change, a de facto cash basis of accounting continued for most companies under ARB 47: this is because pension funds would normally have been in excess of vested benefits at the time of the standard. Prior to the pension reform movement, which began in the 1960s, it was not uncommon for pension plans to have lengthy vesting periods.[13] As a result, plans would normally have been adequately funded for vested benefits. This was due to the fact that accumulated benefits would be predominantly unvested if lengthy vesting periods existed. A plan would have to have been grossly underfunded in order to be affected by ARB 47.

APB 8

A major change in pension accounting occurred with Accounting Principles Board (APB) 8.[14] In this standard (which still guides accounting practice) pension expense must be computed using an acceptable actuarial funding method, regardless of cash contributions.[15] APB 8, then, represents a move from simple cash accounting to a more complex accrual basis. For companies following actuarial funding recommendations, the cash basis of accounting poses no problem. The real concern in APB 8 is for companies not consistently following actuarial funding advice. APB 8 is an attempt to make pension expense recognition consistent between those companies which follow actuarial funding advice and those that do not.

As has been pointed out, annual pension funding was potentially discretionary prior to ERISA. Using a cash basis of accounting, pension expense could vary from year to year, depending on management funding decisions. Companies might fund more in good years and less in bad years. This hypothesis has been supported by one research study based on data preceding adoption of APB 8.[16] The reason for mandating an accrual rests

---

[12]Committee on Accounting Procedure (1956).

[13]Davis and Strasser (1970) report a large Department of Labor survey which indicated that most plans (and particularly larger plans) would not have been radically affected by the vesting requirements of ERISA. However, some plans were significantly affected.

[14]APB (1966).

[15]The methods are the five listed in Exhibit 15-1.

[16]Beidleman (1973).

on the premise that a quantifiable portion of future pension benefits accumulate with each period of employment, regardless of how much is actually funded. The accountant's task is to make a reasonable estimate of the yearly cost of these accumulating pension benefits. Since this is exactly what actuarial funding methods do, it is understandable why APB 8 endorsed their use for pension expense estimation.

For companies which fund an amount equal to the APB 8 accrual, a de facto cash basis of accounting still exists. For companies which fund a different amount, APB 8 standardizes pension expense recognition: pension expense is accrued on the basis of actuarial calculations. In applying APB 8, the first step is to calculate normal cost using one of the acceptable actuarial funding methods. An amount representing interest charges for unfunded pension accruals is added to derive total pension expense.[17] In addition, the effects of actuarial gains or losses require an adjustment of pension expense if normal cost does not implicitly take them into account. If a separate adjustment is required, APB 8, paragraph 30 recommends a period of ten to twenty years to write off the gain or loss.

Because of differences in actuarial funding methods, a range is established into which the actuarially computed pension expense must fall. The minimum expense is composed of three elements: (1) normal cost, (2) the current year's interest on the balance of unfunded accumulated benefits (if they are unfunded), and (3) a 5% reduction of unfunded vested benefits (if they are unfunded).

The first part of minimum expense is normal cost as discussed in the section on pension funding. The second part relates to unfunded accumulated benefits as measured by the actuarial method being used. As indicated in the discussion of pension funding, unfunded accumulated benefits arise (a) when past service credit is granted at a plan's inception, (b) for benefit improvements made retroactive, and (c) for actuarial gains or losses. An interest accrual does not represent a reduction in the unfunded balance; it simply takes into consideration the yearly interest which would have been earned had the amount actually been funded. Since the amount has not been funded, it represents an additional cost to the sponsor which must be funded in the future. The third requirement is complex: if a supplemental contribution is made for unfunded accumulated benefits (as in entry age normal), the requirement is that the beginning balance of the vested portion of unfunded accumulated benefits must decline by 5% for the year. If the actuarial method in use does not require a supplemental contribution (as in individual level premium), the third requirement is assumed to be automatically met. The purpose of the rule is to ensure that the pension expense accrual includes an element of charge for unfunded accumulated benefits, the minimum level being for a reduction of the vested portion of accumulated benefits.

---

[17]If funding in the past has exceeded pension costs, a deduction should be made for the interest effects of the overfunding.

The maximum amount of pension expense is composed of four elements: (1) the normal cost; (2) 10% of the amount of unfunded accumulated benefits at the time a plan is started; (3) 10% of the amount of unfunded accumulated benefits at the time benefit improvements are granted for past service; and (4) the current year's interest on the balance of unfunded pension accruals. The maximum rule is similar to the maximum deduction allowed by the Internal Revenue Service for pension fund contributions. As with the minimum rule, the maximum rule is applicable only to actuarial methods that require a supplemental contribution for unfunded accumulated benefits. The rule is intended to limit the recognition of unfunded accumulated benefits to a minimum period of ten years. It should also be noted that the minimum/maximum rules are not intended to be the rules for determining pension expense; rather, the actuarially calculated pension expense must fall within these guidelines.

The mechanics of APB 8 are to debit pension expense and credit pension liability for the computed pension expense. When funding occurs, the pension liability is debited and cash is credited. It is possible for funding to exceed the accrual, in which case a debit balance will exist in the liability account. This debit would be classified as a deferred charge in the balance sheet. If funding is less than computed pension expense, a deferred credit is recognized in the balance sheet.

When it was adopted, APB 8 was regarded as a successful accounting standard. It utilized a research study as the basis of the accounting standard and brought some uniformity to pension accounting.[18] At the time of its adoption, APB 8 affected companies that were extremely discretionary in funding. However, a major uniformity problem still exists in the measurement of accrued pension expense—because APB 8 permits flexibility in the choice of actuarial funding methods used to accrue pension expense. Funding methods vary significantly in the calculation of yearly normal cost. These differences are material under certain conditions and can materially affect reported income.[19] Appendix 15-A illustrates the yearly variation between actuarial funding methods.

APB 8 is consistent with the revenue–expense approach and with general principles of expense measurement. The accrual requirements based on actuarial methods achieve a "rational and systematic" recognition of pension costs over the working lives of employees. These are the exact words used in APB 8. It will be recalled that expenses are recognized in a rational and systematic manner if direct matching to revenue cannot be achieved. (See Chapter 9 in this text and the discussion of expense recognition, in particular APB Statement 4). Under APB 8, pension costs are

---

[18]APB 8 successfully utilized the two-pronged approach advocated by the Accounting Principles Board. The standard was based on a study of pension accounting by Hicks (1965).

[19]Numerical examples of differences may be found in Hicks (1965), FASB (1981), and Schipper and Weil (1982). Francis (1982) evaluated the yearly differences under a range of simulated conditions and concluded that there can be material effects on the income statement resulting from the choice of actuarial funding method.

allocated to the periods of employee service, and in this way an indirect matching of costs to revenues is considered to be accomplished.

FASB INTERPRETATION 3

FASB Interpretation 3 was issued in response to the passage of ERISA.[20] It reaffirmed APB 8 and concluded that ERISA did not create a pension liability except in the likelihood of plan termination. A liability accrual is required only if termination is probable and if guaranteed termination benefits exceed pension fund assets. This requirement is a reiteration and interpretation of APB 8, paragraph 18, which requires balance sheet recognition of legally unavoidable pension liabilities.

This interpretation is *incorrect* because ERISA created an unavoidable obligation to fund unfunded vested benefits guaranteed by the PBGC. The obligation exists whether the plan is terminated or not. If a plan is not terminated, an obligation still exists in the form of future annual statutory funding requirements (which includes an element representing the funding of unfunded accumulated benefits). Analysis of the pension liability question is made later in the chapter.

SFAS 35

Statement of Financial Accounting Standard (SFAS) 35 defines the pension plan as a reporting entity and establishes accounting standards for the measurement and reporting of plan assets and plan obligations.[21] This is considered a landmark standard because it set accounting and reporting standards for a new entity, the pension plan, as separate and distinct from the sponsoring company. Assets are measured at current market values. Plan obligations are defined as accumulated benefits (both vested and unvested), and are measured using the accrued benefit funding method, without taking future salary increases into consideration.

Great care is taken in SFAS 35 to separate clearly the plan (and pension fund) from the sponsor. The nature of the relationship between the sponsor and employee for the payment of pension benefits is carefully avoided. SFAS 35 represents a subtle way of reporting the sponsoring company's pension obligations. It is far less controversial to report a pension obligation of a plan than to report the obligation of a sponsor. This indirect approach to the liability question is carried through in SFAS 36, which requires information about the "plan's" obligations to be reported as a note in the sponsor's financial statements.

---

[20]FASB (1974).
[21]FASB (1980a).

SFAS 36

SFAS 36 amends the supplemental disclosure requirements of APB 8, paragraph 46.[22] The specific disclosure requirements of SFAS 36 are as follows:

1. Basic plan description.
2. General statement of funding policy (actuarial method not required).
3. Any significant matters affecting comparability between periods; for example, change in accounting methods, changes in actuarial assumptions or funding methods, plan amendments, and actuarial gains or losses.
4. Plan assets, as measured under SFAS 35 requirements (market values).
5. Actuarially calculated accumulated benefits as measured under SFAS 35, separated into vested and unvested amounts.
6. Interest rates used in making the actuarial calculations.
7. Date at which the actuarial calculations were made.

The most significant change is the disclosure of accumulated benefits as measured under SFAS 35, and the segregation of this amount into vested and unvested benefits. It is left to the reader to interpret the significance of the data, and how, if at all, they relate to the sponsor. Disclosure is an effective way of dealing with controversial topics.

SUMMARY OF CURRENT STANDARDS

A revenue–expense approach forms the basis of present pension accounting under APB 8. An accrual of the yearly increase in accumulated benefits is required. Any of the major actuarial funding methods may be chosen. Because of the wide variation in actuarial funding methods, pension expense measurement is not uniform between companies. ERISA has not alleviated the uniformity problem. However, what has happened is that a de facto cash basis of accounting once again exists. Mandatory funding requirements under ERISA have virtually eliminated the incidence of discretionary funding. For most companies, pension expense is equal to the amount funded. In a cash flow sense, then, accounting policies are very uniform between companies. Expense is equal to the amount of cash contribution, although the actuarial basis for determining contributions varies from company to company.

It is only with the accrual approach of measuring pension expense that there is perceived to be a uniformity problem. In other words, the uniformity problem exists because of the way in which accrued pension expense is defined. When it is defined as an increase in accumulated benefits, there is

---

[22]FASB (1980b).

poor uniformity due to choice of actuarial funding methods. Each actuarial funding method calculates accumulated benefits in a different (and arbitrary) manner. The situation is analogous to the arbitrary allocation of costs under alternative depreciation methods. Just as there is no single defensible depreciation method, there is no single defensible actuarial funding method. Therefore, there is no way to eliminate the uniformity problem as long as pension expense is defined and measured the way it presently is. This is a theoretical limitation of the revenue–expense approach to pension accounting.

A LIABILITY APPROACH TO THE PENSION PROBLEM

An alternative approach to pension accounting is to place primacy on the question of an accounting liability to the sponsoring company. It has been argued by the FASB that sponsors should record an accounting liability for unfunded accumulated benefits, with benefits being measured by the accrued benefit actuarial funding method, taking salary increases into consideration.[23] To date, though, no action has been taken to implement such a policy. The accounting in such an approach centers on the definition, recognition, and measurement of a sponsor's pension plan obligation.

Before evaluating the FASB's proposal to record a pension liability, we need to make a brief review of the definition of accounting liabilities.[24] Statement of Financial Accounting Concepts (SFAC) 3 defines accounting liabilities as "... probable future sacrifices of economic benefits arising from present obligations ... (paragraph 28)." The word "obligation" is deliberately used to define an accounting liability and is intended to convey a broader liability concept than legally enforceable claims arising from contracts. Obligations "... refer to duties imposed legally or socially; to do that which one is bound to do by contract, promise, moral responsibility, etc. ... (SFAC 3, footnote 14 to paragraph 28)."

Three separate types of liabilities are mentioned in the SFAC 3 definition: (1) legally enforceable claims arising from contracts, (2) constructive obligations, and (3) equitable obligations. These were discussed at length in Chapter 8. Three tests must also be satisfied before an accounting liability is recognized under the SFAC 3 definition. The tests, set out in paragraph 29, are these: (1) a duty exists to transfer assets in the future (either

---

[23]FASB (1980c).

[24]A preliminary position statement was made in FASB (1982). The details are not included here because they represent nonbinding preliminary views by the FASB. See Francis (1983) for an assessment of the FASB's position. The nonbinding preliminary remarks are interesting, however, from a political perspective. One purpose of the proposal is to put everyone on notice that the FASB is considering adopting a very controversial accounting standard.

on demand, on a fixed date, or on the occurrence of a specified event); (2) the duty is virtually unavoidable, and (3) the obligating event or transaction has already occurred. Recognition occurs in the period when the obligating event or transaction occurs.

Given the definition of an accounting liability in SFAC 3, the next step is to apply it to pensions. A sponsor's potential pension obligation comprises three components: (1) a contractual liability for the current annual statutory funding requirement, (2) a contingent liability for vested benefits guaranteed by the PBGC, and (3) a constructive or equitable obligation to fund accumulated benefits not covered by the first two liabilities.[25] Each of these three possible liabilities is evaluated in terms of the accounting liability definition.

STATUTORY FUNDING REQUIREMENT

The first accounting liability, current contributions due to the pension fund, is not controversial and is presently recognized under FASB Interpretation 3. A sponsor must meet minimum annual funding requirements, or the plan may be terminated by the PBGC. The liability is cleared when the contribution is made to the pension fund. Therefore, this liability is short term in nature and may not even appear in a year-end balance sheet (depending on when the payment is made). For most companies, this same amount also represents pension expense for the period.

VESTED BENEFITS GUARANTEED BY THE PBGC

A contingent legal and accounting liability exists for vested benefits guaranteed by the PBGC. If a pension plan is to be terminated, or if termination is probable, FASB Interpretation 3 requires that a liability must be accrued for any shortfall of pension fund assets relative to guaranteed vested benefits.[26] The termination liability to the PBGC is a contingent legal liability, and this accounting procedure is consistent with the recognition of other contingent liabilities. Under SFAS 5, a contingent liability is recognized when future events confirm that a liability exists.[27] In the case of a pension plan, the critical event which confirms the contingent liability to the PBGC is the probable termination of the plan. A liability is accrued only if there are insufficient pension fund assets to pay the guaranteed benefits.

If a pension plan is not to be terminated, the sponsor still has a contingent liability for vested benefits guaranteed by the PBGC. The event that confirms the liability is the determination of an excess of guaranteed vested

---

[25]The amount represents unfunded, unvested accumulated benefits, plus unfunded vested benefits not guaranteed by the PBGC. For simplicity, the amount will be referred to as unvested accumulated benefits.

[26]As noted in footnote 8, all vested benefits are not guaranteed by the PBGC.

[27]FASB (1975).

benefits over pension fund assets. However, the obligation is not to the PBGC—it is to the pension fund for future contributions. An unavoidable duty exists to fund the unfunded vested benefits, and the duty arises in the period the benefits become guaranteed. The benefits will be funded through the annual statutory funding requirement. If the annual funding requirement is not met, the PBGC may terminate the plan, in which case the unfunded guaranteed vested benefits become an obligation to the PBGC. Either way, then, an obligation exists to transfer assets, and the duty is virtually unavoidable. The SFAC 3 definition and tests are completely satisfied.

At present, the accrual of an accounting liability for vested benefits guaranteed by the PBGC is required only if plan termination is probable. When a liability is accrued, APB 8 paragraph 18 requires that a deferred charge be recorded in the balance sheet. The deferred charge is amortized to income over future periods. However, this procedure is inconsistent with SFAS 5. When a contingent liability is accrued under SFAS 5, the debit is charged immediately to income. There is no reason for deferring such a debit unless there is a benefit in future periods. To defer the charge is implicitly to recognize an asset. SFAC 3 restricts asset recognition to those situations in which there are probable positive cash flows in future periods. The only possible asset that could be argued to exist is increased future labor productivity, owing to the existence of a pension plan. However, an intangible asset, such as increased future productivity, is highly unlikely. After all, the pension plan is being terminated, so the plan itself ceases to have any positive effect on future labor productivity. In addition, since PBGC guaranteed benefits are vested, employees may leave at any time and the benefits will still be guaranteed by the PBGC. Again, there would be no positive effect on future labor productivity. The only reason for deferring the debit is to smooth the income statement. This is not a theoretically valid reason. Pension expense is incurred in the period the contingent liability is confirmed, and the cost should be charged to income in the same period. APB 8, paragraph 18, is inconsistent with SFAS 5, and is theoretically unsound; it should be amended.

If plan termination is not probable, the accrual of an accounting liability for unfunded guaranteed vested benefits should still be made. This is not currently done. As indicated previously, vested benefits guaranteed by the PBGC meet all the requirements of the SFAC 3 liability definition, even if plan termination is not probable. Such a change would have a major impact on present accounting practices and the effect on the balance sheet could be significant. A recent survey of Fortune 500 companies found that 28.5% of the companies had unfunded vested benefits. The dollar amount of the unfunded vested benefits averaged 6.9% of the sponsoring company's net worth.[28] The economic consequences of recording such a liability are considered later in the chapter.

---

[28]Johnson and Higgins (1982).

CONSTRUCTIVE OR EQUITABLE PENSION OBLIGATIONS

A significant controversy concerns the third type of possible accounting liability, a constructive or equitable pension obligation. It has been argued by the FASB that a balance sheet liability should be recognized for all unfunded accumulated benefits of a pension plan, both vested and unvested.[29] Pension benefits contractually come into existence when they vest. There is not a legally enforceable claim for unvested accumulated benefits; therefore, if an accounting liability exists, the obligation must be either constructive or equitable. The controversy centers on the meaning of unvested accumulated benefits and their effect on sponsors. To simplify the discussion, vested benefits not guaranteed by the PBGC will be assumed to be unvested, along with the other unvested accumulated benefits.

Arguments for and against recognition of an accounting liability for unfunded, unvested accumulated benefits are presented in the following paragraphs. In order to simplify terminology, unfunded, unvested accumulated benefits will be referred to as unvested accumulated benefits for the remainder of this section. The word "unfunded" is dropped because the liability recognition question exists only if accumulated benefits are unfunded.

Arguments for Recognition

The central point of the argument favoring recognition is this: the concept of unvested accumulated benefits is valid and is implied by the pension contract. Therefore, the sponsor has a funding obligation to meet the cost of unvested accumulated benefits. Support for this viewpoint is found in the manner in which pension benefits are specified. In final salary plans, the benefit is based on final average salary multiplied by the number of years of service. The value of the pension benefit is a function of each year of service and this is the basis for measuring the value of accumulated benefits.

Until vesting rules are met, accumulated benefits are not binding on a plan. However, unvested benefits still have potential value to employees—based on the probability of surviving in employment and satisfying vesting rules. It also can be argued that the expected value of future vested benefits represents an implied funding obligation to the sponsor. In other words, it represents an estimate of the sponsor's probable cost of meeting future vested benefits arising from employee service to date. The fact that such an amount need not be funded immediately is irrelevant. It will be funded ultimately, given the assumption that both the plan and sponsor continue as going entities. This assumption is normally made about the firm.

The third test of SFAC 3, paragraph 29, requires the recognition of a liability when the obligating duty arises. In the case of a pension plan, the

---

[29]FASB (1982). See also Hall and Landsittel (1977), and Lucas and Hollowell (1981) for further advocacies of liability recognition.

sponsor is argued to be obligated once the employee becomes a member of the plan. Membership is the obligating event and the value of an employee's potential vested benefit increases with each year of service during the prevesting period. For any individual employee, this potential to qualify for a vested benefit is uncertain and will be realized only after vesting occurs. However, for a plan as a whole it is possible to make reliable statistical projections of the probable number of current employees who will survive in employment and satisfy vesting requirements. In this manner it is possible to estimate the total value of accumulated benefits during the prevesting period. The procedures for making the computation of unvested accumulated benefits are very similar to those for making statistical estimates of future warranty costs relating to current period sales.

The argument for recognizing unvested accumulated benefits as a liability is that an implied or moral promise exists in the pension contract. It is necessary to look beyond the formal legal contract to determine the substance of the transaction. A pension contract is interpreted as a promise of future benefits, the potential value of which increases with each year of employee service. A sponsor has an implied obligation to meet the cost of accumulated benefits, both vested and unvested. The obligation transcends the explicit contractual liability in the pension plan and this is what makes unvested accumulated benefits both a constructive and an equitable obligation. It is a constructive obligation because retirement benefits have been met in the past, the sponsor has fully funded the pension fund in the past, and therefore it is reasonable to expect the sponsor to continue funding retirement benefits. It is an equitable obligation because employees expect the receipt of a pension benefit as set out in the plan, even though sponsors legally shelter themselves from such an obligation.

Arguments Against Recognition

The constructive or equitable obligation argument rests on the belief that the implied pension promise transcends the legal terms of the contract. The alternative argument questions if a constructive or equitable obligation can exist when plans quite deliberately limit sponsor liability. The concept of unvested accumulated benefits is contrary to the pension contract. Companies purposely limit the benefits of a pension plan by the use of vesting requirements. Liabilities that are specifically excluded from the pension contract cannot be implied or argued morally to exist. The substance of the pension obligation is explicitly stated in the pension plan. It is not necessary to look beyond the contract for the substance of the transaction.

In terms of the SFAC 3 paragraph 29 requirements, a pension plan obligation for pension benefits does not legally exist until vesting requirements are met. The pension plan (or sponsor) is not obligated for pension benefits when an employee joins a plan. The obligating event occurs when the plan's vesting rules are satisfied. Any other interpretation fails to look at the explicit terms of the pension contract.

There is no legally enforceable claim against the employer for unvested accumulated benefits, either by employees or the PBGC. In addition there is no basis for a constructive or equitable obligation because they have been specifically excluded by the explicit terms of the pension contract. In short, the pension contract shelters the sponsor from a legal obligation for unvested accumulated benefits. An implied obligation cannot be argued to exist because the sponsor has taken deliberate steps to legally avoid one.

The fact that actuaries calculate accumulated benefits to facilitate smooth funding of future benefits does not make accumulated benefits an accounting or legal liability of the sponsor. It is extremely important to distinguish actuarial funding concepts from the concept of an accounting liability. Actuarial methods are funding tools and nothing more. The actuarial measurement of unvested accumulated benefits is a concept created solely for the purpose of funding.

Assessment of the Two Arguments

The stronger argument is against recognition. There is not a legally enforceable claim for unvested accumulated benefits. The argument that a constructive or equitable pension obligation exists is strained. It confuses the actuarial funding concept of accumulated benefits with the concept of an accounting liability. Funding of estimated future vested benefits is good cash flow management and is mandatory under ERISA. But existence of such an actuarial calculation does not make accumulated benefits an accounting liability. The FASB's argument that unvested accumulated benefits should be recognized as an accounting liability cannot be defended.

Given that unvested accumulated benefits can materially affect future cash flows, a strong case does exist for continued supplemental disclosure under SFAS 36. But it is hard to see what would be gained by formally recognizing such a dubious (and large) accounting liability in the balance sheet. Many undesirable economic consequences could result from formal balance sheet recognition. These are reviewed in the next section.

ECONOMIC CONSEQUENCES OF RECOGNIZING A PENSION LIABILITY

The FASB favors a radical change in pension accounting for the sponsors of defined benefit pension plans. Recognition of an accounting liability for unfunded, vested accumulated benefits would be significant, as pointed out earlier. A strong case exists for their recognition. Total accumulated benefits would be even larger and could be enormous compared to other accounting liabilities. For example, a recent survey of Fortune 500 companies found that 42% had unfunded accumulated benefits and that the amount averaged 9.4% of sponsors' owners' equity.[30] Because of the significance of such a proposal, we need to consider some of the possible consequences.

One immediate effect would be on sponsors' debt ratios. Restrictive borrowing covenants in bond trust deeds could technically be violated if a large new pension liability were recognized. This problem might be mitigated by a long-term phase-in period, as occurred with lease capitalization under SFAS 13.[31]

An interesting question to pose is whether companies ought to be concerned with how pensions are reported. If there are no cash flow consequences, alternative accounting policies should be of no interest. However, there may be indirect consequences. One consequence of recognizing pension liabilities might be a shift in wealth between stockholders and debt holders. This would occur if debt covenants restrict dividend payments because of debt levels or if they specify the maintenance of certain debt–equity ratios. Increased pension liabilities may therefore cause a loss of income to stockholders, which should cause lower stock prices. This is an agency theory argument.

Another problem might arise from what is called functional fixation. If unvested accumulated benefits are recognized in the balance sheet and classified with other accounting liabilities, they may be interpreted just like other liabilities. Since most accounting liabilities are legally enforceable contracts, this would be an incorrect interpretation. If unvested accumulated benefits are recognized, users may be misled into automatically grouping them with other liabilities. If lenders and investors were to interpret unvested pension liabilities as being like other balance sheet liabilities, sponsors of pension plans could be unfairly penalized in the capital market. The potential for functional fixation might be reduced by a note that clearly explains the nature of pension obligations and how they differ from contractual liabilities. This argument suggests that the market can be "fooled" sometimes by alternative accounting policies.

Given the preceding arguments, it is very possible that companies would be motivated to reduce or remove unvested pension liabilities from the balance sheet. One way this could be done is to cut back on benefit levels. Another way would be to limit future benefit increases. There might even be a movement back to defined contribution plans. This would eliminate the liability question altogether. In the extreme, companies could even terminate their plans. None of these actions is socially desirable. Yet, there is every reason to expect such behavior if an unvested pension liability is recognized. This is clearly a type of negative economic consequence to be avoided in accounting standards, especially in view of the lack of theoretical support for liability recognition.

[30]Johnson and Higgins (1982).
[31]FASB (1976). A four-year grace period was permitted.

Another consequence of recognizing unvested accumulated benefits is the specification of measurement. The FASB has already struggled with this problem in SFAS 35. The most basic problem is simply trying to define what is meant by an accumulated benefit. Each actuarial method makes an arbitrary (and different) assumption about the annual rate of benefit accumulation and measurement. The choice of method must be arbitrary because the whole concept of an accumulated benefit is artificial. It is an actuarial concept created for the sole purpose of spreading the sponsor's funding burden over time. Other measurement problems concern the inclusion or exclusion of projected future salary increases in calculating the value of accumulated benefits, and the interest rate assumption which is used. Use of projected future salaries makes good sense and is illustrated in Appendix 15-A. Actuarial calculations of accumulated benefits are more sensitive to the interest rate assumption than any of the other actuarial assumptions.[32] A recent survey of Fortune 500 companies found that assumptions ranged from 4 to 14%.[33] Such diversity across companies cannot produce reliable or objective measurements. The measurement problems are substantial, quite separate from the definitional problem of what is meant by accumulated benefits.

RELEVANT SUPPLEMENTAL PENSION DISCLOSURES

The major concern of investors should not be about the existence of unfunded, unvested accumulated benefits. They are a doubtful liability because there is no legally enforceable claim. In the event of bankruptcy there would be no claim against the sponsor for unvested benefits. However, the risks and returns of capital suppliers are indirectly affected through the impact of unfunded accumulated benefits on future cash flows. This is the real consequence of a pension plan on the security of debt holders, on future debt-servicing capacity, and on future income to stockholders. Ironically, information about future funding is not part of the present disclosure requirements under SFAS 36.

There are many ways that projected contributions could be calculated. For example, funding could be projected over twenty years assuming a stationary population in which the number of new entrants and withdrawals are constant each year. In addition, alternative funding levels could be disclosed for a range of future salary projections and interest rate assumptions. All of this information is very feasible for actuaries to produce, given developments in computing. The cost of disclosing funding projections should not be very great and the information would also be useful to management.

---

[32]Winklevoss (1977, p. 197).
[33]Johnson and Higgins (1982).

The controversy in pension accounting concerns the recognition of a liability for unvested accumulated benefits. A strong case does not exist for recognizing the liability. Marginal issues which are also material may be best dealt with through supplemental disclosure. While disclosure should not be used to avoid hard issues, it is important to know the limits of financial statements. In the case of pension liabilities, supplemental disclosure seems to be a better way to report the substance of a pension plan and its effect on the future cash flows of the sponsoring company.

SUMMARY

Pension accounting for the sponsors of defined benefit pension plans has been one of the longstanding problems faced by accounting policy makers. The traditional approach has been based on a revenue–expense orientation in which the objective is to accrue yearly pension expense. This leads to the problem of determining how benefits accumulate with the passage of time, and how these benefits should be measured. APB 8 sanctioned flexibility by permitting one of five actuarial methods to be used to measure yearly pension expense. This results in the same kind of arbitrariness as occurs with multiple depreciation and inventory methods.

An alternative approach is to determine if pension plans create an accounting liability for sponsoring companies. The FASB has tentatively concluded that they do, and that accumulated benefits, both vested and unvested, should be recognized. The FASB is also arguing that the accrued benefit funding method (using future salary levels) should be used to measure both accumulated benefits and yearly pension expense. While this approach would achieve rigid uniformity, it is highly questionable if a liability should be recognized for accumulated benefits which have not vested and which are not guaranteed by the PBGC. This proposal does, however, make good sense for estimating the pension plan obligation under SFAS 35. Standardization of the interest rate assumption would also achieve more uniformity in the application of SFAS 35.

Recognizing a doubtful liability does not appear to be the best way to report relevant information about pension plans. What is needed is information about how the sponsorship of pension plans is likely to affect future cash flows. Funding forecasts under alternative assumptions would be more useful than recognizing a pension liability for unfunded, unvested accumulated benefits. Ironically, this type of information is not reported under the disclosure requirements of SFAS 36.

The pension accounting problem also illustrates the limitation of the accounting classification system. While an argument can be made that an accounting liability should be recognized for unfunded accumulated benefits, the fact remains that a pension liability is quite different from other contractual liabilities, and that to add the two together violates the concept of additivity. This problem shows why disclosure is an attractive solution to this type of reporting dilemma. Yet, the existence of disclosure, per se, should not be used as an excuse to avoid addressing the hard question of whether or not an accounting liability exists for unfunded accumulated benefits. To its credit, the FASB is no longer skirting the hard question.

APPENDIX 15-A: MATHEMATICAL DEFINITIONS AND ILLUSTRATIONS OF ACTUARIAL FUNDING METHODS

A simplified presentation of actuarial pension mathematics is made through use of the following example.[34] Assume a pension plan is started with ten employees on their 62nd birthday. No new employees will be admitted to the plan. Employees withdraw from the plan at the beginning of each year, and pension fund contributions are made at the end of each year. Retirement is assumed to occur at the end of age 64 (the equivalent of age 65). Benefits are a lump sum amount equal to final year's salary times 10% per year of service. Pension fund investments earn 5%. Salary projections are $10,000 at age 62; $20,000 at age 63; and $40,000 at age 64. There are no vested benefits prior to retirement.

Of the ten original members of the plan, ten will survive in employment through age 62, eight will survive in employment through age 63, and four will survive in employment through age 64. At age 62, an employee's probability of surviving to retirement is .4. During age 63, the probability of surviving to retirement is .5, and during age 64, the probability is 1.0. The survival probabilities can also be expressed from entry age to current age. At age 62, the probability of surviving through age 62 is 1.0. The probability of surviving from age 62 through age 63 is .8, and the probability of surviving from age 62 through age 64 is .4.

ACCRUED BENEFIT FUNDING METHODS

The principle of actuarial pension funding is to derive a time series of age-based contribution rates. Actuaries refer to these amounts as normal costs. The simplest actuarial method to use is the accrued funding method, without taking future salary increases into consideration. Age-based normal costs and accumulated benefits are defined in Equations 15.1 and 15.2.

[34]For a good presentation of pension mathematics, see Winklevoss (1977).

$$NC_x = B_x - B_{x-1}\phi_x(1+i)^{-(r-x)} \tag{15.1}$$

where

NC_x	= normal cost at age x;
B_x	= estimated retirement benefits based on current salary and current years of service;
B_{x-1}	= estimated retirement benefits at age $x-1$;
ϕ_x	= probability at age x, of surviving in employment to retirement at age r;
$(1+i)^{-(r-x)}$	= discount rate based on remaining years to retirement.

$$AL_x = B_x\,\phi_x(1+i)^{-(r-x)} \tag{15.2}$$

where

AL_x	= actuarially computed accumulated benefits;
B_x	= estimated retirement benefits based on current salary and current years of service;
ϕ_x	= probability at age x of surviving in employment to retirement age r;
$(1+i)^{-(r-x)}$	= discount rate based on remaining years to retirement.

In applying these two formulae, the current age probabilities of surviving to retirement age are .4 at the end of 62, .5 at the end of age 63, and 1.0 at the end of age 64. The age-based amounts are computed from Equations 15.1 and 15.2, then multiplied by the surviving members each year to derive total pension plan contribution. Plan totals are summarized as shown in Exhibit 15-2.

EXHIBIT 15-2.
Accrued Benefit Method (Using Current Period Salaries)

	Normal Costs	Accumulated Benefits
Age 62	$ 3,628	$ 3,628
Age 63	$11,429	$15,238
Age 64	$32,000	$48,000

EXHIBIT 15-3.
Accrued Benefit Method (Using Projected Salaries)

	Normal Costs	Accumulated Benefits
Age 63	$14,512	$14,512
Age 64	$15,238	$30,476
Age 65	$16,000	$48,000

The FASB is in favor of using salary projections in conjunction with the accrued benefit funding method. In other words, a projected retirement salary of $40,000 is used in Equations 15.1 and 15.2 instead of current salary. This modification of the accrued benefit method results in a different time series of normal costs and actuarial liabilities and is summarized in Exhibit 15-3.

PROJECTED BENEFIT FUNDING METHODS

Pension mathematics are more complicated with projected benefit funding methods. There are two main versions, one in which a survivor-adjusted level annuity per year is calculated, and the other in which contribution levels are calculated as a constant percentage of survivor-adjusted salaries. The level annuity method is illustrated. First it is necessary to define what is called the present value of projected retirement benefits. This is calculated at each age, and is defined as:

$$PVRB_x = B_r \phi_x (1+i)^{-(r-x)} \tag{15.3}$$

where

$PVRB_x$	= present value of projected retirement benefits, age x, based on projected retirement salary and years of service, adjusted by survival probability;
B_r	= estimated retirement benefit based on projected retirement salary and years of service at age r;
ϕ_x	= age-based probability of surviving in employment to age r;
$(1+i)^{-(r-x)}$	= discount rate based on remaining years to retirement.

The function defined in Equation 15.3 is then used to calculate the time series of normal costs and accumulated benefits. These are defined in Equations 15.4 and 15.5, respectively.

$$NC_x = \frac{(PVRB)_y}{a_{\overline{y:r-y}|}} \qquad\qquad (15.4)$$

where

NC_x = normal cost at age x;

$(PVRB)_y$ = PVRB function at entry age y;

$a_{\overline{y:r-y}|}$ = annuity factor representing summation of yearly survival probabilities from entry age y to retirement age r.

$$AL_x = \frac{a_{\overline{y:x-y}|}}{a_{\overline{y:r-y}|}} \times (PVRB)_x \qquad\qquad (15.5)$$

where

AL_x = actuarially computed accumulated benefits;

$a_{\overline{y:x-y}|}$ = annuity factor representing summation of yearly survival probabilities from entry age y, to current age x;

$a_{\overline{y:r-y}|}$ = same as in Equation (15.4);

$(PVRB)_x$ = PVRB function at current age x.

The annuity factors in Equations 15.4 and 15.5, $a_{\overline{y:r-y}|}$ and $a_{\overline{y:x-y}|}$, are necessary in order to determine an age-based level annuity. At age 62, the annuity factor, $a_{\overline{y:r-y}|}$, represents the present value of the survival probabilities from entry age through age 62, age 63, and age 64. These survival probabilities are 1.0, .8, and .4, respectively for ages 62, 63, and 64. To derive present values, the age 64 probability is discounted for two periods, the age 63 probability is discounted for one period, and the age 62 probability is considered to be at present value. This results in a value of 2.125 for the annuity factor, $a_{\overline{y:r-y}|}$.

The value of the annuity factor, $a_{\overline{y:x-y}|}$, is different at ages 62, 63, and 64. At age 62, it represents the present value of the survival probability through age 62, or 1.0. At age 63, it represents the probability of surviving through age 62, plus the probability of surviving through age 63 discounted to present value at age 62. This results in 1.0 plus .8 times $(1.05)^{-1}$, or 1.762. At age 64, the value is the same as the annuity, $a_{\overline{y:r-y}|}$, or 2.125.

As with accrued benefit methods, the age-based calculations must be multiplied by the number of employees at that age, in order to determine the total pension plan contribution. Normal costs and accumulated benefits are summarized in Exhibit 15-4.

To verify that a survivor-adjusted level of annuity has been calculated, divide each of the yearly normal costs by the number of yearly survivors. This results in a level funding of $2049 per surviving employee per year.

Normal costs and accumulated benefits are significantly different under the three actuarial funding methods illustrated above. One way of summarizing these differences is to calculate the cumulative percentage of re-

EXHIBIT 15-4.
Projected Benefit Method (Level Annuity)

	Normal Costs	Accumulated Benefits
Age 62	$20,491	$20,491
Age 63	$16,393	$37,908
Age 64	$ 8,196	$48,000

EXHIBIT 15-5.
Cumulative Percentage of Normal Costs Recognized Through Each Period

	Accrued Benefit (Current Salary)	Accrued Benefit (Future Salary)	Projected Benefit
Age 62	8.3%	33.3%	47.1%
Age 63	33.3%	66.7%	82.9%
Age 64	100.0%	100.0%	100.0%

tirement benefits that have been funded at each age. This is defined as the ratio of $AL_x/PVRB_x$. These results are summarized in Exhibit 15-5.

The allocation of pension cost is quite different under each approach and it is easy to see that material differences in yearly pension expense could occur. While this example is a simplification of pension plan funding calculations, it shows the basic procedure and illustrates the wide variation possible under alternative actuarial funding methods. There is a lack of uniformity under APB 8 because choice is permitted in the use of actuarial methods. The FASB is proposing to solve the uniformity problem by mandating use of the accrued benefit method (with future salary increases). Funding decisions would of course continue to be based on any acceptable actuarial method.

QUESTIONS

1. What do the following terms mean: accumulated benefits, actuarial liability, vested benefits, normal cost, unfunded accumulated benefits, and unfunded actuarial liability? How are they measured?

2. Why is a pension plan a mutually unperformed executory contract? What are the implications, at least in terms of traditional accounting practices?
3. Why is there a potential accounting problem with defined benefit pension plans, but not with defined contribution plans?
4. Explain how current pension accounting standards are based on a revenue–expense approach to the financial statements.
5. Why did APB 8 only minimally improve uniformity between companies?
6. Why does the revenue–expense approach to pension accounting lead to a theoretical impasse?
7. Why is there a uniformity problem with present pension accounting standards, but not under an asset–liability approach or a cash basis of pension accounting?
8. How has ERISA affected the pension accounting problem?
9. What are the difficulties in defining pension liabilities? Why is the accounting classification system very limiting in the case of pensions?
10. Evaluate the arguments for and against the recognition of unfunded accumulated benefits as accounting liabilities. Can you add any of your own?
11. Given the evidence on information efficiency in the securities market, does it matter whether pension information is disclosed in the formal financial statements or as supplemental disclosure?
12. What economic consequences of recognizing a pension liability were suggested in the chapter?
13. Why is information about unfunded, unvested accumulated benefits less relevant than funding projections?
14. What are the main problems in defining and measuring accumulated benefits, holding aside the question of whether recognition should occur at all?
15. Is the FASB's argument favoring recognition of a pension liability for accumulated benefits consistent with the conceptual framework project?

CASES AND PROBLEMS

1. Verify the calculations of normal costs and accumulated benefits in Appendix 15-A. What is the relationship between accumulated benefits and the pension fund?

    Suppose that a plan was introduced in the second year when 8 of the original 10 employees remained, and that one year of past service credit was granted. Calculate the required supplemental contribution needed at the beginning of the second year to make up the deficiency if the original normal costs (as calculated in Appendix 15-A) are used to fund in years 2 and 3. Why is your answer dependent on the actuarial method used for funding? Using the projected benefit method, calculate a new time series of normal costs that will fully fund retirement benefits over the remaining two periods.

2. Assume the following facts concerning a new pension plan: (1) the plan starts with ten employees on their 60th birthday; (2) benefits do not vest until retirement at the end of age 64; (3) no past service credit is granted; (4) funding occurs at the end of each year and investments earn 5%; (5) turnover occurs at the beginning of each year; (6) ten employees survive in service through age 60, eight through age 61, six through age 62, five through age 63, and four through age 64; (7) no new employees enter the plan; (8) at age 60, salaries are $26,000 and increase by $1,000 per year. Benefits accumulate at 10% of final salary per year of service.

   Required:
   (a) Using the actuarial funding method specified by your instructor, prepare the five-year time series of normal costs and accumulated benefits.
   (b) Prove that normal costs compound to the required pension fund balance.

3. Refer to Appendix 15-A. Assume Company A follows the accrued benefit funding schedule in Exhibit 15-2 while Company B funds the entire obligation at retirement date (terminal funding). Assume Company B elects to use the same actuarial method as Company A for the purpose of yearly pension expense accrual. Make the accounting entries required for both companies under APB 8, and explain why they are different between two companies.

4. Presented below is the balance sheet and pension-related disclosures of International Harvester Company for 1981, in $000.

Current Assets	$2,672,003
Total Assets	$5,346,122
Current Liabilities	$1,808,152
Noncurrent Liabilities	$2,056,309
Preferred Stock	$ 196,667
Stockholders' Equity	$1,284,994
Total Liabilities and Stockholders' Equity	$5,346,122

The actuarial present value of accumulated plan benefits and plan net assets for the Company's defined benefit plans at January 1, 1981, are presented below, in thousands of dollars:

Actuarial present value of accumulated plan benefits:	
Vested	$2,481,279
Nonvested	267,554
Total	$2,748,833
Net assets available for benefits	$1,345,740

The weighted average assumed rate of return used in determining the actuarial present value of accumulated plan benefits was 7% for 1981.

Calculate the impact of recognizing unfunded vested benefits and unfunded accumulated benefits in the balance sheet, and the effect on balance sheet ratios. Why might you be motivated to reduce such an accounting liability—if you were the manager of a company? What means would be available to accomplish this?

BIBLIOGRAPHY OF REFERENCED WORKS

Accounting Principles Board (1966). "Accounting for the Cost of Pension Plans," *APB Opinion No. 8* (AICPA).

American Institute of Certified Public Accountants (1981). "Illustrations and Analysis of Disclosure of Pension Information," *Financial Report Survey No. 22* (AICPA).

Beidleman, Carl R. (1973). "Income Smoothing: The Role of Management," *The Accounting Review* (October 1973), pp. 653–667.

Committee on Accounting Procedure (1948). "Pension Plans—Accounting for Annuity Costs Based on Past Services," *ARB No. 36* (AICPA).

—— (1956). "Accounting for the Cost of Pension Plans," *ARB No. 47* (AICPA).

Davis, Harry, and Arnold Strasser (1970). "Private Pension Plans 1960 to 1969—An Overview," *Monthly Labor Review* (July 1970), pp. 45–56.

Financial Accounting Standards Board (1974). "Accounting for the Cost of Pension Plans Subject to the Employee Retirement Income Security Act of 1974," *FASB Interpretation No. 3* (FASB).

—— (1975). "Accounting for Contingencies," *Statement of Financial Accounting Standards No. 5* (FASB).

—— (1976). "Accounting for Leases," *Statement of Financial Accounting Standards No. 13* (FASB).

—— (1980a). "Accounting and Reporting by Defined Benefit Pension Plans," *Statement of Financial Accounting Standards No. 35* (FASB).

—— (1980b). "Disclosure of Pension Information," *Statement of Financial Accounting Standards No. 36* (FASB).

—— (1980c). "Elements of Financial Statements of Business Enterprises," *Statement of Financial Accounting Concepts No. 3* (FASB).

—— (1981). *FASB Discussion Memorandum: An Analysis of Issues Related to Employers' Accounting for Pensions and Other Postemployment Benefits* (FASB).

—— (1982). *Preliminary Views of the Financial Accounting Standards Board on Major Issues Related to Employers' Accounting for Pensions and Other Postemployment Benefits* (FASB).

Francis, Jere R. (1982). "An Analysis of Pension Cost Accruals by Actuarial Methodology." (Ph.D. diss., University of New England).

—— (1983). "FASB's Preliminary Views on Pension Accounting," *The CPA Journal* (May 1983), pp. 44–52.

Hall, William D., and David L. Landsittel (1977). *A New Look at Accounting for Pension Costs* (Richard D. Irwin).

Hicks, Ernest L. (1965). "Accounting for the Cost of Pension Plans," *Accounting Research Study No. 8* (AICPA).

Johnson and Higgins (1982). *Funding Costs and Liabilities of Large Corporate Pension Plans—1982 Executive Report* (Johnson and Higgins).

Lucas, Timothy S., and Betsy Ann Hollowell (1981). "Pension Accounting: The Liability Question," *Journal of Accountancy* (October 1981), pp. 57–66.

McGill, Dan M. (1979). *Fundamentals of Private Pensions*, 4th Ed. (Richard D. Irwin).

Schipper, Katherine, and Roman L. Weil (1982). "Alternative Accounting Treatments for Pensions," *The Accounting Review* (October 1982), pp. 806–824.

Stone, Mary S. (1982). "A Survey of Research on the Effects of Corporate Pension Plan Sponsorship: Implications for Accounting," *Journal of Accounting Literature* (Spring 1982), pp. 1–32.

Winklevoss, Howard E. (1977). *Pension Mathematics with Numerical Illustrations* (Richard D. Irwin).

ADDITIONAL READINGS

Accountants International Study Group (1977). *Accounting for Pension Costs* (AIS Group).

Baker, Roy E. (1964). "The Pension Cost Problem," *The Accounting Review* (January 1964), pp. 52–61.

Basset, Preston C. (1964). "Accounting for Pension-Plan Costs on Corporate Financial Statements," *Transactions of the Society of Actuaries*, Vol. 16, pp. 318–334.

Coutts, W. B., and R. B. Dale-Harris (1963). *Accounting for Costs of Pension Plans* (Canadian Institute of Chartered Accountants).

Danker, Harold; Michael P. Glinsky; John H. Grady; Murray B. Hirsch; and Richard M. Steinberg (1981). *Employer Accounting for Pension Costs and Other Post-Retirement Benefits* (Financial Executives Research Foundation).

Dewhirst, John F. (1971). "A Conceptual Approach to Pension Accounting," *The Accounting Review* (April 1971), pp. 365–373.

Dreher, William (1967). "Alternatives Available Under APB Opinion No. 8; An Actuary's View," *Journal of Accountancy* (March 1967), pp. 37–51.

Drebin, Allan R. (1963). "Recognizing Implicit Interest in Non-funded Pension Plans," *The Accounting Review* (July 1963), pp. 579–583.

Financial Accounting Standards Board (1975). *FASB Discussion Memorandum: An Analysis of Issues Related to Accounting and Reporting for Employee Benefit Plans* (FASB).

——— (1983). *FASB Discussion Memorandum: An Analysis of Additional Issues Related to Employers' Accounting for Pensions and Other Postemployment Benefits* (FASB).

Goodman, Hortense; Frank C. Munn; Anthony Phillips; and Miklos Vasarhelyi (1981). "Illustrations and Analysis of Disclosures of Pension Information," *Financial Report Survey 22* (AICPA).

Hennessey, Vincent L. (1978). "Accounting for Pension Liabilities Created by ERISA," *Journal of Accounting, Auditing and Finance* (Summer 1978), pp. 317–330.

Howitt, Gordon (1968). "Accounting for Pension Plans," *The Australian Accountant* (February 1968), pp. 77–88.

Ijiri, Yuji (1980). *Recognition of Contractual Rights and Obligations: An Exploratory Study of Conceptual Issues* (FASB).

Jenkins, David O. (1964). "Accounting for Funded Industrial Pension Plans," *The Accounting Review* (July 1964), pp. 648–653.

Leo, Mario; Preston C. Basset; and Ernest S. Kachline (1975). *Financial Aspects of Private Pension Plans* (Financial Executives Research Foundation).

Moonitz, Maurice, and Alexander Russ (1966). "Accrual Accounting for Employers' Pension Costs," *Journal of Accounting Research* (Autumn 1966), pp. 155–168.

Nurnberg, Hugo (1974). "Some of the Essential Provisions of Opinion No. 8," *The Accounting Review* (January 1974), pp. 165–176.

Parrott, William H. (1969). "The Allocation of Pension Costs to Periods of Time," *Management Accounting* (April 1969), pp. 39–42.

Philips, G. Edward (1968). "Pension Liabilities and Assets," *The Accounting Review* (January 1968), pp. 10–17.

Phoenix, Julius W., and William D. Bosse (1968). "A Discussion of the Background and Requirements of APB Opinion No. 8," *Accounting Interpretations of APB Opinion No. 8* (AICPA).

Skinner, Ross M. (1980). *Pension Accounting* (Clarkson Gordon Chartered Accountants).

Smith, Jack L. (1977). "Actuarial Cost Methods—Basics for CPA's," *Journal of Accountancy* (February 1977), pp. 62–66.

CHAPTER 16

Leases

Leases have been the subject of more accounting standards than any other single topic. The Committee on Accounting Procedure issued one standard, the Accounting Principles Board (APB) issued five standards, and the Financial Accounting Standards Board (FASB) issued eight. Attention given to leases in accounting standards reflects the increased use of leasing in the business community and the need to clarify and standardize the accounting for this complex transaction. The first lease accounting standard, Accounting Research Bulletin (ARB) 38, was issued in 1949.[1] However, it was only in the 1960s and 1970s that accounting policy makers responded to the lease problem.

Leasing has grown in popularity for a number of operating and financial reasons. From an operating viewpoint, some assets are available only under lease. Others are too expensive for outright purchase. Two significant financing aspects are the taxation advantages (there is full deductibility of lease payments) and the possibility of "off-balance-sheet" financing. This latter occurs when leased assets and lease obligations are not reported in the financial statements. Off-balance-sheet financing results in better debt ratios and higher accounting rates of return than a purchase alternative could produce.

[1]Committee on Accounting Procedure (1949).

The accounting controversy about leases has been concerned with distinguishing the economic substance of leases from their legal form. Prior to ARB 38, the accounting procedure for lease payments was to record them as periodic revenues for lessors and as expenses for lessees. Increasingly, however, some leases came to be viewed as the equivalent of purchases with debt financing. This view now dominates, and the focus of accounting standards has been on defining those situations in which a lease is considered to be a purchase equivalent and in making such leases look like a purchase with debt financing. These types of leases are called **capital leases** and the accounting procedure is called **capitalization.** Noncapitalized leases are called **operating leases** and the lease payments are treated as periodic expenses.

From a lessor's viewpoint, capital leases may be one of two types, sales or financing. A sales-type lease arises when a manufacturer or seller of merchandise uses leasing as a financing instrument to effect what is considered to be the equivalent of a sale. In these situations the accounting standards have first been concerned with defining the criteria for sales recognition, and then making the transaction look like the equivalent of a sale with vendor financing. A financing-type lease occurs when a third party finances a lease rather than a manufacturer or seller. In such situations, the financing party is the lessor and the accounting attempts to make the lease look like a loan with income realized through implicit interest in each lease payment. If a lease is not capitalized by a lessor, the payments are recognized as revenues when received.

The chapter begins with an examination of lease contracts and the capitalization argument. Then the evolution of finite uniformity in lease accounting standards is reviewed, including capitalization criteria and measurement rules. For both lessees and lessors the accounting problem is one of distinguishing between operating and capital leases. Separate accounting rules have been developed for the two types. This approach is defended on the grounds of representational faithfulness, in which a lease is interpreted to be either a simple rental agreement or a more complex capital lease. Finally, the chapter concludes with consideration of the economic consequences of lease accounting standards.

THE LEASE CONTRACT

A **lease** is a legal document conveying use of property for a fixed period of time in exchange for rent or other compensation. From a legal viewpoint, a lease is both a conveyance and a contract, with the contractual element dominating.[2] It is a conveyance because the lessee acquires an interest in

[2]Hawkins and Wehle (1973, p. 51).

EXHIBIT 16-1.

Characteristics of a True Lease

The following factors are considered to be indications that a lease agreement is without doubt a true lease:

1. The absence of a provision for the transfer of the title to the lessee.
2. The absence of any mention of interest as a factor in rental charges.
3. Rental charges that are competitive with those charged by other lessors of similar equipment.
4. Rental charges that are reasonably related to the loss of value due to the lessee's use of the equipment or that are based on production or use and not necessarily related to purchase price.
5. The assumption of the risk of loss by the lessor.
6. The lessor is required to bear the cost of insurance, maintenance and taxes.
7. The lessor retains the right to inspect the equipment during the term of the lease.
8. If the lessee has an option to purchase:
   (a) The option price approximates the predicted fair market value of the equipment at the time the option may be exercised.
   (b) Rentals are not applied to the option price.
9. The rentals charged under leasing plans without an option to purchase approximate the rental charged under plans with such an option.
10. Government agencies recognize the lessor as the owner of the leased asset.
11. The lessee considers by his action that he is a lessee and not a purchaser.

Source: Hawkins and Wehle (1973, pp. 52–53).

property for a fixed period of time. It is a contract because the lessor promises the lessee *quiet enjoyment* of the property during the lease term in exchange for the promise of periodic payments. While it is not possible to define unambiguously a **true lease** in law, Exhibit 16-1 contains a listing of what are regarded as indicators of a true lease. Material variations from the characteristics listed in Exhibit 16-1 may result in a lease being regarded as a conditional sale agreement or a debt instrument rather than a true lease. Capitalization criteria in accounting standards have been concerned with many of these characteristics.

THE EXECUTORY NATURE OF LEASE CONTRACTS

The legal form of a lease contract is an executory (unperformed) contract. A lessor (legal owner) transfers possession of a leased asset to a lessee for a fixed period of time in exchange for a series of rents. A lessee's performance is executory because future rents are due one period at a time. However, the performance question can be argued both ways with respect to the lessor. The distinction is important because it determines whether the contract is mutually unperformed or unilaterally unperformed. As indicated in Chapter 8, mutually unperformed executory contracts have traditionally been excluded from the balance sheet.

It can be argued that a lease contract is fully executed by a lessor when possession of the leased asset is transferred to a lessee. This would make a lease contract unilaterally unperformed by the lessee. Such contracts are recognized in the balance sheet. Possession of a leased asset can be argued to give rise to both an obligation and asset by the lessee. Statement of Financial Accounting Concepts (SFAC) 3 defines assets as probable future economic benefits, and liabilities as probable future sacrifices of economic benefits, both arising from past transactions.[3] A fixed-term lease contract grants property use rights, which may create future economic benefits even though property ownership does not exist. In the same manner, a lease contract also obligates the lessee to make future payments.

If a lease is interpreted as a mutually unperformed executory contract, it can be argued that an asset and liability do not exist for the lessee. In such a situation the lease contract would be interpreted as the lessor permitting use for each period at a time only if the rentals are paid by the lessee. This would simply result in expensing current period lease payments. Mutually unperformed future promises would be excluded from the balance sheet on the grounds that these are future transactions that have not yet occurred.

Legal remedies available to lessors in the event of lessee default treat leases like mutually unperformed executory contracts. A lessee is not liable for future lease payments in the event of default. A lessor must first mitigate the loss of rents by selling the asset or leasing it again. The lessee has a legal obligation to the lessor only for any residual losses after the lessor mitigates the loss. This makes leases significantly different from other debt agreements—for example, corporate bonds in which the borrower is obliged for the full amount of unpaid principal plus any accrued interest in the event of default.

Importance of the executory aspect of lease contracts is evidenced in the second lease accounting standard, APB 5.[4] The fundamental assumption underlying lease capitalization was noncancellability of the lease contract. Existence of noncancellability clauses could be argued to supersede the executory nature of lease contracts. If the promises under a lease contract are noncancellable, the executory nature still exists, but it has been mitigated to some extent; and additional legal rights have been created for both lessee and lessor in the event of nonperformance by the other party.

While the executory nature of lease contracts is an important legal characteristic, its importance has been supplanted by an overriding concern with the economic substance of lease contracts. This basic approach is the one taken by policy makers since the first lease accounting standard in 1949. ARB 38 recommended that where it was obvious a lease contract was

[3]FASB (1980a).
[4]APB (1964).

in substance a purchase, both an asset and obligation should be recognized in the lessee's balance sheet. This general theme has continued in subsequent lease accounting standards.

LEASES COMPARED WITH PURCHASE ARRANGEMENTS

There are legal differences between true leases and purchase arrangements.[5] Purchase arrangements are outright cash sale, credit sale, installment sale, secured credit sale, and a conditional sale agreement. Title passes to the user of the property in all instances except leases and conditional sales. So a lease and conditional sale are very similar in this respect. Title passes in a conditional sale when final payment is made but this does not necessarily occur with a lease. Leases in which the title passes at the end of the lease term or in which a bargain purchase option exists are virtually the same as conditional sales, with respect to legal ownership. Also, leases that are for substantially all of a leased asset's economic life are virtually identical with conditional sales agreements calling for installment payments over the economic life of the asset.

In the event of bankruptcy or default, credit sales and installment sales are identical. With both credit and installment sales the seller is simply a general creditor of the buyer. A secured credit sale gives the seller a preferred claim or lien on the asset, and a general creditor status for any amount of the obligation not covered by the value of the asset. In bankruptcy or default, the seller under a conditional sales agreement has a legal right to recover the property because title has not passed. In addition, the seller has a general creditor status for any difference between the unpaid obligation and asset value. A lessor's claim is limited to provable damages (loss of lease payments), but the lessor must first mitigate these losses either through sale or a new lease of the repossessed property. In this latter way a lease differs from a conditional sales agreement.

Some leases are very similar to a conditional sales agreement, at least in a legal sense. This is particularly true if a lease (1) transfers title at the end of the lease term, or (2) permits a bargain purchase option, or (3) is for a term that represents substantially all of the asset's useful economic life. For leases that resemble conditional sales agreements, a strong argument for capitalization can be made. Of course many of these leases would not be considered to be true leases in the eyes of the law. Even in law, however, the distinction is not always clear between a true lease and a sale. For example, both the Internal Revenue Service and the courts deal with disputes about the two. Some lease contracts are interpreted as conditional sales agreements, and vice versa.

Capitalization of leases that are virtually conditional sales agreements would be consistent with the true legal nature of the transaction rather than

[5]Cook (1963) and Zises (1973).

with the superficial appearance of a lease. Capitalization would be nothing more than treating disguised conditional sales in a manner consistent with other conditional sales.

LEASE CAPITALIZATION

From a lessee's viewpoint, a lease must be accounted for as either (1) a rental agreement or (2) a purchase equivalent with debt financing. For a lessor, the transaction must be treated as either (1) a rental agreement or (2a) a sale equivalent with debt financing (if it is a sales-type lease) or (2b) a loan equivalent (if it is a financing-type lease). Choice (1) for both lessee and lessor interprets the lease contract as an operating lease and recognizes the mutually unperformed executory nature of lease contracts. Choice (2) treats the lease as a capital lease and recognizes the conveyance and financing aspects of leases. The simplicity of the basic accounting classification system forces a lease to be accounted for in one of these two ways.

The accounting policy task has been described in the following manner:

> At one extreme, there is the case of two physically identical items of equipment used by a business, one financed or partly financed by borrowing, and the other financed by a lease that is noncancelable for a period equal to the equipment's useful life. Most every informed person would agree that it doesn't make much sense to report one of these items on the balance sheet and omit the other. At the other end there are ephemeral leases . . . which most everyone agrees should not give rise to a balance sheet item. The problem is to state a principle that will provide a conceptually sound and practical way of drawing a line somewhere between the two extremes.[6]

The heart of the policy problem is classification into operating and capital leases. It represents a classic example of finite uniformity and the attempt to account representationally for the real substance of the lease transaction rather than its superficial legal form.

One of the major arguments made against lease capitalization is a concern for measurement reliability. Specifically, there has been some belief that the use of present-value discounting techniques introduces less reliable accounting numbers into the financial statements. This concern is exaggerated, however, because present-value calculations are only used to make lease financing look like the equivalent of a loan with an equal repayment schedule. The present-value technique as applied to lease accounting is illustrated later in the chapter and it will be seen that only one measure-

---

[6]Anthony (1962).

ment reliability problem exists: the choice of interest rate used to discount the lease payments. There is some inevitable subjectivity in determining a lessee's rate, but it is certainly capable of close approximation. For a lessor, there is no subjectivity because the interest rate implicit in the lease is used. Measurement reliability is not considered to be a major issue with lease accounting today.

CAPITALIZATION FOR LESSEES

Numerous criteria have been proposed to support lease capitalization. A very good survey is found in the FASB's discussion memorandum on leases and is summarized in Exhibit 16-2.[7] In general terms the arguments for lease capitalization invoke the reasoning that certain leases are, in substance, purchases with debt financing. A lease is simply another type of legal instrument to accomplish this end. Different arguments and criteria have been used to define purchase equivalents, but the differences really are little more than alternative points where the line is drawn between operating and capital leases. The many viewpoints can be simplified into three broad approaches: legal, material equity, and substantial transfer of ownership benefits and risks. These represent increasingly broader interpretations of capital leases.

EXHIBIT 16-2.
Lease Capitalization Criteria

---

1. Lessee builds up a material equity in the leased property.
2. Leased property is special purpose to the lessee.
3. Lease term is substantially equal to the estimated useful life of the property.
4. Lessee pays costs normally incident to ownership.
5. Lessee guarantees the lessor's debt with respect to the leased property.
6. Lessee treats the lease as a purchase for tax purposes.
7. Lease is between related parties.
8. Lease passes usual risks and rewards to lessee.
9. Lessee assumes an unconditional liability for lease rentals.
10. Lessor lacks independent economic substance.
11. Residual value at end of lease is expected to be nominal.
12. Lease agreement provides for lessor's recovery of investment plus a fair return.
13. Lessee has the option at any time to purchase the asset for the lessor's unrecovered investment.
14. Lease agreement is noncancellable for a long term.

---

[7]FASB (1974, pp. 40–41).

Legal Approach

One way to resolve the lease classification problem is to treat true leases as described in Exhibit 16-1 as operating leases, and to capitalize leases that are not true leases. This approach to lease capitalization resolves the problem by resorting to legal definitions and concepts. However, such an approach does not address the more fundamental question of whether true leases should be capitalized. It has been argued that all noncancellable leases create legal property rights and obligations that should be in a lessee's balance sheet, even if they do arise from a lease contract.[8] It was also pointed out in Chapter 8 that legal definitions have not proved especially helpful in developing accounting theory or formulating policy.

Material Equity

Historically, the argument for lease capitalization has relied on the concept of **material equity.** This means that the terms of the lease are such that the lessee is clearly paying for more than the current-period rental value of the asset. In other words, the lessee is acquiring an implicit equity in the leased asset through the periodic lease payments. Such a situation would be evidenced by rental payments in excess of yearly economic value or a bargain purchase option. The excess represents payment for the implicit property rights created by the lease. Noncancellability and a lease term for a significant portion of the asset's economic life are attributes of a lease contract that would support the material equity argument. Material equity, as applied in accounting standards, limited capitalization to a small number of leases that were virtually conditional sales agreements with installment payments. As a result, there was very little difference between the legal and material equity approaches.

Transfer of the Benefits and Risks of Ownership

Statement of Financial Accounting Standards (SFAS) 13 took a broader approach to the capitalization argument. Leases that substantially transfer "...all of the benefits and risks incident to the ownership of property should be accounted for as the acquisition of an asset and the incurrence of an obligation by the lessee and as a sale or financing by the lessor."[9] The current definition has dropped noncancellability as a prerequisite for capitalization and de-emphasized the concept of material equity. In spite of the attempt in SFAS 13 to disassociate the standard from earlier standards, the essence of the capitalization argument remains the same as it has been since ARB 38—that a purchase equivalent has occurred. The difficulty of course has been in agreeing on when this occurs. The material equity concept has simply been superseded by a somewhat broader concept and set of tests.

[8]This view is attributed to Myers (1962).
[9]FASB (1976, para. 60).

CAPITALIZATION FOR LESSORS

A basic issue with lessor capitalization is symmetry with lessee accounting. Symmetry means consistent accounting by lessees and lessors for capital and operating leases. There have been arguments both ways. Some feel that symmetry, per se, is not necessary.[10] Others believe that the basic characteristic of a capital lease should be consistently recorded by both lessor and lessee.[11] The absence of symmetry suggests that the basic classification of leases as operating and capital is not being properly done. Accounting standards have moved toward symmetry.

For sales-type leases, the same set of criteria applicable to lessees has been proposed for capitalization. The reason is that if a sales-type lease is a purchase equivalent to the lessee, it must be a sale equivalent to the lessor. However, additional criteria must also exist before a sale is recognized. These criteria have pertained to the usual assumptions underlying revenue recognition, mainly the certainty of cash collection and the absence of uncertainties regarding unincurred costs relating to the sale.

Financing-type leases present a different situation. The capitalization analogy treats such leases as the equivalent of debt financing. There is no sale revenue with financing-type leases, only interest revenue earned from the debt equivalent. Arguments for capitalization of finance-type leases have related more to the debt characteristic of the lease than to the sale characteristic. The main criterion proposed is the concept of *full payout*.[12] This refers to a set of lease payments that returns a lessor's investment in the leased asset plus a reasonable interest on the investment.

EVOLUTION OF LEASE ACCOUNTING STANDARDS

A number of accounting standards have been issued since 1949. These are reviewed chronologically, first as they relate to lessees, and then as they affect lessors.

LESSEE ACCOUNTING

ARB 38

The first lease accounting standard was ARB 38 issued in 1949. It was subsequently codified as Chapter 14 of ARB 43.[13] Capitalization was rec-

---

[10]Hawkins (1970).
[11]Alvin (1970).
[12]FASB (1974, pp. 95–97).
[13]Committee on Accounting Procedure (1953, Chapter 14).

ommended for certain leases which were, in substance, installment purchases. Although the standard referred specifically to the installment purchase analogy, it was more applicable to leases that were de facto conditional sales agreements. The capitalization criteria were any of the following: (1) the existence of a bargain purchase option at the termination of the lease; (2) covenants that permitted the application of lease rentals to the purchase price, or (3) rental payments so high that a purchase plan was evident. The first criterion deals with lease terms that make a lease almost indistinguishable from a conditional sale. The second and third criteria refer to the material equity argument, and could be analagous to either an installment sale or conditional sale, though in legal terms the resemblance is closer to a conditional sale. No details were given in the standard concerning the measurement of either the leased asset or lease obligation.

APB 5

The next accounting standard was APB 5 issued in 1964. As part of the two-pronged approach by the Accounting Principles Board, a research study was commissioned on leases. This resulted in Accounting Research Study (ARS) 4 issued in 1962.[14] ARS 4 took a legalistic perspective in determining whether or not a lease was in substance a purchase. Specifically, the main concern was over the creation of legal property rights. It was argued in ARS 4 that noncancellability of the lease contract creates legal property rights warranting capitalization. APB 5 did not accept the basic argument in ARS 4 and reaffirmed the material equity argument of ARB 38. However, noncancellability, except upon the occurrence of some remote contingency, was introduced as a precondition for capitalization. As suggested earlier in the chapter, this condition could be argued to mitigate the executory nature of lease contracts.

Criteria for capitalization were also modified, though the stated objective was to clarify ARB 43, chapter 14, not change it. The intent was that any lease creating a material equity interest should be capitalized. Either of two primary criteria were listed: (1) a renewal option covering the useful economic life, or (2) existence of a bargain purchase option. Some secondary indicators were also identified: (1) the property was specially acquired by the lessor to meet the needs of the lessee, (2) the lease term corresponded to the useful life, (3) the lessee incurred executory costs (insurance, taxes, and maintenance), (4) the lessee guaranteed any lessor obligation with respect to the leased asset, or (5) the lessee treated the lease as a purchase under tax law. Apparently these secondary criteria were ignored in practice because of the manner in which the standard was worded. As a result, APB 5 caused little change in the number of leases capitalized, even though the opposite effect was intended.[15]

---

[14]Myers (1962).

[15]FASB (1974, pp. 159–160) indicates that there was only a modest increase in the number of leases capitalized after APB 5 was issued, and that most of the increase was due to a new type of lease related to Industrial Development Bonds which met the capitalization criteria.

APB 10

APB 10 was an omnibus opinion issued in 1966.[16] One paragraph dealt with leases and required the consolidation of certain subsidiaries that were principally engaged in leasing assets to parent companies. This standard was partially an amendment of APB 5, paragraph 12, and was concerned with lease contracts between related entities such as parent and subsidiary companies. APB 10 required that subsidiaries engaged in sales-type leases to the parent company must be consolidated. In this way it was not possible to avoid the reporting of leased assets by having unconsolidated subsidiaries write lease contracts. However, the consolidation of subsidiaries engaged in financing-type leases was left unresolved. As a result of APBs 5 and 10, financing-type leases could be treated differently by the lessee, depending on whether the lessor was a subsidiary or an independent entity. Some leases were capitalized and some were not. The Securities and Exchange Commission (SEC) attempted to resolve this inconsistency with Accounting Series Release (ASR) 132, issued in 1972.[17]

APB 31

The next accounting standard for lessees was APB 31, issued in 1973.[18] This standard expanded disclosure of noncapitalized leases. APB 5 had been criticized on the grounds that it excluded many leases which should be capitalized. The disclosures of APB 31 included the amounts of future rentals at both future values and present values. The effect of this disclosure requirement was to create adequate supplemental disclosure to permit users to informally capitalize noncapitalized lease obligations if they desired to do so. While this disclosure expanded the reporting of information concerning noncapitalized lease obligations, it did not go so far as to formally place them in the balance sheet.

The SEC pressured the newly formed FASB to review lease accounting. Shortly after APB 31 was released (it was the last APB Opinion) the SEC issued ASR 147.[19] The SEC was critical of existing lease accounting standards and ASR 147 amended lease disclosure for statutory SEC filings. The main concern of ASR 147 was with financing-type leases. As mentioned above, APBs 5 and 10 were thought to have resulted in inconsistent capitalization of financing-type leases. ASR 147 required supplemental disclosure of noncapitalized financing-type leases on a basis that was equivalent to capitalization.

SFAS 13

The FASB issued a discussion memorandum on leases in 1974. After deliberations, SFAS 13 was issued in 1976. Criteria for lessee capitalization

---

[16] APB (1966b).
[17] SEC (1972). This requirement extended the reporting of capitalized leases between related parties—and represented an interpretation of APB 5, para. 10–12.
[18] APB (1973).
[19] SEC (1973).

were revised again. This time there was a change in concept. Change in the capitalization criteria was substantial. Noncancellability and material equity were abandoned in favor of broader tests representing substantive transfers of ownership benefits and risks—although, as indicated earlier, the underlying objective still seems to be the recognition of purchase equivalents. Perhaps the difference between APB 5 and SFAS 13 is better described as a change in where the line is drawn between operating and capital leases. SFAS 13 is quite clearly intended to capitalize more leases.

There are four tests now applicable to both lessees and lessors:

1. Title passes to the lessee at the end of the lease term.
2. The lease contract contains a bargain purchase option.
3. The lease term is at least 75% of estimated useful life (with the lease term covering more than 25% of the original economic life when new).
4. The present value of minimum lease payments (the sum of minimum rentals excluding executory costs, a bargain purchase payment if one exists, penalty payment for nonrenewal if renewal is unlikely, and any guaranteed residual value at the end of lease term—plus unguaranteed residual value for lessors) is 90% or more of the fair market value of the lease property at the inception of the lease, less any applicable investment tax credit.

For the last test, the discount rate to be used by the lessee is the incremental borrowing rate. However, the lessor's implicit rate in the lease shall be used if it is obtainable and if the implicit rate is lower than the lessee's incremental borrowing rate. This represents conservatism because a lower interest rate will cause a higher present value and could result in lease capitalization under the 90% rule. The lessor's implicit rate is defined in SFAS 13, paragraph 5k, and is illustrated later in the chapter. If *any* one of these four tests or conditions is met, the lease must be treated as a capital lease by the lessee.

SFAS 13 also details how leases should be capitalized. The present value of minimum lease payments (defined previously) is computed using the interest rate determined for test (4) of the list. This amount is debited to leased assets and credited to lease obligations, subject to an upper limit of the asset's fair market value at lease inception. The asset is depreciated over its useful life if tests (1) or (2) are met. Otherwise the depreciation period is the lease term with total amortization equal to the capitalized amount less any guaranteed residual value at the end of the lease term. During the lease term each payment is allocated between interest expense and reduction of the lease obligation. The effective interest method described in APB 21 is used.[20] Finally, any executory costs (taxes, maintenance and insurance) are expensed as incurred. If lease payments include an amount for these costs, it is separated and expensed directly each period.

[20]APB (1971).

In this manner, the prescribed accounting seeks to make the lease resemble a purchase of the asset with debt financing. The leased asset is depreciated over its useful life if it is being leased for substantially all its useful life, with 75% being the materiality threshhold. If the asset is leased for a shorter period, the shorter period is used as the amortization period. Executory costs are separated and expensed in the same manner as would occur with a purchase. Finally, lease payments are separated into the equivalent of principal and interest each period. The purchase analogy is illustrated with a numerical example in Exhibit 16-3.

Real estate leases are accounted for somewhat differently. Leases involving only land are capitalized if either test (1) or test (2) in SFAS 13 is satisfied. Otherwise, land leases are classified as operating. Land under lease is not treated as a purchase equivalent unless title is expected to transfer. The reason for this more limited test is due to the nondepreciable nature of land.

When a lease includes both land and buildings, the capitalization test is more complicated. If tests (1) or (2) are not met, an allocation is made between land and building based on relative fair market values. They are capitalized separately. If a real estate lease involving land does not meet tests (1) or (2), but the fair market value of the land component is less than 25% of the total, the lease is treated as entirely attributable to the building for the purpose of applying tests (3) and (4) of SFAS 13. If either test (3) or (4) is met, the lease is capitalized. In other words, the land component is considered to be immaterial relative to the building component and the entire lease is capitalized. If the land component is 25% or more, the land and building are treated separately with the land being an operating lease and the building being a capital lease if tests (3) or (4) are met. These rules represent somewhat arbitrary ways of dealing with nondepreciable land in real estate leases.

In addition to the prescribed accounting for capital leases, a number of supplemental disclosures are required by SFAS 13: (1) gross amounts of assets under capital lease, (2) future minimum lease payments (excluding executory costs) in aggregate and for each of the five succeeding years, (3) total minimum sublease rentals to be received under noncancellable subleases, and (4) total contingent rentals as they are incurred each period. Leased assets and lease obligations are to be reported separately from other assets and liabilities in the balance sheet. Lease obligations are subject to current and noncurrent classification requirements.

A very important question whenever there is a major change in accounting policy is how it will be implemented. With lease capitalization a generous phase-in period was permitted. For new leases written after 1976, capitalization was required if the new tests are met. However, for existing leases, companies were given until December 31, 1980, to retroactively capitalize the leases and restate prior years financial statements. Supplemental disclosures were required of what the pre-1977 lease assets and obligations would have been during the phase-in period, if they had been capitalized.

EXHIBIT 16-3.

Lease Purchase Analogy

A company may purchase an asset outright for $100,000 with vendor financing. The note payable would be paid off with three year-end payments of $41,634.90. This represents an effective interest of 12%. An alternative is to lease the asset for three years with lease payments of $41,634.90 at the end of each year. The asset's economic life is three years, and no salvage is expected.

Loan/Lease Repayment schedule

(Col. 1) Beginning Principal	(Col. 2) Payment	(Col. 3) Interest (Col. 1 × .12)	(Col. 4) Principal (Col. 2 − Col. 3)	(Col. 5) Ending Principal (Col. 1 − Col. 4)
Year 1 $100,000.00	$41,634.90	$12,000.00	$29,634.90	$70,365.10
Year 2 $ 70,365.10	$41,634.90	$ 8,443.81	$33,191.09	$37,174.01
Year 3 $ 37,174.01	$41,634.90	$ 4,460.89	$37,174.01	- 0 -

Purchase Alternative			*Lease Alternative*		
Year 1			Year 1		
Asset	100,000		Leased Asset	100,000	
Note Payable		100,000	Lease Obligation		100,000
Note Payable	29,634.90		Lease Obligation	29,634.90	
Interest Expense	12,000.00		Interest Expense	12,000.00	
Cash		41,634.90	Cash		41,634.90
Depreciation Expense	33,333.33		Depreciation—Lease	33,333.33	
Accumulated Depreciation		33,333.33	Accumulated Lease Depreciation		33,333.33
Year 2			Year 2		
Note Payable	33,191.09		Lease Obligation	33,191.09	
Interest Expense	8,443.81		Interest Expense	8,443.81	
Cash		41,634.90	Cash		41,634.90
Depreciation Expense	33,333.33		Depreciation—Lease	33,333.33	
Accumulated Depreciation		33,333.33	Accumulated Lease Depreciation		33,333.33
Year 3			Year 3		
Note Payable	37,174.01		Lease Obligation	37,174.01	
Interest Expense	4,460.89		Interest Expense	4,460.89	
Cash		41,634.90	Cash		41,634.90
Depreciation Expense	33,333.34		Depreciation—Lease	33,333.34	
Accumulated Depreciation		33,333.34	Accumulated Lease Depreciation		33,333.34

The reason for a long transition period was due to the potential material effects of lease capitalization on some companies. SFAS 13 was less controversial than expected because the new standard permitted companies some flexibility in complying with the new requirements. There was time to mitigate the impact on the balance sheet of lease capitalization. In the final section of the chapter some evidence is presented that this type of behavior did in fact occur.

A criticism of lessee accounting under SFAS 13 is that some leases that should be capitalized still are not. It can be argued that all leases in excess of one year should be capitalized because assets and liabilities are created which are consistent with definitions of assets and obligations in SFAC 3.[21] One reason for avoiding this policy may be the costs that would be imposed on companies if all leases were capitalized. An apparent compromise exists on this point in the form of supplemental disclosure. For noncancellable operating leases in excess of one year, SFAS 13 requires the following supplemental disclosures:

1. Future minimum rental payments in aggregate and for each of the succeeding five periods.
2. Total minimum rentals to be received under noncancellable subleases.
3. Rental expense with separate totals for minimum rentals, contingent rentals, and sublease rentals.
4. A general description of the lessee's lease contracts.

Supplemental disclosure of noncapitalized leases is not as great under SFAS 13 as it was under APB 31. The noncancellability requirement will exclude some operating leases, and present-value information is not required under SFAS 13. It is unclear why noncancellability was introduced as the overriding criterion for supplemental disclosure of operating leases since it was dropped as a capitalization criterion. Because many more leases will be capitalized under SFAS 13, it may be that the need for supplemental information is not as great as it was prior to the issuance of SFAS 13. Still, it is puzzling why the supplemental disclosures of noncapitalized leases were reduced so much. The weak disclosures of noncapitalized leases create incentives to structure leases in such a way as to avoid both capitalization and supplemental disclosure. If this can be done, off-balance-sheet financing through leases would still be possible. This issue is discussed later in the chapter.

LESSOR ACCOUNTING

The initial impetus for lease capitalization was caused by a concern over lessee balance sheets. In particular, there was a desire to disclose lease

[21]FASB (1980a, paras. 20–36).

obligations as debt equivalents. It was only belatedly that the lessor side of lease transactions came to be considered in accounting standards.

APB 7

APB 7 was issued in 1966 and was the first standard to address lessor accounting.[22] The equivalent of lease capitalization was required but the criteria differed from APB 5. In addition, separate criteria existed for sales-type and financing-type leases. Sales-type leases were capitalized if three conditions were satisfied: (1) credit risks were reasonably predictable, (2) the lessor (seller) did not retain sizable risks of ownership, and (3) there were no important uncertainties regarding either costs or revenues under the lease contract. These three conditions differed from the lessee tests established under APB 5. As a result it was possible for one lease contract to be capitalized by either the lessee or lessor, but not by both. This asymmetry between lessee and lessor accounting was criticized.

Financing-type leases are those which involve a third party that writes the lease contract. The lessor is the third party, with the other two parties being the lessee and the manufacturer (or seller) of the leased asset. *All* financing-type leases were capitalized by lessors under APB 7; however, some financing-type leases were not capitalized by lessees under APBs 5 and 10. As indicated earlier in the chapter, lessee accounting for financing-type leases was inconsistent under APBs 5 and 10.

Leases capitalized under APB 7 were recognized at aggregate future rentals less the interest implicit in each rental. This represented the net present value of lease payments receivable. The effective interest method, as described in APB 21, was prescribed as the basis of interest revenue recognition. Each payment was separated into principal and interest, just as was required for lessees under APB 5.

Initial direct costs incurred by the lessor in originating a lease contract were deferred and recognized on a proportional basis consistent with the recognition of lease revenue. This applied to all leases and was an attempt to match lease-related costs to the revenue generated over the lease term.

APB 27

Criticisms of APB 7 regarding the noncapitalization of many sales-type leases led to the issuance of APB 27 in 1972.[23] The intent in APB 27 was to broaden the criteria for capitalization. The new criteria were these:

1. The collectibility of payments was reasonably assured.
2. No important uncertainties surrounded costs yet to be incurred on the lease.

[22] APB (1966a).
[23] APB (1972).

3. Any one of the following:
   (i)   title passed at end of lease term,
   (ii) a bargain purchase option existed,
   (iii) the leased property or similar property was for sale and the present value of required rentals (excluding executory costs) plus any investment tax credits was equal to or greater than normal selling price, or
   (iv) the lease term was substantially equal to the remaining economic life of the property.

Two of the requirements under both APBs 7 and 27 were similar and dealt with general revenue recognition criteria. Collectibility and the absence of uncertainties are generally assumed when accruing revenue in advance of cash collection. The third requirement of APB 27 replaced the second criterion of APB 7, the transfer of ownership risk, and was satisfied by any one of four conditions. The first two conditions reiterated the capitalization criteria of APB 5 for lessees. The last two were new and provided additional conditions that suggested the lease was a sale equivalent from the lessor's view point. The addition of these two conditions was important because it represented a departure from the material equity argument and looked more broadly at the economic substance of the transaction. However, the newly broadened criteria for lessors was at variance with the narrower criteria for lessees established in APB 5.

SFAS 13

Finally, in SFAS 13 lessee and lessor accounting achieved near symmetry. The four capitalization tests were discussed earlier and apply to both lessees and lessors. It can be seen that the tests are only a slight modification of APB 27. For lessor accounting, the two additional revenue recognition tests of APBs 7 and 27 were also retained in SFAS 13. The existence of these two additional criteria means that it is possible for some leases which are capitalized by lessees to be treated as operating leases by lessors. However, it is unlikely that this would occur very frequently. Inconsistent capitalization of financing-type leases was also eliminated by SFAS 13. It will be recalled that APBs 5, 7, and 10 resulted in the potential for inconsistency.

Some asymmetry still exists between lessor and lessee accounting concerning the choice of interest rate used to calculate the capitalized value of leases. The lessor uses the implicit rate, which equates minimum lease payments plus unguaranteed residual value in excess of any guaranteed amounts, with the sales price of the asset less any applicable investment tax credit. The lessee uses the lower of its incremental borrowing rate or the lessor's implicit rate (if it is obtainable), and only the guaranteed residual value is used. As a result, it is possible for the same lease to be measured differently in the financial statements of lessees and lessors, on account of the use of different interest rates and residual values. This disparity is justified on the grounds of conservatism since a lower interest rate will increase the amount of the capitalized lease obligation. It can also be defended on the grounds that each party may not have the same interest rates, owing to the different risks involved. Different residual values can also be justified because they represent different values to the lessor and lessee.

An area of apparent inconsistency in lessor accounting concerns initial *direct lease costs*. These are costs incurred in arranging the lease. SFAS 13 requires expensing of initial direct lease costs if the lease is a sales type. However, these costs are offset against first year's interest revenue under financing-type leases. When this occurs a new implicit interest rate must be calculated—to recognize the remaining unearned interest revenue using the effective interest method.[24] This will produce lower future interest revenue. So the net result of this rather complex procedure is to allocate initial direct lease costs over the lease term. The justification is that these costs are best matched against interest revenue in the case of financing-type leases because the lessor earns revenue from lease financing. On the other hand, with a sales-type lease, the costs are considered to be selling costs attributable to the arranging of debt finance. The costs are considered necessary to make the sale. This is another example of finite uniformity, in which the same costs are treated differently due to different circumstances. In this case the circumstances relate to the nature of the lessor's operations, and the classification of initial direct lease costs is as either selling costs or as reductions of future interest revenue.

Measurement of capitalized leases for lessors is specified in SFAS 13. The first step is to calculate the implicit interest rate in the lease: the rate of interest that equates minimum lease payments with the asset's fair market value at lease inception, reduced for any lessor investment tax credit. The minimum lease payments are defined as the sum of future rentals (less any amounts for executory costs paid by the lessor), plus amounts to be paid under bargain option purchases, plus penalty payment for nonrenewal if renewal is unlikely, plus guaranteed residual value if the asset reverts to the lessor, plus any unguaranteed residual value. The fair market value of the leased asset would normally be the cash selling price for both sales-type and financing-type leases.

Minimum lease payments receivable plus unguaranteed residual value are recognized at gross amounts, and a contra-account is created to recognize unearned interest. The net balance represents the present value of minimum lease payments receivable. Unearned interest is recognized each period, as the interest component is separated from the lease payment through the effective interest method. Lessor accounting for a financing-type lease is illustrated in Exhibit 16-4.

With a sales-type lease, the same procedures are used to account for the financing aspect of the lease. Present value of minimum lease payments

---

[24]Other methods are permitted if the differences are not material. See SFAS 13, para. 18b.

EXHIBIT 16-4.
Financing-Type Lease

Assume the following:
1. Fair market value at lease inception is $146,156.14.
2. Investment credit of 10% is available.
3. Lease payments are $50,000, at the end of each of the next three years, and include $2,000 for executory costs.
4. Estimated residual value is $13,000, of which $5,000 is guaranteed by the lessee.
5. There are no significant initial direct lease costs.

Step 1—Calculate implicit interest rate.

(Fair Market Value − Investment Tax Credit) = Present Value of (minimum lease payments exclusive of executory costs, guaranteed residual value, and unguaranteed residual value)

$$(\$146,156.14 - \$14,615.61) = \frac{\$48,000}{(1 + i)^1} + \frac{\$48,000}{(1 + i)^2} + \frac{(\$48,000 + \$5,000 + \$8,000)}{(1 + i)^3}$$

or 131,540.53 $i = .09$

Step 2—Record gross amounts of minimum lease payments exclusive of executory costs, guaranteed and unguaranteed residual value, and the unearned interest calculated by the implicit rate.

Taxes Payable	14,615.61	
Lease Payments Receivable	157,000.00	
Unearned Interest		25,459.47
Cash		146,156.14

To record asset payment, capital lease, and reduction of taxes for investment tax credit.

Step 3—Record yearly interest revenue and lease payments.

Year 1

Cash	48,000	
Lease Payments Receivable		48,000
ªUnearned Interest	11,838.65	
Interest Revenue		11,838.65

Year 2

Cash	48,000	
Lease Payments Receivable		48,000
ªUnearned Interest	8,584.13	
Interest Revenue		8,584.13

EXHIBIT 16-4. (Continued).

Year 3

Cash	48,000	
Lease Payments Receivable		48,000
ªUnearned Interest	5,036.69	
Interest Revenue		5,036.69
Asset	13,000	
Lease Payment Receivable		13,000

ªSee Schedule below.

Implicit Principal Repayments Schedule

Beginning Net Lease Investment (Lease payments receivable less unearned interest)	Payment	Interest	Principal	Net Lease Investment Ending Unearned Interest	Net Lease Investment Ending Lease Payment Receivable
Year 1 $131,540.53	$48,000	$11,838.65	$36,161.35	$13,620.82	$109,000
Year 2 $ 95,379.18	$48,000	$ 8,584.13	$39,415.87	$ 5,036.69	$ 61,000
Year 3 $ 55,963.31	$48,000	$ 5,036.69	$42,963.31	- 0 -	$ 13,000

receivable is computed and recognized in the balance sheet. Payments are separated into principal and interest components. However, in addition, revenue is recognized in an amount equal to the fair market value of the asset at lease inception. Normally this would be the cash selling price. The cost of the leased asset is recognized as cost of goods sold. So gross profit on the sales-type lease is recognized in addition to the present value of minimum lease payments receivable and interest revenue on lease payments.

Initial direct lease contract costs are treated differently depending on the type of lease. They are expensed immediately if a lease is a sales type. The rationale is that the costs represent selling costs, rather than financing costs. If a lease is a financing type, the expenses are offset against unearned interest revenue and a new implicit interest rate must be calculated which will recognize the remaining unearned interest using the effective interest method. This latter procedure is illustrated in Exhibit 16-5.

For all noncapitalized leases, the lessor must disclose the cost and book value of leased property (the assets are still recorded in the lessor's balance sheet if they are operating leases). Other supplemental disclosures required of lessors are the same required of lessees and reflect the reciprocal nature of capitalized lease contracts. These are minimum future rentals from non-cancellable leases, in aggregate and for each of the five succeeding years, and contingent rental income as it is recognized.

EXHIBIT 16-5.
Financing-Type Lease with Initial Direct Costs

Assume the same facts as in Exhibit 16-4, except that initial direct lease costs of $1,500 are incurred. The following entry would be made in Year 1:

Unearned Interest	1,500	
Cash		1,500

It is then necessary to calculate a new interest rate which will recognize the remaining unearned interest using the effective interest method:

$$133,040.53 = \frac{48,000}{(1 + i)^1} + \frac{48,000}{(1 + i)^2} + \frac{(48,000 + 5,000 + 8,000)}{(1 + i)^3}$$

By interpolation, $i = .08395$.

Revised Principal Repayment Schedule

Beginning Net Lease Investment	Payment	Interest	Principal	Net Lease Investment Ending Unearned Interest	Net Lease Investment Ending Lease Payments Receivable
Year 1 $133,040.53	$48,000	$11,168.75	$36,831.25	$12,790.72	$109,000.00
Year 2 $ 96,209.28	$48,000	$ 8,076.77	$39,923.23	$ 4,713.95	$ 61,000.00
Year 3 $ 56,286.05	$48,000	$ 4,713.95ᵃ	$43,286.05	- 0 -	$ 13,000.00

ᵃIncludes adjustment for rounding error due to approximation of the effective interest rate.

The FASB has issued a number of amendments and interpretations to SFAS 13.[25] These are all concerned with technical and specific issues. In general, these additional rules have clarified the implementation of lease capitalization arising from complex terms in lease contracts. These additional rules are not reviewed since they pertain to narrower technical issues rather than general standards.

SALE AND LEASEBACK

A sale and leaseback occurs when the owner of an asset legally sells it and enters into a lease agreement to lease the asset back. The lessor (new legal owner) and lessee (original legal owner) both use the standard criteria for classifying such a lease as operating or capital. A principle was established in APB 5 that no immediate recognition should be given to any "book" gains or losses that the lessee might record in such a transaction.

---

[25]The other standards are SFASs 17, 22, 23, 26, 27, 28, and 29. These have been compiled in a single publication (FASB, 1980b).

The general rule was that any gain or loss should be amortized by the lessee as an adjustment of the lease rental if the lease is an operating lease, and an adjustment of lease depreciation if the lease is capitalized. The deferred gain or loss was reported in the balance sheet as a deferred credit or charge, respectively. One exception existed to this rule. A loss was recognized if the asset's book value exceeded the fair market value at the time of the sale–leaseback. This, however, is nothing more than the application of conventional accounting conservatism through the lower-of-cost-or-market rule.

The reason for not recognizing a gain or loss is that the sale and lease-back are considered to be one transaction rather than two. Any book gains or losses therefore arise artificially from the accounting necessity of treating the transaction as having two separate parts. Since the lessee has the same asset as before (but leasing rather than owning), it is argued that no gain or loss should be recognized. To recognize such a gain or loss would be the virtual equivalent of selling something to yourself and recognizing a gain or loss on the transaction. This approach was retained in SFAS 13. If a lease is an operating lease, the deferred gain or loss is recognized proportional to lease payments. If the lease is capitalized, the deferred gain or loss is recognized proportional to lease depreciation. An example of a sale and lease-back involving book gains and losses is illustrated in Exhibit 16-6.

SFAS 13 did establish conditions under which a gain or loss might be immmediately recognized in a sale and leaseback. These tests are concerned with leases in which the original owner retains usage of a substantially smaller part of the total asset. It is argued that there really are two separate and distinct transactions when this occurs. The lessee would no longer have the same asset as before.

LEVERAGED LEASES

Leveraged leases are a special financing-type lease involving four parties instead of the usual three. The procedure is for a lessor to acquire an asset, which is leased to the lessee. However, the lessor borrows some money for the transaction (usually in excess of 50%) from a fourth party. This debt to the fourth party is nonrecourse but the lessor assigns a portion of the lease payments to cover the debt and interest payments. The debt to the fourth party may also be secured by the leased asset, and sometimes by a guarantee from the lessee. At issue is whether this transaction should be accounted for as a conventional financing-type lease with an additional debt transaction, or as a unique transaction warranting separate treatment.

From a lessee's viewpoint, a leveraged lease is not any different from other leases. The more difficult question concerns the effect of a leveraged lease on the lessor. There are two possibilities. One is that a leveraged lease is the same as a conventional financing-type lease with an additional debt transaction between the lessor and the fourth party. The other possibility is to regard a leveraged lease as a unique type of lease warranting special rules applicable to its special circumstances. The FASB concluded in SFAS 13

EXHIBIT 16-6.
Sale–Leaseback

Assume the same facts as in Exhibit 16-3. In addition assume that the lessee was the original asset owner, and sold the asset for $100,000 to the new owner, who is now the lessor.[a] Assuming the asset had a book value of $79,000 to the original owner (now lessee), the following entries would be required by the lessee in addition to those illustrated in Exhibit 16-3.

1. At sale date:

Cash	100,000	
Asset (book value)		79,000
Deferred Gain on Sale-Leaseback		21,000

2. For each of the three years during the lease term:

Deferred Gain on Sale-Leaseback	7,000	
Depreciation-Lease		7,000

---

[a] Normally, any gain or loss would be the difference between the original owner's book value and selling price. In such cases, losses would always be recognized immediately and the gains deferred. However, it is possible for the sales price to be set at some amount other than market value. For example, suppose in this example the selling price was $85,000 and estimated market value was $75,000. The following entry would be made by the original owner at the time of sale.

Loss on Asset	4,000	
Cash	85,000	
Asset (book value)		79,000
Deferred Gain on Sale-Leaseback		10,000

The effect of this entry is to recognize a loss of $4,000 ($79,000 − $75,000) for the adjustment to market value, and to defer the gain of $10,000 representing the payment in excess of market value by the buyer.

---

that the financing-type lease plus debt transaction analogy was inadequate to report leveraged leases. It argued that reporting leveraged leases as two separate transactions, a financing lease and a loan, failed to portray the lessor's net investment in the lease. What is required by SFAS 13 is a complex procedure of reporting all aspects of a leveraged lease in a net amount as part of one transaction. This represents another example of finite uniformity in which relevant circumstances determine the appropriate accounting procedures. The requirements are illustrated in SFAS 13, Appendix E.

ASSESSING SFAS 13

The longstanding criticism of lease accounting is that many leases are not being capitalized but should be. This is no less true of SFAS 13 than it was of ARB 38 or APB 5. An inherent weakness of the finite uniformity approach is that some accounting methods may be preferred by management over others. In these instances, companies will be motivated to manipulate the relevant circumstances in order to get the desired accounting result. With leases, lessees continue to believe that there are advantages of off-balance-sheet financing through leases. This will motivate companies to try to defeat the capitalization tests of lease accounting standards

It is not very difficult to structure a lease contract to defeat the four tests of SFAS 13—because the four tests are not stringent. A more challenging task, though, is to defeat lease capitalization tests for the lessee while satisfying them for the lessor. Lessors normally desire to capitalize leases and recognize sales revenue, but lessees prefer the effects of off-balance-sheet financing. One innovative method to accomplish both objectives is the use of third parties to guarantee residual values to the lessor: such a procedure reduces the lessee's obligation under test (4) of SFAS 13 and, if significant enough, could lead to noncapitalization. However, there is no effect on the lessor because the lessor's accounting deals with the estimated residual value in total. No distinction is made between guaranteed and unguaranteed residual value.

Whenever accounting policies force unpopular results on companies, there will be creative activity to circumvent the unpopular policy. This is certainly the case with lease accounting. Because of the existing "let's beat SFAS 13" attitude, a strong case can be made for rigid uniformity. One solution for this problem would be to capitalize all leases that exceed one year. This unambiguous policy would eliminate the game playing and would also eliminate the somewhat artificial distinction now being made between capital and operating leases. As has been indicated throughout the chapter, it is somewhat arbitrary where the line is drawn between capital and operating leases. Therefore, a rigid policy of capitalizing all leases can be argued to be an improvement by eliminating both the arbitrariness of where the line is drawn and the motivation to circumvent the finite uniformity established in SFAS 13.

ECONOMIC CONSEQUENCES OF LEASE CAPITALIZATION

From the viewpoint of a company preparing financial statements, there are at least two types of economic consequences. One relates to the costs of complying with lease capitalization. More detailed analyses will be required by a company and its auditor in classifying leases as operating and capital. Recall that in Chapter 7 we saw that finite uniformity always imposes a higher compliance cost than rigid uniformity. In addition, the accounting entries for each period will be more complicated if leases are capitalized. There has been no direct study of these types of costs. However, in 1973, one large company estimated it would cost $40,000 to install a lease capitalization system, and $25,000 to $35,000 a year to operate it.[26]

The more critical concern has been whether lease capitalization might provide disincentives for leasing. From a lessee's perspective, leasing offered the possibility of off-balance-sheet financing for most leases prior to SFAS 13. A survey of lessees indicated that the effect on financial statements was a major reason for leasing.[27] Noncapitalization of leases improves debt ratios and accounting rate of return compared with a purchase/debt alternative. Some lessees also believed that noncapitalization of leases increased available capital because these leases do not affect borrowing restrictions in debt covenants. Finally, there was also a belief that the lower debt ratios that would be achieved by noncapitalization would result in better debt ratings and lower interest rates in the capital market.

The argument against lease capitalization was presented to accounting policy makers in the following manner:

> The effects of treating leases as debt would extend beyond lessees to consumers and other parts of the economy. Increases in reported debt would tend to lead to an increase in interest rates and require an increased investment of equity capital requiring an even greater rate of return. This could contribute to inflationary pressures and act as a deterrent to investment in modernized or expanded plant and equipment.[28]

Neutrality tends to mitigate the preceding type of argument. Commenting on lease accounting, a former SEC chairman made these remarks:

> We recognize the usefulness of leases as a financing device. Economic objectives—including tax considerations—of two parties are frequently better satisfied by a lease arrangement than a purchase or sale.
>
> But leasing should not be made more attractive than it really is simply because of the way it is accounted for.[29]

It should not be the accounting, per se, which makes leasing attractive. If it is, the arguments favoring leasing are specious.

The alleged advantages of off-balance-sheet financing have not been entirely supported by research evidence. For example, a survey of analysts indicated that the debt implication of noncapitalized leases is factored into the evaluation of companies.[30] In particular, the debt equivalent of leasing for lease-intensive industries was very well understood by analysts, even prior to SFAS 13. The general feeling by analysts was that lessees were

[26]This evidence is anecdotal, but was reported in Hawkins and Wehle (1973, p. 100),
[27]Hawkins and Wehle (1973).
[28]Committee on Corporate Reporting of the Financial Executives Institute (1971, p. 237).
[29]Cook (1973).
[30]Hawkins and Wehle (1973).

usually within reasonable debt limits, even when lease effects were considered. So the survey evidence suggests that analysts were not "fooled" by off-balance-sheet lease financing even though company management seems to believe otherwise.

The FASB commissioned a comprehensive research study of the economic and behavioral effects of SFAS 13.[31] One finding of the study was that financial ratios and accounting rate of return of companies showed the expected changes due to increased lease capitalization, although the change was smaller than expected. It was suggested that SFAS 13 had less impact than anticipated because pre-1977 leases did not have to be capitalized until 1980. This gave companies time to restructure leases as operating, and to alter their capital structures in order to lessen the effects of capitalization on ratios. There was strong evidence that this type of behavior occurred and it reflects a belief in the naïveté of the market. Yet analysts surveyed in the same study professed not to be fooled by lease accounting differences (operating and capital) having no cash flow differences. The sophisticated user viewpoint is also supported by a capital market study included in the assessment of SFAS 13. The results were that there was no evidence of new information content in lease capitalization; that is, there was no abnormal security price response to the lease capitalization requirement. This is consistent with the efficient markets hypothesis, particularly since similar information was required as footnote disclosure under APB 31 prior to SFAS 13. In other words, the form of disclosure (footnote as in APB 31 or balance sheet as in SFAS 13), is not as important as the existence of disclosure per se.

Two other capital market studies offer additional evidence on lease accounting. One found that APB 31 disclosure requirements caused prices of affected companies to drop.[32] This can be interpreted to mean that the new lease disclosures of APB 31 had information content and that investors responded negatively to the revelation of hidden debt through lease financing. Such a finding is not surprising since the debt equivalent of most leases was not reported very well prior to APB 31. The second study found a negative price response during the time of the FASB's public hearings on leases in late 1974.[33] It is argued that the negative price response may have been due to restrictive debt covenants that would have been violated if leases were capitalized. Such a situation was hypothesized to have possible adverse indirect cash flow consequences on the firm and its stockholders. This is an agency theory type of argument and it does contradict survey evidence that analysts are not fooled by alternative accounting policies. The explanation may be that, prior to APB 31, analysts were really unaware of leases because there was very little reporting of them. But after APB 31 it mattered very little if the disclosures were made in footnotes or in the face of the balance sheet.

[31]Abdel-Khalik (1981).
[32]Ro (1978).
[33]Pfeiffer (1980).

Another study evaluated the usefulness of lease capitalization in bankruptcy prediction.[34] The procedure was to compare financial ratios, with and without lease capitalization, and to determine if the lease-adjusted ratios were better predictors. The study was made prior to both APB 31 and SFAS 13, so the effects of lease capitalization had to be approximated from rather limited footnote information. The results are interesting because they suggest that for bankruptcy prediction, at least, lease capitalization had no significant effect on the usefulness of accounting information. This finding contradicts survey research indicating that users believe lease capitalization is useful in predicting future cash flows and assessing debt paying ability.[35]

Concerns about the adverse effects of lease capitalization seem to have been exaggerated, although the four-year phase-in period may have permitted companies to mitigate the anticipated adverse balance sheet effects. Management continues to believe that noncapitalization offers some advantage, though user surveys and one capital market study suggest that lease capitalization has had no adverse impact. Holding aside the possible impact of lease capitalization on debt covenants, it could be argued that it is irrelevant whether lease information is disclosed as a footnote or in the face of the balance sheet. However, one prominent academic observed that footnote disclosure can give the impression that accountants do not know how to account for leases so they absolve themselves of the problem through extensive disclosures.[36] Difficult accounting problems should not be dealt with through disclosure simply because it is expedient and less controversial. The mandate of standard-setting bodies exists because of technical competency and expertise to decide controversial accounting issues. That mandate could easily be revoked if there is a failure to demonstrate competence and resolve.

SUMMARY

Lease accounting represents a classic example of the search for meaningful finite uniformity. Using a broad classification of leases as operating or capital, the search has been in defining the criteria for classification. This has led to an emphasis on economic substance rather than legal form. The substance of capital leases is argued to be a purchase equivalent with debt financing for the lessee. For the lessor, a capital lease is analogous to a sale with vendor financing if it is a sale-type lease, and to a loan equivalent if it is a financing-type lease. It is somewhat arbitrary where the line is drawn

---

[34]Elam (1975).
[35]Abdel-Khalik (1981).
[36]Anthony (1962).

between operating and capital leases. Over time the criteria have changed, which clearly reflects the subjective nature of the criteria and the difficulty in achieving finite uniformity.

Because the distinction between operating and capital leases is somewhat arbitrary, the economic consequences of lease capitalization are very important in evaluating lease accounting standards. Management attitudes show a belief in the market's naïveté, specifically, the advantages of off-balance-sheet financing. The evidence, however, supports the supposition that users are sophisticated with respect to lease reporting and that they are not fooled by lease accounting differences, at least after APB 31. Finally, there is survey and capital market research to support the position that the reporting of capital leases is useful and relevant. However, a strong case can be made for capitalizing all leases extending beyond one year. This type of rigid uniformity would eliminate the attempts to circumvent SFAS 13 and would solve the uniformity problem in a more reliable and more objective manner.

QUESTIONS

1. What is the argument for finite uniformity in accounting for leases? Why is finite uniformity difficult to achieve? Explain what the relevant circumstances are in accounting for different types of leases.
2. Why is the conveyancing aspect of leases emphasized in capitalization and the contractual element in operating leases?
3. What are the similarities and differences between leases and other means of property acquisition? How can these similarities and differences be reported in the financial statements?
4. Is the executory nature of lease contracts important in assessing lease accounting? How have leases been interpreted? Why might noncancellability override the executory nature?
5. Review the evolution of capitalization criteria in lease accounting standards. Why did APB 5 have little impact? What about SFAS 13? Has there been an underlying theme in the development of lease accounting?
6. It has been suggested that footnote disclosure in lieu of capitalization may give the impression that accountants and policy-making bodies do not know how to account for leases. Evaluate this comment.
7. Does it matter if capital leases are reported in a footnote or in the face of the balance sheet? What research evidence exists to help evaluate this question?

8. Does symmetry exist between lessors and lessees under SFAS 13? Should symmetry be a goal of lease accounting?
9. How is representational faithfulness achieved in the capitalization requirements of SFAS 13?
10. Is there a measurement reliability problem with lease capitalization?
11. Evaluate the manner in which initial direct lease costs are accounted for under SFAS 13.
12. Why are sales–leasebacks considered different from other leases? Explain the rationale for the deferral of gains or losses arising from a sale–leaseback.
13. Why was there some reason to expect negative economic consequences arising from lease capitalization? What is the role of neutrality in such a situation? What has been the response, based on research findings to date?
14. Does the reporting of capital leases have value to users of financial statements? Why are there costs of reporting capital leases?
15. What considerations may have motivated the FASB to grant a four-year transitional period in capitalizing pre-1977 leases meeting the capitalization tests of SFAS 13? What other political behavior is evident in the evolution of lease accounting?

CASES AND PROBLEMS

1. The following information was taken from The Kroger Co. 1977 annual report. As indicated in the notes, leases entered into prior to 1977 were not immediately capitalized. SFAS 13 permitted this deferral until 1980. Evaluate the impact of SFAS 13 on the balance sheet of The Kroger Co. if the pre-1977 leases had been capitalized.

	1977	1976
Property, Plant and Equipment		
Land	$ 14,189,891	$ 14,894,621
Buildings	80,476,555	80,464,968
Equipment	509,969,465	463,184,072
Leaseholds and leasehold improvements	116,939,019	159,936,945
Leased property under capital leases	3,403,527	
Total	774,978,457	718,480,606
Allowance for depreciation and amortization	321,710,959	296,363,852
Property, plant and equipment, net	$453,267,498	$422,116,754

Current Liabilities
  Current portion of long-term
    debt .... $ 5,805,154 $ 5,381,265
  Notes payable   8,900,000
  Accounts payable   343,789,464   289,654,324
  Accrued expenses   149,615,964   140,839,659
  Accrued federal income and other
    taxes   37,569,120   32,336,344
  Current portion of unredeemed
    trading stamps   26,926,973   26,985,895
  Current portion of obligations
    under capital leases   62,853
    Total current liabilities $563,769,528 $504,097,487
Other Liabilities
  Long-term debt $215,578,291 $232,982,894
  Unredeemed trading stamps   26,926,973   216,985,895
  Deferred federal income taxes   79,290,159   69,401,864
  Employees' benefit fund   31,934,419   34,106,565
  Obligations under capital leases ..   3,313,919
    Total other liabilities $357,043,761 $363,477,218

Lease arrangements entered into prior to 1977 have been accounted for as
operating leases. Had such leases been accounted for in accordance with Statement of Financial Accounting Standards No. 13, the following amounts of assets
and liabilities would have been recorded as of the dates indicated:

	Dec. 31, 1977	Jan. 1, 1977
Total capital leases, net of accumulated amortization	$101,057,000	$105,894,000
Total obligations under capital leases	$103,508,000	$108,010,000

Capitalization of lease arrangements entered into prior to 1977, in accordance with Statement of Financial Accounting Standards No. 13, would have
reduced net earnings by an estimated $335,000 for the year ended December
31, 1977 and by an estimated $235,000 for the year ended January 1, 1977.

Source: Accounting Trends and Techniques (American Institutes of Certified Public Accountants, 1978), p. 203.

2. Presented below is a summary of lease accounting for selected years, as
reported in *Accounting Trends and Techniques:*

Year	Both Capital and Operating Leases Reported	All Operating Leases	All Capital Leases	No Lease Reported	Total Companies
1965	26	266	0	308	600
1968	87	238	0	275	600
1971	89	247	52	212	600
1974	130	314	45	111	600
1977	274	194	59	73	600
1980	357	107	83	53	600

On the basis of the numbers of companies in each category, what can you determine about the effect APB5, APB7, APB 31, and SFAS 13 had on financial statements? Support your analysis by careful reference to specific years.

3. Assume the following facts concerning a sales-type lease:

Lease term is three years and qualifies as a capital lease for both lessor and lessee. The asset reverts to the lessor at the end of the lease term. Assume straight-line depreciation by the lessee.

Payments are $50,000 at the beginning of each year, plus a guaranteed residual value of $10,000 at the end of the lease term. The lessor estimates a total residual value of $15,000. Lease payments include $4,000 for executory costs under a maintenance agreement.

Initial direct costs associated with the lease are $2,700.

Cash sales price of the asset is $137,102.50. Lessor's manufacturing cost is $100,000.

The lessee does not know the lessor's implicit rate, but its own incremental borrowing rate is 11%.

Required:

(a) Prepare the accounting entries for both lessor and lessee for the three years. What happens in Year 3 if residual value is only $8,000? (Hint: it may be useful to review an intermediate accounting text).

(b) Assume the same facts as above except that the asset is first sold to a finance company, which then leases the asset to the lessee. Investment tax credit of 10% is available to the lessor. Prepare the required entries in all three years for lessor and lessee.

(c) Evaluate the differences between requirements (a) and (b), as well as the differences between lessor and lessee.

4. One of the four capitalization tests of SFAS 13 is that the lease term is 75% or more of the asset's remaining economic life. Lease term is defined as follows:

The fixed noncancelable term of the lease plus (i) all periods, if any, covered by *bargain renewal options*, (ii) all periods, if any, for which failure to renew the lease imposes a penalty on the lessee in an amount such that renewal appears, at the *inception of the lease*, to be reasonably assured, (iii) all periods, if any, covered by ordinary renewal options during which a guarantee by the lessee of the lessor's debt related to the leased property is expected to be in effect, (iv) all periods, if any, covered by ordinary renewal options preceding the date as of which a *bargain purchase option* is exercisable, and (v) all periods, if any, representing *renewals or extensions* of the lease at the lessor's option; however, in no case shall the lease term extend beyond the date a *bargain purchase option* becomes exercisable. A lease which is cancelable (i) only upon the occurrence of some remote contingency, (ii) only with the permission of the lessor, (iii) only if the lessee enters into a new lease with the same lessor, or (iv) only upon payment by the lessee of a penalty in an amount such that continuation of the lease appears, at *inception*, reasonably assured shall be considered "non-cancelable" for purposes of this definition.

Required:

How can this test be circumvented through either the structuring of the lease contract or interpretation of the test? What are other ways in which lease capitalization could be avoided through the structuring of lease terms or interpretation of the tests? What problem does this exercise illustrate?

BIBLIOGRAPHY OF REFERENCED WORKS

Abdel-Khalik, A. Rashad (1981). *The Economic Effects on Lessees of FASB Statement No. 13, Accounting for Leases* (FASB).

Accounting Principles Board (1954). "Reporting of Leases in the Financial Statements of Lessee," *APB Opinion No. 5* (AICPA).

———— (1966a). "Accounting for Leases in Financial Statements of Lessors," *APB Opinion No. 7* (AICPA).

———— (1966b). "Omnibus Opinion," *APB Opinion No. 10* (AICPA).

———— (1971). "Interest on Receivables and Payables," *APB Opinion No. 21* (AICPA).

———— (1972). "Accounting for Lease Transactions by Manufacturer or Dealer Lessors," *APB Opinion No. 27* (AICPA).

———— (1973). "Disclosure of Lease Commitments by Lessees," *APB Opinion No. 31* (AICPA).

Alvin, Gerald (1970). "Resolving the Inconsistency in Accounting for Leases," *The New York Certified Public Accountant* (March 1970), pp. 223–230.

Anthony, Robert N. (1962). Letter to Weldon Powell, Chairman of the Accounting Principles Board, 25 October 1962. Cited in Financial Accounting Standards Board (1974, p. 39).

Committee on Accounting Procedure (1949). "Disclosure of Long-Term Leases in Financial Statements of Lessees," *ARB 38* (AICPA).

———— (1953). "Restatement and Revision of Accounting Research Bulletins," *ARB No. 43* (AICPA).

Committee on Corporate Reporting of the Financial Executives Institute (1971). Cited in *Proceedings of the Accounting Principles Board of the American Institute of Certified Public Accountants: Public Hearing on Leases* (AICPA).

Cook, Donald C. (1963). "The Case Against Capitalizing Leases," *Harvard Business Review* (January–February 1963), pp. 145–162.

Cook, G. Bradford (1973). "The Commission and the Regulation of Public Utilities" (Paper presented to the Financial Forum of the American Gas Association, Monterey, Ca., 1974), cited in Financial Accounting Standards Board (1974, p. 38).

Elam, Rick (1975). "The Effect of Lease Data on the Predictive Ability of Financial Ratios," *The Accounting Review* (January 1975), pp. 25–43.

Financial Accounting Standards Board (1974). *FASB Discussion Memorandum: An Analysis of Issues Related to Accounting for Leases* (FASB).

—— (1976). "Accounting for Leases," *Statement of Financial Accounting Standards No. 13* (FASB).

—— (1980a). "Elements of Financial Statements of Business Enterprises," *Statement of Financial Accounting Concepts No. 3* (FASB).

—— (1980b). *Accounting for Leases* (FASB).

Hawkins, David (1970). "Objectives, Not Rules, for Lease Accounting," *Financial Executive* (November 1970), pp. 30–38.

Hawkins, David M., and Mary M. Wehle (1973). *Accounting for Leases* (Research Foundation of Financial Executives Institute, 1973).

Myers, John H. (1962). "Reporting of Leases in Financial Statements," *Accounting Research Study No. 4* (AICPA).

Pfeiffer, G. (1980). "The Economic Effects of Accounting Policy Regulation; Evidence on the Lease Accounting Issue" (Ph.D. diss., Cornell University, 1980).

Ro, Byung T. (1978). "The Disclosure of Capitalized Lease Information and Stock Prices," *Journal of Accounting Research* (Autumn 1978), pp. 315–340.

Securities and Exchange Commission (1972). "Reporting Leases in Financial Statements of Lessees," *Accounting Series Release No. 132* (SEC).

—— (1973). "Notice of Adoption of Amendments to Regulation S-X Requiring Improved Disclosure of Leases," *Accounting Series Release No. 147* (SEC).

Zises, Alvin (1973). "The Pseudo-Lease—Trap and Time Bomb," *Financial Executive* (August 1973), pp. 20–25.

ADDITIONAL READINGS

Abdel-Khalik, A. Rashad; Robert B. Thompson; and Robert E. Taylor (1978). "The Impact of Reporting Leases off the Balance Sheet on Bond Risk Premiums: Two Exploratory Studies," *Economic Consequences of Financial Accounting Standards* (FASB), pp. 103–155.

Bevis, Herman W. (1965). "Reporting of Leases: Agreement and Disagreement," *Journal of Accountancy* (April 1965), pp. 27–28.

Bowman, Robert G. (1980). "The Debt Equivalence of Leases: An Empirical Investigation," *The Accounting Review* (April 1980), pp. 237–253.

Clay, Raymond J., and William W. Holder (1977). "A Practitioner's Guide to Accounting for Leases," *Journal of Accountancy* (August 1977), pp. 61–68.

Dieter, Richard (1979). "Is Lessee Accounting Working?" *The CPA Journal* (August 1979), pp. 13–19.

Finnerty, Joseph F.; Rick N. Fitzsimmons; and Thomas W. Oliver (1980). "Lease Capitalization and Systematic Risk," *The Accounting Review* (October 1980), pp. 631–639.

Goodman, Hortense, and Leonard Lorensen (1978). *Illustrations of Accounting for Leases: A Survey of the Application of FASB Statement No. 13* (AICPA).

Ingberman, Monroe; Joshua Ronen; and George H. Sorter (1979). "How Lease Capitalization Under FASB Statement No. 13 will Affect Financial Ratios," *Financial Analysts Journal* (January–February 1979), pp. 28–31.

Ma, Ronald (1972). "Accounting for Long-Term Leases," *Abacus* (June 1972), pp. 21–34.

Nelson, A. Tom (1963). "Capitalizing Leases—The Effect on Financial Ratios," *Journal of Accountancy* (July 1963), pp. 49–58.

Rappaport, Alfred (1965). "Lease Capitalization and the Transaction Concept," *The Accounting Review* (April 1965), pp. 373–376.

Shanno, David F., and Roman L. Weil (1976). "The Separate Phases Method of Accounting for Leveraged Leases: Some Properties of the Allocating Rate and an Algorithm for Finding It," *Journal of Accounting Research* (Autumn 1976), pp. 348–356.

Shillinglaw, Gordon (1958). "Leasing and Financial Statements," *The Accounting Review* (October 1958), pp. 581–592.

Vatter, William J. (1966). "Accounting for Leases," *Journal of Accounting Research* (Autumn 1966), pp. 133–148.

CHAPTER 17

Investments in Equity Securities and Translation of Foreign Operations

In this chapter, two separate but related subjects will be discussed: (1) accounting for investments in equity securities and (2) translation of foreign operations. The related subject of accounting for business combinations is discussed in Chapter 18. It may be beneficial to read both chapters together.

Investments in equity securities are divided into two categories: ownership interests of less than 50%, and those of more than 50%. Within the less than 50% category, there is a nominal break at 20% between the cost and equity methods. The key point here concerns the ability to "influence significantly" the financial and operating policies of the acquired firm. The underlying philosophy of consolidations in which ownership is less than 100% is next examined. The problem of interpreting the minority interest has led to a variety of treatments which have not as yet been successfully resolved.

The second main topic of the chapter is the translation of foreign operations—the consolidation of foreign operations. Statement of Financial

Accounting Standards (SFAS) 8 is reviewed, and we look at the fundamental discrepancy that existed in that document—between accounting and economic (cash flow) gains and losses. The section concludes with a discussion of how SFAS 52 appears to have corrected the inconsistency that existed under SFAS 8.

INVESTMENTS IN EQUITY SECURITIES

Investments in equity securities are accounted for differently depending on the underlying circumstances of the investment. These circumstances relate to the extent of control over the investee that is acquired by the investor.

The point at which one enterprise achieves control of another is not easily determinable and generally requires subjective judgment. Moonitz examined several criteria for establishing control—such as percentage of stock ownership, controlling influence, similarity of operations, and geographical concentration. He concluded that none applied in all situations and that accountants must exercise judgment.[1] Through the years, however, with the guidance of various standard-setting bodies, the accepted norm for establishing control for accounting purposes has become the ownership of more than 50% of the outstanding voting stock of an investee enterprise.

LESS THAN 50% OWNERSHIP

For equity investments of less than 50% of the investee's outstanding voting stock, Accounting Principles Board (APB) 18 and SFAS 12 are the standards governing accounting practice today. APB 18 divides all such investments into two classes: (1) those where the investor does not exercise significant influence over the operating and financial policies of an investee and (2) those where the investor does exercise influence over an investee. In general, with no evidence to the contrary, an investment of 20% or more is presumed to carry with it the ability to exercise significant influence, while one of less than 20% does not permit the exercise of significant influence. This so-called "20% rule" is not rigid; rather, it is an attempt to provide some guidance to the accounting profession to enable it to apply finite uniformity based on the underlying circumstances. There could be situations where significant influence is present with less than 20% ownership and, conversely, is not present with more than 20% ownership.

Unfortunately, many practicing accountants applied the 20% rule as if it represented rigid uniformity, overlooking the underlying circumstances.

---

[1]Moonitz (1944, pp. 22–44).

This resulted in several lawsuits and ultimately led the Financial Accounting Standards Board (FASB) to issue Interpretation 35, which reiterated the importance of the general criterion of significant influence as opposed to the stricter "20% rule."[2] The importance of the classification of a particular investment is that the cost method of accounting is used where no significant influence exists and the equity method is used where significant influence exists (see later discussion of both methods).

SFAS 12 requires that the lower-of-cost-or-market (LCM) rule be applied to investments in marketable equity securities accounted for by the cost method. The LCM rule is applied on a portfolio basis rather than on an individual investment basis. All marketable equity investments are divided into two portfolios:

1. current, which includes those investments that are readily marketable and that management expects to convert into cash within the next year (or within the operating cycle, whichever is longer) and
2. noncurrent, which includes all other equity investments.

For the current portfolio, declines in market prices are reported in the income statement as losses, while increases in market price (above previous declines) are reported in the income statement as reverses of previous losses, rather than gains. In other words, an increase in market price is handled as a change in the estimate of a previously reported loss. The LCM rule is applied similarly to the noncurrent portfolio except that losses (and their reversal) are accumulated in a separate component of the equity section of the balance sheet rather than in the income statement. Presumably, the FASB's logic was that changes in the market price of equity investments in the noncurrent portfolio will not affect cash and, therefore, should not be included in income determination, while similar changes in the current portfolio will affect cash and, therefore, income.

SFAS 12 is a step in the right direction—that is, away from a purely cost basis valuation—but it does not go far enough toward a complete market price valuation for equity investments. The LCM rule, as applied in SFAS 12, is obviously a conservative approach because losses are anticipated while unrealized gains are ignored. Even the terminology denies the anticipation of gains. For example, the recovery of previously recognized losses is assumed to be a correction of a previous estimate rather than the recognition of a gain. Moreover, the practice of accounting for market price declines differently (depending on the classification of the investment) does not appear justified by the underlying circumstances. Certainly a case may be made that market declines in the noncurrent portfolio do not affect cash and, therefore, should not affect earnings. If that argument is accepted, however, then why recognize the market declines at all? The presumption is, after all, that the investment will be held indefinitely and any immediate market declines will not affect ultimate cash flows. Another weakness in

---

[2]FASB (1981a, paras. 2–3).

this dual approach to the recognition of market declines is that it is based on an arbitrary classification of each particular investment, and that classification certainly is susceptible to management manipulation. Market price valuation for all investments would provide more information to financial statement users, be less arbitrary, remove from the balance sheet an undefinable element (i.e., the separate component of equity representing market declines on noncurrent investments), and be less susceptible to management manipulation.

The Cost Method

As we have seen, the cost method of accounting for investments in equity securities is to apply the LCM: this method is used by investors whenever they are unable to exercise significant influence over an investee. Under the cost method, the investment is recorded at cost, including transaction costs. No subsequent adjustments are made to the cost (other than LCM adjustments to valuation accounts) for such events as the investee's income or loss and dividends. Rather, the investee's income or loss is assumed not to affect the investor's underlying equity in the investee (other than possibly to influence the stock price) and, therefore, neither income nor loss is reflected on the investor's financial statements. When an investee declares a cash dividend, the investor records its proportionate amount of that dividend as income on the date of record.

Gains and losses from disposition of an investment are calculated as the selling price less transaction costs minus the cost. Valuation allowances resulting from the application of LCM are ignored in calculating the realized gain or loss. To determine the cost of the investment sold, the investor may use any of three alternatives:

1. Specific identification.
2. First-in-first-out.
3. Weighted average.

Of course, the alternative selected should be applied consistently for all dispositions. There appear to be no theoretical grounds for allowing the three approaches.

The Equity Method

The equity method of accounting for investments in equity securities is used whenever the investor has the ability to exercise significant influence over the investee. If the investor's investment does not establish control (i.e., it is not greater than 50%), full consolidated financial statements (to be discussed later in this chapter and in the next chapter) generally are not required. Rather, what is frequently referred to as a "one line consolidation" takes place: the investment account is used to reflect the investor's underlying equity in the investee. Many of the mechanical adjustments that are required to be made for consolidated financial statements (e.g., recognition and amortization of goodwill) also are required for a one-line consolidation—except that only the net effect of those adjustments is recorded in the investment account rather than all of the individual accounts actually involved.

The investment is recorded at cost plus transaction costs. At the time of the investment, the investor must determine if more (or less) was paid than the underlying book value acquired. For example, assume P Company purchased 25% of S Company's voting stock for $100,000 when S Company's book value was $300,000. P Company paid $25,000 over the underlying book value of S Company ($100,000 − ($300,000)(.25) = $25,000). An attempt should be made to determine what specific assets of S Company are undervalued; however, as is more often the case in a one-line consolidation, the $25,000 is arbitrarily assumed to be attributable to goodwill.

Three events typically must be recorded for each reporting period in the investment account under the equity method: (1) proportionate share of investee's income or loss for the period, (2) proportionate share of investee's cash dividend for the period, and (3) amortization of the amount of the cost of the investment that is different from the underlying book value acquired (e.g., the $25,000 above). The investor's proportionate share of the investee's net income is recorded as a debit to the investment account and a credit to income from equity investments. The investor's proportionate share of the investee's cash dividends is recorded as a debit to cash and a credit to the investment account. The excess cost over book value of the investment is amortized over its estimated useful life by debiting income from equity investments and crediting the investment account. Intercompany profits and losses are eliminated and other adjustments typically made in consolidation (see Chapter 18 for a detailed discussion of these adjustments) also are recorded. The result is that one line on the balance sheet, the investment account, and one line on the income statement, the income from equity investments account, are shown as if consolidation had occurred.

Dispositions of investments accounted for by the equity method are handled similarly to dispositions of investments carried at cost, except that the carrying amount rather than cost is used to determine the gain or loss. When an investment initially is accounted for by the cost method, it sometimes happens that subsequent investments cause the equity method to become applicable (as with a step acquisition); in this situation, the change in method is treated as a change in reporting entity under APB 20. Thus, the investment account must be adjusted retroactively to reflect use of the equity method from the date of the first investment. On the other hand, when the equity method initially is used and then, because of subsequent divestments, the cost method becomes appropriate, the change is not made retroactively. The balance in the investment account at the date of the change is carried forward as if it were cost.

In terms of both relevance and representational faithfulness, one may question the usefulness of the equity method. The investment account represents neither the cost of the investor's investment in the investee nor the market value of that investment. Moreover, it is impossible to determine from the financial statements the amount of dividends received from investees accounted for by the equity method. This information, however, is as important to financial statement users as is the amount displayed as income from equity investments. A market price valuation approach would be superior to the equity method because it would display the current value of the investment as well as its current cash-generating ability. Empirical studies have reached the same conclusion.[3]

MORE THAN 50% OWNERSHIP

In most situations where one entity owns more than 50% of another entity, Accounting Research Bulletin (ARB) 51 requires that consolidated financial statements be prepared. In the last chapter of this book, the subject of consolidated financial statements will be dealt with in connection with a 100% ownership of one entity by another entity. That chapter will discuss most of the accounting issues that must be addressed in order to combine the financial statements of the two entities. This present chapter, on the other hand, will discuss only those accounting issues that must be addressed when more than 50% but less than 100% of an entity is owned by another. Thus, discussion of the issue of pooling of interest versus purchase accounting will be deferred until the next chapter because pooling of interest accounting is proscribed in situations where less than a 90% ownership exists. In practice, pooling usually accompanies a 100% acquisition. The usefulness, or lack thereof, of consolidated financial statements will be discussed in this chapter, as well as the conflicting concepts of accounting for minority interests.

Purpose of Consolidated Financial Statements

The FASB added to its agenda a project on the reporting entity, the purpose of which is to reconsider consolidated financial statements. Until that project is complete, the governing standard is ARB 51, issued in 1959. It states that the purpose of consolidated financial statements is

> ... to present, primarily for the benefit of the shareholders and creditors of the parent company, the results of operations and the financial position of a parent company and its subsidiaries essentially as if the group were a single company.[4]

ARB 51 assumes that consolidated statements are more meaningful than parent-company-only statements or separate company statements of all affiliate companies within the group controlled by a single parent. As shall be seen, that presumption may not be valid. Certainly one reason for

[3]See, for example, Lloyd and Weygandt (1971); and Copeland, Strawser, and Binns (1972).
[4]Committee on Accounting Procedure (para. 2).

questioning the usefulness of consolidated financial statements is that agreement is lacking as to the proper approach to their preparation—and the approach generally followed is not grounded in accounting theory.

Approaches to Consolidated Statements

Whenever minority interests exist, at least three accounting issues arise when the purchase method is used:

1. What amounts should be reported for the investee's identifiable net assets?
2. What amount should be assigned to goodwill?
3. What amount should be assigned to minority interests?

The FASB identified three possible alternative solutions to the preceding questions.[5] However, from a theoretical point of view, a fourth alternative exists. All three alternatives identified by the FASB would recognize a minority interest; but from a purely proprietary theory concept, a minority interest should not be recognized because the minority interest is neither a creditor nor an owner. Exhibit 17-1 summarizes the four approaches to resolving the issues.

EXHIBIT 17-1.
Approaches to Consolidated Statements

Approach	Issue 1 *Identifiable Net Assets*	Issue 2 *Goodwill*	Issue 3 *Minority Interests*
Proprietary	Recognize investor's share of fair value.	Recognize investor's share.	No minority interests would be recognized.
Parent	Recognize investor's share of fair value and minority share of book value.	Recognize investor's share.	Recognize minority share of book value.
Modified Parent	Recognize total fair value.	Recognize investor's share.	Recognize minority share of fair value.
Entity	Recognize total fair value.	Recognize total implied goodwill.	Recognize minority share of fair value and goodwill.

---

[5]FASB (1976b, para. 370).

In order to illustrate the financial statement impact of the four approaches to consolidated financial statements, assume the following:

1. P Company acquires 75% of S Company for $360,000.
2. S Company's book value is $400,000.
3. S Company's fair value of identifiable net assets (excluding goodwill) is $450,000.

Proprietary Approach.   Under the proprietary approach, the parent company owners are paramount. They are the owners of the assets, and the liabilities are their obligations. In preparing consolidated financial statements, only the proportionate amount of the investee's assets and liabilities owned by the investor should be recognized. Similarly only the investor's share of goodwill would be recognized. Because neither the minority interests' share of the identifiable net assets nor its share of goodwill are recognized, it follows that no minority interests would be recognized. The consolidated balance sheet under the proprietary approach would include

1. Identifiable net assets (450,000 × 75%) $337,500
2. Goodwill (360,000 − (450,000 × 75%)) $ 22,500
3. Minority interest   0

In applying the proprietary approach, only the investor's share of unrealized intercompany gains and losses would be eliminated in consolidation. This is because the minority interest is considered outside the consolidated group and, therefore, transactions between the majority and minority must be considered partially (minority percentage) as sales or purchases outside the consolidated group. The proprietary approach to consolidated statements essentially has not been adopted in accounting practice.[6]

Parent Approach.   The parent approach is an extension of the proprietary approach. That is, it maintains the basic theory that the minority interest is outside the consolidated group. However, under this approach, it is assumed that the identifiable assets and liabilities of the investee cannot be separated into majority and minority amounts and, therefore, must be reported on the consolidated statements in their entirety. The measurement of those assets and liabilities is unique. The investor's proportionate amount of the fair value of the investee's identifiable net assets is combined with the minority interest's proportionate amount of the book value of those net assets on the consolidated statements. Only the investor's share of goodwill is recognized. Minority interest is measured as its proportionate share of book value. The consolidated balance sheet under the parent approach would include

1. Identifiable net assets
         (450,000 × 75%) + (400,000 × 25%) $437,500
2. Goodwill (360,000 − (450,000 × 75%)) $ 22,500
3. Minority interest (400,000 × 25%) $100,000

[6]Baxter and Spinney (1975, p. 32).

As with the proprietary approach, only the investor's share of unrealized intercompany gains and losses would be eliminated under the parent approach. Again, the reasoning is that the minority interest is outside the consolidated group and, therefore, sales or purchases to or from it are realized. For the same reason the minority interest is displayed as a liability rather than equity in the consolidated financial statements.

Use of the parent approach is predominant in accounting practice today with the possible exception of the amount of unrealized intercompany gains and losses that are eliminated.[7] The FASB found in a review of published financial statements that this approach was used more than any other.[8] Moreover, it is the approach most often presented and taught in advanced accounting textbooks. It also is the recommended practice of the Accounting Standards Executive Committee (AcSEC) of the AICPA, although that group does favor the elimination of 100% of unrealized intercompany gains and losses regardless of the size of the minority interest.[9]

Modified Parent Approach. The modified parent approach appears not to have any logical theoretical foundation. Rather, it attempts to borrow some advantageous elements from the entity approach while maintaining a semblance of the proprietary approach. Both the investor's and minority interest's share of the fair value of the investee's identifiable assets are recognized, while only the investor's share of goodwill is recognized. Thus, a somewhat illogical result occurs: the price paid by the investor to acquire a controlling interest is said to substantiate the full fair value of the investee's identifiable net assets but not the total fair value of the investee because goodwill is only partially recognized. Minority interest under the modified parent approach is equal to the minority's proportionate amount of the fair value of the investee's identifiable assets. The consolidated balance sheet under the modified parent approach would include

1. Identifiable net assets — $450,000
2. Goodwill (360,000 − (450,000 × 75%)) — $ 22,500
3. Minority interest (450,000 × 25%) — $112,500

Under the modified parent approach, it generally is recommended that 100% of realized intercompany gains and losses be eliminated. The logic of eliminating 100% of intercompany gains and losses rather than only the majority's share presumably is a desire to report assets at their historical cost to the consolidated entity and the uncertainty regarding related party transactions. When 100% of the unrealized intercompany gains and losses is eliminated, an additional issue arises: should the entire elimination be charged (credited) to the majority interest or apportioned between it and the minority interest? A task force of AcSEC found that the latter practice is prevalent today, although the former also occurs. It is AcSEC's recom-

---

[7]ARB 51 requires that all intercompany profit and loss be eliminated regardless of the size of minority interest, although some companies continue to eliminate only the majority's share.
[8]FASB (1976b, para. 371).
[9]AICPA (1981, para. 42).

mendation that the elimination be allocated between majority and minority interests.[10]

Under the modified parent approach, minority interest typically is classified in a no man's land between liabilities and stockholders' equity. Although that classification is unfortunate, one is hard pressed to classify it more precisely. The FASB states that minority interest is equity, but the existence of "ownership rights" in a consolidated enterprise actually held by the various minority interests of that enterprise must be questioned because minority interests are not likely to share in the residual after liquidation of the parent enterprise.[11]

Entity Approach.   Under the entity approach, the entire entity is paramount and both the majority and the minority equity interests are part of that entity. Assets of the enterprise and its liabilities are what make up the entity, and both should be analyzed from the view of the entire enterprise as one operating unit.[12] It follows logically then that the full amount of the fair value of the investee's identifiable net assets as well as goodwill should be recognized in consolidated financial statements. The price paid by the investor to acquire a controlling interest in the investee is used to establish the fair value of the investee. Minority interest is based on that fair value. The consolidated balance sheet under the entity approach would include

1. Identifiable net assets $450,000
2. Goodwill ((360,000 ÷ 75%) − 450,000) $ 30,000
3. Minority interest ((360,000 ÷ 75%) × 25%) $120,000

The entity approach requires eliminating 100% of unrealized intercompany gains and losses because those gains and losses relate to transactions wholly within the same operating entity. The elimination is charged (credited) proportionately to both majority and minority interest because both are considered part of the entity. Likewise, the minority interest is classified as equity because it is simply one of the principal classes of owners' equity. Comparative results of the four approaches are shown in Exhibit 17-2.

EXHIBIT 17-2.
Summary Presentations of Various Approaches to Consolidated Statements

Approach	Identifiable Net Assets	Goodwill	Minority Interests
Proprietary	$337,500	$22,500	$ 0
Parent	437,500	22,500	100,000
Modified Parent	450,000	22,500	112,500
Entity	450,000	30,000	120,000

---

[10] AICPA (1981, para. 42).
[11] FASB (1980, para. 179).
[12] Paton (1922, p. 52).

The Usefulness of Consolidated Statements

As mentioned earlier, the presumption made in accounting standards regarding consolidated statements is that these statements are more useful than separate company statements. We have just seen that wide diversity exists today on consolidation policy.[13] For example, it is possible to report consolidated net assets at four different amounts and to ignore completely minority interest or classify it as a liability, equity, or neither a liability nor equity. The various alternatives for reporting and classifying items arising in consolidation exist even though the underlying circumstances of the transaction that brought about the consolidation are identical. This diversity itself leads one to question the usefulness of the resulting statements. Hopefully the FASB's project on the reporting entity will result in significantly reducing alternative accounting practices for consolidation, which would be an improvement over today's diverse practices, but it should not stop there.

The usefulness of consolidated statements can be challenged on other grounds. Investors primarily motivated by the dividend-paying ability of prospective investees may be misled by consolidated financial statements, whether considering an investment in the parent company or in one of its subsidiaries. If, for example, the parent company is incurring losses consistently while the subsidiaries are earning income in excess of those losses, the consolidated statements would report income and might even show dividends when in fact those dividends are distributed to subsidiaries' stockholders, not parent stockholders. The opposite condition could also exist.

Creditors could be similarly misled by consolidated financial statements. For example, assume a 100% owned subsidiary has current assets of $250,000 and current liabilities of $750,000. Its parent has current assets of $4,000,000 and current liabilities of $1,250,000. The consolidated statements would make it appear that no debt-paying problem exists, while the subsidiary-only statements would indicate that a serious debt-paying problem exists for the subsidiary. Unfortunately, neither approach completely reflects the true situation because of the difference in legal and economic consequences. Subsidiary-only statements reflect the legal problem, but if management chooses to pay all debts of its subsidiary, no economic problem exists. On the other hand, the consolidated statement indicates no economic problem; but if management chooses not to pay debts of its subsidiary, legally the subsidiary is in trouble.

In general, consolidation is a process of adding together assets and liabilities of legally separate enterprises. Unfortunately, the aggregation of the data results in the loss of some information because it is impossible to de-

---

[13]Not only does diversity exist regarding the methods to prepare consolidated statements, but also on whether all subsidiaries should be consolidated. *Accounting Trends & Techniques* (AICPA, 1982) reported that of 600 enterprises surveyed, 423 consolidated all subsidiaries, 168 consolidated only some subsidiaries, and 9 did not consolidate any subsidiaries. The principal types of subsidiaries not consolidated were finance related, real estate, and foreign.

termine whose assets and liabilities are being reported. The real crux of the issue is that the reporting entity does not exist legally. Problems encountered with consolidated statements, such as those listed above, abound and have led some to believe that consolidated statements should be supplemented by separate company statements. In an extensive study of the usefulness of consolidated financial statements, Walker concluded that consolidated statements are not essential and probably not the optimal method of communicating information about a group of affiliated enterprises.[14] The FASB, in SFAS 14, likewise concluded that, although consolidated statements are useful,

> . . . investors and creditors find segment information to be useful in analyzing and understanding consolidated statements and therefore in analyzing overall enterprise results.[15]

It is interesting to note, however, that the Securities and Exchange Commission (SEC) apparently holds the view that consolidated financial statements are less likely to be misinterpreted than separate company financial statements. Prior to March 31, 1982, the parent company of a consolidated group was required to file with the SEC its own separate company financial statements together with consolidated statements. Accounting Series Release (ASR) 302 changed that reporting requirement. Today only consolidated financial statements need be filed by a parent company.

Consolidated statements appear to convey useful information. Consolidation practice alternatives, however, should be reduced because a situation of flexibility exists. Moreover, to overcome the problem of loss of information through aggregation, the data should be disaggregated and separate company statements should be reported together with consolidated statements.

TRANSLATION OF FOREIGN OPERATIONS

Translating foreign-based operations' finances into U.S. dollars has been addressed by all three standard-setting bodies. The Committee on Accounting procedure issued two ARBs on the subject (4 and 43); the Accounting Principles Board issued one APB (6) and discussed the subject at length in 1971 but did not issue a pronouncement; and the FASB has issued three SFASs (1, 8, and 52). The accounting problem is one of reporting foreign-currency-denominated operations in consolidated financial statements that are expressed in U.S. dollars.

---

[14]Walker (1976, pp. 112–113).
[15]FASB (1976a, para. 62).

The problem in accounting for foreign operations is that the historical cost accounting model does not easily accommodate measurements in multiple and unstable units of measure. Thus, the two basic accounting questions that arise are these:

1. At what rate or rates of exchange should foreign operations be translated?
2. What should be done with the amount relating to the effect of a change in the exchange rate?

There are numerous approaches to the translation of foreign operations, but all stem from the basic orientation one adopts. A **U.S. dollar orientation** requires an enterprise to account for foreign operations "as if" those operations actually occurred in U.S. dollars. That is, foreign-currency-denominated assets, liabilities, revenues, and expenses are reported as if originally recorded in U.S. dollars. On the other hand, a **foreign currency orientation** recognizes that the foreign operations occurred in a foreign currency and that those operations may not affect U.S. dollars; therefore, accounting should be consistent with the foreign currency economic impact of the operations. Foreign-currency-denominated assets, liabilities, revenues, and expenses are assumed to be measured in the foreign currency, but are translated to U.S. dollars for reporting purposes. Consistent with the foreign orientation is the notion that exchange rate changes do not affect operations or cash flows until the net assets are exchanged. Therefore, the effects of changing exchange rates should not be reported in income until the net assets are exchanged.

SFAS 8

SFAS 8 and previous standards were consistent with the U.S. dollar orientation. All balance sheet items that were carried at current or future exchange prices (e.g., monetary items, inventories at market price, and investments at market price) were translated at the current exchange rate while items carried at past prices (e.g., fixed assets) were translated at exchange rates existing at the time the item was acquired (i.e., the historical exchange rate). Income statement items were translated at the average exchange rate for the reporting period—except that items related to balance sheet accounts which were translated at historical exchange rates (e.g., cost of goods sold and depreciation) were also translated at the historical rates. The exchange adjustment, the amount required to balance the statements due to different translation rates, was reported each period on the income statement as an exchange gain or loss. This complex translation was necessary to convert foreign currency account balances to their U.S. dollar equivalent; that is, to arrive at the same dollar amount as if dollars had been used as the accounting basis all along.

SFAS 8 was faithful to the historical cost accounting model but it produced illogical results from an economic viewpoint. For example, assume a Swiss subsidiary of a U.S. enterprise borrows $100 million in Swiss francs to finance the construction of a plant that costs $120 million in Swiss francs. Swiss franc revenues generated from use of the new plant will be used to retire the Swiss franc debt, therefore, no U.S. dollars will be used. If the franc appreciates 10% against the U.S. dollar, the liability would be written up to $110 million and an "accounting loss" of $10 million would be reported in the consolidated financial statements in accordance with SFAS 8. Because the cost of the plant is translated at the historical rate, however, no recognition would be given to the fact that the plant may be "worth" more in terms of its future net revenue stream in francs that will be used to retire the debt.

The preceding transaction may be viewed in two ways economically: (1) a gain of $2 million occurred because the building is "worth" $12 million more, while the debt owed is only $10 million more; or (2) no gain or loss occurred because the Swiss subsidiary is self-contained and its operations do not affect the U.S. parent's cash flows, nor do exchange rate changes affect the subsidiary's cash flows. As can be seen, accounting numbers produced by SFAS 8, although faithful to the historical cost model, did not necessarily reflect the perceived economic impact of the foreign operations.

A number of empirical studies were made of the economic impact of SFAS 8 on American multinational enterprises. Although the studies were directed to many facets of the subject, the only aspect where any possible impact was found dealt with foreign exchange risk and management policies regarding hedging of foreign currency exposures. Foreign currency exposure may be defined as either accounting or economic exposure. Accounting exposure is the exposure to exchange gains and losses resulting from translating foreign-currency-denominated financial statements into U.S. dollars (e.g., the $10 million we have just been considering). Economic exposure is the exposure to cash flow changes resulting from dealings in foreign-denominated transactions and commitments (e.g., the necessity to use more U.S. dollars to settle a foreign-currency-denominated debt).

In general, accounting exposure does not affect foreign currency cash flows nor does it affect reporting currency cash flows (i.e., U.S. dollars). Rather, it results in "paper" debits and credits. An example is the translation of the $110 million liability of the preceding example; it would result in reporting a $10 million loss but would not affect either Swiss franc or U.S. dollar cash flows. On the other hand, economic exposure does affect directly consolidated cash flows. An example would be if the $110 million Swiss franc debt were settled using U.S. dollars rather than internationally generated Swiss francs.

Many studies found that multinational enterprises adopted policies of minimizing, through hedging activities, accounting exposure.[16] Unfortu-

---

[16]See, for example, Evans, Folks, and Jilling (1978); and Shank, Dillard, and Murdock (1979).

nately, accounting exposure and economic exposure frequently were opposite; for example, there might be a short accounting exposure and a long economic exposure. The result, then, was that many enterprises were risking cash resources through forward exchange contracts, to hedge a noncash exposure at the sacrifice of economic exposure. Those enterprises, in essence, were transferring a foreign exchange loss under SFAS 8 into an interest cost and simultaneously risking greater economic exposure.

SFAS 52

In May 1978, the FASB requested comments from constituents regarding the first twelve SFASs. Eighty-eight percent of the comments received requested that the Board reconsider SFAS 8. The primary complaints with SFAS 8 were similar to those illustrated in the preceding example: exchange gains and losses are reported when the reverse had occurred from an economic viewpoint.

SFAS 52 changes drastically the means of accounting for foreign currency operations. It adopts a foreign currency orientation rather than a U.S. dollar orientation. The objectives of translation are:

1. To provide information that is generally compatible with the expected economic effects of a rate change on an enterprise's cash flows and equity.
2. To reflect in consolidated statements the results and relationships of the individual consolidated entities as measured in their functional currencies.[17]

The SFAS defines functional currency as:

> ... the currency of the primary economic environment in which the entity operates; normally, that is the currency of the environment in which an entity primarily generates and expends cash.[18]

The objective of translation under SFAS 52, then, is to avoid reporting accounting exchange gains and losses when the opposite (from an economic viewpoint) has occurred, and not to report foreign-currency-denominated operations as if they had occurred in U.S. dollars. Thus, if the results of foreign-currency-denominated operations will not affect U.S. dollar cash flows, no exchange gain or loss is recorded. Moreover, assets, liabilities, revenues, and expenses that are denominated in a foreign currency are measured in that currency, and then translated to U.S. dollars.

To accomplish its objectives, SFAS 52 adopts a net investment approach. This means that net income is measured in the foreign currency, then restated into dollars at the average exchange rate for the period. All balance sheet items are translated at the current exchange rate at the end of the period. Any exchange adjustment resulting from translating balance

[17]FASB (1981b, para. 4).
[18]FASB (1981b, para. 162).

sheet and income statement items at different exchange rates is displayed in a separate component of stockholders' equity, not as a gain or loss on the income statement. The separate component of stockholders' equity is taken into income only upon complete or substantially complete liquidation of the foreign investment by the U.S. parent. At that time, it is included in the gain or loss on disposition of the investment (e.g., net proceeds from sale minus carrying amount of the investment minus debit component of equity, equals gain or loss on disposition).

SFAS 52 does not specify how to determine the functional currency but it does give guidance. Paragraph 6 states:

> For an entity with operations that are relatively self-contained and integrated within a particular country, the functional currency generally would be the currency of that country. However, a foreign entity's functional currency might not be the currency of the country in which the entity is located. For example, the parent's currency generally would be the functional currency for foreign operations that are a direct and integral component or extension of the parent company's operations.[19]

A U.S. parent enterprise may have numerous foreign operations, each with its own functional currency.

If the functional currency of a foreign operation is judged to be U.S. dollars, a different approach is taken. For example, if a foreign subsidiary of a U.S. parent is, in reality, an extension of that parent (i.e., it is nothing more than a sales branch selling the U.S. parent's products and remitting the sales proceeds to the U.S. parent), then although the subsidiary's records are kept in a foreign currency, the functional currency is the U.S. dollar, and the accounting records must be converted into U.S. dollars. This is called "remeasurement" and is done by following the approach in SFAS 8. As a result, exchange gains and losses arising from translation from the currency of record into the functional currency would be recognized on the income statement. Thus, in certain situations, SFAS 52 will result in the same reporting as SFAS 8 (with the exception of monetary liabilities which are translated at current rather than historical rates).

Although remeasurement may appear inconsistent with the approach adopted in SFAS 52, it is entirely consistent on theoretical grounds. The theory behind the functional currency concept is that some foreign subsidiaries are self-contained and that exchange rate fluctuations affect neither them nor their U.S. parent companies until cash is exchanged. On the other hand, however, if the functional currency is really the U.S. dollar, the presumption is that the foreign operation is not self-contained but rather an extension of the parent. Consequently, exchange rate fluctuations will affect cash flows and should be reported on the income statement as was done under SFAS 8.

A problem does occur with the functional currency concept and the use of current exchange rates whenever the functional currency is too unsta-

---

[19]FASB (1981b, para. 6).

ble to be used as a measurement base. This problem is referred to as "the disappearing asset problem" and is present when the functional currency is experiencing rapid inflation much in excess of that experienced in the reporting currency. For example, assume an Argentine subsidiary purchased a fixed asset in December 1974, when the Argentina peso–U.S. dollar exchange rate was $.20. The asset cost 20,000,000 pesos and would be translated as $4,000,000. By September, 1982, the exchange rate was .000040; thus, the asset would be translated at $800.

At least three approaches are available for accounting for the disappearing asset problem. It could be ignored—so the asset would be translated at $800. The original exposure draft (ED) leading up to SFAS 52 adopted this position but it was objected to by most of the comment letters received by the FASB. In the second ED, the FASB proposed to adjust cost of the asset in pesos for the effects of changing prices and translate the adjusted amount at the current exchange rate. Although this approach probably is sound theoretically, it too met with considerable objection. The primary argument opposed to it was that it would result in introducing onto U.S. consolidated financial statements something that is not permitted for changes in prices denominated in U.S. dollars. Finally, the FASB, in SFAS 52, specified that in highly inflationary economies (defined as those with a cumulative inflation rate of approximately 100 percent over three years), the U.S. dollar should be used as if it were the functional currency. Translations, therefore, are similar to the SFAS 8 approach and fixed assets are translated at the historical rate (e.g., .20 in the preceding example).

SUMMARY

Two distinct but related subjects were discussed in this chapter—accounting for investments and translations of foreign operations. Although they are diverse, there is a common element: the usefulness, or lack thereof, of consolidating financial statements that are the result of the methods of accounting used to account for investments and foreign operations.

In accounting for investments, a rather arbitrary rule of 20% is used to determine whether the cost or equity method of accounting should be used. Under the cost method, declines in market price (below cost) on current investments are reported in income, while similar declines on noncurrent investments are reported in the stockholders' equity. Also increases in market price are ignored, except to the extent of previous writedowns. Under the equity method, the investment account represents neither cost nor market price.

For investments greater than 50%, full consolidated financial statements must be prepared. The alternatives for preparing these statements are diverse and may result in different enterprises reporting significantly different amounts even though the underlying circumstances are identical. Moreover, the classification of minority interest arising in consolidation is unsettled and may be classified as either a liability or a stockholders' equity, or neither, depending on the approach taken.

Accounting for the consolidation of a foreign subsidiary's financial statements with those of a U.S. parent has been a controversial subject. The FASB's latest attempt adopts a foreign currency perspective and results in consolidated financial statements that are significantly different from those previously prepared. Only time will tell whether the "new" financial statements are more or less useful than the "old" ones.

QUESTIONS

1. There are two methods of accounting for intercompany investments in stock—the cost and the equity methods. These methods are not alternatives for the same investment. Discuss the theory behind the two methods and how one determines which method to apply.
2. Occasionally it may be necessary to change from the cost method to the equity method or vice versa. Discuss why a change would be necessary and how the change would be treated.
3. The equity method reports neither the investor's cost nor the market value of the investment. Do you believe the equity method provides useful information? Why, or why not?
4. The LCM rule is applied differently depending on the classification of the investment. Do you agree with this finite uniformity? Why, or why not?
5. A separate component of equity is created for certain unrealized adjustments under both SFAS 12 and SFAS 52. Are the adjustments under the two SFASs similar in nature? Why did the FASB create the separate components of equity?
6. What is a one-line consolidation? What differences occur to financial statements when a one-line consolidation is used rather than full consolidation?
7. There are two basic theories of reporting minority interest. Discuss each. Contrast the two theories with the methods generally used in accounting practice.
8. Assume the following:
   P Company acquires 60% of S Company for $750,000.
   S Company book value is $1,000,000.
   Fair value of S Company's identifiable net assets is $1,100,000.

Determine what would be reported for S Company identifiable net assets, goodwill, and minority interest in consolidated financial statements under each of these methods:

(a) Proprietary approach
(b) Parent approach
(c) Modified parent approach
(d) Entity approach

9. Discuss the usefulness of consolidated financial statements as contrasted to separate company financial statements.

10. What are the differences between a foreign currency orientation and a U.S. dollar orientation regarding the translation of foreign currency operations?

11. Why was SFAS 8 criticized?

12. Many believe that SFAS 52 is not in conformity with the historical cost accounting model. Is that true? Why, or why not?

13. Many state that the results reported under SFAS 8 did not reflect economic reality while those reported under SFAS 52 do reflect economic reality. Discuss.

14. Why does hyperinflation invalidate the functional currency approach? How does remeasurement solve the problem?

15. Do you believe that it is possible to prepare useful consolidated financial statements when foreign subsidiaries are included? Why, or why not?

CASES AND PROBLEMS

1. As a result of the volatility in the security markets, the marketable equity securities owned by the insurance operations of Weston Fairfield, Inc. have experienced substantial market value declines after the close of its fiscal year. Weston has not yet issued its financial statements. The marketable equity securities are carried at market with unrealized gains or losses included in the stockholders' equity in accordance with generally accepted accounting principles for insurance companies.

Required:
(a) How do you believe the above situation should be handled in Weston's financial statements in order for those statements to convey useful but not misleading information?
(b) How should the situation be handled in accordance with SFAS 12?

2. Mankeese, Inc., owns approximately 10% of the voting shares of Yankeese, Inc. It has been determined that the equity method of accounting

is not appropriate because Mankeese cannot exert significant influence over Yankeese.

At the end of Mankeese's fiscal year, the quoted market price of Yankeese's shares is less than Mankeese's cost. Mankeese does not want to recognize the decline because it has publicly stated that it intends to acquire at least 15% more of Yankeese's shares. Moreover, it has the financial resources to make the acquisition; however, Yankeese opposes the takeover and plans to fight it.

Required: Should Mankeese be required to apply LCM to its investment in Yankeese? Discuss your position.

3. The following selected amounts pertain to a parent company and its 60%-owned subsidiary at year end.

	Parent	*Subsidiary*
Current Assets	$ 500,000	$1,000,000
Noncurrent Assets		
(Excluding Subsidiary Investment)	5,000,000	2,000,000
Current Liabilities	750,000	250,000
Noncurrent Liabilities	2,000,000	750,000
Revenues	1,700,000	1,500,000
Expenses	1,600,000	900,000
Dividends	100,000	600,000

Required:

(a) Why is consolidation misleading?

(b) What are alternative ways of reporting for the parent company?

BIBLIOGRAPHY OF REFERENCED WORKS

American Institute of Certified Public Accountants (1981). "Certain Issues that Affect Accounting for Minority Interests in Consolidated Financial Statements," *Issues Paper* (AICPA).
——— (1982). *Accounting Trends and Techniques* (AICPA).
Baxter, George C., and James C. Spinney (1975). "A Closer Look at Consolidated Financial Statement Theory," *Canadian Chartered Accountant* (January 1975), pp. 31–36.
Committee on Accounting Procedure (1959). "Consolidated Financial Statements," *Accounting Research Bulletin No. 51* (AICPA).
Copeland, Ronald M.; Robert Strawser; and John G. Binns (1972). "Accounting for Investments in Common Stock," *Financial Executive* (February 1972), pp. 36–46.
Evans, Thomas G.; William R. Folks, Jr.; and Michael Jilling (1978). *The Impact of Financial Accounting Standards No. 8 on the Foreign Exchange Risk Manage-*

ment *Practices of American Multinational Firms: An Economic Impact Study* (FASB).

Financial Accounting Standards Board (1975). "Accounting for the Translation of Foreign Currency Transactions and Foreign Currency Financial Statements," *Statement of Financial Accounting Standards No. 8* (FASB).

———— (1976a). "Financial Reporting for Segments of a Business Enterprise," *Statement of Financial Accounting Standards No. 14* (FASB).

———— (1976b). *Discussion Memorandum: Accounting for Business Combinations and Purchased Intangibles* (FASB).

———— (1980). "Elements of Financial Statements of Business Enterprises," *Statement of Financial Accounting Concepts No. 3* (FASB).

———— (1981a). "Criteria for Applying the Equity Method of Accounting for Investments in Common Stock," *Interpretation No. 35* (FASB).

———— (1981b). "Foreign Currency Translation," *Statement of Financial Accounting Standards No. 52* (FASB).

Lloyd, Michael, and Jerry Weygandt (1971). "Market Value Information for Nonsubsidiary Investments," *The Accounting Review* (October 1971), pp. 756–764.

Moonitz, Maurice (1944). *The Entity Theory of Consolidated Statements* (American Accounting Association).

Paton, William A. (1922). *Accounting Theory* (Ronald Press).

Shank, John K.; Jesse F. Dillard; and Richard J. Murdock (1979). *Assessing the Economic Impact of FASB No. 8* (Financial Executives Research Foundation).

Walker, R. G. (1976). "An Evaluation of the Information Conveyed by Consolidated Statements," *Abacus* (December 1976), pp. 77–115.

ADDITIONAL READINGS

ACCOUNTING FOR INVESTMENTS

Blum, James D., and Herbert L. Jensen (1978). "Accounting for Marketable Securities in Accordance with FASB Statement No. 12," *Management Accounting* (September 1978), pp. 33–41.

Lynch, Thomas Edward (1975). "Accounting for Investments in Equity Securities by the Equity and Market Value Methods," *Financial Analysts Journal* (January–February 1975), pp. 62–69.

O'Connor, Melvin C., and James C. Hamre (1972). "Alternative Methods of Accounting for Long-Term Nonsubsidiary Intercorporate Investments in Common Stock," *The Accounting Review* (April 1972), pp. 308–319.

Storey, Reed K., and Maurice Moonitz (1976). "Market Value Methods for Intercorporate Investments in Stock," *Accounting Research Monograph No. 1* (AICPA).

CONSOLIDATED FINANCIAL STATEMENTS

Walker, R. G. (1978). "International Accounting Compromises: The Case of Consolidation Accounting," *Abacus* (December 1978), pp. 97–111.

FOREIGN CURRENCY TRANSLATION

Dukes, Roland E. (1978). *An Empirical Investigation of the Effects of the Statement of Financial Accounting Standards No. 8 on Security Return Behavior* (FASB).

Lorensen, Leonard (1972). *Reporting Foreign Operations of U.S. Companies in U.S. Dollars* (AICPA).

Peat, Marwick, Mitchell & Co. (1977). *A Survey of the Economic Impacts of FASB Statement No. 8, "Accounting for the Translation of Foreign Currency Transactions and Foreign Currency Financial Statements"* (Peat, Marwick, Mitchell & Co., 1977).

Wyman, Harold E. (1976). "Analysis of Gains or Losses from Foreign Monetary Items: An Application of Purchasing Power Parity Concepts," *The Accounting Review* (July 1976), pp. 545–558.

CHAPTER 18

Business Combinations

A business combination, from an accounting perspective, is defined in the following manner:

> A business combination occurs when a corporation and one or more incorporated or unincorporated businesses are brought together into one accounting entity. The single (accounting) entity carries on the activities of the previously separate, independent enterprises.[1]

There are two general types of business combinations: (1) a statutory merger or statutory consolidation in which two or more companies become one legal and accounting entity, and (2) the acquisition of a wholly or partially owned subsidiary by a parent company.

With a statutory combination (one surviving entity), the actual accounting occurs in the records of the surviving entity. However, separate sets of accounting records exist with a parent-subsidiary type of combination. In order to prepare consolidated (parent-subsidiary) financial statements, it is necessary to combine the separate sets of records, and to make certain other adjustments to arrive at the proper consolidated totals. The focus in this chapter is on the end result of accounting for business combinations, not on the consolidation-adjustment procedures themselves. Adjustment pro-

---

[1]APB (1970a, para. 1).

cedures are covered at length in advanced financial accounting textbooks. Finally, consolidation of partially owned subsidiaries is not addressed in this chapter because the issue was discussed in Chapter 17.

Terminology regarding business combinations is not uniform throughout accounting literature. In this chapter, the terms suggested by the Financial Accounting Standards Board (FASB) are used:

Combined enterprise: The accounting entity that results from a combination.

Constituent companies: The business enterprises that enter into a combination.

Combinor: A constitutent company entering into a combination whose stockholders (owners) as a group end up with control of the voting stock (ownership interests) in the combined enterprise.

Combinee: A constituent company other than the combinor in a combination in which a combinor is identifiable.[2]

The primary accounting issue in a business combination is the valuation of the assets and liabilities of the combinor and combinee at the date the combination is consummated. There are three possibilities. One is to use the book values of both entities. This method is called **pooling of interests accounting.** A second method is to value the assets and liabilities of the combinee at market value and the combinor at book value. This is called **purchase accounting.** The third method, sometimes referred to as the **new entity approach,** results in both combinor's and combinee's assets and liabilities being measured at market values. The central problem faced by standard-setting bodies is whether there are relevant circumstances to justify use of more than one method to account for business combinations.

This chapter is organized in the following manner. First there is an overview of the three possible methods of accounting for business combinations. Then a review is made of the development of accounting standards in the United States. The requirements of Accounting Principles Board (APB) 16 are presented in detail followed by an illustration of the differences between pooling and purchase accounting. Finally, research into the use and effects of pooling and purchase accounting is reviewed and evaluated.

THE THREE ACCOUNTING METHODS

POOLING OF INTERESTS

The pooling of interests concept of a business combination is based on the premise that no substantive transaction occurs between the combinee

[2]FASB (1976, para. 4).

and combinor. Rather, they merely unite their respective ownership interests and continue as a single enterprise. The first applications of the pooling of interests concept resembled more a reorganization than a business combination; for example, the combination of two subsidiaries of the same parent enterprise. In such a situation, no new accountability is established by the combination; the combinor and combinee merely added together their previously separate financial statements to effect the combination. Pooling of interests started just that way, but eventually the method began to be applied to the combination of previously unrelated constituents. It is at this juncture that abuses of the pooling concept began to occur. In very few of these combinations can it really be argued that no *substantive* transaction between the combinor and combinee occurs.

Conceptually a business combination that is a pooling of interests marks the formal unification of two previously separate ownership groups. The combinor and combinee agree to combine, or pool, their equity interests and continue as a single enterprise. There is no purchase by one constituent of the other; thus, the assumption is that no exchange transaction occurs. This is somewhat similar to the concept of a nonmonetary exchange of similar fixed assets. As a result, the "pooled" assets and liabilities have the same basis of accounting after the combination as they did before the combination. The combined enterprise's assets and liabilities after the combination will be equal to the summation of the combinor's and combinee's respective amounts just prior to the combination. Total stockholders' equity of the combined enterprise will be equal to the sum of those of the combinor and combinee immediately prior to the combination. There may be some changes in individual components, depending on the rate of exchange, but in aggregate the total is the sum of the combinor and combinee.

When the assets are sold in an exchange transaction, retained earnings prior to the sale remain with the former owner and are not passed through to the new owner. But because a pooling of interests is not considered a sale, retained earnings of both the combinor and combinee prior to the business combination are passed through to the combined enterprise. Thus, the combined enterprise's income statement for the year that a pooling of interests occurs will include the income of both the combinor and combinee for the full twelve months regardless of when (during that twelve months) the combination occurred. Likewise, the retained earnings from periods prior to the combination for both the combinor and combinee are passed through to the combined enterprise.

PURCHASE METHOD

In purchase accounting, the assumption is that the combinor acquires the combinee and must account for the acquisition as it would for the acquisition of any asset. That is, the asset (the combinee company) is recorded by the combinor at the latter's cost determined as of the date the combination is consummated. This results in recording the combinee's net assets at their fair market value on the date of consummation. Any retained earnings of the combinee prior to the combination, whether in the current fiscal year or prior ones, are attributed to the former owners of the combinee. Thus, the retained earnings of the combined enterprise immediately after the combination as well as the combined income statement include only the combinor's earnings. Accounting for the combination, however, may be complicated for several reasons:

1. If part of the price paid is of a noncash nature, the total cost of the combinee may not be readily obvious.
2. The fair value of the combinee's assets and liabilities probably is not readily available because its statement of financial position reports only book values and, in fact, may not report all assets, such as internally developed patents.
3. Frequently, the total cost of the combinee is not equal to the summation of the fair values of its individual assets less liabilities, and the differential must be dealt with in some manner.

NEW ENTITY APPROACH

Another possible method of accounting for a business combination is to regard the combined enterprise as an entirely new entity. This approach results in the use of current values for all assets and liabilities, both those of the combinor and combinee, as of the date the combination is consummated. The reason for such an approach would be that the business combination results in a substantially new entity. In other words, more is involved than merely one entity purchasing and integrating another into its own operation. The very nature of the combination may be such that an entirely new operation has come into existence. This approach to accounting for business combinations has not been widely considered, but in certain circumstances, a case could be made for its use. It was identified as a possibility in the 1976 FASB discussion memorandum on business combinations.

DEVELOPMENT OF ACCOUNTING STANDARDS FOR BUSINESS COMBINATIONS

Although business combinations occurred in the United States before the passage of the Sherman Act in 1890, accounting for combinations was not a major issue before the 1940s. Most combinations were accounted for as if they were purchases of the combinee by the combinor. The underlying assumption was that the combinee ceased to exist; thus, its net assets were considered liquidated and the proceeds from that liquidation, as distributed to its shareholders. The combinor merely purchased a group of net assets and any profitability from those net assets would accrue in the future. Therefore, the net assets were recorded by the combinor at their current market values at the date the combination was consummated.

Eventually, however, some business combinations were structured differently. They were, in effect, reorganizations of existing ownership interests, with both the combinee's and combinor's stockholders continuing to share in the ownership of the "newly" formed enterprise. The combinee was not assumed to have liquidated as in the earlier combinations, but rather to continue in existence as a partner in the larger combined enterprise. As a result, no new accountability was assumed to have occurred, and the net assets of both the combinor and combinee were simply carried forward to the combined enterprise at their book values. An example of this type of combination was one involving two existing subsidiaries of the same parent corporation. Gradually, this latter method of accounting began to be applied to combinations involving unrelated constituents.[3]

As will be evident from the following discussion, the problem has been and continues to be the identification of what underlying circumstances, if any, surrounding a particular business combination will lead to a certain accounting treatment at the exclusion of another accounting treatment. If the underlying circumstances can be identified conceptually, the problem becomes the establishment of rules or guidelines to aid accounting practice in identifying those circumstances. Several official pronouncements covering accounting for business combinations have been issued. The first was Accounting Research Bulletin (ARB) 40 issued in 1950. This was followed by ARB 48 in 1957, and APB 16 in 1970.

ARB 40 (Codified as ARB 43, Chapter 7c)

ARB 40 recognized that business combinations could be differentiated on the basis of their underlying nature. Accounting for business combinations, therefore, should be in accordance with the nature of the combination and should reflect the underlying circumstances. The primary distinction between a pooling of interests and a purchase was based on the effect on the ownership interests of the constituent enterprises in the combined enterprise. If substantially all equity interests of the constituent enterprises survived in a combined enterprise, a pooling of interests was presumed to have occurred. On the other hand, if the equity interests of one of the constituent enterprises was substantially eliminated in the combined enterprise, a purchase was presumed to have occurred.

---

[3]Wyatt (1963, pp. 20–21).

Additional guidance was provided in ARB 40 to differentiate between a pooling of interests and a purchase. A pooling was more clearly indicated if the relative sizes of the constituent enterprises were similar, if the activities of the constituent enterprises were either similar or complementary, and if the managements of the constituent enterprises (or at least the ability to control management) both survived in the combined enterprise. ARB 40 recognized that some combinations may appear to be pooling of interests but in substance are purchases:

> A plan or firm intention and understanding to retire capital stock issued to the owners of one or more corporate parties, or substantial changes in ownership occurring immediately before or after the combination, would . . . tend to indicate that the combination is a purchase.[4]

Determining whether a business combination is a pooling or a purchase is critical to the accounting and may significantly affect the financial statements of the combined enterprise for many years after the combination. The financial statement ramifications of the two methods of accounting for a business combination will be discussed fully later in the chapter.

ARB 48

Many felt that the criteria established by ARB 40 to distinguish between a business combination that is a pooling of interests and one that is a purchase were not operational because they were too vague. Virtually any business combination could be accounted for as a pooling regardless of the underlying circumstances. That led the Committee on Accounting Procedure to reconsider the subject. It issued ARB 48 in 1957, which superseded Chapter 7C of ARB 43. ARB 48 stated that a pooling of interests combination

> . . . may be described for accounting purposes as a business combination of two or more corporations in which the holders of substantially all of the ownership interests in the constituent corporations become the owners of a single corporation which owns the assets and businesses of the constituent corporations . . .[5]

Certain criteria promulgated in ARB 48 were designed as reliable guides to determine when a business combination was a pooling of interests. Shares of stock received by the owners of the constituent enterprises should be substantially in proportion to their respective interests prior to the combination, and the relative voting rights should not be altered by issuing senior equity or debt securities. As with ARB 40, no intention to retire a substantial portion of the stock issued to effect the combination should exist. The combined enterprise should not sell a significant portion

[4]Committee on Accounting Procedure (1950, para. 2).
[5]Committee on Accounting Procedure (1957, para, 4).

of one of the constituent's assets because to do so would not be consistent with the pooling of all equity interests. Likewise, management of all constituents should carry forward in the combined enterprise. Interestingly, the criterion from ARB 40 that the constituents be relatively of the same size was not retained in ARB 48.

The practical effect of ARB 48 was to broaden rather than narrow the difference between a business combination that was a pooling of interests and one that was a purchase. Many felt that ARB 48 rendered the criteria established by ARB 40 less operational than before. Wyatt stated that ARB 48 "presented the criteria in such a manner than any given combination could be supported as either a purchase or a pooling, depending largely upon the intentions or desires of the parties to the transaction."[6]

APB 16

The controversy over accounting for business combinations contributed to the APB's demise (see discussion in Chapter 2). There were APB members who felt strongly that pooling should be disallowed. Other members felt that it should be acceptable accounting for practically any business combination. These opposite positions eventually came together and resulted in the issuance of APB 16. That document recognizes that both the pooling of interests and purchase methods are acceptable but are not alternative accounting treatments for the same business combination. Any business combination must be accounted for as a purchase unless it meets all of the conditions established by APB 16 for a pooling of interests. If those conditions are met, the business combination must be accounted for as a pooling of interests.

There are three broad conditions established by APB 16 that must be met in order to use pooling of interest accounting: attributes of the combining enterprises, manner of combining interests, and absence of planned transactions. These three conditions are subdivided into twelve strict criteria. The criteria are the result of the deliberations of the opposing forces on the APB and, in many cases, were established arbitrarily. Although perhaps more operational than ARB 48, many of the criteria are so arbitrary that they have resulted in the issuance of thirty-nine AICPA interpretations and numerous SEC and FASB releases regarding the application of the various criteria. The twelve criteria will be examined in detail later in this chapter.

FASB DISCUSSION MEMORANDUM (DM)

Although the FASB has not established any standards other than technical bulletins on accounting for business combinations, it has addressed

---

[6]Wyatt (1963, p. 38).

the subject. Shortly after formation, the FASB issued an open letter to all interested parties requesting views on existing APBs and ARBs. The letter stated in part

> The Board is interested in learning of the experiences of users, preparers, and auditors of financial statements which would indicate that these exist- ing pronouncements need (1) interpretation, (2) amendment or (3) replacement.[7]

The replies to that letter indicated that APBs 16 and 17 (Intangible Assets) most needed the FASB's attention. Accordingly, the FASB added a project to its agenda to encompass a comprehensive reconsideration of accounting for business combinations and purchased intangibles. That project resulted in the issuance of a DM in 1976 entitled "Accounting for Business Combi- nations and Purchased Intangibles." The DM was very comprehensive, cov- ering all relevant areas in accounting for business combinations. After the public hearings in 1977, the FASB deferred action on the project pending development of the conceptual framework project. Subsequent to that de- cision, the FASB dropped the project from its agenda, citing the project's low priority in relation to other existing and potential projects.[8]

APPLICATION OF APB 16

POOLING OF INTERESTS

The underlying assumption of a pooling is that all risks and rewards of ownership of the stockholders of all constituents are unchanged by the combination. These risks and rewards should be no more or less than prior to the combination. The practical problem, however, is identifying when that situation occurs—if indeed it would ever occur in reality.

Pooling of interests accounting has obvious financial statement advan- tages, as will be illustrated. Therefore, pooling is generally desired by man- agement regardless of the underlying circumstances. In fact, a survey by the FASB reported in its 1976 DM on business combinations indicated that the availability of pooling accounting is a strong impetus to business combinations.

The goal of APB 16 was to prevent abuses of the pooling concept that had been the order of the day in the 1960s. To achieve that goal paragraphs 46–48 of APB 16 establish the conditions that a business combination must meet in order to be accounted for as a pooling of interests.

---

[7]FASB (1976, para. 28).
[8]FASB (1981, p. 1).

Paragraph 46–Attributes of the Combining Enterprises

The condition "attributes of the combining enterprises" is presented in paragraph 46. It is subdivided into two criteria:

a. Each of the combining companies is autonomous and has not been a subsidiary or division of another corporation within two years before the plan of combination is initiated.

b. Each of the combining companies is independent of the other combining companies.[9]

The criteria established by paragraph 46 are to assure that the constituents in a pooling of interests are unrelated enterprises. The underlying motive for that requirement is to prevent an enterprise from fragmenting its organization and "pooling" only part of it, thereby circumventing the nature of a pooling of interests, which is a uniting of *all* equity interests.

Paragraph 47–Manner of Combining Interests

Paragraph 47, "manner of combining interests," consists of seven interrelated criteria all established to assure the continuity of ownership interests of the constituent enterprises in the combined enterprise. The criteria are these:

a. The combination is effected in a single transaction or is completed in accordance with a specific plan within one year after the plan is initiated.

b. A corporation offers and issues only common stock with rights identical to those of the majority of its outstanding voting common stock in exchange for substantially all of the voting common stock interest of another company at the date the plan of combination is consummated.

c. None of the combining companies changes the equity interest of the voting common stock in contemplation of effecting the combination either within two years before the plan of combination is initiated or between the dates the combination is initiated and consummated; changes in contemplation of effecting the combination may include distributions to stockholders and additional issuances, exchanges, and retirements of securities.

d. Each of the combining companies reacquires shares of voting common stock only for purposes other than business combinations, and no company reacquires more than a normal number of shares between the dates the plan of combination is initiated and consummated.

e. The ratio of interest of an individual common stockholder to those of other common stockholders in a combining company remains the same as a result of the exchange of stock to effect the combination.

---

[9]APB (1970a, para. 46).

f. The voting rights to which the common stock ownership interests in the resulting combined corporation are entitled are exercisable by the stockholders; the stockholders are neither deprived of nor restricted in exercising those rights for a period.

g. The combination is resolved at the date the plan is consummated and no provisions of the plan relating to the issue of securities or other consideration are pending.[10]

Criteria in paragraphs 47a, c, e, f, and g are aimed directly at ensuring that the stockholder groups of all constituents of the combination receive their proportionate rights in the combined enterprise. Criterion 47a is designed to prevent a situation in which some stockholders of the constituent enterprises receive more (or less) than their proportionate ownership interest in the combined enterprise in a multiple-step pooling. For example, assume 40% of the combinee's stockholders agree to an exchange rate of 2 for 1, while the other 60% hold out for a better exchange offer. If subsequently the latter group gets an exchange rate of other than 2 for 1, the combination could not be treated as a pooling of interest. Criterion 47c is designed to prevent at least two possible situations, both of which are contrary to the nature of a pooling. One situation that would proscribe pooling of interests accounting occurs when one of the constituent enterprises distributes a dividend greater than normal prior to the business combination. The reason for this rule is to prevent an enterprise from distributing part of its assets and pooling the remainder. Another situation proscribing pooling of interests is when one of the constituents reacquires its own stock and then reissues it in order to obtain a new stockholder group that will agree to the business combination.

Criteria 47e and 47f exist to ensure that the constituent stockholder groups maintain their proportionate right to control management of the combined enterprise. They require, for example, that if an individual owns 25% of the combinee enterprise, he must receive 25% of the combinor's shares exchanged for the combinee enterprise. Moreover, those shares must have the same rights as all other combinor shares and the rights must not be restricted for a period of time. Criterion 47g prohibits contingent consideration agreements based on events subsequent to the date the combination is consummated. This criterion is designed to prevent the dilution of either the combinor's or combinee's ownership interests in the combined enterprise.

Criteria 47b, 47c, and 47d are aimed directly at ensuring that all equity interests are combined in order for a business combination to be accounted for as a pooling of interests. Criterion 47b is designed to make certain that substantially all (90%) of the constituents' ownership interests are pooled. Criterion 47d prevents use of treasury stock in pooling of interests business

---

[10] APB (1970a, para. 47).

combinations; this is to ensure that all equity interests are combined and, as with criterion 47c (see earlier discussion), prevents realigning equity interests to obtain a new stockholder group that will agree to the combination.

Paragraph 48–Absence of Planned Transactions

Paragraph 48, "absence of planned transactions," is designed to prevent structuring a business combination as a pooling of interests and then, once that accounting is accomplished, violating the nature of a pooling of interests (that is, not uniting all equity interests). The three criteria in paragraph 47 are these:

a. The combined corporation does not agree directly or indirectly to retire or reacquire all or part of the common stock issued to effect the combination.

b. The combined corporation does not enter into other financial arrangements for the benefit of the former stockholders of a combining company, such as a guaranty of loans secured by stocks issued in the combination, which in effect negates the exchange of equity securities.

c. The combined corporation does not intend or plan to dispose of a significant part of the assets of the combining companies within two years after the combination other than disposals in the ordinary course of business of the formerly separate companies and to eliminate duplicate facilities or excess capacity.[11]

Without criterion 48a the combinor could exchange its stock for the combinee's stock and subsequent to the combination reacquire the stock issued to effect the business combination and treat a purchase as a pooling of interests. Criterion 48b is designed to prevent one of the constituent stockholder groups from being disproportionately rewarded because of the business combination. Although a violation of criterion 48c may not result in a situation that is unfavorable or disproportionate to a particular constituent group, it would be inconsistent with a pooling of all assets and the noncash nature of a pooling.

PURCHASE METHOD

Any business combination that does not qualify as a pooling of interests under APB 16 must be accounted for as a purchase of the combinee by the combinor. In a purchase combination, generally the combinor substantively is the only surviving enterprise. However, identification of the combinor when both (all) constituents are similar in size and the combination

---

[11]APB (1970a, para. 48).

is effected by an exchange of voting common stock may not be obvious. APB 16 provides that unless persuasive evidence to the contrary exists, the former stockholder group of a constituent enterprise that ultimately holds a majority of the voting rights of the combined enterprise is presumed to be the combinor.[12] This decision is critical to the accounting because a new accounting basis is established for the combinee's assets and liabilities as of the date the combination is consummated, while no such new accounting basis is established for the combinor's assets and liabilities.

The resolution of three problems is of critical importance in accounting for a business combination as a purchase. These problems are now discussed.

Measuring the Total Cost of the Combinee

The consideration given by the combinor to acquire the combinee may be one or a combination of numerous forms—such as cash, voting common stock, other types of equity securities, debt securities, or convertible securities. If the total consideration is cash, there is no problem in determining total cost. However, any other type of consideration may result in some valuation problems. If nonconvertible debt securities are given, their fair value can be determined by discounting the securities at an appropriate market rate of interest. When equity securities or convertible debt securities are given, their fair value may not be readily apparent. When an active market exists for the securities given to acquire the combinee, the market price of those securities probably is the best indicator of their fair value if the quantity issued would not have a dilutive effect on that market price. If an active market in the securities does not exist or if the quantity issued would have a dilutive effect, some other means must be used to determine fair value of the consideration. An investment banker may be used to value the securities, or, if the fair value of the net assets acquired is more readily determinable, it could be used instead. In addition the amount determined as the cost of the combinee must include the direct costs of the acquisition, such as finder's fees and legal fees, as well as the fair value of the combinee's liabilities assumed by the combinor. Indirect costs incurred, such as costs of an acquisitions department and registration fees, are not considered part of the cost of the combinee.

Measuring the Fair Value of the Combinee

The fair value of the combinee's assets and liabilities must be determined as of the date the combination is consummated if it is accounted for as a purchase. Unfortunately, the historical cost based accounting system with its many peculiar conventions, such as LIFO and expensing of research and development costs, render the combinee's statement of financial position not particularly helpful in determining the fair value of its net

---

[12]APB (1970a, para. 70).

assets. None of the reported amounts for the following items, for example, would be useful:

1. inventories on the LIFO basis,
2. plant and other long-lived tangible assets,
3. intangibles,
4. long-term debt, particularly in periods of fluctuating interest rates, or
5. pension liabilities.

Paragraph 88 of APB 16 provides general guidelines for determining the fair values of specific categories of assets and liabilities. Exhibit 18-1 provides a summary of these guidelines.

It should be noted that the problem of valuing a going concern is not as simple as merely adding together the fair values of its individual assets less liabilities. Rather, the entire entity must be valued, frequently by use of experts in the field, and the individual fair values of net assets, when summed, may not be equal to the total fair value of the enterprise. Thus, the guidelines provided by paragraph 88 are useful only in allocating total cost, not in determining the fair value of the enterprise acquired.

EXHIBIT 18-1.
APB 16 Guidelines for Determining Fair Values

Marketable securities	Net realizable value
Receivables	Present value determined at current interest rates less an allowance for uncollectibles
Inventories, other than raw materials	Net realizable value less a reasonable profit
Raw materials	Current replacement cost
Plant and Equipment	Current replacement cost for similar assets to be used and net realizable value for assets to be sold
Other assets such as land and natural resources	Appraisal value
Identifiable intangibles	Appraisal value
Goodwill recorded on combinee's books	Ignored
Liabilities	Present value determined at current interest rates
Deferred income taxes on combinee's books	Ignored

Source: APB 16, para. 88.

Allocation of Cost to Assets Acquired

The total cost of the combinee must be recorded by the combinor. That cost is allocated to the combinee's net assets on the basis of their fair values. If the total cost exactly equals the sum of the fair values of the combinee's individual assets less liabilities, no problem exists and the assets and liabilities are recorded by the combinor at their fair values. As is more often the case, however, the total cost does not exactly equal the sum of the fair values of the individual assets less liabilities.

The combinor frequently will be willing to pay an amount greater than the fair value of the combinee's net assets. One reason for this may be the synergistic effect in that the fair value of a going operation may be greater than the sum of the fair values of its components individually. Other reasons may include certain unique intangible assets not recognized as accounting assets; for example, superior managerial skills, outstanding research and development skills, access to a new marketing area or a guaranteed supply of materials. Regardless of the reason, whenever the total cost of the combinee exceeds the fair value of its identifiable net assets, the excess is recorded as **goodwill.** APB 17 requires that goodwill arising in a business combination be amortized to income over a period not to exceed forty years. The straight-line method of amortization should be used unless it can be shown clearly that another method is more appropriate in the circumstances.[13]

Many feel that goodwill represents the value of favorable attitudes toward the enterprise. For example, it could represent the value of customer lists or a good location. Others hold that goodwill represents the discounted value of future excess earnings (over those considered average or normal) that has been acquired. In both situations, however, one cannot point to goodwill as an identifiable accounting asset. Thus, accounting practice has evolved as described above, that is, the goodwill amount "drops out" after all other items have been valued. It is, then, a master valuation account that represents all positive and negative errors in the valuation process for the acquired enterprise.

The amortization of goodwill has equally been a controversial subject. Some believe that its life is unlimited and that it should be carried on financial statements indefinitely. Others believe that it should be amortized but that its life cannot be reasonably determined. Others have suggested that, because its informational value to financial statement users is little, if any, it should be written off immediately to income or retained earnings upon acquisition. The position taken in APB 17 is arbitrary and cannot be defended on any theoretical grounds.

An interesting development pertaining to savings and loan institutions brought the whole question of the existence of goodwill and its amortiza-

---

[13]APB (1970b, paras. 26, 29, and 30).

tion to the forefront in 1982. Many of these thrift institutions were forced by regulators to merge with more financially sound institutions. Frequently, no money exchanged hands, but rather the combinor institution merely assumed the combinee institution's assets and liabilities. The result was that the fair value of the assets assumed was significantly less than the fair value of the liabilities assumed and goodwill was recorded. By amortizing goodwill over forty years (straight-line) and amortizing other assets over a much shorter period, earnings of the combined institution were enhanced.

The FASB questioned the existence of goodwill in such situations. In Statement of Financial Accounting Standard (SFAS) 72, it required the amortization of goodwill in some combinations of thrift institutions to be made over the shorter period in which the other assets are being amortized.[14] This decision by the FASB is in complete contrast with APB 17 and reflects uncertainty about the existence of goodwill and the present accounting for it.

A situation opposite to goodwill may occur: that is, a combinor may be able to acquire a combinee for an amount that is less than the fair value of the combinee's net assets. If this situation does occur, conservatism requires that one cannot record the assets acquired less liabilities at an amount more than their cost. APB 16 assumed that estimates of fair values of the combinee's long-lived assets other than investments are less reliable than those estimates made for current assets, long-term investments, and liabilities. As a result, regardless of the amount paid for the combinee, its current assets, long-term investments, and liabilities are recorded by the combinor at the full amount of their estimated fair values. Any excess of the estimated fair value of the combinee's net assets over the price paid for it is allocated to reduce proportionately the estimated fair values of the combinee's long-lived assets, other than long-term investments. The basis of the allocation is on respective estimated fair values, not book values.[15] Thus there is not a symmetry between positive and negative goodwill; positive goodwill is recognized, but negative goodwill is not. This has a conservative effect on both the income statement and balance sheet.

Although rare, it is possible that the price paid by the combinor will be less than the fair values of the combinee's current assets and long-term investments less liabilities. In such a case, the long-lived assets other than long-term investments would be reduced to zero. Any remaining excess fair value of current assets and long-term investments less liabilities over the price paid by the combinor is recorded as a deferred credit, *negative goodwill*. Negative goodwill is amortized to income over a period not to exceed forty years.[16]

---

[14] FASB (1983, para. 5).
[15] APB (1970b, para. 91).
[16] APB (1970b, para. 91).

ACCOUNTING AND REPORTING DIFFERENCES OF PURCHASE AND POOLING

It is important to understand fully the financial statement ramifications of the method used to account for a business combination. Although the two methods are not alternatives for the same combination (see earlier discussion), if the financial statement results of the combination can be estimated in advance under each approach, the combination possibly could be structured to achieve the desired accounting treatment, be it purchase or pooling. Exhibit 18-2 highlights the primary financial statement differences of the two methods.

Generally, the net assets reported for the combined enterprise will be higher if the purchase method is used than if the pooling of interests method is used. This results because of several factors:

1. The combinee's net assets will be reported at fair value under the purchase method and book value under the pooling of interests method.
2. Some of the combinee's assets, such as internally generated patents, will not be recognized under the pooling of interests method but will be reported at fair value under the purchase method.
3. The price paid by the combinor will be reported at its fair value under the purchase method and at the underlying book value of the combinee's net assets under the pooling of interests method. The effect of this is that goodwill may be reported if the purchase method is used and would not be reported if pooling of interests is used.

On the other hand, reported net income of the combined enterprise generally will be higher if the pooling of interests method is used than if the purchase method is used. At least two factors contribute to this result:

1. The combined income statement for the fiscal year includes the separate enterprises' incomes for the full twelve months regardless of when during that twelve months the combination is consummated under the pooling of interests method. Under the purchase method, the combinee's income prior to consummation of the combination is excluded from the combined income statement.
2. Because the purchase method gradually results in higher net assets than the pooling of interests method, it follows that it generally will result in lower net income because of the write-off of the higher net assets.

EXHIBIT 18-2.
Financial Statement Differences Between Pooling of Interests and Purchase

Item Reported	Amount Reported as Under	
	Pooling of Interests	Purchase
Combinee's Net Assets	Combinee's book value	Fair value determined as of the date the combination is consummated
Combinee's unrecorded assets and liabilities, e.g., internally developed patents and pension liabilities	Ignored	Fair value determined as of the date the combination is consummated
Excess of cost of combinee over fair value of its net assets	Ignored	Goodwill
Securities issued by combinor to combinee as consideration for the combination	Amount of paid-in capital of combinee (some adjustment may be required)	Fair value determined as of the date the combination is consummated
Retained earnings of combinee	Carried forward at same amount	Ignored
Net income for fiscal year in which the combination occurs	Includes net incomes of both combinor and combinee for full twelve months	Includes net income of the combinor for full twelve months but that of the combinee only since the combination was consummated
Net income in years subsequent to the combination	Generally, the summation of the combinor's and combinee's separate pretax incomes. There may be income tax differences	Generally, it will be different than the summation of the combinor's and combinee's pretax incomes because of the write-off of the revaluations of the combinee's net assets when the combination was consummated

The illustration on the following pages is provided to illustrate clearly the financial statement effects of the method used to account for a business combination. It necessarily is kept simple to point out those differences. Also keep in mind that the pooling of interests method and the purchase method are not alternatives for the same business combination, although to simplify the illustration, they are used for the same combination herein.

In the example, Bryce, Inc. is the combinor and Flint, Inc. is the combinee. The consideration given by Bryce to Flint is 5,000 shares of its $10 par value stock that has a current market price of $65 per share. In return, Flint transfers all its outstanding stock to Bryce. The business combination is consummated on January 1, 1984, the first day of both Bryce's and Flint's fiscal year. Exhibit 18-3 presents the statement of financial position of both enterprises immediately prior to the business combination, together with the current fair values of Flint's assets and liabilities.

Exhibit 18-4 presents the combined statement of financial position of Bryce and Flint immediately following the busines combination, using both the pooling of interests and the purchase methods of accounting. Under the pooling of interests method, the combined amounts are determined by adding together the book values on the separate company statements of financial position from Exhibit 18-3. With the exception of stockholders' equity, those amounts would be determined similarly for any pooling of interests, regardless of the terms of the particular business combination. Total stockholders' equity always would be equal to the addition of the separate company amounts; however, the individual component amounts may differ depending on the terms of the stock exchange agreement. For example, if the par values of the separate enterprises' capital stock were different the combined enterprise's capital stock would not equal the separate enterprises' amounts.

Under the purchase method the amounts reported on the combined statement of financial position are determined by adding together the fair values of Flint's assets and liabilities and the book values of Bryce's assets and liabilities. The stockholders' equity is equal to the fair value of the shares issued in the combination plus the book value of Bryce's stockholders' equity immediately prior to the combination.

As can be seen in Exhibit 18-4, the purchase method results in $100,000 more assets than the pooling of interests method ($10,000 current assets + $50,000 plant assets − $15,000 other assets + $55,000 goodwill); it also yields $20,000 less long-term debt and $120,000 more stockholders' equity ($225,000 paid-in capital − $105,000 retained earnings).

When the pooling of interests method is used, the combined income statement for the year in which a combination is consummated includes both the combinor's and the combinee's separate company amounts for the entire twelve months regardless of when during that twelve-month period the combination was consummated. For the purchase method, however, the combinee's income statement amounts only since consummation are included together with the combinor's amounts for the full twelve months. In

---

EXHIBIT 18-3.
Statement of Financial Position for Bryce and Flint and Fair Values for Flint

January 1, 1984

	Flint, Inc.		Bryce, Inc.
	Book Value	Fair Value	Book Value
Current Assets[a]	$ 50,000	$ 60,000	$100,000
Plant Assets[b]	250,000	300,000	500,000
Other Assets[c]	25,000	10,000	40,000
	$325,000		$640,000
Current Liabilities	$ 20,000	20,000	$ 40,000
Long-Term Debt[d]	100,000	80,000	200,000
Capital Stock—$10 Par Value	50,000		200,000
Paid-In Capital	50,000		50,000
Retained Earnings	105,000		150,000
	$325,000		$640,000

[a]Entire difference between book and fair value of current assets attributable to inventory. Both enterprises use FIFO inventory procedures.
[b]Remaining life of plant assets is twenty (20) years.
[c]Remaining life of other assets is ten (10) years.
[d]Remaining period until maturity date of long-term debt is five (5) years.

EXHIBIT 18-4.
Combined Statement of Financial Position for Bryce and Flint, Inc.

	Pooling of Interests	Purchase
Current Assets	$150,000	$ 160,000
Plant Assets	750,000	800,000
Other Assets	65,000	50,000
Goodwill[a]	0	55,000
	$965,000	$1,065,000
Current Liabilities	$ 60,000	$ 60,000
Long-Term Debt	300,000	280,000
Capital Stock—$10 Par Value	250,000	250,000
Paid-In Capital	100,000	325,000
Retained Earnings	255,000	150,000
	$965,000	$1,065,000

[a]Goodwill is assumed to have a life of forty (40) years.

this illustration, we simplified the matter by assuming both constituents have the same fiscal period and that the combination was consummated on the first day of that period.

Exhibit 18-5 presents the separate company income statements for 1984.

Exhibit 18-6 presents the combined income statement for Bryce and Flint, Inc. for 1984 under both the pooling of interests and purchase methods of accounting for the business combination. As was the case with the combined balance sheet, the combined income statement under the pooling of interests method is derived by adding together the separate company income statements. Notice that the combined net income under the pooling of interests is $16,375 higher than that under the purchase method. This is because of the write-off of Flint's fair values under the purchase method, while the book values are written off under the pooling of interests method. Exhibit 18-7 provides a reconciliation of the income statement amounts between the pooling of interests and purchase methods.

EXHIBIT 18-5.
Income Statements for Flint, Inc. and Bryce, Inc. for the Year Ended December 31, 1984

	Flint, Inc.	Bryce, Inc.
Sales	$500,000	$1,000,000
Cost of Sales	250,000	500,000
Gross Profit	$250,000	$ 500,000
Expenses	100,000	200,000
Net Income [a]	$150,000	$ 300,000

[a]Income taxes are ignored in this simplified illustration; however, income tax differences between separate company income statements and the combined income statement may exist under both the pooling of interests and the purchase methods.

EXHIBIT 18-6.
Combined Income Statement for Bryce and Flint, Inc. for The Year Ended December 31, 1984

	Pooling of Interests	Purchase
Sales	$1,500,000	$1,500,000
Cost of Sales	750,000	760,000
Gross Profit	$ 750,000	$ 740,000
Expense	300,000	306,375
Net Income	$ 450,000	$ 433,625

EXHIBIT 18-7.
Reconciliation of Income Statement Amounts
Between the Pooling of Interests and Purchase Methods

Cost of Sales:

Reported on Flint's Income Statement	$250,000
Reported on Bryce's Income Statement	500,000
Reported Under Pooling of Interests Combined Income Statement	$750,000
Increase in Cost of Sales because of higher fair values, all attributed to 1984 under FIFO procedures	10,000
Reported Under Purchase Combined Income Statement	$760,000

Expenses:

Reported on Flint's Income Statement	$100,000
Reported on Bryce's Income Statement	200,000
Reported Under Pooling of Interests Combined Income Statement	$300,000
Depreciation of Excess Fair Value over Book Value of Plant Assets: ($50,000 ÷ 20)	2,500
Depreciation of Excess Book Value over Fair Value of Other Assets: ($15,000 ÷ 10)	(1,500)
Amortization of Goodwill: ($55,000 ÷ 40)	1,375
Amortization of Excess Book Value over Fair Value of Long-term Debt: (20,000 ÷ 5)	4,000
Reported under Purchase Combined Income Statement	$306,375

Cost of sales is $10,000 higher under the purchase method because of the increase in Flint's inventory value at the date the combination is assumed to have been sold in 1984 under the FIFO inventory method. If the combined enterprise used LIFO, this $10,000 may be left in inventory indefinitely and accordingly no adjustment would be required to cost of sales. Expense adjustments include amounts for the depreciation of the increase in Flint's plant assets ($50,000 ÷ 40), and amortization of the decrease in Flint's long-term debt ($20,000 ÷ 5). Similar adjustments to the separate company income statements would be required each year to derive the combined income statement until the original statement of financial position adjustment amounts have been charged or credited to income. In this illustration no year subsequent to 1984 would be affected by the inventory revaluation. However, plant assets would affect nineteen more years; other assets, nine more years; goodwill, thirty-nine more years; and long-term debt, four more years. If any revalued assets or liabilities are disposed of or settled prior to their estimated lives, the amount of the revaluations not previously charged or credited to income would be charged or credited in the year of disposal or settlement. Obviously, no future years would be affected.

RESEARCH ON POOLING AND PURCHASE ACCOUNTING

Earlier in the chapter it was pointed out that management views pooling of interests accounting as an important motivation for business combinations. A FASB survey found that 66% of enterprises having combinations agreed that many combinations would not occur if purchase accounting were required.[17] It was also illustrated in the previous section how pooling of interests can produce more favorable financial statements than purchase accounting. This would certainly explain the preference of management for pooling.

Research has also been conducted concerning the attitude of financial statement users toward the two accounting methods. Interestingly, the two methods are about equally favored. A FASB survey found 40% preferred pooling of interests; 45%, purchase accounting; and 15%, a new accounting basis for both combinor and combinee.[18] Another survey of financial analysts found 46.7% preferred purchase accounting and 43.3% favored pooling of interests.[19] Although some academic researchers have taken a very critical stance on pooling of interests, it is interesting to see that the method has a following with financial analysts.[20] However, *Accounting Trends and Techniques* has reported that, in recent years, approximately 80% of combinations are reported as purchases.[21]

Finally, there has been some limited research to determine how the two accounting methods affect security prices of combinor companies. One study found no evidence that pooling accounting caused higher stock prices. In other words, the stock market did not appear to be fooled by the higher income reported under the pooling method.[22] This finding is con-

---

[17]FASB (1976, para. 138).
[18]FASB (1976, para. 110).
[19]Burton (1970, p. 75).
[20]For example, Briloff (1967).
[21]AICPA (1982, p. 52).
[22]Hong, Kaplan, and Mandelker (1978).

sistent with capital market research regarding the sophistication of users of accounting information.

What insight does empirical research give to the purchase/pooling question? Management seems to prefer pooling because of its favorable financial statement effect. However, security market price research has shown that the market is not fooled or deceived by "book profits" arising solely from the way in which business combinations are accounted for. If the market is not fooled, it could be argued that it makes no difference which method is used, so long as the method is disclosed. This is the efficient market school of thought. Yet if it really makes no difference, why bother having two methods to account for similar but subtly different phenomena. It has proved very difficult to specify the relevant circumstances which justify two radically different accounting methods. Given the continued disquiet about accounting for business combinations, it is disappointing that the FASB has dropped the topic from its agenda.

SUMMARY

Accounting for business combinations has been a controversial subject for many years. Two completely different approaches are used and a third is occasionally mentioned. Under pooling of interests, no new accountability is assumed to occur and the book values of both the combinee's and combinor's net assets are merely carried forward to the combined enterprise. Under purchase, the combinee is assumed to liquidate and its net assets are carried forward to the combined enterprise at fair value, while the combinor's are at book value. The new entity approach assumes that both the combinee and combinor liquidate and the combined enterprise records all assets and liabilities at fair value.

The impact on financial statements of the method used to account for a business combination can be, and often is, significant, while the underlying circumstances are similar or identical. No justifiable reason can be found in accounting theory for such similar events and circumstances to be treated so dissimilarly. It is very difficult to defend the type of finite uniformity which exists in the business combination area.

QUESTIONS

1. What are the underlying circumstance that could justify a pooling of interests business combination as contrasted with a purchase? Discuss.

2. Briefly trace the development of criteria for a pooling of interests. How have those criteria changed from ARB 40 to APB 16? Are these genuine relevant circumstances?

3. What was the objective of ARB 48? Was that objective achieved?

4. What are the accounting and reporting implications of a pooling of interests business combination as contrasted to a purchase?

5. Briefly discuss "attributes of the combining enterprises" and why the APB established it.

6. What does "manner of combining interests" mean, and why did the APB establish it?

7. Briefly discuss "absence of planned transactions" and why the APB established it.

8. What steps must occur to account for a business combination that is a purchase?

9. The logic of pooling rests heavily on the assumption that no substantive economic transaction occurs between the combinor and stockholders of the combinee. How realistic is this assumption?

10. A third accounting method is rarely discussed: a new accounting basis for both combinor and combinee. Under what circumstances might this be the best way to account for a business combination?

11. What insight into business combinations has been provided by empirical research?

12. What are some economic consequences of mandating one accounting method for combinations, probably purchase accounting?

13. In purchase accounting there is not symmetry between positive and negative goodwill. What overriding concept causes this situation?

14. Pooling of interests accounting originated between affiliate companies. APB 16 prohibits pooling for affiliated companies that combine. What has caused this change to occur?

15. Do the differences between pooling and purchase accounting represent real economic differences? Is the nature of the differences consistent with the findings of the capital market study by Hong, Kaplan, and Mandelker (1978)?

CASES AND PROBLEMS

1. The Combinor Company and the Combinee Company are entering into a business combination. The following information about both companies has been collected.

(a) Current balance sheet information:

	Combinee	Combinor
Cash	$ 100,000	$ 6,000,000
Inventory	500,000	8,000,000
Receivables (net)	1,000,000	10,000,000
Land	500,000	5,000,000
Plant (net)	2,000,000	20,000,000
Intangibles (net)	0	1,000,000
	$4,100,000	$50,000,000
Current Liabilities	$ 800,000	$ 1,000,000
Long-term Debt	1,500,000	20,000,000
Deferred Income Tax	100,000	900,000
Common Stock ($100 par value)	1,000,000	20,000,000
Paid-in Capital	200,000	2,100,000
Retained Earnings	500,000	6,000,000
	$4,100,000	$50,000,000

(b) Current fair values of Combinee's assets and liabilities:

Inventory	$ 600,000
Receivables (net)	950,000
Land	600,000
Plant	3,000,000
Intangibles	200,000
Current Liabilities	800,000
Long-term Debt	1,200,000

(c) Estimated remaining lives (both companies):

Inventory (FIFO)	1 year
Receivables	1 year
Plant	20 years
Intangibles	5 years
Current Liabilities	1 year
Long-term Debt	10 years
Goodwill (if any)	40 years

(d) The agreed price of Combinee Company is $4,000,000.

(e) If common stock is used to effect the combination, Combinor will issue 25,000 shares for all of Combinee's shares. The current market price of Combinor's shares is $160 per share.

(f) If cash is used to effect the combination, Combinor will forego approximately $480,000 in interest income.

(g) If debt is used to effect the combination, the debt will bear interest at 15%.

(h) The estimated results of operations of the two separate companies for the next fiscal year are as follows:

	Combinee	Combinor
Sales (including interest)	$6,000,000	$60,000,000
Cost of Sales	2,700,000	33,000,000
Gross Profit	$3,300,000	$27,000,000
Expenses (including depreciation,		
amortization, and interest)	2,100,000	20,000,000
Income	$1,200,000	$ 7,000,000

(i) Income taxes are irrelevant to the business combination and may be ignored.

Required:

(a) Assuming the business combination could be structured as a pooling of interests or a purchase, which method should be used? (Provide calculations in support of your solution).

(b) Assuming the business combination must be accounted for as a purchase, determine the effects of common stock, cash, or long-term debt to effect the combination? Provide calculations in support of your solution.

2. Medical Group (MG) is in the process of acquiring a company that owns and operates health care facilities. MG will acquire the company for cash and assume its liabilities. The acquisition will be accounted for as a purchase. The combinee's ten health care facilities have been appraised independently at $110 million. Replacement cost of these facilities has been determined independently to be $70 million.

Required: Should the $110 million or $70 million be allocated as the cost of the facilities? Discuss your answer. Would your answer be different if replacement cost exceeded appraised value?

3. In 1978 Joseph, Inc. acquired Vollbracht Engineering Co., a manufacturer of commercial refrigeration equipment, in a transaction accounted for as a purchase. The acquisition resulted in $2,000,000 goodwill which is being amortized over 40 years. Vollbracht, which earned $300,000 the fiscal year prior to acquisition, has had disappointing results since acquisition. The following is a summary of results since 1978:

Year	Income (loss) excluding goodwill amortization
1979	180,000
1980	(82,000)
1981	(96,000)
1982	54,000
1983	47,000
1984	7,000

Orders have been improving recently and 1985 projected profits prior to goodwill amortization are $90,000. The in-charge accountant on the audit does not believe that the trend of earnings supports an unamortized balance of goodwill of $1,700,000.

Required: The in-charge accountant has requested your views regarding whether

(a) the above information supports a writedown of goodwill, and

(b) what additional factors should be considered in determining whether there has been a diminution in value.

4. In 1983, the FASB became concerned with procedures used to account for business combinations in the thrift (savings and loan) industry. Purchase-type combinations restate acquired assets and liabilities at current market values at the time of combination. Assets of thrifts are predominantly low-yielding mortgages and must be discounted to present values using current interest rates. The discount is then recognized as income as the mortgages are written up to face value over the remaining period to maturity. This is analogous to a discount on investments in bonds. Liabilities (customer deposits) are likely to be at market values.

Frequently, combiners simply acquired the assets and liabilities (sometimes not even paying any cash). Because of the discounted assets, it was common for liabilities to exceed assets, in which case purchased goodwill was recognized to balance the entry. Under APB 17 goodwill can be amortized over forty years.

The accounting problem was stated in an article which appeared in *Business Week*, April 18, 1983, page 97:

> "Under the old rules," says Bertill A. Gustafson, senior vice-president and controller of Great Western Savings, based in Beverly Hills, California, "the discounted mortgage portfolio would slowly increase in value as maturity approached, usually over about 10 years, creating income each year. Yet the related goodwill would be 'expensed' over a much longer time period, as much as 40 years." The result: bookkeeping profits for the first decade after the acquisition.

In response to this anomaly, the FASB issued SFAS 72, which limits the amortization period of goodwill in the thrift industry to the maturity period of the mortgages. It also requires use of what it called the "interest" method to amortize goodwill. This is not explained, but it appears to mean that goodwill is amortized at the same rate that income is recognized over the period to mortgage maturity.

It has been suggested that the new rule may inhibit future combinations in the thrift industry because of the loss of accounting income.

The *Business Week* article continued:

> "There were a few abuses," acknowledges a senior executive at a New York bank. "Two sick banks got together and all of a sudden both were profitable on paper," he says. "That's why the FASB acted." But the executive says the new rule will effectively discourage numerous transactions that otherwise make economic sense. "I know of many banks that were planning acquisitions, but now they're just baffled."

Required:

(a)   Create a simple illustration to show how accounting income was computed before the change, and how the change will affect income.

(b)   What does "goodwill" represent, here, in the accounting sense? How does it conform to asset definitions? How does this goodwill compare to goodwill in the context of APB 16?

(c)   Evaluate SFAS 72 accounting requirements in terms of accounting theory, particularly the effect on the balance sheet and income statement.

(d)   Why might the new standard inhibit mergers? Is this a desirable economic consequence?

BIBLIOGRAPHY OF REFERENCED WORKS

Accounting Principles Board (1967). "Accounting for Income Taxes," *APB Opinion No. 11* (AICPA).

——— (1970a). "Business Combinations," *APB Opinion No. 16* (AICPA).

——— (1970b). "Intangible Assets," *APB Opinion No. 17* (AICPA).

American Institute of Certified Public Accountants (1982). *Accounting Trends and Techniques* (AICPA).

Briloff, Abraham J. (1967). "Dirty Pooling," *The Accounting Review* (July 1967), pp. 489–496.

Burton, John C. (1970). *Accounting for Business Combinations* (Financial Executives Research Foundation).

Committee on Accounting Procedure (1950). "Business Combinations," *ARB No. 40* (AICPA).

——— (1957). "Business Combinations," *ARB No. 48* (AICPA).

Financial Accounting Standards Board (1976). *FASB Discussion Memorandum: An Analysis of Issues Related to Accounting for Business Combinations and Purchased Intangibles* (FASB).

——— (1980). "Accounting for Preacquisition Contingencies of Purchased Enterprises," *Statement of Financial Accounting Standards No. 38* (FASB).

——— (1981). *Action Alert No. 81-12* (FASB).

——— (1983). "Accounting for Certain Acquisitions of Banking and Thrift Institutions," *Statement of Financial Accounting Standards No. 72* (FASB).

Hong, H.; R. Kaplan; and G. Mandelker (1978). "Pooling vs. Purchase: The Effects of Accounting for Mergers on Stock Prices," *The Accounting Review* (January 1978), pp. 31–47.

Wyatt, Arthur R. (1963). "A Critical Study of Accounting for Business Combinations," *Accounting Research Study No. 5* (AICPA).

ADDITIONAL READINGS

BUSINESS COMBINATIONS

Bachman, Jules (1970). "An Economist Looks at Accounting for Business Combinations," *Financial Analysts Journal* (July–August 1970), pp. 39–48.

Brenner, Vincent C. (1972). "Empirical Study of Support for APB Opinion No. 16," *Journal of Accounting Research* (Spring 1972), pp. 200–208.

Foster, William C. (1974). "The Illogic of Pooling," *Financial Executive* (December 1974), pp. 16–21.

Gagnon, Jean-Marie (1971). "Purchase–Pooling Choice: Some Empirical Evidence," *Journal of Accounting Research* (Spring 1971), pp. 52–72.

Wyatt, Arthur R. (1972). "Inequities in Accounting for Business Combinations," *Financial Executive* (December 1972), pp. 28–35.

GOODWILL

Catlett, George R., and Norman O. Olson (1968). "Accounting for Goodwill," *Accounting Research Study No. 10* (AICPA).

Gynther, Reg S. (1969). "Some Conceptualizing on Goodwill," *The Accounting Review* (April 1969), pp. 247–255.

Miller, Malcolm C. (1973). "Goodwill—An Aggregation Issue," *The Accounting Review* (April 1973), pp. 280–291.

Tearney, Michael G. (1973). "Accounting for Goodwill: A Realistic Approach," *Journal of Accountancy* (July 1973), pp. 41–45.

COMMONLY USED ABBREVIATIONS

AAA American Accounting Association

AICPA American Institute of Certified Public Accountants

APB Accounting Principles Board
(When used with a number it refers to an Accounting Principles Board Opinion.)

ARB Accounting Research Bulletin issued by the Committee on Accounting Procedure

ARS Accounting Research Study issued by the Accounting Principles Board

ASR Accounting Series Release issued by the Securities and Exchange Commission

CAP Committee on Accounting Procedure

FASB Financial Accounting Standards Board

SEC Securities and Exchange Commission

SFAC Statement of Financial Accounting Concepts issued by the Financial Accounting Standards Board

SFAS Statement of Financial Accounting Standards issued by the Financial Accounting Standards Board

SUBJECT INDEX

AUTHOR INDEX